world development report 2010

Development and Climate Change

world development report 2010

Development and Climate Change

THE WORLD BANK
Washington, DC

Softcover
ISBN: 978-0-8213-7987-5
ISSN: 0163-5085
eISBN: 978-0-8213-7988-2
DOI: 10.1596/978-0-8213-7987-5

Hardcover
ISSN: 0163-5085
ISBN: 978-0-8213-7989-5
DOI: 10.1596/978-0-8213-7989-5

Cover design: Rock Creek Strategic Marketing
Cover globe images: Norman Kuring, Ocean Biology Processing Group, National Aeronautics and Space Administration (http://oceancolor.gsfc.nasa.gov)
Interior design: Naylor Design, Inc.
Typesetting: Precision Graphics

Photo credits: Gary Braasch: Overview, chapters 3, 4, 5, 7; Corbis: chapters 1, 2, 6, 8

For more information about the World Development Report 2010, please visit http://www.worldbank.org/wdr.

Contents

Index   399

Boxes

Figures

Maps

Tables

Foreword

Climate change is one of the most complex challenges of our young century. No country is immune. No country alone can take on the interconnected challenges posed by climate change, including controversial political decisions, daunting technological change, and far-reaching global consequences.

As the planet warms, rainfall patterns shift and extreme events such as droughts, floods, and forest fires become more frequent. Millions in densely populated coastal areas and in island nations will lose their homes as the sea level rises. Poor people in Africa, Asia, and elsewhere face prospects of tragic crop failures; reduced agricultural productivity; and increased hunger, malnutrition, and disease.

As a multilateral institution whose mission is inclusive and sustainable development, the World Bank Group has a responsibility to try to explain some of those interconnections across disciplines—development economics, science, energy, ecology, technology, finance, and effective international regimes and governance. With 186 members, the World Bank Group faces the challenge, every day, of building cooperation among vastly different states, the private sector, and civil society to achieve common goods. This 32nd *World Development Report* seeks to apply that experience, combined with research, to advance knowledge about *Development and Climate Change*.

Developing countries will bear the brunt of the effects of climate change, even as they strive to overcome poverty and advance economic growth. For these countries, climate change threatens to deepen vulnerabilities, erode hard-won gains, and seriously undermine prospects for development. It becomes even harder to attain the Millennium Development Goals—and ensure a safe and sustainable future beyond 2015. At the same time, many developing countries fear limits on their critical call to develop energy or new rules that might stifle their many needs—from infrastructure to entrepreneurism.

Tackling the immense and multidimensional challenge of climate change demands extraordinary ingenuity and cooperation. A "climate-smart" world is possible in our time—yet, as this Report argues, effecting such a transformation requires us to act now, act together, and act differently.

We must act now, because what we do today determines both the climate of tomorrow and the choices that shape our future. Today, we are emitting greenhouse gases that trap heat in the atmosphere for decades or even centuries. We are building power plants, reservoirs, houses, transport systems, and cities that are likely to last 50 years or more. The innovative technologies and crop varieties that we pilot today can shape energy and food sources to meet the needs of 3 billion more people by 2050.

We must act together, because climate change is a crisis of the commons. Climate change cannot be solved without countries cooperating on a global scale to improve energy efficiencies, develop and deploy clean technologies, and expand natural "sinks" to grow green by absorbing gases. We need to protect human life and ecological resources. We must act together in a differentiated and equitable way. Developed countries have produced most of the emissions of the past and have high per capita emissions. These countries should lead the way by significantly reducing their carbon footprints and stimulating research into green alternatives. Yet most of the world's future emissions will be generated in the developing world. These countries will need adequate funds and technology transfer so they can pursue lower carbon paths—without jeopardizing their development prospects. And they need assistance to adapt to inevitable changes in climate.

We must act differently, because we cannot plan for the future based on the climate of the past. Tomorrow's climate needs will require us to build infrastructure that can withstand new conditions and support greater numbers of people; use limited land and water resources to supply sufficient food and biomass for fuel while preserving ecosystems; and reconfigure the world's energy systems. This will require adaptation measures that are based on new information about changing patterns of temperature, precipitation, and species. Changes of this magnitude will require substantial additional finance for adaptation and mitigation, and for strategically intensified research to scale up promising approaches and explore bold new ideas.

We need a new momentum. It is crucial that countries reach a climate agreement in December in Copenhagen that integrates development needs with climate actions.

The World Bank Group has developed several financing initiatives to help countries cope with climate change, as outlined in our Strategic Framework for Development and Climate Change. These include our carbon funds and facilities, which continue to grow as financing for energy efficiency and new renewable energy increases substantially. We are trying to develop practical experience about how developing countries can benefit from and support a climate change regime—ranging from workable mechanisms to provide incentives for avoided deforestation, to lower carbon growth models and initiatives that combine adaptation and mitigation. In these ways, we can support the UNFCCC process and the countries devising new international incentives and disincentives.

Much more is needed. Looking forward, the Bank Group is reshaping our energy and environment strategies for the future, and helping countries to strengthen their risk management practices and expand their safety nets to cope with risks that cannot be fully mitigated.

The *2010 World Development Report* calls for action on climate issues: If we act now, act together, and act differently, there are real opportunities to shape our climate future for an inclusive and sustainable globalization.

Robert B. Zoellick
President
The World Bank Group

Acknowledgments

This Report has been prepared by a core team led by Rosina Bierbaum and Marianne Fay and comprising Julia Bucknall, Samuel Fankhauser, Ricardo Fuentes-Nieva, Kirk Hamilton, Andreas Kopp, Andrea Liverani, Alexander Lotsch, Ian Noble, Jean-Louis Racine, Mark Rosegrant, Xiaodong Wang, Xueman Wang, and Michael Ian Westphal. Major contributions were made by Arun Agrawal, Philippe Ambrosi, Elliot Diringer, Calestous Juma, Jean-Charles Hourcade, Kseniya Lvovsky, Muthukumara Mani, Alan Miller, and Michael Toman. Helpful advice and data were provided by Leon Clarke, Jens Dinkel, Jae Edmonds, Per-Anders Enkvist, Brigitte Knopf, and Volker Krey. The team was assisted by Rachel Block, Doina Cebotari, Nicola Cenacchi, Sandy Chang, Nate Engle, Hilary Gopnik, and Hrishikesh Patel. Additional contributions were made by Lidvard Gronnevet and Jon Strand.

Bruce Ross-Larson was the principal editor. The World Bank's Map Design Unit created the maps under the direction of Jeff Lecksell. The Office of the Publisher provided editorial, design, composition, and printing services under the supervision of Mary Fisk and Andres Meneses; Stephen McGroarty served as acquisitions editor.

The *World Development Report 2010* was co-sponsored by Development Economics (DEC) and the Sustainable Development Network (SDN). The work was conducted under the general guidance of Justin Yifu Lin in DEC and Katherine Sierra in SDN. Warren Evans and Alan H. Gelb also provided valuable guidance. A Panel of Advisers comprised of Neil Adger, Zhou Dadi, Rashid Hassan, Geoffrey Heal, John Holdren (until December 2008), Jean-Charles Hourcade, Saleemul Huq, Calestous Juma, Nebojša Nakićenović, Carlos Nobre, John Schellnhuber, Robert Watson, and John Weyant provided extensive and excellent advice at all stages of the Report.

World Bank President Robert B. Zoellick provided comments and guidance.

Many others inside and outside the World Bank contributed with comments and inputs. The Development Data Group contributed to the data appendix and was responsible for the Selected World Development Indicators.

The team benefited greatly from a wide range of consultations. Meetings and regional workshops were held locally or through videoconferencing (using the World Bank's Global Development Learning Network) in: Argentina, Bangladesh, Belgium, Benin, Botswana, Burkina Faso, China, Costa Rica, Côte d'Ivoire, Denmark, Dominican Republic, Ethiopia, Finland, France, Germany, Ghana, India, Indonesia, Kenya, Kuwait, Mexico, Mozambique, the Netherlands, Nicaragua, Norway, Peru, the Philippines, Poland, Senegal, South Africa, Sweden, Tanzania, Thailand, Togo, Tunisia, Uganda, the United Arab Emirates, and the United Kingdom. The team wishes to thank participants in these workshops and videoconferences, which included academics, policy researchers, government officials, and staff of nongovernmental, civil society, and private sector organizations.

Finally, the team would like to acknowledge the generous support of the Government of Norway, the UK Department for International Development, the Government of Denmark, the Government of Germany through Deutsche Gesellschaft für technische Zusammenarbeit, the Swedish Government through Biodiversity Centre/Swedish International Biodiversity Programme (SwedBio), the Trust Fund for Environmentally & Socially Sustainable Development

(TFESSD), the multi-donor programmatic trust fund, and the Knowledge for Change Program (KCP).

Rebecca Sugui served as senior executive assistant to the team—her 17th year with the *WDR*—Sonia Joseph and Jason Victor as program assistants, and Bertha Medina as team assistant. Evangeline Santo Domingo served as resource management assistant.

Abbreviations and Data Notes

Abbreviations

AAU	assigned amount unit
ARPP	Annual Report on Portfolio Performance
BRIICS	Brazil, the Russian Federation, India, Indonesia, China, and South Africa
Bt	*Bacillus thuringiensis*
CCS	carbon capture and storage
CDM	Clean Development Mechanism
CER	certified emission reduction
CGIAR	Consultative Group on International Agricultural Research
CIPAV	Centro para Investigación en Sistemas Sostenibles de Producción Agropecuaria
CH_4	methane
CO_2	carbon dioxide
CO_2e	carbon dioxide equivalent
CPIA	Country Policy and Institutional Assessment
CTF	Clean Technology Fund
EE	energy efficiency
EIT	economies in transition
ENSO	El Niño–Southern Oscillation
ESCO	energy service company
ETF–IW	Environmental Transformation Fund–International Window
EU	European Union
FCPF	Forest Carbon Partnership Facility
FDI	foreign direct investment
FIP	Forest Investment Program
GCCA	Global Climate Change Alliance
GCS	global climate services enterprise
GDP	gross domestic product
GEO	Group on Earth Observation
GEOSS	Global Earth Observation System of Systems
GEEREF	Global Energy Efficiency and Renewable Energy Fund
GEF	Global Environment Facility
GFDRR	Global Facility for Disaster Reduction and Recovery
GHG	greenhouse gas
GM	genetically modified
Gt	gigaton
GWP	global warming potential
IAASTD	International Assessment of Agricultural Science and Technology for Development
IATAL	international air travel adaptation levy

IDA	International Development Association
IEA	International Energy Agency
IFC	International Finance Corporation
IFCI	International Forest Carbon Initiative
IIASA	International Institute for Applied Systems Analysis
IMERS	International Maritime Emission Reduction Scheme
IPCC	Intergovernmental Panel on Climate Change
IPR	intellectual property rights
kWh	kilowatt-hour
JI	Joint Implementation
LDCF	Least Developed Country Fund
LECZ	low-elevation coastal zones
LPG	liquefied petroleum gas
MEA	multilateral environmental agreement
MRGRA	Midwestern Regional GHG Reduction Accord
MRV	measurable, reportable, and verifiable
NAPA	National Adaptation Program of Action
N_2O	nitrous oxide
NGO	nongovernmental organization
O_3	ozone
O&M	operation and maintenance
OECD	Organisation for Economic Co-operation and Development
PaCIS	Pacific Climate Information System
ppb	parts per billion
PPCR	Pilot Program for Climate Resistance
ppm	parts per million
PPP	purchasing power parity
R&D	research and development
RD&D	research, development, and deployment
RDD&D	research, development, demonstration, and deployment
REDD	reduced emissions from deforestation and forest degradation
RGGI	Regional Greenhouse Gas Initiative
SCCF	Strategic Climate Change Fund
SDII	simple daily intensity index
SD-PAMs	sustainable development policies and measures
SO_2	sulfur dioxide
SUV	sports utility vehicle
toe	tons of oil equivalent
TRIPS	Trade-Related Aspects of Intellectual Property Rights
Tt	trillion tons
UN	United Nations
UNFCCC	United Nations Framework Convention on Climate Change
UN-REDD	United Nations Collaborative Program on Reduced Emissions from Deforestation and forest Degradation
WCI	Western Climate Initiative
WGI	World Governance Indicator
WMO	World Meteorological Organization
WTO	World Trade Organization

Data notes

The countries included in regional and income groupings in this Report are listed in the Classification of Economies table at the end of the Selected World Development Indicators. Income classifications are based on gross national product (GNP) per capita; thresholds for income classifications in this edition may be found in the Introduction to Selected World Development Indicators. Figures, maps, and tables (including selected indicators) showing income groupings are based on the World Bank's income classification in 2009. The data shown in the Selected World Development Indicators are based on the classification in 2010. Group averages reported in the figures and tables are unweighted averages of the countries in the group, unless noted to the contrary.

The use of the word *countries* to refer to economies implies no judgment by the World Bank about the legal or other status of a territory. The term *developing countries* includes low- and middle-income economies and thus may include economies in transition from central planning, as a matter of convenience. The terms *industrialized countries* or *developed countries* may be used as a matter of convenience to denote high-income economies.

Dollar figures are current U.S. dollars, unless otherwise specified. *Billion* means 1,000 million; *trillion* means 1,000 billion.

Main Messages of the World Development Report 2010

Poverty reduction and sustainable development remain core global priorities. A quarter of the population of developing countries still lives on less than $1.25 a day. One billion people lack clean drinking water; 1.6 billion, electricity; and 3 billion, adequate sanitation. A quarter of all developing-country children are malnourished. Addressing these needs must remain the priorities both of developing countries and of development aid—recognizing that development will get harder, not easier, with climate change.

Yet climate change must urgently be addressed. Climate change threatens all countries, with developing countries the most vulnerable. Estimates are that they would bear some 75 to 80 percent of the costs of damages caused by the changing climate. Even 2°C warming above preindustrial temperatures—the minimum the world is likely to experience—could result in permanent reductions in GDP of 4 to 5 percent for Africa and South Asia. Most developing countries lack sufficient financial and technical capacities to manage increasing climate risk. They also depend more directly on climate-sensitive natural resources for income and well-being. And most are in tropical and subtropical regions already subject to highly variable climate.

Economic growth alone is unlikely to be fast or equitable enough to counter threats from climate change, particularly if it remains carbon intensive and accelerates global warming. So climate policy cannot be framed as a choice between growth and climate change. In fact, climate-smart policies are those that enhance development, reduce vulnerability, and finance the transition to low-carbon growth paths.

A climate-smart world is within our reach if we act now, act together, and act differently than we have in the past:

- *Acting now* is essential, or else options disappear and costs increase as the world commits itself to high-carbon pathways and largely irreversible warming trajectories. Climate change is already compromising efforts to improve standards of living and to achieve the Millennium Development Goals. Staying close to 2°C above preindustrial levels—likely the best that can be done—requires a veritable energy revolution with the immediate deployment of energy efficiency and available low-carbon technologies, accompanied by massive investments in the next generation of technologies without which low-carbon growth cannot be achieved. Immediate actions are also needed to cope with the changing climate and to minimize the costs to people, infrastructure and ecosystems today as well as to prepare for the greater changes in store.

- *Acting together* is key to keeping the costs down and effectively tackling both adaptation and mitigation. It has to start with high-income countries taking aggressive action to reduce their own emissions. That would free some "pollution space" for developing countries, but more importantly, it would stimulate innovation and the demand for new technologies so they can be rapidly scaled up. It would also help create a sufficiently large and stable carbon market. Both these effects are critical to enable developing countries to move to a lower carbon trajectory while rapidly gaining access to the energy services needed for development, although they will need to be supplemented with financial support. But acting together is also critical to advance development in a harsher environment—increasing climate risks will exceed communities' capacity to adapt. National and international support will be essential to protect the most vulnerable through social assistance programs, to develop international risk-sharing arrangements, and to promote the exchange of knowledge, technology, and information.

- *Acting differently* is required to enable a sustainable future in a changing world. In the next few decades, the world's energy systems must be transformed so that global emissions drop 50 to 80 percent. Infrastructure must be built to withstand new extremes. To feed 3 billion more people without further threatening already stressed ecosystems, agricultural productivity and efficiency of water use must improve. Only long-term, large-scale integrated management and flexible planning can satisfy increased demands on natural resources for food, bioenergy, hydropower, and ecosystem services while conserving biodiversity and maintaining carbon stocks in land and forests. Robust economic and social strategies will be those that take into account increased uncertainty and that enhance adaptation to a variety of climate futures—not just "optimally" cope with the climate of the past. Effective policy will entail jointly evaluating development, adaptation, and mitigation actions, all of which draw on the same finite resources (human, financial, and natural).

An equitable and effective global climate deal is needed. Such a deal would recognize the varying needs and constraints of developing countries, assist them with the finance and technology to meet the increased challenges to development, ensure they are not locked into a permanently low share of the global commons, and establish mechanisms that decouple where mitigation happens from who pays for it. Most emissions growth will occur in developing nations, whose current carbon footprint is disproportionately low and whose economies must grow rapidly to reduce poverty. High-income countries must provide financial and technical assistance for both adaptation and low-carbon growth in developing countries. Current financing for adaptation and mitigation is less than 5 percent of what may be needed annually by 2030, but the shortfalls can be met through innovative financing mechanisms.

Success hinges on changing behavior and shifting public opinion. Individuals, as citizens and consumers, will determine the planet's future. Although an increasing number of people know about climate change and believe action is needed, too few make it a priority, and too many fail to act when they have the opportunity. So the greatest challenge lies with changing behaviors and institutions, particularly in high-income countries. Public policy changes—local, regional, national, and international—are necessary to make private and civic action easier and more attractive.

Overview

Changing the Climate for Development

Thirty years ago, half the developing world lived in extreme poverty—today, a quarter.[1] Now, a much smaller share of children are malnourished and at risk of early death. And access to modern infrastructure is much more widespread. Critical to the progress: rapid economic growth driven by technological innovation and institutional reform, particularly in today's middle-income countries, where per capita incomes have doubled. Yet the needs remain enormous, with the number of hungry people having passed the billion mark this year for the first time in history.[2] With so many still in poverty and hunger, growth and poverty alleviation remain the overarching priority for developing countries.

Climate change only makes the challenge more complicated. First, the impacts of a changing climate are already being felt, with more droughts, more floods, more strong storms, and more heat waves—taxing individuals, firms, and governments, drawing resources away from development. Second, continuing climate change, at current rates, will pose increasingly severe challenges to development. By century's end, it could lead to warming of 5°C or more compared with preindustrial times and to a vastly different world from today, with more extreme weather events, most ecosystems stressed and changing, many species doomed to extinction, and whole island nations threatened by inundation. Even our best efforts are unlikely to stabilize temperatures at anything less than 2°C above preindustrial temperatures, warming that will require substantial adaptation.

High-income countries can and must reduce their carbon footprints. They cannot continue to fill up an unfair and unsustainable share of the atmospheric commons. But developing countries—whose average per capita emissions are a third those of high-income countries (figure 1)—need massive expansions in energy, transport, urban systems, and agricultural production. If pursued using traditional technologies and carbon intensities, these much-needed expansions will produce more greenhouse gases and, hence, more climate change. The question, then, is not just how to make development more resilient to climate change. It is how to pursue growth and prosperity without causing "dangerous" climate change.[3]

Climate change policy is not a simple choice between a high-growth, high-carbon world and a low-growth, low-carbon world—a simple question of whether to grow or to preserve the planet. Plenty of inefficiencies drive today's high-carbon intensity.[4] For example, existing technologies and best practices could reduce energy consumption in industry and the power sector by 20–30 percent, shrinking carbon footprints without sacrificing growth.[5] Many mitigation actions—meaning changes to reduce emissions of greenhouse gases—have significant co-benefits in public health, energy security, environmental sustainability, and financial savings. In Africa, for example, mitigation opportunities are linked to more sustainable land and

Figure 1   Unequal footprints: Emissions per capita in low-, middle-, and high-income countries, 2005

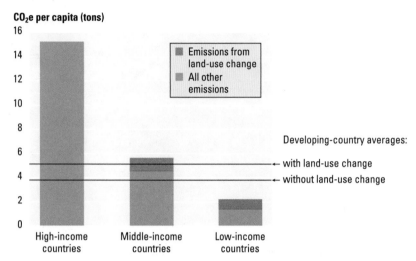

CO$_2$e per capita (tons)

Sources: World Bank 2008c; WRI 2008 augmented with land-use change emissions from Houghton 2009.
Note: Greenhouse gas emissions include carbon dioxide (CO$_2$), methane (CH$_4$), nitrous oxide (N$_2$O), and high-global-warming-potential gases (F-gases). All are expressed in terms of CO$_2$ equivalent (CO$_2$e)—the quantity of CO$_2$ that would cause the same amount of warming. In 2005 emissions from land-use change in high income countries were negligible.

forest management, to cleaner energy (such as geothermal or hydro power), and to the creation of sustainable urban transport systems. So the mitigation agenda in Africa is likely to be compatible with furthering development.[6] This is also the case for Latin America.[7]

Nor do greater wealth and prosperity inherently produce more greenhouse gases, even if they have gone hand in hand in the past. Particular patterns of consumption and production do. Even excluding oil producers, per capita emissions in high-income countries vary by a factor of four, from 7 tons of carbon dioxide equivalent (CO$_2$e)[8] per capita in Switzerland to 27 in Australia and Luxembourg.[9]

And dependence on fossil fuel can hardly be considered unavoidable given the inadequacy of the efforts to find alternatives. While global subsidies to petroleum products amount to some $150 billion annually, public spending on energy research, development, and deployment (RD&D) has hovered around $10 billion for decades, apart from a brief spike following the oil crisis (see chapter 7). That represents 4 percent of overall public RD&D. Private spending on energy RD&D, at $40 billion to $60 billion a year, amounts to 0.5 percent of private revenues—a fraction of what innovative industries such as telecom-

munications (8 percent) or pharmaceuticals (15 percent) invest in RD&D.[10]

A switch to a low-carbon world through technological innovation and complementary institutional reforms has to start with immediate and aggressive action by high-income countries to shrink their unsustainable carbon footprints. That would free some space in the atmospheric commons (figure 2). More important, a credible commitment by high-income countries to drastically reduce their emissions would stimulate the needed RD&D of new technologies and processes in energy, transport, industry, and agriculture. And large and predictable demand for alternative technologies will reduce their price and help make them competitive with fossil fuels. Only with new technologies at competitive prices can climate change be curtailed without sacrificing growth.

There is scope for developing countries to shift to lower-carbon trajectories without compromising development, but this varies across countries and will depend on the extent of financial and technical assistance from high-income countries. Such assistance would be equitable (and in line with the 1992 United Nations Framework Convention on Climate Change, or UNFCCC): high-income countries, with one-sixth of the world's population, are responsible for nearly two-thirds of the greenhouse gases in the atmosphere (figure 3). It would also be efficient: the savings from helping to finance early mitigation in developing countries—for example, through infrastructure and housing construction over the next decades—are so large that they produce clear economic benefits for all.[11] But designing, let alone implementing, an international agreement that involves substantial, stable, and predictable resource transfers is no trivial matter.

Developing countries, particularly the poorest and most exposed, will also need assistance in adapting to the changing climate. They already suffer the most from extreme weather events (see chapter 2). And even relatively modest additional warming will require big adjustments to the way development policy is designed and implemented, to the way people live and make a living, and to the dangers and the opportunities they face.

The current financial crisis cannot be an excuse to put climate on the back burner. On average, a financial crisis lasts less than two years and results in a 3 percent loss in gross domestic product (GDP) that is later offset by more than 20 percent growth over eight years of recovery and prosperity.[12] So for all the harm they cause, financial crises come and go. Not so with the growing threat imposed by a changing climate. Why?

Because time is not on our side. The impacts of greenhouse gases released into the atmosphere will be felt for decades, even millennia,[13] making the return to a "safe" level very difficult. This inertia in the climate system severely limits the possibility of making up for modest efforts today with accelerated mitigation in the future.[14] Delays also increase the costs because impacts worsen and cheap mitigation options disappear as economies become locked into high-carbon infrastructure and lifestyles—more inertia.

Immediate action is needed to keep warming as close as possible to 2°C. That amount of warming is not desirable, but it is likely to be the best we can do. There isn't a consensus in the economic profession that this is the economic optimum. There is, however, a growing consensus in policy and scientific circles that aiming for 2°C warming is the responsible thing to do.[15] This Report endorses such a position. From the perspective of development, warming much above 2°C is simply unacceptable. But stabilizing at 2°C will require major shifts in lifestyle, a veritable energy revolution, and a transformation in how we manage land and forests. And substantial adaptation would still be needed. Coping with climate change will require all the innovation and ingenuity that the human race is capable of.

Inertia, equity, and ingenuity are three themes that permeate this Report. Inertia is the defining characteristic of the climate challenge—the reason we need to act now. Equity is the key to an effective global deal, to the trust needed to find an efficient resolution to this tragedy of the commons—the reason we need to act together. And ingenuity is the only possible answer to a problem that

Figure 2   Rebalancing act: Switching from SUVs to fuel-efficient passenger cars in the U.S. alone would nearly offset the emissions generated in providing electricity to 1.6 billion more people

Emissions (million tons of CO_2)

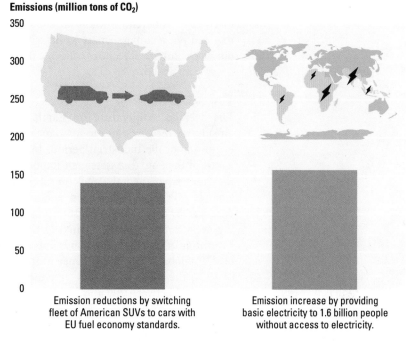

Emission reductions by switching fleet of American SUVs to cars with EU fuel economy standards.

Emission increase by providing basic electricity to 1.6 billion people without access to electricity.

Source: WDR team calculations based on BTS 2008.

Note: Estimates are based on 40 million SUVs (sports utility vehicles) in the United States traveling a total of 480 billion miles (assuming 12,000 miles a car) a year. With average fuel efficiency of 18 miles a gallon, the SUV fleet consumes 27 billion gallons of gasoline annually with emissions of 2,421 grams of carbon a gallon. Switching to fuel-efficient cars with the average fuel efficiency of new passenger cars sold in the European Union (45 miles a gallon; see ICCT 2007) results in a reduction of 142 million tons of CO_2 (39 million tons of carbon) annually. Electricity consumption of poor households in developing countries is estimated at 170 kilowatt-hours a person-year and electricity is assumed to be provided at the current world average carbon intensity of 160 grams of carbon a kilowatt-hour, equivalent to 160 million tons of CO_2 (44 million tons of carbon). The size of the electricity symbol in the global map corresponds to the number of people without access to electricity.

Figure 3   High-income countries have historically contributed a disproportionate share of global emissions and still do

Share of global emissions, historic and 2005

Cumulative CO_2 emissions since 1850: Energy

2%
34%
64%

CO_2 emissions in 2005: Energy

3%
47%
50%

Greenhouse gas emissions in 2005: All sectors, including land-use change

6%
38%
56%

- Low-income countries (1.2 billion people)
- High-income countries (1 billion people)
- Middle-income countries (4.2 billion people)
- ▨ Overuse relative to population share

Sources: DOE 2009; World Bank 2008c; WRI 2008 augmented with land-use change emissions from Houghton 2009.

Note: The data cover over 200 countries for more recent years. Data are not available for all countries in the 19th century, but all major emitters of the era are included. Carbon dioxide (CO_2) emissions from energy include all fossil-fuel burning, gas flaring, and cement production. Greenhouse gas emissions include CO_2, methane (CH_4), nitrous oxide (N_2O), and high-global-warming-potential gases (F-gases). Sectors include energy and industrial processes, agriculture, land-use change (from Houghton 2009), and waste. Overuse of the atmospheric commons relative to population share is based on deviations from equal per capita emissions; in 2005 high-income countries constituted 16 percent of global population; since 1850, on average, today's high-income countries constituted about 20 percent of global population.

is politically and scientifically complex—the quality that could enable us to act differently than we have in the past. Act now, act together, act differently—those are the steps that can put a climate-smart world within our reach. But first it requires believing there is a case for action.

The case for action

The average temperature on Earth has already warmed by close to 1°C since the beginning of the industrial period. In the words of the Fourth Assessment Report of the Intergovernmental Panel on Climate Change (IPCC), a consensus document produced by over 2,000 scientists representing every country in the United Nations: "Warming of the climate system is unequivocal."[16] Global atmospheric concentrations of CO_2, the most important greenhouse gas, ranged between 200 and 300 parts per million (ppm) for 800,000 years, but shot up to about 387 ppm over the past 150 years (figure 4), mainly because of the burning of fossil fuels and, to a lesser extent, agriculture and changing land use. A decade after the Kyoto Protocol set limits on international carbon emissions, as developed countries enter the first period of rigorous accounting of their emissions, greenhouse gases in the atmosphere are still increasing. Worse, they are increasing at an accelerating rate.[17]

The effects of climate change are already visible in higher average air and ocean temperatures, widespread melting of snow and ice, and rising sea levels. Cold days, cold nights, and frosts have become less frequent while heat waves are more common. Globally, precipitation has increased even as Australia, Central Asia, the Mediterranean basin, the Sahel, the western United States, and many other regions have seen more frequent and more intense droughts. Heavy rainfall and floods have become more common, and the damage from—and probably the intensity of—storms and tropical cyclones have increased.

Climate change threatens all, but particularly developing countries

The more than 5°C warming that unmitigated climate change could cause this century[18] amounts to the difference between today's climate and the last ice age, when glaciers reached central Europe and the northern United States. That change occurred over millennia; human-induced climate change is occurring on a one-century time scale giving societies and ecosystems little time to adapt to the rapid pace. Such a drastic temperature shift would cause large dislocations in ecosystems fundamental to human societies and economies—such as the possible dieback of the Amazon rain forest, complete loss of glaciers in the Andes and the Himalayas, and rapid ocean acidification leading to disruption of marine ecosystems and death of coral reefs. The speed and magnitude of change could condemn more than 50 percent of species to extinction. Sea levels could rise by one meter this century,[19] threatening more than 60 million people and $200 billion in assets in developing countries alone.[20] Agricultural

Figure 4   Off the charts with CO_2

Carbon dioxide concentration (ppm)

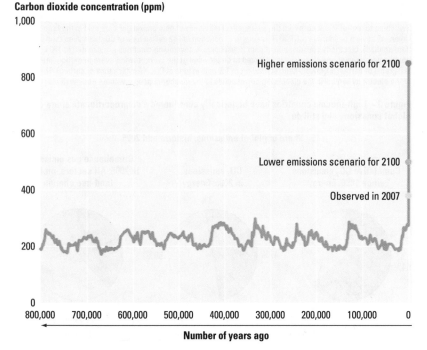

Number of years ago

Source: Lüthi and others 2008.

Note: Analysis of air bubbles trapped in an Antarctic ice core extending back 800,000 years documents the Earth's changing CO_2 concentration. Over this long period, natural factors have caused the atmospheric CO_2 concentration to vary within a range of about 170 to 300 parts per million (ppm). Temperature-related data make clear that these variations have played a central role in determining the global climate. As a result of human activities, the present CO_2 concentration of about 387 ppm is about 30 percent above its highest level over at least the last 800,000 years. In the absence of strong control measures, emissions projected for this century would result in a CO_2 concentration roughly two to three times the highest level experienced in the past 800,000 or more years, as depicted in the two projected emissions scenarios for 2100.

productivity would likely decline throughout the world, particularly in the tropics, even with changes in farming practices. And over 3 million additional people could die from malnutrition each year.[21]

Even 2°C warming above preindustrial temperatures would result in new weather patterns with global consequences. Increased weather variability, more frequent and intense extreme events, and greater exposure to coastal storm surges would lead to a much higher risk of catastrophic and irreversible impacts. Between 100 million and 400 million more people could be at risk of hunger.[22] And 1 billion to 2 billion more people may no longer have enough water to meet their needs.[23]

Developing countries are more exposed and less resilient to climate hazards. These consequences will fall disproportionately on developing countries. Warming of 2°C could result in a 4 to 5 percent permanent reduction in annual income per capita in Africa and South Asia,[24] as opposed to minimal losses in high-income countries and a global average GDP loss of about 1 percent.[25] These losses would be driven by impacts in agriculture, a sector important to the economies of both Africa and South Asia (map 1).

It is estimated that developing countries will bear most of the costs of the damages—some 75–80 percent.[26] Several factors explain this (box 1). Developing countries are particularly reliant on ecosystem services and natural capital for production in climate-sensitive sectors. Much of their population lives in physically exposed locations and economically precarious conditions. And their financial and institutional capacity to adapt is limited. Already

Map 1   Climate change will depress agricultural yields in most countries in 2050, given current agricultural practices and crop varieties

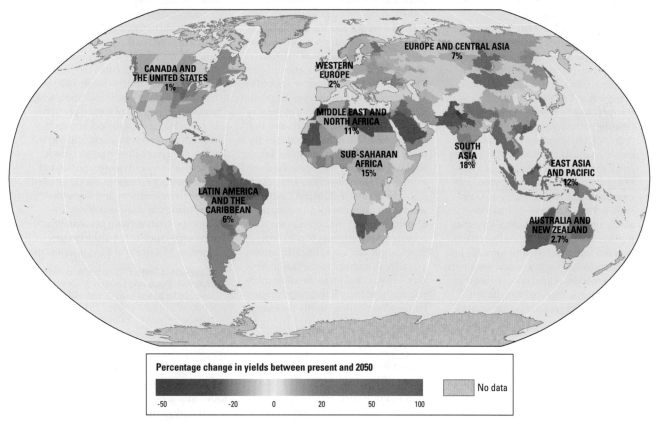

Sources: Müller and others 2009; World Bank 2008c.

Note: The coloring in the figure shows the projected percentage change in yields of 11 major crops (wheat, rice, maize, millet, field pea, sugar beet, sweet potato, soybean, groundnut, sunflower, and rapeseed) from 2046 to 2055, compared with 1996–2005. The yield-change values are the mean of three emission scenarios across five global climate models, assuming no CO$_2$ fertilization (a possible boost to plant growth and water-use efficiency from higher ambient CO$_2$ concentrations). The numbers indicate the share of GDP derived from agriculture in each region. (The share for Sub-Saharan Africa is 23 percent if South Africa is excluded.) Large negative yield impacts are projected in many areas that are highly dependent on agriculture.

BOX 1   *All developing regions are vulnerable to the impacts of climate change—for different reasons*

The problems common to developing countries—limited human and financial resources, weak institutions—drive their vulnerability. But other factors, attributable to their geography and history, are also significant.

Sub-Saharan Africa suffers from natural fragility (two-thirds of its surface area is desert or dry land) and high exposure to droughts and floods, which are forecast to increase with further climate change. The region's economies are highly dependent on natural resources. Biomass provides 80 percent of the domestic primary energy supply. Rainfed agriculture contributes some 23 percent of GDP (excluding South Africa) and employs about 70 percent of the population. Inadequate infrastructure could hamper adaptation efforts, with limited water storage despite abundant resources. Malaria, already the biggest killer in the region, is spreading to higher, previously safe, altitudes.

In **East Asia and the Pacific** one major driver of vulnerability is the large number of people living along the coast and on low-lying islands—over 130 million people in China, and roughly 40 million, or more than half the entire population, in Vietnam. A second driver is the continued reliance, particularly among the poorer countries, on agriculture for income and employment. As pressures on land, water, and forest resources increase—as a result of population growth, urbanization, and environmental degradation caused by rapid industrialization—greater variability and extremes will complicate their management. In the Mekong River basin, the rainy season will see more intense precipitation, while the dry season lengthens by two months. A third driver is that the region's economies are highly dependent on marine resources—the value of

well-managed coral reefs is $13 billion in Southeast Asia alone—which are already stressed by industrial pollution, coastal development, overfishing, and runoff of agricultural pesticides and nutrients.

Vulnerability to climate change in **Eastern Europe and Central Asia** is driven by a lingering Soviet legacy of environmental mismanagement and the poor state of much of the region's infrastructure. An example: rising temperatures and reduced precipitation in Central Asia will exacerbate the environmental catastrophe of the disappearing Southern Aral Sea (caused by the diversion of water to grow cotton in a desert climate) while sand and salt from the dried-up seabed are blowing onto Central Asia's glaciers, accelerating the melting caused by higher temperature. Poorly constructed, badly maintained, and aging infrastructure and housing—a legacy of both the Soviet era and the transition years—are ill suited to withstand storms, heat waves, or floods.

Latin America and the Caribbean's most critical ecosystems are under threat. First, the tropical glaciers of the Andes are expected to disappear, changing the timing and intensity of water available to several countries, resulting in water stress for at least 77 million people as early as 2020 and threatening hydropower, the source of more than half the electricity in many South American countries. Second, warming and acidifying oceans will result in more frequent bleaching and possible diebacks of coral reefs in the Caribbean, which host nurseries for an estimated 65 percent of all fish species in the basin, provide a natural protection against storm surge, and are a critical tourism asset. Third, damage to the Gulf of Mexico's wetlands will make the coast more vulnerable to more intense and more frequent hurricanes. Fourth, the most

disastrous impact could be a dramatic dieback of the Amazon rain forest and a conversion of large areas to savannah, with severe consequences for the region's climate—and possibly the world's.

Water is the major vulnerability in the **Middle East and North Africa**, the world's driest region, where per capita water availability is predicted to halve by 2050 even without the effects of climate change. The region has few attractive options for increasing water storage, since close to 90 percent of its freshwater resources are already stored in reservoirs. The increased water scarcity combined with greater variability will threaten agriculture, which accounts for some 85 percent of the region's water use. Vulnerability is compounded by a heavy concentration of population and economic activity in flood-prone coastal zones and by social and political tensions that resource scarcity could heighten.

South Asia suffers from an already stressed and largely degraded natural resource base resulting from geography coupled with high levels of poverty and population density. Water resources are likely to be affected by climate change through its effect on the monsoon, which provides 70 percent of annual precipitation in a four-month period, and on the melting of Himalayan glaciers. Rising sea levels are a dire concern in the region, which has long and densely populated coastlines, agricultural plains threatened by saltwater intrusion, and many low-lying islands. In more severe climate-change scenarios, rising seas would submerge much of the Maldives and inundate 18 percent of Bangladesh's land.

Sources: de la Torre, Fajnzylber, and Nash 2008; Fay, Block, and Ebinger 2010; World Bank 2007a; World Bank 2007c; World Bank 2008b; World Bank 2009b.

policy makers in some developing countries note that more of their development budget is diverted to cope with weather-related emergencies.[27]

High-income countries will also be affected even by moderate warming. Indeed, damages per capita are likely to be higher in wealthier countries since they

account for 16 percent of world population but would bear 20–25 percent of the global impact costs. But their much greater wealth makes them better able to cope with such impacts. Climate change will wreak havoc everywhere—but it will increase the gulf between developed and developing countries.

Growth is necessary for greater resilience, but is not sufficient. Economic growth is necessary to reduce poverty and is at the heart of increasing resilience to climate change in poor countries. But growth alone is not the answer to a changing climate. Growth is unlikely to be fast enough to help the poorer countries, and it can increase vulnerability to climate hazards (box 2). Nor is growth usually equitable enough to ensure protection for the poorest and most vulnerable. It does not guarantee that key institutions will function well. And if it is carbon intensive, it will cause further warming.

But there is no reason to think that a low-carbon path must necessarily slow economic growth: many environmental regulations were preceded by warnings of massive job losses and industry collapse, few of which materialized.[28] Clearly, however, the transition costs are substantial, notably in developing low-carbon technologies and infrastructure for energy, transport, housing, urbanization, and rural development. Two arguments often heard are that these transition costs are unacceptable given the urgent need for other more immediate investments in poor countries, and that care should be taken not to sacrifice the welfare of poor individuals today for the sake of future, possibly richer, generations. There is validity to these concerns. But the point remains that a strong economic argument can be made for ambitious action on climate change.

The economics of climate change: Reducing climate risk is affordable

Climate change is costly, whatever the policy chosen. Spending less on mitigation will mean spending more on adaptation and accepting greater damages: the cost of action must be compared with the cost of inaction. But, as discussed in chapter 1, the comparison is complex because of the considerable uncertainty about the technologies that will be available in the future (and their cost), the ability of societies and ecosystems to adapt (and at what price), the extent of damages that higher greenhouse gas concentrations will cause, and the temperatures that might constitute

---

BOX 2 *Economic growth: Necessary, but not sufficient*

Richer countries have more resources to cope with climate impacts, and better educated and healthier populations are inherently more resilient. But the process of growth may exacerbate vulnerability to climate change, as in the ever-increasing extraction of water for farming, industry, and consumption in the drought-prone provinces around Beijing, and as in Indonesia, Madagascar, Thailand, and U.S. Gulf Coast, where protective mangroves have been cleared for tourism and shrimp farms.

Growth is not likely to be fast enough for low-income countries to afford the kind of protection that the rich can afford. Bangladesh and the Netherlands are among the countries most exposed to rising sea levels. Bangladesh is already doing a lot to reduce the vulnerability of its population, with a highly effective community-based early warning system for cyclones and a flood forecasting and response program drawing on local and international expertise. But the scope of possible adaptation is limited by resources—its annual per capita income is $450. Meanwhile, the Netherlands government is planning investments amounting to $100 for every Dutch citizen every year for the next century. And even the Netherlands, with a per capita income 100 times that of Bangladesh, has begun a program of selective relocation away from low-lying areas because continuing protection everywhere is unaffordable.

Sources: Barbier and Sathirathai 2004; Deltacommissie 2008; FAO 2007; Government of Bangladesh 2008; Guan and Hubacek 2008; Karim and Mimura 2008; Shalizi 2006; and Xia and others 2007.

---

thresholds or tipping points beyond which catastrophic impacts occur (see Science focus). The comparison is also complicated by distributional issues across time (mitigation incurred by one generation produces benefits for many generations to come) and space (some areas are more vulnerable than others, hence more likely to support aggressive global mitigation efforts). And it is further complicated by the question of how to value the loss of life, livelihoods, and nonmarket services such as biodiversity and ecosystem services.

Economists have typically tried to identify the optimal climate policy using cost-benefit analysis. But as box 3 illustrates, the results are sensitive to the particular assumptions about the remaining uncertainties, and to the normative choices made regarding distributional and measurement issues. (A technology optimist, who expects the impact of climate change to be relatively modest and occurring gradually over time, and who heavily discounts what happens in the future, will favor modest action now. And vice versa for a technology pessimist.) So economists continue to disagree on the economically or socially optimal carbon trajectory. But there are some emerging agreements. In the major models, the benefits of stabilization exceed the costs at 2.5°C warming (though not necessarily at 2°C).[29] And all conclude that business as usual (meaning no mitigation efforts whatsoever) would be disastrous.

Advocates of a more gradual reduction in emissions conclude that the optimal target—the one that will produce the lowest total cost (meaning the sum of impact and mitigation costs)—could be well above

3°C.[30] But they do note that the incremental cost of keeping warming around 2°C would be modest, less than half a percent of GDP (see box 3). In other words, the total costs of the 2°C option is not much more than the total cost of the much less ambitious economic optimum. Why? Partly because the savings from less mitigation are largely offset by the additional costs of more severe impacts or higher adaptation spending.[31] And partly because the real difference between ambitious and modest

---

BOX 3 *The cost of "climate insurance"*

Hof, den Elzen, and van Vuuren examine the sensitivity of the optimal climate target to assumptions about the time horizon, climate sensitivity (the amount of warming associated with a doubling of carbon dioxide concentrations from preindustrial levels), mitigation costs, likely damages, and discount rates. To do so, they run their integrated assessment model (FAIR), varying the model's settings along the range of assumptions found in the literature, notably those associated with two well-known economists: Nicholas Stern, who advocates early and ambitious action; and William Nordhaus, who supports a gradual approach to climate mitigation.

Not surprisingly, their model results in completely different optimal targets depending on which assumptions are used. (The optimal target is defined as the concentration that would result in the lowest reduction in the present value of global consumption.) The "Stern assumptions" (which include relatively high climate sensitivity and climate damages, and a long time horizon combined with low discount rates and mitigation costs) produce an optimum peak CO₂e concentration of 540 parts per million (ppm). The "Nordhaus assumptions" (which assume lower climate sensitivity and damages, a shorter time horizon, and a higher discount rate) produce an optimum of 750 ppm. In both cases, adaptation costs are included implicitly in the climate damage function.

The figure plots the least cost of stabilizing atmospheric concentrations in the range of 500 to 800 ppm for the Stern and Nordhaus assumptions (reported as the difference between the modeled present

value of consumption and the present value of consumption that the world would enjoy with no climate change). A key point evident in the figure is the relative flatness of the consumption loss curves over wide ranges of peak CO₂e concentrations. As a consequence, moving from 750 ppm to 550 ppm results in a relatively small loss in consumption (0.3 percent) with the Nordhaus assumptions. The results therefore suggest that the cost of precautionary mitigation to 550 ppm is small. With the Stern assumptions, a 550 ppm target results in a *gain* in present value of consumption of about 0.5 percent relative to the 750 ppm target.

A strong motivation for choosing a lower peak concentration target is to reduce the risk of catastrophic outcomes linked to global warming. From this perspective, the cost of moving from a high target for peak CO₂e concentrations to a lower target can be viewed as the cost of climate insurance—the amount of welfare the world would sacrifice to reduce the risk of catastrophe. The analysis of Hof, den Elzen, and van Vuuren suggests that the cost of climate insurance is modest under a very wide range of assumptions about the climate system and the cost of mitigating climate change.

Source: Hof, den Elzen, and van Vuuren 2008.

Looking at tradeoffs: The loss in consumption relative to a world without warming for different peak CO₂e concentrations

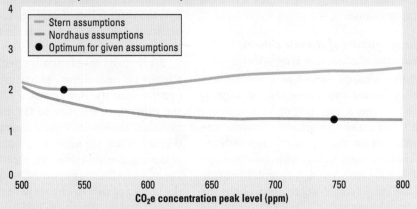

Reduction in net present value of consumption (%)

— Stern assumptions
— Nordhaus assumptions
● Optimum for given assumptions

CO₂e concentration peak level (ppm)

Source: Adapted from Hof, den Elzen, and van Vuuren 2008, figure 10.

Note: The curves show the percentage loss in the present value of consumption, relative to what it would be with a constant climate, as a function of the target for peak CO₂e concentrations. The "Stern assumptions" and "Nordhaus assumptions" refer to choices about the value of key parameters of the model as explained in the text. The dot shows the optimum for each set of assumptions, where the optimum is defined as the greenhouse gas concentration that would minimize the global consumption loss resulting from the sum of mitigation costs and impact damages.

climate action lies with costs that occur in the future, which gradualists heavily discount.

The large uncertainties about the potential losses associated with climate change and the possibility of catastrophic risks may well justify earlier and more aggressive action than a simple cost-benefit analysis would suggest. This incremental amount could be thought of as the insurance premium to keep climate change within what scientists consider a safer band.[32] Spending less than half a percent of GDP as "climate insurance" could well be a socially acceptable proposition: the world spends 3 percent of global GDP on insurance today.[33]

But beyond the question of "climate insurance" is the question of what might be the resulting mitigation costs—and the associated financing needs. In the medium term, estimates of mitigation costs in developing countries range between $140 billion and $175 billion annually by 2030. This represents the incremental costs relative to a business-as-usual scenario (table 1).

Financing needs would be higher, however, as many of the savings from the lower operating costs associated with renewable energy and energy efficiency gains only materialize over time. McKinsey, for example, estimates that while the incremental cost in 2030 would be $175 billion, the upfront investments required would amount to $563 billion over and above business-as-usual investment needs. McKinsey does point out that this amounts to a roughly 3 percent increase in global business-as-usual investments, and as such is likely to be within the capacity of global financial markets.[34] However, financing has historically been a constraint in developing countries, resulting in underinvestment in infrastructure as well as a bias toward energy choices with lower upfront capital costs, even when such choices eventually result in higher overall costs. The search for suitable financing mechanisms must therefore be a priority.

What about the longer term? Mitigation costs will increase over time to cope with growing population and energy needs—but so will income. As a result, the present value of global mitigation costs to 2100 is expected to remain well below 1 percent of global GDP, with estimates ranging

between 0.3 percent and 0.7 percent (table 2). Developing countries' mitigation costs would represent a higher share of their own GDP, however, ranging between 0.5 and 1.2 percent.

There are far fewer estimates of needed adaptation investments, and those that exist are not readily comparable. Some look only at the cost of climate-proofing foreign aid projects. Others include only certain sectors. Very few try to look at overall country needs (see chapter 6). A recent World Bank study that attempts to tackle these issues suggests that the investments needed could be between $75 billion and $100 billion annually in developing countries alone.[35]

Table 1 **Incremental mitigation costs and associated financing requirements for a 2°C trajectory: What will be needed in developing countries by 2030?**
Constant 2005$

Model	Mitigation cost	Financing requirement
IEA ETP		565
McKinsey	175	563
MESSAGE		264
MiniCAM	139	
REMIND		384

Sources: IEA ETP: IEA 2008c; McKinsey: McKinsey & Company 2009 and additional data provided by McKinsey (J. Dinkel) for 2030, using a dollar-to-euro exchange rate of $1.25 to €1; MESSAGE: IIASA 2009 and additional data provided by V. Krey; MiniCAM: Edmonds and others 2008 and additional data provided by J. Edmonds and L. Clarke; REMIND: Knopf and others, forthcoming and additional data provided by B. Knopf.

Note: Both mitigation costs and associated financing requirements are incremental relative to a business-as-usual baseline. Estimates are for the stabilization of greenhouse gases at 450 ppm CO_2e, which would provide a 40–50 percent chance of staying below 2°C warming by 2100 (Schaeffer and others 2008; Hare and Meinshausen 2006). IEA ETP is the model developed by the International Energy Agency, and McKinsey is the proprietary methodology developed by McKinsey & Company; MESSAGE, MiniCAM, and REMIND are the peer-reviewed models of the International Institute for Applied Systems Analysis, the Pacific Northwest Laboratory, and the Potsdam Institute for Climate Impact Research, respectively. McKinsey includes all sectors; other models only include mitigation efforts in the energy sector. MiniCAM reports $168 billion in mitigation costs in 2035, in constant 2000 dollars; this figure has been interpolated to 2030 and converted to 2005 dollars.

Table 2 **In the long term, what will it cost? Present value of mitigation costs to 2100**

Models	Present value of mitigation costs to 2100 for 450 ppm CO_2e (% of GDP)	
	World	Developing countries
DICE	0.7	
FAIR	0.6	
MESSAGE	0.3	0.5
MiniCAM	0.7	1.2
PAGE	0.4	0.9
REMIND	0.4	

Sources: DICE: Nordhaus 2008 (estimated from table 5.3 and figure 5.3); FAIR: Hof, den Elzen, and van Vuuren 2008; MESSAGE: IIASA 2009; MiniCAM: Edmonds and others 2008 and personal communications; PAGE: Hope 2009 and personal communications; REMIND: Knopf and others, forthcoming.

Note: DICE, FAIR, MESSAGE, MiniCAM, PAGE, and REMIND are peer-reviewed models. Estimates are for the stabilization of greenhouse gases at 450 ppm CO_2e, which would provide a 40–50 percent chance of staying below 2°C warming by 2100 (Schaeffer and others 2008; Hare and Meinshausen 2006). The FAIR model result reports abatement costs using the low settings (see table 3 in Hof, den Elzen, and van Vuuren 2008).

A climate-smart world is within reach if we act now, act together, and act differently

Even if the incremental cost of reducing climate risk is modest and the investment needs far from prohibitive, stabilizing warming around 2°C above preindustrial temperatures is extremely ambitious. By 2050 emissions would need to be 50 percent below 1990 levels and be zero or negative by 2100 (figure 5). This would require immediate and Herculean efforts: within the next 20 years global emissions would have to fall, compared to a business-as-usual path, by an amount equivalent to total emissions from high-income countries today. In addition, even 2°C warming would also require costly adaptation—changing the kinds of risks people prepare for; where they live; what they eat; and the way they design, develop, and manage agroecological and urban systems.[36]

So both the mitigation and the adaptation challenges are substantial. But the hypothesis of this Report is that they can be tackled through climate-smart policies that entail acting now, acting together (or globally), and acting differently. Acting now, because of the tremendous inertia in both climate and socioeconomic systems. Acting together, to keep costs down and protect the most vulnerable. And acting differently, because a climate-smart world requires a transformation of our energy, food production, and risk management systems.

Act now: Inertia means that today's actions will determine tomorrow's options

The climate system exhibits substantial inertia (figure 6). Concentrations lag emission reductions: CO_2 remains in the atmosphere for decades to centuries, so a decline in emissions takes time to affect concentrations. Temperatures lag concentrations: temperatures will continue increasing for a few centuries after concentrations have stabilized. And sea levels lag temperature reductions: the thermal expansion of the ocean from an increase in temperature will last 1,000 years or more while the sea-level rise from melting ice could last several millennia.[37]

The dynamics of the climate system therefore limit how much future mitigation can be substituted for efforts today. For example, stabilizing the climate near 2°C (around 450 ppm of CO_2e) would require global emissions to begin declining immediately by about 1.5 percent a year. A five-year delay would have to be offset by faster emission declines. And even longer delays simply could not be offset: a ten-year delay in mitigation would most likely make it impossible to keep warming from exceeding 2°C.[38]

Inertia is also present in the built environment, limiting flexibility in reducing greenhouse gases or designing adaptation responses. Infrastructure investments are lumpy, concentrated in time rather than evenly distributed.[39] They are also long-lived: 15–40 years for factories and power plants, 40–75 years for road, rail, and power distribution networks. Decisions on land use and urban form—the structure and density of cities—have impacts lasting more than a century. And long-lived infrastructure triggers investments in associated capital (cars

Figure 5   What does the way forward look like? Two options among many: Business as usual or aggressive mitigation

Projected annual total global emissions (GtCO₂e)

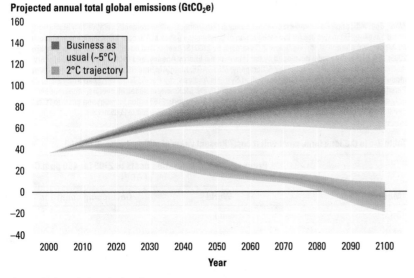

Source: Clarke and others, forthcoming.

Note: The top band shows the range of estimates across models (GTEM, IMAGE, MESSAGE, MiniCAM) for emissions under a business-as-usual scenario. The lower band shows a trajectory that could yield a concentration of 450 ppm of CO_2e (with a 50 percent chance of limiting warming to less than 2°C). Greenhouse gas emissions include CO_2, CH_4, and N_2O. Negative emissions (eventually required by the 2°C path) imply that the annual rate of emissions is lower than the rate of uptake and storage of carbon through natural processes (for example, plant growth) and engineered processes (for example, growing biofuels and when burning them, sequestering the CO_2 underground). GTEM, IMAGE, MESSAGE, and MiniCAM are the integrated assessment models of the Australian Bureau of Agricultural and Resource Economics, the Netherlands Environmental Assessment Agency, International Institute of Applied Systems Analysis, and Pacific Northwest National Laboratory.

for low-density cities; gas-fired heat and power generation capacity in response to gas pipelines), locking economies into lifestyles and energy consumption patterns.

The inertia in physical capital is nowhere close to that in the climate system and is more likely to affect the cost rather than the feasibility of achieving a particular emission goal—but it is substantial. The opportunities to shift from high-carbon to low-carbon capital stocks are not evenly distributed in time.[40] China is expected to double its building stock between 2000 and 2015. And the coal-fired power plants proposed around the world over the next 25 years are so numerous that their lifetime CO_2 emissions would equal those of all coal-burning activities since the beginning of the industrial era.[41] Only those facilities located close enough to the storage sites could be retrofitted for carbon capture and storage (if and when that technology becomes commercially available: see chapters 4 and 7). Retiring these plants before the end of their useful life—if changes in the climate force such action—would be extremely costly.

Inertia is also a factor in research and development (R&D) and in the deployment of new technologies. New energy sources have historically taken about 50 years to reach half their potential.[42] Substantial investments in R&D are needed now to ensure that new technologies are available and rapidly penetrating the marketplace in the near future. This could require an additional $100 billion to $700 billion annually.[43] Innovation is also needed in transport, building, water management, urban design, and many other sectors that affect climate change and are in turn affected by climate change—so innovation is a critical issue for adaptation as well.

Inertia is also present in the behavior of individuals and organizations. Despite greater public concern, behaviors have not changed much. Available energy-efficient technologies that are effective and pay for themselves are not adopted. R&D in renewables is underfunded. Farmers face incentives to over-irrigate their crops, which in turn affects energy use, because energy is a major input in water provision and treatment. Building continues in hazard-prone

areas, and infrastructure continues to be designed for the climate of the past.[44] Changing behaviors and organizational goals and standards is difficult and usually slow, but it has been done before (see chapter 8).

Act together: For equity and efficiency

Collective action is needed to effectively tackle climate change and reduce the costs of mitigation.[45] It is also essential to

Figure 6 Climate impacts are long-lived: Rising temperatures and sea levels associated with higher concentrations of CO_2

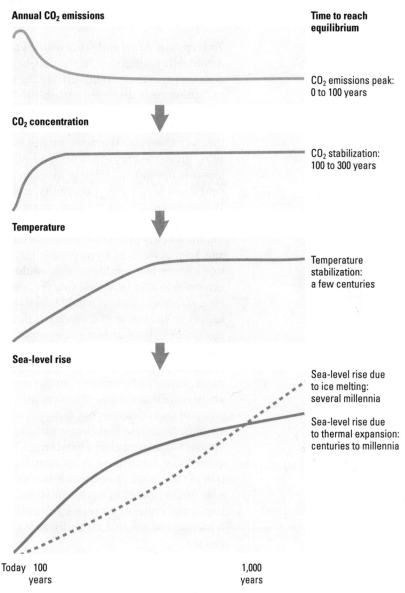

Source: WDR team based on IPCC 2001.
Note: Stylized figures; the magnitudes in each panel are intended for illustrative purposes.

facilitate adaptation, notably through better risk management and safety nets to protect the most vulnerable.

To keep costs down and fairly distributed. Affordability hinges on mitigation being done cost effectively. When estimating the mitigation costs discussed earlier, modelers assume that greenhouse gas emission reductions occur wherever and whenever they are cheapest. *Wherever* means pursuing greater energy efficiency and other low-cost options to mitigate in whatever country or sector the opportunity arises. *Whenever* entails timing investments in new equipment, infrastructure, or farming and forestry projects to minimize costs and keep economies from getting locked into high-carbon conditions that would be expensive to alter later. Relaxing the wherever, whenever rule—as would necessarily happen in the real world, especially in the absence of a global carbon price—dramatically increases the cost of mitigation.

The implication is that there are enormous gains to global efforts—on this point, analysts are unanimous. If any country or group of countries does not mitigate, others must reach into higher-cost mitigation options to achieve a given global target. For example, by one estimate, the nonparticipation of the United States, which is responsible for 20 percent of world emissions, in the Kyoto Protocol increases the cost of achieving the original target by about 60 percent.[46]

Both equity and efficiency argue for developing financial instruments that separate who finances mitigation from where it happens. Otherwise, the substantial mitigation potential in developing countries (65–70 percent of emission reductions, adding up to 45–70 percent of global mitigation investments in 2030)[47] will not be fully tapped, substantially increasing the cost of achieving a given target. Taking it to the extreme, a lack of financing that results in fully postponing mitigation in developing countries to 2020 could more than double the cost of stabilizing around 2°C.[48] With mitigation costs estimated to add up to $4 trillion to $25 trillion[49] over the next century, the losses implied by such

delays are so large that there are clear economic benefits for high-income countries committed to limiting dangerous climate change to finance early action in developing countries.[50] More generally, the total cost of mitigation could be greatly reduced through well-performing carbon-finance mechanisms, financial transfers, and price signals that help approximate the outcome produced by the whenever, wherever assumption.

To manage risk better and protect the poorest. In many places previously uncommon risks are becoming more widespread. Consider floods, once rare but now increasingly common, in Africa and the first hurricane ever recorded in the South Atlantic, which hit Brazil in 2004.[51] Reducing disaster risk—through community-based early warning systems, climate monitoring, safer infrastructure, and strengthened and enforced zoning and building codes, along with other measures—becomes more important in a changing climate. Financial and institutional innovations can also limit risks to health and livelihoods. This requires domestic action—but domestic action will be greatly enhanced if it is supported by international finance and sharing of best-practice.

But as discussed in chapter 2, actively reducing risk will never be enough because there will always be a residual risk that must also be managed through better preparedness and response mechanisms. The implication is that development may need to be done differently, with much greater emphasis on climate and weather risk. International cooperation can help, for example, through pooling efforts to improve the production of climate information and its broad availability (see chapter 7) and through sharing best practices to cope with the changing and more variable climate.[52]

Insurance is another instrument to manage the residual risk, but it has its limitations. Climate risk is increasing along a trend and tends to affect entire regions or large groups of people simultaneously, making it difficult to insure. And even with insurance, losses associated with catastrophic events (such as widespread flooding or severe droughts) cannot be fully absorbed by individuals, communities, and the private sector. In a more volatile climate, governments will increasingly become insurers of last resort and have an implicit responsibility to support disaster recovery and reconstruction. This requires that governments protect their own liquidity in times of crisis, particularly poorer or smaller countries that are financially vulnerable to the impacts of climate change: Hurricane Ivan caused damages equivalent to 200 percent of Grenada's GDP.[53] Having immediate funds available to jump-start the rehabilitation and recovery process reduces the derailing effect of disasters on development.

Multicountry facilities and reinsurance can help. The Caribbean Catastrophe Risk Insurance Facility spreads risk among 16 Caribbean countries, harnessing the reinsurance market to provide liquidity to governments quickly following destructive hurricanes and earthquakes.[54] Such facilities may need help from the international community. More generally, high-income countries have a critical role in ensuring that developing countries have timely access to the needed resources when shocks hit, whether by supporting such facilities or through the direct provision of emergency funding.

But insurance and emergency funding are only one part of a broader risk-management framework. Social policies will become more important in helping people cope with more frequent and persistent threats to their livelihoods. Social policies reduce economic and social vulnerability and increase resilience to climate change. A healthy, well-educated population with access to social protection can better cope with climate shocks and climate change. Social protection policies will need to be strengthened where they exist, developed where they are lacking, and designed so that they can be expanded quickly after a shock.[55] Creating social safety nets in countries that do not yet have them is critical, and Bangladesh shows how it can be done even in very poor countries (box 4). Development agencies could help spread

successful models of social safety nets and tailor them to the needs created by the changing climate.

To ensure adequate food and water for all countries. International action is critical to manage the water and food security challenges posed by the combination of climate change and population pressures—even with improved agricultural productivity and water-use efficiency. One fifth of the world's freshwater renewable resources are shared between countries.[56] That includes 261 transboundary river basins, home to 40 percent of the world's people and governed by over 150 international treaties that do not always include all riparian states.[57] If countries are to manage these resources

---

BOX 4 *Safety nets: From supporting incomes to reducing vulnerability to climate change*

Bangladesh has had a long history of cyclones and floods, and these could become more frequent or intense. The government has safety nets that can be tailored fairly easily to respond to the effects of climate change. The best examples are the vulnerable-group feeding program, the food-for-work program, and the new employment guarantee program.

The vulnerable-group feeding program runs at all times and usually covers more than 2 million households. But it is designed to be ramped up in response to a crisis: following the cyclone in 2008, the program was expanded to close to 10 million households. Targeting, done by the lowest level of local government and monitored by the lowest administrative level, is considered fairly good.

The food-for-work program, which normally operates during the low agriculture season, is ramped up during emergencies. It too is run in collaboration with local governments, but program management has been subcontracted to nongovernmental organizations in many parts of the country. Workers who show up at the work site are generally given work, but there is usually not enough to go around, so the work is rationed through rotation.

The new employment guarantee program provides those with no other means of income (including access to other safety nets) with employment for up to 100 days at wages linked to the low-season agricultural wage. The guarantee element ensures that those who need help get it. If work cannot be provided, the individual is entitled to 40 days of wages at the full rate and then 60 days at half the rate.

Bangladesh's programs, and others in India and elsewhere, suggest some lessons. Rapid response requires rapid access to funding, targeting rules to identify people in need—chronic poor or those temporarily in need—and procedures agreed on well before a shock hits. A portfolio of "shovel-ready" projects can be preidentified as particularly relevant to increasing resilience (water storage, irrigation systems, reforestation, and embankments, which can double as roads in low-lying areas). Experience from India and Bangladesh also suggests the need for professional guidance (engineers) in the selection, design, and implementation of the public works and for equipment and supplies.

Source: Contributed by Qaiser Khan.

more intensively, they will have to scale up cooperation on international water bodies through new international treaties or the revision of existing ones. The system of water allocation will need to be reworked due to the increased variability, and cooperation can be effective only when all riparian countries are involved and responsible for managing the watercourse.

Similarly, increasing arid conditions in countries that already import a large share of their food, along with more frequent extreme events and growth in income and population, will increase the need for food imports.[58] But global food markets are thin—relatively few countries export food crops.[59] So small changes in either supply or demand can have big effects on prices. And small countries with little market power can find it difficult to secure reliable food imports.

To ensure adequate water and nutrition for all, the world will have to rely on an improved trade system less prone to large price shifts. Facilitating access to markets for developing countries by reducing trade barriers, weatherproofing transport (for example, by increasing access to year-round roads), improving procurement methods, and providing better information on both climate and market indexes can make food trade more efficient and prevent large price shifts. Price spikes can also be prevented by investing in strategic stockpiles of key grains and foodstuffs and in risk-hedging instruments.[60]

Act differently: To transform energy, food production, and decision-making systems

Achieving the needed emission reductions will require a transformation both of our energy system and of the way we manage agriculture, land use, and forests (figure 7). These transformations must also incorporate the needed adaptations to a changing climate. Whether they involve deciding which crop to plant or how much hydroelectric power to develop, decisions will have to be robust to the variety of climate outcomes we could face in the future rather than being optimally adapted to the climate of the past.

To ignite a veritable energy revolution. If financing is available, can emissions be cut sufficiently deeply or quickly without sacrificing growth? Most models suggest that they can, although none find it easy (see chapter 4). Dramatically higher energy efficiency, stronger management of energy demand, and large-scale deployment of existing low-CO_2-emitting electricity sources could produce about half the emission reductions needed to put the world on a path toward 2°C (figure 8). Many have substantial co-benefits but are hampered by institutional and financial constraints that have proven hard to overcome.

So known technologies and practices can buy time—if they can be scaled up. For that to happen, appropriate energy pricing is absolutely essential. Cutting subsidies and increasing fuel taxes are politically difficult, but the recent spike and fall in oil and gas prices make the time opportune for doing so. Indeed, European countries used the 1974 oil crisis to introduce high fuel taxes. As a result, fuel demand is about half what it likely would have been had prices been close to those in the United States.[61] Similarly, electricity prices are twice as high

Figure 7   Global CO₂e emissions by sector: Energy, but also agriculture and forestry, are major sources

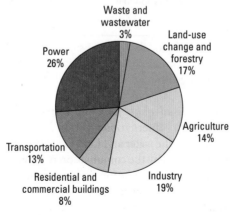

Source: IPCC 2007a, figure 2.1.

Note: Share of anthropogenic (human-caused) greenhouse gas emissions in 2004 in CO_2e (see figure 1 for the definition of CO_2e). Emissions associated with land use and land-use change, such as agricultural fertilizers, livestock, deforestation, and burning, account for about 30 percent of total greenhouse gas emissions. And uptakes of carbon into forests and other vegetation and soils constitute an important carbon sink, so improved land-use management is essential in efforts to reduce greenhouse gases in the atmosphere.

in Europe as they are in the United States and electricity consumption per capita is half.[62] Prices help explain why European emissions per capita (10 tons of CO_2e) are less than half those in the United States (23 tons).[63] Global energy subsidies in developing countries were estimated at $310 billion in 2007,[64] disproportionately benefiting higher-income populations. Rationalizing energy subsidies to target the poor and encourage sustainable energy and transport could reduce global CO_2 emissions and provide a host of other benefits.

But pricing is only one tool for advancing the energy-efficiency agenda, which suffers from market failures, high transaction costs, and financing constraints. Norms, regulatory reform, and financial incentives are also needed—and are cost-effective. Efficiency standards and labeling programs cost about 1.5 cents a kilowatt-hour, much less than any electricity supply options,[65] while industrial energy performance targets

spur innovation and increase competitiveness.[66] And because utilities are potentially effective delivery channels for making homes, commercial buildings, and industry more energy efficient, incentives have to be created for utilities to conserve energy. This can be done by decoupling a utility's profits from its gross sales, with profits instead increasing with energy conservation successes. Such an approach is behind California's remarkable energy conservation program; its adoption has become a condition for any U.S. state to receive federal energy-efficiency grants from the 2009 fiscal stimulus.

For renewable energy, long-term power-purchase agreements within a regulatory framework that ensures fair and open grid access for independent power producers will attract investors. This can be done through mandatory purchases of renewable energy at a fixed price (known as a feed-in tariff) as in Germany and Spain; or through renewable

Figure 8   The full portfolio of existing measures and advanced technologies, not a silver bullet, will be needed to get the world onto a 2°C path

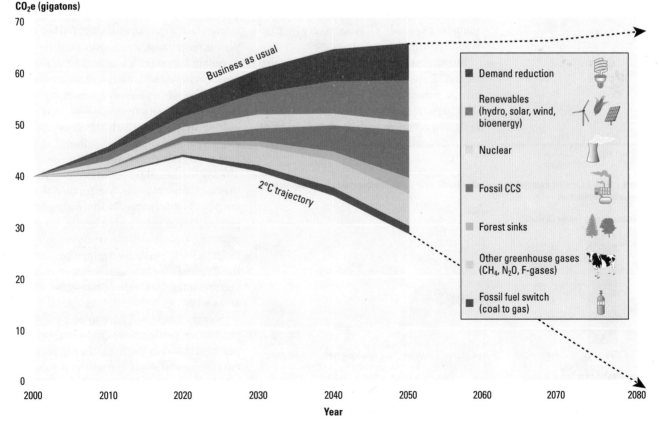

CO_2e (gigatons)

Legend:
- Demand reduction
- Renewables (hydro, solar, wind, bioenergy)
- Nuclear
- Fossil CCS
- Forest sinks
- Other greenhouse gases (CH_4, N_2O, F-gases)
- Fossil fuel switch (coal to gas)

Source: WDR team with data from IIASA 2009.

portfolio standards that require a minimum share of power to come from renewables, as in many U.S. states.[67] Importantly, predictably higher demand is likely to reduce the costs of renewables, with benefits for all countries. In fact, experience shows that expected demand can have an even higher impact than technological innovation in driving down prices (figure 9).

But new technologies will be indispensable: every energy model reviewed for this Report concludes that it is impossible to get onto the 2°C trajectory with only energy efficiency and the diffusion of existing technologies. New or emerging technologies, such as carbon capture and storage, second-generation biofuels, and solar photovoltaics, are also critical.

Few of the needed new technologies are available off the shelf. Ongoing carbon capture and storage demonstration projects currently store only about 4 million tons of CO_2 annually.[68] Fully proving the viability of this technology in different regions and settings will require about 30 full-size plants at a total cost of $75 billion to $100 billion.[69] Storage capacity of 1 billion tons a year of CO_2 is necessary by 2020 to stay within 2°C warming.

Investments in biofuels research are also needed. Expanded production using the current generation of biofuels would displace large areas of natural forests and grasslands and compete with the production of food.[70] Second-generation biofuels that rely on nonfood crops may reduce competition with agriculture by using more marginal lands. But they could still lead to the loss of pasture land and grassland ecosystems and compete for water resources.[71]

Breakthroughs in climate-smart technologies will require substantially more spending for research, development, demonstration, and deployment. As mentioned earlier, global public and private spending on energy RD&D is modest, both relative to estimated needs and in comparison with what innovative industries invest. The modest spending means slow progress, with renewable energy still accounting for only 0.4 percent of all patents.[72] Moreover, developing countries need access to these technologies, which requires boosting domestic capacity to identify and adapt new technologies as well as strengthening international mechanisms for technology transfer (see chapter 7).

To transform land and water management and manage competing demands. By 2050 the world will need to feed 3 billion more people and cope with the changing dietary demands of a richer population (richer people eat more meat, a resource-intensive way to obtain proteins). This must be done in a harsher climate with more storms, droughts, and floods, while also incorporating agriculture in the mitigation agenda—because agriculture drives about half the deforestation every year and directly contributes 14 percent of overall emissions. And ecosystems, already weakened by pollution, population pressure, and overuse, are further threatened by climate change. Producing more and protecting better in a harsher climate while reducing greenhouse gas emissions is a tall order. It will require managing the competing demands for land and water from agriculture, forests and other ecosystems, cities, and energy.

So agriculture will have to become more productive, getting more crop per drop and per hectare—but without the increase in environmental costs currently associated with intensive agriculture. And societies will have to put much more effort into protecting ecosystems. To avoid pulling more land into cultivation and spreading into "unmanaged"

Figure 9   **High expected demand drove cost reductions in solar photovoltaics by allowing for larger-scale production**

Cost reduction by factor ($/watt)

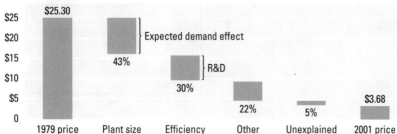

Source: Adapted from Nemet 2006.

Note: Bars show the portion of the reduction in the cost of solar photovoltaic power, from 1979 to 2001, accounted for by different factors such as plant size (which is determined by expected demand) and improved efficiency (which is driven by innovation from R&D). The "other" category includes reductions in the price of the key input silicon (12 percent) and a number of much smaller factors (including reduced quantities of silicon needed for a given energy output, and lower rates of discarded products due to manufacturing error).

land and forests, agricultural productivity will have to increase, perhaps by as much as 1.8 percent a year compared to 1 percent a year without climate change.[73] Most of that increase will have to occur in developing countries because agriculture in high-income countries is already close to maximum feasible yields. Fortunately, new technologies and practices are emerging (box 5). Some improve productivity and resilience as they sequester carbon in the soil and reduce the nutrient runoff that damages aquatic ecosystems. But more research is needed to understand how to scale them up.

Increased efforts to conserve species and ecosystems will need to be reconciled with food production (whether agriculture or fisheries). Protected areas—already 12 percent of the earth's land but only a tiny portion of the ocean and fresh water system—cannot be the only solution to maintaining biodiversity, because species ranges are likely to shift outside the boundaries of such areas. Instead ecoagricultural landscapes, where farmers create mosaics of cultivated and natural habitats, could facilitate the migration of species. While benefiting biodiversity, ecoagriculture practices also increase agriculture's resilience to climate change along with farm productivity and incomes. In Central America farms using these practices suffered half or less of the damage inflicted on others by Hurricane Mitch.[75]

Better management of water is essential for agriculture to adapt to climate change. River basins will be losing natural water storage in ice and snow and in reduced aquifer recharge, just as warmer temperatures increase evaporation. Water can be used more efficiently through a combination of new and existing technologies, better information, and more sensible use. And that can be done even in poor countries and among small farmers: in Andhra Pradesh, India, a simple scheme, in which farmers monitor their rain and groundwater and learn new farming and irrigation techniques, has caused 1 million farmers to voluntarily reduce groundwater consumption to sustainable levels.[75]

Efforts to increase water resources include dams, but dams can be only a part

---

BOX 5 *Promising approaches that are good for farmers and good for the environment*

Promising practices

Cultivation practices such as zero-tillage (which involves injecting seeds directly into the soil instead of sowing on ploughed fields) combined with residue management and proper fertilizer use can help to preserve soil moisture, maximize water infiltration, increase carbon storage, minimize nutrient runoff, and raise yields. Now being used on about 2 percent of global arable land, this practice is likely to expand. Zero tillage has mostly been adopted in high-income countries, but is expanding rapidly in countries such as India. In 2005, in the rice–wheat farming system of the Indo-Gangetic plain, farmers adopted zero-tillage on 1.6 million hectares; by 2008, 20–25 percent of the wheat in two Indian states (Haryana and Punjab) was cultivated using minimum tillage. And in Brazil, about 45 percent of cropland is farmed using these practices.

Promising technologies

Precision agriculture techniques for targeted, optimally timed application of the minimum necessary fertilizer and water could help the intensive, high-input farms of high-income countries, Asia, and Latin America to reduce emissions and nutrient runoff, and increase water-use efficiency. New technologies that limit emissions of gaseous nitrogen include controlled-release nitrogen through the deep placement of supergranules of fertilizer or the addition of biological inhibitors to fertilizers. Remote sensing technologies for communicating precise information about soil moisture and irrigation needs can eliminate unnecessary application of water. Some of these technologies may remain too expensive for most developing-country farmers (and could require payment schemes for soil carbon conservation or changes in water pricing). But others such as biological inhibitors require no extra labor and improve productivity.

Learning from the past

Another approach building on a technology used by indigenous peoples in the Amazon rain forest could sequester carbon on a huge scale while improving soil productivity. Burning wet crop residues or manure (biomass) at low temperatures in the almost complete absence of oxygen produces biochar, a charcoal-type solid with a very high carbon content. Biochar is highly stable in soil, locking in the carbon that would otherwise be released by simply burning the biomass or allowing it to decompose. In industrial settings this process transforms half the carbon into biofuel and the other half into biochar. Recent analysis suggests biochar may be able to store carbon for centuries, possibly millennia, and more studies are underway to verify this property.

Sources: de la Torre, Fajnzylber, and Nash 2008; Derpsch and Friedrich 2009; Erenstein 2009; Erenstein and Laxmi 2008; Lehmann 2007; Wardle, Nilsson, and Zackrisson 2008.

of the solution, and they will need to be designed flexibly to deal with more variable rainfall. Other approaches include using recycled water and desalination, which, while costly, can be worthwhile for high-value use in coastal areas, especially if powered by renewable energy (see chapter 3).

But changing practices and technologies can be a challenge, particularly in poor, rural, and isolated settings, where introducing new ways of doing things requires working with a large number of very risk-averse actors located off the beaten track and facing different constraints and incentives. Extension agencies usually have limited resources to support farmers and are staffed with engineers and agronomists rather than trained communicators. Taking advantage of emerging technologies will also require bringing higher technical education to rural communities.

To transform decision-making processes: Adaptive policy making to tackle a riskier and more complex environment. Infrastructure design and planning, insurance pricing, and numerous private decisions—from planting and harvesting dates to siting factories and designing buildings—have long been based on stationarity, the idea that natural systems fluctuate within an unchanging envelope of variability. With climate change, stationarity is dead.[76] Decision makers now have to contend with the changing climate compounding the uncertainties they already faced. More decisions have to be made in a context of changing trends and greater variability, not to mention possible carbon constraints.

The approaches being developed and applied by public and private agencies, cities, and countries around the world from Australia to the United Kingdom are showing that it is possible to increase resilience even in the absence of expensive and sophisticated modeling of future climate.[77] Of course better projections and less uncertainty help, but these new approaches tend to focus on strategies that are "robust" across a range of possible future outcomes, not just optimal for a particular set of expectations (box 6).[78] Robust strategies can be as simple as picking seed varieties that do well in a range of climates.

Robust strategies typically build flexibility, diversification, and redundancy in response capacities (see chapter 2). They favor "no-regrets" actions that provide benefits (such as water and energy efficiency) even without climate change. They also favor reversible and flexible options to keep the cost of wrong decisions as low as possible (restrictive urban planning for coastal areas can easily be relaxed while forced retreats or increased protection can be difficult and costly). They include safety margins to increase resilience (paying the marginal costs of building a higher bridge or one that can be flooded, or extending safety nets to groups on the brink). And they rely on long-term planning based on scenario analysis and an assessment of strategies under a wide range of possible futures.[79] Participatory design and implementation is critical, because it permits the use of local knowledge about existing vulnerability and fosters ownership of the strategy by its beneficiaries.

Policy making for adaptation also needs to be adaptive itself, with periodic reviews based on the collection and monitoring of information, something increasingly feasible at low cost thanks to better technologies. For example, a key problem in water management is the lack of knowledge about underground water, or about who consumes what. New remote-sensing technology makes it possible to infer groundwater consumption, identify which farmers have low water productivity, and specify when to increase or decrease water applications to maximize productivity without affecting crop yields (see chapter 3).

Making it happen: New pressures, new instruments, and new resources

The previous pages describe the many steps needed to manage the climate change challenge. Many read like the standard fare of a development or environmental science textbook: improve water resource management, increase energy efficiency, promote sustainable agricultural practices, remove perverse subsidies. But these have proven elusive in the past, raising the question of what might make the needed reforms and

BOX 6 *Ingenuity needed: Adaptation requires new tools and new knowledge*

Regardless of mitigation efforts, humanity will need to adapt to substantial changes in the climate—everywhere, and in many different fields.

Natural capital

A diversity of natural assets will be needed to cope with climate change and ensure productive agriculture, forestry, and fisheries. For example, crop varieties are needed that perform well under drought, heat, and enhanced CO_2. But the private-sector- and farmer-led process of choosing crops favors homogeneity adapted to past or current conditions, not varieties capable of producing consistently high yields in warmer, wetter, or drier conditions. Accelerated breeding programs are needed to conserve a wider pool of genetic resources of existing crops, breeds, and their wild relatives. Relatively intact ecosystems, such as forested catchments, mangroves, and wetlands, can buffer the impacts of climate change. Under a changing climate these ecosystems are themselves at risk, and management approaches will need to be more proactive and adaptive. Connections between natural areas, such as

migration corridors, may be needed to facilitate species movements to keep up with the change in climate.

Physical capital

Climate change is likely to affect infrastructure in ways not easily predictable and varying greatly with geography. For example, infrastructure in low-lying areas is threatened by flooding rivers and rising seas whether in Tangier Bay, New York City, or Shanghai. Heat waves soften asphalt and can require road closures; they affect the capacity of electricity transmission lines and warm the water needed to cool thermal and nuclear power plants just as they increase electricity demand. Uncertainties are likely to influence not only investment decisions but the design of infrastructure that will need to be robust to the future climate. Similar uncertainty about the reliability of water supply is leading to both integrated management strategies and improved water-related technologies as hedges against climate change. Greater technical knowledge and engineering capabilities will be needed to design future infrastructure in the light of climate change.

Human health

Many adaptations of health systems to climate change will initially involve practical options that build on existing knowledge. But others will require new skills. Advances in genomics are making it possible to design new diagnostic tools that can detect new infectious diseases. These tools, combined with advances in communications technologies, can detect emerging trends in health and provide health workers with early opportunities to intervene. Innovations in a range of technologies are already transforming medicine. For example, the advent of hand-held diagnostic devices and video-mediated consultations are expanding the prospects for telemedicine and making it easier for isolated communities to connect to the global health infrastructure.

Sources: Burke, Lobell, and Guarino 2009; Ebi and Burton 2008; Falloon and Betts, forthcoming; Guthrie, Juma, and Sillem 2008; Keim 2008; Koetse and Rietveld 2009; National Academy of Engineering 2008; Snoussi and others 2009.

behavior changes possible. The answer lies in a combination of new pressures, new instruments, and new resources.

New pressures are coming from a growing awareness of climate change and its current and future costs. But awareness does not always lead to action: to succeed, climate-smart development policy must tackle the inertia in the behavior of individuals and organizations. Domestic perception of climate change will also determine the success of a global deal—its adoption but also its implementation. And while many of the answers to the climate and development problem will be national or even local, a global deal is needed to generate new instruments and new resources for action (see chapter 5). So while new pressures must start at home with changing behaviors and shifting public opinion, action must be enabled by an efficient and effective international agreement, one that factors in development realities.

New pressures: Success hinges on changing behavior and shifting public opinion

International regimes influence national policies but are themselves a product of domestic factors. Political norms, governance structures, and vested interests drive the translation of international law into domestic policy, while shaping the international regime.[80] And in the absence of a global enforcement mechanism, the incentives for meeting global commitments are domestic.

To succeed, climate-smart development policy has to factor in these local determinants. The mitigation policies that a country will follow depend on domestic factors such as the energy mix, the current and potential energy sources, and the preference for state or market-driven policies. The pursuit of ancillary local benefits—such as cleaner air, technology transfers, and energy security—is crucial to generating sufficient support.

Climate-smart policies also have to tackle the inertia in the behavior of individuals and organizations. Weaning modern economies from fossil fuels and increasing resilience to climate change will require attitudinal shifts by consumers, business leaders, and decision makers. The challenges in changing ingrained behaviors call for a special emphasis on nonmarket policies and interventions.

Throughout the world disaster risk management programs are focused on changing community perceptions of risk. The City of London has made targeted communication and education programs a centerpiece of its "London Warming" Action Plan. And utilities across the United States have begun using social norms and peer community pressure to encourage lower energy demand: simply showing households how they are faring relative to others, and signaling approval of lower than average consumption is enough to encourage lower energy use (see chapter 8).

Addressing the climate challenge will also require changes in the way governments operate. Climate policy touches on the mandate of many government agencies, yet belongs to none. For both mitigation and adaptation, many needed actions require a long-term perspective that goes well beyond those of any elected administration. Many countries, including Brazil, China, India, Mexico, and the United Kingdom, have created lead agencies for climate change, set up high-level coordination bodies, and improved the use of scientific information in policy making (see chapter 8).

Cities, provinces, and regions provide political and administrative space closer to the sources of emissions and the impacts of climate change. In addition to implementing and articulating national policies and regulations, they perform policy-making, regulatory, and planning functions in sectors key to mitigation (transportation, construction, public services, local advocacy) and adaptation (social protection, disaster risk reduction, natural resource management). Because they are closer to citizens, these governments can raise public awareness and mobilize private actors.[81] And at the intersection of the government and the public, they become the space where government accountability for appropriate responses is played out. That is why many local governments have preceded national governments in climate action (box 7).

New instruments and new resources: The role of a global agreement

Immediate and comprehensive action is not feasible without global cooperation, which requires a deal perceived as equitable by all parties—high-income countries, which need to make the most immediate and stringent efforts; middle-income countries, where substantial mitigation and adaptation need to happen; and low-income countries, where the priority is technical and financial assistance to cope with vulnerability to today's conditions, let alone unfolding changes in the climate. The deal must also be effective in achieving climate goals, incorporating lessons from other international agreements and from past successes and failures with large international transfers of resources. Finally, it has to be efficient, which requires adequate funding and financial instruments that can separate where mitigation happens from who funds it—thereby achieving mitigation at least cost.

An equitable deal.   Global cooperation at the scale needed to deal with climate change can happen only if it is based on a global agreement that addresses the needs and constraints of developing countries, only if it can separate where mitigation happens from who bears the burden of this effort, and only if it creates financial instruments to encourage and facilitate mitigation, even in countries that are rich in coal and poor in income or that have contributed little or nothing historically to climate change. Whether these countries seize the opportunity to embark on a more sustainable development path will be heavily influenced by the financial and technical support that higher-income countries can muster. Otherwise the transition costs could be prohibitive.

Global cooperation will require more than financial contributions, however. Behavioral economics and social psychology show that people tend to reject deals they perceive as unfair toward them, even if they stand to benefit.[82] So the fact that

BOX 7 *Cities reducing their carbon footprints*

The movement toward carbon-neutral cities shows how local governments are taking action even in the absence of international commitments or stringent national policies. In the United States, which has not ratified the Kyoto Protocol, close to a thousand cities have agreed to meet the Kyoto Protocol target under the Mayors' Climate Protection agreement. In Rizhao, a city of 3 million people in northern China, the municipal government combined incentives and legislative tools to encourage the large-scale efficient use of renewable energy. Skyscrapers are built to use solar power, and 99 percent of Rizhao's households use solar-power heaters. Almost all traffic signals, street lights, and park illuminations are powered by photovoltaic solar cells. In total the city has over 500,000 square meters of solar water heating panels, the equivalent of about 0.5 megawatts of electric water heaters. As a result of these efforts, energy use has fallen by nearly a third and CO_2 emissions by half.

Examples of movements to carbon-neutral cities are mushrooming well beyond China. In 2008 Sydney became the first city in Australia to become carbon neutral, through energy efficiency, renewable energy, and carbon offsets. Copenhagen is planning to cut its carbon emissions to zero by 2025. The plan includes investments in wind energy and encouraging the use of electric and hydrogen-powered cars with free parking and recharging.

More than 700 cities and local governments around the world are participating in a "Cities for Climate Protection Campaign" to adopt policies and implement quantifiable measures to reduce local greenhouse gas emissions (http://www.iclei.org). Together with other local government associations, such as the C40 Cities Climate Leadership Group and the World Mayors Council on Climate Change, they have embarked on a process that seeks empowerment and inclusion of cities and local governments in the UN Framework Convention on Climate Change.

Sources: Bai 2006; World Bank 2009d; C40 Cities Climate Leadership Group, http://www.c40cities.org (accessed August 1, 2009).

it is in everyone's interest to collaborate is no guarantee of success. There are real concerns among developing countries that a drive to integrate climate and development could shift responsibility for mitigation onto the developing world.

Enshrining a principle of equity in a global deal would do much to dispel such concerns and generate trust (see chapter 5). A long-term goal of per capita emissions converging to a band could ensure that no country is locked into an unequal share of the atmospheric commons. India has recently stated that it would never exceed the average per capita emissions of high-income countries.[83] So drastic action by high-income countries to reduce their own carbon footprint to sustainable levels is essential. This would show leadership, spur innovation, and make it feasible for all to switch to a low-carbon growth path.

Another major concern of developing countries is technology access. Innovation in climate-related technologies remains concentrated in high-income countries, although developing countries are increasing their presence (China is seventh in overall renewable energy patents,[84] and an Indian firm is now the leader in on-road electric cars[85]). In addition, developing countries—at least the smaller or poorer ones—may need assistance to produce new technology or tailor it to their circumstances. This is particularly problematic for adaptation, where technologies can be very location specific.

International transfers of clean technologies have so far been modest. They have occurred in at best one-third of the projects funded through the Clean Development Mechanism (CDM), the main channel for financing investments in low-carbon technologies in developing countries.[86] The Global Environment Facility, which has historically allocated about $160 million a year to climate mitigation programs,[87] is supporting technology needs assessments in 130 countries. About $5 billion has recently been pledged under the new Clean Technology Fund to assist developing countries by supporting large, risky investments involving clean technologies, but there are disputes over what constitutes clean technology.

Building technology agreements into a global climate deal could boost technology innovation and ensure developing-country access. International collaboration is critical for producing and sharing climate-smart technologies. On the production side, cost-sharing agreements are needed for large-scale and high-risk technologies such as carbon capture and storage (see chapter 7). International agreements on standards create markets for innovation. And international support for technology transfer can take the form of joint production and technology sharing—or financial support for the incremental cost of adopting new cleaner technology (as was done through the Multilateral Fund for the Implementation of the Montreal Protocol on Substances that Deplete the Ozone Layer).

A global deal will also have to be acceptable to high-income countries. They worry about the financial demands that could be placed on them and want to ensure that financial transfers deliver the desired adaptation and mitigation results. They also are concerned that a tiered approach allowing developing countries to delay actions might affect their own competitiveness with leading middle-income countries.

An effective deal: Lessons from aid effectiveness and international agreements. An effective climate deal will achieve agreed targets for mitigation and adaptation. Its design can build on the lessons of aid effectiveness and international agreements. Climate finance is not aid finance, but the aid experience does offer critical lessons. In particular, it has become clear that commitments are seldom respected unless they correspond to a country's objectives—the conditionality versus ownership debate. So funding for adaptation and mitigation should be organized around a process that encourages recipient-country development and ownership of a low-carbon development agenda. The aid experience also shows that a multiplicity of funding sources imposes huge transaction costs on recipient countries and reduces effectiveness. And while the sources of funding might be separate, the spending of adaptation and mitigation resources must be fully integrated into development efforts.

International agreements also show that tiered approaches can be an appropriate way of bringing hugely different partners into a single deal. Look at the World Trade Organization: special and differential treatment for developing countries has been a defining feature of the multilateral trading system for most of the postwar period. Proposals are emerging in the climate negotiations around the multitrack framework put forward in the UNFCCC's Bali Action Plan.[88] These proposals would have developed countries commit to output targets, where the "output" is greenhouse gas emissions, and developing countries commit to policy changes rather than emission targets.

This approach is appealing for three reasons. First, it can advance mitigation opportunities that carry development co-benefits. Second, it is well suited to developing countries, where fast population and economic growth is driving the rapid expansion of the capital stock (with opportunities for good or bad lock-in) and increases the urgency of moving energy, urban, and transport systems toward a lower-carbon path. A policy-based track can also offer a good framework for countries with a high share of hard-to-measure emissions from land use, land-use change, and forestry. Third, it is less likely to require monitoring of complex flows—a challenge for many countries. Nevertheless, some overall monitoring and evaluation of these approaches is critical, if only to understand their effectiveness.[89]

An efficient deal: The role of climate finance

Climate finance can reconcile equity and efficiency by separating where climate action takes place from who pays for it. Sufficient finance flowing to developing countries—combined with capacity building and access to technology—can support low-carbon growth and development. If mitigation finance is directed to where mitigation costs are lowest, efficiency will increase. If adaptation finance is directed to where the needs are greatest, undue suffering and loss can be avoided. Climate finance offers the means to reconcile equity, efficiency, and effectiveness in dealing with climate change.

But current levels of climate finance fall far short of foreseeable needs. The estimates presented in table 1 suggest mitigation costs in developing countries could reach $140–$175 billion a year by 2030 with associated financing needs of $265–$565 billion. Current flows of mitigation finance averaging some $8 billion a year to 2012 pale in comparison. And the estimated $30–$100 billion that could be needed annually for adaptation in developing countries dwarfs the less than $1 billion a year now available (figure 10).

Compounding the shortfalls in climate finance are significant inefficiencies in how funds are generated and deployed. Key problems include fragmented sources of finance; high costs of implementing market mechanisms such as the Clean Development Mechanism; and insufficient, distortionary instruments for raising adaptation finance.

Chapter 6 identifies nearly 20 different bilateral and multilateral funds for climate change currently proposed or in operation. This fragmentation has a cost identified in the Paris Declaration on Aid Effectiveness: each fund has its own governance, raising transaction costs for developing countries; and alignment with country development objectives may suffer if sources of finance are narrow. Other tenets of the Paris Declaration, including ownership, donor harmonization, and mutual accountability, also suffer when financing is highly fragmented. An eventual consolidation of funds into a more limited number is clearly warranted.

Looking forward, pricing carbon (whether through a tax or through a cap and trade scheme) is the optimal way of both generating carbon-finance resources and directing those resources to efficient opportunities. In the near future, however, the CDM and other performance-based mechanisms for carbon offsets are likely to remain the key market-based instruments for mitigation finance in developing countries and are therefore critical in supplementing direct transfers from high-income countries.

The CDM has in many ways exceeded expectations, growing rapidly, stimulating learning, raising awareness of mitigation options, and building capacity. But it also has many limitations, including low development co-benefits, questionable additionality (because the CDM generates carbon credits for emission reductions relative to a baseline, the choice of baseline can always be questioned), weak governance, inefficient operation, limited scope (key sectors such as transport are not covered), and concerns about market continuity beyond 2012.[90] For the effectiveness of climate actions it is also important to understand that CDM transactions do not reduce global carbon emissions beyond agreed commitments—they

Figure 10 The gap is large: Estimated annual incremental climate costs required for a 2°C trajectory compared with current resources

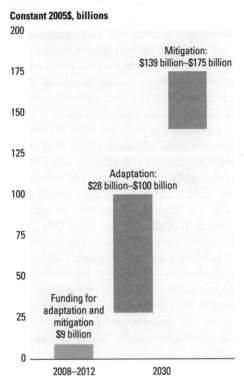

Constant 2005$, billions

Mitigation: $139 billion–$175 billion

Adaptation: $28 billion–$100 billion

Funding for adaptation and mitigation $9 billion

2008–2012   2030

Sources: See table 1 on page 9 and the discussion in chapter 6.
Note: Mitigation and adaptation costs for developing countries only. Bars represent the range of estimates for the incremental costs of the adaptation and mitigation efforts associated with a 2°C trajectory. Mitigation financing needs associated with the incremental costs depicted here are much higher, ranging between $265 billion and $565 billion annually by 2030.

simply change where they occur (in developing rather than developed countries) and lower the cost of mitigation (thereby increasing efficiency).

The Adaptation Fund under the Kyoto Protocol employs a novel financing instrument in the form of a 2 percent tax on certified emission reductions (units of carbon offset generated by the CDM). This clearly raises finance that is additional to other sources, but as pointed out in chapter 6, this approach has several undesirable characteristics. The instrument is taxing a good (mitigation finance) rather than a bad (carbon emissions) and like any tax, there are inevitable inefficiencies (deadweight losses). Analysis of the CDM market suggests that most of the lost gains from trade as a result of the tax would fall on developing-country suppliers of carbon credits.[91] Adaptation finance will also require an allocation mechanism that ideally would embrace the principles of transparency, efficiency, and equity—efficient approaches would direct finance to the most vulnerable countries and those with the greatest capacity to manage adaptation, while equity would require that particular weight be given to the poorest countries.

Strengthening and expanding the climate finance regime will require reforming existing instruments and developing new sources of climate finance (see chapter 6). Reform of the CDM is particularly important in view of its role in generating carbon finance for projects in developing countries. One set of proposals aims at reducing costs through streamlining project approval, including upgrading the review and administrative functions. A key second set of proposals focuses on allowing the CDM to support changes in policies and programs rather than limit it to projects. "Sector no-lose targets" are an example of a performance-based scheme, where demonstrable reductions in sectoral carbon emissions below an agreed baseline could be compensated through the sale of carbon credits, with no penalty if the reductions are not achieved.

Forestry is another area where climate finance can reduce emissions (box 8). Additional mechanisms for pricing forest carbon are likely to emerge from the current climate negotiations. Already several initiatives, including the World Bank's Forest Carbon Partnership Facility, are exploring how financial incentives can reduce deforestation in developing countries and thereby reduce carbon emissions. The major challenges include developing a national strategy and implementation framework for reducing emissions from deforestation and degradation; a reference scenario for emissions; and a system for monitoring, reporting, and verification.

Efforts to reduce emissions of soil carbon (through incentives to change tilling practices, for example) could also be a target of financial incentives—and are essential to ensure natural areas are not converted to food and biofuel production. But the methodology is less mature than for forest carbon, and major monitoring issues would need to be resolved (see box 8). Pilot programs must be developed rapidly to encourage more resilient and sustainable agriculture and to bring more resources and innovation to a sector that has lacked both in recent decades.[92]

Within countries the role of the public sector will be critical in creating incentives for climate action (through subsidies, taxes, caps, or regulations), providing information and education, and eliminating market failures that inhibit action. But much of the finance will come from the private sector, particularly for adaptation. For private infrastructure service providers the flexibility of the regulatory regime will be crucial in providing the right incentives for climate-proofing investments and operations. While it will be possible to leverage private finance for specific adaptation investments (such as flood defenses) experience to date with public-private partnerships on infrastructure in developing countries suggests that the scope will be modest.

Generating additional finance for adaptation is a key priority, and innovative schemes such as auctioning assigned amount units (AAUs, the binding caps that countries accept under the UNFCCC), taxing international transport emissions, and a global carbon tax have the potential to raise tens of billions of dollars of new finance each year. For mitigation it is clear that having an efficient price for carbon, through either a tax or cap-and-trade, will be transformational. Once this is achieved, the private sector will provide much of the needed finance as investors and consumers factor in the price of carbon. But national carbon taxes or carbon markets will not necessarily provide the needed flows of finance to developing countries. If the solution to the climate problem is to be equitable, a reformed CDM and other performance-based schemes, the linking of national carbon markets, the allocation and sale of AAUs, and fiscal transfers will all provide finance to developing countries.

As this Report goes to press, countries are engaged in negotiations on a global climate agreement under the auspices of the UNFCCC. Many of these same countries

BOX 8 *The role of land use, agriculture, and forestry in managing climate change*

Land use, agriculture, and forestry have a substantial mitigation potential but have been contentious in the climate negotiations. Could emissions and uptakes be measured with sufficient accuracy? What can be done about natural fluctuations in growth and losses from fires associated with climate change? Should countries get credits for actions taken decades or centuries before the climate negotiations? Would credits from land-based activities swamp the carbon market and drive down the carbon price, reducing incentives for further mitigation? Progress has been made on many of these issues, and the Intergovernmental Panel on Climate Change has developed guidelines for measuring land-related greenhouse gases.

Net global deforestation averaged 7.3 million hectares a year from 2000 to 2005, contributing about 5.0 gigatons of CO_2 a year in emissions, or about a quarter of the emission reduction needed. Another 0.9 gigaton reduction could come from reforestation and better forest management in developing countries. But improved forest management and reduced deforestation in developing countries are currently not part of the international Clean Development Mechanism of the UNFCCC.

There is also interest in creating a mechanism for payments for improved management of soil carbon and other greenhouse gases produced by agriculture. Technically about 6.0 gigatons of CO_2e in emissions could be reduced through less tillage of soils, better wetland and rice paddy management, and better livestock and manure management. About 1.5 gigatons of emission reductions a year could be achieved in agriculture for a carbon price of $20 a ton of CO_2e (figure).

Forestry and agricultural mitigation would produce many co-benefits. The maintenance of forests keeps open a wider diversity of livelihood options, protects biodiversity, and buffers against extreme events such as floods and landslides. Reduced tillage and better fertilizer management can improve productivity. And the resources generated could be substantial—at least for countries with large forests: if the forest carbon markets meet their full potential, Indonesia could

earn $400 million to $2 billion a year. As for soil carbon, even in Africa, where relatively carbon-poor lands cover close to half the continent, the potential for soil carbon sequestration is 100 million to 400 million tons of CO_2e a year. At $10 a ton, this would be on par with current official development assistance to Africa.

Largely through the efforts of a group of developing countries that formed the Coalition for Rainforests, land use, land-use change, and forestry accounting were reintroduced into the UNFCCC agenda. Those countries seek opportunities to contribute to reducing emissions under their common but differentiated responsibility and to raise carbon finance to better manage their forested systems. Negotiations over what has become known as REDD (Reduced Emissions from Deforestation and Forest Degradation) continue, but most expect some elements of REDD to be part of an agreement in Copenhagen.

Initiatives on soil carbon are not so advanced. While carbon sequestration in agriculture would be an inexpensive, technically simple, and efficient response to climate change, developing a market for it is no easy feat. A pilot project in Kenya (see chapter 3) and soil carbon offsets on the Chicago Climate Exchange point to opportunities. Three steps can help move soil carbon sequestration forward.

First, the carbon monitoring should follow an "activity-based" approach, where emission reductions are estimated based on the activities carried out by the farmer rather than on much more expensive soil analyses. Specific and conservative emission reduction factors can be applied for different agroecological and climatic zones. This is simpler, cheaper, and more predictable for the farmer, who knows up front what the payments, and possible penalties, are for any given activity.

Second, transaction costs can be reduced by "aggregators," who combine activities over many smallholder farms, as in the Kenya pilot project. By working with many farms, aggregators can build up a permanent buffer and average out occasional reversals in sequestration. Pooling over a portfolio of projects with conservative estimates of permanence can make soil carbon sequestration fully equivalent to CO_2 reduction in other sectors.

Third, logistical help, especially for poor farmers who need help to finance up-front costs, must include strengthened extension services. They are key to disseminating knowledge about sequestration practices and finance opportunities.

Sources: Canadell and others 2007; Eliasch 2008; FAO 2005; Smith and others 2008; Smith and others 2009; Tschakert 2004; UNEP 1990; Voluntary Carbon Standard 2007; World Bank 2008c.

It's not just about energy: At high carbon prices the combined mitigation potential of agriculture and forestry is greater than that of other individual sectors of the economy

Potential emission reduction (GtCO₂e/yr)

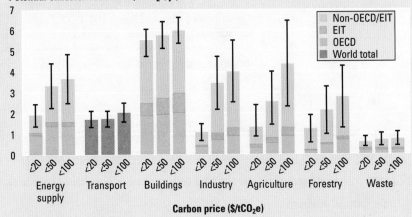

Carbon price ($/tCO₂e)

Source: Barker and others 2007b, figure TS.27.
Note: EIT = economies in transition. The ranges for global economic potentials as assessed in each sector are shown by black vertical lines.

are also in the throes of one of the most severe financial crises of recent decades. Fiscal difficulties and urgent needs could make it difficult to get legislatures to agree to spend resources on what is incorrectly perceived as solely a longer-term threat.

Yet a number of countries have adopted fiscal recovery packages to green the economy while restoring growth, for a global total of more than $400 billion over the next few years in the hope of stimulating the economy and creating jobs.[93] Investments in energy efficiency can produce a triple dividend of greater energy savings, fewer emissions, and more jobs.

The current climate negotiations, to culminate in Copenhagen in December 2009, have been making slow progress—inertia in the political sphere. For all the reasons highlighted in this Report—inertia in the climate system, inertia in infrastructure, inertia in socioeconomic systems—a climate deal is urgently needed. But it must be a smart deal, one that creates the incentives for efficient solutions, for flows of finance and the development of new technologies. And it must be an equitable deal, one that meets the needs and aspirations of developing countries. Only this can create the right climate for development.

Notes

1. Extreme poverty is defined as living on $1.25 a day or less. Chen and Ravallion 2008.

2. FAO 2009b.

3. Article 2 of the United Nations Framework Convention on Climate Change (UNFCCC) calls for stabilizing greenhouse gas concentrations in the atmosphere at a level that "would prevent dangerous anthropogenic [human-caused] inter-

ference with the climate system." http://unfccc .int/resource/docs/convkp/conveng.pdf (accessed August 1, 2009).

4. Defined as carbon emitted per dollar of GDP.

5. On a global scale, this would reduce CO_2 emissions by 4–6 gigatons a year given the current energy mix in the power sector and industry (IEA 2008e). Similar reductions would be possible in the building sector in high-income countries. See, for example, Mills 2009.

6. World Bank 2009b.

7. de la Torre, Fajnzylber, and Nash 2008.

8. Greenhouse gases each have different heat-trapping potential. The carbon dioxide equivalent (CO_2e) concentration can be used to describe the composite global warming effect of these gases in terms of the amount of CO_2 that would have the same heat-trapping potential over a specified period of time.

9. Authors' calculations, based on data from Climate Analysis Indicators Tool (WRI 2008). The range is much greater if small island states such as Barbados (4.6 tons of CO_2e per capita) and oil producers such as Qatar (55 tons of CO_2e per capita) or the United Arab Emirates (39 tons of CO_2e per capita) are included.

10. IEA 2008c.

11. Edmonds and others 2008; Hamilton 2009. Blanford, Richels, and Rutherford (2008) also show substantial savings from countries announcing in advance the date when they will engage in mitigation, because that allows those investing in long-lived assets to factor in the likely change in future regulatory regimes and carbon prices and therefore minimizes the number of stranded assets.

12. Financial crises that are highly synchronized across countries are associated with similar durations and are followed by similar recoveries, although the losses tend to be more severe (5 percent of GDP on average). IMF 2009, table 3.1. Even the Great Depression in the United States lasted only three and a half years, from August 1929 to March 1933. National Bureau of

Many people are taking action to protect our environment. I think that only by working as a team will we succeed in making a difference. Even children can join together to help because we are the next generation and we should treasure our own natural environment.

—Adrian Lau Tsun Yin, China, age 8

Anoushka Bhari, Kenya, age 8

Economic Research Business Cycle Expansion and Contraction database, http://www.nber.org/cycles.html (accessed August 1, 2009).

13. Matthews and Caldeira 2008.

14. Schaeffer and others 2008.

15. While the question of what constitutes dangerous climate change requires value judgments, summaries of recent research by the Intergovernmental Panel on Climate Change (IPCC) suggest that warming by more than 2°C above preindustrial levels sharply increases risks, so that "significant benefits result from constraining temperatures to not more than 1.6°C–2.6°C." Fisher and others 2007; IPCC 2007b; IPCC 2007c; Parry and others 2007. Recent scientific publications further support the notion that warming should be constrained to remain as close as possible to 2°C above preindustrial temperatures. Focus A on science; Mann 2009; Smith and others 2009. The organizers of the 2009 International Scientific Congress on Climate Change concluded that "there is increasing agreement that warming above 2°C would be very difficult for contemporary societies and ecosystems to cope with." http://climatecongress.ku.dk/ (accessed August 1, 2009). Other calls for not allowing warming to exceed 2°C include European Commission 2007; SEG 2007; and International Scientific Steering Committee 2005. The leaders of Australia, Brazil, Canada, China, the European Union, France, Germany, India, Indonesia, Italy, Japan, the Republic of Korea, Mexico, the Russian Federation, South Africa, the United Kingdom, and the United States—meeting at the Major Economies Forum on Energy and Climate in July 2009—recognized "the scientific view that the increase in global average temperature above preindustrial levels ought not to exceed 2°C." http://usclimatenetwork.org/resource-database/MEF_Declarationl-0.pdf (accessed August 1, 2009).

16. IPCC 2007c.

17. Raupach and others 2007.

18. Lawrence and others 2008; Matthews and Keith 2007; Parry and others 2008; Scheffer, Brovkin, and Cox 2006; Torn and Harte 2006; Walter and others 2006.

19. Horton and others 2008.

20. This estimate does not take into account the increase of damages from storm surges, and it uses current population and economic activities. So in the absence of large-scale adaptation, it is likely to be a significant underestimate. Dasgupta and others 2009.

21. Stern 2007.

22. Easterling and others 2007, table 5.6, p 299.

23. Parry and others 2007, table TS.3, p 66.

24. Nordhaus and Boyer 2000. Stern (2007) also finds that losses associated with climate change would be much greater in India and Southeast Asia than the world average.

25. Nordhaus 2008; Stern 2007; Yohe and others 2007, figure 20.3.

26. The PAGE model, used for the Stern Review of Climate Change, estimates that 80 percent of the costs of damages would be borne by developing countries; Hope (2009), with further data breakdowns communicated by the author. The RICE model (Nordhaus and Boyer 2000), as expanded to include adaptation in de Bruin, Dellink, and Agrawala (2009), suggests that about three-quarters of the costs of damages would be borne by developing countries. See also Smith and others (2009); Tol (2008). Note that this may well be an underestimate, since it does not take into account the value of lost ecosystem services. See chapter 1 for a discussion of the limitation of models' ability to capture costs of impacts.

27. Noted during consultations with East African and Latin American countries.

28. Barbera and McConnell 1990; Barrett 2003; Burtraw and others 2005; Jaffe and others 1995; Meyer 1995.

29. Hope 2009; Nordhaus 2008.

30. Nordhaus 2008.

31. Few models incorporate adaptation costs. See de Bruin, Dellink, and Agrawala (2009) for a discussion.

32. Nordhaus 2008, p. 86, figure 5.3. Nordhaus finds the additional cost of stabilizing warming at 2°C rather than his optimal target of 3.5°C to be 0.3 percent of GDP annually. The additonal cost of 2.5°C rather than 3.5°C is less than 0.1 percent of GDP annually.

33. The developing-country average is 1.5 percent of GDP; it includes health insurance and excludes life insurance. Swiss Re 2007.

34. McKinsey & Company 2009.

35. In constant 2005 dollars. World Bank 2009c.

36. Adger and others 2009.

37. IPCC 2001.

38. Mignone and others 2008. This is true in the absence of effective and acceptable geoengineering technology (see chapter 7).

39. This can result from economies of scale in technology provision (as was the case for the French nuclear program and appears to be an issue for concentrated solar power); network effects (for a highway or rail construction program); or demographic or economic shocks. This and the rest of the paragraph are based on Shalizi and Lecocq 2009.

40. Shalizi and Lecocq 2009.

41. Folger 2006; Levin and others 2007.

42. Häfele and others 1981, as cited in Ha-Duong, Grubb, and Hourcade 1997.

43. Davis and Owens 2003; IEA 2008b; Nemet and Kammen 2007; SEG 2007; Stern 2007.

44. Repetto 2008.

45. Stern 2007, part VI.

46. Based on the formula used in Nordhaus 2008.

47. These are rounded values based on the following. The IPCC estimates that at carbon prices up to $50 a ton CO_2e, about 65 percent of emission reduction would take place in developing countries in 2030 (Barker and others 2007a, table 11.3). McKinsey & Company (2009) estimates this share at 68 percent for a 450 ppm scenario if done using a least-cost allocation. As to the least-cost share of global mitigation investments in 2030 taking place in developing countries, it is estimated at 44–67 percent for a 450 ppm CO_2e concentration (see table 4.2: 44 percent, MESSAGE; 56 percent, McKinsey; 67 percent, IEA ETP) although an outlying estimate is offered by REMIND (91 percent). Over the course of the century (using present value of all investments to 2100), the estimated share of developing countries is somewhat higher, with ranges between 66 percent (Edmonds and others 2008) and 71 percent (Hope 2009).

48. Edmonds and others 2008.

49. For a 425–450 ppm CO_2e, or 2°C, stabilization scenario, IIASA (2009) estimates the cost at $4 trillion; Knopf and others (forthcoming) at $6 trillion; Edmonds and others (2008) at $9 trillion; Nordhaus (2008) at $11 trillion; and Hope (2009) at $25 trillion. These are present values, and the large differences among them are largely driven by the different discount rate used. All follow a first-best scenario where mitigation takes place wherever and whenever most cost-effective.

50. Hamilton 2009.

51. The Nameless Hurricane, http://science.nasa.gov/headlines/y2004/02apr_hurricane.htm (accessed March 12, 2009).

52. Rogers 2009; Westermeyer 2009.

53. OECS 2004.

54. World Bank 2008a.

55. Kanbur 2009.

56. FAO 2009a.

57. Worldwatch Institute, "State of the World 2005 Trends and Facts: Water Conflict and Security Cooperation," http://www.worldwatch.org/node/69 (accessed July 1, 2009); Wolf and others 1999.

58. Easterling and others 2007; Fisher and others 2007.

59. FAO 2008.

60. von Braun and others 2008; World Bank 2009a.

61. Sterner 2007. The average fuel price in the Euro area in 2007 was more than twice what it was in the United States ($1.54 a liter as opposed to 63 cents a liter). Variations in emissions not driven by income can be captured by the residuals of a regression of emissions per capita on income. When these residuals are regressed on gasoline prices, the elasticity is estimated at –0.5, meaning that a doubling of fuel prices would halve emissions, holding income per capita constant.

62. Based on average electricity prices for households in 2006–07 from the U.S. Energy Information Agency, http://www.eia.doe.gov/emeu/international/elecprih.html (accessed August 1, 2009).

63. Emission data is from WRI (2008).

64. IEA 2008d; UNEP 2008. A 2004 report by the European Environment Agency (EEA 2004) estimated European subsidies to energy at €30 billion in 2001, two-thirds for fossil fuels, the rest for nuclear and renewables.

65. http://www.eia.doe.gov/emeu/international/elecprih.html (accessed July 2009).

66. Price and Worrell 2006.

67. ESMAP 2006.

68. http://co2captureandstorage.info/index.htm (accessed August 1, 2009).

69. Calvin and others, forthcoming; IEA 2008a.

70. Gurgel, Reilly, and Paltsev 2007; IEA 2006; Wise and others 2009.

71. NRC 2007; Tilman, Hill, and Lehman 2006; WBGU 2009.

72. OECD 2008.

73. Lotze-Campen and others 2009; Wise and others 2009. See chapter 3 for a discussion.

74. Scherr and McNeely 2008.

75. World Bank 2007b.

76. Milly and others 2008.

77. Fay, Block, and Ebinger 2010; Ligeti, Penney, and Wieditz 2007; Heinz Center 2007.

78. Lempert and Schlesinger 2000.

79. Keller, Yohe, and Schlesinger 2008.

80. Cass 2005; Davenport 2008; Dolsak 2001; Kunkel, Jacob, and Busch 2006.

81. Alber and Kern 2008.

82. Guth, Schmittberger, and Schwarze 1982; Camerer and Thaler 1995; Irwin 2009; Ruffle 1998.

83. *Times of India,* http://timesofindia.indiatimes.com/NEWS/India/Even-in-2031-Indias-per-capita-emission-will-be-1/7th-of-US/articleshow/4717472.cms (accessed August 2009).

84. Dechezleprêtre and others 2008.

85. Maini 2005; Nagrath 2007.

86. Haites and others 2006.

87. http://www.gefweb.org/uploadedFiles/Publications/ClimateChange-FS-June2009.pdf (accessed July 6, 2009).

88. http://unfccc.int/meetings/cop_13/items/4049.php (accessed August 1, 2009).

89. The development and aid community has been moving toward impact evaluation and results-based aid, suggesting a degree of frustration with input-based programs (where the quantity of funds disbursed and the number of schools built were monitored, as opposed to the number of children graduating from schools or

improvements in their performance). However, there is some difference in the way "input-based" approaches are defined in this case, because the "inputs" are policy changes rather than narrowly defined financial inputs—adoption and enforcement of a fuel efficiency standard rather than public spending on an efficiency program. Nevertheless, monitoring and evaluation would still be important to learn what works.

90. Olsen 2007; Sutter and Parreno 2007; Olsen and Fenhann 2008; Nussbaumer 2009; Michaelowa and Pallav 2007; Schneider 2007.

91. Fankhauser, Martin, and Prichard, forthcoming.

92. World Bank 2007d.

93. Stimulus packages around the world are expected to inject about $430 billion in key climate change areas over the next few years: $215 billion will be spent on energy efficiency, $38 billion on low-carbon renewables, $20 billion on carbon capture and storage, and $92 billion on smart grids. Robins, Clover, and Singh 2009. See chapter 1 for a discussion of expected job creation.

References

Adger, W. N., S. Dessai, M. Goulden, M. Hulme, I. Lorenzoni, D. R. Nelson, L. O. Naess, J. Wolf, and A. Wreford. 2009. "Are There Social Limits to Adaptation to Climate Change?" *Climatic Change* 93 (3–4): 335–54.

Agrawala, S., and S. Fankhauser. 2008. *Economic Aspects of Adaptation to Climate Change: Costs, Benefits and Policy Instruments.* Paris: Organisation for Economic Cooperation and Development.

Alber, G., and K. Kern. 2008. "Governing Climate Change in Cities: Modes of Urban Climate Governance in Multi-Level Systems." Paper presented at the OECD Conference on Competitive Cities and Climate Change, Milan, October 9–10.

Bai, X. 2006. "Rizhao, China: Solar-Powered City." In *State of the World 2007: Our Urban Future,* ed. Worldwatch Institute. New York: W.W. Norton & Company Inc.

Barbera, A. J., and V. D. McConnell. 1990. "The Impacts of Environmental Regulations on Industry Productivity: Direct and Indirect Effects." *Journal of Environmental Economics and Management* 18 (1): 50–65.

Barbier, E. B., and S. Sathirathai, ed. 2004. *Shrimp Farming and Mangrove Loss in Thailand.* Cheltenham, UK: Edward Elgar Publishing.

Barker, T., I. Bashmakov, A. Alharthi, M. Amann, L. Cifuentes, J. Drexhage, M. Duan, O. Edenhofer, B. Flannery, M. Grubb, M. Hoogwijk, F. I.

Ibitoye, C. J. Jepma, W. A. Pizer, and K. Yamaji. 2007a. "Mitigation From a Cross-Sectoral Perspective." In *Climate Change 2007: Mitigation. Contribution of Working Group III to the Fourth Assessment Report of the Intergovernmental Panel on Climate Change,* ed. B. Metz, O. R. Davidson, P. R. Bosch, R. Dave, and L. A. Meyer. Cambridge, UK: Cambridge University Press.

Barker, T., I. Bashmakov, L. Bernstein, J. E. Bogner, P. R. Bosch, R. Dave, O. R. Davidson, B. S. Fisher, S. Gupta, K. Halsnaes, B. Heij, S. Khan Ribeiro, S. Kobayashi, M. D. Levine, D. L. Martino, O. Masera, B. Metz, L. A. Meyer, G.-J. Nabuurs, A. Najam, N. Nakićenović, H.-H. Rogner, J. Roy, J. Sathaye, R. Schock, P. Shukla, R. E. H. Sims, P. Smith, D. A. Tirpak, D. Urge-Vorsatz, and D. Zhou. 2007b. "Technical Summary." In *Climate Change 2007: Mitigation. Contribution of Working Group III to the Fourth Assessment Report of the Intergovernmental Panel on Climate Change,* ed. B. Metz, O. R. Davidson, P. R. Bosch, R. Dave, and L. A. Meyer. Cambridge, UK: Cambridge University Press.

Barrett, S. 2003. *Environment and Statecraft: The Strategy of Environmental Treaty-Making.* Oxford: Oxford University Press.

Blanford, G. J., R. G. Richels, and T. F. Rutherford. 2008. "Revised Emissions Growth Projections for China: Why Post-Kyoto Climate Policy Must Look East." Harvard Project on International Climate Agreements, Harvard Kennedy School Discussion Paper 08-06, Cambridge, MA.

BTS (Bureau of Transportation Statistics). 2008. *Key Transportation Indicators November 2008.* Washington, DC: U.S. Department of Transportation.

Burke, M., D. B. Lobell, and L. Guarino. 2009. "Shifts in African Crop Climates by 2050 and the Implications for Crop Improvement and Genetic Resources Conservation." *Global Environmental Change* 19 (3): 317–325.

Burtraw, D., D. A. Evans, A. Krupnick, K. Palmer, and R. Toth. 2005. "Economics of Pollution Trading for SO_2 and NO_x." Discussion Paper 05-05, Resources for the Future, Washington, DC.

Calvin, K., J. Edmonds, B. Bond-Lamberty, L. Clarke, P. Kyle, S. Smith, A. Thomson, and M. Wise. Forthcoming. "Limiting Climate Change to 450 ppm CO_2 Equivalent in the 21st Century." *Energy Economics.*

Camerer, C., and R. H. Thaler. 1995. "Anomalies: Ultimatums Dictators and Manners." *Journal of Economic Perspectives* 9 (2): 109–220.

Canadell, J. G., C. Le Quere, M. R. Raupach, C. B. Field, E. T. Buitenhuis, P. Ciais, T. J. Conway,

N. P. Gillett, R. A. Houghton, and G. Marland. 2007. "Contributions to Accelerating Atmospheric CO_2 Growth from Economic Activity, Carbon Intensity, and Efficiency of Natural Sinks." *Proceedings of the National Academy of Sciences* 104 (47): 18866–70.

Cass, L. 2005. "Measuring the Domestic Salience of International Environmental Norms: Climate Change Norms in German, British, and American Climate Policy Debates." Paper presented at the International Studies Association, March 15, Honolulu.

Chen, S, and M. Ravallion. 2008. "The Developing World Is Poorer than We Thought, But No Less Successful in the Fight against Poverty." Policy Research Working Paper 4703, World Bank, Washington, DC.

Clarke, L., J. Edmonds, V. Krey, R. Richels, S. Rose, and M. Tavoni. Forthcoming. "International Climate Policy Architectures: Overview of the EMF 22 International Scenarios." *Energy Economics.*

Dasgupta, S., B. Laplante, C. Meisner, D. Wheeler, and J. Yan. 2009. "The Impact of Sea Level Rise on Developing Countries: A Comparative Analysis." *Climatic Change* 93 (3–4): 379–88.

Davenport, D. 2008. "The International Dimension of Climate Policy." In *Turning Down the Heat: The Politics of Climate Policy in Affluent Democracies,* ed. H. Compston and I. Bailey. Basingstoke, UK: Palgrave Macmillan.

Davis, G., and B. Owens. 2003. "Optimizing the Level of Renewable Electric R&D Expenditures Using Real Options Analysis." *Energy Policy* 31 (15): 1589–1608.

de Bruin, K., R. Dellink, and S. Agrawala. 2009. "Economic Aspects of Adaptation to Climate Change: Integrated Assessment Modeling of Adaptation Costs and Benefits." Environment Working Paper 6, Organisation for Economic Co-operation and Development, Paris.

de la Torre, A., P. Fajnzylber, and J. Nash. 2008. *Low Carbon, High Growth: Latin American Responses to Climate Change.* Washington, DC: World Bank.

Dechezleprêtre, A., M. Glachant, I. Hascic, N. Johnstone, and Y. Ménière. 2008. *Invention and Transfer of Climate Change Mitigation Technologies on a Global Scale: A Study Drawing on Patent Data.* Paris: CERNA.

Deltacommissie. 2008. *Working Together with Water: A Living Land Builds for Its Future.* Netherlands: Deltacommissie.

Derpsch, R., and T. Friedrich. 2009. "Global Overview of Conservation Agriculture Adoption." In *Lead Papers, 4th World Congress on Conservation Agriculture,* February 4–7, 2009, New Delhi, India. New Delhi: World Congress on Conservation Agriculture.

DOE (U.S. Department of Energy). 2009. "Carbon Dioxide Information Analysis Center (CDIAC)." DOE, Oak Ridge, TN.

Dolsak, N. 2001. "Mitigating Global Climate Change: Why Are Some Countries More Committed than Others?" *Policy Studies Journal* 29 (3): 414–36.

Easterling, W., P. Aggarwal, P. Batima, K. Brander, L. Erda, M. Howden, A. Kirilenko, J. Morton, J.-F. Soussana, J. Schmidhuber, and F. Tubiello. 2007. "Food, Fibre and Forest Products." In *Climate Change 2007: Impacts, Adaptation and Vulnerability. Contribution of Working Group II to the Fourth Assessment Report of the Intergovernmental Panel on Climate Change.* ed. M. Parry, O. F. Canziani, J. P. Palutikof, P. J. van der Linden, and C. E. Hanson. Cambridge, UK: Cambridge University Press.

Ebi, K. L., and I. Burton. 2008. "Identifying Practical Adaptation Options: An Approach to Address Climate Change-related Health Risks." *Environmental Science and Policy* 11 (4): 359–69.

Edmonds, J., L. Clarke, J. Lurz, and M. Wise. 2008. "Stabilizing CO_2 Concentrations with Incomplete International Cooperation." *Climate Policy* 8 (4): 355–76.

EEA (European Environment Agency). 2004. "Energy Subsidies in the European Union: A Brief Overview." Technical Report 1/2004, EEA, Copenhagen.

Eliasch, J. 2008. *Climate Change: Financing Global Forests: The Eliasch Review.* London: Earthscan.

Erenstein, O. 2009. "Adoption and Impact of Conservation Agriculture Based Resource Conserving Technologies in South Asia." In *Lead Papers, 4th World Congress on Conservation Agriculture,* February 4–7, 2009, New Delhi, India. New Delhi: World Congress on Conservation Agriculture.

Erenstein, O., and V. Laxmi. 2008. "Zero Tillage Impacts in India's Rice-Wheat Systems: A Review." *Soil and Tillage Research* 100 (1–2): 1–14.

ESMAP (Energy Sector Management Assistance Program). 2006. *Proceedings of the International Grid-Connected Renewable Energy Policy Forum.* Washington, DC: World Bank.

European Commission. 2007. "Limiting Global Climate Change to 2 Degrees Celsius—The Way Ahead for 2020 and Beyond: Impact Assessment Summary." Commission Staff Working Document, Brussels.

Falloon, P., and R. Betts. Forthcoming. "Climate Impacts on European Agriculture and Water Management in the Context of Adaptation and Mitigation: The Importance of an Integrated Approach." *Science of the Total Environment.*

Fankhauser, S., N. Martin, and S. Prichard. Forthcoming. "The Economics of the CDM Levy: Revenue Potential, Tax Incidence and Distortionary Effects." Working paper, London School of Economics.

FAO (Food and Agriculture Organization). 2005. "Global Forest Resources Assessment 2005: Progress towards Sustainable Forest Management." Forestry Paper 147, Rome.

———. 2007. "The World's Mangroves 1980–2005." Forestry Paper 153, Rome.

———. 2008. *Food Outlook: Global Market Analysis.* Rome: FAO.

———. 2009a. "Aquastat." Rome.

———. 2009b. "More People than Ever Are Victims of Hunger." Press release, Rome.

Fay, M., R. I. Block, and J. Ebinger. 2010. *Adapting to Climate Change in Europe and Central Asia.* Washington, DC: World Bank.

Fisher, B. S., N. Nakićenović, K. Alfsen, J. Corfee Morlot, F. de la Chesnaye, J.-C. Hourcade, K. Jiang, M. Kainuma, E. La Rovere, A. Matysek, A. Rana, K. Riahi, R. Richels, S. Rose, D. van Vuuren, and R. Warren. 2007. "Issues Related to Mitigation in the Long-Term Context." In *Climate Change 2007: Mitigation. Contribution of Working Group III to the Fourth Assessment Report of the Intergovernmental Panel on Climate Change,* ed. B. Metz, O. R. Davidson, P. R. Bosch, R. Dave, and L. A. Meyer. Cambridge, UK: Cambridge University Press.

Folger, T. 2006. "Can Coal Come Clean? How to Survive the Return of the World's Dirtiest Fossil Fuel." December. *Discover Magazine.*

Government of Bangladesh. 2008. *Cyclone Sidr in Bangladesh: Damage, Loss and Needs Assessment for Disaster Recovery and Reconstruction.* Dhaka: Government of Bangladesh, World Bank, and European Commission.

Guan, D., and K. Hubacek. 2008. "A New and Integrated Hydro-Economic Accounting and Analytical Framework for Water Resources: A Case Study for North China." *Journal of Environmental Management* 88 (4): 1300–1313.

Gurgel, A. C., J. M. Reilly, and S. Paltsev. 2007. "Potential Land Use Implications of a Global Biofuels Industry." *Journal of Agricultural and Food Industrial Organization* 5 (2): 1–34.

Güth, W., R. Schmittberger, and B. Schwarze. 1982. "An Experimental Analysis of Ultimatum Bargaining." *Journal of Economic Behavior and Organization* 3 (4): 367–88.

Guthrie, P., C. Juma, and H. Sillem, eds. 2008. *Engineering Change: Towards a Sustainable Future in the Developing World.* London: Royal Academy of Engineering.

Ha-Duong, M., M. Grubb, and J.-C. Hourcade. 1997. "Influence of Socioeconomic Inertia and Uncertainty on Optimal CO_2-Emission Abatement." *Nature* 390: 270–73.

Häfele, W., J. Anderer, A. McDonald, and N. Nakićenović. 1981. *Energy in a Finite World: Paths to a Sustainable Future.* Cambridge, MA: Ballinger.

Haites, E., D. Maosheng, and S. Seres. 2006. "Technology Transfer by CDM Projects." *Climate Policy* 6: 327–44.

Hamilton, K. 2009. "Delayed Participation in a Global Climate Agreement." Background note for the WDR 2010.

Hare, B., and M. Meinshausen. 2006. "How Much Warming Are We Committed to and How Much Can Be Avoided?" *Climatic Change* 75 (1–2): 111–49.

Heinz Center. 2007. *A Survey of Climate Change Adaptation Planning.* Washington, DC: John Heinz III Center for Science, Economics and the Environment.

Hof, A. F., M. G. J. den Elzen, and D. P. van Vuuren. 2008. "Analyzing the Costs and Benefits of Climate Policy: Value Judgments and Scientific Uncertainties." *Global Environmental Change* 18 (3): 412–24.

Hope, C. 2009. "How Deep Should the Deep Cuts Be? Optimal CO_2 Emissions over Time under Uncertainty." *Climate Policy* 9 (1): 3–8.

Horton, R., C. Herweijer, C. Rosenzweig, J. Liu, V. Gornitz, and A. C. Ruane. 2008. "Sea Level Rise Projections for Current Generation CGCMs Based on the Semi-Empirical Method." *Geophysical Research Letters* 35: L02715–doi:10.1029/2007GL032486.

Houghton, R. A. 2009. "Emissions of Carbon from Land Management." Background note for the WDR 2010.

ICCT (International Council on Clean Transportation). 2007. *Passenger Vehicle Greenhouse Gas and Fuel Economy Standard: A Global Update.* Washington, DC: ICCT.

IEA (International Energy Agency). 2006. *World Energy Outlook 2006.* Paris: International Energy Agency.

———. 2008a. *CO_2 Capture and Storage—A Key Abatement Option.* Paris: International Energy Agency.

————. 2008b. *Energy Efficiency Policy Recommendations: In Support of the G8 Plan of Action.* Paris: International Energy Agency.

————. 2008c. *Energy Technology Perspective 2008: Scenarios and Strategies to 2050.* Paris: International Energy Agency.

————. 2008d. *World Energy Outlook 2008.* Paris: International Energy Agency.

————. 2008e. *Worldwide Trends in Energy Use and Efficiency: Key Insights from IEA Indicator Analysis.* Paris: International Energy Agency.

IIASA (International Institute for Applied Systems Analysis). 2009. "GGI Scenario Database." Laxenburg, Austria.

IMF (International Monetary Fund). 2009. *World Economic Outlook: Crisis and Recovery.* Washington, DC: IMF.

International Scientific Steering Committee. 2005. *Avoiding Dangerous Climate Change: International Symposium on the Stabilization of Greenhouse Gas Concentrations.* Report of the International Scientific Steering Committee. Exeter, UK: Hadley Centre Met Office.

IPCC (Intergovernmental Panel on Climate Change). 2001. *Climate Change 2001: Synthesis Report. Contribution of Working Groups I, II and III to the Third Assessment Report of the Intergovernmental Panel on Climate Change.* Geneva: IPCC.

————. 2007a. *Climate Change 2007: Synthesis Report. Contribution of Working Groups I, II and II to the Fourth Assessment Report of the Intergovernmental Panel on Climate Change.* Geneva: IPCC.

————. 2007b. "Summary for Policymakers." In *Climate Change 2007: Impacts, Adaptation and Vulnerability. Contribution of Working Group II to the Fourth Assessment Report of the Intergovernmental Panel on Climate Change,* M. L. Parry, O. F. Canziani, J. P. Palutikof, P. J. van der Linden, and C. E. Hanson. Cambridge, UK: Cambridge University Press.

————. 2007c. "Summary for Policymakers." In *Climate Change 2007: The Physical Science Basis. Contribution of Working Group I to the Fourth Assessment Report of the Intergovernmental Panel on Climate Change,* ed. S. Solomon, D. Qin, M. Manning, Z. Chen, M. Marquis, K. B. Averyt, M. Tignor, and H. L. Miller. Cambridge, UK: Cambridge University Press.

Irwin, T. 2009. "Implications for Climate Change Policy of Research on Cooperation in Social Dilemma." Policy Research Working Paper 5006, World Bank, Washington, DC.

Jaffe, A., S. R. Peterson, P. R. Portney, and R. N. Stavins. 1995. "Environmental Regulation and the Competitiveness of U.S. Manufacturing: What Does the Evidence Tell Us?" *Journal of Economic Literature* 33 (1): 132–63.

Kanbur, R. 2009. "Macro Crises and Targeting Transfers to the Poor." Cornell Food and Nutrition Policy Program, Working Paper 236, Ithaca, NY.

Karim, M. F., and N. Mimura. 2008. "Impacts of Climate Change and Sea-Level Rise on Cyclonic Storm Surge Floods in Bangladesh." *Global Environmental Change* 18 (3): 490–500.

Keim, M. E. 2008. "Building Human Resilience: The Role of Public Health Preparedness and Response as an Adaptation to Climate Change." *American Journal of Preventive Medicine* 35 (5): 508–16.

Keller, K., G. Yohe, and M. Schlesinger. 2008. "Managing the Risks of Climate Thresholds: Uncertainties and Information Needs." *Climatic Change* 91: 5–10.

Knopf, B., O. Edenhofer, T. Barker, N. Bauer, L. Baumstark, B. Chateau, P. Criqui, A. Held, M. Isaac, M. Jakob, E. Jochem, A. Kitous, S. Kypreos, M. Leimbach, B. Magné, S. Mima, W. Schade, S. Scrieciu, H. Turton, and D. van Vuuren. Forthcoming. "The Economics of Low Stabilisation: Implications for Technological Change and Policy." In *Making Climate Change Work for Us,* ed. M. Hulme and H. Neufeldt. Cambridge, UK: Cambridge University Press.

Koetse, M., and P. Rietveld. 2009. "The Impact of Climate Change and Weather on Transport: An Overview of Empirical Findings." *Transportation Research Part D: Transport and Environment* 14 (3): 205–21.

Kunkel, N., K. Jacob, and P.-O. Busch. 2006. "Climate Policies : (The Feasibility of) a Statistical Analysis of their Determinants." Paper presented at the Human Dimensions of Global Environmental Change, Berlin.

Lawrence, D. M., A. G. Slater, R. A. Tomas, M. M. Holland, and C. Deser. 2008. "Accelerated Arctic Land Warming and Permafrost Degradation during Rapid Sea Ice Loss." *Geophysical Research Letters* 35: L11506– doi:10.1029/2008GL033985.

Lehmann, J. 2007. "A Handful of Carbon." *Nature* 447: 143–44.

Lempert, R. J., and M. E. Schlesinger. 2000. "Robust Strategies for Abating Climate Change." *Climatic Change* 45 (3–4): 387–401.

Levin, K., B. Cashore, S. Bernstein, and G. Auld. 2007. "Playing It Forward: Path Dependency, Progressive Incrementalism, and the 'Super

Wicked' Problem of Global Climate Change." Paper presented at the International Studies Association 48th Annual Convention, February 28, Chicago.

Ligeti, E., J. Penney, and I. Wieditz. 2007. *Cities Preparing for Climate Change: A Study of Six Urban Regions*. Toronto: Clean Air Partnership.

Lotze-Campen, H., A. Popp, J. P. Dietrich, and M. Krause. 2009. "Competition for Land between Food, Bioenergy and Conservation." Background note for the WDR 2010.

Lüthi, D., M. Le Floch, B. Bereiter, T. Blunier, J.-M. Barnola, U. Siegenthaler, D. Raynaud, J. Jouzel, H. Fischer, K. Kawamura, and T. F. Stocker. 2008. "High-Resolution Carbon Dioxide Concentration Record 650,000–800,000 Years before Present." *Nature* 453 (7193): 379–82.

Maini, C. 2005. "Development of a Globally Competitive Electric Vehicle in India." *Journal of the Indian Insitute of Science* 85: 83–95.

Mann, M. 2009. "Defining Dangerous Anthropogenic Interference." *Proceedings of the National Academy of Sciences* 106 (11): 4065–66.

Matthews, H. D., and K. Caldeira. 2008. "Stabilizing Climate Requires Near-zero Emissions." *Geophysical Research Letters* 35: L04705–doi:10.1029/2007GL032388.

Matthews, H. D., and D. W. Keith. 2007. "Carbon-cycle Feedbacks Increase the Likelihood of a Warmer Future." *Geophysical Research Letters* 34: L09702–doi:10.1029/2006GL028685.

McKinsey & Company. 2009. *Pathways to a Low-carbon Economy. Version 2 of the Global Greenhouse Gas Abatement Cost Curve*. McKinsey & Company.

McNeely, J. A., and S. J. Scherr. 2003. *Ecoagriculture: Strategies to Feed the World and Save Biodiversity*. Washington, DC: Island Press.

Meyer, S. M. 1995. "The Economic Impact of Environmental Regulation." *Journal of Environmental Law and Practice* 3 (2): 4–15.

Michaelowa, A., and P. Pallav. 2007. *Additionality Determination of Indian CDM Projects: Can Indian CDM Project Developers Outwit the CDM Executive Board?* Zurich: University of Zurich.

Mignone, B. K., R. H. Socolow, J. L. Sarmiento, and M. Oppenheimer. 2008. "Atmospheric Stabilization and the Timing of Carbon Mitigation." *Climatic Change* 88 (3–4): 251–65.

Mills, E. 2009. *Building Commissioning: A Golden Opportunity for Reducing Energy Costs and Greenhouse Gas Emissions*. Berkeley, CA: Lawrence Berkeley National Laboratory.

Milly, P. C. D., J. Betancourt, M. Falkenmark, R. M. Hirsch, Z. W. Kundzewicz, D. P. Lettenmaier, and R. J. Stouffer. 2008. "Stationarity Is Dead: Whither Water Management?" *Science* 319 (5863): 573–74.

Müller, C., A. Bondeau, A. Popp, K. Waha, and M. Fader. 2009. "Climate Change Impacts on Agricultural Yields." Background note for the WDR 2010.

Nagrath, S. 2007. "Gee Whiz, It's a Reva! The Diminutive Indian Electric Car Is a Hit on the Streets of London." *Businessworld* 27(2), October 16.

National Academy of Engineering. 2008. *Grand Challenges for Engineering*. Washington, DC: National Academy of Sciences.

Nemet, G. 2006. "Beyond the Learning Curve: Factors Influencing Cost Reductions in Photovoltaics." *Energy Policy* 34 (17): 3218–32.

Nemet, G., and D. M. Kammen. 2007. "U.S. Energy Research and Development: Declining Investment, Increasing Need, and the Feasibility of Expansion." *Energy Policy* 35 (1): 746–55.

Nordhaus, W. 2008. *A Question of Balance: Weighing the Options on Global Warming Policies*. New Haven, CT: Yale University Press.

Nordhaus, W., and J. Boyer. 2000. *Warming the World: Economic Models of Climate Change*. Cambridge, MA: MIT Press.

NRC (National Research Council). 2007. *Water Implications of Biofuels Production in the United States*. Washington, DC: National Academies Press.

Nussbaumer, P. 2009. "On the Contribution of Labeled Certified Emission Reductions to Sustainable Development: A Multi-criteria Evaluation of CDM Projects." *Energy Policy* 37 (1): 91–101.

OECD (Organisation for Economic Co-operation and Development). 2008. *Compendium of Patent Statistics 2008*. Paris: OECD.

OECS (Organization of Eastern Caribbean States). 2004. *Grenada: Macro-Socio-Economic Assessment of the Damages Caused by Hurricane Ivan*. St. Lucia: OECS.

Olsen, K. H. 2007. "The Clean Development Mechanism's Contribution to Sustainable Development: A Review of the Literature." *Climatic Change* 84 (1): 59–73.

Olsen, K. H., and J. Fenhann. 2008. "Sustainable Development Benefits of Clean Development Mechanism Projects. A New Methodology for Sustainability Assessment Based on Text Analysis of the Project Design Documents Submitted for Validation." *Energy Policy* 36 (8): 2819–30.

Parry, M., O. F. Canziani, J. P. Palutikof, and coauthors. 2007. "Technical Summary." In, *Climate Change 2007: Impacts, Adaptation and Vulnerability. Contribution of Working Group II to the Fourth Assessment Report of the Intergovernmental Panel on Climate Change,* ed. M. Parry, O. F. Canziani, J. P. Palutikof, P. J. van der Linden, and C. E. Hanson. Cambridge, UK: Cambridge University Press.

Parry, M., J. Palutikof, C. Hanson, and J. Lowe. 2008. "Squaring Up to Reality." *Nature* 2: 68–71.

Price, L., and E. Worrell. 2006. "Global Energy Use, CO_2 Emissions, and the Potential for Reduction in the Cement Industry." Paper presented at the International Energy Agency Workshop on Cement Energy Efficiency, Paris.

Project Catalyst. 2009. *Adaptation to Climate Change: Potential Costs and Choices for a Global Agreement.* London: ClimateWorks and European Climate Foundation.

Raupach, M. R., G. Marland, P. Ciais, C. Le Quéré, J. G. Canadell, G. Klepper, and C. B. Field. 2007. "Global and Regional Drivers of Accelerating CO_2 Emissions." *Proceedings of the National Academy of Sciences* 104 (24): 10288–93.

Repetto, R. 2008. "The Climate Crisis and the Adaptation Myth." School of Forestry and Environmental Studies Working Paper 13, Yale University, New Haven, CT.

Robins, N., R. Clover, and C. Singh. 2009. *A Climate for Recovery: The Colour of Stimulus Goes Green.* London, UK: HSBC.

Rogers, D. 2009. "Environmental Information Services and Development." Background note for the WDR 2010.

Ruffle, B. J. 1998. "More Is Better, But Fair Is Fair: Tipping in Dictator and Ultimatum Games." *Games and Economic Behavior* 23 (2): 247–65.

Schaeffer, M., T. Kram, M. Meinshausen, D. P. van Vuuren, and W. L. Hare. 2008. "Near-Linear Cost Increase to Reduce Climate Change Risk." *Proceedings of the National Academy of Sciences* 105 (52): 20621–26.

Scheffer, M., V. Brovkin, and P. Cox. 2006. "Positive Feedback between Global Warming and Atmospheric CO_2 Concentration Inferred from Past Climate Change." *Geophysical Research Letters* 33: L10702–doi:10.1029/2005GL025044.

Scherr, S. J., and J. A. McNeely. 2008. "Biodiversity Conservation and Agricultural Sustainability: Towards a New Paradigm of Ecoagriculture Landscapes." *Philosophical Transactions of the Royal Society* 363: 477–94.

Schneider, L. 2007. *Is the CDM Fulfilling Its Environmental and Sustainable Development Objective? An Evaluation of the CDM and Options for Improvement.* Berlin: Institute for Applied Ecology.

SEG (Scientific Expert Group on Climate Change). 2007. *Confronting Climate Change: Avoiding the Unmanageable and Managing the Unavoidable.* Washington, DC: Sigma Xi and the United Nations Foundation.

Shalizi, Z. 2006. "Addressing China's Growing Water Shortages and Associated Social and Environmental Consequences." Policy Research Working Paper 3895, World Bank, Washington, DC.

Shalizi, Z., and F. Lecocq. 2009. "Economics of Targeted Mitigation Programs in Sectors with Long-Lived Capital Stock." Policy Research Working Paper 5063, World Bank, Washington, DC.

Smith, P., D. Martino, Z. Cai, D. Gwary, H. H. Janzen, P. Kumar, B. McCarl, S. Ogle, F. O'Mara, C. Rice, R. J. Scholes, O. Sirotenko, M. Howden, T. McAllister, G. Pan, V. Romanenkov, U. Schneider, S. Towprayoon, M. Wattenbach, and J. U. Smith. 2008. "Greenhouse Gas Mitigation in Agriculture." *Philosophical Transactions of the Royal Society* 363 (1492): 789–813.

Smith, J. B., S. H. Schneider, M. Oppenheimer, G. W. Yohe, W. Hare, M. D. Mastrandrea, A. Patwardhan, I. Burton, J. Corfee-Morlot, C. H. D. Magadza, H.-M. Füssel, A. B. Pittock, A. Rahman, A. Suarez, and J.-P. van Ypersele. 2009. "Assessing Dangerous Climate Change Through an Update of the Intergovernmental Panel on Climate Change (IPCC): Reasons for Concern". *Proceedings of the National Academy of Sciences* 106 (11): 4133–37.

Snoussi, M., T. Ouchani, A. Khouakhi, and I. Niang-Diop. 2009. "Impacts of Sea-level Rise on the Moroccan Coastal Zone: Quantifying Coastal Erosion and Flooding in the Tangier Bay." *Geomorphology* 107 (1–2): 32–40.

Stern, N. 2007. *The Economics of Climate Change: The Stern Review.* Cambridge, UK: Cambridge University Press.

Sterner, T. 2007. "Fuel Taxes: An Important Instrument for Climate Policy." *Energy Policy* 35: 3194–3202.

Sutter, C., and J. C. Parreno. 2007. "Does the Current Clean Development Mechanism (CDM) Deliver its Sustainable Development Claim? An Analysis of Officially Registered CDM Projects." *Climatic Change* 84 (1): 75–90.

Swiss Re. 2007. "World Insurance in 2006: Premiums Came Back to 'Life'." Zurich: Sigma 4/2007.

Tilman, D., J. Hill, and C. Lehman. 2006. "Carbon-Negative Biofuels from Low-Input High-Diversity Grassland Biomass." *Science* 314: 1598–1600.

Tol, R. S. J. 2008. "Why Worry about Climate Change? A Research Agenda." *Environmental Values* 17 (4): 437–70.

Torn, M. S., and J. Harte. 2006. "Missing Feedbacks, Asymmetric Uncertainties, and the Underestimation of Future Warming." *Geophysical Research Letters* 33 (10): L10703–doi:10.1029/2005GL025540.

Tschakert, P. 2004. "The Costs of Soil Carbon Sequestration: An Economic Analysis for Small-Scale Farming Systems in Senegal." *Agricultural Systems* 81 (3): 227–53.

UNEP (United Nations Environment Programme). 1990. *Global Assessment of Soil Degradation.* New York: UNEP.

———. 2008. *Reforming Energy Subsidies: Opportunities to Contribute to the Climate Change Agenda.* Nairobi: UNEP Division of Technology, Industry and Economics.

UNFCCC (United Nations Framework Convention on Climate Change). 2008. *Investment and Financial Flows to Address Climate Change: An Update.* Bonn: UNFCCC.

Voluntary Carbon Standard. 2007. "Guidance for Agriculture, Forestry and Other Land Use Projects." VCS Association, Washington, DC.

von Braun, J., A. Ahmed, K. Asenso-Okyere, S. Fan, A. Gulati, J. Hoddinott, R. Pandya-Lorch, M. W. Rosegrant, M. Ruel, M. Torero, T. van Rheenen, and K. von Grebmer. 2008. "High Food Prices: The What, Who, and How of Proposed Policy Actions." Policy Brief, International Food Policy Research Institute, Washington, DC.

Walter, K. M., S. A. Zimov, J. P. Chanton, D. Verbyla, and F. S. Chapin III. 2006. "Methane Bubbling from Siberian Thaw Lakes as a Positive Feedback to Climate Warming." *Nature* 443: 71–75.

Wardle, D. A., M.-C. Nilsson, and O. Zackrisson. 2008. "Fire-derived Charcoal Causes Loss of Forest Humus." *Science* 320 (5876): 629.

WBGU (German Advisory Council on Global Change). 2009. *Future Bioenergy and Sustainable Land Use.* London: Earthscan.

Westermeyer, W. 2009. "Observing the Climate for Development." Background note for the WDR 2010.

Wise, M. A., K. V. Calvin, A. M. Thomson, L. E. Clarke, B. Bond-Lamberty, R. D. Sands, S. J. Smith, A. C. Janetos, and J. A. Edmonds. 2009.

The Implications of Limiting CO_2 Concentrations for Agriculture, Land Use, Land-use Change Emissions and Bioenergy. Richland, WA: Pacific Northwest National Laboratory (PNNL).

Wolf, A. T., J. A. Natharius, J. J. Danielson, B. S. Ward, and J. K. Pender. 1999. "International Basins of the World." *International Journal of Water Resources Development* 15 (4): 387–427.

World Bank. 2007a. *East Asia Environment Monitor 2007: Adapting to Climate Change.* Washington, DC: World Bank.

———. 2007b. *India Groundwater AAA Midterm Review.* Washington, DC: World Bank.

———. 2007c. *Making the Most of Scarcity: Accountability for Better Water Management Results in the Middle East and North Africa.* Washington, DC: World Bank.

———. 2007d. *World Development Report 2008. Agriculture for Development.* Washington, DC: World Bank.

———. 2008a. *The Caribbean Catastrophe Risk Insurance Facility: Providing Immediate Funding after Natural Disasters.* Washington, DC: World Bank.

———. 2008b. *South Asia Climate Change Strategy.* Washington, DC: World Bank.

———. 2008c. *World Development Indicators 2008.* Washington, DC: World Bank.

———. 2009a. *Improving Food Security in Arab Countries.* Washington, DC: World Bank.

———. 2009b. *Making Development Climate Resilient: A World Bank Strategy for Sub-Saharan Africa.* Washington, DC: World Bank.

———. 2009c. *The Economics of Adaptation to Climate Change.* Washington, DC: World Bank.

———. 2009d. "World Bank Urban Strategy." World Bank, Washington, DC.

WRI (World Resources Institute). 2008. "Climate Analysis Indicators Tool (CAIT)." Washington, DC.

Xia, J., L. Zhang, C. Liu, and J. Yu. 2007. "Towards Better Water Security in North China." *Water Resources Management* 21 (1): 233–47.

Yohe, G. W., R. D. Lasco, Q. K. Ahmad, N. Arnell, S. J. Cohen, C. Hope, A. C. Janetos, and R. T. Perez. 2007. "Perspectives on Climate Change and Sustainability." In *Climate Change 2007: Impacts, Adaptation and Vulnerability. Contribution of Working Group II to the Fourth Assessment Report of the Intergovernmental Panel on Climate Change,* ed. M. L. Parry, O. F. Canziani, J. P. Palutikof, P. J. van der Linden, and C. E. Hanson. Cambridge, UK: Cambridge University Press.

Understanding the Links between Climate Change and Development

In about 2200 BCE a shift in the Mediterranean westerly winds and a reduction in the Indian monsoon produced 300 years of lower rainfall and colder temperatures that hit agriculture from the Aegean Sea to the Indus River. This change in climate brought down Egypt's pyramid-building Old Kingdom and Sargon the Great's empire in Mesopotamia.[1] After only a few decades of lower rainfall, cities lining the northern reaches of the Euphrates, the breadbasket for the Akkadians, were deserted. At the city of Tell Leilan on the northern Euphrates, a monument was halted half-built.[2] With the city abandoned, a thick layer of wind-blown dirt covered the ruins.

Even intensively irrigated southern Mesopotamia, with its sophisticated bureaucracy and elaborate rationing, could not react fast enough to the new conditions. Without the shipments of rainfed grain from the north, and faced with parched irrigation ditches and migrants from the devastated northern cities, the empire collapsed.[3]

Societies have always depended on the climate but are only now coming to grips with the fact that the climate depends on their actions. The steep increase in greenhouse gases since the Industrial Revolution has transformed the relationship between people and the environment. In other words, not only does climate affect development but development affects the climate.

Left unmanaged, climate change will reverse development progress and compromise the well-being of current and future generations. It is certain that the earth will get warmer on average, at unprecedented speed. Impacts will be felt everywhere, but much of the damage will be in developing countries. Millions of people from Bangladesh to Florida will suffer as the sea level rises, inundating settlements and contaminating freshwater.[4] Greater rainfall variability and more severe droughts in semiarid Africa will hinder efforts to enhance food security and combat malnourishment.[5] The hastening disappearance of the Himalayan and Andean glaciers—which regulate river flow, generate hydropower, and supply clean water for over a billion of people on farms and in cities—will threaten rural livelihoods and major food markets (map 1.1).[6]

That is why decisive, immediate action is needed. Even though the debate about the costs and benefits of climate change mitigation continues, the case is very strong for immediate action to avoid unmanageable increases in temperature. The unacceptability of irreversible and potentially catastrophic impacts and the uncertainty about how, and how soon, they could occur

Key messages

Development goals are threatened by climate change, with the heaviest impacts on poor countries and poor people. Climate change cannot be controlled unless growth in both rich and poor countries becomes less greenhouse-gas-intensive. We must act now: country development decisions lock the world into a particular carbon intensity and determine future warming. Business-as-usual could lead to temperature increases of 5°C or more this century. And we must act together: postponing mitigation in developing countries could double mitigation costs, and that could well happen unless substantial financing is mobilized. But if we act now and act together, the incremental costs of keeping warming around 2°C are modest and can be justified given the likely dangers of greater climate change.

Map 1.1 More than a billion people depend on water from diminishing Himalayan glaciers

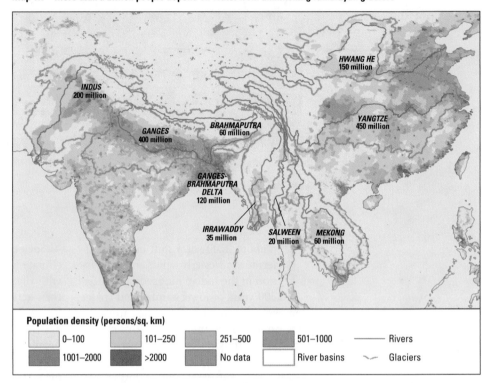

Sources: Center for International Earth Science Information Network, http://sedac.ciesin.columbia.edu/gpw/global.jsp (accessed May 15, 2009); Armstrong and others 2005; ESRI 2002; WDR team.

Note: The glaciers of the Himalayas and Tibetan Plateau regulate the supply of water throughout the year in major river basins supporting large agricultural and urban populations, with meltwater providing between 3 and 45 percent of river flow in the Ganges and Indus, respectively. Reduced storage as ice and snowpack will result in larger flows and flooding during rainy months and water shortages during warmer, drier months when water is most needed for agriculture. Glacier locations shown in the map only include glaciers larger than 1.5 sq. km in area. Numbers indicate how many people live in each river basin.

compel bold actions. The strong inertia in the climate system, in the built environment, and in the behavior of individuals and institutions requires that this action be urgent and immediate.

Over the past two centuries the direct benefits of carbon-intensive development have been concentrated largely in today's high-income countries. The inequity in the global distribution of past and current emissions, and in current and future damages, is stark (figure 1.1; see also focus A figure FA.6 and the overview). But if countries are willing to act, the economic incentives for a global deal exist.

The window of opportunity to choose the right policies to deal with climate change and promote development is closing. The further countries go along current emissions trajectories, the harder it will be to reverse course and alter infrastructures, economies, and lifestyles. High-income countries must face head-on the task of

cutting their own emissions by reshaping their built and economic environments. They also need to promote and finance the transition to low-carbon growth in developing countries. Better application of known practices and fundamental transformations—in natural resource management, energy provision, urbanization, social safety nets, international financial transfers, technological innovation, and governance, both international and national—are needed to meet the challenge.

Increasing people's opportunities and material well-being without undermining the sustainability of development is still the main challenge for large swaths of the world, as a severe financial and economic crisis wreaks havoc across the globe. Stabilizing the financial markets and protecting the real economy, labor markets, and vulnerable groups are the immediate priority. But the world must exploit this moment of opportunity for international cooperation

Figure 1.1   Individuals' emissions in high-income countries overwhelm those in developing countries

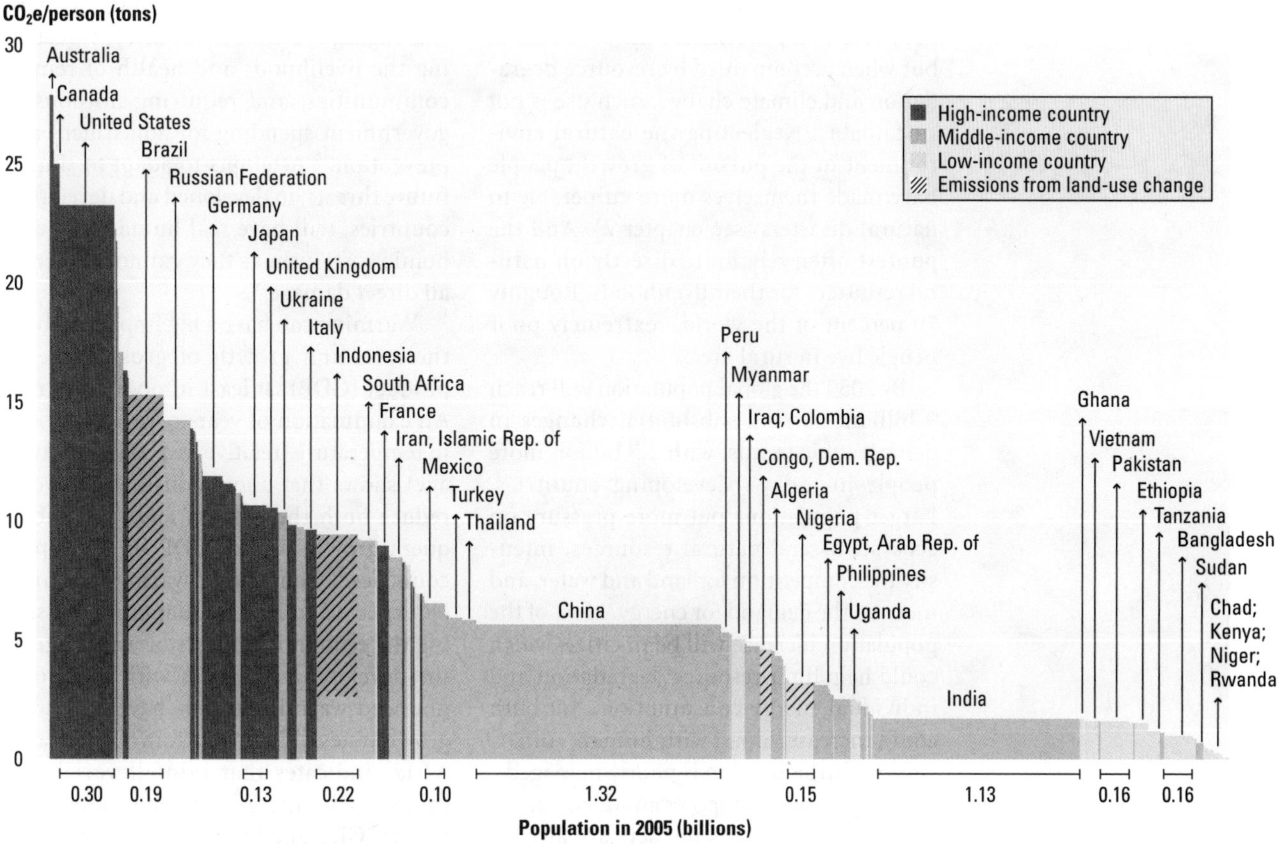

Sources: Emissions of greenhouse gases in 2005 from WRI 2008, augmented with land-use change emissions from Houghton 2009; population from World Bank 2009c.

Note: The width of each column depicts population and the height depicts per capita emissions, so the area represents total emissions. Per capita emissions of Qatar (55.5 tons of carbon dioxide equivalent per capita), UAE (38.8), and Bahrain (25.4)—greater than the height of the y-axis—are not shown. Among the larger countries, Brazil, Indonesia, the Democratic Republic of Congo, and Nigeria have low energy-related emissions but significant emissions from land-use change; therefore, the share from land-use change is indicated by the hatching.

and domestic intervention to tackle the rest of development's problems. Among them, and a top priority, is climate change.

Unmitigated climate change is incompatible with sustainable development

Development that is socially, economically, and environmentally sustainable is a challenge, even without global warming. Economic growth is needed, but growth alone is not enough if it does not reduce poverty and increase the equality of opportunity. And failing to safeguard the environment eventually threatens economic and social achievements. These points are not new. They only echo what still is, after more than 20 years, perhaps the most widely used definition of sustainable development: "development that meets the needs of the present without compromising the ability of future generations to meet their own needs."[7]

By definition, then, unmitigated climate change is incompatible with sustainable development.

Climate change threatens to reverse development gains

An estimated 400 million people escaped poverty between 1990 and 2005, the date of the latest estimate[8]—although the unfolding global financial crisis and the spike in food prices between 2005 and 2008 have reversed some of these gains.[9] Since 1990 infant mortality rates dropped from 106 per 1,000 live births to 83.[10] Yet close to half the population of developing countries (48 percent) are still in poverty, living on less than $2 a day.[11] Nearly a quarter—1.6 billion—lack access to electricity,[12] and one in six lack access to clean water.[13] Around 10 million children under five still die each year from preventable and treatable diseases such as respiratory infections, measles, and diarrhea.[14]

In the last half century the use of natural resources (among them fossil fuels) has supported improvements in well-being, but when accompanied by resource degradation and climate change, such use is not sustainable. Neglecting the natural environment in the pursuit of growth, people have made themselves more vulnerable to natural disasters (see chapter 2). And the poorest often rely more directly on natural resources for their livelihoods. Roughly 70 percent of the world's extremely poor people live in rural areas.

By 2050 the global population will reach 9 billion, barring substantial changes in demographic trends, with 2.5 billion more people in today's developing countries. Larger populations put more pressure on ecosystems and natural resources, intensify the competition for land and water, and increase the demand for energy. Most of the population increase will be in cities, which could help limit resource degradation and individual energy consumption. But both could increase, along with human vulnerability, if urbanization is poorly managed.

Climate change imposes an added burden on development.[15] Its impacts are already visible, and the most recent scientific evidence shows the problem is worsening fast, with current trajectories of greenhouse gas (GHG) emissions and sea-level rise outpacing previous projections.[16] And the disruptions to socioeconomic and natural systems are happening even now—that is, even sooner than previously thought (see focus A on science).[17] Changing temperature and precipitation averages and a more variable, unpredictable, or extreme climate can alter today's yields, earnings, health, and physical safety and ultimately the paths and levels of future development.

Climate change will affect numerous sectors and productive environments, including agriculture, forestry, energy, and coastal zones, in developed and developing countries. Developing economies will be more affected by climate change, in part because of their greater exposure to climate shocks and in part because of their low adaptive capacity. But no country is immune. The 2003 summer heat wave killed more than 70,000 people in a dozen European countries (map 1.2). The mountain pine beetle

epidemic in western Canadian forests, partly a consequence of milder winters, is ravaging the timber industry, threatening the livelihoods and health of remote communities, and requiring millions in government spending for adjustment and prevention.[18] Attempts to adapt to similar future threats, in developed and developing countries, will have real human and economic costs even as they cannot eliminate all direct damage.

Warming can have a big impact on both the level and growth of gross domestic product (GDP), at least in poor countries. An examination of year-to-year variations in temperature (relative to a country's average) shows that anomalously warm years reduce both the current level and subsequent growth rate of GDP in developing countries.[19] Consecutive warm years might be expected to lead to adaptation, lessening the economic impacts of warming, yet the developing countries with more pronounced warming trends have had lower growth rates.[20] Evidence from Sub-Saharan Africa indicates that rainfall variability, projected to increase substantially, also reduces GDP and increases poverty.[21]

Agricultural productivity is one of many factors driving the greater vulnerability of developing countries (see chapter 3, map 3.3). In northern Europe and North America crop yields and forest growth might increase under low levels of warming and carbon dioxide (CO_2) fertilization.[22] But in China and Japan yields of rice, a major global staple, will likely decline, while yields of wheat, maize, and rice in Central and South Asia will be particularly hard hit.[23] Prospects for crops and livestock in rainfed semiarid lands in Sub-Saharan Africa are also bleak, even before warming reaches 2–2.5°C above preindustrial levels.[24]

India's post-1980 deceleration in the increase of rice productivity (from the Green Revolution in the 1960s) is attributable not only to falling rice prices and deteriorating irrigation infrastructure, as previously postulated, but also to adverse climate phenomena from local pollution and global warming.[25] Extrapolating from past year-to-year variations in climate and agricultural outcomes, yields of major crops in India are projected to decline by 4.5 to

Map 1.2 Rich countries are also affected by anomalous climate: The 2003 heat wave killed more than 70,000 people in Europe

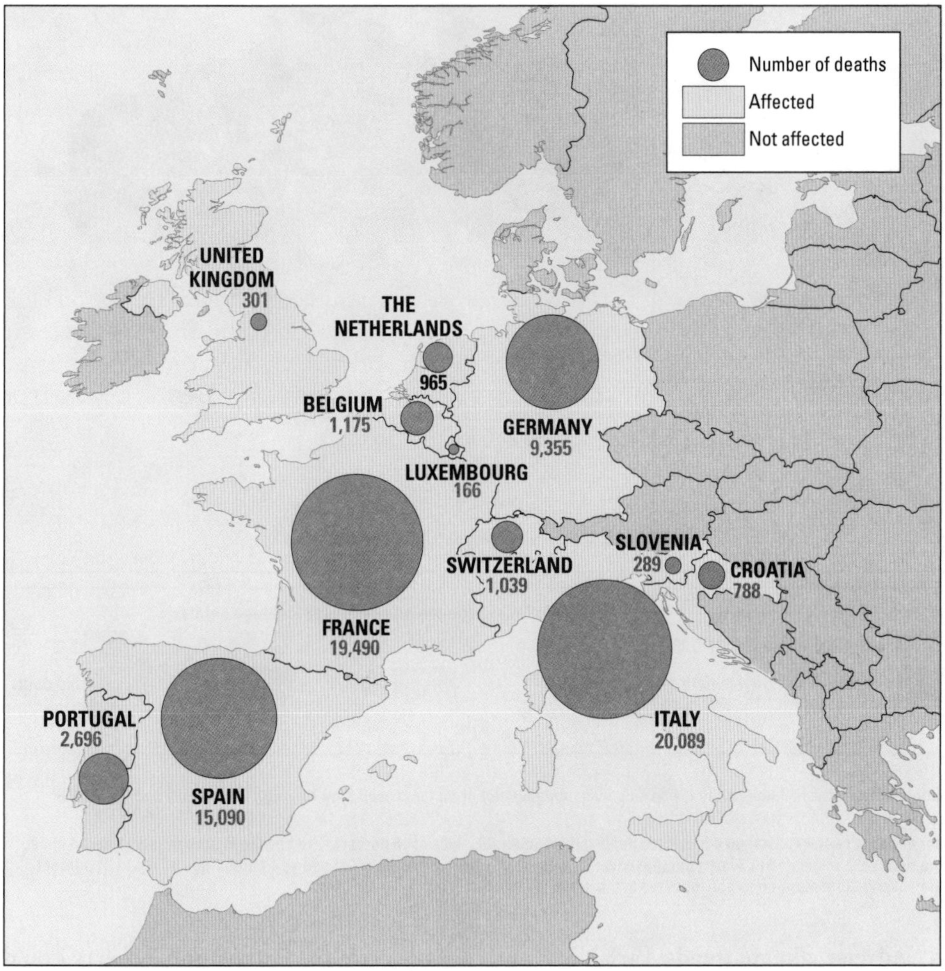

Number of deaths

Affected

Not affected

UNITED KINGDOM
301

THE NETHERLANDS
965

BELGIUM
1,175

GERMANY
9,355

LUXEMBOURG
166

SWITZERLAND
1,039

SLOVENIA
289

CROATIA
788

FRANCE
19,490

ITALY
20,089

PORTUGAL
2,696

SPAIN
15,090

Source: Robine and others 2008.

Note: Deaths attributed to the heat wave are those estimated to be in excess of the deaths that would have occurred in the absence of the heat wave, based on average baseline mortality trends.

9 percent within the next three decades, even allowing for short-term adaptations.[26] The implications of such climate change for poverty—and GDP—could be enormous given projected population growth and the evidence that one percentage point of agricultural GDP growth in developing countries increases the consumption of the poorest third of the population by four to six percentage points.[27]

The impacts of climate change on health add to the human and economic losses, especially in developing countries. The World Health Organization estimates that climate change caused a loss of 5.5 million disability-adjusted life years in 2000—84 percent of them in Sub-Saharan Africa and East and South Asia.[28] As temperatures rise, the number of people exposed to malaria and dengue will increase, with the burden most pronounced in developing countries.[29] The incidence of drought, projected to increase in the Sahel and elsewhere, is strongly correlated with past meningitis epidemics in Sub-Saharan Africa.[30] Declining agricultural yields in some regions will increase malnutrition, reducing people's resistance to illness. The burden of diarrheal diseases from climate change alone is projected to increase up to 5 percent by 2020 in countries with per capita incomes below $6,000. Higher temperatures are likely to increase cardiovascular illness, especially in the tropics but also in higher-latitude (and higher-income) countries—more than offsetting the relief from fewer cold-related deaths.[31]

Map 1.3   Climate change is likely to increase poverty in most of Brazil, especially its poorest regions

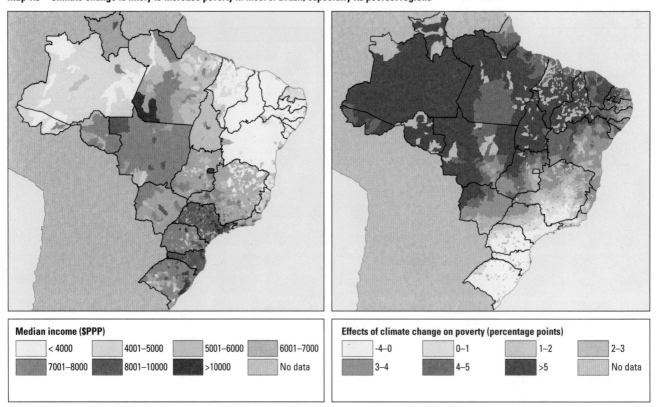

Median income ($PPP)

< 4000	4001–5000	5001–6000	6001–7000
7001–8000	8001–10000	>10000	No data

Effects of climate change on poverty (percentage points)

-4–0	0–1	1–2	2–3
3–4	4–5	>5	No data

Sources: Center for International Earth Science Information Network, http://sedac.ciesin.columbia.edu/gpw/global.jsp (accessed May 15, 2009); Dell, Jones, and Olken 2009; Assunçao and Chein 2008.

Note: Climate-change poverty impact estimates for mid-21st century based on a projected decline in agricultural yields of 18 percent. The change in poverty is expressed in percentage points; for example, the poverty rate in the northeast, estimated at 30 percent (based on $1 a day with year 2000 data), could rise by 4 percentage points to 34 percent. The estimates allow for internal migration, with the poverty outcomes of migrants counted in the sending municipality.

Adverse climate trends, variability, and shocks do not discriminate by income, but better-off people and communities can more successfully manage the setbacks (map 1.3). When Hurricane Mitch swept through Honduras in 1998, more wealthy households than poor ones were affected. But poor households lost proportionally more: among affected households, the poor lost 15 to 20 percent of their assets, while the richest lost only 3 percent.[32] The longer-term impacts were greater too: all affected households suffered a slowdown in asset accumulation, but the slump was greater for poorer households.[33] And impacts varied by gender (box 1.1): male-headed households, with greater access to new lodging and work, spent shorter periods in postdisaster shelters compared with female-headed households, which struggled to get back on their feet and remained in the shelters longer.[34]

A cycle of descent into poverty could emerge from the confluence of climate change, environmental degradation, and market and institutional failures. The cycle could be precipitated by the gradual collapse of a coastal ecosystem, less predictable rainfall, or a more severe hurricane season.[35] While large-scale natural disasters cause the most visible shocks, small but repeated shocks or subtle shifts in the distribution of rainfall throughout the year can also produce abrupt yet persistent changes in welfare.

Empirical evidence on poverty traps—defined as consumption *permanently* below a given threshold—is mixed.[36] But there is growing evidence of slower physical asset recovery and human capital growth among the poor after shocks. In Ethiopia a season with starkly reduced rainfall depressed consumption even after four to five years.[37] Instances of drought in Brazil have been

BOX 1.1   *Empowered women improve adaptation and mitigation outcomes*

Women and men experience climate change differently. Climate-change impacts and policies are not gender neutral because of differences in responsibility, vulnerability, and capacity for mitigation and adaptation. Gender-based patterns of vulnerability are shaped by the value of and entitlement to assets, access to financial services, education level, social networks, and participation in local organizations. In some circumstances, women are more vulnerable to climate shocks to livelihoods and physical safety—but there is evidence that in contexts where women and men have equal economic and social rights, disasters do not discriminate. Empowerment and participation of women in decision making can lead to improved environmental and livelihood outcomes that benefit all.

Women's participation in disaster management saves lives

Community welfare before, during, and after extreme climatic events can be improved by including women in disaster preparedness and rehabilitation. Unlike other communities that witnessed numerous deaths, La Masica, Honduras, reported no deaths during and after Hurricane Mitch in 1998. Gender-sensitive community education on early warning systems and hazard management provided by a disaster agency six months before the hurricane contributed to this achievement. Although both men and women participated in hazard management activities, ultimately, women took over the task of continuously monitoring the early warning system. Their enhanced risk awareness and management capacity enabled the municipality to evacuate promptly. Additional lessons from postdisaster recovery indicate that putting women in charge of food distribution systems results in less corruption and more equitable food distribution.

Women's participation boosts biodiversity and improves water management

Between 2001 and 2006 the Zammour locality in Tunis saw an increase in vegetal area, biodiversity preservation, and stabilization of eroding lands in the mountainous ecosystem—the result of an antidesertification program that invited women to share their perspectives during consultations, incorporated local women's knowledge of water management, and was implemented by women. The project assessed and applied innovative and effective rainwater collection and preservation methods, such as planting in stone pockets to reduce the evaporation of irrigation water, and planting of local species of fruit trees to stabilize eroded lands.

Women's participation enhances food security and protects forests

In Guatemala, Nicaragua, El Salvador, and Honduras women have planted 400,000 maya nut trees since 2001. Beyond enhanced food security, women and their families can benefit from climate change finance, as the sponsoring Equilibrium Fund pursues carbon-trading opportunities with the United States and Europe. In Zimbabwe, women lead over half of the 800,000 farm households living in communal areas, where women's groups manage forest resources and development projects through tree planting, nursery development, and woodlot ownership and management.

Women represent at least half of the world's agricultural workers, and women and girls remain predominantly responsible for water and firewood collection. Adaptation and mitigation potential, especially in the agriculture and forestry sectors, cannot be fully realized without employing women's expertise in natural resource management, including traditional knowledge and efficiency in using resources.

Women's participation supports public health

In India indigenous peoples know medicinal herbs and shrubs and apply these for therapeutic uses. Indigenous women, as stewards of nature, are particularly knowledgeable and can identify almost 300 useful forest species.

Globally, whether in Central America, North Africa, South Asia, or Southern Africa, gender-sensitive climate change adaptation and mitigation programs show measurable results: women's full participation in decision making can and will save lives, protect fragile natural resources, reduce greenhouse gases, and build resilience for current and future generations. Mechanisms or financing for disaster prevention, adaptation, and mitigation will remain insufficient unless they integrate women's full participation—voices and hands—in design, decision making, and implementation.

Sources: Contributed by Nilufar Ahmad, based on Parikh 2008; Lambrou and Laub 2004; Neumayer and Plumper 2007; Smyth 2005; Aguilar 2006; UNISDR 2007; UNDP 2009; and Martin 1996.

followed by significantly reduced rural wages in the short term, with the wages of affected workers catching up with their peers' only after five years.[38]

In addition limited access to credit, insurance, or collateral hampers poor households' opportunities to make productive investments or leads them to choose investments with low risk and low returns to guard against future shocks.[39] In villages throughout India poorer farmers have mitigated climatic risk by investing in assets and technologies with low sensitivity to rainfall variation but also with low average returns, locking in patterns of inequality in the country.[40]

Climate shocks can also permanently affect people's health and education. Research in Côte d'Ivoire linking rainfall patterns and investment in children's education shows that in regions experiencing greater-than-usual weather variability, school enrollment rates declined by 20 percent for both boys and girls.[41] And when coupled with other problems, environmental shocks can have long-term effects. People exposed to drought and civil strife in Zimbabwe during early childhood (between 12 and 24 months of age) suffered from a height loss of 3.4 centimeters, close to 1 fewer years of schooling, and a nearly six-month delay in starting school. The estimated effect on lifetime earnings was 14 percent, a big difference to someone near the poverty line.[42]

Balancing growth and assessing policies in a changing climate

Growth: Changing carbon footprints and vulnerabilities.   By 2050 a large share of the population in today's developing countries will have a middle-class lifestyle. But the planet cannot sustain 9 billion people with the carbon footprint of today's average middle-class citizen. Annual emissions would nearly triple. Moreover, not all development increases resilience: growth may not happen fast enough and can create new vulnerabilities even as it reduces others. And poorly designed climate change policies could themselves become a threat to sustainable development.

But it is ethically and politically unacceptable to deny the world's poor the opportunity to ascend the income ladder simply because the rich reached the top first. Developing countries now contribute about half of annual greenhouse gas emissions but have nearly 85 percent of the world's population; the energy-related carbon footprint of the average citizen of a low- or middle-income country is 1.3 or 4.5 metric tons of carbon dioxide equivalent (CO_2e), respectively, compared with 15.3 in high-income countries.[43] Moreover, the bulk of past emissions—and thus the bulk of the existing stock of greenhouse gases in the atmosphere—is the responsibility of developed countries.[44] Resolving the threat of climate change to human well-being thus not only depends on climate-smart development—increasing incomes and resilience while reducing emissions relative to projected increases. It also requires climate-smart prosperity in the developed countries—with greater resilience and absolute reductions in emissions.

Evidence shows that policy can make a big difference in how carbon footprints change when incomes grow.[45] The average carbon footprint of citizens in rich countries, including oil producers and small island states, varies by a factor of twelve, as does the energy intensity of GDP,[46] suggesting that carbon footprints do not always increase with income. And today's developing economies use much less energy per capita than developed countries such as the United States did at similar incomes, showing the potential for lower-carbon growth.[47]

Adaptation and mitigation need to be integrated into a climate-smart development strategy that increases resilience, reduces the threat of further warming, and improves development outcomes. Adaptation and mitigation measures can advance development, and prosperity can raise incomes and foster better institutions. A healthier population living in better-built houses and with access to bank loans and social security is better equipped to deal with a changing climate and its consequences. Advancing robust, resilient development policies that promote adaptation is needed today because changes in the climate, already begun, will increase even in the short term.

The spread of economic prosperity has always been intertwined with adaptation to changing ecological conditions. But as growth has altered the environment and as environmental change has accelerated, sustaining growth and adaptability demands greater capacity to understand our environment, generate new adaptive technologies and practices, and diffuse them widely. As economic historians have explained, much of humankind's creative potential has been directed at adapting to the changing world.[48] But adaptation cannot cope with all the impacts related to climate change, especially as larger changes unfold in the long term (see chapter 2).[49]

Countries cannot grow out of harm's way fast enough to match the changing climate. And some growth strategies, whether driven by the government or the market, can also add to vulnerability—particularly if they overexploit natural resources. Under the Soviet development plan, irrigated cotton cultivation expanded in water-stressed

Central Asia and led to the near disappearance of the Aral Sea, threatening the livelihoods of fishermen, herders, and farmers.[50] And clearing mangroves—natural coastal buffers against storm surges—to make way for intensive shrimp farming or housing development increases the physical vulnerability of coastal settlements, whether in Guinea or in Louisiana.

Climate shocks can strain normally adequate infrastructure or reveal previously untested institutional weaknesses, even in fast-growing and high-income countries. For example, despite impressive economic growth for more than two decades, and in part because of accompanying labor-market transitions, millions of migrant workers in China were stranded during the unexpectedly intense snow storms in January 2008 (map 1.4). The train system collapsed as workers returned home for the Chinese New Year, stranding millions, while the southern and central provinces suffered food shortages and power failures. Hurricane Katrina exposed the United States as unprepared and ill equipped, showing that even decades of steady prosperity do not always produce good planning (and by extension, good adaptation). Nor do high average incomes guarantee protection for the poorest communities.

Mitigation policies—for better or worse. Mitigation policies can be exploited to provide economic co-benefits in addition to emission reductions and can create local and regional opportunities. Biofuels could make Brazil the world's next big energy supplier—its ethanol production has more than doubled since the turn of the century.[51] A large share of unexploited hydropower potential is in developing countries, particularly in Sub-Saharan Africa (map 1.5). North Africa and the Middle East, with year-round exposure to sunlight, could benefit from increased European demand for solar energy (see chapter 4, box 4.15).[52] Yet comparative advantage in renewable energy production in many countries still is not optimally exploited, evidenced by the proliferation of solar power production in Northern Europe rather than North Africa.

But mitigation policies can also go wrong and reduce welfare if ancillary effects are not considered in design and execution. Relative to cleaner cellulosic ethanol production and even gasoline, corn-based biofuel production in the United States imposes higher health costs from local pollution and offers only dubious CO_2 emission reductions (figure 1.2).[53] Moreover, biofuel policies in the United States and Europe have diverted inputs from food to fuel production and

Map 1.4   The January 2008 storm in China severely disrupted mobility, a pillar of its economic growth

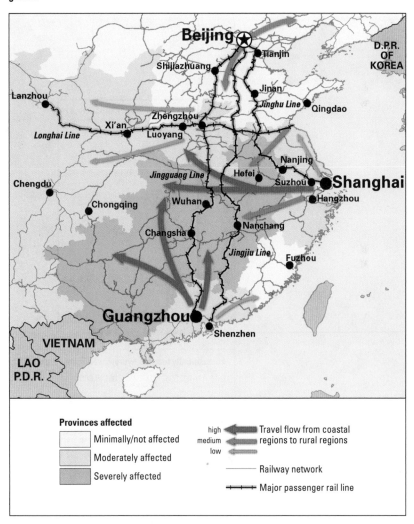

Sources: ACASIAN 2004; Chan 2008; Huang and Magnoli 2009; United States Department of Agriculture Foreign Agricultural Service, Commodity Intelligence Report, February 1 2008, http://www.pecad.fas.usda.gov/high-lights/2008/02/MassiveSnowStorm.htm (accessed July 14, 2009); Ministry of Communications, Government of the People's Republic of China, "The Guarantee Measures and Countermeasures for Extreme Snow and Rainfall Weather," February 1 2008, http://www.china.org.cn/e-news/news080201-2.htm (accessed July 14, 2009).

Note: Width of arrows reflects estimates of size of travel flows during the Chinese New Year holiday, based on reversal of estimated labor migration flows. Total internal migration is estimated between 130 million and 180 million people. Assessment of severity of the storm's impact is based on cumulative precipitation in the month of January and Chinese news and government communications at the time of the storm.

Map 1.5   Africa has enormous untapped hydropower potential, compared to lower potential but more exploitation of hydro resources in the United States

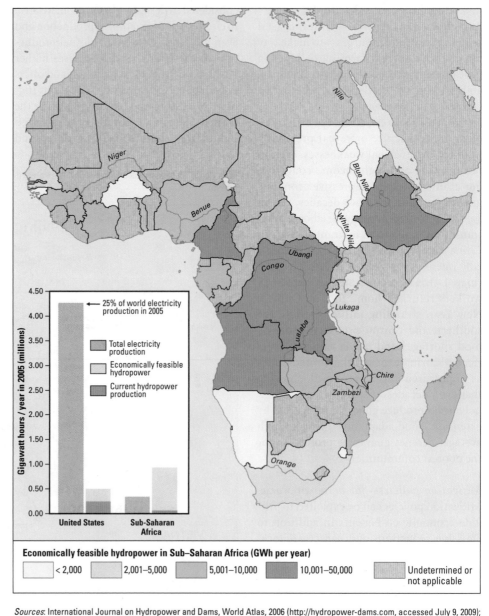

Economically feasible hydropower in Sub–Saharan Africa (GWh per year)

| < 2,000 | 2,001–5,000 | 5,001–10,000 | 10,001–50,000 | Undetermined or not applicable |

Sources: International Journal on Hydropower and Dams, World Atlas, 2006 (http://hydropower-dams.com, accessed July 9, 2009); IEA Energy Balances of OECD Countries 2008; and IEA Energy Balances of Non-OECD Countries 2007 (http://www.oecd.org/document/10/0,3343,en_21571361_33915056_39154634_1_1_1,00.html, accessed July 9, 2009).

Note: The United States has exploited over 50 percent of its hydropower potential, compared to only 7–8 percent in the countries of Sub-Saharan Africa. Total electricity production in the United States is shown for scale.

contributed to increases in global food prices.[54] Such food price hikes often increase poverty rates.[55] The overall impact on poverty depends on the structure of the economy, because net producers will benefit from higher prices, and net buyers will be worse off. But many governments in food-surplus countries, including Argentina, India, and Ukraine, have responded with export bans and other protectionist measures, limiting the gains for domestic producers, reducing grain supplies, and narrowing the scope for future market solutions.[56]

The interrelationship of trade and mitigation policies is not straightforward. It has been suggested that the carbon content of exports be counted in the carbon tally of the destination country, so that the exporting countries are not punished for specializing in the heavy industrial goods consumed by others. But if importers place a border tax on the carbon content of goods to equalize the carbon price, exporting countries would still bear some of the burden through a loss in competitiveness (see focus C on trade).

Green taxes. As outlined in chapter 6, carbon taxes can be an efficient instrument for controlling carbon emissions—but changes in the tax system to incorporate environmental costs (green taxes) could be regressive, depending on the country's economic structure, the quality of targeting, and the distribution of burden sharing. In the United Kingdom a carbon tax imposed equally on all households would be very regressive, consistent with findings from other OECD countries.[57] The reason is

that spending on energy constitutes a larger share of total expenditures for poor households than for rich ones. But the regressive effect could be offset either through scaled tariff design or a targeted program based on existing social policy mechanisms.[58]

And green taxes in developing countries could even be progressive, as suggested by a recent study for China. Most poor households in China reside in rural areas and consume products much less carbon intensive than those consumed by generally better-off urban households. If revenues from a carbon tax were recycled into the economy on an equal per capita basis, the progressive effect would be larger still.[59]

Gaining political support for green taxes and ensuring they do not harm the poor will not be easy. Revenue recycling would be critical for Latin America and Eastern Europe, where a significant share of the poor live in urban areas and would be directly hurt by green taxes. But such revenue recycling, as well as the targeting suggested by the Great Britain study, would require a strong commitment to such a policy shift, difficult in the many developing countries where regressive subsidies for energy and other infrastructure services are politically entrenched. Without revenue recycling, the impact of carbon pricing or green taxes—even if progressive—is likely to harm the poor because poor households spend as much as 25 percent of their income on electricity, water, and transport. It is also likely to be politically difficult because even the average household spends about 10 percent of its income on these services.[60]

The real income of the poorest will also be reduced in the near term as the higher up-front costs of greener infrastructure construction, operation, and services hit the supply side of the economy.[61] A green tax could have a direct effect on households (caused by the increase in energy prices) and an indirect effect (on total household expenditure as a result of higher costs of production and thus prices of consumer goods). A study in Madagascar found that the indirect effects could represent 40 percent of the welfare losses through higher prices of food, textiles, and transport.[62] Despite the greater direct consumption of

Figure 1.2   Corn-based biofuels in the United States increase CO$_2$ emissions and health costs relative to gasoline

Nonmarket costs ($/liter)

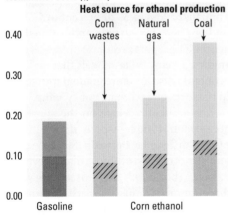

Source: Hill and others 2009.

Note: Costs are in terms of dollar per liter of gasoline or gasoline equivalent. Health costs (green) are estimated costs because of particulate matter emissions, from the production and end-use combustion of an additional liter of ethanol. Greenhouse-gas emission costs (blue) assume a carbon price of $120 a ton, based on the estimated price of carbon capture and storage. A portion (diagonal hatching in figure) of the greenhouse gas emissions associated with corn ethanol production comes from clearing, conversion, or cultivation of land.

infrastructure services by the middle class, the poorest quintile was projected to suffer the biggest loss in real income.

There is ample scope around the world for better energy tariff and subsidy design that both increases cost recovery and better targets benefits to the poor.[63] Climate change (and green tax proceeds) may make it worthwhile and feasible to expand income support programs to countries that now rely on energy and water pricing as part of their social policy. Greater energy efficiency reduces costs for everyone, while greener technologies can be less expensive than traditional carbon-intensive ones. For example, upgrading to improved wood-fired cook stoves in rural Mexico could reduce emissions by 160 million tons of CO_2 over the next 20 years, with net economic gains (from lower direct energy costs and better health) of $8 to $24 for each ton of avoided CO_2 emissions.[64]

Evaluating the tradeoffs

While few still debate the need for action to mitigate climate change, controversy remains over how much and how soon to mitigate. Holding the changes in global average temperatures below "dangerous" levels (see focus A on science) would require immediate and global actions—actions that are costly—to reduce emissions from projected levels by 50 to 80 percent by 2050.

A growing literature shows that the case for immediate and significant mitigation is stronger when taking into account the inertia in the climate system, meaning that warming and its impacts cumulate slowly but are to a considerable extent irreversible; the inertia of the built environment, which implies a higher cost of reducing emissions in the future if higher-emission fixed capital is put into place today; and the benefit of reducing the greater uncertainty and risk of catastrophic outcomes associated with higher temperatures.[65]

Any response to climate change involves some weighing of pros and cons, strengths and weaknesses, benefits and costs. The question is *how* this evaluation is to be undertaken. Cost-benefit analysis is a crucial tool for policy evaluation in the unavoidable context of competing priorities

and scarce resources. But monetizing costs and benefits can too easily omit nonmarket environmental goods and services and becomes impossible if future risks (and attitudes toward risk) are highly uncertain.

Additional decision tools, complementing cost-benefit analysis, are needed to establish overall goals and acceptable risks. Multicriteria approaches can provide insights about tradeoffs that are not all expressed in monetary terms. In the face of risk aversion and uncertainty about future climate risks, the "tolerable windows" approach can identify emissions paths that stay within chosen boundaries of acceptable risk and then evaluate the cost of doing so.[66] "Robust decision making" can highlight policies that provide an effective hedge against undesirable future outcomes.[67]

The cost-benefit debate: Why it's not just about the discount rate

The economic debate about the cost-benefit analysis of climate change policy has been particularly active since the publication of the *Stern Review of the Economics of Climate Change* in 2007. That report estimated the potential cost of unmitigated climate change to be very high—a permanent annualized loss of 5–20 percent of GDP—and argued for strong and immediate action. The report's recommendations contradicted many other models that make an economic case for more gradual mitigation in the form of a "climate policy ramp."[68]

The academic debate on the appropriate discount rate—which drives much of the difference between Stern's result and the others—will most likely never be resolved (box 1.2).[69] Stern used a very low discount rate. In this approach, commonly justified on ethical grounds, the fact that future generations will likely be richer is the only factor that makes the valuation of future welfare lower than that of today; in all other ways, the welfare of future generations is just as valuable as the welfare of the current generation.[70] Good arguments can be presented in favor of both high and low discount rates. Unfortunately, intergenerational welfare economics cannot help solve the debate—because it raises more questions than it can answer.[71]

BOX 1.2   *The basics of discounting the costs and benefits of climate change mitigation*

The evaluation of resource allocation across time is a staple of applied economics and project management. Such evaluations have been used extensively to analyze the problem of costs and benefits of climate change mitigation. But big disagreements remain about the correct values of the parameters.

The social discount rate expresses the monetary costs and benefits incurred in the future in terms of their present value, or their value to decision makers today. By definition, then, the primary tool of intergenerational welfare analysis—total expected net present value—collapses the distribution of welfare over time. Determining the appropriate value for the elements of the discount rate in the context of a long-term problem like climate change involves deep economic and ethical considerations (see box 1.4).

Three factors determine the discount rate. The first is how much weight to give to the welfare enjoyed in the future, strictly because it comes later rather than sooner. This pure rate of time preference can be thought of as a measure of impatience. The second factor is the growth rate in per capita consumption: if growth is rapid, future generations will be much wealthier, reducing the value assigned today to losses from future climate damages compared with costs of mitigation borne today. The third factor is how steeply the marginal utility of consumption (a measure of how much an additional dollar is enjoyed) declines as income rises.[a]

There is no universal agreement on how to choose the numerical values for each of the three factors that determine the social discount rate. Both ethical

judgments and empirical information that attempt to assess preferences from past behavior are used, sometimes in combination. Because the costs of mitigation policies are borne immediately, and the possibly large benefits of such policies (avoided damages) are enjoyed far in the future, the choice of parameters for the social discount rate strongly influences climate-policy prescriptions.

Sources: Stern 2007; Stern 2008; Dasgupta 2008; Roemer 2009; Sterner and Persson 2008.

a. The marginal utility of consumption declines as income rises because an additional dollar of consumption provides more utility to a poor person than to a person already consuming a lot. The steepness of the change—known as the elasticity of the marginal utility of consumption with respect to changes in income level—also measures tolerance of risk and inequality.

Yet the call for rapid and significant action to mitigate greenhouse gas emissions is not solely dependent on a low discount rate. While its role in determining the relative weight of costs and benefits is important, other factors raise the benefits of mitigation (avoided damages) in ways that also strengthen the case for rapid and significant mitigation, even with a higher discount rate.[72]

Broader impacts.   Most economic models of climate change impacts do not adequately factor in the loss of biodiversity and associated ecosystem services—a paradoxical omission that amounts to analyzing the tradeoffs between consumption goods and environmental goods without including environmental goods in individuals' utility function.[73] Although the estimated market value of lost environmental services may be difficult to calculate and may vary across cultures and value systems, such losses do have a cost. The losses increase the relative price of environmental services as they become relatively and absolutely scarcer. Introducing environmental losses into a standard integrated assessment model significantly increases the overall cost of

unmitigated climate change.[74] In fact, factoring the loss of biodiversity into a standard model results in a strong call for more rapid mitigation, even with a higher discount rate.

More accurately modeled dynamics: Threshold effects and inertia.   The damage function, which links changes in temperatures to associated monetized damages, is usually modeled in cost-benefit analysis as rising smoothly. But mounting scientific evidence suggests that natural systems could exhibit nonlinear responses to climate change as a consequence of positive feedbacks, tipping points, and thresholds (box 1.3). Positive feedbacks could occur, for example, if warming causes the permafrost to thaw, releasing the vast amounts of methane (a potent greenhouse gas) it contains and further accelerating warming. Thresholds or tipping points are relatively rapid and large-scale changes in natural (or socioeconomic) systems that lead to serious and irreversible losses. Positive feedbacks, tipping points, and thresholds mean that there might be great value to keeping both the pace and magnitude of climate change as low as possible.[75]

BOX 1.3 *Positive feedbacks, tipping points, thresholds, and nonlinearities in natural and socioeconomic systems*

Positive feedbacks in the climate system

Positive feedbacks amplify the effects of greenhouse gases. One such positive feedback is the change in reflectiveness, or albedo, of the earth's surface: highly reflective surfaces like ice and snow bounce the sun's warming rays back out to the atmosphere, but as higher temperatures cause ice and snow to melt, more energy is absorbed on the earth's surface, leading to further warming and more melting, as the process repeats itself.

Tipping points in natural systems

Even smooth, moderate changes in the climate can lead a natural system to a point beyond which relatively abrupt, possibly accelerating, irreversible, and ultimately very damaging changes occur. For example, regional forest die-off could result from the combination of drought, pests, and higher temperatures that combine to exceed physiological limits. A possible tipping point of global concern is the melting of the ice sheet that covers much of Greenland. Past a certain level of warming, summer melt will not refreeze in winter, dramatically increasing the rate of melting and leading to a sea-level rise of 6 meters.

Thresholds in socioeconomic systems

The economic cost of direct impacts could also present strong threshold effects—a result of the fact that current infrastructures and production practices are engineered to be robust only to previously experienced variation in weather conditions. This suggests that any increases in impacts will be driven primarily by rising concentrations of population and assets rather than by climate—so long as weather events remain within the envelope of past variations—but that impacts could increase sharply if climate conditions consistently exceed these boundaries in the future.

Nonlinearities and indirect economic effects

The economic response to these impacts is itself nonlinear, in part because climate-change impacts will simultaneously increase the need for adaptation and potentially decrease adaptive capacity. Direct impacts can also beget indirect effects (macroeconomic feedbacks, business interruptions, and supply-chain disruptions) that increase more than dollar for dollar in response to greater direct damages. This effect is evident in some natural disasters. Recent evidence in Louisiana shows that the economy has the capacity to absorb up to $50 billion of direct losses with minimal indirect losses. But indirect losses increase rapidly with more destructive disasters (figure). Direct losses from Hurricane Katrina reached $107 billion, with indirect losses adding another $42 billion; a simulated disaster with direct losses of $200 billion would cause an additional $200 billion in indirect losses.

Sources: Schmidt 2006; Kriegler and others 2009; Adams and others 2009; Hallegatte 2008; personal communication from Stéphane Hallegatte, May 2009.

Indirect losses increase even more steeply as direct damages rise: Estimates from Louisiana

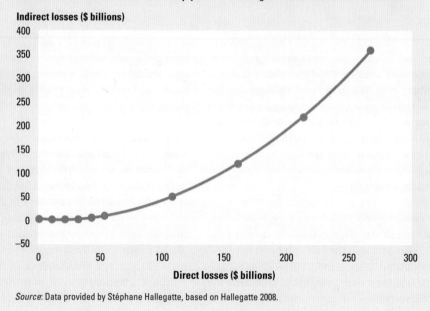

Source: Data provided by Stéphane Hallegatte, based on Hallegatte 2008.

Substantial inertia in the climate system adds to the concern about positive feedbacks, threshold effects, and irreversibility of climate change impacts. Scientists have found that the warming caused by increases in greenhouse gas concentration may be largely irreversible for a thousand years after emissions stop.[76] Postponing mitigation forgoes the option of a lower warming trajectory: for example, a delay of more than 10 years would likely preclude stabilization of the atmosphere at any less than 3°C of warming.[77] In addition, the climate system will keep changing for several centuries even after concentrations of greenhouse gases stabilize (see overview). So only immediate mitigation preserves the option value—that is, avoids the loss of options in stabilization outcomes.

Inertia is also substantial in the built environment—transport, energy, housing, and the urban form (the way cities are designed). In response to this inertia, some argue for postponing mitigation investments to avoid getting locked into higher cost, lower-carbon investments unnecessarily, instead waiting until better, less expensive technology allows quick ramping up of mitigation and more is known about the risks societies will need to protect against.

But it is not possible in practice to postpone major investments in infrastructure and energy provision without compromising economic development. Energy demand is likely to triple in developing countries between 2002 and 2030. In addition, many power plants in high-income countries were built in the 1950s and 1960s so are coming to the end of their useful life, implying that many new plants will need to be built over the next 10–20 years even with constant demand. Currently, coal plants remain among the cheapest option for many countries—in addition to offering energy security for those with ample coal reserves. If all coal-burning power plants scheduled to be built in the next 25 years come into operation, their lifetime CO_2 emissions would be equal to those of all coal-burning activities since the beginning of industrialization.[78] Consequently, the absence of stronger emission reduction commitments by the power sector today will lock in relatively high emission trajectories.

Nor is it always possible to cost-effectively retrofit such investments on a large scale. Retrofits are not always possible, and they can be prohibitively costly. Staying with the coal example, carbon capture and storage—a technology that is being developed to capture the CO_2 produced by a fossil-fuel power plant and store it underground—requires that the plant be located within 50 to 100 miles of an appropriate CO_2 storage site or else the cost of transporting the carbon becomes prohibitively high.[79] For countries endowed with an abundance of potential storage sites, this is not an issue: about 70 percent of China's power plants happen to be close enough to storage sites and therefore could reasonably be retrofitted if and when the technology

becomes commercially available. This is not the case in India, South Africa, or many other countries, where retrofits will prove unaffordable unless new plants are sited close to the few existing storage sites (see chapters 4 and 7).

Developing countries, with less existing infrastructure than developed countries, have a flexibility advantage and could potentially leapfrog to cleaner technologies. Developed countries must provide leadership in bringing new technologies to market and sharing knowledge from their experiences of deployment. The ability to change emissions trajectories depends on the availability of appropriate and affordable technology, which will not be in place at some future date without research and development (R&D) investment, dissemination, and learning-by-doing starting today.

Opportunities to shift from higher- to lower-carbon long-lived capital stock are not equally available over time.[80] The choice to switch to a more energy and economically efficient system realistically cannot be made in the future if the required technologies are not yet on the shelf and at sufficient scale to be affordable and if people do not yet have the know-how to use them (see chapter 7).[81] Effective, affordable backstop mitigation technologies for transforming energy systems will not be available in the future without active research and demonstration initiatives that move potential technologies along the cost and learning curves. To that end, developed countries need to provide leadership in developing and bringing new technologies to market and in sharing knowledge from their experiences of deployment.

Accounting for uncertainties. Economic assessments of climate change policies must factor in the uncertainties about the size and timing of adverse impacts and about the feasibility, cost, and time profiles of mitigation efforts. A key uncertainty missed by most economic models is the possibility of large catastrophic events related to climate change (see focus A on science), a topic that is at the center of an ongoing debate.[82] The underlying probability distribution of such catastrophic risks is unknown and will likely remain so. More aggressive mitigation almost surely will reduce their likelihood, though it is very difficult to assess by how much. The possibility of a global catastrophe, even one with very low probability, should increase society's willingness to pay for faster and more aggressive mitigation to the extent that it helps to avoid calamity.[83]

Even without considering these catastrophic risks, substantial uncertainties remain around climate change's ecological and economic impacts. The likely pace and ultimate magnitude of warming are unknown. How changes in climate variability and extremes—not just changes in mean temperature—will affect natural systems and human well-being is uncertain. Knowledge is limited about people's ability to adapt, the costs of adaptation, and the magnitude of unavoided residual damages. Uncertainty about the speed of discovering, disseminating, and adopting new technologies is also substantial.

These uncertainties only increase with the pace and amount of warming—a major argument for immediate and aggressive action.[84] Greater uncertainty requires adaptation strategies that can cope with many different climates and outcomes. Such strategies exist (and are discussed below), but they are less efficient than strategies that could be designed with perfect knowledge. So uncertainty is costly. And more uncertainty increases costs.

Without inertia and irreversibility, uncertainty would not matter so much, because decisions could be reversed and adjustments would be smooth and costless. But tremendous inertia—in the climate system, in the built environment, and in the behavior of individuals and institutions—makes it costly, if not impossible, to adjust in the direction of more stringent mitigation if new information is revealed or new technologies are slow to be discovered. So inertia greatly increases the potential negative implications of climate policy decisions under uncertainty. And uncertainty combined with inertia and irreversibility argue for greater precautionary mitigation.

The economics of decision making under uncertainty makes a case that uncertainty about the effects of climate change calls for more rather than less mitigation.[85] Uncertainty makes a strong argument for adopting an iterative approach to selecting targets—starting with an aggressive stance. This is not lessened by the prospect of learning (acquiring new information that changes our assessment of uncertainty).

Normative choices on aggregation and values. Climate change policies require tradeoffs between short-term actions and long-term benefits, between individual choices and global consequences. So climate change policy decisions are driven fundamentally by ethical choices. Indeed, such decisions are about concern for the welfare of others.

Directly including the benefits from nonmarket environmental goods—and their existence for future generations—in economic models of well-being is one approach for capturing these tradeoffs.[87] In practice the ability to quantify such tradeoffs has been limited, but this framework does provide a point of departure for further assessment of the increased value that societies assign to the environment as income increases, of possible tradeoffs between current consumption and costly efforts to safeguard the welfare—and existence—of future generations.[88]

Moreover, the way a model aggregates impacts across individuals or countries of different income levels significantly affects the value of estimated losses.[89] To capture a dimension of equity additional to the intergenerational concerns expressed in the discount rate, equity weights can be applied to reflect that the loss of a dollar means more to a poor person than to a rich one. Such an approach better captures human welfare (rather than just income). And because poor people and poor countries are more exposed to climate change, this approach substantially increases estimated aggregate losses from climate change. By contrast, summing up global damages in dollars and expressing them as a share of global GDP—implicitly weighting damages by contribution to total output—amounts to giving a much lower weight to the losses of poor people.

Value systems also play a role in environmental policy decisions. Recently climate change has emerged as a human rights issue (box 1.4). And most societies have ethical or religious systems that value nature and identify human responsibilities for the stewardship of the earth and its natural riches—though the results often fall short of the espoused ideals. In the first half of the 1600s, Japan was hurtling toward an environmental catastrophe through massive deforestation. But as early as 1700 it had an elaborate system of woodland management in place.[90] One reason the Tokugawa shogunate, the rulers at the time, decided to act was concern for future family generations—a concern that resulted from Confucian cultural traditions[91]—and a desire to maintain the hereditary political system. Today, Japan's territory is almost 80 percent forested.[92]

BOX 1.4 *Ethics and climate change*

The complexity of climate change highlights several ethical questions. Issues of fairness and justice are particularly important given the long temporal and geographical disconnect between greenhouse gas emissions and their impacts. At least three major ethical dimensions arise in the climate change problem: evaluating impacts, considering intergenerational equity, and distributing responsibilities and costs.

Evaluating impacts
Several disciplines, economics included, argue that welfare should be the overarching criterion in policy evaluation. But even within a "discounted utilitarianism" framework, there are large disagreements, most notably about which discount rate to use and how to aggregate welfare across individuals in the present and future. One common argument is that there is no sound ethical reason to discount economic and human impacts just because they are anticipated to happen 40—or even 400—years hence. A counterargument is that it is not equitable for the current generation to allocate resources to mitigating future climate change if other investments are seen to have a higher return, thus coming back to the problem of weighing costs and benefits of alternative uncertain options.

Recent discussion has focused on human rights as the relevant criterion for evaluating impacts. Some human rights—particularly economic and social rights—will be jeopardized by climate-change impacts and possibly some policy responses. These include the right to food, the right to water, and the right to shelter. Climate impacts may also have direct and indirect effects on exercising and realizing civil and political rights. But establishing causation and attribution is a serious problem and may limit the scope for applying human rights law to international or domestic disputes.

Because the causes of climate change are diffuse, the direct link between the emissions of a country and the impacts suffered in another are difficult to establish in a litigation context. A further obstacle to defining responsibility and harm in legal terms is the diffusion of emissions and impacts over time: in some cases, the source of the harm has occurred over multiple generations, and the damages felt today may also by felt by many future generations.

Considering intergenerational equity
Intergenerational equity is an integral part of the evaluation of impacts. How intergenerational equity is incorporated in an underlying economic model has significant implications. As noted in box 1.2, standard present-value criteria discount future costs and benefits, collapsing the distribution of welfare over time to the present moment. Alternative formulations include maximizing the current generation's utility, incorporating its altruistic concerns for future generations, and taking into account the uncertainty of the existence of future generations.

Distributing responsibilities and costs
Probably the most contentious issue is who should bear the burden of solving the climate change problem. One ethical response is the "polluter pays" principle: responsibilities should be allocated according to each country's or group's contribution to climate change. A particular version of this view is that cumulative historical emissions need to be taken into account when establishing responsibilities. A counterargument holds that "excusable ignorance" grants immunity to past emitters, because they were not aware of the consequences of their actions, but this argument has been criticized on the grounds that the potential negative effects of greenhouse gases on the climate have been understood for some time.

A further dimension of responsibility concerns how people have benefited from the past emissions of greenhouse gases (see overview figure 3). While these benefits clearly have been enjoyed by the developed countries, which have contributed the bulk of atmospheric CO_2 so far, developing countries also gained some benefits from the resulting prosperity. One response is to ignore the past and allot equal per capita entitlements to all future emissions. Yet another view recognizes that what is ultimately important is not the distribution of emissions but rather the distribution of economic welfare, including climate change damages and mitigation costs. This suggests that in a world of unequal wealth, greater responsibility for bearing costs falls to the better off—although this conclusion does not preclude mitigation actions being undertaken in poorer countries with external finance provided by high-income countries (see chapter 6).

Sources: Singer 2006; Roemer 2009; Caney 2009; World Bank 2009b.

Alternative frameworks for decision making

Uncertainty, inertia, and ethics point to the need for caution and thus to the need for more immediate and aggressive mitigation, but the analytical debate over how much more continues among economists and policy makers. The conclusions of different cost-benefit analyses are very sensitive to initial assumptions such as the baseline scenario, the abatement and damage functions, and the discount rate, including implicit assumptions embedded in model formulations[93]—which can lead to decision-making gridlock.

Alternative decision-making frameworks that incorporate broader-based assessments of costs and benefits, allowance for risk aversion, and the implications of ethical judgments can more effectively support decision making in the face of numerous knowledge gaps and obstacles. Including some of the valuation issues noted above (option values, ecosystem services, risks of discontinuities) into a broader cost-benefit analysis is desirable (albeit difficult). More, however, is needed to make the normative consequences of policy choices as transparent as possible to inform decision makers aiming to establish concrete environmental and development targets and policies. That can help them win the support of the myriad stakeholders who will experience the real-world costs and benefits.

One alternative is a tolerable windows, or "guardrail," approach. A window of mitigation goals, or a range bounded by guardrails, is chosen to limit temperature change and the rate of change to what are considered—heuristically or on the basis of expert judgment—to be tolerable levels.[94] The window is defined by constraints derived from several climate-sensitive systems. One constraint could be determined by society's aversion to a given GDP loss, associated with a given amount and rate of temperature change. A second could be defined by society's aversion to social strife and inequitable impacts. A third could be concern about warming thresholds, beyond which certain ecosystems collapse.[95]

The guardrails approach does not require a monetary estimate of the damages, because the constraints are determined by what is judged to be tolerable in each system (for instance, it might be difficult to translate into GDP figures the number of people displaced after a severe drought). Drivers of the value of emission guardrails include scientific analysis of the potential for threshold effects, as well as nonmonetized judgments about residual risks and vulnerabilities that would remain under different mitigation and adaptation strategies. The costs of remaining within proposed sets of guardrails need to be considered in relation to the judgments surrounding the levels of climate safety provided by the different guardrails. On this sort of multicriteria basis, decision makers can make an informed and more comprehensive assessment of where it is best to set the guardrails (and this assessment can be periodically revisited over time).

This approach can be complemented by decision support techniques, such as robust decision making, to address difficult-to-evaluate uncertainties.[96] In the context of unknown probabilities and a highly uncertain future, a robust strategy answers the question, "What actions should we take, given that we cannot predict the future, to reduce the possibility of an undesirable outcome to an acceptable level?"[97] In the context of climate change, policy becomes a contingency problem—what is the best strategy given a variety of possible outcomes?—rather than a traditional optimization problem. The intellectual underpinnings of this approach are not new; they can be traced back to the work by Savage in the early 1950s on "minimizing the maximum regret."[98]

Looking for robust rather than just optimal strategies is done through what essentially amounts to scenario-based planning. Different scenarios are created, and alternative policy options are compared based on their robustness—the ability to avoid a given outcome—across the different scenarios. Such analysis includes "shaping actions" that influence the future, "hedging actions" that reduce future vulnerability, and "signposts" that indicate the need for a reassessment or change of strategies.

Robust decision analysis can also be done with more formal quantitative tools, in an exploratory modeling approach, using mathematical methods for characterizing decisions and outcomes under conditions of deep uncertainty.

Under robust decision making, costs, benefits, and the tradeoffs inherent in climate policies are assessed under all scenarios. The policy prescription is not to pursue an "optimal" policy—in the traditional sense of maximizing utility—that performs, on average, better than the others. Instead, sound policies are those that withstand unpredictable futures in a robust way. In this framing near-term policies can be understood as a hedge against the cost of policy adjustments—lending support to efforts to invest in R&D and infrastructure today to keep open the option of a low-carbon future tomorrow.[99]

The costs of delaying the global mitigation effort

Today's global warming was caused overwhelmingly by emissions from rich countries.[100] Developing countries are rightly concerned about the consequences of imposing limitations on their growth. This supports the argument, embodied in the principle of "common but differentiated responsibilities" in the United Nations Framework Convention on Climate Change (UNFCCC), which holds that high-income countries should lead in reducing emissions, given both their historical responsibility and their significantly higher per capita emissions today. Developed countries' much greater financial and technological resources further argue for their taking on the bulk of mitigation costs, regardless of where the mitigation occurs.

But emission reductions by rich countries alone will not be enough to limit warming to tolerable levels. While cumulative per capita past emissions are small especially in low-income but also in middle-income countries,[101] total annual energy-related CO_2 emissions in middle-income countries have caught up with those of rich countries, and the largest share of current emissions from land-use change comes from tropical countries.[102] More important, projected changes in fossil-fuel use in middle-income countries suggest that their CO_2 emissions will continue to increase and will exceed the cumulative emissions of developed countries in the coming decades.[103]

The implication, as stated in the UNFCCC and the Bali Action Plan,[104] is that all nations have a role in an agreement that reduces global emissions and that this role has to be commensurate with their development status. In this approach, developed countries take the lead in meeting significant reduction targets, and they assist developing countries in laying the foundations for lower-carbon growth pathways and meeting their citizens' adaptation needs. The UNFCC also calls for developed countries to compensate developing countries for the additional mitigation and adaptation costs developing countries will incur.

A critical component of global action is a global mechanism allowing those who mitigate to differ from those who pay (the subject of chapter 6). Negotiated international financial transfers can enable the direct financing—*by* high-income countries—of mitigation measures undertaken *in* developing countries. (In developing countries, mitigation will often entail reorienting future emission trajectories to more sustainable levels, not reducing absolute emission levels.) Unlocking large-scale finance from the high-income countries seems a great challenge. However, *if* high-income countries are committed to achieving lower total global emissions, it is in their interest to provide the financing to ensure that significant mitigation takes place in developing countries. Estimates of global mitigation costs usually assume that mitigation will happen wherever or whenever it is cheapest. Many low-cost measures to reduce emissions relative to projected trajectories are in developing countries. So global least-cost mitigation paths always imply that a large share of mitigation is in developing countries—regardless of who pays.[105]

Delayed action by any country to significantly lower emission trajectories implies a higher global cost for any chosen mitigation target. For example, delaying mitigation actions in developing countries until

2050 could more than double the total cost of meeting a particular target, according to one estimate.[106] Another estimate suggests that an international agreement that covers only the five countries with the highest total emissions (covering two-thirds of emissions) would triple the cost of achieving a given target, compared with full participation.[107] The reason is that shrinking the pool of mitigation opportunities available for reaching a set target requires pursuing not only the negative- and low-cost measures but also high-cost measures.

Although developed and developing countries have similar potential for negative cost (net benefit) measures and high-cost measures, the middle range of low-cost mitigation options is predominantly in developing countries (with many in agriculture and forestry). Exploiting all available measures will be crucial for achieving substantial mitigation. This point is illustrated by the McKinsey analysis (figure 1.3a), but the results are not exclusive to it. If developing countries do not reduce their emission trajectories, the total cost of any chosen amount of mitigation will be much higher (the marginal cost of abatement in developed countries alone—the red line in figure 1.3b—is always higher than if the global portfolio of options—the orange line in figure 1.3b—is considered). The decline in total mitigation potential and the increase in global mitigation costs stemming from an approach involving mitigation mostly in high-income countries do not depend on any particular model.[108] Nor do they depend on any differences in opportunities and costs between developed and developing countries: if the developed countries declined to reduce their emissions, similarly global costs would rise and some amount of potential abatement would be forgone (figure 1.3c).

These increases in global abatement costs represent pure deadweight losses—wasted additional costs that yield zero welfare gains. Avoiding such losses (the shaded wedges between the marginal cost curves in figures 1.3b and 1.3c) creates plenty of incentives and space to negotiate the location and financing of mitigation actions while making all participants better off. It

is much cheaper for the world as a whole to reach a given mitigation goal with a full portfolio of measures occurring in all countries. It is so much cheaper that, provided enough countries are committed to a global mitigation objective, all will be better off if the developed countries bear the cost of financing scaled-up measures in developing countries today.

Developed countries have the means and incentives to transfer enough finance to non-Annex I countries[109] to make them at least as well off by receiving transfers and scaling up their mitigation efforts immediately, compared with delaying commitment a decade or more before phasing in their own national targets and policies. For a given mitigation target, each dollar transferred to that end could yield an average of three dollars in welfare gains by eliminating deadweight losses—gains that can be shared according to negotiated terms. In other words, the participation of developing countries in reaching a global target is worth a lot. Sharing the large recovered deadweight losses can form a strong incentive for universal participation in a fair deal. It is not a zero-sum game.[110]

That said, it is crucial not to underestimate the difficulties of reaching agreement on global emissions targets. The reason is that such agreement suffers from a kind of international "tragedy of the commons": all countries can benefit from global participation, but unilateral incentives to participate are weak for most countries. This is the case not only because all countries would like to free ride, enjoying the benefits without bearing the costs.[111] Most countries are small enough that if one decided to defect from a global agreement, the agreement would not unravel. When applied to all countries, however, this reasoning undermines the possibility of reaching a deal in the first place.[112]

In fact, simulations exploring a variety of coalition structures and international resource transfers to persuade reluctant participants to stay in the coalition reveal the difficulty in reaching a stable agreement (one that is consistent with self-interest) to undertake deep and costly cuts in global emissions. Stable and effective coalitions

Figure 1.3   Assessing deadweight losses from partial participation in a climate deal

a. Global greenhouse gas mitigation marginal cost curve beyond 2030 business-as-usual

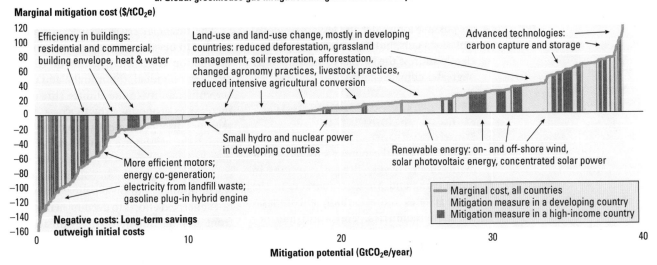

Marginal mitigation cost ($/tCO$_2$e)

Efficiency in buildings: residential and commercial; building envelope, heat & water

Land-use and land-use change, mostly in developing countries: reduced deforestation, grassland management, soil restoration, afforestation, changed agronomy practices, livestock practices, reduced intensive agricultural conversion

Advanced technologies: carbon capture and storage

Small hydro and nuclear power in developing countries

More efficient motors; energy co-generation; electricity from landfill waste; gasoline plug-in hybrid engine

Renewable energy: on- and off-shore wind, solar photovoltaic energy, concentrated solar power

Negative costs: Long-term savings outweigh initial costs

— Marginal cost, all countries
☐ Mitigation measure in a developing country
■ Mitigation measure in a high-income country

Mitigation potential (GtCO$_2$e/year)

b. Deadweight loss from only mitigating in developed countries: a limited participation marginal cost curve

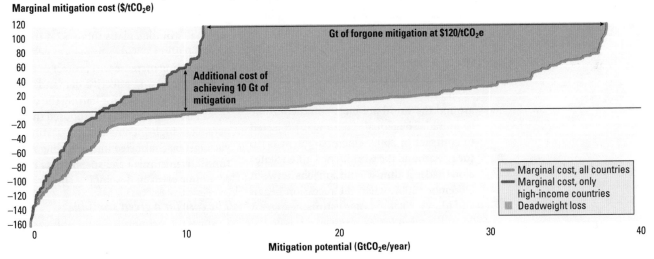

Marginal mitigation cost ($/tCO$_2$e)

Gt of forgone mitigation at $120/tCO$_2$e

Additional cost of achieving 10 Gt of mitigation

— Marginal cost, all countries
— Marginal cost, only high-income countries
☐ Deadweight loss

Mitigation potential (GtCO$_2$e/year)

c. Deadweight loss from only mitigating in developing countries: a limited participation marginal cost curve

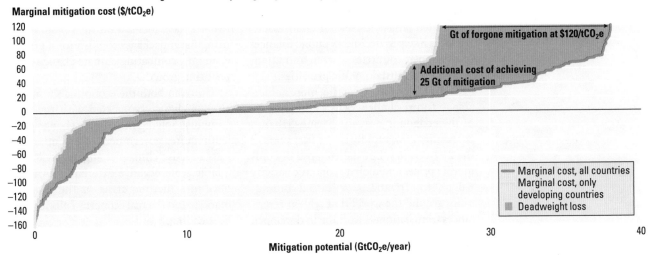

Marginal mitigation cost ($/tCO$_2$e)

Gt of forgone mitigation at $120/tCO$_2$e

Additional cost of achieving 25 Gt of mitigation

— Marginal cost, all countries
— Marginal cost, only developing countries
☐ Deadweight loss

Mitigation potential (GtCO$_2$e/year)

Source: McKinsey & Company 2009 with further data breakdown provided for WDR 2010 team.

Note: The bars in (a) represent various mitigation measures, with the width indicating the amount of emission reduction each measure would achieve and the height indicating the cost, per ton of avoided emissions, of the measure. Tracing the height of the bars creates a marginal mitigation cost curve. Panels (b) and (c) show the marginal mitigation cost curve if mitigation only takes place in high-income countries (b) or only in developing countries (c), as well as the resulting deadweight losses associated with these scenarios. Such deadweight losses could be avoided or minimized through financial mechanisms that allow a separation between who pays and who mitigates, and ensure the most cost-effective mitigation measures are adopted.

are possible for milder and less costly global emissions cuts, but such cuts do not sufficiently address the threats to sustainability of greater climate change.[113]

Seizing the moment: Immediate stimulus and long-term transformations

In 2008 the global economy suffered a dramatic shock, triggered by disruptions in the housing and financial markets in the United States and eventually encompassing many countries. The world had not experienced such a financial and economic upheaval since the Great Depression. Credit markets froze, investors fled to safety, scores of currencies realigned, and stock markets dropped sharply. At the height of the financial volatility the stock market in the United States lost $1.3 trillion in value in one session.[114]

The ongoing consequences for the real economy and development indicators around the world are huge—and continue to unfold. The global economy is projected to contract in 2009. Unemployment is on the rise around the world. The United States alone had lost almost 5 million jobs between December 2007, when the recession began and March 2009.[115] Some estimates suggest 32 million job losses in developing countries.[116] Between 53 million and 90 million people will fail to escape poverty because of the fallout during 2009.[117] Official development assistance—already well below the committed targets for several donor countries—is likely to decline as public finances in developed countries worsen and attention shifts toward domestic priorities.

Some regions are becoming more vulnerable to future challenges as a consequence of the economic downturn: Sub-Saharan economies grew rapidly in the first years of the 21st century, but the collapse of commodity prices and global economic activity will test this trend. Countries and communities around the world that rely on remittances from nationals working in developed countries are severely affected as these financial transfers fall.[118] In Mexico remittances fell by $920 million in the six months leading up to March 2009—a decline of 14 percent.[119]

The financial crisis presents an added burden to development efforts and a likely distraction from the urgency of climate change. Individual, community, and country vulnerability to the climate threat will increase as economic growth slows down, revenues disappear, and assistance shrinks. While the economic slowdown will be matched by a temporary deceleration in emissions, people remain vulnerable to the warming already in the pipeline; and without concerted efforts to decouple emissions from growth, emissions will again accelerate as economic recovery takes hold.

Governments in many developed and developing countries are responding to the crisis by expanding public spending. Spending proposed in several national and regional stimulus plans totals $2.4 trillion to $2.8 trillion.[120] Governments expect that this spending increase will protect or create jobs by increasing effective demand—one of the main priorities for halting the downturn. The World Bank has proposed that 0.7 percent of high-income countries' stimulus packages be channeled into a "vulnerability fund" to minimize the social costs of the economic crisis in developing countries.[122]

The case for a green stimulus

Despite the economic chaos the case for urgent action against climate change remains. And it becomes more pressing given the increase in poverty and vulnerability around the world. Thus recent public debates have focused on the possibility of using fiscal packages to push for a greener economy, combating climate change while restoring growth.

How can both the economic slump and climate change be tackled with the fiscal stimulus? Solving the climate change problem requires government intervention, not least because climate change is created by a large-scale negative externality. And the once-in-a-lifetime crisis in the financial markets and the real economy calls for public spending.

Investment in climate policy can be an efficient way to deal with the economic crisis in the short term. Low-carbon technologies could generate a net increase in jobs, because they can be more labor intensive than high-carbon sectors.[122] Some estimates suggest that $1 billion in government spending on green projects in the United States can create 30,000 jobs in a year, 7,000 more than generated by traditional infrastructure.[123] Other estimates suggest that spending $100 billion would generate almost 2 million jobs—about half of them directly.[124] But as with any short-term stimulus, the job gains might not be sustained in the long run.[125]

Green spending around the world

Several governments have included a share of "green" investments in their stimulus proposals—including low-carbon technologies, energy efficiency, research and development, and water and waste management (figure 1.4). The Republic of Korea will devote 80.5 percent of its fiscal plan to green projects. Some $100 billion to $130 billion of the U.S. stimulus package has been allocated to climate-change-related investments. Overall, some $436 billion will be disbursed in green investments as part of fiscal stimuli around the world, with half expected to be used during 2009.[126]

The efficiency of these investments will depend on how quickly they can be implemented; how well targeted they can be in creating jobs and utilizing underused resources; and how much they shift economies toward long-lived, low-carbon infrastructure, reduced emissions, and increased resilience.[127] Investments in energy efficiency in public buildings, for instance, are appealing because they are usually "shovel ready," are very labor intensive, and generate

long-term savings for the public sector.[128] Similar virtues can be found in helping to finance other energy-efficiency measures that reduce the social cost of energy in private buildings, as well as in water and sanitation facilities and in improved traffic flows.

In each country the portfolio of projects and investments varies widely, according to the specific conditions of the economy and the needs for job creation. Most stimulus packages in Latin America, for instance, will be spent on public works—including highways—with limited mitigation potential.[129] In the Republic of Korea, where 960,000 jobs are expected to be created in the next four years, a large part of the investment—$13.3 billion of $36 billion—will be allocated to three projects: river restoration, expansion of mass transit and railroads, and energy conservation in villages and schools, programs projected to create 500,000 jobs.[130] China will devote $85 billion to rail transport as a low-carbon alternative to road and air transport that can also help alleviate transportation bottlenecks. Another $70 billion will be allocated for a new electricity grid that improves the efficiency and availability of electricity.[131] In the United States two fairly inexpensive projects—$6.7 billion for renovating federal buildings, and another $6.2 billion for weatherizing homes—will create an estimated 325,000 jobs a year.[132]

In most developing countries the projects in stimulus packages do not have a strong emission-reduction component, but they could improve resilience to climate change

Figure 1.4   Global green stimulus spending is rising

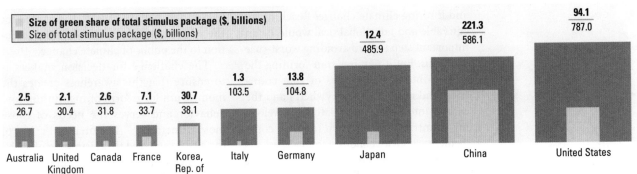

| | Size of green share of total stimulus package ($, billions) |
| | Size of total stimulus package ($, billions) |

Australia	United Kingdom	Canada	France	Korea, Rep. of	Italy	Germany	Japan	China	United States
2.5 / 26.7	2.1 / 30.4	2.6 / 31.8	7.1 / 33.7	30.7 / 38.1	1.3 / 103.5	13.8 / 104.8	12.4 / 485.9	221.3 / 586.1	94.1 / 787.0

Source: Robins, Clover, and Singh 2009.

and create jobs. Improving water and sanitation networks in Colombia, for example, is estimated to create 100,000 direct jobs per $1 billion invested while reducing the risk of water-borne illnesses.[133] Both developing and developed countries should consider adaptation measures such as streambed and wetland restoration, which can be particularly labor intensive and thus reduce both the physical and financial vulnerability of some groups. The challenge would be to ensure that the adaptation measures are sustained after the expenditure program ends.

These preliminary figures will likely change as the crisis unfolds. There is no guarantee that the green elements of the fiscal stimulus will succeed in either generating jobs or changing the carbon mix of the economy. And even in the best-case scenario, the fiscal interventions will not be enough to eliminate the risk of high-carbon lock-in and climate vulnerability. But the opportunity to jump-start green investments and lay the foundation for low-carbon economies is real and needs to be seized.

Fundamental transformations in the medium and long term

Incorporating sound low-carbon and high-resilience investment components in fiscal expansions to combat the financial crisis will not be enough to thwart the long-term problems posed by climate change. Fundamental transformations are needed in social protection, in carbon finance, in research and development, in energy markets, and in the management of land and water.

Over the medium and long terms the challenge is to find new paths to reach the twin goals of sustaining development and limiting climate change. Reaching an equitable and fair global deal would be an important step toward avoiding worst-case scenarios. But it requires transforming the carbon-intensive lifestyles of rich countries (and rich people everywhere) and the carbon-intensive growth paths of developing countries. This in turn requires complementary socioeconomic changes.

Modifications in social norms that reward a low-carbon lifestyle could prove a powerful element of success (see chapter 8).

But behavioral change needs to be matched with institutional reform, additional finance, and technological innovation to avoid irreversible, catastrophic increases in temperature. In any case and under any scenario, strong public policy can help economies absorb the shocks of unavoidable climate impacts, minimize net social losses, and protect the welfare of those who most stand to lose.

The response to climate change could generate momentum to improve the development process and promote welfare-enhancing reforms that need to happen anyway. For example, the joint efforts to increase energy efficiency and promote development could find a policy—and physical—expression in greener, more resilient cities. Improving urban design to promote energy efficiency—through, say, more public transportation and a congestion charge—can increase physical security and the quality of life. Much depends on the degree to which existing inadequate institutional mechanisms and policies can be strengthened or replaced thanks to greater political space for change brought about by the threat of global warming and to increased international technical and financial assistance.

Individual citizens will have a large role in the public debate and implementation of solutions. Opinion surveys show that people around the world are concerned about climate change, even in the recent financial turmoil[134] (though evidence on recent trends in the United States is mixed).[135] Most governments also recognize, at least in discourse, the enormity of the danger. And the international community has acknowledged the problem, as exemplified by the 2007 Nobel Peace prize awarded for the scientific assessment and communication to the public of climate change.

The challenge for decision makers is to ensure that this awareness creates the momentum for reform of institutions and behavior and serves the needs of those most vulnerable.[136] The financial crises of the 1990s catalyzed the revamping of social safety nets in Latin America, giving birth to Progresa–Oportunidades in Mexico and Bolsa Escola–Bolsa Familia in Brazil, among the best innovations in social policy in decades.[138]

The current crisis has eroded faith in unregulated markets. As a consequence, better regulation, more intervention, and greater government accountability are expected. For dealing with climate change, additional climate-smart regulation is needed to induce innovative approaches to mitigation and adaptation. Such policies create an opening for the scale and scope of government interventions needed to correct climate change—the biggest market failure in human history.

Notes

1. Weiss and Bradley 2001.
2. Ristvet and Weiss 2000.
3. Weiss 2000.
4. Harrington and Walton 2008; IWM and CEGIS 2007.
5. Schmidhuber and Tubiello 2007.
6. Bates and others 2008.
7. WCED 1987.
8. Chen and Ravaillon 2008.
9. World Bank 2009a.
10. United Nations 2008.
11. Chen and Ravaillon 2008.
12. IEA 2007.
13. United Nations 2008.
14. United Nations 2008.
15. UNDP 2008.
16. IARU 2009.
17. Smith and others 2009.
18. Patriquin and others 2005; Patriquin, Wellstead, and White 2007; Pacific Institute for Climate Solutions 2008.
19. Note that this relationship holds even when controlling for the fact that poorer countries tend to be warmer on average. Dell, Jones, and Olken 2008.
20. Dell, Jones, and Olken 2008.
21. Brown and others 2009.

22. IPCC 2007b.
23. Cruz and others 2007.
24. Easterling and others 2007.
25. Auffhammer, Ramanathan, and Vincent 2006.
26. Guiteras 2007.
27. Ligon and Sadoulet 2007.
28. Campbell-Lendrum, Corvalan, and Pruss-Ustun 2003.
29. Among the many diverse regions and countries affected are Colombia (Vergara 2009), the Caucasus (Rabie and others 2008), Ethiopia (Confalonieri and others 2007), and the islands of the South Pacific (Potter 2008).
30. Molesworth and others 2003.
31. Confalonieri and others 2007.
32. Confalonieri and others 2007; Morris and others 2002.
33. Carter and others 2007.
34. World Bank 2001.
35. Azariadis and Stachurski 2005.
36. Lokshin and Ravallion 2000; Jalan and Ravallion 2004; Dercon 2004.
37. Dercon 2004.
38. Mueller and Osgood 2007.
39. Azariadis and Stachurski 2005.
40. Rosenzweig and Binswanger 1993.
41. Jensen 2000.
42. Alderman, Hoddinott, and Kinsey 2006.
43. Figures include all greenhouse gases but do not include emissions from land-use change. If estimates of land-use change emissions are added, the share of developing countries in global emissions is closer to 60 percent.
44. WRI 2008.
45. Chomitz and Meisner 2008.
46. Authors' calculations, based on data from CAIT (WRI 2008). Greenhouse gas emissions (excluding land-use change) per capita range from 4.5 to 55.5 metric tons CO_2e (7 to 27, if small-island states and oil producers are excluded) among high-income countries. Emissions per \$1,000 of output at market exchange rates range from 0.15 to 1.72 metric tons in high-income

"Take care of your earth,

Look after its creatures.

Don't leave your children,

A planet that's dead."

—Lakshmi Shree, India, age 12

countries; measuring output at purchasing power parity, the range is 0.20 to 1.04 metric tons.

47. Marcotullio and Schulz 2007.

48. Rosenberg 1971.

49. IPCC 2007a.

50. Lipovsky 1995.

51. "Annual Brazilian Ethanol Exports" and "Brazilian Ethanol Production," http://english .unica.com.br/dadosCotacao/estatistica/ (accessed December 2008).

52. Ummel and Wheeler 2008.

53. Hill and others 2009.

54. Mitchell 2008.

55. Ivanic and Martin 2008.

56. Ng and Aksoy 2008; World Bank 2008.

57. Cramton and Kerr 1999.

58. Ekins and Dresner 2004.

59. Brenner, Riddle, and Boyce 2007.

60. Benitez and others 2008.

61. Estache 2009.

62. Andriamihaja and Vecchi 2007.

63. Komives and others 2005.

64. Johnson and others 2008.

65. Pindyck 2007; Weitzman 2009a; Hallegatte, Dumas, and Hourcade 2009.

66. Yohe 1999; Toth and Mwandosya 2001.

67. Lempert and Schlesinger 2000.

68. Nordhaus 2008a. For a discussion of models and their results, see, for example, Heal 2008; Fisher and others 2007; Tol 2005; and Hourcade and Ambrosi 2007.

69. The 5 percent estimate is largely driven by the discount rate, but the margin between 5 percent and 20 percent is based on the inclusion of nonmarket impacts (health and environment), possibly higher sensitivity of the climate to greenhouse gases, and the use of equity weighting. Stern 2007; Dasgupta 2007; Dasgupta 2008.

70. For a discussion, see Dasgupta 2007; Dasgupta 2008; and box 1.4.

71. Dasgupta 2008.

72. Heal 2008; Sterner and Persson 2008.

73. Guesnerie 2004; Heal 2005; Hourcade and Ambrosi 2007.

74. Sterner and Persson 2008.

75. Hourcade and others (2001) explore the sensitivity of seven different integrated assessment models to the shape of the damage function and find that optimal concentration trajectories can imply significant departure from current emission trends if significant damages occur with warming of 3°C or 500 parts per milion (ppm) CO_2 concentration. More generally, they note that early action can be justified if a nonzero probability is assigned to damages increasing very rapidly with warming, so that damages grow more rapidly than the rate at which discounting shaves down their weight.

76. Solomon and others 2009.

77. Mignone and others 2008.

78. Folger 2006; Auld and others 2007.

79. Carbon capture and storage technology is described in chapter 4, box 4.6.

80. Shalizi and Lecocq 2009.

81. For a general discussion, see Arthur 1994; for a more specific application of increasing returns and the need to invest in innovation in the area of energy efficiency, see Mulder 2005.

82. Weitzman 2007; Weitzman 2009a; Weitzman 2009b; Nordhaus 2009.

83. Gjerde, Grepperud, and Kverndokk 1999; Kousky and others 2009.

84. Hallegatte, Dumas, and Hourcade 2009.

85. See Pindyck (2007) and Quiggin (2008) for recent reviews.

86. O'Neill and others 2006.

87. In their model, Sterner and Persson (2008) include environmental goods in the utility function.

88. Portney and Weyant 1999.

89. Fisher and others 2007; Hourcade and Ambrosi 2007; Tol 2005.

90. Diamond 2005.

91. Komives and others 2007; Diamond 2005.

92. Diamond 2005.

93. Hof, den Elzen, and van Vuuren 2008.

94. Bruckner and others 1999.

95. Yohe 1999.

96. Toth and Mwandosya 2001.

97. Lempert and Schlesinger 2000.

98. Savage 1951; Savage 1954.

99. Klaus, Yohe, and Schlesinger 2008.

100. IPCC 2007a.

101. See overview figure 3 for cumulative emissions relative to population share.

102. According to the IEA (2008), non-OECD (Organisation for Economic Co-operation and Development) countries reached the same level of annual energy-related emissions as OECD countries in 2004 (approximately 13 gigatons of CO_2 a year). The World Resource Institute's CAIT emission indicator database suggests the same conclusion using the World Bank's definition of developed and developing countries; WRI 2008.

103. Wheeler and Ummel 2007.

104. Chapter 5, box 5.1, describes the Bali Action Plan in detail.

105. For 2030, this has been estimated at 65–70 percent of the emission reduction, or 45–70 percent of the investment cost. Over the course of the century (using net present value to 2100) the estimated share of investments that should take place in developing countries is 65–70 percent. See overview note 47 for sources.

106. Edmonds and others 2008.

107. Nordhaus 2008b.

108. See, for example, Edmonds and others 2008.

109. See note 108 above and chapter 5, box 5.1.

110. Hamilton 2009.

111. Barrett 2006; Barrett 2007.

112. Barrett and Stavins 2003.

113. Carraro, Eykmans, and Finus 2009; personal communication with Carlo Carraro, 2009.

114. Brinsley and Christie 2009.

115. Bureau of Labor Statistics 2009.

116. ILO 2009.

117. World Bank 2009a.

118. Ratha, Mohapatra, and Xu 2008.

119. Banco de México, http://www.banxico .org.mx/SieInternet/consultarDirectorioInternet Action.do?accion=consultarCuadro&idCuadro =CE99&locale=es (accessed May 15, 2009).

120. Robins, Clover, and Singh 2009.

121. Robert B. Zoellick, "A Stimulus Package for the World," *New York Times*, January 22, 2009.

122. Fankhauser, Sehlleier, and Stern 2008.

123. Houser, Mohan, and Heilmayr 2009.

124. Pollin and others 2008.

125. Fankhauser, Sehlleier, and Stern 2008.

126. Robins, Clover, and Singh 2009.

127. Bowen and others 2009.

128. Bowen and others 2009; Houser, Mohan, and Heilmayr 2009.

129. Schwartz, Andres, and Dragoiu 2009.

130. Barbier 2009.

131. Barbier 2009.

132. Authors' calculations based on Houser, Mohan, and Heilmayr 2009.

133. Schwartz, Andres, and Dragoiu 2009.

134. Accenture 2009.

135. Pew Research Center for People and the Press 2009.

136. Ravallion 2008.

137. These programs pionered the use of incentive-based transfers to poor households to supplement incomes while directly encouraging poverty-combating behaviors. In contrast to traditional income support, these programs provide cash to poor households conditional on their participation in nutrition and health programs (immunizations, pre-natal care) or on their children's school attendance. Fiszbein and Schady 2009.

References

ACASIAN (Australian Consortium for the Asian Spatial Information and Analysis Network). 2004. "China Rail Transport Network database." Griffith University, Brisbane.

Accenture. 2009. *Shifting the Balance from Intention to Action: Low Carbon, High Opportunity, High Performance*. New York: Accenture.

Adams, H. D., M. Guardiola-Claramonte, G. A. Barron-Gafford, J. C. Villegas, D. D. Breshears, C. B. Zou, P. A. Troch, and T. E. Huxman. 2009. "Temperature Sensitivity of Drought-Induced Tree Mortality Portends Increased Regional Die-Off under Global-Change-Type Drought." *Proceedings of the National Academy of Sciences* 106 (17): 7063–66.

Aguilar, L. 2006. "Climate Change and Disaster Mitigation: Gender Makes a Difference." International Union for Conservation of Nature, Gland, Switzerland.

Alderman, H., J. Hoddinott, and B. Kinsey. 2006. "Long-Term Consequences of Early Childhood Malnutrition." *Oxford Economic Papers* 58 (3): 450–74.

Andriamihaja, N., and G. Vecchi. 2007. "An Evaluation of the Welfare Impact of Higher Energy Prices in Madagascar." Working Paper Series 106, World Bank, Africa Region, Washington, DC.

Armstrong, R., B. Raup, S. J. S. Khalsa, R. Barry, J. Kargel, C. Helm, and H. Kieffer. 2005. "GLIMS Glacier Database." National Snow and Ice Data Center, Boulder, CO.

Arthur, W. B. 1994. *Increasing Returns and Path-Dependence in the Economy*. Ann Arbor, MI: University of Michigan Press.

Assunçao, J. J., and F. Chein. 2008. "Climate Change, Agricultural Productivity and Poverty." Background Paper for de la Torre and others, 2008, *Low Carbon, High Growth: Latin America Responses to Climate Change*. Washington, DC: World Bank.

Auffhammer, M., V. Ramanathan, and J. R. Vincent. 2006. "Integrated Model Shows that Atmospheric Brown Clouds and Greenhouse Gases Have Reduced Rice Harvests in India." *Proceedings of the National Academy of Sciences* 103 (52): 19668–72.

Auld, G, S. Bernstein, B. Cashore, and K. Levin. 2007. "Playing It Forward: Path Dependency, Progressive Incrementalism, and the 'Super Wicked' Problem of Global Climate Change." Paper presented at the International Studies Association annual convention, February 28, Chicago.

Azariadis, C., and J. Stachurski. 2005. "Poverty Traps." In *Handbook of Economic Growth, vol. 1,* ed. P. Aghion and S. Durlauf. Amsterdam: Elsevier.

Barbier, E. B. 2009. *A Global Green New Deal*. Nairobi: United Nations Environment Programme.

Barrett, S. 2006. "The Problem of Averting Global Catastrophe." *Chicago Journal of International Law* 6 (2): 1–26.

———. 2007. *Why Cooperate? The Incentive to Supply Global Public Goods.* Oxford, UK: Oxford University Press.

Barrett, S., and R. Stavins. 2003. "Increasing Participation and Compliance in International Climate Change Agreements." *International Environmental Agreements: Politics, Law and Economics* 3 (4): 349–76.

Bates, B., Z. W. Kundzewicz, S. Wu, and J. Palutikof. 2008. "Climate Change and Water." Technical Paper, Intergovernmental Panel on Climate Change, Geneva.

Benitez, D., R. Fuentes Nieva, T. Serebrisky, and Q. Wodon. 2008. "Assessing the Impact of Climate Change Policies in Infrastructure Service Delivery: A Note on Affordability and Access." Background note for the WDR 2010.

Bowen, A., S. Fankhauser, N. Stern, and D. Zenghelis. 2009. *An Outline of the Case for a "Green" Stimulus.* London: Grantham Research Institute on Climate Change and the Environment and the Centre for Climate Change Economics and Policy.

Brenner, M. D., M. Riddle, and J. K. Boyce. 2007. "A Chinese Sky Trust? Distributional Impacts of Carbon Charges and Revenue Recycling in China." *Energy Policy* 35 (3): 1771–84.

Brinsley, J., and R. Christie. 2009. "Paulson to Work Quickly with Congress to Revive Plan (Update 1)." Bloomberg, September 29.

Brown, C., R. Meeks, Y. Ghile, and K. Hunu. 2009. "An Empirical Analysis of the Effects of Climate Variables on National Level Economic Growth." Background paper for the WDR 2010.

Bruckner, T., G. Petschel-Held, F. L. Toth, H.-M. Füssel, C. Helm, M. Leimbach, and H.-J. Schellnhuber. 1999. "Climate Change Decision Support and the Tolerable Windows Approach." *Environmental Modeling and Assessment* 4: 217–34.

Bureau of Labor Statistics. 2009. "Employment Situation Summary." Washington, DC.

Campbell-Lendrum, D. H., C. F. Corvalan, and A. Pruss-Ustun. 2003. "How Much Disease Could Climate Change Cause?" In *Climate Change and Human Health: Risks and Responses,* ed. A. J. McMichael, D. H. Campbell-Lendrum, C. F. Corvalan, K. L. Ebi, A. Githeko, J. D. Scheraga, and A. Woodward. Geneva: World Health Organization.

Caney, S. 2009. "Ethics and Climate Change." Background paper for the WDR 2010.

Carraro, C., J. Eykmans, and M. Finus. 2009. "Optimal Transfers and Participation Decisions in International Environmental Agreements." *Review of International Organizations* 1 (4): 379–96.

Carter, M. R., P. D. Little, T. Mogues, and W. Negatu. 2007. "Poverty Traps and Natural Disasters in Ethiopia and Honduras." *World Development* 35 (5): 835–56.

Chan, K. W. 2008. "Internal Labor Migration in China: Trends, Geographical Distribution and Policies." Paper presented at the Proceedings of United Nations Expert Group Meeting on Population Distribution, Urbanization, Internal Migration and Development, New York.

Chen, S., and M. Ravaillon. 2008. "The Developing World Is Poorer than We Thought, But No Less Successful in the Fight against Poverty." Policy Research Working Paper 4703, World Bank, Washington, DC.

Chomitz, K., and C. Meisner. 2008. "A Simple Benchmark for CO_2 Intensity of Economies." Washington, DC: Background Note for the World Bank Internal Evaluation Group on Climate Change and the World Bank Group.

Confalonieri, U., B. Menne, R. Akhtar, K. L. Ebi, M. Hauengue, R. S. Kovats, B. Revich, and A. Woodward. 2007. "Human Health." In *Climate Change 2007: Impacts, Adaptation and Vulnerability. Contribution of Working Group II to the Fourth Assessment Report of the Intergovernmental Panel on Climate Change,* ed. M. L. Parry, O. F. Canziani, J. P. Palutikof, P. J. van der Linden, and C. E. Hanson. Cambridge, UK: Cambridge University Press.

Cramton, P., and S. Kerr. 1999. "The Distributional Effect of Carbon Regulation: Why Auctioned Carbon Permits Are Attractive and Feasible." In *The Market and the Environment,* ed. T. Sterner. Northampton, UK: Edward Elgar Publishing.

Cruz, R. V., H. Harasawa, M. Lal, S. Wu, Y. Anokhin, B. Punsalmaa, Y. Honda, M. Jafari, C. Li, and N. Huu Ninh. 2007. "Asia." In *Climate Change 2007: Impacts, Adaptation and Vulnerability. Contribution of Working Group II to the Fourth Assessment Report of the Intergovernmental Panel on Climate Change,* ed. M. L. Parry, O. F. Canziani, J. P. Palutikof, P. J. van der Linden, and C. E. Hanson. Cambridge, UK: Cambridge University Press.

Dasgupta, P. 2007. "Comments on the Stern Review's Economics of Climate Change." *National Institute Economic Review* 199: 4–7.

———. 2008. "Discounting Climate Change." *Journal of Risk and Uncertainty* 37 (2): 141–69.

Dell, M., B. F. Jones, and B. A. Olken. 2008. "Climate Change and Economic Growth: Evidence from the Last Half Century." Working Paper 14132, National Bureau of Economic Research, Cambridge, MA.

———. 2009. "Temperature and Income: Reconciling New Cross-Sectional and Panel Estimates." *American Economic Review* 99 (2): 198–204.

Dercon, S. 2004. "Growth and Shocks: Evidence from Rural Ethiopia." *Journal of Development Economics* 74 (2): 309–29.

Diamond, J. 2005. *Collapse: How Societies Choose to Fail or Succeed*. New York: Viking.

Easterling, W., P. Aggarwal, P. Batima, K. Brander, L. Erda, M. Howden, A. Kirilenko, J. Morton, J.-F. Soussana, J. Schmidhuber, and F. Tubiello. 2007. "Food, Fibre and Forest Products." In *Climate Change 2007: Impacts, Adaptation and Vulnerability. Contribution of Working Group II to the Fourth Assessment Report of the Intergovernmental Panel on Climate Change,* ed. M. Parry, O. F. Canziani, J. P. Palutikof, P. J. van der Linden, and C. E. Hanson. Cambridge, UK: Cambridge University Press.

Edmonds, J., L. Clarke, J. Lurz, and M. Wise. 2008. "Stabilizing CO_2 Concentrations with Incomplete International Cooperation." *Climate Policy* 8 (4): 355–76.

Ekins, P., and S. Dresner. 2004. *Green Taxes and Charges: Reducing their Impact on Low-income Households*. York, UK: Joseph Rowntree Foundation.

ESRI (Environmental Systems Research Institute). 2002. "ESRI Data and Maps." Redlands, CA.

Estache, A. 2009. "How Should the Nexus between Economic and Environmental Regulation Work for Infrastructure Services?" Background note for the WDR 2010.

Fankhauser, S., F. Sehlleier, and N. Stern. 2008. "Climate Change, Innovation and Jobs." *Climate Policy* 8: 421–29.

Fisher, B. S., N. Nakićenović, K. Alfsen, J. Corfee Morlot, F. de la Chesnaye, J.-C. Hourcade, K. Jiang, M. Kainuma, E. La Rovere, A. Matysek, A. Rana, K. Riahi, R. Richels, S. Rose, D. van Vuuren, and R. Warren. 2007. "Issues Related to Mitigation in the Long-Term Context." In *Climate Change 2007: Mitigation. Contribution of Working Group III to the Fourth Assessment Report of the Intergovernmental Panel on Climate Change,* ed. B. Metz, O. R. Davidson, P. R. Bosch, R. Dave, and L. A. Meyer. Cambridge, UK: Cambridge University Press.

Fiszbein, A., and N. Schady. 2009. *Conditional Cash Transfers: Reducing Present and Future Poverty*. Washington, DC: World Bank.

Folger, T. 2006. "Can Coal Come Clean? How to Survive the Return of the World's Dirtiest Fossil Fuel." December. *Discover Magazine.*

Gjerde, J., S. Grepperud, and S. Kverndokk. 1999. "Optimal Climate Policy under the Possibility of a Catastrophe." *Resource and Energy Economics* 21 (3–4): 289–317.

Guesnerie, R. 2004. "Calcul Economique et Développement Durable." *La Revue Economique* 55 (3): 363–82.

Guiteras, R. 2007. "The Impact of Climate Change on Indian Agriculture." Department of Economics Working Paper, Massachusetts Institute of Technology, Cambridge, MA.

Hallegatte, S. 2008. "An Adaptive Regional Input-Output Model and its Application to the Assessment of the Economic Cost of Katrina." *Risk Analysis* 28 (3): 779–99.

Hallegatte, S., P. Dumas, and J.-C. Hourcade. 2009. "A Note on the Economic Cost of Climate Change and the Rationale to Limit it to 2°K." Background paper for the WDR 2010.

Hamilton, K. 2009. "Delayed Participation in a Global Climate Agreement." Background note for the WDR 2010.

Harrington, J., and T. L. Walton. 2008. "Climate Change in Coastal Areas in Florida: Sea Level Rise Estimation and Economic Analysis to Year 2080." Florida State University, Tallahassee, FL.

Heal, G. 2005. "Intertemporal Welfare Economics and the Environment." In *Handbook of Environmental Economics, Vol. 3,* ed. K.-G. Maler and J. R. Vincent. Amsterdam: Elsevier.

———. 2008. "Climate Economics: A Meta-Review and Some Suggestions." Working Paper 13927, National Bureau of Economic Research, Cambridge, MA.

Hill, J., S. Polasky, E. Nelson, D. Tilman, H. Huo, L. Ludwig, J. Neumann, H. Zheng, and D. Bonta. 2009. "Climate Change and Health Costs of Air Emissions from Biofuels and Gasoline." *Proceedings of the National Academy of Sciences* 106 (6): 2077–82.

Hof, A. F., M. G. J. den Elzen, and D. P. van Vuuren. 2008. "Analyzing the Costs and Benefits of Climate Policy: Value Judgments and Scientific Uncertainties." *Global Environmental Change* 18 (3): 412–24.

Houghton, R. A. 2009. "Emissions of Carbon from Land Management." Background note for the WDR 2010.

Hourcade, J.-C., and P. Ambrosi. 2007. "Quelques Leçons d'un Essai à Risque, l'evaluation des Dommages Climatiques par Sir Nicholas Stern." *Revue d'economie politique* 117 (4): 33–46.

Hourcade, J.-C., M. Ha-Duong, A. Grübler, and R. S. J. Tol. 2001. "INASUD Project Findings on Integrated Assessment of Climate Policies." *Integrated Assessment* 2 (1): 31–35.

Houser, T., S. Mohan, and R. Heilmayr. 2009. "A Green Global Recovery? Assessing U.S. Economic Stimulus and the Prospects for International Coordination." Policy Brief PB09-03, World Resources Institute, Washington, DC.

Huang, Y., and A. Magnoli, eds. 2009. *Reshaping Economic Geography in East Asia.* Washington, DC: World Bank.

IARU (International Alliance of Research Universities). 2009. "Climate Change: Global Risks, Challenges and Decisions." IOP Conference Series: Earth and Environmental Science. Copenhagen.

IEA (International Energy Agency). 2007. *World Energy Outlook 2007.* Paris: IEA.

———. 2008. *World Energy Outlook 2008.* Paris: IEA.

ILO (International Labour Organization). 2009. *Global Employment Trends: January 2009.* Geneva: ILO.

IPCC (Intergovernmental Panel on Climate Change). 2007a. *Climate Change 2007: Synthesis Report. Contribution of Working Groups I, II, and II to the Fourth Assessment Report of the Intergovernmental Panel on Climate Change.* Geneva: IPCC.

———. 2007b. "Summary for Policymakers." In *Climate Change 2007: Impacts, Adaptation and Vulnerability. Contribution of Working Group II to the Fourth Assessment Report of the Intergovernmental Panel on Climate Change,* ed. M. L. Parry, O. F. Canziani, J. P. Palutikof, P. J. van der Linden, and C. E. Hanson. Cambridge, UK: Cambridge University Press.

Ivanic, M., and W. Martin. 2008. "Implications of Higher Global Food Prices for Poverty in Low-Income Countries." Policy Research Working Paper 4594, World Bank, Washington, DC.

IWM (Institute of Water Modelling) and CEGIS (Center for Environmental and Geographical Information Services). 2007. *Investigating the Impact of Relative Sea-Level Rise on Coastal Communities and Their Livelihoods in Bangladesh.* Dhaka: IWM, CEGIS.

Jalan, J., and M. Ravallion. 2004. "Household Income Dynamics in Rural China." In *Insurance against Poverty,* ed. S. Dercon. Oxford, UK: Oxford University Press.

Jensen, R. 2000. "Agricultural Volatility and Investments in Children." *American Economic Review* 90 (2): 399–404.

Johnson, T., F. Liu, C. Alatorre, and Z. Romo. 2008. "Mexico Low-Carbon Study—México: Estudio Para la Disminución de Emisiones de Carbono (MEDEC)." World Bank, Washington, DC.

Klaus, K., G. Yohe, and M. Schlesinger. 2008. "Managing the Risks of Climate Thresholds: Uncertainties and Information Needs." *Climatic Change* 91: 5–10.

Komives, K., V. Foster, J. Halpern, Q. Wodon, and R. Abdullah. 2005. *Water, Electricity, and the Poor: Who Benefits from Utility Subsidies?* Washington, DC: World Bank.

Komives, K., V. Foster, H. Halpern, Q. Wodon, and R. Krznaric. 2007. *Food Coupons and Bald Mountains: What the History of Resource Scarcity Can Teach Us about Tackling Climate Change.* New York: United Nations Development Programme.

Kousky, C., O. Rostapshova, M. A. Toman, and R. Zeckhauser. 2009. "Responding to Threats of Climate Change Catastrophes." Background paper for the *Economics of Natural Disasters,* Global Facility for Disaser Reduction and Recovery, World Bank, Washington, DC.

Kriegler, E., J. W. Hall, H. Held, R. Dawson, and H. J. Schellnhuber. 2009. "Imprecise Probability Assessment of Tipping Points in the Climate System." *Proceedings of the National Academy of Sciences* 106 (13): 5041–46.

Lambrou, Y., and R. Laub. 2004. *Gender Perspectives on the Conventions on Biodiversity, Climate Change and Desertification.* Rome: Food and Agriculture Organization.

Lempert, R. J., and M. E. Schlesinger. 2000. "Robust Strategies for Abating Climate Change." *Climatic Change* 45 (3–4): 387–401.

Ligon, E., and E. Sadoulet. 2007. "Estimating the Effects of Aggregate Agricultural Growth on the Distribution of Expenditures." Background paper for the WDR 2008.

Lipovsky, I. 1995. "The Central Asian Cotton Epic." *Central Asian Survey* 14 (4): 29–542.

Lokshin, M., and M. Ravallion. 2000. "Short-lived Shocks with Long-lived Impacts?

Household Income Dynamics in a Transition Economy." Policy Research Working Paper 2459, World Bank, Washington, DC.

Marcotullio, P. J., and N. B. Schulz. 2007. "Comparison of Energy Transitions in the United States and Developing and Industrializing Economies." *World Development* 35 (10): 1650–83.

Martin, A. 1996. "Forestry: Gender Makes the Difference." International Union for Conservation of Nature, Gland, Switzerland.

McKinsey & Company. 2009. *Pathways to a Low-carbon Economy: Version 2 of the Global Greenhouse Gas Abatement Cost Curve.* McKinsey & Company.

Mignone, B. K., R. H. Socolow, J. L. Sarmiento, and M. Oppenheimer. 2008. "Atmospheric Stabilization and the Timing of Carbon Mitigation." *Climatic Change* 88 (3 -4): 251–65.

Mitchell, D. 2008. "A Note on Rising Food Prices." Policy Research Working Paper 4682, World Bank, Washington, DC.

Molesworth, A. M., L. E. Cuevas, S. J. Connor, A. P. Morse, and M. C. Thomson. 2003. "Environmental Changes and Meningitis Epidemics in Africa." *Emerging Infectious Diseases* 9 (10): 1287–93.

Morris, S., O. Neidecker-Gonzales, C. Carletto, M. Munguia, J. M. Medina, and Q. Wodon. 2002. "Hurricane Mitch and Livelihoods of the Rural Poor in Honduras." *World Development* 30 (1): 39–60.

Mueller, V., and D. Osgood. 2007. "Long-term Impacts of Droughts on Labor Markets in Developing Countries: Evidence from Brazil." Earth Institute at Columbia University, New York.

Mulder, P. 2005. *The Economics of Technology Diffusion and Energy Efficiency.* Cheltenham, UK: Edward Elgar.

Neumayer, E., and T. Plumper. 2007. "The Gendered Nature of Natural Disasters: The Impact of Catastrophic Events on the Gender Gap in Life Expectancy, 1981–2002." *Annals of the Association of American Geographers* 97 (3): 551–66.

Ng, F., and M. A. Aksoy. 2008. "Who Are the Net Food Importing Countries?" Policy Research Working Paper 4457, World Bank, Washington, DC.

Nordhaus, W. 2008a. *A Question of Balance: Weighing the Options on Global Warming Policies.* New Haven, CT: Yale University Press.

———. 2008b. "The Role of Universal Participation in Policies to Slow Global Warming." Paper presented at the Third Atlantic Workshop on Energy and Environmental Economics, A Toxa, Spain.

———. 2009. "An Analysis of the Dismal Theorem." Cowles Foundation Discussion Paper 1686, New Haven, CT.

O'Neill, B. C., P. Crutzen, A. Grübler, M. Ha-Duong, K. Keller, C. Kolstad, J. Koomey, A. Lange, M. Obersteiner, M. Oppenheimer, W. Pepper, W. Sanderson, M. Schlesinger, N. Treich, A. Ulph, M. Webster, and C. Wilson. 2006. "Learning and Climate Change." *Climate Policy* 6: 585–89.

Pacific Institute for Climate Solutions. 2008. "Climate Change and Health in British Columbia." University of Victoria, Victoria.

Parikh, J. 2008. *Gender and Climate Change: Key Issues.* New Delhi: Integrated Research and Action for Development.

Patriquin, M., A. M. Wellstead, and W. A. White. 2007. "Beetles, Trees, and People: Regional Economic Impact Sensitivity and Policy Considerations Related to the Mountain Pine Beetle Infestation in British Columbia, Canada." *Forest Policy and Economics* 9 (8): 938–46.

Pindyck, R. 2007. "Uncertainty in Environmental Economics." *Review of Environmental Economics and Policy* 1 (1): 45–65.

Pollin, R., H. Garrett-Peltier, J. Heintz, and H. Scharber. 2008. *Green Recovery: A Program to Create Good Jobs and Start Building a Low Carbon Economy.* Washington, DC: Center for American Progress.

Portney, P. R., and J. P. Weyant. 1999. *Discounting and Intergenerational Equity.* Washington, DC: Resources for the Future.

Potter, S. 2008. *The Sting of Climate Change: Malaria and Dengue Fever in Maritime Southeast Asia and the Pacific Islands.* Sydney: Lowy Institute for International Policy.

Quiggin, J. 2008. "Uncertainty and Climate Policy." *Economic Analysis and Policy* 38 (2): 203–10.

Rabie, T., S. el Tahir, T. Alireza, G. Sanchez Martinez, K. Ferl, and N. Cenacchi. 2008. "The Health Dimension of Climate Change." Background Paper for *Adapting to Climate Change in Europe and Central Asia,* ed. M. Fay, R. I. Block, and J. Ebinger, 2010, World Bank, Washington, DC.

Ratha, D., S. Mohapatra, and Z. Xu. 2008. *Outlook for Remittance Flows 2008–2010.* Washington, DC: World Bank.

Ravallion, M. 2008. "Bailing Out the World's Poorest." Policy Research Working Paper 4763, World Bank, Washington, DC.

Ristvet, L., and H. Weiss. 2000. "Imperial Responses to Environmental Dynamics at Late Third Millennium Tell Leilan." *Orient-Express* 2000 (4): 94–99.

Robine, J.-M., S. L. K. Cheung, S. Le Roy, H. Van Oyen, C. Griffiths, J.-P. Michel, and F. R. Herrmann. 2008. "Death Toll Exceeded 70,000 in Europe during Summer of 2003." *Comptes Rendus Biologies* 331 (2): 171–78.

Robins, N., R. Clover, and C. Singh. 2009. *A Climate for Recovery: The Colour of Stimulus Goes Green.* London: HSBC.

Roemer, J. 2009. "The Ethics of Distribution in a Warming Planet." Cowles Foundation Discussion Paper 1693, New Haven, CT.

Rosenberg, N. 1971. "Technology and the Environment: An Economic Exploration." *Technology and Culture* 12 (4): 543–61.

Rosenzweig, M. R., and H. P. Binswanger. 1993. "Wealth, Weather Risk and the Composition and Profitability of Agricultural Investments." *Economic Journal* 103 (416): 56–78.

Savage, L. J. 1951. "The Theory of Statistical Decision." *Journal of the American Statistical Association* 46 (253): 55–67.

———. 1954. *The Foundations of Statistics.* New York: John Wiley & Sons.

Schmidhuber, J., and F. N. Tubiello. 2007. "Global Food Security under Climate Change." *Proceedings of the National Academy of Sciences* 104 (50): 19703–08.

Schmidt, G. 2006. "Runaway Tipping Points of No Return." Real Climate, July 5, 2009.

Schwartz, J., L. Andres, and G. Dragoiu. 2009. "Crisis in LAC: Infrastructure Investment, Employment and the Expectations of Stimulus." World Bank, LCSSD Economics Unit, Washington, DC.

Shalizi, Z., and F. Lecocq. 2009. "Economics of Targeted Mitigation Programs in Sectors with Long-Lived Capital Stock." Policy Research Working Paper 5063, World Bank, Washington, DC.

Singer, P. 2006. "Ethics and Climate Change: Commentary." *Environmental Values* 15: 415–22.

Smith, J. B., S. H. Schneider, M. Oppenheimer, G. W. Yohe, W. Hare, M. D. Mastrandrea, A. Patwardhan, I. Burton, J. Corfee-Morlot, C. H. D. Magadza, H.-M. Füssel, A. B. Pittock, A. Rahman, A. Suarez, and J.-P. van Ypersele. 2009. "Assessing Dangerous Climate Change through an Update of the Intergovernmental Panel on Climate Change (IPCC) 'reasons for concern.'" *Proceedings of the National Academy of Sciences* 106 (11): 4133–37.

Smyth, I. 2005. "More than Silence: The Gender Dimensions of Tsunami Fatalities and Their Consequences." Paper presented at the WHO Conference on Health Aspects of the Tsunami Disaster in Asia, Phuket, Thailand.

Solomon, S., G.-K. Plattner, R. Knutti, and P. Friedlingstein. 2009. "Irreversible Climate Change due to Carbon Dioxide Emissions." *Proceedings of the National Academy of Sciences* 106 (6): 1704–09.

Stern, N. 2007. *The Economics of Climate Change: The Stern Review.* Cambridge, UK: Cambridge University Press.

———. 2008. *Key Elements of a Global Deal on Climate Change.* London: London School of Economics and Political Science.

Sterner, T., and U. M. Persson. 2008. "An Even Sterner Review: Introducing Relative Prices into the Discounting Debate." *Review of Environmental Economics and Policy* 2 (1): 61–76.

Tol, R. S. J. 2005. "The Marginal Damage Cost of Carbon Dioxide Emissions: An Assessment of the Uncertainties." *Energy Policy* 33: 2064–74.

Toth, F., and M. Mwandosya. 2001. "Decision-making Frameworks." In *Climate Change 2001: Mitigation. Contribution of Working Group III to the Third Assessment Report of the Intergovernmental Panel on Climate Change,* ed. B. Metz, O. Davidson, R. Swart, and J. Pan. Cambridge, UK: Cambridge University Press.

Ummel, K., and D. Wheeler. 2008. "Desert Power: The Economics of Solar Thermal Electricity for Europe, North Africa, and the Middle East." Working Paper 156, Center for Global Development, Washington, DC.

UNDP (United Nations Development Programme). 2008. *Human Development Report 2007/2008. Fighting Climate Change: Human Solidarity in a Divided World.* New York: UNDP.

———. 2009. *Resource Guide on Gender and Climate Change.* New York: UNDP.

UNISDR (United Nations International Strategy for Disaster Risk Reduction). 2007. *Gender Perspective: Working Together for Disaster Risk Reduction. Good Practices and Lessons Learned.* Geneva: UNISDR.

United Nations. 2008. *The Millennium Development Goals Report 2008.* New York: UN.

Vergara, W. 2009. "Assessing the Potential Consequences of Climate Destabilization in Latin America." Sustainable Development Working Paper 32, World Bank, Latin America and Caribbean Region, Washington, DC.

WCED (World Commission on Environment and Development). 1987. *Our Common Future.* Oxford, UK: WCED.

Weiss, H. 2000. "Beyond the Younger Dryas: Collapse as Adaptation to Abrupt Climate Change in Ancient West Asia and the Eastern Mediterranean." In *Environmental Disaster and the Archaeology of Human Response,* ed. G. Bawden and R. M. Reycraft. Albuquerque: Maxwell Museum of Anthropology.

Weiss, H., and R. S. Bradley. 2001. "What Drives Societal Collapse?" *Science* 291: 609–10.

Weitzman, M. 2007. "A Review of the *Stern Review on the Economics of Climate Change*." *Journal of Economic Literature* 45 (3): 703–24.

———. 2009a. "On Modeling and Interpreting the Economics of Catastrophic Climate Change." *Review of Economics and Statistics* 91 (1): 1–19.

———. 2009b. "Reactions to the Nordhaus Critique." Harvard University. Cambridge, MA.

Wheeler, D., and K. Ummel. 2007. "Another Inconvenient Truth: A Carbon-Intensive South Faces Environmental Disaster, No Matter What the North Does." Working Paper 134, Center for Global Development, Washington, DC.

World Bank. 2001. "Hurricane Mitch: The Gender Effects of Coping and Crises." Notes of the Development Economics Vice Presidency and Poverty Reduction and Economic Management Network 56, Washington, DC.

———. 2008. "Double Jeopardy: Responding to High Food and Fuel Prices." Working Paper 44951, Washington, DC.

———. 2009a. *Global Monitoring Report 2009: A Development Emergency*. Washington, DC: World Bank.

———. 2009b. "World Bank Statement to the Tenth Session of the United Nations Human Rights Council." Geneva.

———. 2009c. *World Development Indicators 2009*. Washington, DC: World Bank.

WRI (World Resources Institute). 2008. "The Climate Analysis Indicators Tool (CAIT)." Washington, DC.

Yohe, G. W. 1999. "The Tolerable Windows Approach: Lessons and Limitations." *Climatic Change* 41 (3–4): 283–95.

The science of climate change

The climate is changing—that is now indisputable. There is a scientific consensus that the world is becoming a warmer place principally attributable to human activities. In the words of the Intergovernmental Panel on Climate Change (IPCC) in its fourth assessment report: "Warming of the climate system is unequivocal."[1] For nearly 1 million years before the Industrial Revolution, the carbon dioxide (CO_2) concentration in the atmosphere ranged between 170 and 280 parts per million (ppm). Levels are now far above that range—387 ppm—higher than the highest point in at least the past 800,000 years, and the rate of increase may be accelerating.[2] Under high-emissions scenarios, concentrations by the end of the 21st century could exceed those experienced on the planet for tens of millions of years.

Article 2 of the United Nations Framework Convention on Climate Change sets the objective of achieving a "stabilization of greenhouse gas emissions at a level that would prevent dangerous anthropogenic interference with the climate system."[3] To the extent that avoiding "dangerous" interference is defined in the convention, it is described as keeping emissions to levels that "allow ecosystems to adapt naturally to climate change, ensure that food production is not threatened and enable economic development to proceed in a sustainable manner." It is not clear that this objective is fully achievable because the warming already observed has been linked to increases in droughts, floods, heat waves, forest fires, and intense rainfall events that are already threatening human and natural systems.

There is convincing evidence that the capacity of societies and ecosystems to adapt to global warming is severely tested beyond warming of 2°C.[4] If the world is able to limit the human-caused temperature increase to about 2°C above its preindustrial level, it might be possible to limit significant loss from the Greenland and West Antarctic ice sheets and subsequent sea-level rise; to limit the increase of floods, droughts, and forest fires in many regions; to limit the increase of death and illness from the spread of infectious and diarrheal diseases and from extreme heat; to avoid extinction of more than a quarter of all known species; and to prevent significant declines in global food production.[5]

But, even stabilizing global temperatures at 2°C above preindustrial levels will significantly change the world. Earth has warmed 0.8°C on average from preindustrial times, and high-latitude regions are already experiencing environmental and cultural disruption; further impacts will be unavoidable as warming continues. A 2°C warming will cause more frequent and stronger extreme weather events, including heat waves, increased water stress in many world regions, declining food production in many tropical regions, and damaged ecosystems, including widespread loss of coral reefs from warming and ocean acidification.

Unless the world acts quickly to alter emissions pathways, models project that by 2100 the global average temperature will increase to 2.5–7°C above preindustrial levels,[6] depending on the amount and rate of energy growth, limits on fossil-fuel energy sources, and the pace of development of carbon-free energy technologies (see chapter 4). Although this temperature may seem like a modest increase compared with seasonal variations, the lower end of this range is the equivalent of moving from Oslo to Madrid. The upper end is equivalent to the warming that has occurred since the peak of the last glacial age, which led to the melting of two-kilometer thick ice that covered northern Europe and North America.[7] For the next few decades, the global average temperature is projected to increase 0.2–0.3°C a decade,[8] a rate of change that will tax the ability of species and ecosystems to adapt (see focus B on biodiversity).

Defining "dangerous anthropogenic interference" will be a political decision, not a scientific determination. A decade after the Kyoto Protocol, as we enter the first period of rigorous accounting of emissions by developed countries, the world is negotiating the course of action for the coming decades that will largely determine whether our children inherit a planet that has stabilized around 2°C warmer or is on a path to much higher temperatures. The term "dangerous" involves several components—the total magnitude of change, the rate of change, the risk of sudden or abrupt change, and the likelihood of crossing irreversibly harmful thresholds. What is determined to be a dangerous degree of climate change can be expected to depend on the effects on human and natural systems and their capacity to adapt. This focus looks at how the climate system works, at the changes observed to date, what a 2°C warmer world versus a 5°C or warmer world portends, the risks of crossing irreversible thresholds, and the challenge to limit warming to 2°C.

How the climate system works

The climate of Earth is determined by the incoming energy from the Sun, the outgoing energy radiated from Earth, and exchanges of energy among the atmosphere, land, oceans, ice, and living things. The composition of the atmosphere is particularly important because some gases and aerosols (very small particles) affect the flow of incoming solar radiation and outgoing infrared radiation. Water vapor, CO_2, methane

(CH₄), ozone (O₃), and nitrous oxide (N₂O) are all greenhouse gases (GHGs) naturally present in the atmosphere. They warm Earth's surface by impeding the escape of infrared (heat) energy into space. The warming effect created by the natural levels of these gases is "the natural greenhouse effect." This effect warms the world about 33°C more than it would be otherwise, keeps most of the world's water in the liquid phase, and allows life to exist from the equator to near the poles.

Gases released from human activities have greatly amplified the natural greenhouse effect. The global average atmospheric CO_2 concentration has increased significantly since the beginning of the Industrial Revolution, especially in the past 50 years. Over the 20th century, the CO_2 concentration increased from about 280 ppm to 387 ppm—almost 40 percent—mainly because of the burning of carbon-based fossil fuels and, to a lesser extent, deforestation and changes in land use (box

FA.1). The combustion of coal, oil, and natural gas now contributes about 80 percent of the CO_2 emitted annually, with land-use changes and deforestation accounting for the remaining 20 percent. In 1950 the contributions from fossil fuels and land use were about equal; since then, energy use has grown by a factor of 18. The concentrations of other heat-trapping gases, including methane and nitrous oxide, have also increased significantly as a result of fossil-fuel combustion, farm-

---

BOX FA.1 *The carbon cycle*

The amount of carbon dioxide (CO_2) in the atmosphere is controlled by biogeochemical cycles that redistribute carbon among the ocean, land, living material, and atmosphere. The atmosphere currently contains about 824 gigatons (Gt) of carbon. Human-caused emissions of carbon in 2007 totaled about 9 Gt of carbon, of which about 7.7 Gt (or 28.5 Gt of CO_2) were from the combustion of fossil fuel and the rest were from changes in land cover. (One Gt equals a billion metric tons. To convert carbon emissions and fluxes to CO_2 amounts, multiply the amount of carbon by 3.67.)

The atmospheric concentration of CO_2 is currently increasing at a rate of about 2 parts per million (ppm) a year, which is equivalent to an increase in the atmospheric loading of carbon by about 4 Gt of carbon a year (in other words, about half of the fossil-fuel emissions of CO_2 lead to a long-term increase in the atmospheric concentration). The rest of the CO_2 emissions are being taken up by "carbon sinks"—the ocean and terrestrial ecosystems. The oceans take up about 2 Gt of carbon a year (the difference between the 90.6 and 92.2 indicated in the figure, plus a small land-to-ocean flux). The net uptake of carbon by oceans and by terrestrial systems (photosynthesis minus respiration) and the estimates of emissions from land-use change and fossil-fuel combustion would result in atmospheric concentrations higher than are recorded. It appears that terrestrial ecosystems are currently taking up the excess. A 2.7 Gt "residual sink," as it is

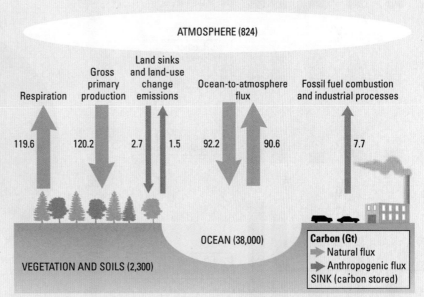

Source: Adapted from IPCC 2007b.

termed, is assumed to result mainly from changes in land cover (net increases in forest cover from reforestation and afforestation in excess of deforestation) and increased carbon uptake because of enhanced growth of the world's forests in response to higher CO_2 concentrations (known as the CO_2 fertilization effect).

Terrestrial ecosystems hold about 2,300 Gt of carbon—roughly 500 Gt in above-ground biomass and about three times that amount in the soils. Reducing deforestation needs to be an important component of slowing emissions growth. While every effort should be made to increase land storage of carbon, there will be challenges as the climate changes

and the frequency of fire, pest infestations, drought, and heat stress increases. If fossil-fuel emissions continue on a business-as-usual path, uptake of emissions by forests and other terrestrial ecosystems may slow and even reverse, with these ecosystems becoming a net source of emissions by the end of the century, according to some models. And warmer oceans will absorb CO_2 more slowly, so a greater fraction of fossil-fuel emissions will remain in the atmosphere.

Sources: Fischlin and others 2007; IPCC 2000; IPCC 2001; Canadell and others 2007; Houghton 2003; Prentice and others 2001; Sabine and others 2004.

ing and industrial activities, and land-use changes (figure FA.1).[9]

Some of the pollutants introduced by humans warm Earth, and some cool it (figure FA.2). Some are long-lived, and some short-lived. By trapping infrared radiation, carbon dioxide, nitrous oxide, and halocarbons[10] warm Earth, and because the increased concentrations of these gases persist for centuries, their

warming influence causes long-term climate change. In contrast, the warming influence of methane emissions persists for only a few decades, and the climatic influences of aerosols—which can either be heat-trapping such as black carbon (soot) or heat-reducing such as reflective sulfates[11]—persist for only days to weeks.[12] So while a sharp decline in the CO_2 emissions from the

combustion of coal in coming decades would reduce long-term warming, the associated reduction in the cooling effect from sulfur emissions caused mainly by coal combustion would lead to an increase of perhaps 0.5°C.

Temperatures today are already 0.8°C above preindustrial levels (figure FA.3). Were it not for the cooling influence of reflective particles (such as sul-

Figure FA.1   Global emissions of greenhouse gases have been increasing

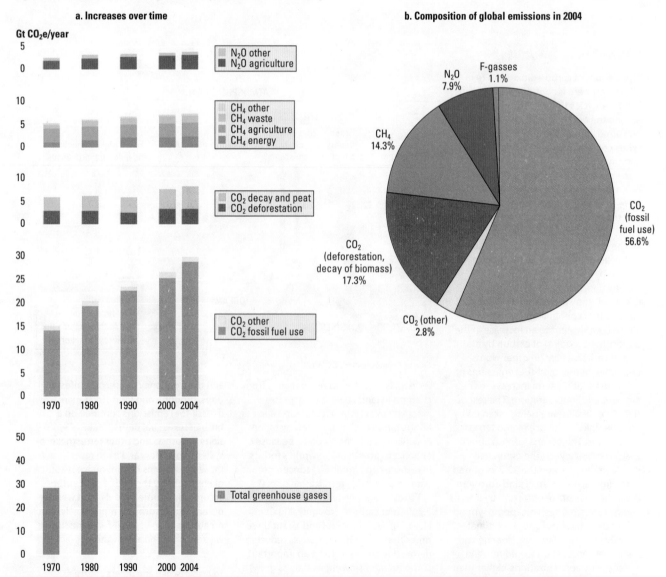

a. Increases over time

b. Composition of global emissions in 2004

Source: Reproduced from Barker and others 2007.

Note: This figure shows the sources and growth rates of some of the medium- to long-term greenhouse gases. Fossil fuels and land-use change have been the major sources of CO_2, while energy and agriculture contribute about equally to emissions of CH_4. N_2O comes mainly from agriculture. Additional greenhouse gases not included in the figure are black carbon (soot), tropospheric ozone, and halocarbons. The comparisons of the equivalent emissions of different gases are based on the use of the 100-year Global Warming Potential; see note 9 for explanation.

Figure FA.2 Major factors affecting the climate since the Industrial Revolution

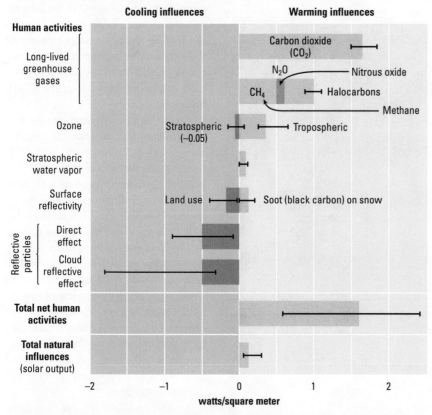

Source: Adapted from Karl, Melillo, and Peterson 2009.

Note: The figure above shows the amount of warming influence (orange bars) or cooling influence (blue bars) that different factors have had on Earth's climate since the beginning of the industrial age (from about 1750 to the present). Results are in watts per square meter. The top part of the box includes all the major human-induced factors, while the second part of the box includes the Sun, the only major natural factor with a long-term effect on climate. The cooling effect of individual volcanoes is also natural but is relatively short-lived (2 to 3 years), thus their influence is not included in this figure. The bottom part of the box shows that the total net effect (warming influences minus cooling influences) of human activities is a strong warming influence. The thin lines on each bar provide an estimate of the range of uncertainty.

Figure FA.3 Global annual average temperature and CO$_2$ concentration continue to climb, 1880–2007

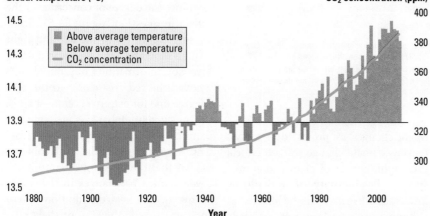

Source: Adapted from Karl, Melillo, and Peterson 2009.

Note: Orange bars indicate temperature above the 1901–2000 average, blue bars are below average temperatures. The green line shows the rising CO$_2$ concentration. While there is a clear long-term global warming trend, each individual year does not show a temperature increase relative to the previous year, and some years show greater changes than others. These year-to-year fluctuations in temperature are attributable to natural processes, such as the effects of El Niños, La Niñas, and volcanic eruptions.

fate aerosols) and the decades that it takes ocean temperatures to come into equilibrium with the increased trapping of infrared radiation, the global average temperature increase caused by human activities would likely already be about 1°C warmer than it is today. Thus the current elevated concentrations of greenhouse gases alone are near to committing the world to a 2°C warming, a level beyond which the world can expect to experience very disruptive, even "dangerous" consequences.[13]

Changes observed to date and the implications of our changing understanding of the science

The effects of changes in climate since the mid-19th century are particularly evident today in the observations of higher average air and ocean temperatures; the widespread melting of snow and ice around the world, particularly in the Arctic and Greenland (figure FA.4); and the increase in global sea level. Cold days, cold nights, and frosts have become less frequent, while the frequency and intensity of heat waves have increased. Both floods and droughts are occurring more frequently.[14] The interiors of continents have tended to dry out despite an overall increase in total precipitation. Globally, precipitation has increased, as the water cycle of the planet has been sped up by warmer temperatures, even while the Sahel and Mediterranean regions have seen more frequent and more intense droughts. Heavy rainfall and floods have become more common, and there is evidence that the intensities of storms and tropical cyclones have increased.[15]

These impacts are not distributed evenly across the globe (map FA.1). As expected, temperature changes are greater at the poles, with some regions of the Arctic warming 0.5°C in just the past 30 years.[16] At low latitudes—those close to the equator—a greater fraction of the trapped infrared energy goes into evaporation, limiting warming but providing

Figure FA.4   Greenland's melting ice sheet

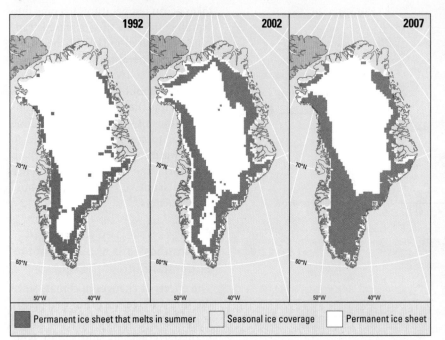

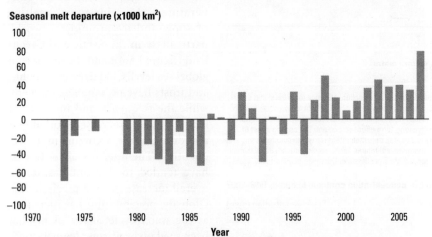

Sources: Top panel: Adapted from ACIA 2005 and Cooperative Institute for Environmental Sciences (CIRES), http://cires.colorado.edu/steffen/greenland/melt2005/ (accessed July, 2009). Bottom panel: Reproduced from Mote 2007.

Note: The orange areas on the maps of Greenland show the extent of summer ice melt, which has increased dramatically in recent years. Ten percent more ice was lost in 2007 than in 2005. The bar chart shows that despite annual variation in ice cover, significant loss has occurred for more than a decade.

an increase in water vapor that pours out as more intense rains from convective storms and tropical cyclones.

The resilience of many ecosystems is likely to be exceeded in the coming decades by a combination of the effects of climate change and other stresses, including habitat degradation, invasive species, and air and water pollution.

Major changes are projected in ecosystems as climate change shifts the ideal geographic ranges of plant and animal species. Productivity of agriculture, forests, and fisheries will be affected as will other ecological services.[17] Already 20,000 datasets show a wide range of species on the move, with changes averaging about six kilometers a decade toward the

poles or six meters a decade up mountains as an apparent result of the increase in temperatures.[18] These rapid changes are leading to asynchrony in many of the long-established predator-prey relationships, with some species arriving too early or too late to find their traditional food sources.

Over the past 20 years, our understanding of the science of climate change has greatly improved. In 1995, for example, the IPCC concluded: "The balance of evidence suggests a discernible human influence on global climate."[19] In 2001 the IPPC concluded: "There is new and stronger evidence that most of the warming observed over the last 50 years is attributable to human activities."[20] Six years later, in 2007, the IPCC concluded: "Warming of the climate system is unequivocal. Most of the observed increase in globally-averaged temperatures since the mid-20th century is very likely due to the observed increase in anthropogenic greenhouse gas concentrations."[21]

In 2001 and 2007 the scientific community summarized the best understanding of climate change impacts or reasons for concern in five categories: unique species/threatened ecosystems, extreme events, breadth of impacts, total economic impacts, and large-scale discontinuities. In the "burning ember" charts, the intensity of the red shading signifies the degree of concern over the effect in question (figure FA.5). Comparing column B in the left and right panels shows how the change in the best available information from 2001 to 2007 moved the red area closer to the zero degree line for extreme events—that is, at the current global average temperature, extreme events are already increasing. A comparison of the two E columns shows that the threat of discontinuous events, such as changes in the ocean conveyor-belt heat-distribution system or catastrophic thawing of the Arctic leading to massive releases of methane, becomes much larger if the world warms another 2°C over today's levels.

Map FA.1 Regional variation in global climate trends over the last 30 years

a. Temperature

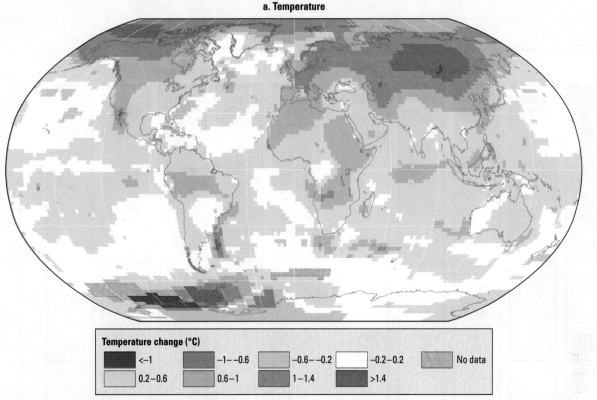

Temperature change (°C)

<–1	–1––0.6	–0.6––0.2	–0.2–0.2	No data
0.2–0.6	0.6–1	1–1.4	>1.4	

Source: Goddard Institute for Space Studies, http://data.giss.nasa.gov/cgi-bin/gistemp/do_nmap.py?year_last=2009&month_last=07&sat=4&sst=1&type=anoms&mean_gen=07&year1=1990&year2=2008&base1=1951&base2=1980&radius=1200&pol=reg (accessed July 2009).

Note: Yellow, orange, and red colors denote average increases in temperatures (°C) from 1980 to the present compared with the previous three decades. Warming has been greatest at high latitudes, especially in the Northern Hemisphere.

b. Precipitation

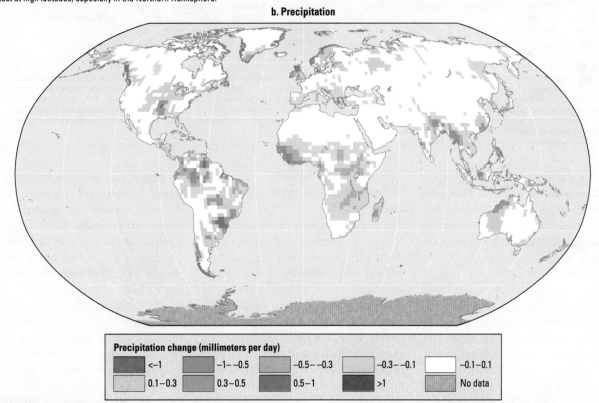

Precipitation change (millimeters per day)

<–1	–1––0.5	–0.5––0.3	–0.3––0.1	–0.1–0.1
0.1–0.3	0.3–0.5	0.5–1	>1	No data

Source: Goddard Institute for Space Studies, http://data.giss.nasa.gov/cgi-bin/precipcru/do_PRCmap.py?type=1&mean_gen=0112&year1=1980&year2=2000&base1=1951&base2=1980 (accessed May 2009).

Note: Yellow denotes increased precipitation in millimeters a day; blue denotes decreases from 1980 to present compared with the previous three decades. Drying has been greatest in continental interiors, while rainfall has become more intense in many coastal areas. The changing geographic distribution of rainfall has serious implications for agriculture.

Figure FA.5   Embers burning hotter: Assessment of risks and damages has increased from 2001 to 2007

2001 assessment

2007 assessment

Increase in global mean temperature above circa 1990 (°C)

A	B	C	D	E		A	B	C	D	E
Risks to many	Large increase	Negative for most regions	Net negative in all metrics	Higher		Risks to many	Large increase	Negative for most regions	Net negative in all metrics	High

Negative for some regions; positive for others — Positive or negative market impacts; majority of people adversely affected

Risks to some — Increase — Negative for some regions; positive for others — Positive or negative market impacts; majority of people adversely affected — Very low

Risks to some — Increase — Low

A — Risks to unique and threatened systems
B — Risk of extreme weather events
C — Distribution of impacts
D — Aggregate impacts
E — Risks of large scale discontinuities

Future

Past

Source: Reproduced from Smith and others 2009.

Notes: The figure shows risks from climate change, as described in 2001 (left) compared with updated data (right). Climate-change consequences are shown as bars and the increases in global mean temperature (°C) above today's levels (0 degrees to 5 degrees). Each column corresponds to a specific kind of impact. For example, "unique and threatened systems," such as alpine meadows or arctic ecosystems, are the most vulnerable (illustrated by the shading in column A) and only a small change in temperature may lead to great loss. The color scheme represents progressively increasing levels of risk from yellow to red. Between 1900 and 2000 global average temperature increased by ~0.6°C (and by nearly 0.2°C in the decade since) and has already led to some impacts. Since 2001 the assessed risk of damages has increased even for temperatures of an additional 1°C above today's levels, or about 2°C total above preindustrial levels.

Since the finalization of the IPCC's fourth assessment report in 2007, new information has further advanced scientific understanding. This information includes updated observations of recent changes in climate, better attribution of observed climate change to human and natural causal factors, improved understanding of carbon-cycle feedbacks, and new projections of future changes in extreme weather events and the potential for catastrophic change.[22] Many risks are now assessed to be greater than previously thought, particularly the risks of large sea-level rise in the current century and of increases in extreme weather events.

Future changes if the temperature increase exceeds 2°C

The physical impacts of future climate change on humans and the environment will include increasing stresses on and even collapses of ecosystems, biodiversity loss, changing timing of growing seasons, coastal erosion and aquifer salinization, permafrost thaw, ocean acidification,[23] and shifting ranges for pests and diseases. These impacts are shown for different temperatures and world regions in figure FA.6.

The physical effects of future climate change will have varying impacts on people and the environment at different temperature increases and in different regions (see figure FA.6). If temperatures reach 2°C above preindustrial levels, water availability will be reduced for another 0.4–1.7 billion people in midlatitudes and semiarid low latitudes. Those affected by severe water shortages will be mainly in Africa and Asia. At these higher temperatures, most coral reefs would die (box FA.2), and some crops, particularly cereals, could not be successfully grown in the altered climates prevailing in low-latitude regions. About a quarter of plant and animal species are likely to be at increased risk of extinction (see

Figure FA.6　Projected impacts of climate change by region

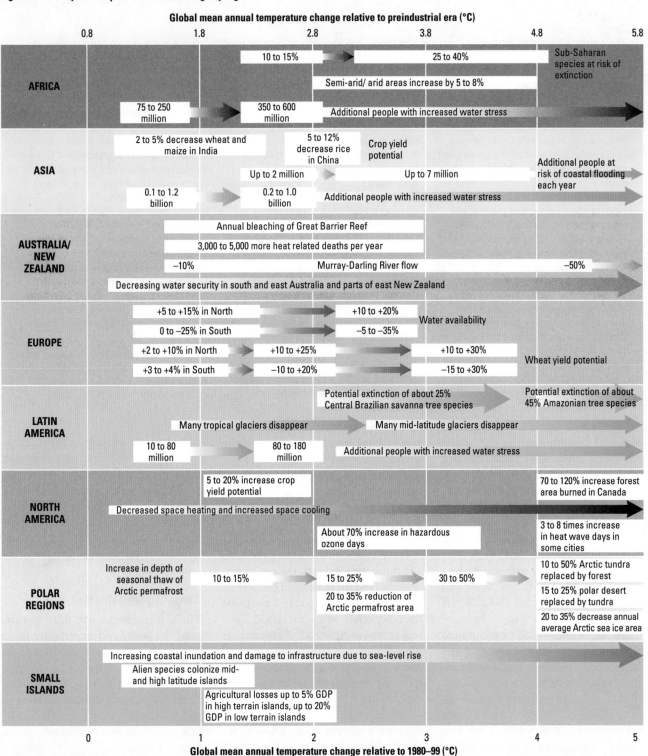

Global mean annual temperature change relative to preindustrial era (°C)

| | | 0.8 | | 1.8 | | 2.8 | | 3.8 | | 4.8 | | 5.8 |

AFRICA
- 10 to 15% → 25 to 40%
- Semi-arid/ arid areas increase by 5 to 8%
- 75 to 250 million → 350 to 600 million → Additional people with increased water stress
- Sub-Saharan species at risk of extinction

ASIA
- 2 to 5% decrease wheat and maize in India
- 5 to 12% decrease rice in China — Crop yield potential
- Up to 2 million → Up to 7 million
- Additional people at risk of coastal flooding each year
- 0.1 to 1.2 billion → 0.2 to 1.0 billion → Additional people with increased water stress

AUSTRALIA/ NEW ZEALAND
- Annual bleaching of Great Barrier Reef
- 3,000 to 5,000 more heat related deaths per year
- −10% — Murray-Darling River flow — −50%
- Decreasing water security in south and east Australia and parts of east New Zealand

EUROPE
- +5 to +15% in North → +10 to +20% — Water availability
- 0 to −25% in South → −5 to −35%
- +2 to +10% in North → +10 to +25% → +10 to +30%
- +3 to +4% in South → −10 to +20% → −15 to +30% — Wheat yield potential

LATIN AMERICA
- Potential extinction of about 25% Central Brazilian savanna tree species → Potential extinction of about 45% Amazonian tree species
- Many tropical glaciers disappear → Many mid-latitude glaciers disappear
- 10 to 80 million → 80 to 180 million → Additional people with increased water stress

NORTH AMERICA
- 5 to 20% increase crop yield potential
- Decreased space heating and increased space cooling
- About 70% increase in hazardous ozone days
- 70 to 120% increase forest area burned in Canada
- 3 to 8 times increase in heat wave days in some cities

POLAR REGIONS
- Increase in depth of seasonal thaw of Arctic permafrost
- 10 to 15% → 15 to 25% → 30 to 50%
- 20 to 35% reduction of Arctic permafrost area
- 10 to 50% Arctic tundra replaced by forest
- 15 to 25% polar desert replaced by tundra
- 20 to 35% decrease annual average Arctic sea ice area

SMALL ISLANDS
- Increasing coastal inundation and damage to infrastructure due to sea-level rise
- Alien species colonize mid- and high latitude islands
- Agricultural losses up to 5% GDP in high terrain islands, up to 20% GDP in low terrain islands

| | 0 | | 1 | | 2 | | 3 | | 4 | | 5 |

Global mean annual temperature change relative to 1980–99 (°C)

Source: Adapted from Parry and others 2007.

BOX FA.2 *Ocean health: Coral reefs and ocean acidification*

The oceans will become more acidic over the coming decades and centuries as a direct chemical consequence of the increasing atmospheric concentration of CO_2. Absorption of approximately one-third of manmade emissions of CO_2 over the past 200 years has decreased the pH of surface seawater by 0.1 units (pH, the degree of acidity or alkalinity, is measured on a logarithmic scale, and a 0.1 decrease in pH represents a 30 percent increase in ocean acidity). Projected pH decreases in ocean surface waters over the next 100 years range from 0.3 to 0.5 units, which would make the ocean more acidic than it has been in many tens of millions of years.[a] One of the most important implications of the changing acidity of the oceans is the problem that it may cause for the many marine photosynthetic organisms and animals, such as corals, bivalves, and some plankton species that make their shells and plates out of calcium carbonate. The process of "calcification" will be inhibited as the water becomes more acidic. Some of the most abundant life forms that will be affected are plankton, which form the base of the marine food chain and are a major food source for fish and marine mammals. From the evidence available, there is significant uncertainty about whether marine species and ecosystems will be able to acclimate or evolve in response to such rapid changes in ocean chemistry. At this stage, research into the impacts of high concentrations of CO_2 in the oceans is still in its infancy.

But for coral reefs, the adverse consequences are already becoming evident. Coral reefs are among the marine ecosystems most vulnerable to the changing climate and atmospheric composition and are threatened by a combination of direct human impacts and global climate change. Their loss would directly affect millions of people. Coral reefs, both tropical and deep cold water, are global centers of biodiversity. They provide goods and services of roughly $375 billion a year to nearly 500 million people. About 30 million of the world's poorest people directly rely on coral reef ecosystems for food.

Coral reefs are already being pushed to their thermal limits by recent temperature increases. Higher sea surface temperatures stress corals and cause coral bleaching (the loss or death of symbiotic algae), frequently resulting in large-scale mortality. An ecological "tipping point" is likely to be crossed in many areas if ocean temperatures increase to more than 2°C above their preindustrial levels, especially as ocean acidification reduces carbonate concentrations, inhibiting reef accretion. Once the corals die, macroalgae colonize the dead reefs and prevent regrowth of corals. Poor management can amplify these dynamics, because overfishing of herbivore reef fish leads to greater macroalgae abundance, and sediment and nutrient runoff from deforestation and poor agricultural practices promote macroalgae growth, exacerbating damage to corals.

Sources: Barange and Perry 2008; Doney 2006; Fabry and others 2008; Wilkinson 2008.
a. Monaco Declaration, http://ioc3.unesco.org/oanet/Symposium2008/Monaco Declaration.pdf (accessed May 2009).

---

focus B).[24] Communities will suffer more heat stress, and coastal areas will be more frequently flooded.[25]

What if temperatures rise to 5°C above preindustrial levels? About 3 billion additional people would suffer water stress, corals would have mostly died off, some 50 percent of species worldwide would eventually go extinct, productivity of crops in both temperate and tropical zones would fall, about 30 percent of coastal wetlands would be inundated, the world would be committed to several meters of sea-level rise, and there would be substantial burden on health systems from increasing malnutrition and diarrheal and cardiorespiratory diseases.[26] Terrestrial ecosystems are expected to shift from being carbon "sinks" (storage) to being a source of carbon; whether this carbon is released as carbon dioxide or methane it would still accelerate global warming.[27] Many

small island states and coastal plains would be flooded by storm surges and sea-level rise as the major ice sheets deteriorate and the traditional ways of life of Arctic peoples would be lost as the sea ice retreats.

Recent evidence indicates that loss of sea ice, the melting of the Greenland and Antarctic ice sheets, the rate of sea-level rise, and the thawing of the permafrost and mountain glaciers are faster than expected when the IPCC 2007 report was completed.[28] New analyses suggest that droughts in West Africa[29] and a drying of the Amazon rain forest[30] may be more probable than previously thought.[31]

While scientific uncertainty has often been cited as a reason to wait for more evidence before acting to control climate change, these recent surprises all illustrate that uncertainty can cut the other way as well and that out-

comes can be worse than expected. As the overview and chapter 1 highlight, the existence of uncertainties warrant a precautionary approach to climate change given the potential for irreversible impacts and the inertia in the climate system, in infrastructure and technology turnover, and in socioeconomic systems.

Crossing thresholds?

These impacts do not fully capture the probability and uncertainty of an increase in extreme events or define the thresholds of irreversible catastrophic events. Although climate change is often characterized as a gradual increase in global average temperature, this depiction is inadequate and misleading in at least two ways.

First, the historical and paleo-climatic records both suggest that the projected changes in the climate could well occur in jumps and shifts rather than gradually. As mentioned, the Greenland and West Antarctic ice sheets are particularly at risk from global warming, and there appear to be mechanisms that could lead to large and rapid changes in the amount of ice they store.[32] This is important because total loss of the ice now stored in both sheets would eventually raise the global sea level by about 12 meters. Some analyses indicate that this process would proceed slowly in a warming world, taking as much as several millennia or more. But recent studies indicate that because these ice sheets are largely below sea level and surrounded by warming water, their deterioration could happen much faster, conceivably in only a few centuries.[33] Sharply increased melting of either or both of these ice sheets, with accompanying changes in ocean circulation, is only one of several possibilities for tipping points in the climate system of a warming world, where changes could mean passing a point of no return—one where a system will shift to a different state, causing the potential for severe environmental and societal dislocations to go up accordingly.[34]

Second, no one lives in the global average temperature. Climate change impacts will differ sharply from region to region and often will interact with other environmental stresses. For example, evaporation and precipitation are both increasing and will continue to increase globally, but as the atmospheric circulation shifts, the changes will vary regionally, with some places become wetter and some drier. Among the likely additional consequences will be shifts in storm tracks, more intense tropical cyclones and extreme rainfall events, a higher snow line leading to less spring snowpack, further shrinkage of mountain glaciers,[35] reduced coverage of winter snowfall and sea ice, faster evaporation of soil moisture leading to more frequent and more intense droughts and fires, less extensive permafrost, and more frequent air pollution episodes. Shifts in the timing and patterns of the world's monsoons and ocean-atmosphere oscillations (as in the El Niño/Southern Oscillation and the North Atlantic Oscillation) are also likely. Map FA.2 and table FA.1 show some of the possible tipping points, their location, and the temperatures that might trigger change as well as the likely impacts.

Can we aim for 2°C warming and avoid 5°C or beyond?

Many studies conclude that stabilizing atmospheric concentrations of greenhouse gases at 450 ppm CO_2 or its equivalent will yield only a 40–50 percent chance of limiting the global average temperature increase to 2°C above preindustrial levels.[36] Many emission paths can get us there, but all require emissions to peak in the next decade and then to decline worldwide to half of today's levels by 2050, with further emissions reductions thereafter. However, for greater confidence that a particular temperature will not be exceeded, the emissions reductions must be even steeper. As indicated in figure FA.7c, the "best guess" of a 2°C path cannot exclude the possibility of hitting 4°C.

A more robust way of thinking about the problem is in terms of an emissions budget. Keeping warming caused by CO_2 alone to 2°C will require limiting cumulative CO_2 emissions to 1 trillion tons (Tt) of carbon (3.7 Tt CO_2).[37] The world has already emitted half that amount over the previous two-and-a-half centuries. For the 21st century, a business-as-usual path would release the remaining half trillion tons in 40 years, requiring future generations to live in a world in which essentially zero carbon was emitted.

The concept of a cumulative budget provides a framework for thinking about targets for the short and long term. For example, the higher emissions are in 2020, the lower they will need to be in 2050 to stay within the same overall budget. If carbon emissions are allowed to increase another 20–40 percent before reductions begin, the rate of decline would need to be between 4 percent (the orange path in figure FA.7a) and 8 percent (blue path) each year to keep to the carbon budget. For comparison, at Kyoto the wealthy countries agreed to reduce emissions on average by 5.2 percent from 1990 levels over the 2008–12 period, whereas total global emissions would need to decline by 4–8 percent each and every year in order to limit warming to about 2°C.

Warming caused by other greenhouse gases such as methane, black carbon, and nitrous oxide—which currently contribute about 25 percent of total warming—means that an even lower limit for CO_2 will be necessary to stay near 2°C warming from human activities. These other greenhouse gases could account for about 125 billion of the remaining 500 billion tons in our emissions budget, meaning that the carbon dioxide that can be emitted—measured in carbon—is really only about 375 billion tons total.[38] Short-term measures that reduce 2020 emissions of potent, but short-lived gases, such as methane and black carbon or tropospheric ozone, slow the rate of warming. Indeed, reducing black carbon by 50 percent or ozone by 70 percent,[39] or halting deforestation would each offset about a decade of fossil-fuel emissions and would help to limit warming in concert with reductions in CO_2 emissions. To really reduce the risk of excessive warming, moving to negative emissions may also be required. Accomplishing this—that is, having no new emissions and also removing CO_2 from the atmosphere—may be possible using biomass to supply energy, followed by sequestration of the carbon (see chapter 4).

Map FA.2   Potential tipping elements in the climate system: Global distribution

Source: Adapted from Lenton and others 2008.

Note: Several regional-scale features of the climate system have tipping points, meaning that a small climate perturbation at a critical point could trigger an abrupt or irreversible shift in the system. These could be triggered this century depending on the pace and magnitude of climate change.

Table FA.1   Potential tipping elements in the climate system: Triggers, time-scale, and impacts

Tipping element	Triggering level of warming	Transition timescale	Key impacts
Disappearance of Arctic summer sea-ice	+0.5–2°C	~10 years (rapid)	Amplified warming, ecosystem change
Melting of Greenland ice sheet	+1–2°C	>300 years (slow)	Sea-level rise of 2–7 meters
Melting of West Antarctic ice sheet	+3–5°C	>300 years (slow)	Sea-level rise of 5 meters
Collapse of Atlantic thermohaline circulation	+3–5°C	~100 years (gradual)	Regional cooling in Europe
Persistence of El Niño-Southern Oscillation (ENSO)	+3–6°C	~100 years (gradual)	Drought in Southeast Asia and elsewhere
Indian summer monsoon	N/A	~1 year (rapid)	Drought
Sahara/Sahel and West African Monsoon	+3–5°C	~10 years (rapid)	Increased carrying capacity
Drying and dieback of Amazon rainforest	+3–4°C	~50 years (gradual)	Biodiversity loss, decreased rainfall
Northward shift of boreal forest	+3–5°C	~50 years (gradual)	Biome switch
Warming of Antarctic bottom water	Unclear	~100 years (gradual)	Changed ocean circulation, reduced carbon storage
Melting of tundra	Ongoing	~100 years (gradual)	Amplified warming, biome switch
Melting of permafrost	Ongoing	<100 years (gradual)	Amplified warming from release of methane and carbon dioxide
Release of marine methane hydrates	Unclear	1,000 to 100,000 years	Amplified warming from release of methane

Source: Adapted from Lenton and others 2008.

Note: An expert elicitation of opinions about the probability of passing a tipping point in a subset of these systems—the melting of the West Antarctic ice sheet, melting of Greenland ice sheet, Amazon drying, and ocean circulation (Kriegler and others 2009)—estimated at least a 16 percent probability of one of these events for a warming of 2–4°C. The probability would rise to greater than 50 percent for a global mean temperature change above 4°C relative to year 2000 levels. In many cases, these numbers are considerably higher than the probability allocated to catastrophic events in current climate-damage assessments; for example, Stern (2007) assumed a 5–20 percent loss of the ice sheets with a 10 percent probability for a warming of 5°C.

Figure FA.7   Ways to limit warming to 2°C above preindustrial levels

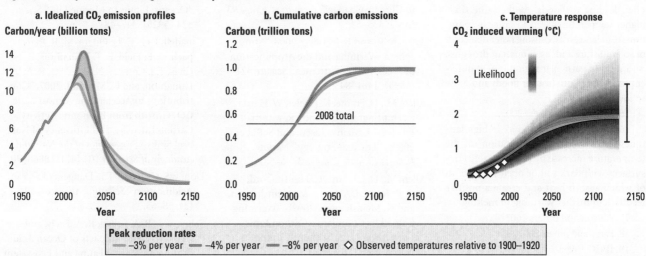

Source: Allen and others 2009a.

Note: Three idealized CO₂ emission paths (FA.7a) each consistent with total cumulative emissions (b) of 1 trillion tonnes of carbon. Each of the paths yields the same range of projected temperature increase (c) relative to uncertainty in the climate system's response (grey shading and red error bar), provided the cumulative total is unaffected. The blue, green, and red curves in FA.7a are all consistent with the 1 trillion tonne budget, but the higher and later the emissions peak, the faster the emissions have to decline to stay within the same cumulative emissions budget. Diamonds in FA.7c indicate observed temperatures relative to 1900–1920. While 2°C is the most likely outcome, temperature increases as high as 4° degrees above preindustrial levels cannot be ruled out.

Notes

1. IPCC 2007b. The Intergovernmental Panel on Climate Change (IPCC) was organized in 1988 as a joint effort of the World Meteorological Organization and the UN Environment Programme to summarize the state of scientific knowledge about climate change in a periodic series of major assessments. The first of these was completed in 1990, the second in 1995, the third in 2001, and the fourth in 2007.

2. Raupach and others 2007.

3. http://unfccc.int/essential_background/convention/background/items/1353.php (accessed August 30, 2009).

4. Smith and others 2009.

5. Parry and others 2007.

6. Temperature increases at the poles will be about double the global average.

7. Schneider von Deimling and others 2006.

8. The observed increases have averaged about 0.2°C per decade since 1990, which give us confidence in the future projections. See IPCC 2007a, table 3.1, which gives a range of 0.1–0.6°C a decade across all scenarios.

9. According to the latest estimates from the World Meteorological Organization, the average CO₂ concentration in 2008 was 387 parts per million (ppm). Methane and nitrous oxide concentrations have also increased, reaching new highs of 1,789 and 321 parts per billion (ppb), respectively. The carbon dioxide equivalent concentration (CO₂e) is a quantity that describes, for a given mixture and amount of greenhouse gases, the amount of CO₂ that would have the same potential to contribute to global warming measured over a specified period. For example, for the same mass of gas, the Global Warming Potential (GWP) for methane over a 100-year period is 25, and for nitrous oxide, 298. This means that emissions of 1 metric ton of methane and nitrous oxide, respectively, would cause the same warming influence as emissions of 25 and 298 metric tons of carbon dioxide. Fortunately, the mass of the emissions of these gases is not as great as for CO₂, so their effective warming influence is less. Note, however, that over different periods, the GWPs can vary; for example, the near-term (20-year) GWP for methane is 75, indicating that over short periods of time, methane emissions are very important and controlling them can slow the pace of climate change.

10. Halocarbon compounds are chemicals containing carbon atoms bonded to halogen atoms (fluorine, chlorine, bromine, or iodine). These compounds tend to be very persistent and nonreactive. Until they were banned to protect the ozone layer, many were commonly used as refrigerants and to form insulating materials. Because these compounds also lead to global warming, the banning of them under the Montreal Protocol and subsequent amendments has helped to limit global warming (in fact, even more so than the Kyoto Protocol). While the replacement compounds that have been introduced do contribute less to global warming and ozone depletion, greatly increased use of the replacements could exert a significant warming influence over time, and so emissions of such compounds should be reduced over coming decades.

11. Natural removal of the sulfate particles from the atmosphere over the few weeks following their formation is also the primary contributor to acidification of precipitation (acid rain), which reduces soil fertility, damages plants and buildings, and adversely affects human health.

12. Forster and others 2007.

13. Adger and others 2008; SEG 2007.

14. Millennium Ecosystem Assessment 2005. These seemingly contradictory changes are possible because, as temperature goes up, both evaporation and the capacity of the atmosphere to hold water vapor increase. With increased atmospheric water vapor,

convective rains become more intense, more often leading to floods. At the same time, higher temperatures lead to faster evaporation from land areas, causing faster depletion of soil moisture and faster onset of droughts. As a result a particular region can, at different times, face both heavier floods and more serious droughts.

15. Webster and others 2005.

16. Melting of snow and ice in high latitudes leads to "polar amplification" of the temperature increase by replacing reflective surfaces with dark soil or open water, both of which absorb heat and create a positive feedback of further warming or melting.

17. Allison and others 2005.

18. Parry and others 2007.

19. IPCC 1995.

20. IPCC 2001.

21. IPCC 2007a. "Very likely" is used by the IPCC to denote greater than 90 percent certainty.

22. Füssel 2008; Ramanathan and Feng 2008.

23. Brewer and Peltzer 2009; McNeil and Matear 2008; Silverman and others 2009.

24. Parry and others 2007.

25. Parry and others 2007, table TS3.

26. Battisti and Naylor 2009; Lobell and Field 2007.

27. Global Forest Expert Panel on Adaptation of Forests to Climate Change 2009.

28. US National Snow and Ice Data Center, http://nsidc.org (accessed August 2009); Füssel 2008; Rahmstorf 2007.

29. Shanahan and others 2009.

30. Phillips and others 2009.

31. Allan and Soden 2008.

32. Rignot and Kanagaratnam 2006; Steffensen and others 2008.

33. Füssel 2008.

34. Lenton and others 2008.

35. UNEP-WGMS 2008.

36. See also discussions in the overview and in chapter 4.

37. Allen and others 2009b.

38. Meinshausen and others 2009.

39. Wallack and Ramanathan 2009.

References

ACIA. 2005. *Arctic Climate Impact Assessment*. New York: Cambridge University Press.

Adger, W. N., S. Dessai, M. Goulden, M. Hulme, I. Lorenzoni, D. R. Nelson, L. O. Naess, J. Wolf, and A. Wreford. 2008. "Are There Social Limits to Adaptation to Climate Change?" *Climatic Change* 93 (3–4): 335–54.

Allan, R. P., and B. J. Soden. 2008. "Atmospheric Warming and the Amplification of Precipitation Extremes." *Science* 321 (5895): 1481–84.

Allen, M., D. Frame, K. Frieler, W. Hare, C. Huntingford, C. Jones, R. Knutti, J. Lowe, M. Meinshausen, and S. Raper. 2009a. "The Exit Strategy." *Nature Reports Climate Change* 3: 56–58.

Allen, M., D. J. Frame, C. Huntingford, C. D. Jones, J. A. Lowe, M. Meinshausen, and N. Meinshausen. 2009b. "Warming Caused by Cumulative Carbon Emissions towards the Trillionth Tonne." *Nature* 458: 1163–66.

Allison, E. H., W. N. Adger, M. Badjeck, K. Brown, D. Conway, N. K. Dulvy, A. S. Halls, A. Perry, and J. D. Reynolds. 2005. *Effects of Climate Change on the Sustainability of Capture and Enhancement Fisheries Important to the Poor: Analysis of the Vulnerability and Adaptability of Fisherfolk Living in Poverty*. London: UK. Department for International Development (DfID).

Barange, M., and R. I. Perry. 2008. "Physical and Ecological Impacts of Climate Change Relevant to Marine and Inland Capture Fisheries and Aquaculture." Paper presented at FAO conference on Climate Change and Fisheries and Aquaculture. Rome.

Barker, T., I. Bashmakov, L. Bernstein, J. E. Bogner, P. R. Bosch, R. Dave, O. R. Davidson, B. S. Fisher, S. Gupta, K. Halsnaes, B. Heij, S. Khan Ribeiro, S. Kobayashi, M. D. Levine, D. L. Martino, O. Masera, B. Metz, L. A. Meyer, G.-J. Nabuurs, A. Najam, N. Nakićenović, H.-H. Rogner, J. Roy, J. Sathaye, R. Schock, P. Shukla, R. E. H. Sims, P. Smith, D. A. Tirpak, D. Urge-Vorsatz, and D. Zhou. 2007. "Technical Summary." In B. Metz, O. R. Davidson, P. R. Bosch, R. Dave, and L. A. Meyer, ed., *Climate Change 2007: Mitigation. Contribution of Working Group III to the Fourth Assessment Report of the Intergovernmental Panel on Climate Change*. Cambridge, UK: Cambridge University Press.

Battisti, D. S., and R. L. Naylor. 2009. "Historical Warnings of Future Food Insecurity with Unprecedented Seasonal Heat." *Science* 323 (5911): 240–44.

Brewer, P. G., and E. T. Peltzer. 2009. "Oceans: Limits to Marine Life." *Science* 324 (5925): 347–48.

Canadell, J. G., C. Le Quere, M. R. Raupach, C. B. Field, E. T. Buitenhuis, P. Ciais, T. J. Conway, N. P. Gillett, R. A. Houghton, and G. Marland. 2007. "Contributions to Accelerating Atmospheric CO_2 Growth from Economic Activity, Carbon Intensity, and Efficiency of Natural Sinks." *Proceedings of the National Academy of Sciences* 104 (47): 18866–70.

Doney, S. C. 2006. "The Dangers of Ocean Acidification." *Scientific American* 294 (3): 58–65.

Fabry, V. J., B. A. Seibel, R. A. Feely, and J. C. Orr. 2008. "Impacts of Ocean Acidification on Marine Fauna and Ecosystem Processes." *ICES Journal of Marine Sciences* 65 (3): 414–32.

Fischlin, A., G. F. Midgley, J. T. Price, R. Leemans, B. Gopal, C. Turley, M. D. A. Rounsevell, O. P. Dube, J. Tarazona, and A. A. Velichko. 2007. "Ecosystems, Their Properties, Goods and Services." In *Climate Change 2007: Impacts, Adaptation and Vulnerability. Contribution of Working Group II to the Fourth Assessment Report of the Intergovernmental Panel on Climate Change*, ed. M. Parry, O. F. Canziani, J. P. Palutikof, P. J. van der Linden, and C. E. Hanson. Cambridge, UK: Cambridge University Press.

Forster, P., V. Ramaswamy, P. Artaxo, T. Bernsten, R. Betts, D. W. Fahey, J. Haywood, J. Lean, D. C. Lowe, G. Myhre, J. Nganga, R. Prinn, G. Raga, M. Schulz, and R. Van Dorland. 2007. "Changes in Atmospheric Constituents and in Radiative Forcing." In *Climate Change 2007: The Physical Science Basis. Contribution of Working Group I to the Fourth Assessment Report of the Intergovernmental Panel on Climate Change*, ed. S. Solomon, D. Qin, M. Manning, Z. Chen, M. Marquis, K. B. Averyt, M. Tignor, and H. L. Miller. Cambridge, UK: Cambridge University Press.

Füssel, H. M. 2008. "The Risks of Climate Change: A Synthesis of New Scientific Knowledge Since the Finalization of the IPCC Fourth Assessment Report." Background note for the WDR 2010.

Global Forest Expert Panel on Adaptation of Forests to Climate Change. 2009. *Adaptation of Forests and People* to Climate Change: A Global Assessment Report. Vienna: International Union of Forest Research Organizations.

Houghton, R. A. 2003. "The Contemporary Carbon Cycle." In *Treatise on Geochemistry*, vol 8, *Biogeochemistry*, ed. W. H. Schlesinger. New York: Elsevier.

IPCC (Intergovernmental Panel on Climate Change). 1995. *Climate Change 1995: Synthesis Report. Contribution of Working Groups I, II, and III to the Second Assessment Report of the Intergovernmental Panel on Climate Change.* Geneva: IPCC.

———. 2000. *IPCC Special Report: Methodological and Technological Issues in Technology Transfer—Summary for Policymakers.* Cambridge, UK: Cambridge University Press.

———. 2001. *Climate Change 2001: Synthesis Report. Contribution of Working Groups I, II and III to the Third Assessment Report of the Intergovernmental Panel on Climate Change.* Cambridge, UK: Cambridge University Press.

———. 2007a. *Climate Change 2007: Synthesis Report. Contribution of Working Groups I, II and II to the Fourth Assessment Report of the Intergovernmental Panel on Climate Change.* Geneva: IPCC.

———. 2007b. "Summary for Policymakers." In *Climate Change 2007: The Physical Science Basis. Contribution of Working Group I to the Fourth Assessment Report of the Intergovernmental Panel on Climate Change,* ed. S. Solomom, D. Qin, M. Manning, Z. Chen, M. Marquis, K. B. Averyt, M. Tignor, and H. L. Miller. Cambridge, UK: Cambridge University Press.

Karl, T. R., J. M. Melillo, and T. C. Peterson. 2009. *Global Climate Change Impacts in the United States.* Washington, DC: U.S. Climate Change Science Program and the Subcommittee on Global Change Research.

Kriegler, E., J. W. Hall, H. Held, R. Dawson, and H. J. Schellnhuber. 2009. "Imprecise Probability Assessment of Tipping Points in the Climate System." *Proceedings of the National Academy of Sciences* 106 (13): 5041–46.

Lenton, T. M., H. Held, E. Kriegler, J. W. Hall, W. Lucht, S. Rahmstorf, and H. J. Schellnhuber. 2008. "Tipping Elements

in the Earth's Climate System." *Proceedings of the National Academy of Sciences* 105 (6): 1786–93.

Lobell, D. B., and C. B. Field. 2007. "Global Scale Climate-Crop Yield Relationships and the Impacts of Recent Warming." *Environmental Research Letters* 2: 1–7.

McNeil, B. I., and R. J. Matear. 2008. "Southern Ocean Acidification: A Tipping Point at 450-ppm Atmospheric CO_2." *Proceedings of the National Academy of Sciences* 105 (48): 18860–64.

Meinshausen, M., N. Meinshausen, W. Hare, S. C. B. Raper, K. Frieler, R. Knutti, D. J. Frame, and M. R. Allen. 2009. "Greenhouse-Gas Emission Targets for Limiting Global Warming to 2°C." *Nature* 458 (7242): 1158–62.

Millennium Ecosystem Assessment. 2005. *Ecosystems and Human Well-Being: Synthesis Report.* Washington, DC: World Resources Institute.

Mote, T. L. 2007. "Greenland Surface Melt Trends 1973–2007: Evidence of a Large Increase in 2007." *Geophysical Research Letters* 34 (22): L22507–doi:10.1029/2007GL031976.

Parry, M., O. F. Canziani, J. P. Palutikof, and Co-authors. 2007. "Technical Summary." In *Climate Change 2007: Impacts, Adaptation and Vulnerability. Contribution of Working Group II to the Fourth Assessment Report of the Intergovernmental Panel on Climate Change,* ed. M. Parry, O. F. Canziani, J. P. Palutikof, P. J. van der Linden, and C. E. Hanson. Cambridge, UK: Cambridge University Press.

Phillips, O. L., L. E. O. C. Aragao, S. L. Lewis, J. B. Fisher, J. Lloyd, G. Lopez-Gonzalez, Y. Malhi, A. Monteagudo, J. Peacock, C. A. Quesada, G. van der Heijden, S. Almeida, I. Amaral, L. Arroyo, G. Aymard, T. R. Baker, O. Banki, L. Blanc, D. Bonal, P. Brando, J. Chave, A. C. A. de Oliveira, N. D. Cardozo, C. I. Czimczik, T. R. Feldpausch, M. A. Freitas, E. Gloor, N. Higuchi, E. Jimenez, G. Lloyd, P. Meir, C. Mendoza, A. Morel, D. A. Neill, D. Nepstad, S. Patino, M. C. Penuela, A. Prieto, F. Ramirez, M. Schwarz, J. Silva, M. Silveira, A. S. Thomas, H. Steege, J. Stropp, R. Vasquez, P. Zelazowski, E. A. Davila, S. Andelman, A. Andrade, K. J. Chao, T. Erwin, A. Di Fiore, H. Euridice, H. Keeling, T. J. Killeen, W. F. Laurance, A. P.

Cruz, N. C. A. Pitman, P. N. Vargas, H. Ramirez-Angulo, A. Rudas, R. Salamao, N. Silva, J. Terborgh, and A. Torres-Lezama. 2009. "Drought Sensitivity of the Amazon Rainforest." *Science* 323 (5919): 1344–47.

Prentice, I. C., G. D. Farquhar, M. J. R. Fasham, M. L. Goulden, M. Heimann, V. J. Jaramillo, H. S. Kheshgi, C. Le Quere, R. J. Scholes, and D. W. R. Wallace. 2001. "The Carbon Cycle and Atmospheric Carbon Dioxide." In *Climate Change 2001: The Scientific Basis. Contribution of Working Group I to the Third Assessment Report of the Intergovernmental Panel on Climate Change,* ed. J. T. Houghton, Y. Ding, D. J. Griggs, M. Noguer, P. J. van der Linden, X. Dai, K. Maskell, and C. A. Johnson. Cambridge, UK: Cambridge University Press.

Rahmstorf, S. 2007. "A Semi-Empirical Approach to Projecting Future Sea-level Rise." *Science* 315: 368–70.

Ramanathan, V., and Y. Feng. 2008. "On Avoiding Dangerous Anthropogenic Interference with the Climate System: Formidable Challenges Ahead." *Proceedings of the National Academy of Sciences* 105 (38): 14245–50.

Raupach, M. R., G. Marland, P. Ciais, C. Le Quere, J. G. Canadell, G. Klepper, and C. B. Field. 2007. "Global and Regional Drivers of Accelerating CO_2 Emissions." *Proceedings of the National Academy of Sciences* 104 (24): 10288–93.

Rignot, E., and P. Kanagaratnam. 2006. "Changes in the Velocity Structure of the Greenland Ice Sheet." *Science* 311 (5763): 986–90.

Sabine, C. L., M. Heiman, P. Artaxo, D. C. E. Bakker, C.-T. A. Chen, C. B. Field, N. Gruber, C. Le Quere, R. G. Prinn, J. E. Richey, P. Romero-Lankao, J. A. Sathaye, and R. Valentini. 2004. "Current Status and Past Trends of the Carbon Cycle." In *The Global Carbon Cycle: Integrating Humans, Climate, and the Natural World,* ed. C. B. Field and M. R. Raupach. Washington, DC: Island Press.

Schneider von Deimling, T., H. Held, A. Ganopolski, and S. Rahmstorf. 2006. "How Cold Was the Last Glacial Maximum?" *Geophysical Research Letters* 33: L14709, doi:10.1029/2006GL026484.

SEG (Scientific Expert Group on Climate Change). 2007. *Confronting Climate*

Change: Avoiding the Unmanageable and Managing the Unavoidable. Washington, DC: Sigma Xi and the United Nations Foundation.

Shanahan, T. M., J. T. Overpeck, K. J. Anchukaitis, J. W. Beck, J. E. Cole, D. L. Dettman, J. A. Peck, C. A. Scholz, and J. W. King. 2009. "Atlantic Forcing of Persistent Drought in West Africa." *Science* 324 (5925): 377–80.

Silverman, J., B. Lazar, L. Cao, K. Caldiera, and J. Erez. 2009. "Coral Reefs May Start Dissolving When Atmospheric CO_2 Doubles." *Geophysical Research Letters* 36 (5): L05606–doi:10.1029/2008GL036282.

Smith, J. B., S. H. Schneider, M. Oppenheimer, G. W. Yohe, W. Hare, M. D. Mastrandrea, A. Patwardhan, I. Burton, J. Corfee-Morlot, C. H. D. Magadza, H.-M. Füssel, A. B. Pittock, A. Rahman, A. Suarez, and J.-P. van Ypersele. 2009.

"Assessing Dangerous Climate Change through an Update of the Intergovernmental Panel on Climate Change (IPCC) 'Reasons for concern'." *Proceedings of the National Academy of Sciences* 106 (11): 4133–37.

Steffensen, J. P., K. K. Andersen, M. Bigler, H. B. Clausen, D. Dahl-Jensen, H. Fischer, K. Goto-Azuma, M. Hansson, S. J. Johnsen, J. Jouzel, V. Masson-Delmotte, T. Popp, S. O. Rasmussen, R. Rothlisberger, U. Ruth, B. Stauffer, M. L. Siggaard-Andersen, A. E. Sveinbjornsdottir, A. Svensson, and J. W. C. White. 2008. "High-Resolution Greenland Ice Core Data Show Abrupt Climate Change Happens in Few Years." *Science* 321 (5889): 680–84.

Stern, N. 2007. *The Economics of Climate Change: The Stern Review.* Cambridge, UK: Cambridge University Press.

UNEP-WGMS (United Nations Environment Programme–World Glacier Monitoring Service). 2008. *Global Glacier Changes: Facts and Figures.* Chatelaine, Switzerland: DEWA/GRID-Europe.

Wallack, J. S., and V. Ramanathan. 2009. "The Other Climate Changers." *Foreign Affairs* 5 (88): 105–13.

Webster, P. J., G. J. Holland, J. A. Curry, and H. R. Chang. 2005. "Changes in Tropical Cyclone Number, Duration, and Intensity in a Warming Environment." *Science* 309 (5742): 1844–46.

Wilkinson, C., ed. 2008. *Status of Coral Reefs of the World 2008.* Townsville: Australian Institute of Marine Science.

PART 1

Reducing Human Vulnerability: Helping People Help Themselves

Families in Bangladesh are deciding whether to rebuild their homes and livelihoods after yet another flood—once occasional, now every few years—or to take their chances in Dhaka, the crowded capital. In the tall forests of southern Australia, families are deciding whether to rebuild their homes after the most damaging fires in history—aware that they are still in the grip of the longest and most severe drought on record. With losses from extreme climate events inevitable, societies have explicitly or implicitly chosen the risk they bear and the coping strategies to deal with them. Some losses are so high and the coping so insufficient that development is impeded. As the climate changes, more and more people risk falling into what is called the "adaptation deficit."

Reducing vulnerability and increasing resilience to the climate has traditionally been the responsibility of households and communities[1] through their livelihood choices, asset allocations, and locational preferences. Experience shows that local decision making, diversity, and social learning are key features of flexible, resilient communities[2] and that vulnerable communities can be effective agents of innovation and adaptation.[3] But climate change threatens to overwhelm local efforts, requiring more from national and global supporting structures.

People's vulnerability is not static, and the effects of climate change will amplify many forms of human vulnerability. Crowded cities expand into hazardous zones. Natural systems are transformed through modern agriculture. Infrastructure development—dams and roads—create new opportunities but can also create new risks for people. Climate change, superimposed on these processes, brings additional stress for natural, human, and social systems. People's livelihoods need to function under conditions that will almost certainly change but cannot be predicted with certainty.

Whichever mitigation pathway is followed, the temperature and other climate changes over the next decades will be very similar. Temperatures are already about 1°C above those of the preindustrial era, and all realistic mitigation scenarios suggest that we may expect another 1°C by midcentury. The world of 2050 and beyond, however, will be much different from today's—just how different depends on mitigation. Consider two possibilities for this generation's children and grandchildren. In the first scenario the world is on track to limiting

Key messages

Further climate change is unavoidable. It will stress people physically and economically, particularly in poor countries. Adapting requires robust decision making—planning over a long time horizon and considering a broad range of climate and socioeconomic scenarios. Countries can reduce physical and financial risks associated with variable and extreme weather. They can also protect the most vulnerable. Some established practices will have to be expanded—such as insurance and social protection—and others will have to be done differently—such as urban and infrastructure planning. These adaptation actions would have benefits even without climate change. Promising initiatives are emerging, but applying them on the necessary scale will require money, effort, ingenuity, and information.

temperature increases to 2–2.5°C above preindustrial levels. In the second the emissions are much higher, leading eventually to temperatures about 5°C or more above preindustrial levels.[4]

Even on the lower temperature trajectory many ecosystems will come under increasing stress, patterns of pests and disease will continue to change, and agriculture will require significant changes in practice or displacement in location. On the higher temperature trajectory most of the negative trends will be even worse, and the few positive trends, such as increases in agricultural productivity in cooler cropping regions, will be reversed. Agriculture will undergo transformational change in practices and locations. Storm intensity will be higher. And sea levels are likely to rise by about one meter.[5] Floods, droughts, and extreme temperatures will be much more common.[6] The past decade has been the hottest on record, but by 2070 even the coolest years are likely to be hotter than now. As the physical and biological stresses arising from climate change increase, so will social tension.

On the higher trajectory, warming could trigger feedbacks in Earth systems that would make it difficult to further constrain temperature increases, regardless of mitigation. These feedbacks could rapidly collapse ecosystems, as some are predicting for the Amazon and the boreal peat lands (see focus A). People in that higher-track world would see rapidly accelerating losses and costs reverberate through their societies and economies—requiring adaptation at a scale unprecedented in human history. International tensions could be expected to rise over resources, and migration away from the areas most affected would increase.[7]

On the lower track, adaptation will be challenging and costly, and business-as-usual development will be far from sufficient. Broader and accelerated implementation of policies that have proved successful is paramount as is adaptation that harnesses the ingenuity of people, institutions, and markets. On the higher track the question is whether warming may be approaching, or already exceeding, levels to which we can adapt.[8] Some argue

convincingly that ethics, culture, knowledge, and attitudes toward risk limit human adaptation more than physical, biological, or economic thresholds.[9] The adaptation effort that will be required by future generations is thus determined by how effectively climate change is mitigated.

Incremental environmental impacts imply stronger physical constraints on future development. Climate-smart policies will have to address the challenges of a riskier and more complex environment. Development practice has to be more adaptive to shifting baselines, grounded in strategies robust to imperfect knowledge.[10] Cropping strategies need to be robust under more volatile weather conditions by seeking to maintain long-term consistency in output rather than to maximize production. Urban planners in coastal cities need to anticipate demographic developments and new risks from rising seas or flooding. Public health workers need to prepare for surprising changes in climate-linked disease patterns.[11] Information is crucial to support risk-based planning and strategies—it is the basis of good policy and better risk management.

Managing ecosystems and their services will be more important and more difficult. Well-managed landscapes can modulate flood waters. Intact coastal wetlands can buffer against storm damage. But management of natural resources will face a rapidly changing climate with more extreme events and with ecosystems under increasing threats from stresses other than climate (such as land-use and demographic change).[12] Managing such physical risks is an integral part of climate-smart development—an essential step to avoid avoidable impacts on people.

However, not all physical impacts are avoidable, particularly those linked to extreme and catastrophic events whose probability is difficult to assess under climate change. Eliminating the risk of the most extreme events is not possible, and attempting to do so would be extremely costly given the uncertainty about the location and timing of impacts. Being financially prepared to cope with climate impacts is critical for both households and government. This requires flexible risk-spreading mechanisms.

As chapter 1 discusses, the poor have the least capacity to manage physical and financial risk and to make longer-term adaptation decisions. Their lives are affected more by climate, whether they practice subsistence farming or are landless squatters in a floodplain at the urban fringe. Other social groups share many of the vulnerabilities of the poor stemming from their lack of entitlements, productive assets, and voice.[13] Social policy, a critical complement to physical and financial risk management, provides many tools to help manage the risk affecting the most vulnerable and to empower communities to become agents in climate-change management.

This chapter focuses on measures that will assist people in handling today's variable climate and the climate changes that occur over the next few decades. It first describes a policy framework based on strategies that are robust to climate uncertainty and management practices that are adaptive in the face of dynamic conditions. It then looks at managing physical risks, financial risks, and social risks.

Adaptive management: Living with change

Climate change adds an additional source of unknowns for decision makers to manage. Real-world decision makers make decisions under uncertainty every day, even in the absence of climate change. Manufacturers invest in flexible production facilities that can be profitable across a range of production volumes to compensate for unpredictable demand. Military commanders insist on overwhelming numerical superiority. Financial investors protect themselves against fluctuations in markets by diversifying. All these forms of hedging are likely to lead to suboptimal results for any fixed expectation about the future, but they are robust in the face of uncertainty.[14]

A compounding set of uncertainties—about demographics, technology, markets, and climate—requires policies and investment decisions to be based on imperfect and incomplete knowledge. Local and national decision makers face even greater

uncertainties because projections tend to lose precision at finer scales—an inherent problem of downscaling from coarse, aggregate models. If decision parameters cannot be observed and measured,[15] robust strategies (see chapter 1) that directly address the reality of a world of shifting baselines and intermittent disturbances[16] are the appropriate framework in a context of unknown probabilities.

Accepting uncertainty as inherent to the climate change problem and robustness as a decision criterion implies changing decision-making strategies for long-lived investment and long-term planning. It demands rethinking traditional approaches that assume a deterministic model of the world in which the future is predictable.

First, priority should be given to no-regrets options: investment and policy options that provide benefits even without climate change. Such options exist in almost every domain—in water and land management (see chapter 3), in sanitation to reduce water-borne diseases (controlling sewer leakage), in disaster risk reduction (avoiding high-risk zones), in social protection (providing assistance to the poor). But such options often are not implemented, partly because of a lack of information and transaction costs but also because of cognitive and political failures (see chapter 8).[17]

Second, buying "safety margins" in new investments can increase climate resilience, often at low cost. For instance, the marginal cost of building a higher dam or including additional groups in a social protection scheme can be small.[18] Safety margins account not only for possible impacts of climate change (more severe events) but also for the uncertainty in socioeconomic development (changes in demand).

Third, reversible and flexible options need to be favored, accepting that decisions can be wrong and thus keeping the cost of reversing them as low as possible. Restrictive urban planning because of uncertain flooding outcomes can be reversed more easily and cheaply than future retreat or protection options. Insurance provides flexible ways of managing risk and protecting necessary investment when the direction and magnitude of change are uncertain.[19]

Farmers transitioning to drought-tolerant varieties (rather than investing in irrigation) can use insurance to protect their seasonal investment in new seeds from an exceptionally severe drought. For storm-prone areas a combination of early warning systems, evacuation plans, and (possibly expensive) property insurance can provide more flexibility to save lives and replace homes than can protecting entire coastal areas with infrastructure or depopulating them unnecessarily.[20]

Fourth, institutionalizing long-term planning requires forward-looking scenario analysis and an assessment of strategies under a wide range of possible futures. This leads to periodic reviews of investment (and, if necessary, revisions), and it improves policies and practices by iterative learning from outcomes. Widening the spatial scope of planning is equally critical to be prepared for changes that may propagate over longer distances, such as the melting of glaciers that change the water supply of urban zones hundreds of kilometers downstream, widespread droughts that affect regional grain markets, or accelerated rural-urban migration caused by environmental degradation. But the required structural changes can be difficult because of the inertia in prevailing management practices.[21]

Implementing such strategies through adaptive management entails continuous information development, flexible and robust planning and design, participatory implementation, and monitoring and evaluation of feedback. It realigns decisions and management with the scale of ecological and social contexts and processes, such as watersheds and ecoregions, and can be driven by local or community management systems.[22] It stresses management informed by scientific and local knowledge, as well as policy experiments that develop understanding, set learning as an objective, and improve the ability to make decisions under uncertainty (box 2.1).[23]

Involving stakeholders in planning increases ownership and the likelihood that actions will be sustained.[24] Boston and London both have climate-change strategies. In Boston the process was research-led, with inconsistent stakeholder engagement. The completed study, seen as overly technical, has had little impact. London used a bottom-up approach, engaging many stakeholders. And after the London Warming Report was released, the Climate Change Partnership evolved from the stakeholder organization to continue adaptation planning.[25]

A risk-based decision-making model favoring robustness and longer-term planning, and appropriate local, community, and national governance structures is essential for adaptation to climate change.[26] Increasing pressure on scarce resources (land, water), combined with major socio-demographic transformations (population growth, urbanization, globalization) and a shifting climate, provide much less room to leave risks unmanaged. A storm hitting a modern, rapidly growing coastal city has the potential to cause a lot more damage than in the past when the coast was less populated and built up. In the face of the uncertainty arising from climate change, robust strategies and adaptive management provide the appropriate framework to better manage physical, financial, and social risks.

Managing physical risks: Avoiding the avoidable

Natural systems, when well managed, can reduce human vulnerability to climate risks

---

BOX 2.1 *Characteristics of adaptive management*

Adaptive management is an approach to guide intervention in the face of uncertainty. The principal idea is that management actions are informed by explicit learning from policy experiments and the use of new scientific information and technical knowledge to improve understanding, inform future decisions, monitor the outcome of interventions, and develop new practices. This framework establishes mechanisms to evaluate alternative scenarios and structural and nonstructural measures, understand and challenge assumptions, and explicitly consider uncertainties. Adaptive management has a long time horizon for planning and capacity building, and is aligned with ecological processes at appropriate spatial scale. It creates an enabling framework for cooperation between administrative levels, sectors, and line departments; broad stakeholder participation (including research centers and non-government organizations) in problem solving and decisionmaking; and adaptable legislation to support local action and respond to new information.

Sources: Adapted from Raadgever and others 2008; Olsson, Folke, and Berkes 2004.

and deliver developmental co-benefits, reduce poverty, conserve biodiversity, and sequester carbon. Ecosystem-based adaptation—maintaining or restoring natural ecosystems to reduce human vulnerability—is a cost-effective approach to reducing climate risks and one that offers multiple benefits (see focus B). For example, forested catchments buffer water flows from moderate rains far better than nonforested catchments, but heavier rains quickly saturate the sponge, so most water moves quickly over the land.[27] Well-vegetated wetlands downstream may be needed to further buffer water flows while natural drainage systems carry it away. But wetlands converted to agriculture or urban settlements and simplified drainage systems inevitably fail, leading to flooding. A comprehensive response to flood management includes maintaining catchment cover, managing wetlands and river channels, and siting infrastructure and planning urban expansion appropriately. Similarly, coastal mangrove forests protect against storm surges partly by absorbing the flows and partly by keeping human settlements behind the mangroves farther from the sea.

Build climate-smart cities

Half the world's people now live in cities, a share that will rise to 70 percent by 2050.[28] Of urban population growth (5 million new residents a month), 95 percent will be in the developing world, with small cities growing fastest.[29] Urban areas concentrate people and economic assets, often in hazard-prone areas as cities have historically prospered in coastal areas and at the confluence of rivers. In fact, low-elevation coastal zones at risk from rising sea levels and coastal surges are home to about 600 million people globally and 15 of the world's 20 megacities (map 2.1).[30]

Map 2.1 At risk: Population and megacities concentrate in low-elevation coastal zones threatened by sea level rise and storm surges

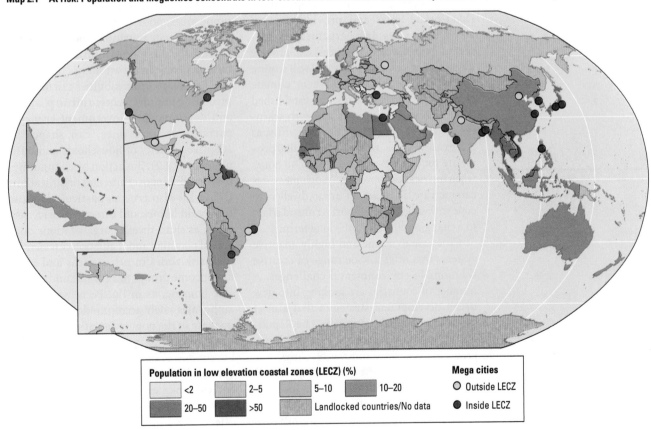

Population in low elevation coastal zones (LECZ) (%)

<2 · 2–5 · 5–10 · 10–20 · 20–50 · >50 · Landlocked countries/No data

Mega cities
○ Outside LECZ
● Inside LECZ

Source: United Nations 2008a.
Note: Megacities in 2007 included Beijing, Bombay, Buenos Aires, Cairo, Calcutta, Dhaka, Istanbul, Karachi, Los Angeles, Manila, Mexico City, Moscow, New Delhi, New York, Osaka, Rio de Janeiro, São Paulo, Seoul, Shanghai, and Tokyo. Megacities are defined as urban areas with more than 10 million inhabitants.

Climate change is only one of many factors that determine urban vulnerability. For many coastal cities, migration increases the population exposed to rising sea levels, storm surges, and floods,[31] as in Shanghai, where the net annual influx of people exceeds the natural growth rate by a factor of four.[32] And many cities in river deltas are sinking as a result of groundwater extraction and declining sediment deposits caused by dams upstream. While subsiding land has been an issue for some time in many coastal cities (New Orleans, Shanghai), it is an emerging threat for Hanoi, Jakarta, and Manila.[33] Urban development farther inland increases the water demand upstream, and many rivers, including the Nile, no longer reach their delta.

Urbanization, done well, can increase resilience to climate-related risks. Higher population densities lower the per capita costs of providing piped treated water, sewer systems, waste collection, and most other infrastructure and public amenities. Sound urban planning restricts development in flood-prone areas and provides critical access to services. Infrastructure developments (embankments or levees) can provide physical protection for many and will require additional safety margins where climate change increases risk. And well-established communication, transport, and early warning systems help evacuate people swiftly, as is the case in Cuba, where up to 800,000 people are routinely evacuated within 48 hours when hurricanes approach.[34] Such measures can increase the ability of urban dwellers to cope with shocks in the short term and adapt to a changing climate in the long term.[35]

Cities are dynamic and highly adaptive systems that offer a wide range of creative solutions to environmental challenges. A number of countries are looking into new urban development strategies that aim at spreading regional prosperity. The Republic of Korea has embarked on an ambitious program to develop "Innovation Cities" as a way to decentralize the country's economic activities.[36] Many of these efforts focus on technological innovation and offer new opportunities to redesign future cities to deal with the climate-change challenges.

Attempts to influence the spatial patterns of urban areas through public policy interventions show mixed results, however. The Arab Republic of Egypt's attempt to create satellite cities to decongest Cairo never attracted the projected population and did little to stop population growth in Cairo, partly because of the lack of policies to promote regional integration.[37] Successful policies facilitate concentration and migration during the early stages of urbanization and interurban connectivity during the later stages. Public investments in infrastructure are most effective when they increase social equity (through broader access to services) and integrate the urban space (through the transport system).[38]

Urbanization seldom is harmonious, generating pollution and pockets of wrenching poverty and social dislocation. Today, urban areas in developing countries are home to 746 million people living below the poverty line (a quarter of the world's poor),[39] and the urban poor suffer from more than low income and consumption. Overcrowding, insecure tenure, illegal settlements sited in landslide- and flood-prone areas, poor sanitation, unsafe housing, inadequate nutrition, and poor health exacerbate the vulnerabilities of the 810 million people in urban slums.[40]

These many vulnerabilities call for comprehensive improvements in urban planning and development. Government agencies, particularly local ones, can shape the adaptive capacity of households and businesses (box 2.2). But action by community-based and nongovernmental organizations (NGOs) is also crucial, particularly those that build homes and directly provide services, as slum-dweller organizations do.[41] Sound planning and regulation can identify high-risk zones in urban areas and allow low-income groups to find safe and affordable housing, as in Ilo, Peru, where local authorities safely accommodated a fivefold increase in the population after 1960.[42] But hard investments in infrastructure may also be required to protect urban zones, such as coastal cities in North Africa, with seawalls and embankments (box 2.3).

A major risk for urban areas is flooding—often caused by buildings, infrastructure, and paved areas that prevent infiltration, exacerbated by overwhelmed drainage systems. In well-managed cities flooding is

---

BOX 2.2   *Planning for greener and safer cities: The case of Curitiba*

Despite a sevenfold population increase between 1950 and 1990, Curitiba, Brazil, has proven itself to be a clean and efficient city, thanks to good governance and social cooperation. The cornerstone of Curitiba's success lies in its innovative Plano Director, adopted in 1968 and implemented by the Instituto de Pesquisa Planejamento Urbano de Curitiba (IPPUC). Rather than use high-tech solutions for urban infrastructure, like subways and expensive mechanical garbage separation plants, the IPPUC pursued appropriate technology that is effective both in cost and application.

Land use and mobility were planned in an integrated fashion, and the city's radial (or axial) layout was designed to divert traffic from the downtown area (three-fourths of the city's people use a highly efficient bus system). The industrial center is built close to the city center to minimize the commute for workers. Numerous natural preservation areas are situated around the industrial area to buffer flooding.

Another part of the city's success is its waste management; 90 percent of its residents recycle at least two-thirds of their trash. In low-income areas where conventional waste management is difficult, the "Garbage Purchase" program exchanges garbage for bus tokens, surplus food, and school notebooks.

Replications are under way. In Juarez, Mexico, for example, the Municipal Planning Institute is building new homes and transforming the previously inhabited flood zone into a city park.

Source: Roman 2008.

---

rarely a problem because surface drainage is built into the urban fabric to accommodate floodwaters from extreme events that exceed the capacity of protective infrastructure (see box 2.3). Inadequate solid waste management and drain maintenance, by contrast, can quickly clog drainage channels and cause local flooding with even light rainfall; in Georgetown, Guyana, such a situation led to 29 local floods between 1990 and 1996.[43]

Cities also have to look beyond their borders to prepare for climate change.

Many Andean cities are reengineering their water supplies to accommodate the shrinking and eventual disappearance of glaciers. Melting means that dry-season water supply is no longer reliable, and reservoirs will need to compensate for the lost water storage and regulation function of glaciers.[44] In the deltas in Southeast Asia, the rapidly spreading suburbs of cities such as Bangkok and Ho Chi Minh City are encroaching on rice fields, reducing water retention capacity and increasing

---

BOX 2.3   *Adapting to climate change: Alexandria, Casablanca, and Tunis*

Alexandria, Casablanca, and Tunis, each with 3 million to 5 million people, are assessing the extent of the projected impacts of climate change and devising adaptation scenarios for 2030 through an ongoing regional study. The cities' early responses to their increasing vulnerability show uneven paths toward adaptation.

In Alexandria the recent construction of the corniche, a major six-lane highway built right on the coast, has worsened coastal erosion and steepened the profile of the seabed, causing storm surges to reach farther into the city. Sea defenses are being built without sufficient engineering studies or coordination among the responsible institutions. A lake near the city, a natural receptacle for drainage waters, is suffering acute pollution and real-estate pressures to reclaim it for construction purposes.

Casablanca responded to recent devastating urban flooding episodes with works to improve upstream watershed management and to broaden the main drainage canals. Leaks in the household water distribution network have been repaired, with the water saving equal to the consumption of about 800,000 people. But coastal zone management remains a concern, given the limited tools to control construction and reduce sand extraction from beaches.

Tunis is also addressing its urban flooding risks by improving drainage canals and controlling informal construction around some natural reservoirs. Seawalls are being built to defend the most threatened coastal neighborhoods, and the new master plan directs urban development away from the sea. But the city center, already below sea level, is subsiding, and harbor and logistic facilities, as well as power-generation and water-treatment plants, are under threat. Major urban redevelopment projects, if carried out, also risk increasing the city's vulnerability to rising seas.

Adaptation to climate change in Alexandria, Casablanca, and Tunis should occur primarily through improving urban planning; identifying land-use and expansion scenarios that would minimize vulnerability; addressing the vulnerability of key infrastructure assets, such as ports, roads, bridges, and water-treatment plants; and improving the capacity of responsible institutions to coordinate responses and manage emergencies. In addition, energy efficiency in buildings and municipal systems can be consistent with increasing resilience to climate change while reducing greenhouse gas emissions.

Source: Bigio 2008.

the risk of floods.[45] The risk can get worse when upstream storage areas reach their capacity and have to discharge water. Peak river discharges in South and Southeast Asian river basins are projected to increase with climate change, requiring greater upstream efforts to protect urban centers downstream (map 2.2).[46]

Local city governments can promote risk reduction and risk-based planning. Creating a risk information database, developed jointly with citizens, businesses, and officials, is the first step in setting priorities for intervention and identifying hotspots. And establishing a city mandate through executive orders and council legislation can

Map 2.2   A complex challenge: managing urban growth and flood risk in a changing climate in South and Southeast Asia

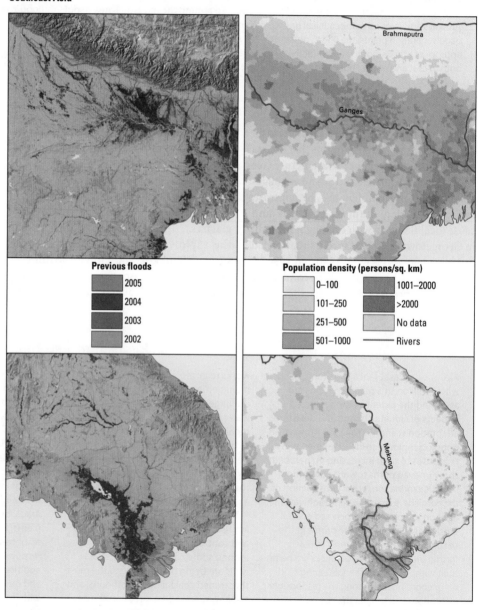

Sources: WDR team analysis. Flood data: Dartmouth Flood Observatory 2009. Population data: CIESIN 2005.
Note: Living with floods is engrained in the economic activities and culture of people in South and Southeast Asia. The floodplains of some of the major river basins (Ganges, top; Mekong, bottom) concentrate a large number of people and expose agriculture and growing urban centers to seasonal flood risk. Climate change is likely to bring more intense flooding, partly caused by the melting of glaciers in the upper catchment of the Himalaya region and partly by the shorter and more intense monsoon rains, which will likely change flood patterns in the region. At the same time urban centers are rapidly encroaching into agricultural areas that serve as natural retention zones for flood waters, bringing new complexity to managing flood water and urban expansion in the future.

facilitate mainstreaming, as in storm- and flood-prone Makati City, Philippines, where the Disaster Coordination Council plans the city's disaster risk management.[47]

Many municipal actions to promote local development and resilience to extreme events and disasters overlap with the measures for adaptation, including water supply and sanitation, drainage, prevention-focused health care, and disaster preparedness (box 2.4). Such interventions are likely to be in the immediate interest of decision makers in urban contexts (see chapter 8).[48] It is evidently easier to cast adaptation-oriented initiatives as being in the city's immediate interests, in order to break political logjams for climate action.[49]

Building climate-smart cities will involve considerable use of emerging technologies. However, much of the available technical expertise in developing countries is concentrated in the central government, with local authorities often left to draw from a small pool of expertise.[50] Urban universities can play a key role in supporting efforts by cities to adopt and implement climate-smart practices through changes in curriculum and teaching methods that enable students to spend more time in the practical world solving local problems.

Keep people healthy

Diseases linked to climate, namely malnutrition, diarrheal diseases, and vector-borne illnesses (especially malaria), already represent a huge health burden in some regions, particularly Africa and South Asia. Climate change will increase that burden and will be most consequential for the poor (see chapter 1).[51] The estimated additional 150,000 deaths a year attributable to climate change in recent decades may be just the tip of the iceberg.[52] The indirect effects of climate change mediated by water and sanitation, ecosystems, food production, and human habitation could be far higher. Children are especially susceptible, with malnutrition and infectious diseases (mostly diarrheal diseases) part of a vicious cycle causing cognitive and learning disabilities that permanently affect future productivity. In Ghana and Pakistan the costs associated with malnutrition and diarrheal diseases are estimated to be as high as 9 percent of gross domestic product (GDP) when accounting for long-term productivity losses in later years. These costs will only increase with climate change, if adaptation to these conditions is slow.[53]

The recent heat waves, such as the one that killed about 70,000 people in Europe in 2003, showed that even high-income countries can be vulnerable.[54] Heat waves are likely to increase in frequency and intensity (map 2.3),[55] with urban heat islands producing temperatures up to 3.5–4.5°C higher than in surrounding rural areas.[56] For better preparedness several countries and metropolitan areas now have heat-health warning systems (box 2.5).

Vector-borne diseases are increasing their geographic spread and are reappearing

BOX 2.4 *Fostering synergies between mitigation and adaptation*

The spatial organization of cities, or their urban form, determines energy use and efficiency. The concentration of population and consumption tends to increase rapidly during the early stage of urbanization and development. Denser urban areas have higher energy efficiency and shorter travel distances (see chapter 4, box 4.7). But increasing the density of people, economic activity, and infrastructure tends to amplify the effects of climate on cities. For instance, green space can reduce the urban heat-island effects, but it can also fall victim to building developments. Similarly, increased density combined with the paving of infiltration areas hampers urban drainage that mitigates flooding.

Climate-smart urban design can foster synergies between mitigation and adaptation. Promoting renewable energy sources tends to favor the decentralization of energy supply. Green spaces provide shading and cooling, reducing the need to air-condition buildings or to leave the city during heat waves. Green-roofing can save energy, attenuate storm water, and provide cooling. Synergies between adaptation and mitigation are often related to building height, layout, spacing, materials, shading, ventilation, and air-conditioning.

Many climate-smart designs, combining ecological principles, social sensibilities, and energy efficiency, are planned for urban areas in China, such as Dongtan, close to Shanghai, but so far the plans have largely remained blueprints.

Sources: Girardet 2008; Laukkonen and others 2009; McEvoy, Lindley, and Handley 2006; Wang and Yaping 2004; World Bank 2008g; Yip 2008.

Map 2.3   Northern cities need to prepare for Mediterranean climate—now

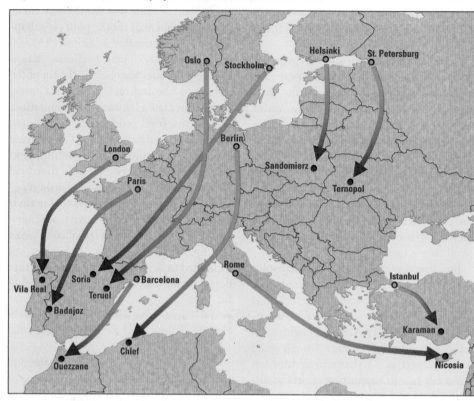

Source: WDR team, reproduced from Kopf, Ha-Duong, and Hallegatte 2008.

Note: With increasing global temperatures, climate zones will shift north, and by the middle of the 21st century many central and northern European cities will "feel" Mediterranean. This is not good news and has major implications: water utilities will need to adjust management plans, and health services will need to be prepared for more extreme heat episodes (similar to the 2003 European heat wave). While a few degrees of warming may seem appealing on a cold winter day in Oslo (the scenario shown in the map corresponds approximately to a global temperature increase of 1.2°C relative to today), the necessary changes in planning, public health management, and urban infrastructure are substantial. Buildings that were designed and engineered for cold harsh winters will need to function in a drier and hotter climate, and heritage buildings may suffer irreparable damages. Even more challenging is the construction of new buildings today as their design needs to be highly flexible to gradually adjust to drastically different conditions over the coming decades.

BOX 2.5   *Preparing for heat waves*

After heat waves in 2003 the Spanish Ministry of Health and CatSalut (the regional Catalan health service) implemented a comprehensive interministerial and interagency action plan to blunt the effects of future heat waves on health.[a] The plan incorporates health responses and communications (at all levels of health care) triggered by a heat-health warning system.

The plan has three levels of action during the summer season:

- Level 0 starts on June 1 and focuses on preparedness.
- Level 1 is triggered during July and August and focuses on meteorological assessments (including daily recordings of temperature and humidity), disease surveillance, assessment of preventive actions, and protection of at-risk populations.
- Level 2 is activated only if the temperature rises above the warning threshold (35°C in coastal areas and 40°C in inland areas), at which point health and social care and emergency service responses are initiated.

The action plan and its health system response hinge on using primary health care centers (including social services) in the region. The centers identify and localize vulnerable populations to strengthen outreach to them and disseminate public health information during the summer. They also collect health data to monitor and evaluate the health impacts of heat waves and the effectiveness of interventions.

Similar actions are under way elsewhere. Wales has a framework for heatwave preparedness and response. It establishes guidelines for preventing and treating heat-related illnesses, operates an early warning system during the summer months, and has communication mechanisms with the meteorological office.[b] Metropolitan Shanghai has a heat-health warning system as part of its multi-hazard management plan.[c]

Sources:

a. CatSalut 2008.

b. Welsh Assembly Government 2008.

c. Shanghai Multi-Hazard Early Warning System Demonstration Project, http://smb.gov.cn/SBQXWebInEnglish/TemplateA/Default/index.aspx (accessed March 13, 2009).

in Eastern Europe and Central Asia.[57] Malaria already strains economies in tropical areas,[58] killing almost 1 million people a year (mostly children), and climate change is projected to expose 90 million more people (a 14 percent increase) to the disease by 2030 in Africa alone.[59] Dengue has been expanding its geographic range (map 2.4), and climate change is expected to double the rate of people at risk from 30 percent to up to 60 percent of the world population (or 5 billion to 6 billion people) by 2070.[60] To detect and monitor epidemic-prone diseases, national health systems need better surveillance and

early warning systems.[61] Today, surveillance in many parts of the world fails to anticipate new disease pressure, for example, in Africa, where malaria is reaching urban dwellers with the expansion of urban settlements into areas of transmission.[62] Satellite remote-sensing and biosensors can improve the accuracy and precision of surveillance systems and prevent disease outbreaks through early detection of changes in climate factors.[63] Advanced seasonal climate forecast models can now predict peak times for malaria transmission and give regional authorities in Africa information to operate

Map 2.4   Climate change accelerates the comeback of dengue in the Americas

Source: PAHO 2009.

Note: Infectious and vector-borne diseases have been expanding into new geographic areas all over the world. In the Americas the incidence of dengue fever has been rising because of increasing population density and widespread international travel and trade. Changes in humidity and temperature brought about by climate change amplify this threat and allows disease vectors (mosquitoes) to thrive in locations previously unsuitable for the disease; see Knowlton, Solomon, and Rotkin-Ellman 2009.

an early warning system and longer lead-times to respond more effectively.[64]

Most measures to prevent these diseases are not new, but climate change makes the better implementation of well-established public health approaches even more urgent.[65] Breaking the transmission pathways requires better management of water (urban drainage), improved sanitation and hygiene (sewerage systems, sanitation facilities, hand-washing behaviors), and effective vector control to limit or eradicate insects that transmit disease pathogens.[66]

Such interventions require coordinated intersectoral action and public expenditures. For water-borne diseases, interventions should include the health agency, public works, and utilities.[67] Jointly managed water, sanitation, hygiene, and food security—combined with health and disaster management—can yield high returns. So can engaging the private sector, if it improves performance. Privatizing water services in Argentina in the 1990s dramatically reduced the child mortality linked to water-borne diseases.[68]

Monitoring and managing the health impacts of climate change will require greater use of new diagnostic tools. Advances in genomics and information technology are accelerating the design of a wide range of diagnostic tools that can help in monitoring the spread of diseases and the emergence of new ones. New communications tools will make it easier to collect, analyze, and share health information in a timely manner.[69] But having such tools will not be sufficient without extensive programs to train health care workers. Similarly, major institutional reforms will need to be introduced to integrate health care into other activities. Schools, for example, can be major centers for the provision of basic health care as well as sources of medical information and education.

Prepare for extreme events

Natural disasters are taking an increasing economic toll, and managing them better is essential for adapting to climate change. While deaths from weather-related natural disasters are on the decline,[70] economic losses caused by storms, floods, and droughts are all rising (from about $20 billion a year in the early 1980s to $70 billion in the early 2000s for high-income countries and from $10 billion a year to $15 billion for low- and middle-income countries).[71] But this increase is largely explained by higher exposure of economic value per area rather than changes in climate.[72] The number of affected people (people requiring humanitarian assistance after disasters) continues to increase, with the largest share in lower-middle-income countries characterized by rapid urban growth (figure 2.1).[73] About 90 percent of the economic losses in developing

Figure 2.1   The number of people affected by climate-related disasters is increasing

Number of people killed per five-year period (millions)

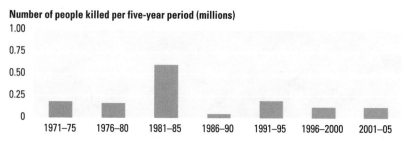

Number of people affected per five-year period (billions)

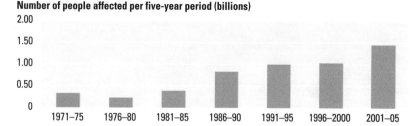

People affected as a share of population (%)

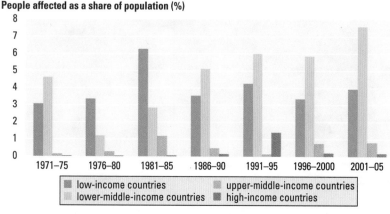

- low-income countries
- lower-middle-income countries
- upper-middle-income countries
- high-income countries

Sources: WDR team; CRED 2009.

Note: Over the past 40 years the death toll has fallen but the number of people affected has doubled every decade. (*People affected* are those requiring immediate assistance during a period of emergency and can also include displaced or evacuated people.) In lower-middle-income countries almost 8 percent of the population is affected each year. The increase cannot be attributed only to climate change; much results from population increase, greater exposure of infrastructure and improved reporting of disasters. However, the impacts on people are just as real and show why it is so essential to begin focusing on the current adaptation deficit while looking ahead to a more climatically stressful future.

countries are borne by households, businesses, and governments with the rest covered by insurance or donor funds.

Unless disaster impacts are systematically reduced, past development gains will be at risk. So the focus is shifting from coping with disaster events to forward-looking disaster risk management and toward preventive rather than reactive measures. In line with the Hyogo Framework of Action for reducing disaster risks (the 2005 policy framework defined by the United Nations), recovery and reconstruction are being designed to reduce risks of future disasters, bridging the humanitarian and development agendas.[74] The private sector is instrumental in this framework, providing financial (insurance, risk assessments) and technical (communication, construction, service provision) solutions.[75]

Climate change greatly increases the need for effective management of extreme weather events and for disaster risk management that increases preparedness and prevents losses (box 2.6).[76] In many places previously uncommon risks are becoming more

---

BOX 2.6 *Beating the odds and getting ahead of impacts: Managing the risk of extreme events before they become disasters*

Recurrent extreme climate events—storms, floods, droughts, wildfires—characterize many parts of the world and are part of the climate system. Climate change is likely to change patterns of extreme events, but negative impacts can be reduced through systematic risk management. The basic steps are assessing risk, reducing risk, and mitigating risk.[a]

Assessing risk, a prerequisite for risk management, is the basis for informed decision making. It focuses action and resources. Identifying pertinent risk is the first step and generally does not require sophisticated techniques. Rice farmers in Asia readily point out their most flood-prone fields. Water reservoir managers know the difficulties of managing the competing demands for electricity and water supply when water levels are low. And communities can identify social groups and individuals who tend to be affected first when adverse weather events occur.

Quantifying risk is the next step, and a variety of approaches exist depending on the scope of a risk assessment. Communities use simple participatory techniques based on readily observable indicators (such as the market price for staple crops during droughts) to trigger action at the household and community level, or they use community-based mapping to determine flood-prone areas. Risk assessments at the sector level (agriculture or hydropower) or for a country generally require more systematic and quantitative data analysis (mapping agricultural extent or regional hydrology).

Understanding risk requires investment in scientific, technical, and institutional capacity to observe, record, research, analyze, forecast, model, and map natural hazards and vulnerabilities. Geographic information systems can integrate these sources of information and give decision makers a powerful tool to understand risk—both at the national agencies and the local level. Many low- and middle-income countries are now performing risk assessments and are systematically strengthening their capacity to manage disasters better.[b]

Reducing risk requires mainstreaming risk in the overall strategic framework of development, a task more important than ever as the density of people and infrastructure increases. Since the late 1990s there has been increasing recognition of the need to address risks emanating from natural hazards in medium-term strategic development frameworks, in legislation and institutional structures, in sectoral strategies and policies, in budgetary processes, in individual projects, and in monitoring and evaluation. Mainstreaming requires analysis of how potential hazard events could affect policies, programs, and projects and vice versa.

Development initiatives do not necessarily reduce vulnerability to natural hazards, and they can unwittingly create new vulnerabilities or heighten existing ones. Solutions for jointly sustaining development, reducing poverty, and strengthening resilience to hazards thus need to be explicitly sought. Disaster risk reduction should promote resilience and help communities adapt to new and increased risks. But even this cannot be guaranteed. For instance, investments in structural flood control designed according to current probabilities could add to future losses by encouraging development in flood-prone areas today but leaving them more prone to future major damages. So climate-change predictions have to be taken into account in current decision making and longer-term planning.

Mitigating risk entails actions to minimize impacts during an event and its immediate aftermath. Early warning and surveillance systems harness information technology and communication systems to provide advance warnings of extreme events. For such information to save lives, disaster management agencies need mechanisms in place to receive and communicate information to communities well ahead of the event. This requires systematic preparedness training; capacity building and awareness raising; and coordination between national, regional, and local entities. Taking swift and targeted action after a disaster is equally important, including social protection for the most vulnerable and a strategy for recovery and reconstruction.

Sources: WDR team; Ranger, Muir-Wood, and Priya 2009; United Nations 2007; United Nations 2009; NRC 2006; Benson and Twigg 2007.

a. Here the term *mitigation* refers to avoidance of losses from extreme weather events, for example, by evacuating people from a flood plain, through short-term measures in anticipation of an immediate threat.

b. Global Facility for Disaster Reduction and Recovery, www.gfdrr.org (accessed May 15, 2009); Prevention, www.proventionconsortium.org (accessed May 15, 2009).

widespread, as in Africa, where the number of floods is increasing rapidly (figure 2.2), and in Brazil, which experienced the first South Atlantic hurricane ever in 2004.[77]

Generating information about where extreme weather impacts are likely and the consequences they may have requires socioeconomic data (maps showing population density or land values) as well as physical information (records of precipitation or extreme events).[78] But in a changing climate the past is no longer prologue (oncerare events may become more frequent), and uncertainty about the future climate is an important element in assessing risk and evaluating planning decisions. Equally important are monitoring and periodic updates in socioeconomic data to reflect

changes in land use and demographics. Satellite and geographic information technology provide powerful means to generate physical and socioeconomic information rapidly and cost-effectively (box 2.7; see also chapters 3 and 7).

Many developed countries provide detailed flood-risk maps as a public service to homeowners, businesses, and local authorities.[79] In China the government has drawn such maps since 1976 and publishes flood-risk maps that delineate high-risk zones for the most populated river basins. With such tools, residents can have information on when, how, and where to evacuate. The maps can also be used for land-use planning and building design.[80] Put in the hands of local communities, such services foster local action, as in Bogota, where similar risk-based information for earthquake-prone zones strengthens the resilience of communities.[81]

Risk can never be eliminated, and being prepared to cope with extreme events is vital for protecting people. Warning systems and response plans (say, for evacuation in an emergency) save lives and prevent avoidable losses. Engaging communities in preparedness and emergency communication protects their livelihoods. For example, in Mozambique communities along the Búzi River use radios to warn communities downstream of flooding.[82] Even in remote, isolated communities local action can reduce risk, create jobs, and address poverty

Figure 2.2   Floods are increasing, even in drought-prone Africa

Events per five-year period

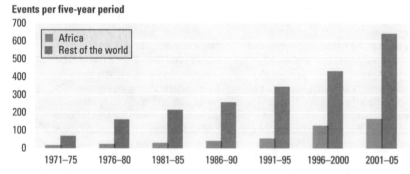

Source: WDR team analysis from CRED 2009.
Note: Flood events are increasing everywhere but particularly in Africa, with new regions being exposed to flooding and with less recovery time between events. Reporting of events may have improved since the 1970s, but this is not the main cause of rising numbers of reported floods, because the frequency of other disaster events in Africa, such as droughts and earthquakes, has not shown a similar increase.

BOX 2.7   *Satellite data and geo-information are instrumental in managing risk—and inexpensive*

Satellite data and geo-information technology are often available for free or at moderate cost, and the software and tools to use such technology operate on desktop computers.

Satellites monitor moisture and vegetation and provide invaluable information to agricultural extension services. They track tropical storms and provide early warning to coastal communities. By mapping flood impacts they support recovery and reconstruction operations. They map forests and biomass and

empower indigenous forest dwellers with information. High-resolution sensors identify urban encroachment into hazardous zones. Geographic positioning devices used in surveys can reveal new information about how households interact with the natural environment. Geo-information systems streamline data management, ensure information is available when it is needed, and provide a cost-effective and rapid tool to build the knowledge base for informed policy making and for understanding risk patterns in

places where such data and knowledge are currently limited.

The use of such services and technology broadly and effectively in developing countries does not require hard investments—investments in higher education, institutional capacity building, mission-focused regional research centers, and promoting private enterprise are the main elements.

Sources: ESA 2002; NRC 2007a, 2007b.

(box 2.8). At the national level, being financially prepared to provide immediate assistance after disasters is critical for avoiding long-term losses for communities.

Managing financial risks: Flexible instruments for contingencies

Public policy creates a framework that delineates clear roles and responsibilities for the public sector, private sector, households, and individuals. Core to such a framework is a spectrum of risk management practices with layered responsibilities. A minor drought that causes small losses in crop production can be managed by households through informal and community-based risk sharing unless several small droughts occur in short sequence (see chapter 1). A more severe drought, one that occurs, say, every 10 years, can be managed through risk transfer instruments in the private sector. But for the most severe and widespread events the government has to act as the insurer of last resort. It has to develop a framework that allows communities to help themselves and the private sector to play an active and commercially viable role, while making provisions to cover its liabilities arising from catastrophic events.

Provide layers of protection

The use and support of insurance mechanisms has gained much attention in the context of adaptation.[83] Insurance can protect against losses associated with extreme climate events and manage costs that cannot be covered by international aid, by governments, or by citizens.[84] Some novel approaches have been developed and tested, such as weather-based derivatives and microinsurance products on the private market. Consider the weather-index insurance for smallholder farmers in India that provides compensation to hundreds of thousands of farmers in case of severe precipitation shortfall—and the Caribbean common insurance pool that quickly provides governments with liquidity after disasters.[85]

But insurance is not a silver bullet—it is only one element in a broader risk management framework that promotes risk reduction (avoiding avoidable losses) and rewards sound risk management practices (just as

---

BOX 2.8   *Creating jobs to reduce flood risk*

Heavy rains are common in Liberia, yet drainage systems have not been maintained for decades because of years of neglect and civil war. As a result, flooding has triggered recurrent disasters in both rural and urban settings. Cleaning the drains was not a priority for government officials or citizens, because nobody had the resources. But after Mercy Corps, an international nongovernmental organization, raised the possibility of cash-for-work options, government officials embraced it. In September 2006 a one-year project to clear and rehabilitate drainage systems was launched in five counties. This significantly increased the flow of rainwater and reduced flooding and related health risks. The project also rehabilitated wells and improved market access by clearing roads and building small bridges.

Source: Mercy Corps 2008.

---

homeowners receive a premium reduction if they install fire alarms). If climate is trending in a predictable fashion (toward hotter or drier weather conditions, for instance), insurance is not viable. Insurance is appropriate when impacts are random and rare, helping households, businesses, and governments spread risk over time (by paying regular premiums rather than covering the full costs at once) and geographically (by sharing risk with others). So, it does not eliminate risk, but it does reduce the variance of losses borne by individuals in the insurance pool.

Insurance against storms, floods, and droughts, whether provided to governments or individuals, is difficult to manage. Climate risk tends to affect entire regions or large groups of people simultaneously; for example, thousands of breeders in Mongolia saw their livestock decimated in 2002, when a dry summer was followed by an extremely cold winter (box 2.9). Such covariant events characterize many climate risks and make insurance very difficult to provide because claims tend to cluster and require large backup capital and administrative efforts.[86] That is one reason major climate risks are not widely covered by insurance, particularly in the developing world. Indeed, microfinance institutions often limit the share of agricultural loans in their portfolio in case widespread weather impacts cause their clients to default.[87]

The provision of financial services has been a long-standing challenge in development for reasons unrelated to climate change. Access to insurance products is generally much

BOX 2.9   *Public-private partnerships for sharing climate risks: Mongolia livestock insurance*

An important concept of climate-risk management is risk-sharing by communities, governments, and businesses. In Mongolia livestock herders, the national government, and insurance companies developed a scheme to manage the financial risks arising from severe winter-spring cold episodes (*dzuds*) that periodically result in widespread livestock mortality. Such episodes killed 17 percent of livestock in 2002 (in some areas up to 100 percent), amounting to losses of $200 million (16 percent of GDP).

In this scheme herders retain the responsibility for smaller losses that do not affect the viability of their business or household, and they often use arrangements with community members to buffer against smaller losses. Larger losses (of 10–30 percent) are covered through commercial livestock insurance provided by Mongolian insurers. A social insurance program through the government bears the losses associated with catastrophic livestock mortality that would overwhelm herders and insurers alike. This tiered approach defines a clear framework for self-insurance by herders, commercial insurance, and social insurance.

An important innovation is the use of index insurance rather than individual livestock insurance, which had been ineffective because the verification of individual losses tends to be fraught with moral hazard and often prohibitively high costs. With this new type of insurance, herders are compensated based on the average livestock mortality rate in their district, and an individual loss assessment is not required. This gives Mongolian insurers incentives to offer commercial insurance to herders, which they had been reluctant to do.

The scheme provides advantages for all. Herders can buy insurance against unavoidable losses. Insurers can expand their business in rural areas, strengthening the rural financial service infrastructure. The government, by providing a well-structured social insurance, can better manage its fiscal risk. Even though a catastrophic event exposes the government to significant potential risk, the government had been compelled politically to absorb even greater risk in the past. Because the government covers catastrophic outcomes, the commercial insurance, limited to moderate levels of mortality, can be offered at affordable rates.

Sources: Mahul and Skees 2007; Mearns 2004.

---

weaker in developing countries (figure 2.3), a fact reflected in the generally lower penetration of financial services in rural areas. The Philippines Crop Insurance Corporation, for example, reaches only about 2 percent of farmers, largely in the more productive and richer zones.[88] Providing financial services to rural populations is challenging and risky, because many rural households are not part of the monetized economy and have weather-sensitive livelihoods. In urban settings people are more concentrated, but it is still difficult to reach the poor in the informal economy.

Climate change could further erode the insurability of climate-related risk. Unchecked climate change could make many climate risks uninsurable or the premiums unaffordable. Insurability requires the ability to identify and quantify (or at least estimate partially) the likelihood of an event and the associated losses, to set premiums, and to diversify risk among individuals or collectives.[89] Meeting all three conditions makes a risk insurable but not necessarily profitable (as reflected in the low premium-to-claims ratio of many agricultural insurance programs) and the transaction costs of operating an insurance program can be considerable.[90] The uncertainties arising from climate change confound the actuarial processes that underlie

insurance markets.[91] And diversifying risk will be more difficult as climate change leads to more synchronized, widespread, and systemic effects globally and regionally—effects that are difficult to offset in other regions or market segments.

The erosion of market-based insurability implies a strong reliance on governments as insurers of last resort, a role that many governments have implicitly taken. But the track record of governments has not been stellar, in either the developing world or the developed. For instance, Hurricane Katrina in 2005 bankrupted the U.S. flood insurance program 10 times over, with more claims in one year than in its 37-year history. And few government-sponsored crop insurance programs are financially sustainable without major subsidies.[92] At the same time, if the magnitude of losses associated with recent catastrophic events is any indication of the insurability of future losses from climate change, it suggests a more explicit role of the public sector to absorb the damages that are beyond the private sector's capacity.[93]

Insurance is no panacea for adapting to climate risks and is only *one* strategy to address *some* of the impacts of climate change. It generally is not appropriate for long-term and irreversible impacts, such as sea-level

Figure 2.3   Insurance is limited in the developing world

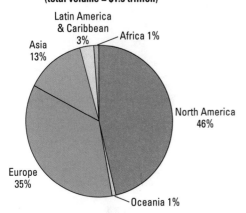

Non–life insurance premium volume in 2006
(total volume = $1.5 trillion)

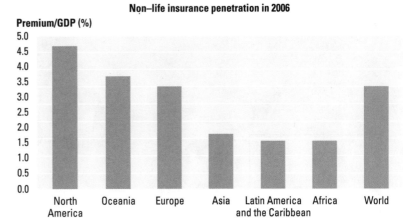

Non–life insurance penetration in 2006

Source: Swiss Re 2007.

Note: Insurance is primarily a developed-country market as indicated by the regional share of premiums (left), and penetration (premium as percent of GDP) of non–life insurance (right). Non–life insurance includes property, casualty, and liability insurance (also referred to as general insurance), health insurance, and insurance products not defined as life insurance.

rise and desertification, trends that would lead to massive losses for insurers and thus be uninsurable. Insurance must also be considered within an overall risk-management and adaptation strategy, including sound regulation of land-use and building codes, to avoid counterproductive behavior—or maladaptation (such as continued settlement on a storm-prone coast)—because of the security in an insurance contract.[94]

Keep governments liquid

Financial planning prepares governments for catastrophic climate impacts and maintains essential government services in the immediate aftermath of disasters.[95] Prearranged financing arrangements—such as catastrophe reserve funds, contingent lines of credit, and catastrophe bonds—allow governments to respond swiftly, scale up social protection programs, and avoid longer-term losses that accrue to households and communities while people are homeless, out of work, and experience basic deprivations.[96] Having immediate funds available to jumpstart the rehabilitation and recovery process reduces the derailing effect of disasters on development.

Many small countries are financially more vulnerable to catastrophic events because of the magnitude of disaster-related losses relative to the size of their economy (map 2.5); in Grenada in 2004,

for example, the winds of Hurricane Ivan caused losses equivalent to more than 200 percent of GDP.[97] Because outside aid is not always immediately available, 16 Caribbean countries have developed a well-structured financial risk-management scheme to streamline emergency funding and minimize service interruptions. Operating since 2007, it provides rapid liquidity to governments following destructive hurricanes and earthquakes, using innovative access to international reinsurance markets that can diversify and offset risk globally (box 2.10).

Even poor economies can manage climate risks more effectively by harnessing information, markets, good planning, and technical assistance. By forming partnerships with insurers and international financial institutions, governments can overcome the private sector's reluctance to commit capital and expertise to the low-income market. In 2008 Malawi pioneered a weather-based risk management contract to protect itself against droughts that would lead to national maize production shortfalls (often accompanied by high volatility in regional commodity prices and food insecurity). In exchange for a premium an international reinsurance company committed to pay an agreed amount to the government in case of predefined severe drought conditions, as measured and reported by

Map 2.5 Small and poor countries are financially vulnerable to extreme weather events

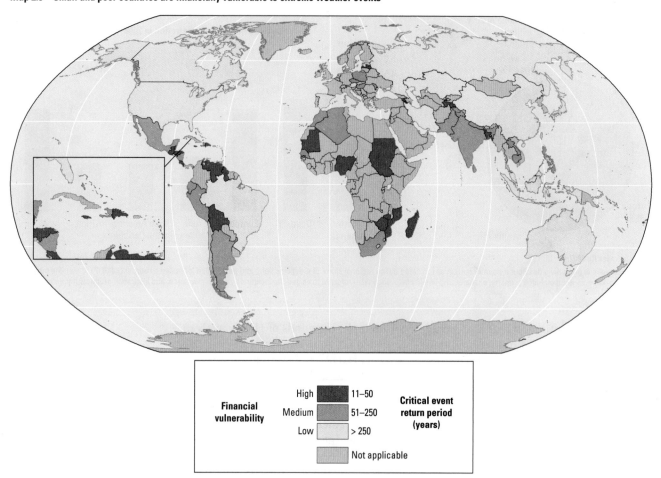

Financial vulnerability

High — 11–50

Medium — 51–250

Low — > 250

Critical event return period (years)

Not applicable

Source: Mechler and others 2009.

Note: The map shows degree to which countries are financially vulnerable to floods and storms. For example, in countries shaded dark red a severe weather event that would exceed the public sector's financial ability to restore damaged infrastructure and continue with development as planned is expected about once every 11 to 50 years (an annual probability of 2–10 percent). The high financial vulnerability of small economies underscores the need for financial contingency planning to increase governments' resilience against future disasters. Only the 74 most disaster-prone countries that experienced direct losses of at least 1 percent of GDP due to floods, storms, and droughts during the past 30 years were included in the analysis.

the Malawian weather service. The World Bank Treasury acted as a trusted intermediary to the market, increasing confidence in the transaction on both sides. Because payment and drought parameters were defined beforehand, disbursement from such a financial product could be rapid, and the government could forward-purchase maize on regional commodity markets to secure food as soon as possible before drought would affect the most vulnerable, which reduces response costs significantly, and decreases dependence on international appeals for assistance.[98]

For these initiatives to be affordable and sustainable, disaster risk reduction needs to be systematically promoted to minimize government reliance on such financial arrangements for more routine losses. Contingent financing has opportunity costs and should cover only the most urgent government financial needs and most extreme losses. Agricultural extension services, building code enforcement, and strategic urban planning are a few examples showing where government action can reduce avoidable consequences and the likelihood of the most extreme outcomes. Equally important are early warning systems that provide advance warning and prevent the loss of human life and economic damages. Such systems, supported by governments, can have dramatic effects, as in Bangladesh, where they have reduced human deaths from floods and storms and therefore the need for the government to finance the losses.[99]

Managing social risks: Empower communities to protect themselves

Climate change does not affect everyone equally.[100] For poor households even moderate climate stress can result in irreversible losses of human and physical capital.[101] The impacts on children can be long term and affect lifetime earnings through education (withdrawal from school after a shock), health (compounding effect of poor sanitation and water- or vector-borne diseases), and stunting.[102] Women in the developing world experience the effects of climate disproportionately because many of their household responsibilities (gathering and selling wild products) are affected by the vagaries of the weather.[103] Households and communities adapt through their livelihood choices, asset allocations, and locational preferences, often relying on traditional knowledge to inform these decisions.[104] People will be both more willing and more able to change if they have social support systems that combine community sharing, publicly provided social insurance (such as pensions), privately supplied finance and insurance, and publicly provided safety nets.

Build resilient communities

Building on local and traditional knowledge about managing climate risk is important for two reasons.[105] First, many communities, notably indigenous peoples, already have context-relevant knowledge and strategies for addressing climate risks. Efforts to marry development and climate adaptation for vulnerable communities will benefit from the ways people have always responded to environmental risks, as in Africa where communities have adapted to extended periods of drought.[106] But those traditional coping and adaptation strategies can prepare communities only for some perceived risks, not for the uncertain and possibly different risks brought by climate change.[107] In this way communities might be well adapted to their

BOX 2.10   *The Caribbean Catastrophe Risk Insurance Facility: Insurance against service interruption after disasters*

Among the many challenges facing the governments of small island states in the aftermath of natural disasters, the most urgent is obtaining access to cash to implement urgent recovery efforts and maintain essential government services. This challenge is particularly acute for Caribbean countries, whose economic resilience is limited by mounting vulnerability and high indebtedness.

The new Caribbean Catastrophe Risk Insurance Facility provides Caribbean Community governments with an insurance instrument akin to business interruption insurance. It furnishes short-term liquidity if they suffer catastrophic losses from a hurricane or earthquake.

A wide range of instruments exists to finance long-term recovery, but this facility fills a gap in financing short-term needs through parametric insurance. It disburses funds based on the occurrence of a predefined event of a particular intensity, without having to wait for onsite loss assessments and formal confirmations. This type of insurance is generally less expensive and settles claims quickly, because measuring the strength of an event is almost instantaneous. The facility allows participating countries to pool their individual risks into one better-diversified portfolio and facilitates access to the reinsurance market, further spreading risks outside the region.

Such insurance mechanisms should be part of a comprehensive financial strategy using an array of instruments to cover different types of events and probabilities.

Sources: Ghesquiere, Jamin, and Mahul 2006; World Bank 2008e.

climates but less able to adapt to climate change.[108] Second, the local nature of adaptation means that sweeping policies with one-size-fits-all prescriptions are not suited to serving the needs of different urban and rural locations.[109]

Building blocks of community resilience—the capacity to retain critical functions, self-organize, and learn when exposed to change—are evident throughout the world.[110] In coastal Vietnam storm surges and rising sea levels are already putting stress on coping mechanisms. After cutbacks of many state services in the late 1990s, local collective decision making and credit and exchange networks substituted social capital and learning for government planning and infrastructure. (In recent years, however, the government has recognized its role to support community resilience and infrastructure development and now promotes a broad agenda of disaster risk management).[111]

In the western Arctic the Inuit, experiencing diminished sea ice and shifting wildlife distributions, have adjusted the timing of subsistence activities and are hunting a greater variety of species. They are increasing the resilience of their communities by sharing food, trading more with one another, and by developing new local institutions.[112] Similarly, indigenous communities in developing countries are adapting to climate change—for instance, through rainwater harvesting, crop and livelihood diversification, and changes in seasonal migration—to alleviate adverse impacts and take advantage of new opportunities.[113]

In general, communities have better time-, place-, and event-specific knowledge of local climate hazards and of how such hazards affect their assets and productive activities. Communities also have greater capacity to manage local social and ecological relationships that will be affected by climate change. And they typically incur lower costs than external actors in implementing development and environmental projects (figure 2.4). A recent review of more than 11,000 fisheries found that the likelihood of stock collapse can be dramatically reduced by moving away from overall harvest limits

and introducing individual transferable catch quotas with local enforcement.[114] Active participation of local communities and primary stakeholders in comanagement of fisheries is a key to success.[115]

Beyond resilience-enhancing benefits, decentralized resource management can have synergistic benefits for mitigation and adaptation. For example, forest commons management in tropical regions has produced simultaneous livelihood benefits (adaptation) and carbon storage gains (mitigation) when local communities own their forests, have greater decision-making autonomy, and ability to manage larger forest patches.[116] In many developing countries decentralized governance of forests based on principles of common-pool resources has given local populations the authority to manage forests, use their time- and place-specific knowledge to create appropriate rules and institutions, and work with government agencies to implement the rules they have created.[117] Enhancing indigenous peoples' land rights and ensuring their role in management has resulted in more sustained and cost-effective management

Figure 2.4 Turning back the desert with indigenous knowledge, farmer action, and social learning

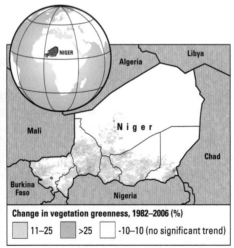

Change in vegetation greenness, 1982–2006 (%)

☐ 11–25   ■ >25   ☐ -10–10 (no significant trend)

Sources: WRI and others 2008; Botoni and Reij 2009; Herrmann, Anyamba, and Tucker 2005.

Note: In Niger farmers have turned back the encroaching desert; landscapes that were denuded in the 1980s are now densely studded with trees, shrubs, and crops. This transformation, so vast that its effects can be observed from satellites, has affected 5 million hectares of land (about the size of Costa Rica), which amounts to almost half of the cultivated land in Niger. The new economic opportunities created by the regreening have benefited millions of people through increased food security and resilience to drought. Key to this success was a low-cost technique known as farmer-managed natural regeneration that adapts a centuries-old technique of woodland management. After some earlier success with the reintroduction of this indigenous technique in the 1980s, farmers saw the benefits and spread the word. The social learning effect was enhanced by donors supporting farmer study tours and farmer-to-farmer exchanges. The central government's role was pivotal in reforming land tenure and forest policies.

of forests and biodiversity resources, as in Mexico and Brazil.[118]

Effective community-based adaptation builds on social learning, the process of exchanging knowledge about existing experiences, and incorporating it with technical scientific information.[119] When people migrate between urban and rural areas for seasonal employment or in the wake of natural disasters, their movements follow flows of earlier movements of relatives and friends.[120] When people adopt new technologies or change cropping patterns, their decisions depend on information flows in social networks.[121] When people choose different areas to strengthen their skills and education, their decisions are tied to those of their peers.[122]

Community and experience-based social learning has been a principal means to cope with climate risks in the past, but it may prove insufficient for climate change. Consequently, effective community-oriented climate adaptation strategies must balance the assets of communities (greater local capacity and knowledge, potential reserves of social capital, lower costs) against the deficits (limited scientific knowledge, narrow scope for action).

While numerous community-based adaptation activities are supported by a wide range of NGOs and other intermediaries, they reach only a minuscule fraction of those at risk. A pressing challenge is to replicate their successes far more widely. Scaling up has often been limited by poor links, and sometimes tensions, between local stakeholders and government institutions. Issues of authority, responsibility, and funding often impede cooperation. Successfully scaling up community-driven development will require that its supporters and governments think of the process beyond the project and of transformation or transition to avoid projects coming to a brutal end when funding stops. Capacity, pivotal to success, includes motivation and commitment, which in turn require appropriate incentives at all levels.[123] The new Adaptation Fund can greatly increase the support for scaling up because it is expected to manage resources on the order of $0.5 billion to $1.2 billion by 2012 and to directly support governments at all levels, NGOs, and other intermediary agencies.[124]

Provide safety nets for the most vulnerable

Climate change will amplify vulnerabilities and expose more people to climate threats more frequently and for longer periods. This requires social policies to assist groups whose livelihoods may gradually erode with climate change. Extreme events may also directly affect households and require safety nets (social assistance) to prevent the most vulnerable from falling economically. Protracted episodes of climate stress (as is common with drought) can contribute to commodity price increases and volatility, disproportionally affecting the poor and vulnerable, as was the case in the 2008 food crises.[125] High food prices increase poverty for those who need to purchase food to support their families, and worsen nutrition, reduce use of health and education services, and deplete the productive assets of the poor.[126] In parts of the developing world food insecurity and associated food price fluctuations already represent a systemic source of risk that is expected to increase with climate change.[127]

Climate shocks have two important characteristics. First, there is uncertainty about who exactly will be affected and where. The affected population is often not identified until a crisis is well advanced, when it is difficult to respond swiftly and effectively. Second, the timing of possible shocks is not known ahead of time. Both aspects have implications for conceptualizing and designing social policies in response to future climate threats. Social protection should be thought of as a system, rather than isolated interventions, and should be put in place during good times. Safety nets need to have flexible financing and contingent targeting so they can be ramped up to provide effective responses for episodic shocks.[128]

To address chronic vulnerabilities, a wide set of safety net instruments provides cash or in-kind transfers to poor households.[129] Used effectively, they have an immediate impact on reducing inequality and are the first-best approach to addressing the poverty implications of commodity price increases; they allow households to invest in their future livelihoods and manage risk by reducing the incidence of negative coping strategies (such as selling of livestock during droughts). Safety nets can be designed to encourage households to invest in human capital (education, training, nutrition) that increases resilience in the long term.

In response to shocks, safety nets can have an insurance function if they are designed to be scalable and flexible. They are often phased, with the priorities shifting from immediate provision of food, sanitation, and cleanup to eventual recovery, rebuilding, and, possibly, disaster prevention and mitigation. To fulfill an insurance function, safety nets need countercyclical and scalable budgets, targeting rules to identify people with transitory needs, flexible implementation that allows rapid response following a shock, and basic organizational procedures and responsibilities agreed on well before a disaster.[130] Early warnings provided through seasonal forecasts and bulletins can mobilize safety nets ahead of time and prepare logistics and food deliveries.[131]

Safety nets will need to be strengthened substantially where they exist and developed where they are lacking. Many low-income countries cannot afford permanent transfers to their poor, but scalable safety nets that provide a basic form of noncontributory insurance can represent a core social protection that prevents mortality and excessive depletion of assets, even in poor countries where they have not commonly been used.[132]

For instance, the Productive Safety Net in Ethiopia combines permanent social assistance (a longer-term workfare program targeted at 6 million food-insecure households) and scalable safety nets that can be rapidly expanded to serve millions of transitory poor households during a major drought. An important innovation is the use of indexes based on observed weather impacts to quickly provide more scalable and targeted assistance to food-insecure

areas and insurance-based mechanisms to access contingent financing.[133]

Workfare programs can be part of a safety net's response.[134] They are labor-intensive public works programs that provide income to a target population while building or maintaining public infrastructure. These programs focus on assets and high-return activities that can increase the resilience of communities, such as water storage, irrigation systems, and embankments. To be fully effective, however, they need clear objectives, suitable and well-conceived projects, predictable funding, professional guidance in selection and implementation, and credible monitoring and evaluation (box 2.11).

Safety nets can also facilitate the reform of energy policy. Raising fuel prices brings energy efficiency, economic gains, and fiscal savings, but also brings significant political and social risks. Safety nets can protect the poor from high energy prices and help eliminate large, burdensome, regressive, and climate-damaging energy subsidies (see chapter 1).[135] Energy subsidies, a common response to high fuel prices, are often inefficient and not well targeted, but eliminating them is often problematic. Several middle-income countries (Brazil, China, Colombia, India, Indonesia, Malaysia, and Turkey) have recently used safety nets to facilitate the removal of fossil-fuel subsidies.[136] Cash transfer payments following the removal of subsidies must be carefully targeted to ensure that the poor are reasonably compensated—the reform in Indonesia showed that, even with substantial mistargeting, the bottom four deciles of the population still gained during the transfer period.[137]

Facilitate migration in response to climate change

Migration will often be an effective response to climate change—and unfortunately the only response in some cases. Estimates of the number of people at risk of migration, displacement, and relocation by 2050 vary from to 200 million to as high as 1 billion.[138] (But these estimates are based on broad assessments of people exposed to increasing risks rather than

---

BOX 2.11 *Workfare in India under the Indian National Rural Employment Guarantee Act*

India over time has developed an employment guarantee program built on an earlier successful scheme in the state of Maharashtra. The program establishes, through self-selection, the right of up to 100 days of employment at the statutory minimum wage for every household that volunteers. Households do not have to demonstrate need, and some wages are paid even if work cannot be provided.

The program makes provision for at least a third of the work to be available to women, on-site child care, and medical insurance for work injuries; work must be provided promptly and within five kilometers of the household where possible. The operation is transparent with lists of works and contractors publicly available and on the program's Web site, allowing public oversight against corruption and inefficiency. Since the program's inception in 2005, 45 million households have contributed 2 billion days of labor and undertaken 3 million tasks.[a]

With appropriate guidance, the program can support climate-smart development. It operates at scale and can direct significant labor toward appropriate adaptive works, including water conservation, catchment protection, and plantations. It provides funds for tools and other items necessary to complete activities and technical support for designing and implementing the projects. It can thus become a core part of village development through productive, climate-resilient asset creation and maintenance.[b]

Sources:

a. National Rural Employment Guarantee Act—2005, http://nrega.nic.in/ (accessed May 2009).

b. CSE India, http://www.cseindia.org/programme/nrml/update_january08.htm (accessed May 15, 2009); CSE 2007.

---

analyses of whether exposure will lead them to migrate.[139]) Adaptation, such as coastal protection, will offset climate impacts and reduce migration.[140]

Today's movements are a crude guide to the geography of movements in the near future (box 2.12). Migration related to climate change is likely to be predominantly from rural areas in developing countries to towns and cities. Policies to facilitate migration should consider that most of the world's migrants move within their own countries and that the migration routes used by economic and involuntary migrants overlap significantly.

Little evidence suggests that migration caused by climate change provokes or exaggerates conflict, but that could change. People migrating because of environmental changes are likely disempowered, with little capacity to wage conflict.[141] Where migration coincides with conflict, the relationship may not be causal.[142] Similarly, the link between violent conflict and resource scarcity (water wars)[143] or degradation has rarely been substantiated (poverty and dysfunctional institutions have more explanatory power).[144] But uncertainty about the causal chains does not imply that future climate-induced migration would not increase the potential for conflict when coinciding with pressure on resources, food insecurity, catastrophic events, and lack of governance in the receiving region.[145]

The negative portrayal of migration can foster policies that seek to reduce and control its incidence and do little to address the needs of those who migrate, when migration may be the only option for those affected by climate hazards. Indeed, policies designed to restrict migration rarely succeed, are often self-defeating, and increase the costs to migrants and to communities of origin and destination.[146] In facilitating migration as a response to climate impacts, it is better to formulate integrated migration and development policies that address the needs of voluntary migrants and support their entrepreneurial abilities and technical skills.

To the extent possible, policies should discourage settlement of migrants in areas with high exposure to persistent climate hazards (map 2.6). Between 1995 and 2005, 3 million people were displaced by civil unrest in Colombia, mostly to small or mid-sized cities. Many have moved to marginal city areas prone to flooding or landslides or near waste dumps, while their lack of education and job skills leaves them earning only 40 percent of the minimum salary.[147] Anticipating involuntary migration and resettlement, forward-looking plans should identify alternative sites, apply compensation formulas that allow migrants to relocate and develop new sources of livelihoods, and build public and social infrastructure for community life. Again, such policies

BOX 2.12 *Migration today*

The estimates of climate-change-induced migration are highly uncertain and ambiguous. In the short term climate stress is likely to add incrementally to existing migration patterns (map at left) rather than generating entirely new flows of people. The majority of the world's migrants move within their own countries. For example, there are nearly as many internal migrants in China alone (about 130 million) as there are international migrants in all countries (estimated to be 175 million in 2000). Most internal migrants are economic migrants, moving from rural to urban areas. There is also significant, if poorly estimated, rural-rural migration, which tends to smooth demand and supply in rural labor markets, and which serves as a step in the migration path of rural migrants.

International migration is largely a phenomenon in the developed world. Of international migrants, about two-thirds move between developed countries. The growth in new arrivals is higher in the developed than the developing countries,

and about half of all international migrants are women. Half of the world's international migrants originate from 20 countries. Less than 10 percent of the world's international migrants are people forced to cross an international border for fear of persecution (the definition of refugees). Many forced migrants, however, fall under the definition of internally displaced persons (map at right), estimated to number 26 million people globally. The routes and intermediaries used by migrants fleeing conflicts, ethnic strife, and human rights violations are increasingly the same as those used by economic migrants. The available international statistics do not allow a specific attribution of internal displacement due to environmental degradation or natural disasters, but most of the forced migration linked to climate change is likely to remain internal and regional.

Migration flows are not random, but patterned, with flows of migrants concentrating around places where existing migrants have demonstrated that a life can be established and can help future

migrants to overcome the barriers to movement. These patterns are largely explained by barriers to movement and the requirements to overcome them. Barriers include financial ones as the costs of transport, housing on arrival, and living expenses while developing new income streams. Observations suggest that there is a "migration hump," where the rate of migration from a community increases as incomes rise beyond a level necessary to meet subsistence needs, and then decreases again as the gap between incomes at the place of origin and the main destination closes. The migration hump explains why the poorest of the poor do not migrate or migrate only very short distances.

Sources: Tuñón 2006; World Bank 2008f; United Nations 2005; United Nations 2006; Migration DRC 2007; de Haas 2008; Lucas 2006; Sorensen, van Hear, and Engberg-Pedersen 2003; Amin 1995; Lucas 2006; Lucas 2005; Massey and Espana 1987; de Haan 2002; Kolmannskog 2008.

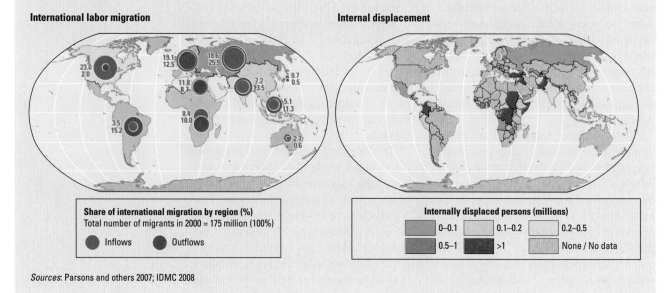

Sources: Parsons and others 2007; IDMC 2008

stand in sharp contrast to many ongoing efforts to address the needs of involuntary migrants and refugees—whether they are internally displaced or cross international borders.

Recent experience has suggested some lessons for resettling migrants. The first is to involve the communities to be resettled

in planning the move and in reconstruction—and to rely as little as possible on outside contractors and agencies. Those being resettled must receive compensation at the standards and prices in the receiving region, and they should be involved in the design and construction of infrastructure in the new location. Where possible, the

Map 2.6   Senegalese migrants settle in flood-prone areas around urban Dakar

Population change between 1999 and 2008 (number of inhabitants/pixel)

<0	0–50	51–100	101–250	251–500	>500

Flood risk

Low   Medium   High   Very high flood risk

Source: Geoville Group 2009.

Note: Slow economic growth in the agricultural sector has made Dakar the destination of an exodus from the rest of the country. Forty percent of Dakar's new inhabitants between 1988 and 2008 have moved into zones of high flood potential, twice as high as that of Dakar's urban (19 percent) and rural communes (23 percent). Because urban expansion is geographically limited, the influx of migrants has resulted in a very high concentration of people in urban and peri-urban zones (in the map, 16 pixels constitute one square kilometer).

decision-making structures in the community being resettled should be respected to the fullest extent.

Looking ahead to 2050: Which world?

A recurring theme of this Report is that the inertia in social, climate, and biological systems supports the case for action now. Some children alive today will be in leadership positions in 2050. On a path to a 2°C warmer world, they will face dramatic changes. However, managing these changes will be but one of their many challenges. Heading toward a 5°C warmer world, the outlook will be far more dismal. It will be clear that mitigation efforts over more than half a century have been inadequate. Climate change will not be simply one of many challenges—it will be the dominant challenge.

"I would like to reach out to our world leaders to help initiate educational awareness and local government efforts to empower children to protect and restore the environment. Social and Political Institutions must respond and adapt strategies to protect public health, particularly for children. As a fifth grader, I think these are possible ways in order to ensure the survival of our Mother Earth."

—Dave Laurence A. Juntilla, Philippines, age 11

Raisa Kabir, Bangladesh, age 10

Notes

1. WRI and others 2008; Heltberg, Siegel, and Jorgensen 2009.

2. Tompkins and Adger 2004.

3. Enfors and Gordon 2008.

4. The first is approximately the B1 SRES scenario where the world is on track to stabilization of greenhouse gases at 450–550 ppm CO_2e and eventually a temperature of about 2.5°C above preindustrial levels, and the second where emissions are significantly higher is approximately the A1B SRES scenario, which would lead to stabilization at about 1,000 ppm and eventually temperatures about 5°C above preindustrial levels; see Solomon and others 2007.

5. Horton and others 2008; Parry and others 2007; Rahmstorf and others 2007.

6. Allan and Soden 2008.

7. WBGU 2008.

8. Adger and others 2008.

9. Repetto 2008.

10. Lempert and Schlesinger 2000.

11. Keim 2008.

12. Millennium Ecosystem Assessment 2005.

13. Ribot, forthcoming.

14. Lempert and Schlesinger 2000; Lempert 2007.

15. Lewis 2007.

16. Lempert and Schlesinger 2000; Lempert and Collins 2007.

17. Bazerman 2006.

18. Groves and Lempert 2007.

19. Ward and others 2008.

20. Hallegatte 2009.

21. Pahl-Wostl 2007; Brunner and others 2005; Tompkins and Adger 2004; Folke and others 2002.

22. Cumming, Cumming, and Redman 2006.

23. Olsson, Folke, and Berkes 2004; Folke and others 2005; Dietz, Ostrom, and Stern 2003.

24. Dietz and Stern 2008.

25. Ligeti, Penney, and Wieditz 2007.

26. Pahl-Wostl 2007.

27. FAO and CIFOR 2005.

28. United Nations 2008b.

29. United Nations 2008a.

30. Balk, McGranahan, and Anderson 2008. Low-elevation coastal zones are defined as coastal land below 10 meters elevation; see Socioeconomic Data and Application Center, http://sedac.ciesin.columbia.edu/gpw/lecz.jsp (accessed January 8, 2009).

31. McGranahan, Balk, and Anderson 2007.

32. The net migration rate in Shanghai has been 4–8 percent, compared with approximately minus 2 percent attributable to natural growth between 1995 and 2006; see United Nations 2008a.

33. Nicholls and others 2008.

34. Simms and Reid 2006.

35. World Bank 2008a.

36. Seo 2009.

37. World Bank 2008g.

38. World Bank 2008g.

39. Using a $2.15 a day poverty line; see Ravallion, Chen, and Sangraula 2007.

40. United Nations 2008a.

41. Satterthwaite 2008.

42. Díaz Palacios and Miranda 2005.

43. Pelling 1997.

44. World Bank 2008c.

45. Hara, Takeuchi, and Okubo 2005.

46. Bates and others 2008.

47. World Bank 2008a.

48. Satterthwaite and others 2007.

49. McEvoy, Lindley, and Handley 2006.

50. Laryea-Adjei 2000.

51. Confalonieri and others 2007.

52. Only includes major cause-specific mortality and excludes indirect effects and morbidity; see McMichael and others 2004; Global Humanitarian Forum 2009.

53. World Bank 2008b.

54. Robine and others 2008.

55. Solomon and others 2007; Luber and McGeehin 2008.

56. Corburn 2009.

57. Fay, Block, and Ebinger 2010.

58. Gallup and Sachs 2001.

59. Hay and others 2006; this estimation only accounts for the expansion of the disease vector; population growth will compound this effect and increase the population at risk by 390 million people (or 60 percent) relative to the 2005 population baseline.

60. Hales and others 2002; without climate change only 35 percent of the projected global population in 2085 would be at risk.

61. WHO 2008; de la Torre, Fajnzylber, and Nash 2008.

62. Keiser and others 2004.

63. Rogers and others 2002.

64. World Climate Programme 2007.

65. WHO 2005; Frumkin and McMichael 2008.

66. Better sanitation and hygiene are good for health, as evidenced by the impact of sanitation improvements on urban child health in Salvador, Brazil, a city with 2.4 million people. The program reduced the prevalence of diarrheal diseases by 22 percent across the city in 2003–04 and by 43 percent in high-risk communities. The improvements were mostly attributable to new infrastructure (Barreto and others 2007).

67. AMWA 2007.

68. Galiani, Gertler, and Schargrodsky 2005.

69. Richmond 2008.

70. A growing body of evidence suggests that existing disaster loss data miss most of the small events that may account for as much as a quarter of deaths attributed to natural hazards, and that decision makers in many municipalities have relatively low awareness of the risks climate change poses for their cities' populations and infrastructure; see Awuor, Orindi, and Adwera 2008; Bull-Kamanga and others 2003; Roberts 2008.

71. Hoeppe and Gurenko 2006.

72. United Nations 2009.

73. United Nations 2008a.

74. International Strategy for Disaster Reduction, http://www.unisdr.org/eng/hfa/hfa.htm (accessed March 12, 2009).

75. World Economic Forum 2008.

76. Milly and others 2002.

77. The Nameless Hurricane, http://science.nasa.gov/headlines/y2004/02apr_hurricane.htm (accessed March 12, 2009).

78. Ranger, Muir-Wood, and Priya 2009.

79. An example is the information services provided by the Scottish Environment Protection Agency, www.sepa.org.uk/flooding (accessed March 12, 2009).

80. Lin 2008.

81. Ghesquiere, Jamin, and Mahul 2006.

82. Ferguson 2005.

83. Linnerooth-Bayer and Mechler 2006.

84. Mills 2007.

85. Manuamorn 2007; Giné, Townsend, and Vickery 2008; World Bank 2008e.

86. Hochrainer and others 2008.

87. Christen and Pearce 2005.

88. Llanto, Geron, and Almario 2007.

89. Kunreuther and Michel-Kerjan 2007; Tol 1998.

90. World Bank 2005.

91. Mills 2005; Dlugolecki 2008; ABI 2004.

92. Skees 2001.

93. This raises important issues: land-use regulation and codes are required and need to be enforced. Mandatory insurance may be required by law in high-risk areas. There are also equity concerns: what to do with people who have lived in high-risk areas all along but cannot afford true risk-based premiums?

94. Kunreuther and Michel-Kerjan 2007.

95. Cummins and Mahul 2009.

96. See Cardenas and others 2007 for an example of the use of market instruments for sovereign financial risk management for natural disasters in Mexico.

97. Mechler and others 2009.

98. World Bank to Offer Index-based Weather Derivative Contracts, http://go.worldbank.org/9GXG8E4GP1 (accessed May 15, 2009).

99. Government of Bangladesh 2008.

100. Bankoff, Frerks, and Hilhorst 2004.

101. Dercon 2004.

102. Alderman, Hoddinott, and Kinsey 2006; Bartlett 2008; UNICEF 2008; del Ninno and Lundberg 2005.

103. Francis and Amuyunzu-Nyamongo 2008; Nelson and others 2002.

104. Ensor and Berger 2009; Goulden and others 2009; Gaillard 2007.

105. Adger and others 2005; Orlove, Chiang, and Cane 2000; Srinivasan 2004; Wilbanks and Kates 1999.

106. Stringer and others, forthcoming; Twomlow and others 2008.

107. Nelson, Adger, and Brown 2007.

108. Walker and others 2006.

109. Gaiha, Imai, and Kaushik 2001; Martin and Prichard 2009.

110. Gibbs 2009.

111. Adger 2003.

112. Berkes and Jolly 2002.

113. Macchi 2008; Tebtebba Foundation 2008.

114. Costello, Gaines, and Lynham 2008.

115. Pomeroy and Pido 1995.

116. Chhatre and Agrawal, forthcoming.

117. Ostrom 1990; Berkes 2007; Agrawal and Ostrom 2001; Larson and Soto 2008.

118. Sobrevila 2008; White and Martin 2002.

119. Bandura 1977; Levitt and March 1988; Ellison and Fudenberg 1993; Ellison and Fudenberg 1995.

120. Granovetter 1978; Kanaiaupuni 2000; Portes and Sensenbrenner 1993.

121. Buskens and Yamaguchi 1999; Rogers 1995.

122. Foskett and Helmsley-Brown 2001.

123. Gillespie 2004.

124. World Bank 2009.

125. Ivanic and Martin 2008.

126. Grosh and others 2008.

127. Lobell and others 2008.

128. Kanbur 2009; Ravallion 2008.

129. Grosh and others 2008.

130. Grosh and others 2008; Alderman and Haque 2006.

131. Famine Early Warning Systems Network, www.fews.net (accessed May 15, 2009).

132. Alderman and Haque 2006; Vakis 2006.

133. Hess, Wiseman, and Robertson 2006.

134. del Ninno, Subbarao, and Milazzo 2009.

135. IEG 2008; Komives and others 2005.

136. World Bank 2008d.

137. World Bank 2006.

138. Myers 2002; Christian Aid 2007.
139. Barnett and Webber 2009.
140. Black 2001; Anthoff and others 2006.
141. Gleditsch, Nordås, and Salehyan 2007.
142. Reuveny 2007.
143. Barnaby 2009.
144. Theisen 2008; Nordås and Gleditsch 2007.
145. WBGU 2008; Campbell and others 2007.
146. de Haas 2008.
147. Bartlett and others 2009.

References

ABI (Association of British Insurers). 2004. *A Changing Climate for Insurance: A Summary Report for Chief Executives and Policymakers.* London: ABI.

Adger, W. N. 2003. "Social Capital, Collective Action, and Adaptation to Climate Change." *Economic Geography* 79 (4): 387–404.

Adger, W. N., S. Dessai, M. Goulden, M. Hulme, I. Lorenzoni, D. R. Nelson, L. O. Naess, J. Wolf, and A. Wreford. 2008. "Are There Social Limits to Adaptation to Climate Change?" *Climatic Change* 93 (3–4): 335–54.

Adger, W. N., T. P. Hughes, C. Folke, S. R. Carpenter, and J. Rockstrom. 2005. "Social-ecological Resilience to Coastal Disasters." *Science* 309 (5737): 1036–39.

Agrawal, A., and E. Ostrom. 2001. "Collective Action, Property Rights, and Decentralization in Resource Use in India and Nepal." *Politics and Society* 29 (4): 485–514.

Alderman, H., and T. Haque. 2006. "Counter-cyclical Safety Nets for the Poor and Vulnerable." *Food Policy* 31 (4): 372–83.

Alderman, H., J. Hoddinott, and B. Kinsey. 2006. "Long Term Consequences of Early Childhood Malnutrition." *Oxford Economic Papers* 58 (3): 450–74.

Allan, R. P., and B. J. Soden. 2008. "Atmospheric Warming and the Amplification of Extreme Precipitation Events." *Science* 321: 1481–84.

Amin, S. 1995. "Migrations in Contemporary Africa: A Retrospective View." In *The Migration Experience in Africa*, ed. J. Baker and T. A. Aina. Uppsala: Nordic Africa Institute.

AMWA (Association of Metropolitan Water Agencies). 2007. *Implications of Climate Change for Urban Water Utilities.* Washington, DC: AMWA.

Anthoff, D., R. J. Nicholls, R. S. J. Tol, and A. T. Vafeidis. 2006. "Global and Regional Exposure to Large Rises in Sea-level: A Sensitivity Analysis." Research Working Paper 96, Tyndall Center for Climate Change, Norwich, UK.

Awuor, C. B., V. A. Orindi, and A. Adwera. 2008. "Climate Change and Coastal Cities: The Case of Mombasa, Kenya." *Environment and Urbanization* 20 (1): 231–42.

Balk, D., G. McGranahan, and B. Anderson. 2008. "Urbanization and Ecosystems: Current Patterns and Future Implications." In *The New Global Frontier: Urbanization, Poverty and Environment in the 21st Century,* ed. G. Martine, G. McGranahan, M. Montgomery, and R. Fernandez-Castilla. London: Earthscan.

Bandura, A. 1977. *Social Learning Theory.* New York: General Learning Press.

Bankoff, G., G. Frerks, and D. Hilhorst. 2004. *Mapping Vulnerability: Disasters, Development and People.* London: Earthscan.

Barnaby, W. 2009. "Do Nations Go to War over Water?" *Nature* 458: 282–83.

Barnett, J., and M. Webber. 2009. *Accommodating Migration to Promote Adaptation to Climate Change.* Stockholm: Commission on Climate Change and Development.

Barreto, M. L., B. Genser, A. Strina, A. M. Assis, R. F. Rego, C. A. Teles, M. S. Prado, S. M. Matos, D. N. Santos, L. A. dos Santos, and S. Cairncross. 2007. "Effect of City-wide Sanitation Programme on Reduction in Rate of Childhood Diarrhoea in Northeast Brazil: Assessment by Two Cohort Studies." *Lancet* 370: 1622–28.

Bartlett, S. 2008. "Climate Change and Urban Children: Impacts and Implications for Adaptation in Low and Middle Income Countries." *Environment and Urbanization* 20 (2): 501–19.

Bartlett, S., D. Dodman, J. Haroy, D. Satterthwaite, and C. Tacoli. 2009. "Social Aspects of Climate Change in Low and Middle Income Nations." Paper presented at the Cities and Climate Change: Responding to an Urgent Agenda. World Bank Fifth Urban Research Symposium, Marseille, June 28–30.

Bates, B., Z. W. Kundzewicz, S. Wu, and J. Palutikof. 2008. "Climate Change and Water." Technical paper, Intergovernmental Panel on Climate Change, Geneva.

Bazerman, M. H. 2006. "Climate Change as a Predictable Surprise." *Climatic Change* 77: 179–93.

Benson, C., and J. Twigg. 2007. *Tools for Main-streaming Disaster Risk Reduction: Guidance Notes for Development Organizations*. Geneva: ProVention Consortium.

Berkes, F. 2007. "Understanding Uncertainty and Reducing Vulnerability: Lessons from Resilience Thinking." *Natural Hazards* 41 (2): 283–95.

Berkes, F., and D. Jolly. 2002. "Adapting to Climate Change: Social Ecological Resilience in a Canadian Western Arctic Community." *Ecology and Society* 5 (2): 18.

Bigio, A. G. 2008. "Concept Note: Adapting to Climate Change in the Coastal Cities of North Africa." World Bank, Middle East and Northern Africa Region, Washington, DC.

Black, R. 2001. "Environmental Refugees: Myth or Reality?" New Issues in Refugee Research Working Paper 34, United Nations High Commissioner for Refugees, Geneva.

Botoni, E., and C. Reij. 2009. "La Transformation Silencieuse de l'Environnement et des Systèmes de Production au Sahel : Impacts des Investissements Publics et Privés dans la Gestion des Ressources Naturelles." Technical report, Free University Amsterdam and Comité Permanent Inter-États de Lutte contre la Sécheresse dans le Sahel (CILSS), Ouagadougou, Burkina Faso.

Brunner, R. D., T. A. Steelman, L. Coe-Juell, C. M. Cromley, C. M. Edwards, and D. W. Tucker. 2005. *Adaptive Governance: Integrating Science, Policy, and Decisions Making*. New York: Columbia University Press.

Bull-Kamanga, L., K. Diagne, A. Lavell, F. Lerise, H. MacGregor, A. Maskrey, M. Meshack, M. Pelling, H. Reid, D. Satterthwaite, J. Songsore, K. Westgate, and A. Yitambe. 2003. "Urban Development and the Accumulation of Disaster Risk and Other Life-Threatening Risks in Africa." *Environment and Urbanization* 15 (1): 193–204.

Buskens, V., and K. Yamaguchi. 1999. "A New Model for Information Diffusion in Heterogeneous Social Networks." *Socio-logical Methodology* 29 (1): 281–325.

Campbell, K. M., J. Gulledge, J. R. McNeill, J. Podesta, P. Ogden, L. Fuerth, R. J. Woolsey, A. T. J. Lennon, J. Smith, R. Weitz, and D. Mix. 2007. *The Age of Consequences: The Foreign Policy and National Security Implications of Global Climate Change*. Washington, DC: Center for a New American Security and the Center for Strategic and International Studies.

Cardenas, V., S. Hochrainer, R. Mechler, G. Pflug, and J. Linnerooth-Bayer. 2007. "Sovereign Financial Disaster Risk Management: The Case of Mexico." *Environmental Hazards* 7 (1): 40–53.

CatSalut. 2008. *Action Plan to Prevent the Effects of a Heat Wave on Health*. Barcelona: Generalitat de Catalunya Departament de Salut.

Chhatre, A., and A. Agrawal. Forthcoming. "Carbon Storage and Livelihoods Generation through Improved Governance of Forest Commons." *Science*.

Christen, R. P., and D. Pearce. 2005. *Managing Risks and Designing Products for Agricultural Microfinance: Feature of an Emerging Model*. Washington, DC: CGAP; Rome: IFAD.

Christian Aid. 2007. *Human Tide: The Real Migration Crisis*. London: Christian Aid.

CIESIN (Center for International Earth Science Information Network). 2005. "Gridded Population of the World (GPWv3)." CIESIN, Columbia University, and Centro Internacional de Agricultura Tropical, Palisades, NY.

Confalonieri, U., B. Menne, R. Akhtar, K. L. Ebi, M. Hauengue, R. S. Kovats, B. Revich, and A. Woodward. 2007. "Human Health." In *Climate Change 2007: Impacts, Adaptation and Vulnerability. Contribution of Working Group II to the Fourth Assessment Report of the Intergovernmental Panel on Climate Change*, ed. M. L. Parry, O. F. Canziani, J. P. Palutikof, P. J. van der Linden, and C. E. Hanson. Cambridge, UK: Cambridge University Press.

Corburn, J. 2009. "Cities, Climate Change and Urban Heat Island Mitigation: Localising Global Environmental Science." *Urban Studies* 46 (2): 413–27.

Costello, C., S. D. Gaines, and J. Lynham. 2008. "Can Catch Shares Prevent Fisheries Collapse?" *Science* 321 (5896): 1678–81.

CRED (Centre for Research on the Epidemiology of Disasters). 2009. "EM-DAT: The International Emergency Disasters Database." CRED, Université Catholique de Louvain, Ecole de Santé Publique, Louvain.

CSE (Center for Science and Environment). 2007. "An Ecological Act: A Backgrounder to the National Rural Employment Guarantee Act (NREGA)," CSE, New Delhi.

Cumming, G. S., D. H. M. Cumming, and C. L. Redman. 2006. "Scale Mismatches in Social-Ecological Systems: Causes, Consequences, and Solutions." *Ecology and Society* 11 (1): 14.

Cummins, J. D., and O. Mahul. 2009. *Catastrophe Risk Financing in Developing Countries. Principles for Public Intervention.* Washington, DC: World Bank.

Dartmouth Flood Observatory. 2009. "Global Active Archive of Large Flood Events." Dartmouth College, Hanover, NH. Available at www.dartmouth.edu/~floods. Accessed January 19, 2009.

de Haan, A. 2002. "Migration and Livelihoods in Historical Perspectives: A Case Study of Bihar, India." *Journal of Development Studies* 38 (5): 115–42.

de Haas, H. 2008. "The Complex Role of Migration in Shifting Rural Livelihoods: A Moroccan Case Study." In *Global Migration and Development,* ed. T. van Naerssen, E. Spaan, and A. Zoomers. London: Routledge.

de la Torre, A., P. Fajnzylber, and J. Nash. 2008. *Low Carbon, High Growth: Latin American Responses to Climate Change.* Washington, DC: World Bank.

del Ninno, C., and M. Lundberg. 2005. "Treading Water: The Long-term Impact of the 1998 Flood on Nutrition in Bangladesh." *Economics and Human Biology* 3 (1): 67–96.

del Ninno, C., K. Subbarao, and A. Milazzo. 2009. "How to Make Public Works Work: A Review of the Experiences." Discussion Paper 0905, Social Protection and Labor, World Bank, Washington, DC.

Dercon, S. 2004. *Insurance against Poverty.* Oxford, UK: Oxford University Press.

Díaz Palacios, J., and L. Miranda. 2005. "Concertación (Reaching Agreement) and Planning for Sustainable Development in Ilo, Peru." In *Reducing Poverty and Sustaining the Environment: The Politics of Local Engagement,* ed. S. Bass, H. Reid, D. Satterthwaite, and P. Steele. London: Earthscan.

Dietz, T., E. Ostrom, and P. C. Stern. 2003. "The Struggle to Govern the Commons." *Science* 302 (5652): 1907–12.

Dietz, T., and P. C. Stern, eds. 2008. *Public Participation in Environmental Assessment and Decision Making.* Washington, DC: National Academies Press.

Dlugolecki, A. 2008. "Climate Change and the Insurance Sector." *Geneva Papers on Risk and Insurance—Issues and Practice* 33 (1): 71–90.

Ellison, G., and D. Fudenberg. 1993. "Rules of Thumb for Social Learning." *Journal of Political Economy* 101 (4): 612–43.

———. 1995. "Word-of-Mouth Communication and Social Learning." *Quarterly Journal of Economics* 110 (1): 93–125.

Enfors, E. I., and L. J. Gordon. 2008. "Dealing with Drought: The Challenge of Using Water System Technologies to Break Dryland Poverty Traps." *Global Environmental Change* 18 (4): 607–16.

Ensor, J., and R. Berger. 2009. "Community-Based Adaptation and Culture in Theory and Practice." In *Adapting to Climate Change: Thresholds, Values, Governance,* ed. N. Adger, I. Lorenzoni, and K. L. O'Brien. Cambridge, UK: Cambridge University Press.

ESA (European Space Agency). 2002. *Sustainable Development: The Space Contribution: From Rio to Johannesburg—Progress Over the Last 10 Years.* Paris: ESA for the Committee on Earth Observation Satellites.

Fankhauser, S., N. Martin, and S. Prichard. Forthcoming. "The Economics of the CDM Levy: Revenue Potential, Tax Incidence, and Distortionary Effects." Working Paper, London School of Economics.

FAO (Food and Agriculture Organization) and CIFOR (Center for International Forestry Research). 2005. "Forests and Floods: Drowning In Fiction or Thriving On Facts?" FAO Regional Office for Asia and the Pacific Publication 2005/03, Bangkok.

Fay, M., R. I. Block, and J. Ebinger, eds. 2010. *Adapting to Climate Change in Europe and Central Asia.* Washington, DC: World Bank.

Ferguson, N. 2005. *Mozambique: Disaster Risk Management Along the Rio Búzi. Case Study on the Background, Concept, and Implementation of Disaster Risk Management in the Context of the GTZ-Programme for Rural Development (PRODER).* Duren: German Gesellschaft für Technische Zusammenarbeit, Governance and Democracy Division.

Folke, C., S. Carpenter, T. Elmqvist, L. Gunderson, C. S. Holling, B. Walker, J. Bengtsson, F. Berkes, J. Colding, K. Danell, M. Falkenmark, L. Gordon, R. Kasperson, N. Kautsky, A. Kinzig, S. Levin, K.-G. Mäler, F. Moberg, L. Ohlsson, P. Olsson, E. Ostrom, W. Reid, J. Rockström, H. Savenije, and U. Svedin. 2002. *Resilience and Sustainable Development: Building Adaptive Capacity in a World of Transformations.* Stockholm: Environmental Advisory Council to the Swedish Government.

Folke, C., T. Hahn, P. Olsson, and J. Norberg. 2005. "Adaptive Governance of Social-ecological Systems." *Annual Review of Environment and Resources* 30: 441–73.

Foskett, N., and J. Hemsley-Brown. 2001. *Choosing Futures: Young People's Decision-Making in Education, Training and Career Markets*. London: RoutledgeFalmer.

Francis, P., and M. Amuyunzu-Nyamongo. 2008. "Bitter Harvest: The Social Costs of State Failure in Rural Kenya." In *Assets, Livelihoods, and Social Policy,* ed. C. Moser and A. A. Dani. Washington, DC: World Bank.

Frumkin, H., and A. J. McMichael. 2008. "Climate Change and Public Health: Thinking, Communicating, Acting." *American Journal of Preventive Medicine* 35 (5): 403–10.

Gaiha, R., K. Imai, and P. D. Kaushik. 2001. "On the Targeting and Cost Effectiveness of Anti-Poverty Programmes in Rural India." *Development and Change* 32 (2): 309–42.

Gaillard, J.-C. 2007. "Resilience of Traditional Societies in Facing Natural Hazards." *Disaster Prevention and Management* 16 (4): 522–44.

Galiani, S., P. Gertler, and E. Schargrodsky. 2005. "Water for Life: The Impact of the Privatization of Water Services on Child Mortality." *Journal of Political Economy* 113 (1): 83–120.

Gallup, J. L., and J. D. Sachs. 2001. "The Economic Burden of Malaria." *American Journal of Tropical Medicine and Hygiene* 64 (1–2): 85–96.

Geoville Group. 2009. "Spatial Analysis of Natural Hazard and Climate Change Risks in Peri-Urban Expansion Areas of Dakar, Senegal." Paper presented at the World Bank Urban Week 2009. Washington, DC.

Ghesquiere, F., L. Jamin, and O. Mahul. 2006. "Earthquake Vulnerability Reduction Program in Colombia: A Probabilistic Cost-Benefit Analysis." Policy Research Working Paper 3939, World Bank, Washington, DC.

Gibbs, M. T. 2009. "Resilience: What Is It and What Does It Mean for Marine Policymakers?" *Marine Policy* 33 (2): 322–31.

Gillespie, S. 2004. "Scaling Up Community-Driven Development: A Synthesis of Experience." FCND Discussion Paper 181, Food Consumption and Nutrition Division, International Food Policy Research Institute, Washington, DC.

Giné, X., R. Townsend, and J. Vickery. 2008. "Patterns of Rainfall Insurance Participation in Rural India." *World Bank Economic Review* 22 (3): 539–66.

Girardet, H. 2008. *Cities People Planet: Urban Development and Climate Change*. 2nd ed. Chichester, UK: John Wiley & Sons.

Gleditsch, N., R. Nordås, and I. Salehyan. 2007. "Climate Change and Conflict: The Migration Link." Coping with Crisis Working Paper Series, International Peace Academy, New York (May).

Global Humanitarian Forum. 2009. *The Anatomy of A Silent Crisis*. Geneva: Global Humanitarian Forum.

Goulden, M., L. O. Naess, K. Vincent, and W. N. Adger. 2009. "Accessing Diversification, Networks and Traditional Resource Management as Adaptations to Climate Extremes." In *Adapting to Climate Change: Thresholds, Values, Governance,* ed. N. Adger, I. Lorenzoni, and K. O'Brien. Cambridge, UK: Cambridge University Press.

Government of Bangladesh. 2008. *Cyclone Sidr in Bangladesh: Damage, Loss and Needs Assessment for Disaster Recovery and Reconstruction*. Dhaka: Government of Bangladesh, World Bank, and the European Commission.

Granovetter, M. 1978. "Threshold Models of Collective Behavior." *American Journal of Sociology* 83 (6): 1420–43.

Grosh, M. E., C. del Ninno, E. Tesliuc, and A. Ouerghi. 2008. *For Protection and Promotion: The Design and Implementation of Effective Safety Nets*. Washington, DC: World Bank.

Groves, D. G., and R. J. Lempert. 2007. "A New Analytic Method for Finding Policy-Relevant Scenarios." *Global Environmental Change* 17 (1): 73–85.

Hales, S., N. de Wet, J. Maindonald, and A. Woodward. 2002. "Potential Effect of Population and Climate Changes on Global Distribution of Dengue Fever: An Emperical Model." *Lancet* 360: 830–34.

Hallegatte, S. 2009. "Strategies to Adapt to an Uncertain Climate Change." *Global Environmental Change* 19 (2): 240–47.

Hara, Y., K. Takeuchi, and S. Okubo. 2005. "Urbanization Linked with Past Agricultural Landuse Patterns in the Urban Fringe of a Deltaic Asian Mega-City: A Case Study in Bangkok." *Landscape and Urban Planning* 73 (1): 16–28.

Hay, S. I., A. J. Tatem, C. A. Guerra, and R. W. Snow. 2006. *Population at Malaria Risk in Africa: 2005, 2015, and 2030*. London: Centre for Geographic Medicine, KEMRI/Welcome Trust Collaborative Programme, University of Oxford.

Heltberg, R., P. B. Siegel, and S. L. Jorgensen. 2009. "Addressing Human Vulnerability to Climate Change: Toward a 'No-Regrets'

Approach." *Global Environmental Change* 19 (1): 89–99.

Herrmann, S. M., A. Anyamba, and C. J. Tucker. 2005. "Recent Trends in Vegetation Dynamics in the African Sahel and Their Relationship to Climate." *Global Environmental Change* 15 (4): 394–404.

Hess, U., W. Wiseman, and T. Robertson. 2006. *Ethiopia: Integrated Risk Financing to Protect Livelihoods and Foster Development.* Rome: World Food Programme.

Hochrainer, S., R. Mechler, G. Pflug, and A. Lotsch. 2008. "Investigating the Impact of Climate Change on the Robustness of Index-Based Microinsurance in Malawi." Policy Research Working Paper 4631, World Bank, Washington, DC.

Hoeppe, P., and E. N. Gurenko. 2006. "Scientific and Economic Rationales for Innovative Climate Insurance Solutions." *Climate Policy* 6: 607–20.

Horton, R., C. Herweijer, C. Rosenzweig, J. Liu, V. Gornitz, and A. C. Ruane. 2008. "Sea Level Rise Projections for Current Generation CGCMs Based on the Semi-Empirical Method." *Geophysical Research Letters* 35:L02715. DOI:10.1029/2007GL032486.

IDMC (Internal Displacement Monitoring Centre). 2008. *Internal Displacement: Global Overview of Trends and Developments in 2008.* Geneva: IDMC.

IEG (Independent Evaluation Group). 2008. *Climate Change and the World Bank Group-Phase I: An Evaluation of World Bank Win-Win Energy Policy Reforms.* Washington, DC: IEG Knowledge Programs and Evaluation Capacity Development.

Ivanic, M., and W. Martin. 2008. "Implications of Higher Global Food Prices for Poverty in Low-Income Countries." Policy Research Working Paper 4594, World Bank, Washington, DC.

Kanaiaupuni, S. M. 2000. "Reframing the Migration Question: An Analysis of Men, Women, and Gender in Mexico." *Social Forces* 78 (4): 1311–47.

Kanbur, R. 2009. "Macro Crises and Targeting Transfers to the Poor." Cornell University, Ithaca, NY.

Keim, M. E. 2008. "Building Human Resilience: The Role of Public Health Preparedness and Response as an Adaptation to Climate Change." *American Journal of Preventive Medicine* 35 (5): 508–16.

Keiser, J., J. Utzinger, M. C. Castro, T. A. Smith, M. Tanner, and B. H. Singer. 2004. "Urbanization in Sub-Saharan Africa and Implications for Malaria Control." *American Journal of Tropical Medicine and Hygiene* 71 (S2): 118–27.

Knowlton, K., G. Solomon, and M. Rotkin-Ellman. 2009. "Fever Pitch: Mosquito-Borne Dengue Fever Threat Spreading in The Americas." Issue Paper, Natural Resources Defense Council, New York (July).

Kolmannskog, V. O. 2008. *Future Floods of Refugees: A Comment on Climate Change, Conflict and Forced Migration.* Oslo: Norwegian Refugee Council.

Komives, K., V. Foster, J. Halpern, Q. Wodon, and R. Abdullah. 2005. *Water, Electricity, and the Poor: Who Benefits from Utility Subsidies?* Washington, DC: World Bank.

Kopf, S., M. Ha-Duong, and S. Hallegatte. 2008. "Using Maps of City Analogues to Display and Interpret Climate Change Scenarios and Their Uncertainty." *Natural Hazards and Earth System Science* 8 (4): 905–18.

Kunreuther, H., and E. Michel-Kerjan. 2007. "Climate Change, Insurability of Large-Scale Disasters and the Emerging Liability Challenge." Working Paper 12821, National Bureau of Economic Research, Cambridge, MA.

Larson, A., and F. Soto. 2008. "Decentralization of Natural Resource Governance Regimes." *Annual Review of Environment and Resources* 33: 213–39.

Laryea-Adjei, G. 2000. "Building Capacity for Urban Management in Ghana: Some Critical Considerations." *Habitat International* 24 (4): 391–402.

Laukkonen, J., P. K. Blanco, J. Lenhart, M. Keiner, B. Cavric, and C. Kinuthia-Njenga. 2009. "Combining Climate Change Adaptation and Mitigation Measures at the Local Level." *Habitat International* 33 (3): 287–92.

Lempert, R. J. 2007. "Creating Constituencies for Long-term Radical Change." Wagner Research Brief 2, New York University, New York.

Lempert, R. J., and M. T. Collins. 2007. "Managing the Risk of Uncertain Threshold Responses: Comparison of Robust, Optimum, and Precautionary Approaches." *Risk Analysis* 27 (4): 1009–26.

Lempert, R. J., and M. E. Schlesinger. 2000. "Robust Strategies for Abating Climate Change." *Climatic Change* 45 (3–4): 387–401.

Levitt, B., and J. G. March. 1988. "Organizational Learning." *Annual Review of Sociology* 14: 319–38.

Lewis, M. 2007. "In Nature's Casino." *New York Times Magazine,* August 26, 2007.

Ligeti, E., J. Penney, and I. Wieditz. 2007. *Cities Preparing for Climate Change: A Study of Six Urban Regions.* Toronto: The Clean Air Partnership.

Lin, H. 2008. *Proposal Report on Flood Hazard Mapping Project in Taihu Basin.* China: Taihu Basin Authority of Ministry of Water Resources.

Linnerooth-Bayer, J., and R. Mechler. 2006. "Insurance for Assisting Adaptation to Climate Change in Developing Countries: A Proposed Strategy." *Climate Policy* 6: 621–36.

Llanto, G. M., M. P. Geron, and J. Almario. 2007. "Developing Principles for the Regulation of Microinsurance (Philippine Case Study)." Discussion Paper 2007-26, Philippine Institute for Development Studies, Makati City.

Lobell, D. B., M. Burke, C. Tebaldi, M. D. Mastrandrea, W. P. Falcon, and R. L. Naylor. 2008. "Prioritizing Climate Change Adaptation Needs for Food Security in 2030." *Science* 319 (5863): 607–10.

Luber, G., and M. McGeehin. 2008. "Climate Change and Extreme Heat Events." *American Journal of Preventive Medicine* 35 (5): 429–35.

Lucas, R. E. B. 2005. *International Migration and Economic Development: Lessons from Low-Income Countries: Executive Summary.* Stockholm: Almkvist & Wiksell International, Expert Group on Development Issues.

———. 2006. "Migration and Economic Development in Africa: A Review of Evidence." *Journal of African Economies* 15 (2): 337–95.

Macchi, M. 2008. *Indigenous and Traditional People and Climate Change: Vulnerability and Adaptation.* Gland, Switzerland: International Union for Conservation of Nature.

Mahul, O., and J. Skees. 2007. "Managing Agricultural Risk at the Country Level: The Case of Index-based Livestock Insurance in Mongolia." Policy Research Working Paper 4325, World Bank, Washington, DC.

Manuamorn, O. P. 2007. "Scaling Up Microinsurance: The Case of Weather Insurance for Smallholders in India." Agriculture and Rural Development Discussion Paper 36, World Bank, Washington, DC.

Massey, D., and F. Espana. 1987. "The Social Process of Internationl Migration." *Science* 237 (4816): 733–38.

McEvoy, D., S. Lindley, and J. Handley. 2006. "Adaptation and Mitigation in Urban Areas: Synergies and Conflicts." *Proceedings of the Institution of Civil Engineers* 159 (4): 185–91.

McGranahan, G., D. Balk, and B. Anderson. 2007. "The Rising Tide: Assessing the Risks of Climate Change and Human Settlements in Low Elevation Coastal Zones." *Environment and Urbanization* 19 (1): 17–37.

McMichael, A., D. Campbell-Lendrum, S. Kovats, S. Edwards, P. Wilkinson, T. Wilson, R. Nicholls, S. Hales, F. Tanser, D. Le Sueur, M. Schlesinger, and N. Andronova. 2004. "Global Climate Change." In *Comparative Quantification of Health Risks: Global and Regional Burden of Disease Attributable to Selected Major Risk Factors,* vol. 2, ed. M. Ezzati, A. D. Lopez, A. Rodgers, and C. J. L. Murray. Geneva: World Health Organization.

Mearns, R. 2004. "Sustaining Livelihoods on Mongolia's Pastoral Commons: Insights from a Participatory Poverty Assessment." *Development and Change* 35 (1): 107–39.

Mechler, R., S. Hochrainer, G. Pflug, K. Williges, and A. Lotsch. 2009. "Assessing Financial Vulnerability to Climate-Related Natural Hazards." Background paper for the WDR 2010.

Mercy Corps. 2008. "Reducing Flood Risk through a Job Creation Scheme." In *Linking Disaster Risk Reduction and Poverty Reduction: Good Practices and Lessons Learned: 2008,* ed. Global Network of NGOs for Disaster Risk Reduction. Geneva: United Nations Development Programme and International Strategy for Disaster Reduction (ISDR).

Migration DRC. 2007. "Global Migrant Origin Database." Development Research Centre on Migration, Globalisation and Poverty, University of Sussex, Brighton.

Millennium Ecosystem Assessment. 2005. *Ecosystems and Human Well-Being: Synthesis.* Washington, DC: World Resources Institute.

Mills, E. 2005. "Insurance in a Climate of Change." *Science* 309 (5737): 1040–44.

———. 2007. "Synergism between Climate Change Mitigation and Adaptation: Insurance Perspective." *Mitigation and Adaptation Strategies for Global Change* 12: 809–42.

Milly, P. C. D., R. T. Wetherald, K. A. Dunne, and T. L. Delworth. 2002. "Increasing Risk of

Great Floods in a Changing Climate." *Nature* 415 (6871): 514–17.

Myers, N. 2002. "Environmental Refugees: A Growing Phenomenon of the 21st Century." *Philosophical Transactions of the Royal Society B* 357 (1420): 609–13.

NRC (National Research Council of the National Academies). 2006. *Facing Hazards and Disasters. Understanding Human Dimension.* Washington, DC: National Academies Press.

———. 2007a. *Contributions of Land Remote Sensing for Decisions about Food Security and Human Health.* Washington, DC: National Academies Press.

———. 2007b. *Earth Science and Application from Space: National Imperatives for the Next Decade and Beyond.* Washington, DC: National Academies Press.

Nelson, D. R., W. N. Adger, and K. Brown. 2007. "Adaptation to Environmental Change: Contributions of a Resilience Framework." *Annual Review of Environment and Resources* 32: 395–419.

Nelson, V., K. Meadows, T. Cannon, J. Morton, and A. Martin. 2002. "Uncertain Prediction, Invisible Impacts, and the Need to Mainstream Gender in Climate Change Adaptations." *Gender and Development* 10 (2): 51–59.

Nicholls, R. J., P. P. Wong, V. Burkett, C. D. Woodroffe, and J. Hay. 2008. "Climate Change and Coastal Vulnerability Assessment: Scenarios for Integrated Assessment." *Sustainability Science* 3 (1): 89–102.

Nordås, R., and N. Gleditsch. 2007. "Climate Change and Conflict." *Political Geography* 26 (6): 627–38.

Olsson, P., C. Folke, and F. Berkes. 2004. "Adaptive Comanagement for Building Resilience in Social-Ecological Systems." *Environmental Management* 34 (1): 75–90.

Orlove, B. S., J. H. Chiang, and M. A. Cane. 2000. "Forecasting Andean Rainfall and Crop Yield from the Influence of El Niño on Pleiades Visibility." *Nature* 403 (6765): 68–71.

Ostrom, E. 1990. *Governing the Commons: The Evolution of Institutions for Collective Action.* New York: Cambridge University Press.

Pahl-Wostl, C. 2007. "Transitions toward Adaptive Management of Water Facing Climate and Global Change." *Water Resources Management* 21: 49–62.

PAHO (Pan American Health Organization). 2009. "Dengue." Washington, DC, http://new.paho.org/hq/index.php?option=com_content&task=view&id=264&Itemid=363 (accessed July 2009).

Parry, M., O. F. Canziani, J. P. Palutikof, and others. 2007. "Technical Summary." In *Climate Change 2007: Impacts, Adaptation and Vulnerability. Contribution of Working Group II to the Fourth Assessment Report of the Intergovernmental Panel on Climate Change,* ed. M. Parry, O. F. Canziani, J. P. Palutikof, P. J. van der Linden, and C. E. Hanson. Cambridge, UK: Cambridge University Press.

Parsons, C. R., R. Skeldon, T. L. Walmsley, and L. A. Winters. 2007. "Quantifying International Migration: A Database of Bilateral Migrant Stocks." Policy Research Working Paper 4165, World Bank, Washington, DC.

Pelling, M. 1997. "What Determines Vulnerability to Floods: A Case Study in Georgetown, Guyana." *Environment and Urbanization* 9 (1): 203–26.

Pomeroy, R. S., and M. D. Pido. 1995. "Initiatives towards Fisheries Co-management in the Philippines: The Case of San Miguel Bay." *Marine Policy* 19 (3): 213–26.

Portes, A., and J. Sensenbrenner. 1993. "Embeddedness and Immigration: Notes on the Social Determinants of Economic Actions." *American Journal of Sociology* 98 (6): 13–20.

Raadgever, G. T., E. Mostert, N. Kranz, E. Interwies, and J. G. Timmerman. 2008. "Assessing Management Regimes in Transboundary River Basins: Do They Support Adaptive Management." *Ecology and Society* 13 (1): 14.

Rahmstorf, S., A. Cazenave, J. A. Church, J. E. Hansen, R. F. Keeling, D. E. Parker, and R. C. J. Somerville. 2007. "Recent Climate Observations Compared to Projections." *Science* 316 (5825): 709.

Ranger, N., R. Muir-Wood, and S. Priya. 2009. "Assessing Extreme Climate Hazards and Options for Risk Mitigation and Adaptation in the Developing World." Background paper for the WDR 2010.

Ravallion, M. 2008. "Bailing Out the World's Poorest." Policy Research Working Paper 4763, World Bank, Washington, DC.

Ravallion, M., S. Chen, and P. Sangraula. 2007. "New Evidence on the Urbanization of Poverty." Policy Research Working Paper 4199, World Bank, Washington, DC.

Repetto, R. 2008. "The Climate Crisis and the Adaptation Myth." Yale School of Forestry and Environmental Studies Working Paper 13, Yale University, New Haven, CT.

Reuveny, R. 2007. "Climate Change Induced Migration and Violent Conflict." *Political Geography* 26 (6): 656–73.

Ribot, J. C. Forthcoming. "Vulnerability Does Not Just Fall from the Sky: Toward Multi-Scale Pro-Poor Climate Policy." In *The Social Dimensions of Climate Change: Equity and Vulnerability in a Warming World,* ed. R. Mearns and A. Norton. Washington, DC: World Bank.

Richmond, T. 2008. "The Current Status and Future Potential of Personalized Diagnostics: Streamlining a Customized Process." *Biotechnology Annual Review* 14: 411–22.

Roberts, D. 2008. "Thinking Globally, Acting Locally: Institutionalizing Climate Change at the Local Government Level in Durban, South Africa." *Environment and Urbanization* 20 (2): 521–37.

Robine, J.-M., S. L. K. Cheung, S. Le Roy, H. Van Oyen, C. Griffiths, J.-P. Michel, and F. R. Herrmann. 2008. "Death Toll Exceeded 70,000 in Europe during the Summer of 2003." *Comptes Rendus Biologies* 331 (2): 171–78.

Rogers, D., S. E. Randolph, R. W. Snow, and S. I. Hay. 2002. "Satellite Imagery in the Study and Forecast of Malaria." *Nature* 415 (6872): 710–15.

Rogers, E. 1995. *Diffusion of Innovations.* New York: Free Press.

Roman, A. 2008. "Curitiba, Brazil." In *Encyclopedia of Earth—Environmental Information Coalition.* Washington, DC: National Council for Science and the Environment.

Satterthwaite, D. 2008. "The Social and Political Basis for Citizen Action on Urban Poverty Reduction." *Environment and Urbanization* 20 (2): 307–18.

Satterthwaite, D., S. Huq, M. Pelling, A. Reid, and R. Lankao. 2007. *Adapting to Climate Change in Urban Areas: The Possibilities and Constraints in Low and Middle Income Countries.* London: International Institutte for Environment and Development.

Seo, J.-K. 2009. "Balanced National Development Strategies: The Construction of Innovation Cities in Korea." *Land Use Policy* 26 (3): 649–61.

Simms, A., and H. Reid. 2006. *Up in Smoke? Latin America and the Caribbean: The Threat from Climate Chnage to the Environment and Human Development.* London: Working Group on Climate Change and Development, International Institute for Environment and Development, New Economics Foundation.

Skees, J. R. 2001. "The Bad Harvest: Crop Insurance Reform Has Become a Good Idea Gone Awry." *Regulation* 24 (1): 16–21.

Sobrevila, C. 2008. *The Role of Indigenous People in Biodiversity Conservation: The Natural but Often Forgotten Partners.* Washington, DC: World Bank.

Solomon, S., D. Qin, M. Manning, R. B. Alley, T. Berntsen, N. L. Bindoff, Z. Chen, A. Chidthaisong, J. M. Gregory, G. C. Hegerl, M. Heimann, B. Hewitson, B. J. Hoskins, F. Joos, J. Jouzel, V. Kattsov, U. Lohmann, T. Matsuno, M. Molina, N. Nicholls, J. Overpeck, G. Raga, V. Ramaswamy, J. Ren, M. Rusticucci, R. Somerville, T. F. Stocker, P. Whetton, R. A. Wood, and D. Wratt. 2007. "Technical Summary." In *Climate Change 2007: The Physical Science Basis. Contribution of Working Group I to the Fourth Assessment Report of the Intergovernmental Panel on Climate Change,* ed. S. Solomon, D. Qin, M. Manning, Z. Chen, M. Marquis, K. B. Averyt, M. Tignor, and H. L. Miller. Cambridge, UK: Cambridge University Press.

Sorensen, N., N. van Hear, and P. Engberg-Pedersen. 2003. "Migration, Development and Conflict: State-of-the-Art Overview." In *The Migration-Development Nexus,* ed. N. van Hear and N. Sorensen. New York and Geneva: United Nations and International Organization for Migration.

Srinivasan, A. 2004. "Local Knowledge for Facilitating Adaptation to Climate Change in Asia and the Pacific: Policy Implications." Working Paper 2004-002, Institute for Global Environmental Strategies, Kanagawa, Japan.

Stringer, L. C., J. C. Dyer, M. S. Reed, A. J. Dougill, C. Twyman, and D. Mkwambisi. Forthcoming. "Adaptations to Climate Change, Drought and Desertification: Local Insights to Enhance Policy in Southern Africa." *Environmental Science and Policy.*

Swiss Re. 2007. "World Insurance in 2006: Premiums Came Back to Life." Zurich: Sigma (April).

Tebtebba Foundation. 2008. *Guide on Climate Change and Indigenous Peoples.* Baguio City, the Philippines: Tebtebba Foundation.

Theisen, O. M. 2008. "Blood and Soil? Resource Scarcity and Internal Armed Conflict Revisited." *Journal of Peace Research* 45 (6): 801–18.

Tol, R. S. J. 1998. "Climate Change and Insurance: A Critical Appraisal." *Energy Policy* 26 (3): 257–62.

Tompkins, E. L., and W. N. Adger. 2004. "Does Adaptive Management of Natural Resources Enhance Resilience to Climate Change?" *Ecology and Society* 9 (2): 10.

Tuñón, M. 2006. *Internal Labour Migration in China*. Beijing: International Labour Organisation.

Twomlow, S., F. T. Mugabe, M. Mwale, R. Delve, D. Nanja, P. Carberry, and M. Howden. 2008. "Building Adaptive Capacity to Cope with Increasing Vulnerability Due to Climatic Change in Africa: A New Approach." *Physics and Chemistry of the Earth* 33 (8–13): 780–87.

UNICEF (United Nations Children's Fund). 2008. *Climate Change and Children: A Human Security Challenge*. Florence: UNICEF.

United Nations. 2005. *Trends in Total Migrant Stock: The 2005 Revision*. New York: United Nations Population Division, Department of Economic and Social Affairs.

———. 2006. *The State of the World's Refugees: Human Displacement in the New Millennium*. Oxford, UK: United Nations High Commissioner for Refugees.

———. 2007. *Drought Risk Reduction Framework and Practices: Contribution to the Implementation of the Hyogo Framework for Action*. Geneva: United Nations International Strategy for Disaster Reduction.

———. 2008a. *State of the World's Cities 2008/9. Harmonious Cities*. London: Earthscan.

———. 2008b. *World Urbanization Prospects: The 2007 Revision*. New York: United Nations Population Division, Department of Economic and Social Affairs.

———. 2009. *2009 Global Assessment Report on Disaster Risk Reduction: Risk and Poverty in a Changing Climate*. Geneva: United Nations International Strategy for Disaster Reduction.

Vakis, R. 2006. "Complementing Natural Disasters Management: The Role of Social Protection." Social Protection Discussion Paper 0543, World Bank, Washington, DC.

Walker, B., L. H. Gunderson, A. Kinzig, C. Folke, S. Carpenter, and L. Schultz. 2006. "A Handful of Heuristics and Some Propositions for Understanding Resilience in Social-Ecological Systems." *Ecology and Society* 11 (1):13.

Wang, R., and Y. E. Yaping. 2004. "Eco-city Development in China." *Ambio: A Journal of the Human Environment* 33 (6): 341–42.

Ward, R. E. T, C. Herweijer, N. Patmore, and R. Muir-Wood. 2008. "The Role of Insurers in Promoting Adaptation to the Impacts of Climate Change." *Geneva Papers on Risk and Insurance Issues and Practice* 33 (1): 133–39.

WBGU (German Advisory Council on Global Change). 2008. *Climate Change as a Security Risk*. London: Earthscan.

Welsh Assembly Government. 2008. *Heatwave Plan for Wales: A Framework for Preparedness and Response*. Cardiff, UK: Welsh Assembly Government Department for Public Health and Health Professions.

White, A., and A. Martin. 2002. *Who Owns the World's Forests? Forest Tenure and Public Forests in Transition*. Washington, DC: Forest Trends and Center for International Environmental Law.

WHO (World Health Organization). 2005. *Health and Climate Change: The Now and How. A Policy Action Guide*. Geneva: WHO.

———. 2008. *Protecting Health from Climate Change: World Health Day 2008*. Geneva: WHO.

Wilbanks, T. J., and R. W. Kates. 1999. "Global Change in Local Places: How Scale Matters." *Climatic Change* 43 (3): 601–28.

World Bank. 2005. *Managing Agricultural Production Risk: Innovations in Developing Countries*. Washington, DC: World Bank.

———. 2006. *Making the New Indonesia Work for the Poor*. Washington, DC: World Bank.

———. 2008a. *Climate Resilient Cities: A Primer on Reducing Vulnerabilities to Climate Chnage Impacts and Strengthening Disaster Risk Management in East Asian Cities*. Washington, DC: World Bank.

———. 2008b. *Environmental Health and Child Survival: Epidemiology, Economics, Experiences*. Washington, DC: World Bank.

———. 2008c. *Project Appraisal Document: Regional Adaptation to the Impact of Rapid Glacier Retreat in the Tropical Andes*. Washington, DC: World Bank.

———. 2008d. *Reforming Energy Price Subsidies and Reinforcing Social Protection: Some Design Issues*. Washington, DC: World Bank.

———. 2008e. *The Caribbean Catastrophe Risk Insurance Facility: Providing Immediate Funding after Natural Disasters*. Washington, DC: World Bank.

———. 2008f. *World Development Indicators 2008*. Washington, DC: World Bank.

———. 2008g. *World Development Report 2009. Reshaping Economic Geography*. Washington, DC: World Bank.

————. 2009. *Development and Climate Change: A Strategic Framework for the World Bank Group: Technical Report.* Washington, DC: World Bank.

World Climate Programme. 2007. *Climate Services Crucial for Early Warning of Malaria Epidemics.* Geneva: World Climate Programme.

World Economic Forum. 2008. *Building Resilience to Natural Disasters: A Framework for Private Sector Engagement.* Geneva: World Economic Forum, World Bank, and United Nations International Strategy for Disaster Reduction.

WRI (World Resources Institute), United Nations Development Programme, United Nations Environment Programme, and World Bank. 2008. *World Resources 2008: Roots of Resilience: Growing the Wealth of the Poor.* Washington, DC: WRI.

Yip, S. C. T. 2008. "Planning for Eco-Cities in China: Visions, Approaches and Challenges." Paper presented at the 44th ISOCARP Congress. The Netherlands.

Biodiversity and ecosystem services in a changing climate

Earth supports a complex web of 3 million to 10 million species of plants and animals[1] and an even greater number of micro-organisms. For the first time a single species, humankind, is in a position to preserve or destroy the very functioning of that web.[2] In people's daily lives only a few species appear to matter. A few dozen species provide most basic nutrition—20 percent of human calorie intake comes from rice,[3] 20 percent comes from wheat;[4] a few species of cattle, poultry, and pigs supply 70 percent of animal protein. Only among the 20 percent of animal protein from fish and shell fish is a diversity of dietary species found.[5] Humans are estimated to appropriate a third of the Sun's energy that is converted to plant material.[6]

But human well-being depends on a multitude of species whose complex interactions within well-functioning ecosystems purify water, pollinate flowers, decompose wastes, maintain soil fertility, buffer water flows and weather extremes, and fulfill social and cultural needs, among many others (box FB.1). The Millennium Ecosystem Assessment concluded that of 24 ecosystem services examined, 15 are being degraded or used unsustainably (table FB.1). The main drivers of degradation are land-use conversion, most often to agriculture or aquaculture; excess nutrients; and climate change. Many consequences of degradation are focused in particular regions, with the poor disproportionately affected because they depend most directly on ecosystem services.[7]

Threats to biodiversity and ecosystem services

In the past two centuries or so, humankind has become the driver of one of the major extinction events on Earth. Appropriating major parts of the energy flow through the food web and altering the fabric of the land cover to favor the species of greatest value have increased the rate of species extinction 100 to 1,000 times the rate before human dominance of Earth.[8] In the past few decades people have become aware of their impacts on biodiversity and the threats of those impacts. Most countries have biodiversity protection programs of varying degrees of effectiveness, and several international treaties and agreements coordinate measures to slow or halt the loss of biodiversity.

Climate change imposes an additional threat. Earth's biodiversity has adjusted to past changes in climate—even to rapid changes—through a mix of species migration, extinctions, and opportunities for new species. But the rate of change that will continue over the next century or so, whatever the mitigation efforts, far exceeds past rates, other than catastrophic extinctions such as after major meteorite events. For example, the rates of tree species migration during the waxing and waning of the most recent ice age about 10,000 years ago were estimated to be about 0.3–0.5 kilometers a year. This is only a tenth the rate of change in climate zones that will occur over the coming century.[9] Some species will migrate fast enough to thrive in a new location, but many will not keep up, especially in the fragmented landscapes of today, and many more will not survive the dramatic reshuffling of ecosystem composition that will accompany climate change (map FB.1). Best estimates of species losses suggest that about 10 percent of species will be condemned to extinction for each 1°C temperature rise,[10] with even greater numbers at risk of significant decline.[11]

Efforts to mitigate climate change through land-based activities may support the maintenance of biodiversity and ecosystem services or threaten them further. Carbon stocks in and on the land can be increased through reforesta-

---

BOX FB.1 *What is biodiversity? What are ecosystem services?*

Biodiversity is the variety of all forms of life, including genes, populations, species, and ecosystems. Biodiversity underpins the services that ecosystems provide and has value for current uses, possible future uses (option values), and intrinsic worth.

The number of species is often used as an indicator of the diversity of an area, though it only crudely captures the genetic diversity and the complexity of ecosystem interactions. There are 5 million to 30 million distinct species on Earth; most are microorganisms and only about 1.75 million have been formally described. Two-thirds of the diversity is in the tropics; a 25 hectare plot in Ecuador was found to have more tree species than exist in all of the United States and Canada, along with more than half the number of mammal and bird species in those two countries.

Ecosystem services are the ecosystem processes or functions that have value to individuals or society. The Millennium Ecosystem Assessment described five major categories of ecosystem services: *provisioning,* such as the production of food and water; *regulating,* such as the control of climate and disease; *supporting,* such as nutrient cycles and crop pollination; *cultural,* such as spiritual and recreational benefits; and *preserving,* such as the maintenance of diversity.

Sources: Millennium Ecosystem Assessment 2005; Kraft, Valencia, and Ackerly 2008; Gitay and others 2002.

Table FB.1   Assessment of the current trend in the global state of major services provided by ecosystems

Service	Subcategory	Status	Notes
Provisioning services			
Food	Crops	↑	Substantial production increase
	Livestock	↑	Substantial production increase
	Capture fisheries	↓	Declining production due to overharvest
	Aquaculture	↑	Substantial production increase
	Wild foods	↓	Declining production
Fiber	Timber	+/−	Forest loss in some regions, growth in others
	Cotton, hemp, silk	+/−	Declining production of some fibers, growth in others
	Wood fuel	↓	Declining production
Genetic resources		↓	Lost through extinction and crop genetic resource loss
Biochemicals, natural medicines, pharmaceuticals		↓	Lost through extinction, overharvest
Fresh water		↓	Unsustainable use for drinking, industry, and irrigation; amount of hydro energy unchanged, but dams increase ability to use that energy
Regulating services			
Air quality regulation		↓	Decline in ability of atmosphere to cleanse itself
Climate regulation	Global	↑	Globally, ecosystems have been a net sink for carbon since mid-century
	Regional and local	↓	Preponderance of negative impacts (for example, changes in land cover can affect local temperature and precipitation)
Water regulation		+/−	Varies depending on ecosystem change and location
Erosion regulation		↓	Increased soil degradation
Water purification and waste treatment		↓	Declining water quality
Disease regulation		+/−	Varies depending on ecosystem change
Pest regulation		↓	Natural control degraded through pesticide use
Pollination		↓	Apparent global decline in abundance of pollinators
Natural hazard regulation		↓	Loss of natural buffers (wetlands, mangroves)
Cultural services			
Spiritual and religious values		↓	Rapid decline in sacred groves and species
Aesthetic values		↓	Decline in quantity and quality of natural lands
Recreation and ecotourism		+/−	More areas accessible but many degraded

Source: Millennium Ecosystem Assessment 2005.

tion and revegetation and through such agricultural practices as reduced soil tillage. These activities can create complex and diverse landscapes supportive of biodiversity. But poorly planned mitigation actions, such as clearing forest or woodland to produce biofuels, can be counterproductive to both goals. Large dams can provide multiple benefits through irrigation and energy production but also can threaten biodiversity through direct inundation and dramatic changes in downstream river flows and the dependent ecosystems.

What can be done?
Changes in priorities and active and adaptive management will be needed to maintain biodiversity under a changing climate. In some places, active management will take the form of further improving protection from human interference, while in others conservation may need to include interventions in species and ecosystem processes that are stronger and more hands-on than today's. In all cases biodiversity values must be actively considered—in the face of climate

change and in the context of competing uses for land or sea.

This requires an ongoing process to anticipate how ecosystems will respond to a changing climate while interacting with other environmental modifiers. Some species will die out, others will persist, and some will migrate, forming new combinations of species. The ability to anticipate such change will always be incomplete and far from perfect, so any management actions must be within a framework that is flexible and adaptive.

Map FB.1   While many of the projected ecosystem changes are in boreal or desert areas that are not biodiversity hotspots, there are still substantial areas of overlap and concern

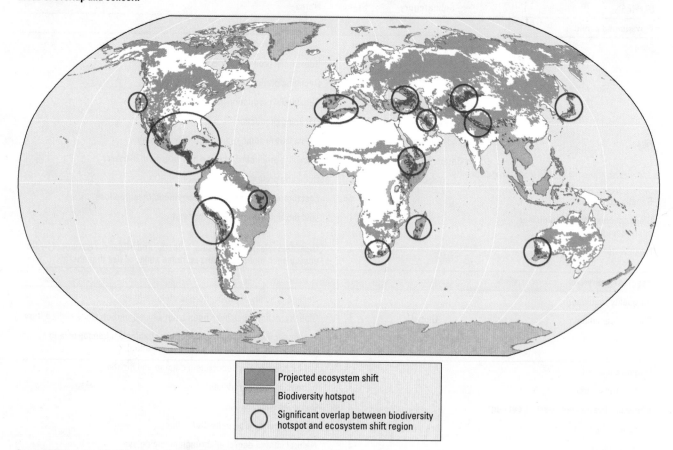

Projected ecosystem shift

Biodiversity hotspot

○ Significant overlap between biodiversity hotspot and ecosystem shift region

Source: WDR team based on Myers and others (2000) and Fischlin and others (2007).

Note: The map shows the overlap between biodiversity hotspots—regions with exceptional concentrations of endemic species undergoing exceptional loss of habitat (Conservation International and Myers and others 2000)—and the projected changes in terrestrial ecosystems by 2100 relative to the year 2000, as presented by the Intergovernmental Panel on Climate Change in Fischlin and others (2007), figure 4.3 (a), p. 238. The changes should be taken as only indicative of the range of possible ecosystem changes and include gains or losses of forest cover, grassland, shrub- and woodland, herbaceous cover, and desert amelioration.

Some species loss is inevitable, and some species may need to be protected in botanical and zoological gardens or in seed banks. It is essential that key species in the delivery of ecosystem services are identified and, if necessary, actively managed. Proactive management of land and the seas under a changing climate is a fairly new and ill-defined process. Relatively little knowledge has been developed on identifying realistic management responses, so significant sharing of learning, best practices, and capacity building will be necessary.

Conservation reserves

Any extensions or modifications to the conservation priority areas (conservation reserves) need to capture altitudinal, lati-tudinal, moisture, and soil gradients. Proposals to expand or modify conservation reserves could lead to clashes over priorities for land allocation and for resources within biodiversity management (such as money for land acquisition versus that for active habitat manipulation). Powerful tools exist for selecting the optimal allocation of lands to achieve particular conservation goals that could balance competing demands.[12]

But protected areas alone are not the solution to climate change. The current reserve network has increased rapidly over the past decade to cover about 12 percent of Earth's land area,[13] but it is still inadequate to conserve biodiversity. Given demographic pressures and competing land uses, protected areas are not likely to grow significantly. This means that the lands that surround and connect areas with high conservation values and priorities (the environmental matrix), and the people who manage or depend on these lands will be of increasing importance for the fate of species in a changing climate.

There will be a greater need for more flexible biodiversity conservation strategies that take the interests of different social groups into account in biodiversity management strategies. So far the principal actors in creating protected areas have been nongovernmental organizations and central governments. To ensure the flexibility needed to maintain biodiversity, a wide range of managers, owners, and stakeholders of these matrix lands and waters will need to be engaged in management partnerships. Incentives and compensation for these actors may be required to maintain a matrix that provides refugia and corridors for species. Some of the options include extending payments for environmental services, "habitat banking,"[14] and further exploration of "rights-based approaches to resources access," as used in some fisheries.

Biodiversity planning and management

A plan for actively managing the viability of ecosystems as the climate changes should be developed for all conservation lands and waters and significant areas of habitat. Elements include:

- Climate-smart management plans for coping with major stressors, such as fire, pests, and nutrient loads.

- Decision procedures and triggers for changing management priorities in the face of climate change. For example, if a conservation area is affected by two fires within a short period, making the reestablishment of the previous habitat and values unlikely, then a program to actively manage the transition to an alternative ecosystem structure should be implemented.

- Integration into the plans of the rights, interests, and contributions of indigenous peoples and others directly dependent on these lands or waters.

Such proactive planning is rare even in the developed world.[15] Canada has a proactive management approach to climate change in the face of rapid warming in its northern regions.[16] Other countries are outlining some of the core principles of proactive management: forecasting changes; managing regional biodiversity, including conservation areas and their surrounding landscape; and setting priorities to support decision making in the face of inevitable change.[17] But in many parts of the world, basic biodiversity management is still inadequate. In 1999 the International Union for Conservation of Nature determined that less than a quarter of protected areas in 10 devel-oping countries were adequately managed and that more than 10 percent of protected areas were already thoroughly degraded.[18]

Community-based conservation

Community-based conservation programs could be adopted on a much larger scale. These programs attempt to enhance local user rights and stewardship over natural resources, allowing those nearest to natural resources, who already share in the costs of conservation (such as wildlife depredation of crops) to share in its benefits as well. But such programs are not panaceas, and more effort needs to go into designing effective programs.

Community participation is the sine qua non of successful biodiversity conservation in the developing world, but long-term success stories (such as harvesting sea turtle eggs in Costa Rica and Brazil) are rare.[19] Certain elements clearly contribute to the success that some programs have had regionally, such as the wildlife-focused programs in southern Africa. These elements include stable governments, high resource value (iconic wildlife), strong economies that support export-oriented resource use (including tourism and safari hunting), low human population densities, good local governance, and government policies that offer a social safety net to buffer against lean years. Even when these conditions are met, the benefits in some countries typically do not accrue to the poor.[20]

Managing marine ecosystems

Effective land management also has benefits for marine ecosystems. Sedimentation and eutrophication caused by land-based runoff reduce the resilience of marine ecosystems such as coral reefs.[21] The economic value of coral reefs is often greater than the value of the agriculture on the land that affects them.[22]

For fisheries the main tools for managing biodiversity are ecosystem-based fisheries management,[23] integrated coastal zone management including protected marine areas,[24] and binding international cooperation within the framework of the Law of the Sea.[25] Fisheries are seen as being in crisis, and fisheries mismanagement is blamed. But the fundamental requirements for fisheries management are known.[26] Climate change may provide an additional impetus to implement reforms, primarily by reducing fishing fleet overcapacity and fishing effort to sustainable levels.[27] A sustainable, long-term harvesting strategy must be implemented—one that assesses stock exploitation in relation to reference points that take uncertainty and climate change into account.[28] The key challenge is to translate high-level policy goals into operational actions for sustainable fisheries.[29]

Payment for ecosystem services

Payment for ecosystem services has for some time been considered an efficient and equitable way to achieve many outcomes related to conservation and the provision of ecosystem services. Examples include paying upstream land managers to manage the watershed in ways that protect ecosystem services such as flows of clean water, sharing profits from game reserves with surrounding landholders whose property is damaged by the game, and most recently paying landholders to increase or maintain the carbon stocks on their land. Box FB.2 provides examples of the provision of multiple services of conservation and carbon sequestration.

Experience suggests that, because payments are provided only if a service is rendered, user-financed schemes tend to be better tailored to local needs, better monitored, and better enforced than similar government-financed programs.[30]

A significant opportunity for additional payments for conservation and improved land management may flow from the scheme for Reduced Emissions from Deforestation and forest Degradation (REDD) under consideration by the United Nations Framework Convention on Climate Change. REDD seeks to lower emissions by paying countries for reducing deforestation and degrada-

BOX FB.2   *Payment for ecosystem and mitigation services*

Two successful payment programs are the Moldova Soil Conservation project and the bird conservation and watershed protection program in Bolivia's Los Negros Valley, both funded through the World Bank BioCarbon Fund. In Moldova, 20,000 hectares of degraded and eroded state-owned and communal agricultural lands are being reforested, reducing erosion and providing forest products to local communities.

The project is expected to sequester about 2.5 million tons of carbon dioxide equivalent by 2017. In Bolivia, farmers bordering Amboró National Park are paid to protect a watershed containing the threatened cloud forest habitat of 11 species of migratory birds, with benefits both for local biodiversity and for dry-season water supplies.

Source: World Bank Carbon Finance Unit.

tion. These payments could be part of a market-based mechanism within an enhanced Clean Development Mechanism process, or they could be non-market payments from a new financial mechanism that does not impinge on the emissions compliance mechanisms. The challenge of REDD is in its implementation, which is discussed in more detail in chapter 6.

REDD could make a significant contribution to both the conservation of biodiversity and mitigation of climate change if it protects biologically diverse areas that have high carbon stocks and are at high risk of deforestation. Techniques for identifying such areas are available and could be used to guide the allocation of financial resources (map FB.2).[31]

To deal effectively with the changing impacts and competing uses of ecosystems under a changing climate, governments will need to introduce strong, locally appropriate policies, measures, and incentives to change long-established behaviors, some of which are already illegal. These actions will run counter to some community preferences, so the balance between appropriate regulation and incentives is critical. REDD holds potential benefits for forest-dwelling indigenous and local communities, but a number of conditions will need to be met for these benefits to be achieved. Indigenous peoples, for example, are unlikely to benefit from REDD if their identities and rights are

not recognized and if they do not have secure rights to their lands, territories, and resources (box FB.3). Experience from community-based natural resource management initiatives has shown that the involvement of local people, including indigenous peoples, in participatory monitoring of natural resources can provide accurate, cost-effective, and locally anchored information on forest biomass and natural resource trends.

Ecosystem-based adaptation

"Hard" adaptation measures such as coastal defense walls, river embankments, and dams to control river flows all present threats to biodiversity.[32] Adaptation goals can often be achieved through better management of ecosystems rather than through physical and engineering interventions; for example, coastal ecosystems can be more effective as buffer zones against storm surges than sea walls. Other options include catchment and flood plain management to adjust downstream water flows and the introduction of climate-resilient agroecosystems and dry-land pastoralism to support robust livelihoods.

Ecosystem-based adaptation aims to increase the resilience and reduce the vulnerability of people to climate change through the conservation, restoration, and management of ecosystems. When integrated into an overall adaptation strategy, it can deliver a cost-effective contribution to adaptation and generate societal benefits.

In addition to the direct benefits for adaptation, ecosystem-based adaptation activities can also have indirect benefits for people, biodiversity, and mitigation. For example, the restoration of mangrove systems to provide shoreline protection from storm surges

BOX FB.3   *Excerpts from the Declaration of Indigenous Peoples on Climate Change*

"All initiatives under Reducing Emissions from Deforestation and Degradation (REDD) must secure the recognition and implementation of the rights of Indigenous Peoples, including security of land tenure, recognition of land title according to traditional ways, uses and customary laws and the multiple benefits of forests for climate, ecosystems, and peoples before taking any action." (Article 5)

"We call for adequate and direct funding in developed and developing States and for a fund to be created to enable Indigenous Peoples' full and effective participation in all climate processes, including adaptation, mitigation, monitoring, and transfer of appropriate technologies, in order to foster our empowerment, capacity building, and

education. We strongly urge relevant United Nations bodies to facilitate and fund the participation, education, and capacity building of Indigenous youth and women to ensure engagement in all international and national processes related to climate change." (Article 7)

"We offer to share with humanity our Traditional Knowledge, innovations, and practices relevant to climate change, provided our fundamental rights as intergenerational guardians of this knowledge are fully recognized and respected. We reiterate the urgent need for collective action." (Concluding Para).

The declaration was issued during the Indigenous Peoples Global Summit on Climate Change held in Anchorage on April 24, 2009.

Map FB.2   Unprotected areas at high risk of deforestation and with high carbon stocks should be priority areas to benefit from a REDD mechanism.

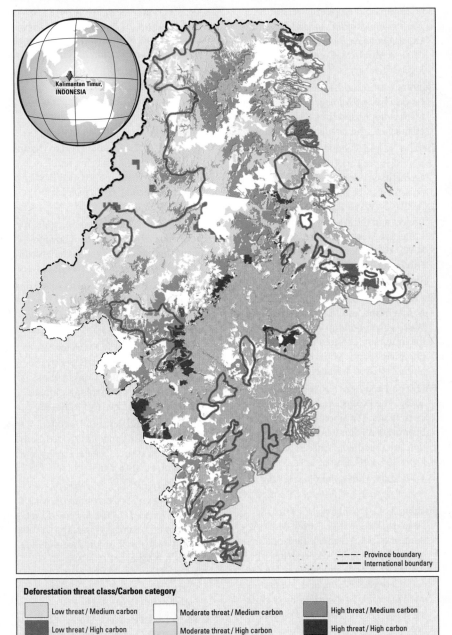

Deforestation threat class/Carbon category

Low threat / Medium carbon	Moderate threat / Medium carbon	High threat / Medium carbon
Low threat / High carbon	Moderate threat / High carbon	High threat / High carbon
Protected area	Non-forest in 2003	No data

- - - - Province boundary
— - — International boundary

Sources: Brown and others 1993; Harris and others 2009.

Note: A recent study for the East Kalimantan region of Indonesia used GEOMOD and a database of carbon stocks in Indonesia's tropical forests to identify the best areas for REDD activities. The resulting map identifies areas with high deforestation threat that also have high carbon stocks. The overlay of the existing or proposed protected areas allows decision makers to see where to direct financial resources and focus the protection efforts to get the most benefits under a REDD mechanism (namely, the dark red areas—high threat/high carbon—not included within the boundaries of already existing protected areas).

can also increase fishery opportunities and sequester carbon. Ecosystem-based adaptation options are often more accessible to the rural poor, women, and other vulnerable groups than options based on infrastructure and engineering. Consistent with community-based approaches to adaptation, ecosystem-based adaptation builds effectively on local knowledge and needs.

Ecosystem-based adaptation may require giving priority to some ecosystem services at the expense of others. Using wetlands for coastal protection may require emphasis on silt accumulation and stabilization, for example, possibly at some expense to wildlife and recreation. Slope stabilization with dense shrubbery is an effective ecosystem-based adaptation to increasing rainfall intensity under climate change. However, in the dry periods often associated with the increasingly variable rainfall patterns under climate change the slopes may be exposed to wildfires that destroy the shrubs and lead to disastrous reversals of the adaptation goals. So, ecosystem-based adaptation must be assessed for risk and cost-effectiveness.

Notes

1. McGinley 2007.
2. Vitousek and others 1999.
3. Fitzgerald, McCouch, and Hall 2009.
4. Brown 2002.
5. WHO and FAO 2009.
6. Haberl 1997.
7. Millennium Ecosystem Assessment 2005.
8. Lawton and May 1995.
9. England and others (2004) estimated the average rate of glacial retreat to be 0.1 kilometer a year about 8,000 years ago during the last ice age, which ultimately placed a constraint on how fast species could migrate poleward.
10. Convention on Biological Diversity 2009; Fischlin and others 2007.
11. Foden and others 2008.
12. Bode and others 2008; Joseph, Maloney, and Possingham 2008; McCarthy and Possingham 2007.
13. UNEP-WCMC 2008.
14. This is a form of trading high-conservation-value lands. Some holders of such lands will choose to place them in a habitat bank. If a need arises to damage similar land elsewhere, such as for highway easements, the project proponents must buy the rights to land of equivalent conservation value from the bank.
15. Heller and Zavaleta 2009.
16. Welch 2005.

17. Hannah and others 2002; Hannah, Midgley, and Miller 2002.

18. Dudley and Stolton 1999.

19. Campbell, Haalboom, and Trow 2007.

20. Bandyopadhyay and Tembo 2009.

21. Smith, Gilmour, and Heyward 2008.

22. Gordon 2007.

23. FAO 2003; FAO 2005; Stiansen and others 2005.

24. Halpern 2003; Harmelin-Vivien and others 2008.

25. Lodge and others 2007.

26. Cunningham and Bostock 2005.

27. OECD 2008; World Bank 2008.

28. Beddington, Agnew, and Clark 2007.

29. FAO 2003; FAO 2005; ICES 2008a; ICES 2008b.

30. Wunder, Engel, and Pagiola 2008.

31. Brown and others 1993; Harris and others 2009.

32. This section draws upon material being prepared by the Ad Hoc Technical Expert Group on Biodiversity and Climate Change 2009 for the Convention on Biological Diversity and the UN Framework Convention on Climate Change.

References

Bandyopadhyay, S., and G. Tembo. 2009. "Household Welfare and Natural Resource Management around National Parks in Zambia." Policy Research Working Paper Series 4932, World Bank, Washington, DC.

Beddington, J. R., D. J. Agnew, and C. W. Clark. 2007. "Current Problems in the Management of Marine Fisheries." *Science* 316 (5832): 1713–16.

Bode, M., K. A. Wilson, T. M. Brooks, W. R. Turner, R. A. Mittermeier, M. F. McBride, E. C. Underwood, and H. P. Possingham. 2008. "Cost-Effective Global Conservation Spending Is Robust to Taxonomic Group." *Proceedings of the National Academy of Sciences* 105 (17): 6498–501.

Brown, S., L. R. Iverson, A. Prasad, and L. Dawning. 1993. "Geographical Distribution of Carbon in Biomass and Soils of Tropical Asian Forests." *Geocarto International* 4: 45–59.

Brown, T. A. 2002. *Genomes.* Oxford: John Wiley & Sons.

Campbell, L. M., B. J. Haalboom, and J. Trow. 2007. "Sustainability of Community-Based Conservation: Sea Turtle Egg Harvesting in Ostional (Costa Rica) Ten Years Later." *Environmental Conservation* 34 (2): 122–31.

Convention on Biological Diversity. 2009. *Draft Findings of the Ad Hoc Technical Expert Group on Biodiversity and Climate Change.* Montreal: Convention on Biological Diversity.

Cunningham, S., and T. Bostock. 2005. *Successful Fisheries Management. Issues, Case Studies and Perspectives.* Delft, The Netherlands: Eburon Academic Publishers.

Dudley, N., and S. Stolton. 1999. "Conversion of Paper Parks to Effective Management: Developing a Target." Paper presented at the Joint Workshop of the IUCN/WWF Forest Innovations Project and the World Commission on Protected Areas in association with the WWF-World Bank Alliance and the Forests for Life Campaign. June 14. Turrialba, Costa Rica.

England, J. H., N. Atkinson, A. S. Dyke, D. J. A. Evans, and M. Zreda. 2004. "Late Wisconsinan Buildup and Wastage of the Innuitian Ice Sheet across Southern Ellesmere Island, Nunavut." *Canadian Journal of Earth Sciences* 41 (1): 39–61.

FAO (Food and Agriculture Organization). 2003. "The Ecosystem Approach to Fisheries: Issues, Terminology, Principles, Institutional Foundations, Implementation and Outlook." Fisheries Technical Paper 443, FAO, Rome.

———. 2005. *Putting Into Practice the Ecosystem Approach to Fisheries.* Rome: FAO.

Fischlin, A., G. F. Midgley, J. T. Price, R. Leemans, B. Gopal, C. Turley, M. D. A. Rounsevell, O. P. Dube, J. Tarazona, and A. A. Velichko. 2007. "Ecosystems, Their Properties, Goods and Services." In *Climate Change 2007: Impacts, Adaptation and Vulnerability. Contribution of Working Group II to the Fourth Assessment Report of the Intergovernmental Panel on Climate Change,* ed. M. Parry, O. F. Canziani, J. P. Palutikof, P. J. van der Linden, and C. E. Hanson. Cambridge, UK: Cambridge University Press.

Fitzgerald, M. A., S. R. McCouch, and R. D. Hall. 2009. "Not Just a Grain of Rice: The Quest for Quality." *Trends in Plant Science* 14 (3): 133–39.

Foden, W., G. Mace, J.-C. Vie, A. Angulo, S. Butchart, L. DeVantier, H. Dublin, A. Gutsche, S. Stuart, and E. Turak. 2008. "Species Susceptibility to Climate Change Impacts." In *The 2008 Review of the IUCN Red List of Threatened Species,* ed. J.-C. Vie, C. Hilton-Taylor, and S. N. Stuart. Gland, Switzerland: International Union for Conservation of Nature.

Gitay, H., A. Suarez, R. T. Watson, and D. J. Dokken, eds. 2002. *Climate Change and Biodiversity.* Technical Paper of the Intergovernmental Panel on Climate Change, IPCC Secretariat, Geneva.

Gordon, I. J. 2007. "Linking Land to Ocean: Feedbacks in the Management of Socio-Ecological Systems in the Great Barrier Reef Catchments." *Hydrobiologia* 591 (1): 25–33.

Haberl, H. 1997. "Human Appropriation of Net Primary Production as an Environmental Indicator: Implications for Sustainable Development." *Ambio* 26 (3): 143–46.

Halpern, B. S. 2003. "The Impact of Marine Reserves: Do Reserves Work and Does Reserve Size Matter?" *Ecological Applications* 13 (1): S117–37.

Hannah, L., T. Lovejoy, G. Midgley, W. Bond, M. Bush, J. Lovett, D. Scott, and F. I. Woodward. 2002. "Conservation of Biodiversity in a Changing Climate." *Conservation Biology* 16 (1): 264–68.

Hannah, L., G. Midgley, and D. Miller. 2002. "Climate Change-Integrated Conservation Strategies." *Global Ecology and Biogeography* 11 (6): 485–95.

Harmelin-Vivien, M., L. Le Direach, J. Bayle-Sempere, E. Charbonnel, J. A. Garcia-Charton, D. Ody, A. Perez-Ruzafa, O. Renones, P. Sanchez-Jerez, and C. Valle. 2008. "Gradients of Abundance and Biomass across Reserve Boundaries in Six Mediterranean Marine Protected Areas: Evidence of Fish Spillover?" *Biological Conservation* 141 (7): 1829–39.

Harris, N. L., S. Petrova, F. Stolle, and S. Brown. 2009. "Identifying Optimal Areas for REDD Intervention: East Kalimantan, Indonesia, as a Case Study." *Environmental Research Letters* 3:035006, doi:10.1088/1748-9326/3/3/035006.

Heller, N. E., and E. S. Zavaleta. 2009. "Biodiversity Management in the Face of Climate Change: A Review of 22 Years of Recommendations." *Biological Conservation* 142 (1): 14–32.

ICES (International Council for the Exploration of the Sea). 2008a. *ICES Advice*

Book 9: Widely Distributed and Migratory Stocks. Copenhagen: ICES Advisory Committee.

———. 2008b. *ICES Insight Issue No. 45.* Copenhagen: ICES.

Joseph, L. N., R. F. Maloney, and H. P. Possingham. 2008. "Optimal Allocation of Resources among Threatened Species: A Project Prioritization Protocol." *Conservation Biology* 23 (2): 328–38.

Kraft, N. J. B., R. Valencia, and D. D. Ackerly. 2008. "Functional Traits and Niche-Based Tree Community Assembly in an Amazonian Forest." *Science* 322 (5901): 580–82.

Lawton, J. H., and R. M. May. 1995. *Extinction Rates.* Oxford, UK: Oxford University Press.

Lodge, M. W., D. Anderson, T. Lobach, G. Munro, K. Sainsbury, and A. Willock. 2007. *Recommended Best Practices for Regional Fisheries Management Organizations.* London: Chatham House for the Royal Institute of International Affairs.

McCarthy, M. A., and H. P. Possingham. 2007. "Active Adaptive Management for Conservation." *Conservation Biology* 21 (4): 956–63.

McGinley, M. 2007. *Species Richness.* Washington, DC: Encyclopedia of Earth—Environmental Information Coalition, National Council for Science and Environment.

Millennium Ecosystem Assessment. 2005. *Ecosystems and Human Well-Being: Synthesis Report.* Washington, DC: World Resources Institute.

Myers, N., R. A. Mittermeier, C. G. Mittermeier, G. A. B. da Fonseca, and J. Kent. 2000. "Biodiversity Hotspots for Conservation Priorities." *Nature* 403: 853–58.

OECD (Organisation for Economic Cooperation and Development). 2008. *Recommendation of the Council on the Design and Implementation of Decommissioning Schemes in the Fishing Sector.* Paris: OECD.

Smith, L. D., J. P. Gilmour, and A. J. Heyward. 2008. "Resilience of Coral Communities on an Isolated System of Reefs following Catastrophic Mass-Bleaching." *Coral Reefs* 27 (1): 197–205.

Stiansen, J. E., B. Bogstad, P. Budgell, P. Dalpadado, H. Gjosaeter, K. Hiis Hauge, R. Ingvaldsen, H. Loeng, M. Mauritzen, S. Mehl, G. Ottersen, M. Skogen, and E. K. Stenevik. 2005. *Status Report on the Barents Sea Ecosystem 2004–2005.* Bergen, Norway: Institute of Marine Research (IMR).

UNEP-WCMC ((United Nations Environment Program–World Conservation Monitoring Center). 2008. *State of the World's Protected Areas 2007: An Annual Review of Global Conservation Progress.* Cambridge, UK: UNEP-WCMC.

Vitousek, P. M., H. A. Mooney, J. Lubchenco, and J. M. Melillo. 1999. "Human Domination of Earth's Ecosystems." *Science* 277 (5325): 494–99.

Welch, D. 2005. "What Should Protected Area Managers Do in the Face of Climate Change?" *The George Wright Forum* 22 (1): 75–93.

WHO and FAO (World Health Organization and Food and Agriculture Organization). 2009. "Global and Regional Food Consumption Patterns and Trends." In *Diet, Nutrition and the Prevention of Chronic Diseases.* Geneva and Rome: WHO and FAO.

World Bank. 2008. *The Sunken Billions: The Economic Justification for Fisheries Reform.* Washington, DC: World Bank and FAO.

Wunder, S., S. Engel, and S. Pagiola. 2008. "Taking Stock: A Comparative Analysis of Payments for Environmental Services Programs in Developed and Developing Countries." *Ecological Economics* 65 (4): 834–52.

CHAPTER 3

Managing Land and Water to Feed Nine Billion People and Protect Natural Systems

Climate change is already affecting the natural and managed systems—forests, wetlands, coral reefs, agriculture, fisheries—that societies depend on to provide food, fuel, and fiber, and for many other services. It will depress agricultural yields in many regions, making it harder to meet the world's growing food needs. It comes as the world faces intensified competition for land, water, biodiversity, fish, and other natural resources. At the same time, societies will be under pressure to reduce the 30 percent of greenhouse gas emissions that come from agriculture, deforestation, land-use change, and forest degradation.

To meet the competing demands and reduce vulnerability to climate change, societies will need to balance producing more from their natural resources with protecting these resources. That means managing water, land, forests, fisheries, and biodiversity more efficiently to obtain the services and products societies need without further damaging these resources through overuse, pollution, or encroachment.

Water will have to be used more efficiently. To do that, managers need to think on basin-wide scales and to devise efficient and flexible ways to allocate water among competing quantity and quality demands for human use (such as energy, agriculture, fisheries, and urban consumption) and for healthy ecosystems (such as forests, wetlands, and oceans).

Countries also need to get more from their agriculture. The rate of increase in yields for key agricultural commodities has been declining since the 1960s. Countries will have to reverse that trend if the world is to meet its food needs in the face of climate change. Models vary, but all show the need for a marked increase in productivity.[1] That increase in productivity cannot come at the expense of soil, water, or biodiversity as it has so often in the past. So countries will need to accelerate research, enhance extension services, and improve market infrastructure to get crops to market. But they also need to give farmers incentives to reduce carbon emissions from soil and deforestation. And they need to help farmers hedge against an uncertain climate by diversifying income sources and genetic traits of crops, and better integrate biodiversity into the agricultural landscape.

Key messages

Climate change will make it harder to produce enough food for the world's growing population, and will alter the timing, availability, and quality of water resources. To avoid encroaching into already-stressed ecosystems, societies will have to almost double the existing rate of agricultural productivity growth while minimizing the associated environmental damage. This requires dedicated efforts to deploy known but neglected practices, identify crop varieties able to withstand climate shocks, diversify rural livelihoods, improve management of forests, and invest in information systems. Countries will need to cooperate to manage shared water resources and fisheries and to improve food trade. Getting basic policies right matters, but new technologies and practices are also emerging. Financial incentives will help. Some countries are redirecting their agricultural subsidies to support environmental actions, and future credits for carbon stored in trees and soils could benefit emission reductions and conservation goals.

Applying climate-smart practices will hinge on managing biodiversity better—integrating natural habitats into rural landscapes, protecting wetlands, and maintaining the water storage provided by aquifers. Increasingly, countries are making use of techniques that improve soil and water productivity. But these innovations will bear fruit only if decisions are based on solid intersectoral analysis and only if users have the right incentives—stemming from policies, institutions, and market conditions.

Many natural resources cross borders. As climate change makes resources harder to manage, and growing populations increase demand, countries will need to cooperate more intensively to manage international waters, forests, and fisheries. All countries will turn more frequently to the international agricultural market and so will benefit from a number of measures—from stock management to more competitive procurement techniques to customs and port logistics—that make food trade more reliable and efficient.

Climate change also puts a premium on information about natural resources. Information—traditional and new, international and local—will have a high payoff under a more variable and more uncertain climate, where the stakes are higher and making decisions is more complicated. Information supports resource management, food production, and better trade. If societies generate information they can trust about their resources and can get it to the people who can use it, from international river basin authorities to farmers in their fields, those people can make more informed choices.

Many of these solutions, long advocated in the natural resource literature, have been frustratingly slow in coming to fruition. But three new factors, all related to climate change, could provide new incentives. First, food prices are expected to increase as a result of more climate shocks as well as from growing demand. Increasing food prices should spur innovation to increase productivity. Second, it may be possible to extend carbon markets to pay farmers to store carbon in soil. This step would create

incentives to conserve forests and adopt more sustainable farming techniques. The techniques are not yet proven at the needed scale, but the potential is great, and the additional benefits for agricultural productivity and poverty reduction are substantial. At a high enough carbon price, global emission reductions from agriculture could equal reductions from the energy sector (see overview, box 8).[2] Third, countries could change the way they support agriculture. Rich countries provide $258 billion annually in agriculture support,[3] more than half of which depends only on the amount of crop produced or input used. Though politically difficult, countries are beginning to change the terms of these subsidies to encourage implementation of climate-smart practices on a large scale.

This chapter first discusses what can be done at the national level to increase productivity of agriculture and fisheries while more effectively protecting natural resources. It next discusses what can be done to support national efforts, focusing on international cooperation and the essential role of information both at the global and the local level. Then it focuses on how incentives might change to accelerate implementation of beneficial practices and to help societies balance the need for increased production with better protection of natural resources.

Put in place the fundamentals for natural resource management

An extensive literature recommends strengthening the policy and institutional conditions that influence how people manage agriculture, aquaculture, and healthy ecosystems. Several measures can increase productivity in all sectors, while protecting long-term ecological health. None of these approaches functions alone. All require the support of the others to work effectively, and any change in one can alter the whole system.

Several themes recur across sectors, climates, and income groups.

- *Innovative decision-making tools* allow users to determine the impacts of different actions on natural resources.

- *Research and development* that produce new technologies and adapt them to local conditions can improve resource management, as can *advisory services* that help users learn about the options available to them.
- *Property rights* give users incentives to protect or invest in their resources.
- *Pricing resources* in a way that reflects their full value gives incentives to use them efficiently.
- *Well-regulated markets* are important for many agricultural and natural resource functions; infrastructure is also critical so that producers can access those markets effectively.
- *Strong institutions* are important for setting and enforcing rules.
- *Information*, at all levels, permits users and managers to make better choices.

These fundamentals apply to water, agriculture, and fisheries, as discussed in this chapter.

To understand how these drivers affect the incentives of a particular community, consider farmers on the plains of the Oum Er Rbia river basin in Morocco. Engineers have designed a feasible drip irrigation system that would allow these farmers to generate higher revenue from the water they receive (by increasing yields or switching to higher-value crops). Economists have figured out that it will be profitable. Hydrologists have calculated how much water they can safely allocate to these farmers without neglecting environmental needs. Sociologists have talked to the farmers and found that 80 percent of them want to invest in this technology. Marketing specialists have talked to agroprocessors who want to buy the new crops. And the government is willing to pay for a large share. But even here, getting things moving is fiendishly difficult.

It is not worth investing in new, improved pipes between the dam and the field unless most farmers will install the drip irrigation on their fields. Yet the farmers will not put down a deposit on the drip systems until they are convinced that the new pipes will really be laid and the water will really flow. They also need information about how to use the new systems. The irrigation agency, used to providing advice to farmers, is moving toward contracting advisory services out to private firms. It will have to find, contract, and supervise these firms—tasks that require a very different set of skills. And the farmers will need to trust these new advisors as well.

Farmers' choices of crops are determined in part by government price supports for sugar and wheat, which reduce the incentives to switch to other crops such as higher-value fruits and vegetables. If international trade agreements make it easier to ensure a reliable market for new crops, the farmers might make the switch. But without good roads, refrigerated transport, and state-of-the-art packaging facilities, the fruit and vegetables will rot before reaching their destination.

If the new advisory services are good, farmers will learn how they can get higher incomes by switching to growing fruit and vegetables for export. The extension services will also help them to organize and interact with European buyers. New infrastructure (a reliable weigh station, a cold-storage facility) will make it feasible to assume the risk of switching crops. If the farmers can get information they trust about the impacts of their actions on their aquifer, they may determine as a group to use water more responsibly. If the river basin agency has new planning tools, it can allocate water more effectively across different users' priorities, including the environment. In the long term new initiatives that set a price on soil carbon or change water allocation may provide the incentives for farmers to grow crops using different soil management techniques. Each step in the process is feasible, and in the long run will benefit every player. The challenge comes in coordinating all the efforts across multiple institutions and in persisting to see things through over a long time.

Natural resources cannot be managed separately, especially with climate change. New ways are needed to put water, agriculture, forests, and fisheries into a broader context with a web of related outcomes. In some communities, farmers have begun to moderate their fertilizer use to protect aquatic ecosystems, and fisheries managers are considering how setting catch limits for one species will affect others. These management tools appear under a wide variety of names: ecosystem-based management, integrated soil-fertility management, adaptive management, to name a few. But all share key features: they coordinate a broader range of variables (wider landscapes, longer time frames, and learning by experience) than do traditional approaches. And they stress the need for reliable information about the managed resource to ensure that recommendations are accurate, site specific, and adaptable to changing conditions. By increasing climate variability, climate change will make ecosystems'

responses less predictable; resource managers will need to cope with that uncertainty with robust plans that consider the potential outcomes of multiple actions under multiple conditions.

Adaptive management (as described in chapter 2) will need to be applied at all levels of resource management. Individual farmers can monitor their soil to tailor fertilizer use to local soil, water, climate, and crop conditions without harming ecosystems. Rural communities can tailor their cropping choices to the amount of water they can safely extract from their groundwater year after year, and go back to using the aquifer only as insurance against

Figure 3.1   Climate change in a typical river basin will be felt across the hydrological cycle

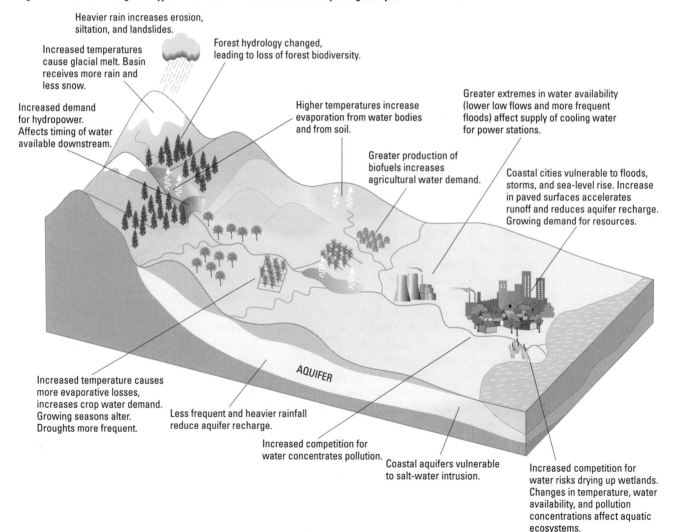

Heavier rain increases erosion, siltation, and landslides.

Increased temperatures cause glacial melt. Basin receives more rain and less snow.

Forest hydrology changed, leading to loss of forest biodiversity.

Increased demand for hydropower. Affects timing of water available downstream.

Higher temperatures increase evaporation from water bodies and from soil.

Greater extremes in water availability (lower low flows and more frequent floods) affect supply of cooling water for power stations.

Greater production of biofuels increases agricultural water demand.

Coastal cities vulnerable to floods, storms, and sea-level rise. Increase in paved surfaces accelerates runoff and reduces aquifer recharge. Growing demand for resources.

AQUIFER

Increased temperature causes more evaporative losses, increases crop water demand. Growing seasons alter. Droughts more frequent.

Less frequent and heavier rainfall reduce aquifer recharge.

Increased competition for water concentrates pollution.

Coastal aquifers vulnerable to salt-water intrusion.

Increased competition for water risks drying up wetlands. Changes in temperature, water availability, and pollution concentrations affect aquatic ecosystems.

Sources: WDR team based on World Bank, forthcoming d; Bates and others 2008.

drought. And policy makers can use robust decision-making tools to forge more resilient international agreements for sharing resources. This chapter offers specifics on applying new tools and technologies to manage water, agriculture, and fisheries and advocates a systemwide approach for coping with climate change across all three sectors.

Produce more from water and protect it better

Climate change will make it harder to manage the world's water

People will feel many of the effects of climate change through water. The entire water cycle will be affected (figure 3.1). While the world as a whole will get wetter as warming speeds up the hydrological cycle, increased evaporation will make drought conditions more prevalent (map 3.1). Most places will experience more intense and variable precipitation, often with longer dry periods in between (map 3.2).[4] The effects on human activity and natural systems will be widespread. Areas that now depend on glaciers and snowmelt will have more fresh water initially, but supply will then decline over time.[5] The shifts may be so rapid and unpredictable that traditional agricultural and water management practices are no longer useful. This is already the case for the indigenous communities in the Cordillera Blanca in Peru, where farmers are facing such rapid changes that their traditional practices are failing. The government and scientists are starting to work with them to try to find new solutions.[6]

Map 3.1   Water availability is projected to change dramatically by the middle of the 21st century in many parts of the world

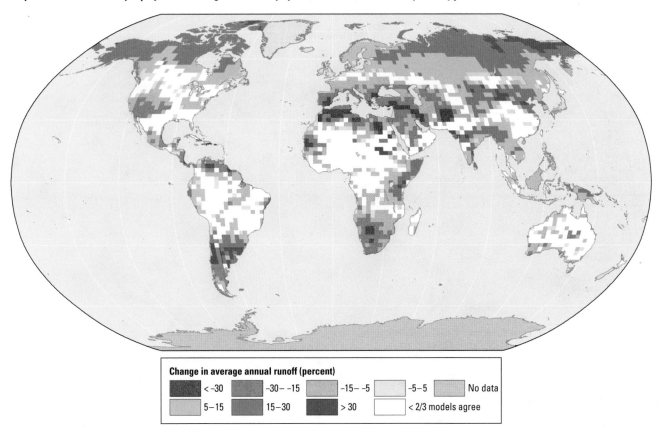

Change in average annual runoff (percent)

< –30	–30– –15	–15– –5
–5–5	No data	
5–15	15–30	> 30
< 2/3 models agree		

Sources: Milly and others 2008; Milly, Dunne, and Vecchia 2005.

Note: The colors indicate percentage changes in annual runoff values (based on the median of 12 global climate models using the IPCC SRES A1B scenario) from 2041–2060 compared with 1900–1970. The white denotes areas where less than two-thirds of the models agree on whether runoff will increase or decrease. Runoff is equal to precipitation minus evaporation, but the values shown here are annual averages, which could mask seasonal variability in precipitation such as an increase in both floods and droughts.

Map 3.2   The world will experience both longer dry spells and more intense rainfall events

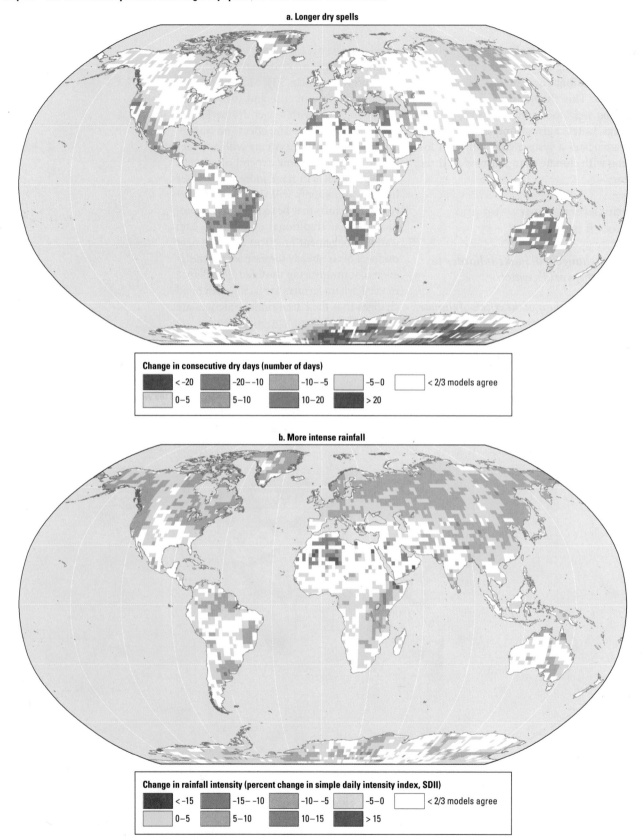

a. Longer dry spells

Change in consecutive dry days (number of days)

< –20	–20– –10	–10– –5	–5–0
0–5	5–10	10–20	> 20

< 2/3 models agree

b. More intense rainfall

Change in rainfall intensity (percent change in simple daily intensity index, SDII)

< –15	–15– –10	–10– –5	–5–0
0–5	5–10	10–15	> 15

< 2/3 models agree

Source: The World Climate Research Program CMIP3 Multi-model Database (http://www-pcmdi.llnl.gov/ipcc/about_ipcc.php). Analysis by the World Bank.

Note: The maps show the median change (based on 8 climate models using SRES A1B) in annual values in 2030–2049, compared with 1980–1999. A "dry" day is defined as one with precipitation less than 1millimeter whereas a "rainy" day has more than 1 millimeter. Precipitation intensity (SDII, or simple daily intensity index) is the total projected annual precipitation divided by the number of "rainy" days. White areas show areas of high model disagreement (fewer than two-thirds of the models agree on the sign of change).

Increasing knowledge about the world's water will improve management. To manage water well, it is critical to know how much water is available in any basin and what it is used for. This may sound straightforward, but it is not. The UN's World Water Development Report states: "Few countries know how much water is being used and for what purposes, the quantity and quality of water that is available and can be withdrawn without serious environmental consequences, and how much is being invested in water infrastructure."[7] Water accounting is complex. Definitions and methods vary, and confusion is common. For example, the Pacific Institute puts the Arab Republic of Egypt's annual renewable water resources in 2007 at 86.8 cubic kilometers, whereas Earthtrends reports it at 58 cubic kilometers. Both reports cite the same source of information. The confusion stems from different interpretations of the term *use* (the higher figure includes water reuse within Egypt, while the lower figure does not).[8]

The planet contains a fixed amount of water, with the form and location varying over space and time.[9] Humans have little control over most of it—saltwater in oceans, freshwater in glaciers, water in the atmosphere. Most investment concentrates on water in rivers and lakes, but soil moisture and groundwater together account for 98 percent of the world's available freshwater (figure 3.2).[10] Many people worry about how much drinking water is available,

Figure 3.2   Freshwater in rivers makes up a very small share of the water available on the planet—and agriculture dominates water use

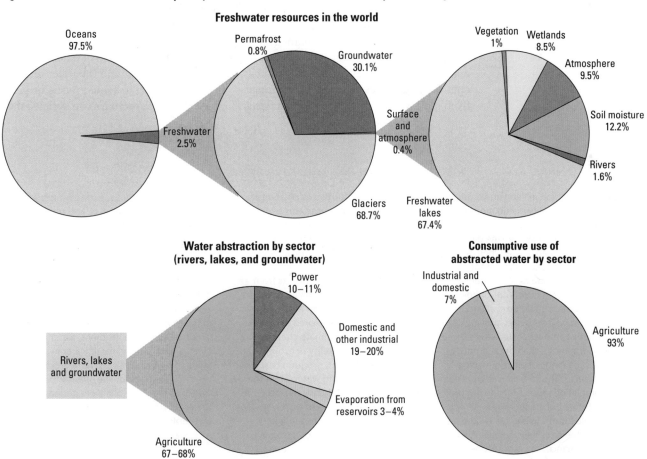

Source: Shiklomanov 1999; Shiklomanov and Rodda 2003; Vassolo and Döll 2005.

Note: When humans use water, they affect the quantity, timing, or quality of water available for other users. Water for human use typically involves withdrawing water from lakes, rivers, or groundwater and either consuming it so that it reenters the atmospheric part of the hydrological cycle or returning it to the hydrological basin. When irrigated crops use water, it is a consumptive use—it becomes unavailable for use elsewhere in the basin. In contrast, releasing water from a dam to drive hydroelectric turbines is a nonconsumptive use because the water is available for downstream users but not necessarily at the appropriate time. Withdrawals by a city for municipal supplies are mainly nonconsumptive, but if the returning water is inadequately treated, the quality of water downstream is affected.

not realizing that agriculture dominates human water use. Each day, a person drinks 2–4 liters of water but eats food that requires 2,000–5,000 liters of water in its production.[11] These averages mask considerable variation. In some basins, industrial and urban use dominates, and more and more basins will be in that situation given the pace of urban growth.[12]

Climate change will reduce the natural water storage of snow and glaciers, which will in turn affect aquifer storage and require water managers to design and operate reservoirs differently. Water managers will have to manage the entire water cycle. They can no longer afford to concentrate on the small share of water in rivers and lakes and leave groundwater and soil moisture to be managed by landowners. Many basins will experience increased demand, reduced availability, and increased variability all at the same time. Water managers in those places will have less room to maneuver if their decisions are not robust to a variety of outcomes. Tools are available to help societies cope with these changes. They range from policy reform to decision-making protocols, from data collection technologies to new infrastructure design.

The effects of climate change on hydrological patterns mean that the past can no longer be used as a guide for future hydrological conditions. So, like other natural resource managers, water engineers are developing new tools that consider impacts across a number of scales and time frames to help evaluate tradeoffs and make choices robust to an uncertain future (box 3.1).[13]

Climate change will make applying and enforcing sound water policies even more important

Allocating water efficiently and limiting water consumption to safe levels will become increasingly important with climate change. When water is scarce, individual users can take too much, making water unavailable to others or harming ecosystems and the services they provide. When consumption in a basin exceeds the amount of water available, users must use less, and the water must be shared according to some process or principles. Policy makers have two options: they

---

BOX 3.1   *Robust decision making: Changing how water managers do business*

Traditional decision making under uncertainty uses probability distributions to rank different options for action, based on the envelope of risk from the past. But this approach is inadequate when decision makers do not know or cannot agree on how actions relate to consequences, how likely different events are, or how different outcomes should be evaluated. As chapter 2 shows, robust decision making is an alternative. Robust strategies are those that perform better than the alternatives across a wide range of plausible future circumstances. They are derived from computer simulation models that do not predict the future but create large ensembles of plausible futures to identify candidate robust strategies and systematically assess their performance. The process does not choose an optimal solution; instead, it finds the strategy that minimizes vulnerability to a range of possible risks.

Southern California's Inland Empire Utilities Agency has used this technique to respond to the effects of climate change on its long-term urban water management plan First, the agency derived probable regional climate projections by combining outputs from 21 climate models. Coupled with a water management simulation model, hundreds of scenarios explored assumptions about future climate change, the quantity and availability of groundwater, urban development, program costs, and the cost of importing water. Then the agency calculated the present value of costs of different ways to supply water under 200 scenarios. They rejected any strategy that gave costs above $3.75 billion over 35 years. Scenario discovery analysis concluded that the costs would be unacceptable if three things happened at the same time: large

precipitation declines, large changes in the price of water imports, and reductions of natural percolation into the groundwater basin.

The goal of the process is to reduce the agency's vulnerability if those three things happen at the same time. The agency identified new management responses including increasing water-use efficiency, capturing more storm water for groundwater replenishment, water recycling, and importing more water in wet years so that in dry years more groundwater can be extracted. The agency found that, if all these actions were undertaken, the costs would almost never exceed the threshold of $3.75 billion.

Source: Groves and others 2008; Groves and Lempert 2007; Groves, Yates, and Tebaldi 2008.

can either set and enforce fixed quantities for specific users, or they can use prices to encourage users to cut back and even trade among themselves. Either way, designing and enforcing good policies require accurate information and strong institutions.

Quantitative allocations are most common, and it is difficult to do them well. South Africa has one of the most sophisticated schemes, though it is still a work in progress. Its 1998 National Water Act stipulates that water is public property and cannot be privately owned.[14] All users must register and license their water use and pay for it, including river or groundwater extracted at their own expense. *Streamflow reduction activity* is a category of water use, which means that owners of plantation forests must apply for a license just like an irrigator or a town's water utility. Only plantation forestry has so far been categorized as a streamflow reduction activity, but rainfed agriculture or water harvesting techniques could follow. Counting forestry as a water user makes land use compete squarely with other water users. The only guaranteed rights to water are for ecological reserves and to ensure that each person has at least 25 liters daily for basic human needs.[15]

Water is almost always priced below its value, giving users little incentive to use it efficiently.[16] The literature is virtually unanimous in calling for economic instruments to reduce demand.[17] Charging for water services (irrigation, drinking water, wastewater collection and treatment) can also recover the cost of providing the service and maintaining infrastructure.[18]

The role of pricing to influence demand varies for different types of water use. For municipal water, pricing tends to be effective at reducing demand, especially when combined with user outreach. When the price is high, many utilities and users fix leaks and use only what they need.[19] But because urban consumption accounts on average for only 20 percent of water abstractions, the effects on overall use are limited (figure 3.2). And because municipal use is basically nonconsumptive, the impact of reduced use in cities does little to increase availability elsewhere in the basin.

For irrigation, a consumptive use, pricing is more complex. First, the amount of water actually consumed is difficult to measure. Second, experience shows that farmers do not reduce consumption until the price is several multiples of the cost of providing the service. Yet most countries find it politically unacceptable to charge much more than is required to recover the operational costs. Third, too steep an increase in the price of surface water will encourage any farmer who can drill into an aquifer to switch to groundwater, shifting but not eliminating the problem of overuse.[20]

In most countries the state or another owner of the water charges the city utility or irrigation agency for the water extracted from the river or aquifer. This is known as bulk water. For a host of technical and political reasons few countries charge enough for bulk water to affect the way resources are allocated between competing uses.[21] Indeed, no country allocates surface water by price,[22] although Australia is moving toward such a system.[23] Although far from straightforward, fixed quotas on the combined quantity of surface and groundwater allocated to irrigation, or, better, the amount of water actually consumed (evapotranspiration), seem to be politically and administratively more realistic than pricing to limit overall consumptive use.[24]

Tradable water rights could improve water management in the long term but are not realistic short-term options in most developing countries. Tradable rights have great potential for making water allocation more efficient and for compensating people who forgo their water use.[25] Formal tradable water rights schemes are in place in Australia, Chile, South Africa, and the western United States. In Australia, evaluations indicate that trading rights has helped farmers withstand droughts and spurred innovation and investment without government intervention.

But the details of the design greatly affect the success of the venture, and establishing the necessary institutions is a lengthy process. It took decades to develop this capacity in Australia, a country with a long history of good governance, where customers were educated and accustomed to following rules, and where allocation rules were broadly in place and enforced before the rights system was established.[26] Countries that allow water trading when they do not have the institutional ability to enforce the quotas assigned to each user tend to increase overextraction considerably (box 3.2).

Climate change, which makes future water resources less predictable, complicates the already challenging task of establishing tradable water rights.[27] Even in a stable climate, sophisticated agencies find it difficult to determine in advance how much water can safely be allocated to different users, and how much should be set aside for environmental purposes.[28] By not properly accounting for certain uses (such as plantation forestry and natural vegetation) or for changes in user behavior, the schemes in Australia and Chile assigned rights for more water than was actually available. They had to undergo the painful process of reassigning or reducing the allocations.[29] Properly regulated markets for fixed quantities of water are a good long-term goal, but most developing countries need to take a number

of crucial interim steps before adopting such a system.[30]

Climate change will require investing in new technologies and improving the application of existing technologies

Water storage can help with increased variability.   Storage in rivers, lakes, soil, and aquifers is a key aspect of any strategy to manage variability—both for droughts (storing water for use in dry periods) and for floods (keeping storage capacity available for excess flows). Because climate change will reduce natural storage in the form of ice and snow and in aquifers (by reducing recharge), many countries will need increased artificial storage.

Water planners will need to consider storage options across the entire landscape. Water stored in soil can be used more efficiently by managing land cover, particularly by improving the productivity of rainfed agriculture. Managing groundwater, already challenging, will be more important as surface water becomes less reliable. Groundwater is a cushion for coping with unreliable public supplies and rainfall. For example, it supplies 60 percent of irrigated agriculture and 85 percent of rural drinking

---

BOX 3.2   *The dangers of establishing a market for water rights before the institutional structures are in place*

A review based on the Australian experience concludes that "with the benefit of hindsight and emerging experience, it is becoming clearer that . . . it is necessary to attend to many design issues. Water trading is likely to be successful unambiguously if and only if allocation and use management regimes are designed for trading and associated governance arrangements prevent over-allocation from occurring. Opposition to the development of markets without attention to design detail is justified."

Design concerns include accounting (proper assessment of the interconnected surface- and groundwater, planning for climatic shifts to drier conditions, and expanded consumption by plantation forestry because of public subsidies), and institutional issues (designing separate

rules and agencies to define entitlements, manage allocations, and control the use of water; developing accurate registers early in the process; allowing unused water to be carried over from year to year; developing a private brokerage industry; and ensuring timely flow of information to all parties).

Some countries have long-standing informal water-trading arrangements. The ones that work are often based on customary practices. Farmers in Bitit, Morocco, for example, have traded water for decades, based on rules established by customary practices. The system operates from a detailed list available to the entire community, which identifies each shareholder and specifies the amount of water each is entitled to, expressed as hours of flow.

Schemes that allow trading in the absence of established and enforced water rights can worsen overexploitation. Farmers near the city of Ta'iz, in the Republic of Yemen, sell their groundwater to tankers to supply the city. Before this market existed, the farmer withdrew only as much water from the aquifer as his crops needed. By increasing the price of a unit of water, the trading increases the benefits of using groundwater. And because the farmer's extraction from his well is not controlled, there is no limit to the amount he can extract. As a result, the unregulated market accelerates the depletion of the aquifer.

Sources: CEDARE 2006; World Bank 2007b; Young and McColl, forthcoming.

water in India as well as half the drinking water received by households in Delhi. Well managed, groundwater can continue to act as a natural buffer. But it is far from well managed. In arid regions across the world, aquifers are overexploited. Up to a quarter of India's annual agricultural harvest is estimated to be at risk because of groundwater depletion.[31]

Improving groundwater management requires actions to enhance both supply (artificial recharge, accelerated natural recharge, barriers within aquifers to retard underground flows) and demand. And groundwater cannot be managed alone—it must be integrated with regulation of surface water.[32] Supply enhancing techniques are not straightforward. For example, artificial recharge is of limited use when water and suitable aquifer storage sites are not in the same places as the overstressed aquifers; 43 percent of the funds allocated for India's $6 billion artificial recharge program is likely to be spent recharging aquifers that are not overexploited.[33]

Dams will be an important part of the story of climate change and water. And they will need to be designed with built-in flexibility to deal with potential precipitation and runoff changes in their basins. Many of the best sites for dams are already exploited, yet the potential for new dams does exist, particularly in Africa. Managed well, dams provide hydropower and protect against droughts and floods. Comprehensive analyses of the economic impacts of dams are rare, but four case studies indicate positive direct economic effects and large indirect effects, with the poor sometimes benefiting disproportionately.[34] The High Dam at Aswan in Egypt, for example, has generated net annual economic benefits equivalent to 2 percent of Egypt's gross domestic product (GDP).[35] It has generated 8 billion kilowatt-hours of energy, enough to electrify all of the country's towns and villages. It has allowed the expansion of agriculture and year-round navigation (stimulating investments in Nile cruises) and has saved the country's crops and infrastructure from droughts and floods. But dams have well-known negative effects as well,[36] and the tradeoffs need to be weighed carefully. Climate change puts a premium on identifying robust designs: where countries face uncertainty about even whether their rainfall will increase or decrease, it can be cost-effective to build structures that are specifically designed to be changed in the future. As hydraulic systems increase in complexity, countries need solid hydrological, operational, economic, and financial analyses and capable institutions all the more (box 3.3).

Nonconventional technologies can increase water availability in some water-scarce regions. Water supplies can be enhanced by desalinating seawater or brackish water and reusing treated wastewater. Desalination, which accounted for less than 0.5 percent of all water use in 2004,[37] is set to become more widely used.

Technical developments, including energy-efficient filters, are causing desalination prices to fall, and pilot schemes are beginning to power desalination plants with renewable energy.[38] Depending on the

---

BOX 3.3 *Managing water resources within the margin of error: Tunisia*

Tunisia is a good example of the demands on water managers in countries that are approaching the limits of their resources. With only 400 cubic meters of renewable resources per capita, which are highly variable and distributed unevenly over time and space, Tunisia has a huge challenge managing its water. Yet in contrast to its Maghreb neighbors, it has withstood consecutive droughts without rationing water to farmers or resorting to supplying cities from barges. It has built dams with conduits to connect them and to transfer water between different areas of the country.

As the most promising schemes were developed, the government built additional infrastructure in more marginal areas. Rivers that flowed to the sea have been dammed even when water demand in those basins is not intense. The stored water can be pumped across the mountain range into the country's principal river basin. The new water both increases supply and dilutes the salinity in the area where water demand is highest. In addition, Tunisia treats and reuses one-third of its urban wastewater for agriculture and wetlands, and recharges aquifers artificially. Tunisian water managers now face a complex set of decisions: they must optimize water quantity, timing, quality, and energy costs, showing the importance of human capacity to manage resources so intensively.

Source: Louati 2009.

scale of the plant and the technology, desalinated water can be produced and delivered to the utility for as little as $0.50 per cubic meter. This remains more expensive than conventional sources when freshwater is available.[39] Therefore, desalinated water usually makes sense only for the highest-value uses, such as urban water supply or tourist resorts.[40] It also tends to be limited to coastal areas, because inland distribution of desalinated water adds to the costs.[41]

Producing more food without more water will not be easy, but some new approaches will help.   Managing water to meet future needs will also involve making water use more efficient, particularly in agriculture, which accounts for 70 percent of freshwater withdrawals from rivers and groundwater (figure 3.2).[42]

There appears to be scope for increasing the productivity of water in rainfed agriculture, which provides livelihoods for the majority of the world's poor, generates more than half of the gross value of the world's crops, and accounts for 80 percent of the world's crop water use.[43] Options, described in the next section, include mulching, conservation tillage, and similar techniques that retain water in the soil so that less is lost to evaporation and more is available to plants. Other options involve small-scale rainwater storage, sometimes called water harvesting.

Of the various interventions to increase rainfed production, some (mulching, conservation tillage) divert some water that would otherwise evaporate unproductively. Others (water harvesting, groundwater pumps) divert some water that would otherwise have been available to users downstream. When water is plentiful, impacts on other users are imperceptible, but as water becomes scarcer, the impacts become more important. Once again, comprehensive accounting for water and integrated planning of land and water at local, watershed, and regional scales can make these interventions productive, by ensuring that the tradeoffs are properly evaluated.

Irrigated agriculture is expected to produce a greater share of the world's food in the future, as it is more resilient to climate change in all but the most water-scarce basins.[44] Crop productivity per hectare will have to increase, because there is little scope for increasing the total area under irrigation. Indeed, irrigated land is expected to increase by just 9 percent between 2000 and 2050.[45] And water productivity (in this case, agricultural output per unit of water allocated to irrigation) will also have to improve, given the increasing water demands of cities, industries, and hydropower. New technologies have the potential to increase water productivity when combined with strong policies and institutions.[46]

Getting more "crop per drop" involves a complex combination of investments and institutional changes. Countries from Armenia to Zambia are investing in new infrastructure that delivers the water efficiently from the reservoir to the crops, reducing evaporative losses. However, as the example of the Moroccan farmers described earlier indicates, the investments can work only if local institutions deliver the water reliably, farmers have a voice in decision making, and they can get the advice they need on how to make the most of the new infrastructure or technological developments. New infrastructure will help water management only if combined with strong quantitative limits on each individual's water consumption, covering both ground and surface water. Otherwise, the increased profitability of irrigation will tempt farmers to expand their cultivated area or double- or triple-crop their fields, drawing ever more water from their wells. This is good for the individual farmer, certainly, but not for the other water users in the basin.[47]

Good crop management can increase water productivity by developing varieties resistant to cold so that crops can be grown in the winter, when less water is required.[48] Growing crops in greenhouses or under shade screens also can reduce the evaporative demand of open fields, though it does increase production costs.[49] When crops die before they produce their yields, the water they have consumed is wasted. Therefore more widespread adoption of drought- and heat-tolerant varieties will increase water as well as agricultural productivity.[50]

Well-timed applications of irrigation water can also help. If farmers do not know exactly how much water is needed, they often overirrigate because a little extra water is less harmful to yields than too little water. By monitoring water intake and growth throughout the growing season, farmers can deliver the exact amount of water that their crops need and irrigate only when really necessary. Remote-sensing systems are beginning to allow farmers to see the water needs of plants with great accuracy even before the plants show signs of stress.[51] But because of the technological requirements, precision agriculture of this type is limited to a small number of the world's farmers.[52]

Even before this technology becomes widely available, it is possible to apply simple automated systems to help poorer farmers increase the precision of applying irrigation water. The Moroccan farmers who convert to drip irrigation under the government scheme discussed earlier will benefit from a simple technology that uses a standard irrigation formula adapted to local growing conditions. Depending on the weather in the area, the system will deliver a message to

farmers' cell phones telling them how many hours they should irrigate that day. Acting on this information will allow them to avoid overirrigating.[53]

Producing more in agriculture while protecting the environment

Climate change will push societies to accelerate agricultural productivity growth

Climate change will depress agricultural yields. Climate change adds several conflicting pressures to agricultural production. It will affect agriculture directly through higher temperatures, greater crop water demand, more variable rainfall, and extreme climate events such as floods and droughts. It will increase yields in some countries but lower them in most of the developing world, reducing global average yields (map 3.3).

Map 3.3   Climate change will depress agricultural yields in most countries by 2050 given current agricultural practices and crop varieties

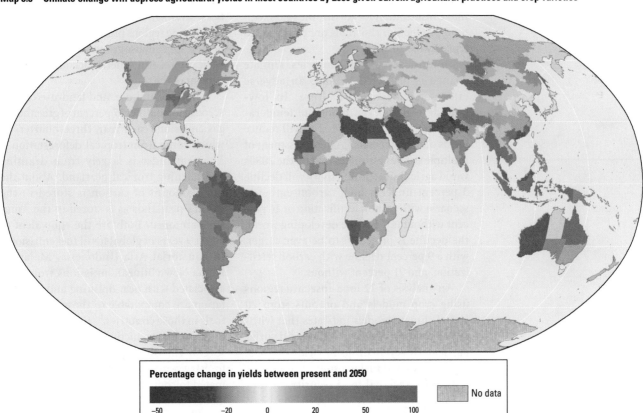

Percentage change in yields between present and 2050

−50   −20   0   20   50   100   No data

Source: Müller and others 2009.

Note: The figure shows the projected percentage change in yields of 11 major crops (wheat, rice, maize, millet, field pea, sugar beet, sweet potato, soybean, groundnut, sunflower, and rapeseed) from 2046 to 2055, compared with 1996–2005. The values are the mean of three emission scenarios across five global climate models, assuming no CO_2 fertilization (see note 54). Large negative yield impacts are projected in many areas that are highly dependent on agriculture.

In mid to high latitudes, local increases in temperature of only 1–3°C, along with associated carbon fertilization[54] and rainfall changes, may have small beneficial impacts on crop yields.[55] Kazakhstan, the Russian Federation, and Ukraine are all geographically positioned to benefit from these temperature increases, but they may not be able to capitalize fully on the opportunities. Since the breakup of the Soviet Union, together they have removed 23 million hectares of arable land from production, almost 90 percent of which was used for grain production.[56] Although world grain yields have been rising on average by about 1.5 percent a year since 1991, yields in Kazakhstan and Ukraine have fallen, and Russia's yields have risen only slightly. If these countries are to take advantage of the warming temperatures to increase agricultural production, they will have to build stronger institutions and better infrastructure.[57] Even if they do, extreme climate events may wipe out the improved average conditions: when the increased likelihood of extreme climate events is taken into consideration for Russia, the years with food production shortfalls are projected to triple by the 2070s.[58]

In most developing countries, climate change is projected to have an adverse effect on current agriculture. In low-latitude regions even moderate temperature increases of another 1–2°C will reduce yields of major cereals.[59] One assessment of multiple studies estimates that by the 2080s world agricultural productivity will decline 3 percent under a high-carbon-emission scenario with carbon fertilization or 16 percent without it.[60] For the developing world, the decline is projected to be even larger, with a 9 percent decline with carbon fertilization, and 21 percent without.

An analysis of 12 food-insecure regions using crop models and outputs from 20 global climate models indicates that without adaptation Asia and Africa will suffer particularly severe drops in yields by 2030. These losses will include some of the crops critical for regional food security, including wheat in South Asia, rice in Southeast Asia, and maize in southern Africa.[61] These projections are likely to underestimate the impact: models that project the effect of climate change on agriculture typically look at average changes and exclude the effects of extreme events, variability, and agricultural pests, all of which are likely to increase. Climate change will also make some land less suitable for agriculture, particularly in Africa.[62] One study projects that by 2080 land with severe climate or soil constraints in Sub-Saharan Africa will increase by 26 million to 61 million hectares.[63] That is 9–20 percent of the region's arable land.[64]

Efforts to mitigate climate change will put more pressure on land. In addition to reducing yields, climate change will put pressure on farmers and other land managers to reduce greenhouse gas emissions. In 2004 about 14 percent of global greenhouse gas emissions came from agricultural practices. This includes nitrous oxide from fertilizers; methane from livestock, rice production, and manure storage; and carbon dioxide (CO_2) from burning biomass, but excludes CO_2 emissions from soil management practices, savannah burning, and deforestation.[65] Developing regions produce the largest share of these greenhouse gas emissions, with Asia, Africa, and Latin America accounting for 80 percent of the total.

Forestry, land use, and land-use change account for another 17 percent of greenhouse gas emissions each year, three-quarters of which come from tropical deforestation.[66] The remainder is largely from draining and burning tropical peatland. About the same amount of carbon is stored in the world's peatlands as is stored in the Amazon rainforest. Both are the equivalent of about 9 years of global fossil fuel emissions. In equatorial Asia (Indonesia, Malaysia, Papua New Guinea), emissions from fires associated with peat draining and deforestation are comparable to those from fossil fuels in those countries.[67] Emissions related to livestock production are counted across several emissions categories (agriculture, forestry, waste), and overall they are estimated to contribute up to 18 percent of the global total, mostly through methane emissions from the animals, manure waste, and clearing for pasture.[68]

The cultivation of biofuels to mitigate climate change will create even more competition for land. Current estimates indicate that dedicated energy crop production takes place on only 1 percent of global arable land, but biofuel legislation in developed and developing countries supports expanding production. Global ethanol production increased from 18 billion liters a year in 2000 to 46 billion in 2007, while biodiesel production increased nearly eightfold to 8 billion liters. Land allocated to biofuels is projected to increase fourfold by 2030, with most of the growth in North America (accounting for 10 percent of arable land in 2030) and Europe (15 percent).[69] Projections indicate that only 0.4 percent of arable land in Africa and about 3 percent in Asia and Latin America will be dedicated to biofuel production by 2030.[70] Under some scenarios for mitigating climate change, projections beyond 2030 suggest that land allocated to producing biofuels by 2100 will grow to more than 2 billion hectares—a huge figure given that current cropland covers "only" 1.6 billion hectares. These scenarios project that most of the land for such large-scale biofuel production will originate from conversion of natural forests and pastureland.[71]

If demand increases rapidly, biofuels will be a significant factor in agricultural markets, increasing commodity prices. Much of the current demand for biofuel crops is spurred by government targets and subsidies and by high oil prices. Without artificial support the competitiveness of biofuels is still poor, with the exception of Brazil's sugarcane ethanol. Nor is it clear how much biofuels reduce greenhouse gas emissions because of the fossil fuels used during production and the emissions from land clearing. Despite the potential that biofuels have to decrease greenhouse gas emissions, the actual net carbon savings of current-generation biofuels is under debate, when production processes and associated land-use changes are factored in to the calculations. In addition, demand for land for biofuels already competes with biodiversity conservation. As a result, it is important to establish guidelines for expansion of biofuels so that other environmental goals are not squeezed out (box 3.4). Comprehensive life-cycle accounting for biofuels—which includes their contribution to emission reductions as well as their water and fertilizer use—may slow the pace of conversion.

Second-generation biofuels now under development, such as algae, *jatropha*, sweet sorghum, and willows, could reduce competition with agricultural land for food crops by using less land or marginal land, although some of these developments could still lead to the loss of pasture land and grassland ecosystems. Perennial crops with deeper root systems, such as switchgrass, can better combat soil and nutrient erosion, require fewer nutrient inputs, and sequester higher rates of carbon than current biofuel feedstocks.[72] But their water needs may prohibit their sustainable production in arid regions. More research is needed to improve the productivity and emission reduction potential of future generations of biofuels.

Growing populations, more carnivorous palates, and climate change will require large increases in agricultural productivity. The amount of land needed to feed the world in 2050 will depend significantly on how much meat people eat. Meat is a resource-intensive way for humans to consume protein, because it requires land for pasture and grain feed. The resource implications vary with the type of meat and how it is produced. Producing 1 kg of beef can take as much as 15,000 liters of water if it is produced in industrial feedlots in the United States (figure 3.3).[73,74] But extensive beef production in Africa requires only 146–300 liters per kilogram depending on the weather.[75] Per kilogram, beef production is also greenhouse-gas intensive, even compared with other meat production, emitting 16 kilograms of CO_2 equivalent (CO_2e) for every kilogram of meat produced (figure 3.4).[76]

Despite the resource implications, demand for meat is expected to increase as population and incomes grow. Eating more

BOX 3.4   *Palm oil, emission reductions, and avoided deforestation*

Palm oil plantations represent the convergence of many current land-use issues. Palm oil is a high-yielding crop with food and biofuel uses, and its cultivation creates opportunities for smallholders. But it infringes on tropical forests and their many benefits, including greenhouse gas mitigation. Cultivation of palm oil has tripled since 1961 to cover 13 million hectares, with most of the expansion in Indonesia and Malaysia and more than half on recently deforested lands. Recent announcements for new palm oil concessions in the Brazilian Amazon, Papua New Guinea, and Madagascar raise concerns that the trend is likely to continue.

Smallholders currently manage 35 to 40 percent of the land under palm oil cultivation in Indonesia and Malaysia, providing a profitable diversification in livelihoods. However, harvested palm nuts must be delivered to mills for processing within 24 hours of harvesting, so holdings tend to cluster around mills. Thus a high proportion of the area around mills is converted to palm oil, either as large tract commercial plantations or densely clustered smallholdings. Certain landscape design practices, such as the creation of agroforestry belts to smooth the transition between palm oil plantations and forest patches, can help make the plantation landscape less inimical to biodiversity while providing further diversification for smallholders.

The mitigation value of biodiesel derived from palm oil is also questionable. Detailed life-cycle analysis shows that the net reduction in carbon emissions depends on the land cover existing before the palm oil plantation (figure). Significant emission reductions derive from plantations developed on previous grasslands and cropland, whereas net emissions will increase greatly if peatland forests are cleared for producing palm oil.

The expansion of the carbon market to include REDD (Reduced Emissions from Deforestation and forest Degradation) is an important tool to balance the relative values of palm oil production and deforestation on one hand, and forest protection on the other. This balance will be critical to ensure biodiversity protection and emission reduction.

Recent studies show that converting land to palm oil production may be between six to ten times more profitable than maintaining the land and receiving payments for carbon credits through REDD, should this mechanism be limited to the voluntary market. If REDD credits are given the same price as carbon credits traded in compliance markets, the profitability of land conservation would increase dramatically, perhaps even exceeding profits from palm oil, making agricultural conversion less attractive. Therefore, done right, REDD could realistically reduce deforestation and thereby contribute to a global mitigation effort.

Emission reductions from biodiesel derived from palm oil differ greatly according to the previous land use on the palm oil plantation site.

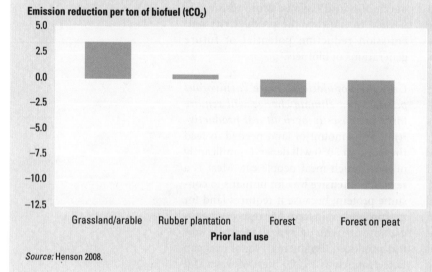

Emission reduction per ton of biofuel (tCO_2)

Prior land use: Grassland/arable, Rubber plantation, Forest, Forest on peat

Source: Henson 2008.

Sources: Butler, Koh, and Ghazoul, forthcoming; Henson 2008; Koh, Levang, and Ghazoul, forthcoming; Koh and Wilcove 2009; Venter and others 2009.

meat will be beneficial for poor consumers who need the protein and micronutrients.[77] But by 2050 the production of beef, poultry, pork, and milk is expected to at least double from 2000 levels to respond to the demand of larger, wealthier, and more urban populations.[78]

The world will have to meet the growing demand for food, fiber, and biofuel in a changing climate that reduces yields—while at the same time conserving ecosystems that store carbon and provide other essential services. Obtaining more land suitable for agricultural production is unlikely. Studies indicate that globally the amount of land suitable for agriculture will remain the same in 2080 as it is today,[79] because increases in suitable land in the higher latitudes will be largely offset by losses in the lower latitudes.

Therefore agriculture productivity (tons per hectare) will need to increase. Models vary but one study indicates that annual increases of 1.8 percent a year will be needed

Figure 3.3   Meat is much more water intensive than major crops
(liters of water per kilogram of product)

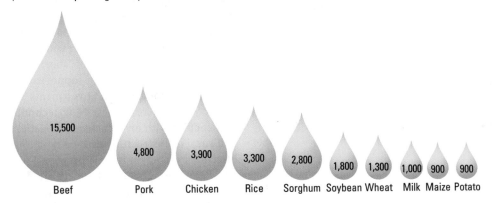

Source: Waterfootprint (https://www.waterfootprint.org), accessed May 15, 2009; Gleick 2008.

Note: Figure shows liters of water needed to produce one kilogram of product (or one liter for milk). Water use for beef production only characterizes intensive production systems.

up to 2055—almost twice the 1 percent a year that would be needed under business as usual (figure 3.5).[80] This means that yields will have to more than double over 50 years. Many of the world's breadbaskets, such as North America, are approaching maximum feasible yields for major cereals,[81] so a significant portion of this yield growth will need to occur in developing countries. This means not just an acceleration of yield growth but a reversal of recent slowing: the yield growth rate for all cereals in developing countries slipped from 3.9 percent a year between 1961 and 1990 to 1.4 percent a year between 1990 and 2007.[82]

Climate change will require highly productive and diverse agricultural landscapes

Productivity gains must not come at the expense of soil, water, and biodiversity. Intensive agriculture often damages natural systems. Highly productive agriculture, such as is practiced in much of the developed world, is usually based on farms that specialize in a particular crop or animal and on the intensive use of agrochemicals. This kind of farming can damage water quality and quantity. Fertilizer runoff has increased the number of low-oxygen "dead zones" in coastal oceans exponentially since the 1960s: they now cover about 245,000 square kilometers, mostly in coastal waters of the developed world (map 3.4).[83] Intensive irri-

gation often causes salt to build up in soils, reducing fertility and limiting food production. Salinization currently affects between 20 million and 30 million of the world's 260 million hectares of irrigated land.[84]

Less environmentally deleterious agricultural intensification is essential, particularly considering the environmental problems associated with further extensification of agriculture. Without increased crop and livestock yields per hectare, pressure on land resources will accelerate as crop and pasture areas expand under extensive production. Since the middle of the 20th century, 680 million hectares, or 20 percent of the world's grazing lands, have been

Figure 3.4   Intensive beef production is a heavy producer of greenhouse gas emissions

Food item (1 kg)	Emissions (kg CO_2e)	Driving distance equivalent (km)
Potato	0.24	1.2
Wheat	0.80	4.0
Chicken	4.60	22.7
Pork	6.40	31.6
Beef	16.00	79.1

Source: Williams, Audsley, and Sandars 2006.

Note: The figure shows CO_2 equivalent emissions in kilograms resulting from the production (in an industrial country) of 1 kilogram of a specific product. The driving distance equivalent conveys the number of kilometers one must drive in a gasoline-powered car averaging 11.5 kilometers a liter to produce the given amount of CO_2e emissions. For example, producing 1 kilogram of beef and driving 79.1 kilometers both result in 16 kilograms of emissions.

Figure 3.5 Agricultural productivity will have to increase even more rapidly because of climate change

Agricultural productivity index (2005 = 100)

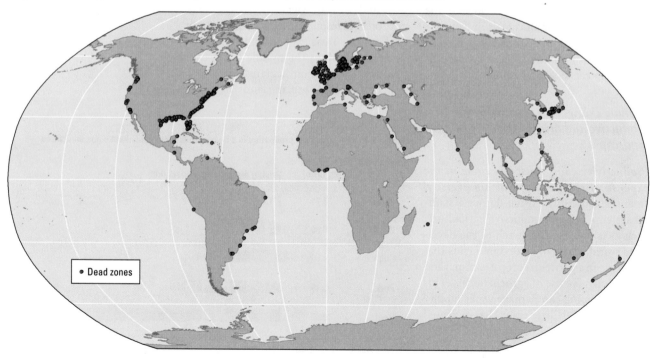

Source: Lotze-Campen and others 2009.

Note: The figure shows the required annual growth in an agricultural productivity index under two scenarios. In this index, 100 indicates productivity in 2005. The projections include all major food and feed crops. The green line represents a scenario without climate change of global population increasing to 9 billion in 2055; total calorie consumption per capita and the dietary share of animal calories increasing in proportion to rising per capita income from economic growth; further trade liberalization (doubling the share of agricultural trade in total production over the next 50 years); cropland continuing to grow at historical rates of 0.8 percent a year; and no climate change impacts. The orange line represents a scenario of climate change impacts and associated societal responses (IPCC SRES A2): no CO_2 fertilization, and agricultural trade reduced to 1995 levels (about 7 percent of total production) on the assumption that climate change-related price volatility triggers protectionism and that mitigation policy curbs the expansion of cropland (because of forest conservation activities) and increases demand for bioenergy (reaching 100 EJ [10^{18} joules] globally in 2055).

degraded.[85] Converting land for agriculture has already significantly reduced the area of many ecosystems (figure 3.6).

The Green Revolution illustrates both the immense benefits from increasing agricultural productivity and the shortcomings when technology is not supported by appropriate policies and investments to protect natural resources. New technology, coupled with investments in irrigation and rural infrastructure, drove a doubling of cereal production in Asia between 1970 and 1995. The agricultural growth and the associated decline in food prices during this time led to a near doubling of real per capita income, and the number of poor people fell from about 60 percent of the population to 30 percent, even as the population increased 60 percent.[86] Latin America also experienced significant gains. But in Africa, poor infrastructure, high transport costs, low investment in irrigation, and pricing and marketing policies that penalized farmers all impeded adoption of the new technologies.[87] Despite its overall success,

Map 3.4   Intensive agriculture in the developed world has contributed to the proliferation of dead zones

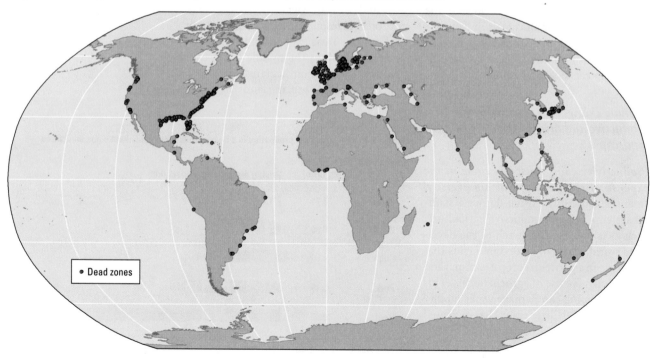

Source: Diaz and Rosenberg 2008.

Note: In the developed world intensive agriculture has often come at high environmental cost, including runoff of excess fertilizers leading to dead zones in coastal areas. Dead zones are defined as extreme hypoxic zones, that is, areas where oxygen concentrations are lower than 0.5 milliliters of oxygen per liter of water. These conditions normally lead to mass mortality of sea organisms, although in some of these zones organisms have been found that can survive at oxygen levels of 0.1 milliliter per liter of water.

the Green Revolution in many parts of Asia was accompanied by environmental damages stemming from overuse of fertilizer, pesticides, and water. Perverse subsidies and pricing and trade policies that encouraged monoculture of rice and wheat and heavy use of inputs contributed to these environmental problems.[88]

Climate-resilient farming requires diverse income sources, production choices, and genetic material. Climate change will create a less predictable world. Crops will fail more often. One way to buffer the uncertainty is to diversify on all levels (box 3.5). The first type of diversification relates to sources of income, including some outside of agriculture.[89] As farms get smaller and input prices increase, farmers will do this anyway. Indeed, in much of Asia smallholders and landless workers typically earn more than half their total household income from nonagricultural sources.[90]

A second type of diversification involves increasing the types of production on the farm. The market opportunities for crop diversification are expanding in many intensively farmed areas as a result of more open export markets and buoyant national demand in rapidly growing economies, especially in Asia and Latin America.[91] In these regions farmers may be able to diversify into livestock, horticulture, and specialized agricultural production.[92] These activities typically give high returns per unit of land and are labor intensive, which makes them suitable to small farms.

The third type of diversification involves increasing the genetic variability within individual crop varieties. Most high-yielding varieties in use on highly productive farms were bred on the assumption that the climate varied within a stable envelope; the breeders aimed for seed to be increasingly homogenous. In a changing climate, however, farmers can no longer rely on a handful of varieties that work under a narrow set of environmental conditions. Farmers will need each batch of seeds to contain genetic material able to deal with a variety of climatic conditions. Each year, some plants flourish whatever the climate that year. Over a number of years the average

Figure 3.6 Ecosystems have already been extensively converted for agriculture

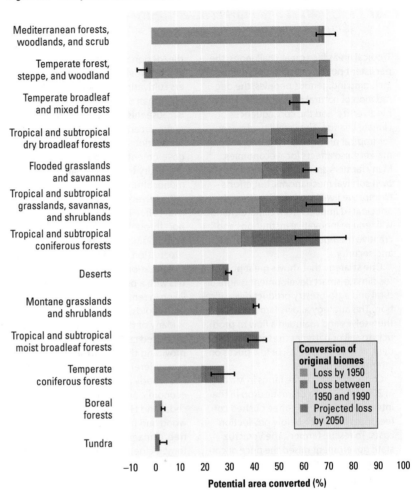

Source: Millennium Ecosystem Assessment 2005.

Note: The projections are based on four scenarios of how the world will approach ecosystem services and include assumptions about ecosystem management, trade liberalization, technology, and the treatment of public goods.

yields will be higher from diverse seeds than from uniform seeds, even though yields in a "normal" year may be lower.

Experiments using standard cultivation practices indicate that under increased CO_2 concentrations and higher temperatures (reflecting projections of the Intergovernmental Panel on Climate Change for 2050) older varieties of wheat or barley may grow faster and have an advantage over more modern varieties introduced in the late 20th century.[93] Furthermore, the wild relatives of today's crops contain genetic material that may be useful to make commercial crops more adaptable to changing conditions. Increased temperatures and CO_2 levels have a greater positive effect on

BOX 3.5 *Product and market diversification: An economic and ecological alternative for marginal farmers in the tropics*

Tropical areas face great challenges: the persistent poverty of rural populations, including indigenous peoples; the degradation of natural resources; the loss of biodiversity; and the consequences of climate change. The volatility of prices for tropical products on the international markets also affects local economies. Many farmers around the world have their own survival mechanisms, but efforts to improve livelihoods and address the anticipated impacts from climate change will require innovative institutions and creative methods for income generation and security.

One strategy that shows great potential for climate-smart development is agricultural and agroforestry product diversification. This strategy allows farmers to feed themselves and maintain a flow of products to sell or barter at the local market despite droughts, pests, or low prices on international markets.

Consider small coffee farms in Mexico. In 2001 and 2002 a dramatic drop in the international price of coffee pushed coffee prices in Mexico below production costs. To rescue farmers, the Veracruz state government raised the price of coffee produced in the area by establishing the "designation of origin of Veracruz" and by providing subsidies only to farmers cultivating high-quality coffee in areas more than 600 meters above sea level. Because this policy would hurt thousands of producers living in the low-quality production area below 600 meters, the government invited the Veracruzana University to find alternatives to coffee monoculture.

The diversification of productive lowland coffee lands found financial support through the UN Common Fund for Commodities, with the sponsorship and supervision of the International Coffee Organization. It started in two municipalities with a pilot group of 1,500 farmers, living in remote communities with 25–100 households.

Many of the farmers had traditionally produced coffee in a multicrop system, providing the opportunity to test in each plot different configurations of alternative woody and herbaceous species of economic and cultural value: Spanish cedar and Honduras mahogany trees (for wood and furniture), the Panama rubber tree, cinnamon, guava (as food and phytomedicine), *jatropha* (for food and biofuel), allspice, cocoa, maize, vanilla, chile, passion fruit, alongside coffee. All trees, herbs, and produce were locally familiar, except the cinnamon tree. There is a potentially large market for cinnamon, which is usually imported. The farmers are now learning which practices and configurations hold the best production potential in this innovative diversified system.

A cooperative company pooled different agricultural products in groups with similar market values but with different exposures to climate, pests, and market risks. Early results indicate that this bundling seems to work well, improving livelihoods and increasing the resilience of the communities. The company has been able to sell all product types, several of them at a better price than before the project started. And in the first two years the project introduced a million native timber trees.

Locals report that the practices have reduced erosion and improved soils, benefiting the surrounding ecosystem while buffering against potential future flooding associated with climate change.

Source: Contributed by Arturo Gomez-Pompa.

some weeds than on their cultivated relatives.[94] The genetic material of the weeds could therefore be used to enhance cultivars of commercial crops to produce more resilient varieties.[95]

Productive landscapes can integrate biodiversity. While protected areas may be the cornerstones of conservation, they will never be enough to conserve biodiversity in the face of climate change (see focus B on biodiversity). The world's reserve network roughly quadrupled between 1970 and 2007 to cover about 12 percent of Earth's land,[96] but even that is inadequate to conserve biodiversity. To adequately represent the continent's species in reserves, while capturing a large proportion of their geographic ranges, Africa would have to protect an additional 10 percent of its land, almost twice its current protection.[97] Geographically fixed and often isolated by habitat destruction, reserves are ill-equipped to accommodate species range shifts due to climate change. One study of protected areas in South Africa, Mexico, and Western Europe estimates that between 6 and 20 percent of species may be lost by 2050.[98] Moreover, existing land reserves remain under threat given future economic pressures and frequently weak regulatory and enforcement systems. In 1999 the International Union for the Conservation of Nature determined that less than a quarter of protected areas in 10 developing countries were adequately managed and that more than 10 percent of protected areas were already thoroughly degraded.[99] At least 75 percent of protected forest areas surveyed in Africa lacked long-term funding, even though international donors were involved in 94 percent of them.[100]

A landscape-scale approach to land use can encourage greater biodiversity outside protected areas, which is essential to allow for ecosystem shifts, species dispersal and the promotion of ecosystem services. The field of ecoagriculture holds promise.[101] The idea is to improve the farmland's productivity and simultaneously conserve biodiversity and improve environmental conditions on surrounding lands. Through the methods of ecoagriculture, farmers can increase their agricultural output and reduce their costs, reduce agricultural pollution, and create habitat for biodiversity (figure 3.7).

Effective policies to conserve biodiversity give farmers strong incentives to minimize conversion of natural areas to farmland and to protect or even expand high quality habitat on their land. Other options include incentives to develop ecological networks and corridors between protected areas and other habitats. Studies in North America and Europe show that lands withdrawn from conventional agricultural production (set-asides) unequivocally increase biodiversity.[102]

Agriculture practices that enhance biodiversity often have many co-benefits, such as reducing vulnerability to natural disasters, enhancing farm income and productivity, and providing resilience to climate change. During Hurricane Mitch in 1998 farms using ecoagricultural practices suffered 58 percent, 70 percent, and 99 percent less damage in Honduras, Nicaragua, and Guatemala, respectively, than farms using conventional techniques.[103] In Costa Rica, vegetative windbreaks and fence rows boosted farmers' income from pasture and coffee while also increasing bird diversity.[104] In Zambia the use of leguminous trees[105] and herbaceous cover crops in improved fallow practices increased soil fertility, suppressed weeds, and controlled erosion, thereby almost trebling annual net farm incomes.[106] Bee pollination is more effective when agricultural fields are closer to natural or seminatural habitat,[107] a finding that matters because 87 of the world's 107 leading food crops depend on animal pollinators.[108] Shade-grown coffee systems can protect crops from extreme temperature and drought.[109]

In Costa Rica, Nicaragua, and Colombia silvopastoral systems that integrate trees with pastureland are improving the sustainability of cattle production and diversifying and increasing farmers' incomes.[110] Such systems will be particularly useful as a climate-change adaptation, because trees retain their foliage in most droughts, providing fodder and shade and thus stabilizing milk and meat production. They also can improve water quality. Agricultural production and revenues can go together with

Figure 3.7   Computer simulation of integrated land use in Colombia.

Source: Photograph by Walter Galindo, from the files of Fundación CIPAV (Centro para Investigación en Sistemas Sostenibles de Producción Agropecuaria), Colombia. The photograph represents the Finca "La Sirena," in the Cordillera Central, Valle del Cauca. Arango 2003.

Note: The first photo is the real landscape. The second figure is computer generated and shows what the area would look like if farm productivity were increased by using ecoagricultural principles. The increased productivity would reduce grazing pressure on hillsides, protecting watersheds, sequester carbon through afforestation, and increase habitat for biodiversity between fields.

biodiversity conservation. Indeed, in many cases intact ecosystems generate more revenues than converted ones. In Madagascar managing a 2.2 million hectare forest over 15 years cost $97 million, when accounting for the forgone economic benefits that would have occurred if the land had been converted to agriculture. But the benefits of the well-managed forest (half of which come from watershed protection and reduced soil erosion) were valued between $150 million and $180 million over the same period.[111]

Decades of development experience show how difficult it is in practice to protect habitats for biodiversity. New schemes are however emerging to give landowners strong financial incentives to stop land conversion. These include ways to generate revenues from the services that ecosystems provide to society (see focus B), conservation easements (which pay farmers to take sensitive land out of production),[112] and tradable development rights.[113]

Climate change will require faster adoption of technologies and approaches that increase productivity, cope with climate change, and reduce emissions

Several options will need to be pursued simultaneously to increase productivity. Agricultural research and extension has been underfunded in the past decade. The share of official development assistance for agriculture dropped from 17 percent in 1980 to 4 percent in 2007,[114] despite estimates that rates of return to investment in agricultural research and extension are high (30–50 percent).[115] Public expenditures on agricultural research and development (R&D) in low- and middle-income countries have increased slowly since 1980, from $6 billion in 1981 to $10 billion in 2000 (measured in 2005 purchasing power dollars), and private investments remain a small share (6 percent) of agricultural R&D in those countries.[116] Those trends will have to be reversed if societies are to meet their food needs.

The recently concluded Integrated Assessment of Agricultural Knowledge, Science, and Technology for Development (IAASTD) showed that successful agricultural development under climate change will involve a combination of existing and new approaches.[117] First, countries can build on the traditional knowledge of farmers. Such knowledge embodies a wealth of location-specific adaptation and risk management options that can be applied more widely. Second, policies that change the relative prices that farmers face have great potential to encourage practices that will help the world adapt to climate change (by increasing productivity) and mitigate it (by reducing agricultural emissions).

Third, new or unconventional farming practices can increase productivity and reduce carbon emissions. Farmers are beginning to adopt "conservation agriculture," which includes minimum tillage (where seeds are sowed with minimum soil disturbance and residue coverage on the soil surface is at least 30 percent), crop residue retention, and crop rotations. These tillage methods can increase yields,[118] control soil erosion and runoff,[119] increase water and nutrient-use efficiency,[120] reduce production costs, and in many cases sequester carbon.[121]

In 2008, 100 million hectares, or about 6.3 percent of global arable land, were farmed with minimum tillage—about double the amount in 2001.[122] Most takeup has been in developed countries, because the technique has heavy equipment requirements and has not been modified for conditions in Asia and Africa.[123] Minimum tillage also makes the control of weeds, pests, and diseases more complex, requiring better management.[124]

Nevertheless, in the rice-wheat farming system of the Indo-Gangetic plain of India, farmers adopted zero-tillage on 1.6 million hectares in 2005.[125] In 2007–08 an estimated 20–25 percent of the wheat in two Indian states alone (Haryana and Punjab) was cultivated under minimum tillage, corresponding to 1.26 million hectares.[126] Yields increased by 5–7 percent, and costs came down by $52 a hectare.[127] About 45 percent of Brazilian cropland is farmed using these practices.[128] The use of minimum tillage will probably continue to grow, particularly if the technique becomes eligible for payments for soil carbon sequestration in a compliance carbon market.

Biotechnology could provide a transformational approach to addressing the tradeoffs between land and water stress and agricultural productivity, because it could improve crop productivity, increase crop adaptation to climatic stresses such as drought and heat, mitigate greenhouse gas emissions, reduce pesticide and herbicide applications, and modify plants for better biofuel feedstocks (box 3.6). There is, however, little likelihood of genetic modification affecting water productivity in the short term.[129]

Climate-smart farming practices improve rural livelihoods while mitigating and adapting to climate change. New crop varieties, extended crop rotations (notably for perennial crops), reduced use of fallow land, conservation tillage, cover crops, and biochar can all increase carbon storage (box 3.7). Draining rice paddies at least once during the growing season and applying rice straw waste to the soil in the off-season could reduce methane emissions by 30 percent.[130] Methane emissions from livestock can also be cut by using higher-quality feeds, more precise feeding strategies, and improved grazing practices.[131] Better pasture management alone could achieve about 30 percent of the greenhouse gas abatement potential from agriculture (1.3 gigatons of CO_2e a year by 2030 over 3 billion hectares globally).[132]

As countries intensify agricultural production, the environmental impacts of soil fertility practices will come to the fore.[133] The developed world and many places in Asia

---

BOX 3.6 *Biotech crops could help farmers adapt to climate change*

Conventional selection and plant breeding have produced modern varieties and major productivity gains. In the future a combination of plant breeding and selection of preferred traits through genetic techniques (genetic modification, or GM) is likely to contribute most to producing crops better adapted to pests, droughts, and other environmental stresses accompanying climate change.

A number of crops with genetically modified traits have been broadly commercialized in the last 12 years. In 2007 an estimated 114 million hectares were planted with transgenic crop varieties, mostly with insect-resistant or herbicide-tolerant traits. More than 90 percent of this acreage was planted in only four countries (Argentina, Brazil, Canada, and the United States). These technologies will significantly reduce environmental pollution, increase crop productivity, cut production costs, and reduce nitrous oxide emissions. To date successful breeding programs have produced crop varieties, including cassava and maize, that resist a number of pests and diseases, and herbicide-tolerant varieties of soybean, rapeseed, cotton, and maize are available. Farmers using insect-resistant GM crops have reduced the amount of pesticides they use and the number of active ingredients in the herbicides they apply.

Genes affecting crop yield directly and those associated with adaptation to various types of stress have been identified and are being evaluated in the field. New varieties could improve the way crops cope with unreliable water supplies and potentially improve how they convert water. Breeding plants that can survive longer periods of drought will be even more critical in adapting to climate change. Initial experiments and field testing with GM crops suggest that progress may be possible without interfering with yields during nondrought periods, a problematic tradeoff for drought-tolerant varieties developed through conventional breeding. Drought-tolerant maize is nearing commercialization in the United States and is under development for African and Asian conditions.

Nevertheless, GM crops are controversial, and public acceptance and safety must be addressed. The public is concerned about the ethics of deliberately altering genetic material as well as about potential risks to food safety and the environment, and ethical concerns. After more than 10 years of experience, there has been no documented case of negative human health impacts from GM food crops, yet popular acceptance is still limited. Environmental risks include the possibility of GM plants cross-pollinating with wild relatives, creating aggressive weeds with higher disease resistance and the rapid evolution of new pest biotypes adapted to GM plants. However, scientific evidence and 10 years of commercial use show that safeguards, when appropriate, can prevent the development of resistance in the targeted pests and the environmental harm from commercial cultivation of transgenic crops, such as gene flow to wild relatives. Crop biodiversity may decrease if a small number of GM cultivars displace traditional cultivars, but this risk also exists with conventionally bred crop varieties. Impacts on biodiversity can be reduced by introducing several varieties of a GM crop, as in India, where there are more than 110 varieties of Bt (*Bacillus thuringiensis*) cotton. Although the track record with GM crops is good, establishing science-based biosafety regulatory systems is essential so that risks and benefits can be evaluated on a case-by-case basis, comparing the potential risks with alternative technologies and taking into account the specific trait and the agroecological context for using it.

Source: Benbrook 2001; FAO 2005; Gruere, Mehta-Bhatt, and Sengupta 2008; James 2000; James 2007; James 2008; Normile 2006; Phipps and Park 2002; Rosegrant, Cline, and Valmonte-Santos 2007; World Bank 2007c.

BOX 3.7   *Biochar could sequester carbon and increase yields on a vast scale*

Scientists investigating some unusually fertile soils in the Amazon basin found that the soil was altered by ancient charcoal-making processes. The indigenous people burned wet biomass (crop residues and manure) at low temperatures in the almost complete absence of oxygen. The product was a charcoal-type solid with a very high carbon content, called biochar. Scientists have reproduced this process in modern industrial settings in several countries.

Biochar appears to be highly stable in soil. Studies on the technical and economic viability of the technique are continuing, with some results indicating that biochar may lock carbon into the soil for hundreds or even thousands

of years, while others suggest that in some soils the benefits are far less. Nevertheless, biochar can sequester carbon that would otherwise be released into the atmosphere through burning or decomposition.

So biochar could have great carbon mitigation potential. To give an idea of scale, in the United States waste biomass from forestry and agriculture, plus biomass that could be grown on land that is currently idle, would provide enough material for the United States to sequester 30 percent of its fossil fuel emissions using this technique. Biochar can also increases soil fertility. It binds to nutrients and could thus help regenerate degraded lands as well as reduce

the need for artificial fertilizers and thus the pollution of rivers and streams. The potential is there. But there are two challenges: to demonstrate the chemical properties and to develop mechanisms for application on a large scale.

Research is needed in a number of areas, including methodologies to measure biochar's potential for long-term carbon sequestration; environmental risk assessment; biochar's behavior in different soil types; economic viability; and the potential benefits in developing countries.

Sources: Lehmann 2007a; Lehmann 2007b; Sohi and others 2009; Wardle, Nilsson, and Zackrisson 2008; Wolf 2008.

and Latin America may reduce fertilizer use to reduce both greenhouse gas emissions and the nutrient runoff that harms aquatic ecosystems. Changing the rate and timing of fertilizer applications reduces the emissions of nitrous oxide from soil microbes. Controlled-release nitrogen[134] improves efficiency (yield per unit of nitrogen), but so far it has proved too expensive for many farmers in developing countries.[135] New biological inhibitors that reduce the volatilization of nitrogen could achieve many of the same goals more cheaply. They are likely to be popular with farmers because they involve no extra farm labor and little change in management.[136] If producers and farmers have incentives to apply new fertilizer technology and to use fertilizers efficiently, many countries could maintain agricultural growth even as they reduce emissions and water pollution.

In Sub-Saharan Africa, by contrast, natural soil fertility is low, and countries cannot avoid using more inorganic fertilizer. Integrated adaptive management programs with site-specific testing and monitoring can reduce the risk of overfertilizing. But such programs are still rare in most developing countries because there has not been enough public investment in the research, extension, and

information services necessary for effective implementation—a recurring theme of this chapter.

Part of achieving the necessary increase in agricultural productivity in the developing world, sound fertilizer policy includes measures to make fertilizers affordable to the poor.[137] It also includes broader programs, such as the Farm Inputs Promotion program in Kenya that works with local companies and subsidiaries of international seed companies to improve agricultural inputs (by formulating fertilizers using locally available minerals, providing improved seed varieties, and distributing fertilizer in rural areas) and to promote sound agronomic practices (correct fertilizer placement, soil management, and effective weed and pest control).

Produce more and protect better in fisheries and aquaculture

Marine ecosystems will have to cope with stresses as least as great as those on land

The oceans have absorbed about half the anthropogenic emissions released since 1800,[138] and more than 80 percent of the heat of global warming.[139] The result is a warming, acidifying ocean, changing at an unprecedented pace with impacts across the aquatic realm (see focus A on the science of climate change).[140]

Ecosystem-based management can help coordinate an effective response to fisheries in crisis. Even without climate change, between 25 and 30 percent of marine fish stocks are overexploited, depleted, or recovering from depletion—and are thus yielding less than their maximum potential. About 50 percent of stocks are fully exploited and producing catches at or close to their maximum sustainable limits, with no room for further expansion. The proportion of underexploited or moderately exploited stocks declined from 40 percent in the mid-1970s to 20 percent in 2007.[141] It may be possible to get more value from the fish caught—for example, by reducing the fish caught unintentionally, estimated at one-quarter of the world fish catch.[142] It is likely that the maximum potential of fisheries in the world's oceans has been reached, and only more sustainable practices can maintain the productivity of the sector.[143]

Ecosystem-based management, which considers an entire ecosystem rather than a particular species or site and recognizes humans as integral elements in the system, can effectively protect the structure, functioning, and key processes of coastal and marine ecosystems.[144] Policies include coastal management, area-based management, marine protected areas, limits on fishing effort and gear, licensing, zoning, and coastal law enforcement. Managing marine ecosystems effectively also involves managing activities on land to minimize the eutrophication episodes that stress marine ecosystems, such as coral reefs, in many parts of the world.[145] The economic value of coral reefs can be many times that of the agriculture that caused the problems.[146]

The developing world already has some success stories. A program at Danajon Bank reef in the central Philippines has begun increasing fish biomass over the historical level.[147] Indeed, some developing countries implement ecosystem-based management more effectively than many developed countries.[148]

Climate change will create new pressures—an expected increase in food prices, increased demand for fish protein, and the need to protect marine ecosystems—that could prompt governments to implement long-advocated reforms. These include reducing catch to sustainable levels, and getting rid of perverse subsidies, which fuel the overcapacity of fishing fleets.[149] The annual number of newly built fishing vessels is less than 10 percent of the level in the late 1980s, but overcapacity is still a problem.[150] The global cost of poor governance of marine capture fisheries is an estimated $50 billion a year.[151] Rights-based catch shares can provide individual and community incentives for sustainable harvests. These schemes can grant rights to various forms of dedicated access, including community-based fishing, as well as impose individual fishing quotas.[152]

Aquaculture will help meet growing demand for food

Fish and shellfish currently supply about 8 percent of the world animal protein consumed.[153] With the world population growing by about 78 million people a year,[154] fish and shellfish production must grow by about 2.2 million metric tons every year to maintain current consumption of 29 kilograms per person each year.[155] If capture fish stocks fail to recover, only aquaculture will be able to fill the future demand.[156]

Aquaculture contributed 46 percent of the world's fish food supply in 2006,[157] with average annual growth (7 percent) outpacing population growth over the last decades. Productivity has increased by an order of magnitude for some species, driving down prices and expanding product markets.[158] Developing countries, mostly in the Asia-Pacific region, dominate production. Of the fish eaten in China, 90 percent comes from aquaculture.[159]

Demand for fish from aquaculture is projected to increase (figure 3.8), but climate change will affect aquaculture operations worldwide. Rising seas, more severe storms, and saltwater intrusion in the main river deltas of the tropics will damage aquaculture, which is based on species with limited saline tolerance, such as catfish in the

Figure 3.8   Demand for fish from aquaculture will increase, particularly in Asia and Africa

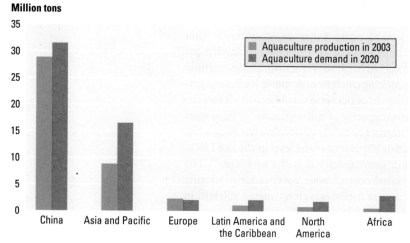

Million tons

Source: De Silva and Soto 2009.

Mekong Delta. Higher water temperatures in temperate zones may exceed the optimal temperature range of cultivated organisms. And as temperatures rise, diseases affecting aquaculture are expected to increase both in incidence and impact.[160]

Aquaculture is expected to grow at a rate of 4.5 percent a year between 2010 and 2030.[161] But sustainable growth for the sector entails overcoming two major obstacles. First is the extensive use of fish proteins and oils as fishmeal, which keeps the pressure on capture fisheries.[162] The growth in aquaculture will have to come from species not dependent on feed derived from fishmeal; today, 40 percent of aquaculture depends on industrial feeds, much from marine and coastal ecosystems, which are already stressed.[163] Plant-based aquaculture feeds (such as oil-seed-based feed) are promising,[164] and some operations have completely replaced fishmeal with plant-based feeds in the diets of herbivorous and omnivorous fish, without compromising growth or yields.[165] The emphasis on cultivating herbivorous and omnivorous species—currently about 7 percent of total production—makes sense for resource efficiency.[166] For example, production of one kilogram of salmon, marine finfish, or shrimp in aquaculture systems is highly resource-intensive, requiring between 2.5–5 kilograms of wild fish as feed for one kilogram of food produced.[167]

Second, aquaculture can cause environmental problems. Coastal aquaculture has been responsible for 20 to 50 percent of the loss of mangroves worldwide;[168] further losses compromise climate resiliency of the ecosystems and make coastal populations more vulnerable to tropical storms. Aquaculture also can result in the discharge of wastes into marine ecosystems that in some areas contributes to eutrophication. New effluent management techniques—such as recirculation of water,[169] better calibration of feed, and integrated and polyculturing in which complementary organisms are raised together to reduce wastes[170]—can lessen the environmental impacts. So can appropriate aquaculture development in underexploited bodies of water, such as rice paddies, irrigation canals, and seasonal ponds. Integrated agriculture-aquaculture schemes promote recycling of nutrients, so that wastes from aquaculture can become an input (fertilizer) for agriculture and vice-versa, thereby optimizing resource use and reducing pollution.[171] These systems have diversified income and provided protein for households in many parts of Asia, Latin America, and Sub-Saharan Africa.[172]

Building flexible international agreements

Managing natural resources in order to cope with climate change entails better international collaboration. It also demands more reliable international food trade so that countries are better placed to cope with climate shocks and reduced agricultural potential.

Countries that share watercourses will need to agree on how to manage them

About one-fifth of the world's renewable freshwater resources cross or form international borders, and in some regions, particularly in developing countries, the share is far higher. However, only 1 percent of such waters is covered by any kind of treaty.[173] Moreover, few of the existing treaties on international watercourses encompass all the countries touching the watercourse in question.[174] The United Nations Convention on the Law of the Non-Navigational

Uses of International Watercourses, which was adopted by the UN General Assembly in 1997, has yet to command sufficient ratifications to enter into force.[175]

Cooperation among riparian countries is essential to address water challenges caused by climate change. Such cooperation can be achieved only through inclusive agreements that make all the riparian countries responsible for the joint management and sharing of the watercourse and that are designed to address increased variability from both droughts and floods. Typically water agreements are based on allocating fixed quantities of water to each party; climate change makes this concept problematic. Allocations based on percentages of flow volume would better address variability. Even better would be a "benefit- sharing" approach, where the focus is not on water volumes but on the economic, social, political, and environmental values derived from water use.[176]

Countries will need to work together to better manage fisheries

Fish is the most international of food commodities. One-third of global fish production is traded internationally, the highest ratio for any primary commodity.[177] As their fish stocks have declined, European, North American, and many Asian nations have begun importing more fish from developing countries.[178] This increased demand, combined with the overcapitalization of some fishing fleets (the European fleet is 40 percent larger than the fish stocks can accommodate), is spreading the depletion of marine resources to the southern Mediterranean, West Africa, and South America. And despite the multibillion dollar-a-year international trade in fisheries, developing countries receive relatively little in fees from foreign fishing fleets operating in their waters. Even in the rich tuna fishery of the western Pacific, small island developing states receive only about 4 percent of the value of the tuna taken.[179] By modifying the distribution of fish stocks, changing food webs, and disrupting the physiology of already stressed fish species, climate change will only make things worse.[180] Fleets facing further declines in stocks may venture even farther afield, and

new agreements on resource sharing will need to be negotiated.

To facilitate adaptation and regulate fishery rights, it is important to develop international resource management regimes, both legal and institutional, and associated monitoring systems. Such agreements might be facilitated by strengthening regional fisheries management organizations.[181] The Benguela Current's Large Marine Ecosystem Programme is a promising development. Running along the west coast of Angola, Namibia, and South Africa, the Benguela ecosystem is one of the most highly productive in the world, supporting a reservoir of biodiversity including fish, seabirds, and sea mammals. Within the ecosystem there is already evidence that climate change is shifting the ranges of some key commercial species poleward from the tropics.[182] This shift compounds existing stresses from overfishing, diamond mining, and oil and gas extraction. Angola, Namibia, and South Africa established the Benguela Current Commission in 2006, the first such institute created for a large marine ecosystem. The three countries committed to integrated management of the fishery in order to adapt to climate change.[183]

More reliable trade in agricultural commodities will help countries experiencing unexpected weather extremes

Even if farmers, businesses, governments, and water managers dramatically increase the productivity of land and water, some parts of the world will not have enough water to always grow all of their food. Deciding how much food to import and how much to grow domestically has implications for agricultural productivity and water management (box 3.8). Seeking food self-sufficiency when resource endowments and growth potential are inadequate will impose heavy economic and environmental costs.

Many countries already import a large share of their food—most Arab countries import at least half of the food calories they consume—and increasingly harsh conditions mean that all countries need to prepare

BOX 3.8 *Policy makers in Morocco face stark tradeoffs on cereal imports*

Morocco, with severe water constraints and a growing population, imports half its cereals. Even without climate change, if it wishes to maintain cereal imports at no more than 50 percent of demand without increasing water use, Morocco would have to make technical improvements to achieve a combination of two options: either 2 percent more output per unit of water allocated to irrigated cereals or 1 percent more output per unit of land in rainfed areas (blue line in figure).

Adding in the effects of higher temperatures and reduced precipitation makes the task more challenging: technological progress will need to be 22–33 percent faster than without climate change (depending on the policy instruments selected) (green line in figure). But if the country wants more protection against domestic climate shocks to agriculture and against market price shocks and decides to increase the share of its consumption produced domestically from 50 percent to 60 percent, it has to increase water efficiency every year by 4 percent in irrigated agriculture, or by 2.2 percent

in rainfed areas, or any combination in between (orange line). In other words, a robust response to climate change could require Morocco to implement technical improvements between 100 percent and 140 percent faster than it would have

had to without climate change. Reducing net imports could only be achieved if Morocco made much higher efficiency gains domestically.

Source: World Bank, forthcoming a.

Achieving cereal self-sufficiency without increasing water use in Morocco

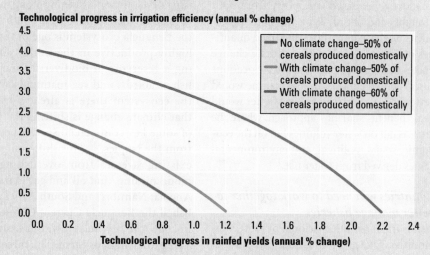

Technological progress in irrigation efficiency (annual % change)

No climate change–50% of cereals produced domestically
With climate change–50% of cereals produced domestically
With climate change–60% of cereals produced domestically

Technological progress in rainfed yields (annual % change)

for failure of domestic crops.[184] Climate change will make today's arid countries drier, compounding the increased demand from growing income and populations. Therefore, more people will live in regions that consistently import a large share of their food every year. In addition, more people will live in countries that experience shocks to domestic agriculture, as climate change increases the likelihood and severity of extreme climate events. Several global scenarios project a 10–40 percent increase in net imports by developing countries as a result of climate change.[185] Trade in cereals is projected to more than double in volume by 2050, and trade in meat products to more than quadruple.[186] And most of the increased dependence on food imports will come in developing countries.[187]

As the sharp rise of food prices in 2008 illustrated, the global food market is volatile. Why did the prices spike? First, grain markets are thin: only 18 percent of world wheat and 6 percent of world rice are

exported. The rest is consumed where it is grown.[188] And only a few countries export grain (map 3.5). In thin markets, small shifts in either supply or demand can make a big difference in price. Second, per capita global food stocks were at one of the lowest levels on record. Third, as the market for biofuel increased, some farmers shifted out of food production, contributing significantly to increases in world food prices.

When countries do not trust international markets, they respond to price hikes in ways that can make things worse. In 2008 many countries restricted exports or controlled prices to try to minimize the effects of higher prices on their own populations, including Argentina, India, Kazakhstan, Pakistan, Russia, Ukraine, and Vietnam. India banned exports of rice and pulses, and Argentina raised export taxes on beef, maize, soybeans, and wheat.[189]

Export bans or high export tariffs make the international market smaller and more volatile. For example, export restrictions on

Map 3.5   World grain trade depends on exports from a few countries

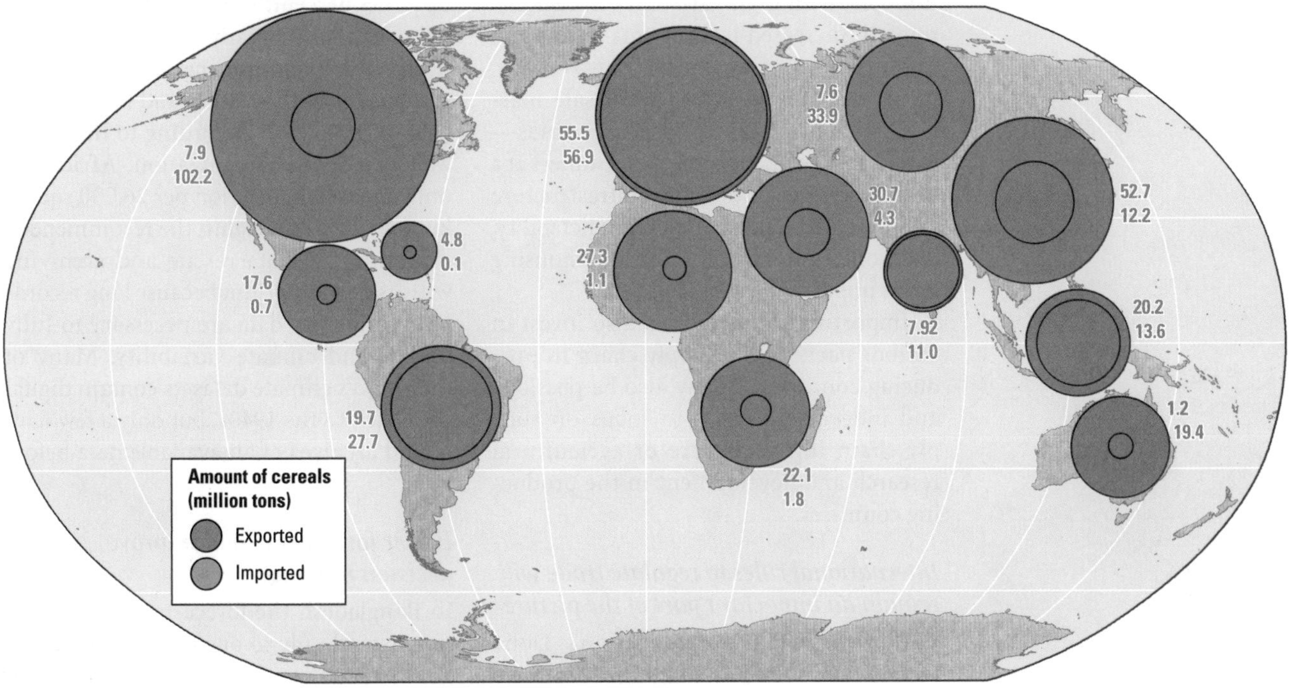

Amount of cereals
(million tons)
Exported
Imported

Source: FAO 2009c.
Note: Annual exports and imports are based on the average over four years (2002–2006).

rice in India affect Bangladeshi consumers adversely and dampen the incentives for rice farmers in India to invest in agriculture, a long-term driver of growth. In addition, export bans stimulate the formation of cartels, undermine trust in trade, and encourage protectionism. Domestic price controls can also backfire by diverting resources from those who need them most and by reducing incentives for farmers to produce more food.

Countries can take measures to improve access to markets

Countries can take unilateral action to improve their access to international food markets, a particularly important step for small countries whose actions do not affect the market but that nonetheless import a large share of their food. One of the simplest ways is to improve procurement methods. Sophisticated measures for issuing tenders to import food, such as electronic tendering and bidding and advanced credit and hedging products, could all help governments get a better deal. Another option would be to relax national laws that prohibit

multinational procurement so that small countries can group together for economies of scale.[190]

A third measure is active management of stocks. Countries need robust national stockpiling and the latest instruments in risk hedging, combining small physical stockpiles with virtual stockpiles purchased through futures and options. Models indicate that futures and options could have saved Egypt between 5 and 24 percent of the roughly $2.7 billion it spent purchasing wheat between November 2007 and October 2008, when prices were soaring.[191] Global collective action in managing stocks would also help prevent extreme price spikes. A small physical food reserve could allow a smooth response to food emergencies. An international coordinated global food reserve could reduce pressures to achieve grain self-sufficiency. And an innovative virtual reserve could prevent market price spikes and keep prices closer to levels suggested by long-run market fundamentals without putting the coordinated global reserves at risk.[192]

Weatherproofing transport services is also critical to ensure year-round access to markets, particularly in countries such as Ethiopia, with high variability in regional rainfall. Increased investments in improving logistics in the supply chain—roads, ports, customs facilities, wholesale markets, weighbridges, and warehouses—would help get more food to consumers at a lower price. But institutional infrastructure is also needed. Transparency, predictability, and honesty in customs and warehousing are as important as the facilities.

Importing countries can also invest in various parts of the supply chain in producing countries. It may also be possible, and indeed less risky, to focus on supply chain infrastructure or agricultural research and development in the producing countries.

International rules to regulate trade will remain an important part of the picture

The World Trade Organization's Doha Development Agenda sought to eliminate trade barriers and improve market access for developing countries. But negotiations were suspended in 2008. One study concludes there would be a potential loss of at least $1.1 trillion in world trade if world leaders fail to conclude the Doha Round.[193] Completing this agreement would be a key first step in improving international food trade. Key measures include pulling down effective tariff rates and reducing agricultural subsidies and protection by developed countries.[194]

Reliable information is fundamental for good natural resource management

Investments in weather and climate services pay for themselves many times over, yet these services are sorely lacking in the developing world

Typically the ratio of the economic benefits to the costs of national meteorological services is in the range of 5–10 to 1,[195] and a 2006 estimate suggests it could be 69 to 1 in China.[196] Weather and climate services can ameliorate the impacts of extreme events to some degree (see chapters 2 and 7). According to the United Nations International Strategy for Disaster Reduction, advance

flood warnings can reduce flood damage by up to 35 percent.[197] Much of the developing world, particularly in Africa, urgently needs better monitoring and forecasting systems for both weather and hydrological change (map 3.6). According to the World Meteorological Organization, Africa has only one weather station per 26,000 square kilometers—one-eighth the recommended minimum.[198] Data rescue and archiving will also be important because long records of high-quality data are necessary to fully understand climate variability. Many of the world's climate datasets contain digital data back to the 1940s, but only a few have digital archives of all available data before then.[199]

Better forecasts would improve decision making

In Bangladesh the forecasts for precipitation extend only to one to three days; longer forecasts would allow farmers time to modify planting, harvesting, and fertilizer applications, especially in rainfed cropping areas where food crises can last for many months. There have been significant improvements in seasonal climate forecasts (how precipitation and temperature over the course of a few months will vary from the norm), particularly in the tropics and in areas affected by the El Niño Southern Oscillation (ENSO).[200] The onset of monsoon rainfall in Indonesia and the Philippines and the number of rainy days in a season in parts of Africa, Brazil, India, and Southeast Asia can now be predicted with greater precision.[201] ENSO-based seasonal forecasts in South America, South Asia, and Africa have good potential for improving agricultural production and food security.[202] For example, in Zimbabwe subsistence farmers increased yields (ranging from 17 percent in good rainfall years to 3 percent in poor rainfall years) when they used seasonal forecasts to modify the timing or variety of the crops planted.[203]

New remote-sensing and monitoring technologies hold great promise for sustainability

One reason that policy makers have found it so difficult to curb the overexploitation of

Map 3.6   Developed countries have more data collection points and longer time series of water monitoring data

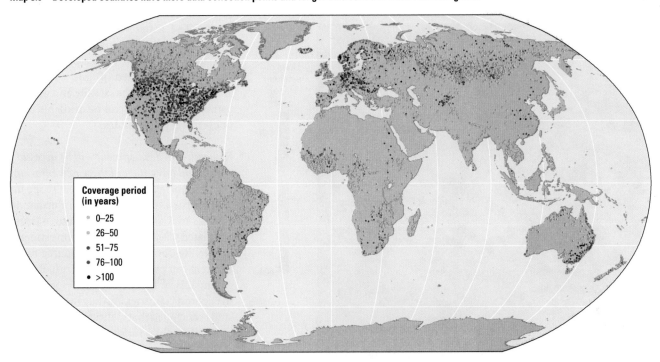

Source: Dataset for global distribution and time series coverage was provided by the Global Runoff Data Center.
Note: The map shows the discharge monitoring stations that provide information on river runoff.

land and water and their related ecosystems is that neither the managers nor the users of the resources have accurate and timely information. They don't know how much of the resource is present, how much is being used, or how their actions will affect quantities in the future. But new remote-sensing technologies are beginning to fill some of that gap, informing decisions about more efficient allocations of water and helping with enforcement of water limits.

One of the most promising applications of remote sensing measures water's productivity.[204] When thermal images from satellites are combined with field data on crop types and linked to maps from geographic information systems, scientists can measure yields on any geographic scale (the farm, the basin, or the country). That allows water managers to make better decisions about water allocations and to target advisory services to the farmers with lowest water productivity. It also guides important investment decisions—say, between increasing the productivity of rainfed or irrigated agriculture. And it can help managers measure the actual results of invest-

ments in irrigation water-saving techniques, difficult in the past (figure 3.9).

Until recently, measuring groundwater consumption was difficult and expensive in all countries, and it simply was not done in many developing countries. Taking inventories of hundreds of thousands of private wells and installing and reading meters was too costly. But new remote-sensing technology can measure total evaporation and transpiration from a geographic area. If the surface water applied to that area through precipitation and surface-water irrigation deliveries is known, the net consumption of groundwater can be imputed.[205] Various countries are experimenting with using information from new remote-sensing technologies to enforce groundwater limits, including those Moroccan farmers who are considering converting to drip irrigation (discussed at the beginning of the chapter). Options for enforcement include pumps that shut off automatically when the farmer exceeds the evapotranspiration limit and systems that simultaneously send text messages to farmers' cell phones, warning them

Figure 3.9   Remote-sensing techniques are used in the vineyards of Worcester (West Cape, South Africa) to gauge water productivity

Liters of water per liter of wine

150

300

450

600

Source: Water Watch, www.waterwatch.nl (accessed May 1, 2009).

Note: Farmers whose fields are red are using one-fourth as much water per liter of wine than those whose fields are shown in blue. In addition to gauging water productivity, governments can also use these techniques to target the activities of advisory and enforcement services.

they are about to exceed their allocation of groundwater, and alert inspectors to monitor those particular farms.[206]

Digital maps created from remote-sensing information will help resource managers at many levels.   Using information from remote sensing to create digital maps of all of Africa's soils will be very useful for sustainable land management. Current soil maps are 10–30 years old and generally not digitized, making them inadequate to inform policies to address soil fertility and erosion. An international consortium is using the latest technologies to prepare a digitized global map, starting with the African continent.[207] Satellite imagery and new applications now allow scientists to measure streamflow, soil moisture and water storage (lakes, reservoirs, aquifers, snow, and ice) and to forecast floods. They also make it possible to show crop yields, crop stress, CO_2 uptake, species composition and richness, land cover and land-cover change (such as deforestation), and

primary productivity. They can even map the spread of individual invasive plant species.[208] The scales vary, as does the timing of updates. But rapid advances allow managers to measure with a precision and regularity undreamed of only a few years ago. Depending on the satellite and weather conditions, the data can be available daily or even every 15 minutes.

Research and development will be necessary to take full advantage of these new information technologies.   There is great scope for applying new technologies and information systems to manage natural resource issues associated with climate change. Investments in satellite data for natural resource management can pay off in the long run. But the potential is far from being met, especially in the poorest countries. A study in the Netherlands concluded that additional investments in satellite observations for water quality management (eutrophication, algal blooms, turbidity), including the capital costs of the satellite, has a 75 percent probability of producing financial benefits.[209] Research and development of these tools and their application in developing countries are thus ripe for public and private investment.[210]

More reliable information can empower communities and change the governance of natural resources

Natural resource management often requires governments to set and enforce laws, limits, or prices. Political and socio-economic pressures make this very difficult, especially where formal institutions are weak. But when resource users have the right information about the impacts of their actions, they can bypass governments and work together to reduce overexploitation, often increasing their revenues. Making a strong economic case for reform can help, as in a recent study that highlighted the global cost of poor governance in marine capture fisheries.[211]

India offers several examples of better information resulting in more efficient agricultural production and welfare gains. In the state of Madhya Pradesh a subsidiary of Indian Tobacco Company (ITC) developed a system called eChoupals to lower its procurement cost and improve the quality of soybeans that it received from farmers. The eChoupals are village Internet kiosks run by local entrepreneurs who provide price information on soybean futures to farmers and enable them to sell their produce directly to ITC, bypassing the middlemen and wholesale market yards (*mandis*). Through the eChoupals ITC spends less per ton of produce, and farmers immediately know the price they will receive, reducing waste and inefficiency. The payback period for the initial capital cost of developing the kiosks is about four to six years.[212]

A project sponsored by the UN's Food and Agriculture Organization in Andhra Pradesh, India, has dramatically reduced the overexploitation of aquifers. It used low-tech and low-cost approaches to enable communities to assess the state of their own resources. Rather than use expensive equipment and specialist hydrogeologists, the project brought in sociologists and psychologists to assess how best to motivate the villagers to cut current water consumption. It created "barefoot hydrogeologists," to teach local people about the aquifer that sustained their livelihoods (figure 3.10). These non-specialist, often illiterate, farmers are generating such good data that they even sell it to the government hydrogeological services. Through this project, awareness of the impacts of their actions, social regulation, and information about new crop varieties and techniques led the villagers to agree to change crops and adopt practices to reduce evaporative losses.

With almost 1 million farmers, the project is entirely self-regulating, and there are no financial incentives or penalties for noncompliance. Participating villages have reduced withdrawals, while withdrawals from neighboring villages continue to increase. For an undertaking of this scale, the cost is remarkably low—$2,000 a year for each of the 65 villages.[213] It has great potential for replication, but principally in the hard-rock aquifers that empty and refill quickly and that do not have vast lower layers common in other geological formations.[214]

These initiatives to encourage users to reduce overexploitation of natural resources can reduce dependence on overstretched government agencies and overcome broader governance issues. They can also be tools for governments, working with communities, to change user behavior. The Hai basin, the most water-scarce in China, is extremely important for agriculture. Together with two neighboring basins, it produces half of China's wheat. Water resources in the Hai basin are polluted, wetland ecosystems threatened, and groundwater severely overexploited. Every year the basin uses 25 percent more groundwater than it receives as precipitation.[215]

In this same basin, the Chinese government worked with 300,000 farmers to innovate in water management. This initiative focused on reducing overall water consumption rather than simply increasing water productivity. It combined investments in irrigation infrastructure with advisory services to help optimize soil water. It limited the use of aquifer water. It introduced new institutional arrangements, such as transferring responsibility for managing irrigation services to groups of farmers and improving cost-recovery for surface water irrigation. And it used the latest monitoring techniques, by measuring water productivity and groundwater consumption at the plot level with satellite data, combined with more traditional agronomic services. The monitoring provides real-time

Figure 3.10   In Andhra Pradesh, India, farmers generate their own hydrological data, using very simple devices and tools, to regulate withdrawals from aquifers

Source: Bank staff.

Note: Armed with information, each farmer sets his or her own limit for how much water to safely extract each growing season. Technical assistance helps them get higher returns for the water they use by managing soil water better, switching crops, and adopting different crop varieties.

information to policy makers and farmers so that they can adjust their practices, and detect noncompliance.[216]

The results have been impressive. Farmers increased their incomes while reducing water consumption by switching to higher-value crops. Cash crop production tripled, farm incomes increased up to fivefold in many areas, and agricultural production per unit of water consumed increased 60–80 percent. Total water use in the area fell by 17 percent, with the rate of groundwater depletion at 0.02 meters a year, compared with 0.41 meters a year outside the project areas.

In summary, technologies and tools exist or are being developed to help farmers and other resource managers manage water, land, farms, and fisheries. In an ideal world the right people would have access to these technologies and tools. But they will be effective only with the right policies and infrastructure. This ideal world is represented pictorially in figures 3.11 and 3.12. Many of the steps toward this ideal world

have frustrated societies for decades in the past. But circumstances are changing in ways that might accelerate progress.

Pricing carbon, food, and energy could be the springboard

This chapter suggests many new approaches to help developing countries cope with the additional stress that climate change will put on efforts to manage land and water resources well. It emphasizes repeatedly that new technologies and new investments will bear fruit only in a context of strong institutions and sensible policies—when the "fundamentals" are right. Yet the fundamentals are not right in many of the world's poorest countries. And getting them right—building strong institutions, changing subsidy regimes, changing the way valuable commodities are allocated—is a long-term process even in the best of circumstances.

To compound the problems, many of the responses this chapter proposes to help countries improve land and water

Figure 3.11   An ideal climate-smart agricultural landscape of the future would enable farmers to use new technologies and techniques to maximize yields and allow land managers to protect natural systems, with natural habitats integrated into agriculturally productive landscapes

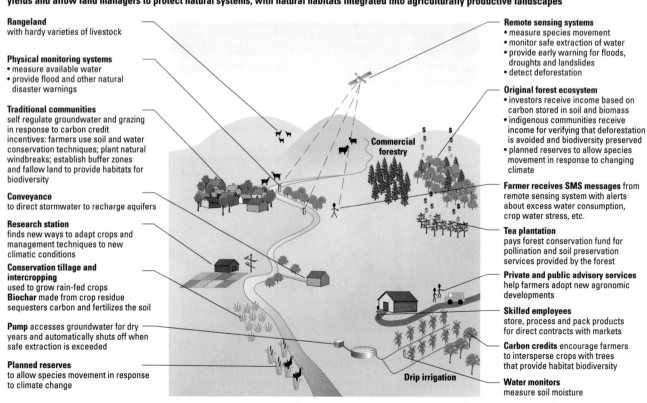

Rangeland
with hardy varieties of livestock

Physical monitoring systems
• measure available water
• provide flood and other natural disaster warnings

Traditional communities
self regulate groundwater and grazing in response to carbon credit incentives: farmers use soil and water conservation techniques; plant natural windbreaks; establish buffer zones and fallow land to provide habitats for biodiversity

Conveyance
to direct stormwater to recharge aquifers

Research station
finds new ways to adapt crops and management techniques to new climatic conditions

Conservation tillage and intercropping
used to grow rain-fed crops
Biochar made from crop residue sequesters carbon and fertilizes the soil

Pump accesses groundwater for dry years and automatically shuts off when safe extraction is exceeded

Planned reserves
to allow species movement in response to climate change

Commercial forestry

Remote sensing systems
• measure species movement
• monitor safe extraction of water
• provide early warning for floods, droughts and landslides
• detect deforestation

Original forest ecosystem
• investors receive income based on carbon stored in soil and biomass
• indigenous communities receive income for verifying that deforestation is avoided and biodiversity preserved
• planned reserves to allow species movement in response to changing climate

Farmer receives SMS messages from remote sensing system with alerts about excess water consumption, crop water stress, etc.

Tea plantation
pays forest conservation fund for pollination and soil preservation services provided by the forest

Private and public advisory services
help farmers adopt new agronomic developments

Skilled employees
store, process and pack products for direct contracts with markets

Carbon credits encourage farmers to intersperse crops with trees that provide habitat biodiversity

Drip irrigation

Water monitors
measure soil moisture

Source: WDR team.

Figure 3.12   An ideal climate-smart landscape of the future would use flexible technology to buffer against climate shocks through natural infrastructure, built infrastructure, and market mechanisms

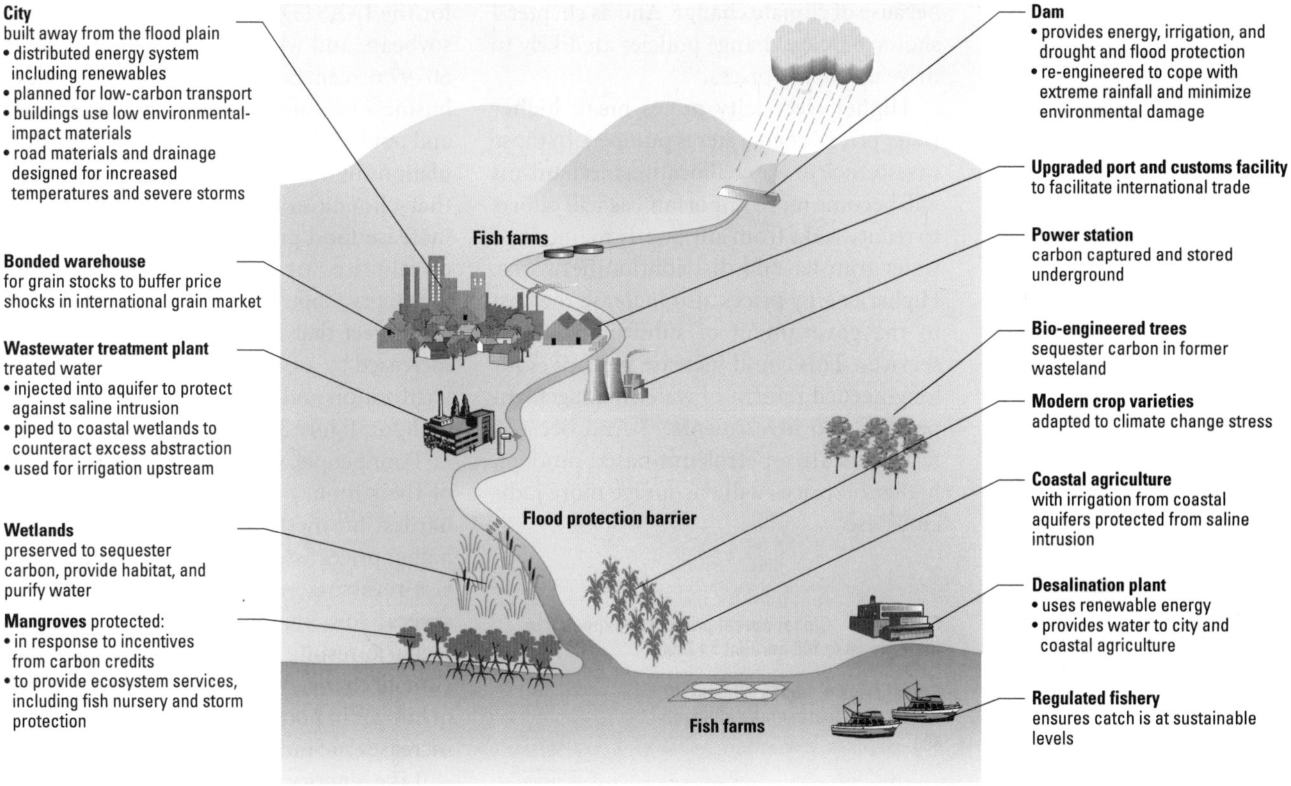

City
built away from the flood plain
• distributed energy system including renewables
• planned for low-carbon transport
• buildings use low environmental-impact materials
• road materials and drainage designed for increased temperatures and severe storms

Bonded warehouse
for grain stocks to buffer price shocks in international grain market

Wastewater treatment plant
treated water
• injected into aquifer to protect against saline intrusion
• piped to coastal wetlands to counteract excess abstraction
• used for irrigation upstream

Wetlands
preserved to sequester carbon, provide habitat, and purify water

Mangroves protected:
• in response to incentives from carbon credits
• to provide ecosystem services, including fish nursery and storm protection

Fish farms

Flood protection barrier

Fish farms

Dam
• provides energy, irrigation, and drought and flood protection
• re-engineered to cope with extreme rainfall and minimize environmental damage

Upgraded port and customs facility
to facilitate international trade

Power station
carbon captured and stored underground

Bio-engineered trees
sequester carbon in former wasteland

Modern crop varieties
adapted to climate change stress

Coastal agriculture
with irrigation from coastal aquifers protected from saline intrusion

Desalination plant
• uses renewable energy
• provides water to city and coastal agriculture

Regulated fishery
ensures catch is at sustainable levels

Source: WDR team.

management in the face of climate change require farmers, many of them among the world's poorest, to change their practices. It also requires people operating beyond the law (illegal loggers, illegal miners) and wealthy, influential people (including property developers) to stop practices that have brought them extreme profits. This chapter is proposing accelerating actions that have at best seen slow progress in the past few decades. Is it realistic to expect change on a sufficient scale to really tackle the challenge climate change confronts us with?

Three new factors might provide the stimulus for change and overcome some of the barriers that have hampered these improvements in the past. First, climate change is expected to increase the price of energy, water, and land and thus of food and other agricultural commodities. That will increase the pace of innovation and accelerate the adoption of practices that increase productivity. Of course higher prices will also make it more profitable to overexploit resources or

encroach on natural habitats. Second, a carbon price applied to carbon in the landscape, may encourage landowners to conserve natural resources. If implementation difficulties could be overcome, this would buy down the risk to farmers of adopting new practices. It might also give landowners the right incentives to protect natural systems. Third, if the world's $258 billion a year in agricultural subsidies were even partially redirected to carbon sequestration and biodiversity conservation, it would demonstrate the techniques and approaches outlined in this chapter on the necessary scale.

Rising energy, water, and agricultural prices could spur innovation and investment in increasing productivity

A combination of factors will drive up food prices in the next few decades. They include increased demand for food from growing and increasingly rich populations. They also include increased production of biofuels, which could result in competition for agricultural land and water. Furthermore, it will become more difficult to grow food because of climate change. And as chapter 4 shows, climate change policies are likely to drive up energy prices.[217]

Higher electricity prices mean higher water prices when water is pumped. In those cases, efficient water allocation mechanisms will become more important, as will efforts to reduce leaks from any poorly maintained water transfer and distribution networks. Higher energy prices also increase the cost to the government of subsidizing water services. This could increase incentives for long-needed reform of water management policies and investments.[218] And because fertilizers are a petroleum-based product, higher oil prices will encourage more judicious use.

Food prices are expected to be higher and more volatile in the long run. Modeling for the IAASTD projected that maize, rice, soybean, and wheat prices will increase by 60–97 percent between 2000 and 2050 under business as usual, and prices for beef, pork, and poultry, by 31–39 percent.[219] Other simulations of the world food system also show that climate-induced shortfalls of cereals increase food prices.[220] In most estimates, cereal prices are projected to increase, even if farmers adapt.[221] By 2080 different scenarios project that world food prices will have increased by around 7–20 percent with CO_2 fertilization and by around 40–350 percent without (figure 3.13).[222]

Poor people, who spend up to 80 percent of their money on food, probably will be hardest hit by the higher food prices. The higher prices associated with climate change risk reversing progress in food security in several low-income countries. Although scenario results differ, nearly all agree that climate change will put more people at risk of hunger in poorer nations, with the largest increases in South Asia and Africa.[223]

Like energy prices, high food prices have profound effects on the potential adjustments in land and water use stemming from climate change. Investments in agriculture, land, and water become more profitable for farmers as well as the public and private sectors. Private agricultural companies, international aid donors, international development banks, and national governments can see and act on the higher international prices fairly quickly. But the transmission of increases in international food prices to farmers is imperfect, as shown in the 2007–08 food price crisis. For example, farmers in most of Sub-Saharan Africa saw higher food prices only after some lag, and the transmission of higher prices was slower and less complete than in most of Asia and Latin America.[224]

The better the quality of rural infrastructure, the more farmers benefit from higher international prices. High food prices can spur land conversion to crops and livestock, with negative impacts on ecosystems. But they can also induce significant new investments in agricultural research, irrigation development, and rural

Figure 3.13 Global cereal prices are expected to increase 50 to 100 percent by 2050

Cereal price increase without CO_2
fertilization (percentage change)

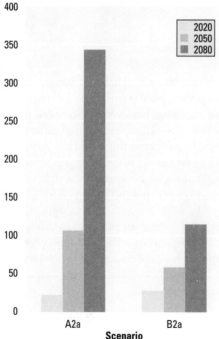

Source: Parry and others 2004.

Note: The IPCC SRES A2 family of emission scenarios describes a world where population continues to grow, and the trends of per capita income growth and technological change vary between regions and are slower than in other story lines. The B2 scenario family describes a world where global population grows at a rate lower than in A2, economic development is intermediate, and technological change is moderate.

infrastructure to intensify production. The simultaneous rise in energy and food prices will also make some big investments profitable again, including large multipurpose dams for power and irrigation. It will be important to channel the incentives from high food prices into innovative investments and policy reforms to boost agricultural productivity while making land and water use sustainable.

An international price that paid for avoiding emissions and sequestering carbon in agriculture could encourage better protection of natural systems

Under the Clean Development Mechanism of the Kyoto Protocol, agricultural soil carbon sequestration projects in the developing world are not eligible for selling carbon credits to investors in the developed world. If they were, incentives for farmers and other land users would change fundamentally. Carbon markets that cover greenhouse gases from agricultural and other land-management practices could be one of the most important mechanisms to drive sustainable development in a world affected by climate change. The potential is huge: one source estimates 4.6 gigatons of CO_2 or more a year by 2030, which is more than half of the potential from forestry (7.8 gigatons of CO_2 a year).[225] At $100 a ton of CO_2e, potential emission reductions from agriculture are on par with those from energy (see overview, box 8). Models show that pricing carbon in agriculture and land-use change would help prevent the conversion of intact ecosystems ("unmanaged land" in figure 3.14) to meet rising demand for biofuel.

Although the mechanisms for conserving soil carbon through a carbon price are not yet developed, the potential to reduce emissions from agriculture is large. Even in Africa, where relatively carbon-poor drylands make up 44 percent of the continent, the possibility for agricultural carbon sequestration is great.[226] The projected mean agricultural mitigation potential across the continent is 100 million to 400 million metric tons of CO_2e a year by 2030.[227] With a relatively low price of $10 a metric ton in 2030, this financial flow would be comparable to the annual official development assistance to Africa.[228] A study of African pastoralists shows that even modest improvements in natural resource management could produce additional carbon sequestration of 0.50 metric ton of carbon a year per hectare. A price of $10 per metric ton of CO_2 would increase their incomes by 14 percent.[229]

Carbon sequestration in agriculture would be a relatively inexpensive and efficient response to climate change. The abatement cost in agriculture in 2030 is estimated to be almost an order of magnitude lower than that in the forestry sector ($1.8 per metric ton of CO_2 equivalent compared with $13.5 per metric ton of CO_2 equivalent).[230] One reason for this is that many agricultural techniques that improve carbon sequestration also increase agricultural yields and revenues.

So, the techniques for storing more carbon in soil already exist, but they are not being adopted. The list of causes is long—inadequate knowledge of management techniques appropriate to tropical and subtropical soils, weak extension infrastructure to deliver the available innovations, lack of property rights to encourage investments with long-term payoffs but short-term costs, inappropriate fertilizer taxation policies, and poor transport infrastructure.

The world community could take four practical steps to expand the carbon market. First, rather than attempt to monitor detailed emissions and uptakes in each field, the people involved in the carbon markets (local and international) need to agree on a simplified actuarial-based accounting system that monitors the activities of farmers and conservatively estimates the associated carbon sequestration.[231] It would not be cost-effective or feasible to measure carbon sequestration across multiple, dispersed smallholder parcels in the developing world. Moreover, the approach is transparent and would allow the farmer to know up front what the payments and penalties would be for various activities.

The processes by which soils take up or emit carbon are complex. They vary from place to place (even within a field) and depend on soil properties, climate, farming system, and land-use history. Further,

Figure 3.14 A carbon tax applied to emissions from agriculture and land-use change would encourage protection of natural resources.

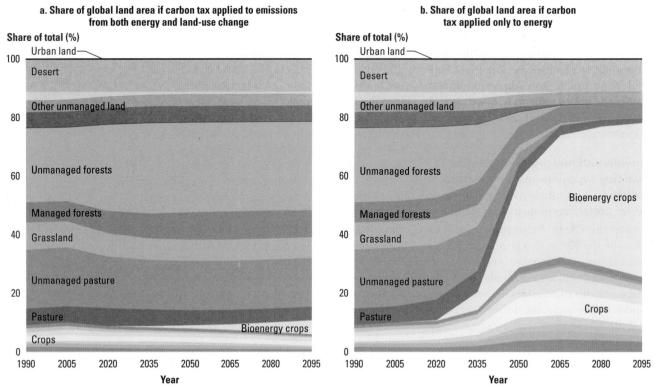

a. Share of global land area if carbon tax applied to emissions from both energy and land-use change

b. Share of global land area if carbon tax applied only to energy

Source: Wise and others 2009.

Note: Projections based on the MiniCAM Global Integrated Assessment Model. Both scenarios represent a path to achieve a CO_2 concentration of 450 ppm by 2095. In figure 3.14a, a price is put on carbon emissions from fossil fuels, industry, and land-use change. In figure 3.14b, the same price is applied but only to fossil-fuel and industry emissions. When a price is not applied to terrestrial emissions, growers are likely to encroach into natural habitats, mainly in response to the demand for biofuels.

annual changes are usually small relative to existing stocks. And the sequestration plateaus quickly. Carbon accumulation in soil saturates after about 15–30 years, depending on the type of agriculture, and few emission reductions would occur after that time.[232] Furthermore, no-till agriculture in heavy clay soils can result in releases of nitrous oxide—a powerful greenhouse gas. These emissions would more than outweigh the carbon storage benefits of adopting the new techniques over the first five years. No-till may therefore not be a good greenhouse gas emission reduction technique in some soils.[233] But it is possible, based on existing data and modeling, to broadly estimate carbon sequestration per agricultural practice for agroecological and climatic zones. Moreover, cost-effective techniques for measuring soil carbon in the field (using lasers, ground-penetrating radar, and gamma ray spectroscopy) now allow for faster measurement of carbon sequestration and the updating of model estimates at smaller spatial scales.[234]

In the meantime, programs could use conservative estimates of sequestration across soil types and focus on regions where there is more certainty about soil carbon stocks and flows (such as the more productive agricultural areas). Moreover, no carbon sequestration technique (such as conservation tillage) is a panacea in every cropping system and across every soil type.

A model for such a system may be the Conservation Reserve Program administered by the U.S. Department of Agriculture on nearly 14 million hectares of land since 1986.[235] This voluntary program was initially established to reduce soil erosion, with landowners and agricultural producers entering contracts to retire highly erodible and environmentally sensitive cropland and pasture from production for 10–15 years in return for payments. Over time the program expanded its objective to include the conservation of wildlife habitat and water quality, and the payments are based on an aggregate Environmental

Benefits Index of the parcel and of the specific activity (such as riparian buffers and shelterbelts). The actual environmental benefits of each parcel are not directly measured but rather estimated based on activities, and a similar activity-based system could apply to agricultural carbon sequestration.[236]

The second practical step involves developing "aggregators"—typically private or nongovernmental organizations that reduce transaction costs of the activities by integrating them over multiple smallholder farmers, forest dwellers, and pastoralists. Without them the market will tend to favor large reforestation projects, because the land of the average individual smallholder farmer in the developing world cannot sequester very large amounts. Scaling up spatially will also reduce concerns related to the uncertainty and impermanence of the carbon stock. Adopting an actuarial approach, pooling across a portfolio of projects, and applying conservative estimates could make soil carbon sequestration fully equivalent to CO_2 reductions in other sectors.[237]

Third, the up-front costs for carbon-sequestering management practices must be addressed. Adopting new practices is risky, especially for poor farmers.[238] Carbon finance is typically delivered only after the farmers have actually reduced emissions (as in pilot projects in Kenya described in box 3.9). But the promise of future carbon finance can be used to make up-front payments to buy down farmers' risks either as collateral for loans, or by having investors make some of the payments up front.

Fourth, farmers need to know about their options. This will involve better agricultural advisory services in the developing world. Agricultural extension services are good investments: the average rate of return globally is 85 percent.[239] Companies or organizations that can measure or verify results will also be required.

The Chicago Climate Exchange, one subset of the voluntary market, shows the possible benefits of trading the carbon sequestration from landscape-related activities.[240] It allows emitters to receive carbon credits for continuous conservation tillage, grassland planting, and rangeland management. For agricultural carbon trading, the exchange requires that members place 20 percent of all earned offsets in a reserve to insure against possible future reversals. The Exchange shows that simplified rules and modern monitoring techniques can overcome technical barriers. However, some critics claim that "additionality" has not been fully assessed: the net emission reductions may not be greater than they would have been in the absence of a market.

In the near term the voluntary market incubates methods for agricultural and landscape-level sequestration. But for these measures to really expand in this direction, the market for them will need to be linked to the future global compliance market. The economies of scale that landscape-level sequestration promises will be more readily accessed if there are no divisions separating sequestration in agriculture and forestry.

Because carbon sequestration activities tend to have a positive impact on soil and water management as well as on yields,[241] the most important aspect of carbon finance applied to soil management may be to serve as a "lever" to execute the sustainable agricultural practices that also have many other benefits. From 1945 to 1990 soil degradation in Africa reduced agricultural productivity by an estimated 25 percent.[242] And about 86 percent of the land in Sub-Saharan Africa is moisture-stressed.[243] Effective carbon finance mechanisms would help reduce the rate of land degradation. A soil compliance carbon market holds great potential for helping to achieve the necessary balance between intensifying productivity, protecting natural resources, and simultaneously helping rural development in some of the world's poorest communities. Such a market is not yet ready. Technical issues regarding verification, scale, and time frame remain to be solved. The United Nations Framework Convention on Climate Change proposes a phased approach starting with capacity building and financial support. The first phase would demonstrate techniques, monitoring approaches, and financing mechanisms. In the second phase soil carbon techniques would be incorporated into the broader compliance carbon market.[244]

BOX 3.9 *Pilot projects for agricultural carbon finance in Kenya*

Preliminary results from two pilot projects in western Kenya indicate that smallholder agriculture can be integrated into carbon finance. One involves mixed cropping systems across 86,000 hectares, using a registered association of 80,000 farmers as the aggregator. Another smaller coffee project encompasses 7,200 hectares thus far, and a 9,000-member farmer cooperative serves as the aggregator. The average size of landholdings for both projects is small (about 0.3 hectare).

The amount of carbon sequestration is estimated to be 516,000 tons and 30,000 tons of CO_2e a year, respectively,

The sequestration activities include reduced tillage, cover crops, residue management, mulching, composting, green manure, more targeted application of fertilizers, reduced biomass burning, and agroforestry. The projects use activity-based monitoring. The estimates of carbon sequestration over 20 years are derived from a model known as RothC. The World Bank BioCarbon Fund is purchasing the carbon credits based on a price per ton mutually agreed on by the fund and the project developers, VI Agroforestry and Swedish Cooperative Centre and ECOM Agroindustrial Group. Of the total revenues that the communities

receive, 80 percent will go to the community and 20 percent to monitoring and project development.

Two lessons are emerging. First, a good aggregator is essential, especially one that can also advise on agricultural practices. Second, the method for monitoring must be simple and accessible and transparent to the farmer. In these cases, the farmer can easily consult a table to determine the exact payment he or she will receive for each activity, a system that encourages participation.

Sources: Kaonga and Coleman 2008; Woelcke and Tennigkeit 2009.

Redirecting agricultural subsidies could be an important mechanism for achieving climate-smart land and water management

The member countries of the Organisation for Economic Co-operation and Development provide $258 billion every year in support to their farmers, which amounts to 23 percent of farm earnings.[245] Of this support 60 percent is based on the quantity of a specific commodity produced and on variable inputs with no constraints attached to their use—only 2 percent is for noncommodity services (such as creating buffer strips to protect waterways, preserving hedgerows, or protecting endangered species).

The political imperatives of climate change offer an opportunity to reform those subsidy schemes, to focus them more on climate change mitigation and adaptation measures that would also benefit domestic soil, water, and biodiversity resources as well as increase farm productivity. In addition to these direct benefits, allocating resources on that scale would also demonstrate whether these climate-smart techniques can be applied on a large scale in the developing world and attract entrepreneurial ingenuity and energy to find new ways of solving the technical and monitoring problems that will arise.

The European Union has already reformed its Common Agricultural Policy so that any income support to farmers is contingent on their meeting good environmental and agricultural standards, and any rural development support goes to measures that improve competitiveness, manage the environment and the land, improve the quality of life, and increase diversification. Through the rural development support category, farmers can be compensated if they provide environmental services that go beyond the mandatory standards.[246] This reform is a promising initiative to jump-start climate- and farmer-smart agricultural and natural resource policies, and the European Union could serve as a testbed for mechanisms that could be applied for sustainable land and water management in the developing world.

————

To cope with the effects of climate change on natural resources and simultaneously reduce emissions of greenhouse gases, societies need to produce more from land and water and protect their resources better. To produce more, they need to increase investment in agriculture and water management, particularly in developing countries. For agriculture that means investing in roads and research and development as well as adopting better policies and institutions. For water, it means using new decision-making tools and better data, strengthening policies and institutions, and investing in infrastructure. The expected increase in prices of agricultural production will give farmers and other resource users an incentive to innovate and invest. But the increased profitability will also increase incentives to overexploit resources. Protection needs the same increase in effort as production.

A number of tools, techniques, and approaches exist that can help users protect natural resources better. But users often do not have the right incentives to apply them. There are disparities in space and in time. What is best for a farmer is not best for the whole landscape or watershed. What is optimal over a short time period is not optimal over decades. Doing things differently also involves asking poor farmers and rural dwellers to take risks they may not be willing to take.

Governments and public organizations can take three types of actions to make the incentives for resource users more climate-smart. First, they can provide information so that people can make informed choices and can enforce cooperative agreements. This can be high-tech information. It can also be information that communities themselves gather. Second, they can set a price for retaining or storing carbon in the soil. Done right, this will reduce the risks to farmers of adopting new practices. It will also help resource users consider a longer time horizon in their decisions. Third, they can redirect agricultural subsidies, particularly in rich countries, so that they encourage climate-smart rural development practices. These subsidies can be transformed to show

how the new techniques can be adopted on a large scale, and they can be used to make individual actions fit better with the needs of the landscape as a whole. Finally, they can attract the ingenuity and creativity needed to achieve the delicate balancing act of feeding the world of nine billion people, reducing greenhouse gas emissions, and protecting the natural resource base.

Notes

1. See for example Lotze-Campen and others 2009.

2. IPCC 2007b.

3. OECD 2008.

4. Burke and Brown 2008; Burke, Brown, and Christidis 2006.

5. Milly and others 2008; Barnett, Adam, and Lettenmaier 2005.

6. de la Torre, Fajnzylber, and Nash 2008.

7. World Water Assessment Programme 2009.

8. Perry and others, forthcoming.

9. World Water Assessment Programme 2009.

10. World Bank, forthcoming d.

11. World Bank, forthcoming d.

12. Molden 2007.

13. Milly and others 2008; Ritchie 2008; Young and McColl 2005.

14. As the public trustee of the nation's water resources, the national government, acting through the minister of water affairs, must ensure that water is protected, used, developed, conserved, managed, and controlled in a sustainable and equitable manner, for the benefit of all persons and in accordance with its constitutional mandate. Salman M. A. Salman, World Bank Staff, personal communication, July 2009.

15. Dye and Versfeld 2007.

16. Bates and others 2008.

17. Molle and Berkoff 2007.

18. Molle and Berkoff 2007; OECD 2009.

"Our globe is facing environmental problems due to human behavior—cutting down trees, air pollution, use of plastics cannot be reused or recycled, chemical hazards in agriculture. . . . Tree planting would reduce CO_2."

—Netpakaikarn Netwong, Thailand, age 14

19. Olmstead, Hanemann, and Stavins 2007.

20. Molle and Berkoff 2007.

21. Asad and others 1999.

22. Bosworth and others 2002.

23. See Murray Darling Basin Agreement Schedule E, http://www.mdbc.gov.au/about/the_mdbc_agreement.

24. Molle and Berkoff 2007.

25. Rosegrant and Binswanger 1994.

26. World Bank 2007b.

27. Bates and others 2008; Molden 2007.

28. Young and McColl 2005.

29. http://www.environment.gov.au/water/mdb/overallocation.html (accessed May 7, 2009).

30. Molden 2007.

31. World Bank, forthcoming b.

32. World Bank, forthcoming b.

33. World Bank, forthcoming b.

34. Bhatia and others 2008.

35. Strzepek and others 2004.

36. World Commission on Dams 2000. For discussion of the impacts of the High Dam at Aswan on soil fertility and coastlines in the Nile Delta, see Ritchie 2008.

37. World Water Assessment Programme 2009.

38. Danfoss Group Global. http://www.danfoss.com/Solutions/Reverse+Osmosis/Case+stories.htm (accessed May 9, 2009).

39. FAO 2004b.

40. Desalination is also viable for high-value agriculture in some parts of the world, such as Spain. Gobierno de España 2009.

41. World Water Assessment Programme 2009.

42. Molden 2007.

43. Molden 2007.

44. Molden 2007.

45. Rosegrant, Cai, and Cline 2002.

46. For example, see the reference to the *Indian Financial Express* on December 1 2008, cited in Perry and others, forthcoming.

47. De Fraiture and Perry 2007; Molden 2007; Ward and Pulido-Velazquez 2008.

48. Perry and others, forthcoming.

49. Moller and others 2004; Perry and others, forthcoming.

50. Perry and others, forthcoming.

51. www.fieldlook.com (accessed May 5, 2009).

52. Perry and others, forthcoming.

53. World Bank, forthcoming c.

54. Carbon dioxide (CO_2) is an input in photosynthesis, the process by which plants use sunlight to produce carbohydrates. Thus, higher CO_2 concentrations will have a positive effect on many crops, enhancing biomass accumulation and final yield. In addition, higher CO_2 concentrations reduce plant stomatal openings—the pores through which plants transpire, or release water—and thus reduce water loss. The so-called C3 crops, such as rice, wheat, soybeans, legumes, as well as trees, should benefit more than the C4 crops, such as maize, millet, and sorghum. However, recent field experiments indicate that past laboratory tests have overstated the positive effect. For example, one study indicates that at CO_2 concentrations of 550 parts per million, yield increases amounted to 13 percent for wheat, not 31 percent; 14 percent for soybeans, not 32 percent; and 0 percent, not 18 percent, for C4 crops. Cline 2007. For this reason, the graphics in this chapter show only yields without CO_2 fertilization.

55. Easterling and others 2007.

56. EBRD and FAO 2008.

57. Fay, Block, and Ebinger 2010.

58. A food production shortfall is a situation in which the weather makes annual potential production of the most important crops in an administrative region less than 50 percent of the region's average production level during 1961–1990. The greater likelihood of shortfalls occurring in more than one region in a given year may reduce the potential for exports from other regions to compensate for food production deficiencies, thus leading to food security concerns. Alcamo and others 2007.

59. Easterling and others 2007.

60. Cline 2007. The high-emission scenario is the IPCC's SRES A2 scenario, which, over a range of models, leads to a mean temperature increase of 3.13°C from 2080 to 2099 relative to 1980–99. Meehl and others 2007.

61. Lobell and others 2008.

62. Schmidhuber and Tubiello 2007.

63. Based on five climate models and the high-emission SRES A2 scenario. Fischer and others 2005.

64. Calculation based on FAO 2009c.

65. IPCC 2007a.

66. Emissions come from converting unmanaged land to agriculture, and from soil erosion.

67. van der Werf and others 2008.

68. Steinfeld and others 2006.

69. This 18 percent sums the estimated contribution of livestock production to emissions across several categories, such as land use, land-use change, and forestry, to get the total contribution of livestock. It comprises livestock greenhouse gas emissions from land-use change (36 percent); manure management (31 percent); direct emission by animals (25 percent); feed production (7 percent); and processing and transport (1 percent). Steinfeld and others 2006.

70. IEA 2006. This estimate assumes that current trade restrictions are maintained. If those restrictions change, particularly those that restrict imports of biofuels into the United States, there could be a large regional shift in production.

71. Gurgel, Reilly, and Paltsev 2008.

72. NRC 2007; Tilman, Hill, and Lehman 2006.

73. Beckett and Oltjen 1993.

74. Hoekstra and Chapagain 2007. Pimentel and others (2004) give an estimate of 43,000 liters per kilogram of beef.

75. Peden, Tadesse, and Mammo 2004. In this system one head of cattle consumes 25 liters of water a day over a two-year period to produce 125 kilograms of dressed weight and consumes crop residues for which no additional water input is required.

76. Williams, Audsley, and Sandars 2006. Moreover, some sources give higher emission estimates for meat production—up to 30 kilogram of CO_2e per kilogram of beef produced, for example (Carlsson-Kanyama and Gonzales 2009).

77. Randolph and others 2007; Rivera and others 2003.

78. Delgado and others 1999; Rosegrant and others 2001; Rosegrant, Fernandez, and Sinha 2009; Thornton 2009; World Bank 2008e.

79. One study projects that total "good" and "prime" agricultural land available will remain virtually unchanged at 2.6 billion and 2 billion hectares, respectively, in 2080 compared with the average during 1961–1990 (based on the Hadley Centre HadCM3 climate model and assuming the very high emission scenario, SRES A1F1). Fischer, Shah, and van Velthuizen 2002; Parry and others 2004.

80. Lotze-Campen and others 2009.

81. Cassman 1999; Cassman and others 2003.

82. Calculated from FAO 2009c.

83. Diaz and Rosenberg 2008.

84. Schoups and others 2005.

85. Delgado and others 1999.

86. Hazell 2003.

87. Hazell 2003; Rosegrant and Hazell 2000.

88. Pingali and Rosegrant 2001.

89. Reardon and others 1998.

90. Rosegrant and Hazell 2000.

91. Rosegrant and Hazell 2000.

92. One form of specialized agricultural products is known as functional foods. These are products in food or drink form that influence functions in the body and thereby offer benefits for health, well-being, or performance beyond their regular nutritional value. Examples include antioxidant foods, such as guarana and açaí berry, vitamin A-rich golden rice and orange-fleshed sweet potato, margarine fortified with plant sterols to improve cholesterol levels, and eggs with increased omega-3 fatty acids for heart health. Kotilainen and others 2006.

93. Ziska 2008.

94. T. Christopher, "Can Weeds Help Solve the Climate Crisis?" *New York Times*, June 29, 2008.

95. Ziska and McClung 2008.

96. UNEP-WCMC 2008. In the oceans the share of total area under protection is even more paltry. Approximately 2.58 million square kilometers, or 0.65 percent of the world's oceans and 1.6 percent of the total marine area within Exclusive Economic Zones, are marine protected areas. Laffoley 2008.

97. Gaston and others 2008.

98. Hannah and others 2007.

99. Dudley and Stolton 1999.

100. Struhsaker, Struhsaker, and Siex 2005.

101. Scherr and McNeely 2008; McNeely and Scherr 2003.

102. van Buskirk and Willi 2004.

103. McNeely and Scherr 2008.

104. Chan and Daily 2008.

105. Leguminous trees contain symbiotic bacterial nodules that fix atmospheric nitrogen thereby enhancing the nutrients load in the plants and in the soil.

106. McNeely and Scherr 2003.

107. Ricketts and others 2008.

108. Klein and others 2007.

119. Lin, Perfecto, and Vandermeer 2008.

110. World Bank 2008a.

111. World Bank 2008a.

112. Of the $6 billion spent annually on land trusts and conservation easements, a third is in the developing world. Scherr and McNeely 2008.

113. A typical system of zoning for conservation allows development in some areas and limits it in conservation areas. Tradable development rights are an alternative to pure zoning that allows for substitutability between areas in meeting conservation goals and provides incentives for compliance. Some landowners agree to limits on development—that is, restrictions on their property rights—in return for payments. For instance, a government law may prescribe that 20 percent of each private property be maintained as natural forest. Landowners would be permitted to deforest beyond the 20 percent threshold only if they purchase from other landowners who keep more than 20 percent of their property forested and sell the development rights of this "surplus" forest, which is irreversibly placed under forest reserve status. Chomitz 2004.

114. World Bank 2008c.

115. Alston and others 2000; World Bank 2007c.

116. Beintema and Stads 2008.

117. IAASTD 2009.

118. Blaise, Majumdar, and Tekale 2005; Govaerts, Sayre, and Deckers 2005; Kosgei and others 2007; Su and others 2007.

119. Thierfelder, Amezquita, and Stahr 2005; Zhang and others 2007.

120. Franzluebbers 2002.

121. Govaerts and others 2009.

122. Derpsch and Friedrich 2009.

123. Derpsch 2007; Hobbs, Sayre, and Gupta 2008.

124. World Bank 2005.

125. Derpsch and Friedrich 2009; Erenstein and Laxmi 2008.

126. Erenstein 2009.

127. Erenstein and others 2008.

128. de la Torre, Fajnzylber, and Nash 2008.

129. Passioura 2006.

130. Yan and others 2009.

131. Thornton 2009.

132. Smith and others 2009.

133. Doraiswamy and others 2007; Perez and others 2007; Singh 2005.

134. Such as the deep placement of urea briquettes or supergranules.

135. Singh 2005.

136. Singh 2005.

137. Poulton, Kydd, and Dorward 2006; Dorward and others 2004; Pender and Mertz 2006.

138. Hofmann and Schellnhuber 2009; Sabine and others 2004.

139. Hansen and others 2005.

140. FAO 2009e.

141. FAO 2009e.

142. Delgado and others 2003.

143. FAO 2009e.

144. Arkema, Abramson, and Dewsbury 2006.

145. Smith, Gilmour, and Heyward 2008.

146. Gordon 2007.

147. Armada, White, and Christie 2009.

148. Pitcher and others 2009.

149. OECD 2008; World Bank 2008d.

150. FAO 2009e.

151. World Bank 2008d.

152. Costello, Gaines, and Lynham 2008; Hardin 1968; Hilborn 2007a; Hilborn 2007b.

153. FAO 2009c. Fish and seafood include both marine and freshwater fish and invertebrates. Total animal protein includes the former, plus all terrestrial meat, milk, and other animal products. The data are for 2003.

154. United Nations 2009.

155. FAO 2009c (2003 data).

156. FAO 2009e.

157. FAO 2009e.

158. World Bank 2006.

159. De Silva and Soto 2009.

160. De Silva and Soto 2009.

161. FAO 2004a.

162. Gyllenhammar and Hakanson 2005.

163. Deutsch and others 2007.

164. Gatlin and others 2007.

165. Tacon, Hasan, and Subasinghe 2006.

166. Tacon, Hasan, and Subasinghe 2006.

167. Naylor and others 2000.

168. Primavera 1997.

169. Tal and others 2009.

170. Naylor and others 2000.

171. FAO 2001; Lightfoot 1990.

172. Delgado and others 2003.

173. FAO 2009b.

174. For example, China and Nepal are not parties to an agreement between Bangladesh and India for the water of the Ganges basin and receive no allocation.

175. Salman 2007.

176. Qaddumi 2008.

177. Kurien 2005.

178. FAO 2009e.

179. Duda and Sherman 2002.

180. FAO 2009d; Sundby and Nakken 2008.

181. Lodge 2007.

182. BCLME Programme 2007.

183. GEF 2009.

184. World Bank 2009.

185. Fischer and others 2005.

186. Rosegrant, Fernandez, and Sinha 2009.

187. Easterling and others 2007.

188. FAO 2008.

189. Mitchell 2008. Climate shocks have led to restrictive domestic food trade policies and exacerbated price increases in the past as well; for examples, see Battisti and Naylor 2009.

190. World Bank 2009.

191. World Bank 2009.

192. von Braun and others 2008.

193. Bouet and Laborde 2008.

194. Other issues need a case-by-case assessment, such as exemptions from tariff cuts on special products, as sought by developing countries for products specified as important for food security, livelihood security, and rural development. World Bank 2007c.

195. WMO 2000.

196. Xiaofeng 2007.

197. United Nations 2004.

198. "Africa's Weather Stations Need 'Major Effort,'" Science and Development Network. www.SciDev.net, November 7, 2006.

199. WMO 2007.

200. Barnston and others 2005; Mason 2008.

201. Moron and others, forthcoming; Moron, Robertson, and Boer 2009; Moron, Robertson, and Ward 2006; Moron, Robertson, and Ward 2007.

202. Sivakumar and Hansen 2007.

203. Patt, Suarez, and Gwata 2005.

204. Bastiaanssen 1998; Menenti 2000.

205. WaterWatch, www.waterwatch.nl (accessed May 9, 2009).

206. Bastiaansen, W., WaterWatch, personal communication, May 2009.

207. http://www.globalsoilmap.net/ (accessed May 15, 2009).

208. Bindlish, Crow, and Jackson 2009; Frappart and others 2006; Turner and others 2003.

209. Bouma, van der Woerd, and Kulik 2009.

210. UNESCO 2007.

211. World Bank 2008d.

212. Kumar 2004.

213. World Bank 2007a.

214. World Bank, forthcoming b.

215. World Bank 2008b.

216. World Bank 2008b.

217. Mitchell 2008.

218. Zilberman and others 2008.

219. Rosegrant, Fernandez, and Sinha 2009.

220. Parry and others 1999; Parry, Rosenzweig, and Livermore 2005; Rosenzweig and others 2001.

221. Rosenzweig and others 2001.

222. Parry and others 2004.

223. Fischer and others 2005; Parry and others 1999; Parry and others 2004; Parry 2007; Parry, Rosenzweig, and Livermore 2005; Schmidhuber and Tubiello 2007.

224. Dawe 2008; Robles and Torero, forthcoming; Simler 2009.

225. McKinsey & Company 2009.

226. Perez and others 2007.

227. Smith and others 2009.

228. The official development assistance flow to Africa from 1996 to 2004 was about $1.30 billion a year: World Bank 2007c.

229. Perez and others 2007.

230. McKinsey & Company 2009.

231. The sequestration benefits of those activities would be regularly updated based on the state-of-the-art measurement and model-based approaches.

232. West and Post 2002.

233. Rochette and others 2008.

234. Johnston and others 2004.

235. Sullivan and others 2004.

236. In the Conservation Reserve Program, however, landowners bid on the payments and the government accepts or rejects the bids, which is quite different than a carbon emissions trading market.

237. McKinsey & Company 2009.

238. Tschakert 2004.

239. Alston and others 2000.

240. Chicago Climate Exchange, http://www.chicagoclimatex.com/index.jsf (accessed February 10, 2009).

241. Lal 2005.

242. UNEP 1990.

243. Swift and Shepherd 2007.

244. FAO 2009a.

245. OECD 2008.

246. http://ec.europa.eu/agriculture/capreform/infosheets/crocom_en.pdf (accessed May 12, 2009).

References

Alcamo, J., N. Dronin, M. Endejan, G. Golubev, and A. Kirilenko. 2007. "A New Assessment of Climate Change Impacts on Food Production Shortfalls and Water Availability in Russia." *Global Environmental Change* 17 (3–4): 429–44.

Alston, J. M., C. Chan-Kang, M. C. Marra, P. G. Pardey, and T. Wyatt. 2000. *A Meta-Analysis of Rates of Return to Agricultural R&D: Ex Pede Herculem?* Washington, DC: International Food Policy Research Institute.

Arango, H. 2003. *Planificación Predial Participativa, Fundación Centro para la Investigación en Sistemas Sostenibles de Producción Agropecuaria.* Cali, Colombia: Fundación CIPAV, Ingeniero Agrícola.

Arkema, K. K., S. C. Abramson, and B. M. Dewsbury. 2006. "Marine Ecosystem-Based Management: From Characterization to Implementation." *Ecology and the Environment* 4 (10): 525–32.

Armada, N., A. T. White, and P. Christie. 2009. "Managing Fisheries Resources in Danajon Bank, Bohol, Philippines: An Ecosystem-Based Approach." *Coastal Management* 307 (3–4): 308–30.

Asad, M., L. G. Azevedo, K. E. Kemper, and L. D. Simpson. 1999. "Management of Water Resources: Bulk Water Pricing in Brazil." Technical Paper 432, World Bank, Washington, DC.

Barnett, T. P., J. C. Adam, and D. P. Lettenmaier. 2005. "Potential Impacts of a Warming Climate on Water Availability in Snow-dominated Regions." *Nature* 438: 303–09.

Barnston, A. G., A. Kumar, L. Goddard, and M. P. Hoerling. 2005. "Improving Seasonal Prediction Practices through Attribution of Climate Variability." *Bulletin of the American Meteorological Society* 86 (1): 59–72.

Bastiaanssen, W. G. M. 1998. *Remote Sensing in Water Resources Management: The State of the Art.* Colombo: International Water Management Institute.

Bates, B., Z. W. Kundzewicz, S. Wu, and J. Palutikof. 2008. "Climate Change and Water." Technical Paper, Intergovernmental Panel on Climate Change, Geneva:.

Battisti, D. S., and R. L. Naylor. 2009. "Historical Warnings of Future Food Insecurity with Unprecedented Seasonal Heat." *Science* 323 (5911): 240–44.

BCLME Programme. 2007. "The Changing State of the Benguela Current Large Marine Ecosystem." Paper presented at the Expert Workshop on Climate Change and Variability and Impacts Thereof in the BCLME Region, May 15. Kirstenbosch Research Centre, Cape Town.

Beckett, J. L., and J. W. Oltjen. 1993. "Estimation of the Water Requirement for Beef Production in the United States." *Journal of Animal Science* 7 (4): 818–26.

Beintema, N. M., and G.-J. Stads. 2008. "Measuring Agricultural Research Investments: A Revised Global Picture." Agricultural Science and Technology Indicators Background Note, International Food Policy Research Institute, Washington, DC.

Benbrook, C. 2001. "Do GM Crops Mean Less Pesticide Use?" *Pesticide Outlook* 12 (5): 204–07.

Bhatia, R., R. Cestti, M. Scatasta, and R. P. S. Malik. 2008. *Indirect Economic Impacts of Dams: Case Studies from India, Egypt and Brazil.* New Delhi: Academic Foundation.

Bindlish, R., W. T. Crow, and T. J. Jackson. 2009. "Role of Passive Microwave Remote Sensing in Improving Flood Forecasts." *IEEE Geoscience and Remote Sensing Letters* 6 (1): 112–16.

Blaise, D., G. Majumdar, and K. U. Tekale. 2005. "On-Farm Evaluation of Fertilizer Application and Conservation Tillage on Productivity of Cotton and Pigeonpea Strip Intercropping on Rainfed Vertisols of Central India." *Soil and Tillage Research* 84 (1): 108–17.

Bosworth, B., G. Cornish, C. Perry, and F. van Steenbergen. 2002. *Water Charging in Irrigated Agriculture: Lessons from the Literature.* Wallingford, UK: HR Wallingford Ltd.

Bouët, A., and D. Laborde. 2008. "The Cost of a Non-Doha." Briefing note, International Food Policy Research Institute, Washington, DC.

Bouma, J. A., H. J. van der Woerd, and O. J. Kulik. 2009. "Assessing the Value of Information for Water Quality Management in the North Sea." *Journal of Environmental Management* 90 (2): 1280–88.

Burke, E. J., and S. J. Brown. 2008. "Evaluating Uncertainties in the Projection of Future Drought." *Journal of Hydrometeorology* 9 (2): 292–99.

Burke, E. J., S. J. Brown, and N. Christidis. 2006. "Modeling the Recent Evolution of Global Drought and Projections for the 21st Century with the Hadley Centre Climate Model." *Journal of Hydrometeorology* 7: 1113–25.

Butler, R. A., L. P. Koh, and J. Ghazoul. Forthcoming. "REDD in the Red: Palm Oil Could Undermine Carbon Payment Schemes." *Conservation Letters.*

Carlsson-Kanyama, A., and A. D. Gonzales. 2009. "Potential Contributions of Food Consumption Patterns to Climate Change." *American Journal of Clinical Nutrition* 89 (5):1704S–09S.

Cassman, K. G. 1999. "Ecological Intensification of Cereal Production Systems: Yield Potential, Soil Quality, and Precision Agriculture." *Proceedings of the National Academy of Sciences* 96 (11): 5952–59.

Cassman, K. G., A. Dobermann, D. T. Walters, and H. Yang. 2003. "Meeting Cereal Demand While Protecting Natural Resources and Improving Environmental Quality." *Annual Review of Environment and Resources* 28: 315–58.

CEDARE (Center for Environment and Development in the Arab Region and Europe). 2006. *Water Conflicts and Conflict Management Mechanisms in the Middle East and North Africa Region.* Cairo: CEDARE.

Chan, K. M. A., and G. C. Daily. 2008. "The Payoff of Conservation Investments in Tropical Countryside." *Proceedings of the National Academy of Sciences* 105 (49): 19342–47.

Chomitz, K. M. 2004. "Transferable Development Rights and Forest Protection: An Exploratory Analysis." *International Regional Science Review* 27 (3): 348–73.

Cline, W. R. 2007. *Global Warming and Agriculture: Impact Estimates by Country.* Washington, DC: Center for Global Development and Peterson Institute for International Economics.

Costello, C., S. D. Gaines, and J. Lynham. 2008. "Can Catch Shares Prevent Fisheries Collapse?" *Science* 321 (5896): 1678–81.

Dawe, D. 2008. "Have Recent Increases in International Cereal Prices Been Transmitted to Domestic Economies? The Experience in Seven Large Asian Countries." Agricultural Development Economics Division Working Paper 08-03, Food and Agriculture Organization, Rome.

De Fraiture, C., and C. Perry. 2007. "Why Is Agricultural Water Demand Unresponsive at Low Price Ranges?" In *Irrigation Water Pricing: The Gap between Theory and Practice,* ed. F. Molle and J. Berkoff. Oxfordshire, UK: CAB International.

de la Torre, A., P. Fajnzylber, and J. Nash. 2008. *Low Carbon, High Growth: Latin American Responses to Climate Change.* Washington, DC: World Bank.

De Silva, S., and D. Soto. 2009. "Climate Change and Aquaculture: Potential Impacts, Adaptation and Mitigation." Technical Paper 530, Food and Agriculture Organization, Rome.

Delgado, C. L., M. W. Rosegrant, H. Steinfeld, S. Ehui, and C. Courbois. 1999. "Livestock to 2020: The Next Food Revolution." Food, Agriculture, and Environment Discussion Paper 28, International Food Policy Research Institute, Washington, DC.

Delgado, C. L., N. Wada, M. Rosegrant, S. Meijer, and M. Ahmed. 2003. *Outlook for Fish to 2020:*

Meeting Global Demand. Washington, DC: International Food Policy Research Institute.

Derpsch, R. 2007. "No-Tillage and Conservation Agriculture: A Progress Report." In *No-Till Farming Systems,* ed. T. Goddard, M. A. Zoebisch, Y. T. Gan, W. Elli, A. Watson, and S. Sombatpanit. Bangkok: World Association of Soil and Water Conservation.

Derpsch, R., and T. Friedrich. 2009. "Global Overview of Conservation Agriculture Adoption." In *Lead Papers 4th World Congress on Conservation Agriculture.* New Delhi: World Congress on Conservation Agriculture.

Deutsch, L., S. Graslund, C. Folke, M. Troell, M. Huitric, N. Kautsky, and L. Lebel. 2007. "Feeding Aquaculture Growth through Globalization: Exploitation of Marine Ecosystems for Fishmeal." *Global Environmental Change* 17 (2): 238–49.

Diaz, R. J., and R. Rosenberg. 2008. "Spreading Dead Zones and Consequences for Marine Ecosystems." *Science* 321 (5891): 926–29.

Doraiswamy, P., G. McCarty, E. Hunt, R. Yost, M. Doumbia, and A. Franzluebbers. 2007. "Modeling Soil Carbon Sequestration in Agricultural Lands of Mali." *Agricultural Systems* 94 (1): 63–74.

Dorward, A., S. Fan, J. Kydd, H. Lofgren, J. Morrison, C. Poulton, N. Rao, L. Smith, H. Tchale, S. Thorat, I. Urey, and P. Wobst. 2004. "Institutions and Policies for Pro-Poor Agricultural Growth." *Development Policy Review* 22 (6): 611–22.

Duda, A. M., and K. Sherman. 2002. "A New Imperative for Improving Management of Large Marine Ecosystems." *Ocean and Coastal Management* 45: 797–833.

Dudley, N., and S. Stolton. 1999. *Conversion of "Paper Parks" to Effective Management: Developing a Target.* Gland, Switzerland: Report to the WWF-World Bank Alliance from the International Union for the Conservation of Nature and WWF, Forest Innovation Project.

Dye, P., and D. Versfeld. 2007. "Managing the Hydrological Impacts of South African Plantation Forests: An Overview." *Forest Ecology and Management* 251 (1–2): 121–28.

Easterling, W., P. Aggarwal, P. Batima, K. Brander, L. Erda, M. Howden, A. Kirilenko, J. Morton, J.-F. Soussana, J. Schmidhuber, and F. Tubiello. 2007. "Food, Fibre and Forest Products." In *Climate Change 2007: Impacts, Adaptation and Vulnerability. Contribution of Working Group II to the Fourth Assessment Report of the Intergovernmental Panel on Climate Change,* ed. M. Parry, O. F. Canziani, J. P. Palutikof, P. J. van der Linden, and C. E. Hanson. Cambridge, UK: Cambridge University Press.

EBRD (European Bank for Reconstruction and Development) and FAO (Food and Agriculture Organization). 2008. "Fighting Food Inflation through Sustainable Investment." EBRD and FAO, London.

Erenstein, O. 2009. "Adoption and Impact of Conservation Agriculture Based Resource Conserving Technologies in South Asia." In *Lead Papers, 4th World Congress on Conservation Agriculture, February 4–7, 2009, New Delhi, India.* New Delhi: WCCA.

Erenstein, O., U. Farooq, R. K. Malik, and M. Sharif. 2008. "On-Farm Impacts of Zero Tillage Wheat in South Asia's Rice-Wheat Systems." *Field Crops Research* 105 (3): 240–52.

Erenstein, O., and V. Laxmi. 2008. "Zero Tillage Impacts in India's Rice-Wheat Systems: A Review." *Soil and Tillage Research* 100 (1-2): 1–14.

FAO (Food and Agriculture Organization). 2001. "Integrated Agriculture-Aquaculture." Fisheries Technical Paper 407, Rome.

———. 2004a. *The State of World Fisheries and Aquaculture 2004.* Rome: FAO.

———. 2004b. "Water Desalination For Agricultural Applications." Land and Water Discussion Paper 5, FAO, Rome.

———. 2005. *Agricultural Biodiversity in FAO.* Rome: FAO.

———. 2008. *Food Outlook: Global Market Analysis.* Rome: FAO.

———. 2009a. "Anchoring Agriculture within a Copenhagen Agreement: A Policy Brief for UNFCCC Parties by FAO." FAO, Rome.

———. 2009b. "Aquastat." FAO, Rome.

———. 2009c. "FAOSTAT." FAO, Rome.

———. 2009d. "Fisheries and Aquaculture in a Changing Climate." FAO, Rome.

———. 2009e. *The State of World Fisheries and Aquaculture 2008.* Rome: FAO.

Fay, M., R. I. Block, and J. Ebinger, ed. 2010. *Adapting to Climate Change in Europe and Central Asia.* Washington, DC: World Bank.

Fischer, G., M. Shah, F. Tubiello, and H. T. Van Velthuizen. 2005. "Socio-economic and Climate Change Impacts on Agriculture: An Integrated Assessment, 1990–2080." *Philosophical Transactions of the Royal Society B: Biological Sciences* 360: 2067–83.

Fischer, G., M. Shah, and H. van Velthuizen. 2002. "Climate Change and Agricultural Vulnerability." Paper presented at the World Summit on Sustainable Development, Johannesburg.

Franzluebbers, A. J. 2002. "Water Infiltration and Soil Structure Related to Organic Matter and Its Stratification with Depth." *Soil and Tillage Research* 66: 197–205.

Frappart, F., K. D. Minh, J. L'Hermitte, A. Cazenave, G. Ramillien, T. Le Toan, and N. Mognard-Campbell. 2006. "Water Volume Change in the Lower Mekong from Satellite Altimetry and Imagery Data." *Geophysical Journal International* 167 (2): 570–84.

Gaston, K. J., S. F. Jackson, L. Cantu-Salazar, and G. Cruz-Pinon. 2008. "The Ecological Performance of Protected Areas." *Annual Review of Ecology, Evolution, and Systematics* 39: 93–113.

Gatlin, D. M., F. T. Barrows, P. Brown, K. Dabrowski, T. G. Gaylord, R. W. Hardy, E. Herman, G. Hu, A. Krogdahl, R. Nelson, K. Overturf, M. Rust, W. Sealey, D. Skonberg, E. J. Souza, D. Stone, R. Wilson, and E. Wurtele. 2007. "Expanding the Utilization of Sustainable Plant Products in Aquafeeds: A Review." *Aquaculture Research* 38 (6): 551–79.

Gleick, P. 2008. *The World's Water 2008–2009: The Biennial Report on Freshwater Resources.* Washington, DC: Island Press.

GEF (Global Environment Facility). 2009. *From Ridge to Reef: Water, Environment, and Community Security: GEF Action on Transboundary Water Resources.* Washington, DC: GEF.

Gobierno de España. 2009. *La Desalinización en España.* Madrid: Ministerio de Medio Ambiente y Medio Rural y Marino.

Gordon, I. J. 2007. "Linking Land to Ocean: Feedbacks in the Management of Socio-Ecological Systems in the Great Barrier Reef Catchments." *Hydrobiologia* 591 (1): 25–33.

Govaerts, B., K. Sayre, and J. Deckers. 2005. "Stable High Yields With Zero Tillage and Permanent Bed Planting?" *Field Crops Research* 94: 33–42.

Govaerts, B., N. Verhulst, A. Castellanos-Navarrete, K. D. Sayre, J. Dixon, and L. Dendooven. 2009. "Conservation Agriculture and Soil Carbon Sequestration: Between Myth and Farmer Reality." *Critical Reviews in Plant Sciences* 28 (3): 97–122.

Groves, D. G., M. Davis, R. Wilkinson, and R. Lempert. 2008. "Planning for Climate Change in the Inland Empire: Southern California." *Water Resources Impact* 10 (4): 14–17.

Groves, D. G., and R. J. Lempert. 2007. "A New Analytic Method for Finding Policy-Relevant Scenarios." *Global Environmental Change* 17 (1): 73–85.

Groves, D. G., D. Yates, and C. Tebaldi. 2008. "Developing and Applying Uncertain Global

Climate Change Projections for Regional Water Management Planning." *Water Resources Research* 44 (12): 1–16.

Gruere, G. P., P. Mehta-Bhatt, and D. Sengupta. 2008. "Bt Cotton and Farmer Suicides in India: Reviewing the Evidence." Discussion Paper 00808, International Food Policy Research Institute, Washington, DC.

Gurgel, A. C., J. M. Reilly, and S. Paltsev. 2008. *Potential Land Use Implications of a Global Biofuels Industry.* Cambridge, MA: Massachusetts Institute of Technology Joint Program on the Science and Policy of Global Change.

Gyllenhammar, A., and L. Hakanson. 2005. "Environmental Consequence Analyses of Fish Farm Emissions Related to Different Scales and Exemplified by Data from the Baltic: A Review." *Marine Environmental Research* 60: 211–43.

Hannah, L., G. Midgley, S. Andelman, M. Araujo, G. Hughes, E. Martinez-Meyer, R. Pearson, and P. Williams. 2007. "Protected Areas Needs in a Changing Climate." *Frontiers in Ecology and Evolution* 5 (3): 131–38.

Hansen, J., L. Nazarenko, R. Ruedy, M. Sato, J. Willis, A. Del Genio, D. Koch, A. Lacis, K. Lo, S. Menon, T. Novakov, J. Perlwitz, G. Russell, G. A. Schmidt, and N. Tausnev. 2005. "Earth's Energy Imbalance: Confirmation and Implications." *Science* 308 (5727): 1431–35.

Hardin, G. 1968. "The Tragedy of the Commons." *Science* 162 (3859): 1243–48.

Hazell, P. B. R. 2003. "The Green Revolution: Curse or Blessing?" In *Oxford Encyclopedia of Economic History,* ed. J. Mokyr. New York: Oxford University Press.

Henson, I. E. 2008. "The Carbon Cost of Palm Oil Production in Malaysia." *The Planter* 84: 445–64.

Hilborn, R. 2007a. "Defining Success in Fisheries and Conflicts in Objectives." *Marine Policy* 31 (2): 153–58.

———. 2007b. "Moving to Sustainability by Learning from Successful Fisheries." *Ambio* 36 (4): 296–303.

Hobbs, P. R., K. Sayre, and R. Gupta. 2008. "The Role of Conservation Agriculture in Sustainable Agriculture." *Philosophical Transactions of the Royal Society* 363 (1491): 543–55.

Hoekstra, A. Y., and A. K. Chapagain. 2007. "Water Footprints of Nations: Water Use by People as a Function of Their Consumption Pattern." *Water Resources Management* 21 (1): 35–48.

Hofmann, M., and H.-J. Schellnhuber. 2009. "Oceanic Acidification Affects Marine Carbon Pump and Triggers Extended Marine Oxygen Holes." *Proceedings of the National Academy of Sciences* 106 (9): 3017–22.

IAASTD (International Assessment of Agricultural Knowledge, Science and Technology for Development). 2009. *Summary for Decision Makers of the Global Report*. Washington, DC: IAASTD.

IEA (International Energy Agency). 2006. *World Energy Outlook 2006*. Paris: IEA.

IPCC (Intergovernmental Panel on Climate Change). 2007a. *Climate Change 2007: Synthesis Report. Contribution of Working Groups I, II and II to the Fourth Assessment Report of the Intergovernmental Panel on Climate Change*. Geneva: IPPC.

———. 2007b. "Summary for Policymakers." In *Climate Change 2007: Mitigation. Contribution of Working Group III to the Fourth Assessment Report of the Intergovernmental Panel on Climate Change,* ed. B. Metz, O. R. Davidson, P. R. Bosch, R. Dave, and L. A. Meyer. Cambridge, UK: Cambridge University Press.

James, C. 2000. *Global Review of Commercialized Transgenic Crops*. Ithaca, NY: International Service for the Acquisition of Agri-Biotech Applications.

———. 2007. *Global Status of Commercialized Biotech/GM Crops: 2007*. Ithaca, NY: International Service for the Acquisition of Agri-Biotech Applications.

———. 2008. *Global Status of Commercialized Biotech/GM Crops: 2008*. Ithaca, NY: International Service for the Acquisition of Agri-Biotech Applications.

Johnston, C. A., P. Groffman, D. D. Breshears, Z. G. Cardon, W. Currie, W. Emanuel, J. Gaudinski, R. B. Jackson, K. Lajtha, K. Nadelhoffer, D. Nelson, W. MacPost, G. Retallack, and L. Wielopolski. 2004. "Carbon Cycling in Soil." *Frontiers in Ecology and the Environment* 2 (10): 522–28.

Kaonga, M. L., and K. Coleman. 2008. "Modeling Soil Organic Carbon Turnover in Improved Fallows in Eastern Zambia Using the RothC-26.3 Model." *Forest Ecology and Management* 256 (5): 1160–66.

Klein, A. M., B. E. Vaissiere, J. H. Cane, I. Steffan-Dewenter, S. A. Cunningham, C. Kremen, and T. Tscharntke. 2007. "Importance of Pollinators in Changing Landscapes for World Crops." *Proceedings of the Royal Society* 274 (1608): 303–13.

Koh, L. P., P. Levang, and J. Ghazoul. Forthcoming. "Designer Landscapes for Sustainable Biofuels." *Trends in Ecology and Evolution*.

Koh, L. P., and D. S. Wilcove. 2009. "Is Oil Palm Agriculture Really Destroying Tropical Biodiversity." *Conservation Letters* 1 (2): 60–64.

Kosgei, J. R., G. P. W. Jewitt, V. M. Kongo, and S. A. Lorentz. 2007. "The Influence Of Tillage on Field Scale Water Fluxes and Maize Yields in Semi-Arid Environments: A Case Study of Potshini Catchment, South Africa." *Physics and Chemistry of the Earth , Parts A/B/C* 32 (15–18): 1117–26.

Kotilainen, L., R. Rajalahti, C. Ragasa, and E. Pehu. 2006. "Health Enhancing Foods: Opportunities for Strengthening the Sector in Developing Countries." Agriculture and Rural Development Discussion Paper 30, World Bank, Washington, DC.

Kumar, R. 2004. "eChoupals: A Study on the Financial Sustainability of Village Internet Centers in Rural Madhya Pradesh." *Information Technologies and International Development* 2 (1): 45–73.

Kurien, J. 2005. "International Fish Trade and Food Security: Issues and Perspectives." Paper presented at the 31st Annual Conference of the International Association of Aquatic and Marine Science Libraries, Rome.

Laffoley, D. d'A. 2008. "Towards Networks of Marine Protected Areas: The MPA Plan of Action for IUCN's World Commission on Protected Areas." International Union for Conservation of Nature, World Commission on Protected Areas, Gland, Switzerland.

Lal, R. 2005. "Enhancing Crop Yields in the Developing Countries through Restoration of the Soil Organic Carbon Pool in Agricultural Lands." *Land Degradation and Development* 17 (2): 197–209.

Lehmann, J. 2007a. "A Handful of Carbon." *Nature* 447: 143–44.

———. 2007b. "Bio-Energy in the Black." *Frontiers in Ecology and the Environment* 5 (7): 381–87.

Lightfoot, C. 1990. "Integration of Aquaculture and Agriculture: A Route Towards Sustainable Farming Systems." *Naga: The ICLARM Quarterly* 13 (1): 9–12.

Lin, B. B., I. Perfecto, and J. Vandermeer. 2008. "Synergies between Agricultural Intensification and Climate Change Could Create Surprising Vulnerabilities for Crops." *BioScience* 58 (9): 847–54.

Lobell, D. B., M. Burke, C. Tebaldi, M. D. Mastrandrea, W. P. Falcon, and R. L. Naylor. 2008. "Prioritizing Climate Change Adaptation Needs for Food Security in 2030." *Science* 319 (5863): 607–10.

Lodge, M. W. 2007. "Managing International Fisheries: Improving Fisheries Governance by Strengthening Regional Fisheries Management Organizations." Chatham House Energy, Environment and Development Programme Briefing Paper EEDP BP 07/01, London.

Lotze-Campen, H., A. Popp, J. P. Dietrich, and M. Krause. 2009. "Competition for Land between Food, Bioenergy and Conservation." Background note for the WDR 2010.

Louati, Mohamed El Hedi. "Tunisia's Experience in Water Resource Mobilization and Management." Background note for the WDR 2010.

Mason, S. J. 2008. "'Flowering Walnuts in the Wood' and Other Bases for Seasonal Climate Forecasting." In *Seasonal Forecasts, Climatic Change and Human Health: Health and Climate.* ed. M. C. Thomson, R. Garcia-Herrera, and M. Beniston. Amsterdam: Springer Netherlands.

McKinsey & Company. 2009. *Pathways to a Low-Carbon Economy: Version 2 of the Global Greenhouse Gas Abatement Cost Curve.* Washington, DC: McKinsey & Company.

McNeely, J. A., and S. J. Scherr. 2003. *Ecoagriculture: Strategies to Feed the World and Save Biodiversity.* Washington, DC: Island Press.

Meehl, G. A., T. F. Stocker, W. D. Collins, P. Friedlingstein, A. T. Gaye, J. M. Gregory, A. Kitoh, R. Knutti, J. M. Murphy, A. Noda, S. C. B. Raper, I. G. Watterson, A. J. Weaver, and Z.-C. Zhao. 2007. "Global Climate Projections." In *Climate Change 2007: The Physical Science Basis. Contribution of Working Group I to the Fourth Assessment Report of the Intergovernmental Panel on Climate Change,* ed. S. Solomon, D. Qin, M. Manning, Z. Chen, M. Marquis, K. B. Averyt, M. Tignor, and H. L. Miller. Cambridge, UK: Cambridge University Press.

Menenti, M. 2000. "Evaporation." In *Remote Sensing in Hydrology and Water Management,* ed. G. A. Schultz and E. T. Engman. Berlin: Springer-Verlag.

Millennium Ecosystem Assessment. 2005. *Ecosystems and Human Well-Being: Biodiversity Synthesis.* Washington, DC: World Resources Institute.

Milly, P. C. D., J. Betancourt, M. Falkenmark, R. M. Hirsch, Z. W. Kundzewicz, D. P. Lettenmaier, and R. J. Stouffer. 2008. "Stationarity Is Dead: Whither Water Management?" *Science* 319 (5863): 573–74.

Milly, P. C. D., K. A. Dunne, and A. V. Vecchia. 2005. "Global Pattern of Trends in Streamflow and Water Availability in a Changing Climate." *Nature* 438 (17): 347–50.

Mitchell, D. 2008. "A Note on Rising Food Prices." Policy Research Working Paper 4682, World Bank, Washington, DC.

Molden, D. 2007. *Water for Food, Water for Life: A Comprehensive Assessment of Water Management in Agriculture.* London: Earthscan and International Water Management Institute.

Molle, F., and J. Berkoff. 2007. *Irrigation Water Pricing: The Gap between Theory and Practice.* Wallingford, UK: CAB International.

Moller, M., J. Tanny, Y. Li, and S. Cohen. 2004. "Measuring and Predicting Evapotranspiration in an Insect-Proof Screenhouse." *Agricultural and Forest Meteorology* 127 (12): 35–51.

Moron, V., A. Lucero, F. Hilario, B. Lyon, A. W. Robertson, and D. DeWitt. Forthcoming. "Spatio-Temporal Variability and Predictability of Summer Monsoon Onset over the Philippines." *Climate Dynamics.*

Moron, V., A. W. Robertson, and R. Boer. 2009. "Spatial Coherence and Seasonal Predictability of Monsoon Onset over Indonesia." *Journal of Climate* 22 (3): 840–50.

Moron, V., A. W. Robertson, and M. N. Ward. 2006. "Seasonal Predictability and Spatial Coherence of Rainfall Characteristics in the Tropical Setting of Senegal." *Monthly Weather Review* 134 (11): 3248–62.

———. 2007. "Spatial Coherence of Tropical Rainfall at Regional Scale." *Journal of Climate* 20 (21): 5244–63.

Müller, C., A. Bondeau, A. Popp, K. Waha, and M. Fader. 2009. "Climate Change Impacts on Agricultural Yields." Background note for the WDR 2010.

NRC (National Research Council). 2007. *Water Implications of Biofuels Production in the United States.* Washington, DC: National Academies Press.

Naylor, R. L., R. J. Goldburg, J. H. Primavera, N. Kautsky, M. C. M. Beveridge, J. Clay, C. Folke, J. Lubchenco, H. Mooney, and M. Troell. 2000. "Effects of Aquaculture on World Fish Supplies." *Nature* 405 (6790): 1017–24.

Normile, D. 2006. "Agricultural Research: Consortium Aims to Supercharge Rice Photosynthesis." *Science* 313 (5786): 423.

OECD (Organisation for Economic Cooperation and Development). 2008. *Agricultural Policies in OECD Countries: At a Glance 2008.* Paris: OECD.

————. 2009. *Managing Water for All: An OECD Perspective on Pricing and Financing.* Paris: OECD.

Olmstead, S., W. M. Hanemann, and R. N. Stavins. 2007. "Water Demand under Alternative Price Structures." Working Paper 13573, National Bureau of Economic Research, Cambridge, MA.

Parry, M. 2007. "The Implications of Climate Change for Crop Yields, Global Food Supply and Risk of Hunger." *SAT e-Journal* 4 (1), Open Access e-Journal, International Crops Research Institute for the Semi-Arid Tropics (ICRISAT). http://www.icrisat.org/Journal/SpecialProject/sp14.pdf.

Parry, M., C. Rosenzweig, A. Iglesias, G. Fischer, and M. Livermore. 1999. "Climate Change and World Food Security: A New Assessment." *Global Environmental Change* 9 (S1): S51–S67.

Parry, M., C. Rosenzweig, A. Iglesias, M. Livermore, and G. Fischer. 2004. "Effects of Climate Change on Global Food Production under SRES Emissions and Socio-Economic Scenarios." *Global Environmental Change* 14 (1): 53–67.

Parry, M., C. Rosenzweig, and M. Livermore. 2005. "Climate Change, Global Food Supply and Risk of Hunger." *Philosophical Transactions of the Royal Society B* 360 (1463): 2125–38.

Passioura, J. 2006. "Increasing Crop Productivity When Water Is Scarce: From Breeding to Field Management." *Agricultural Water Management* 80 (1-3): 176–96.

Patt, A. G., P. Suarez, and C. Gwata. 2005. "Effects of Seasonal Climate Forecasts and Participatory Workshops among Subsistence Farmers in Zimbabwe." *Proceedings of the National Academy of Sciences* 102 (35): 12623–28.

Peden, D., G. Tadesse, and M. Mammo. 2004. "Improving the Water Productivity of Livestock: An Opportunity for Poverty Reduction." Paper presented at the Integrated Water and Land Management Research and Capacity Building Priorities for Ethiopia Conference. Addis Ababa.

Pender, J., and O. Mertz. 2006. "Soil Fertility Depletion Sub-Saharan Africa: What Is the Role of Organic Agriculture." In *Global Development or Organic Agriculture: Challenges and Prospects,* ed. N. Halberg, H. F. Alroe, M. T. Knudsen, and E. S. Kristensen. Wallingford, UK: CAB International.

Perez, C., C. Roncoli, C. Neely, and J. Steiner. 2007. "Can Carbon Sequestration Markets Benefit Low-Income Producers in Semi-Arid Africa? Potentials and Challenges." *Agricultural Systems* 94 (1): 2–12.

Perry, C., P. Steduto, R. G. Allen, and C. M. Burt. Forthcoming. "Increasing Productivity in Irrigated Agriculture: Agronomic Constraints and Hydrological Realities." *Agricultural Water Management.*

Phipps, R., and J. Park. 2002. "Environmental Benefits of Genetically Modified Crops: Global and European Perspectives on Their Ability to Reduce Pesticide Use." *Journal of Animal and Feed Science* 11: 1–18.

Pimentel, D., B. Berger, D. Filiberto, M. Newton, B. Wolfe, E. Karabinakis, S. Clark, E. Poon, E. Abbett, and S. Nandagopal. 2004. "Water Resources: Agricultural and Environmental Issues." *BioScience* 54 (10): 909–18.

Pingali, P. L., and M. W. Rosegrant. 2001. "Intensive Food Systems in Asia: Can the Degradation Problems Be Reversed?" In *Tradeoffs or Synergies? Agricultural Intensification, Economic Development and the Environment,* ed. D. R. Lee and C. B. Barrett. Wallingford, UK: CAB International.

Pitcher, T., D. Kalikoski, K. Short, D. Varkey, and G. Pramod. 2009. "An Evaluation of Progress in Implementing Ecosystem-Based Management of Fisheries in 33 Countries." *Marine Policy* 33 (2): 223–32.

Poulton, C., J. Kydd, and A. Dorward. 2006. "Increasing Fertilizer Use in Africa: What Have We Learned?" Discussion Paper 25, World Bank, Washington, DC.

Primavera, J. H. 1997. "Socio-economic Impacts of Shrimp Culture." *Aquaculture Research* 28: 815–27.

Qaddumi, H. 2008. "Practical Approaches to Transboundary Water Benefit Sharing." Working Paper 292, Overseas Development Institute, London.

Randolph, T. F., E. Schelling, D. Grace, C. F. Nicholson, J. L. Leroy, D. C. Cole, M. W. Demment, A. Omore, J. Zinsstag, and M. Ruel. 2007. "Invited Review: Role of Livestock in Human Nutrition and Health for Poverty Reduction in Developing Countries." *Journal of Animal Science* 85 (11): 2788–2800.

Reardon, T., K. Stamoulis, M. E. Cruz, A. Balisacan, J. Berdugue, and K. Savadogo. 1998. "Diversification of Household Incomes into Nonfarm Sources: Patterns, Determinants and Effects." Paper presented at the IFPRI/

World Bank Conference on Strategies for Stimulating Growth of the Rural Nonfarm Economy in Developing Countries, Airlie House, Virginia.

Ricketts, T. H., J. Regetz, I. Steffan-Dewenter, S. A. Cunningham, C. Kremen, A. Bogdanski, B. Gemmill-Herren, S. S. Greenleaf, A. M. Klein, M. M. Mayfield, L. A. Morandin, A. Ochieng, and B. F. Viana. 2008. "Landscape Effects on Crop Pollination Services: Are There General Patterns?" *Ecology Letters* 11(5):499–515.

Ritchie, J. E. 2008. "Land-Ocean Interactions: Human, Freshwater, Coastal and Ocean Interactions under Changing Environments." Paper presented at the Hydrology Expert Facility Workshop: Hydrologic Analysis to Inform Bank Policies and Projects: Bridging the Gap, November 24, Washington, DC.

Rivera, J. A., C. Hotz, T. Gonzalez-Cossio, L. Neufeld, and A. Garcia-Guerra. 2003. "The Effect of Micronutrient Deficiencies on Child Growth: A Review of Results from Community-Based Supplementation Trials." *Journal of Nutrition* 133 (11): 4010S–20S.

Robles, M., and M. Torero. Forthcoming. "Understanding the Impact of High Food Prices in Latin America." *Economia.*

Rochette, P., D. A. Angers, M. H. Chantigny, and N. Bertrand. 2008. "Nitrous Oxide Emissions Respond Differently to No-Till in a Loam and a Heavy Clay Soil." *Soil Science Society of America Journal* 72: 1363–69.

Rosegrant, M. W., and H. Binswanger. 1994. "Markets in Tradable Water Rights: Potential for Efficiency Gains in Developing Country Water Resource Allocation." *World Development* 22 (11): 1613–25.

Rosegrant, M. W., X. Cai, and S. Cline. 2002. *World Water and Food to 2025: Dealing with Scarcity.* Washington, DC: International Food Policy Research Institute.

Rosegrant, M. W., S. A. Cline, and R. A. Valmonte-Santos. 2007. "Global Water and Food Security: Emerging Issues." In *Proceedings of the International Conference on Water for Irrigated Agriculture and the Environment: Finding a Flow for All,* ed. A. G. Brown. Canberra: ATSE Crawford Fund.

Rosegrant, M. W., M. Fernandez, and A. Sinha. 2009. "Looking into the Future for Agriculture and KST." In *IAASTD Global Report,* ed. B. McIntyre, H. R. Herren, J. Wakhungu, and R. T. Watson. Washington, DC: Island Press.

Rosegrant, M. W., and P. B. R. Hazell. 2000. *Transforming the Rural Asian Economy: The Unfinished Revolution.* New York: Oxford University Press.

Rosegrant, M. W., M. Paisner, S. Meijer, and J. Witcover. 2001. *Global Food Projections to 2020: Emerging Trends and Alternative Futures.* Washington, DC: International Food Policy Research Institute.

Rosenzweig, C., A. Iglesias, X. Yang, P. R. Epstein, and E. Chivian. 2001. "Climate Change and Extreme Weather Events: Implications for Food Production, Plant Diseases and Pests." *Global Change and Human Health* 2 (2): 90–104.

Sabine, C. L., R. A. Feely, N. Gruber, R. M. Key, K. Lee, J. L. Bullister, R. Wanninkhof, C. S. Wong, D. W. R. Wallace, B. Tilbrook, F. J. Millero, T.-H. Peng, A. Kozyr, T. Ono, and A. F. Rios. 2004. "The Oceanic Sink for Anthropogenic CO_2." *Science* 305: 367–71.

Salman, S. M. A. 2007. "The United Nations Watercourses Convention Ten Years Later: Why Has Its Entry into Force Proven Difficult?" *Water International* 32 (1): 1–15.

Scherr, S. J., and J. A. McNeely. 2008. "Biodiversity Conservation and Agricultural Sustainability: Towards a New Paradigm of Ecoagriculture Landscapes." *Philosophical Transactions of the Royal Society B* 363: 477–94.

Schmidhuber, J., and F. N. Tubiello. 2007. "Global Food Security under Climate Change." *Proceedings of the National Academy of Sciences* 104 (50): 19703–08.

Schoups, G., J. W. Hopmans, C. A. Young, J. A. Vrugt, W. W. Wallender, K. K. Tanji, and S. Panday. 2005. "Sustainability of Irrigated Agriculture in the San Joaquin Valley, California." *Proceedings of the National Academy of Sciences* 102 (43): 15352–56.

Shiklomanov, I. A. 1999. *World Water Resources: An Appraisal for the 21st Century.* Paris: UNESCO International Hydrological Programme.

Shiklomanov, I. A., and J. C. Rodda. 2003. *World Water Resources at the Beginning of the 21st Century.* Cambridge, UK: Cambridge University Press.

Simler, K. R. 2009. "The Impact of Higher Food Prices on Poverty in Uganda." World Bank, Washington, DC.

Singh, U. 2005. "Integrated Nitrogen Fertilization for Intensive and Sustainable Agriculture." *Journal of Crop Improvement* 15 (2): 259–88.

Sivakumar, M. V. K., and J. Hansen, ed. 2007. *Climate Prediction and Agriculture: Advances and Challenges.* New York: Springer.

Smith, L. D., J. P. Gilmour, and A. J. Heyward. 2008. "Resilience of Coral Communities on an Isolated System of Reefs Following Catastrophic Mass-bleaching." *Coral Reefs* 27 (1): 197–205.

Smith, P., D. Martino, Z. Cai, D. Gwary, H. H. Janzen, P. Kumar, B. McCarl, S. Ogle, F. O'Mara, C. Rice, R. J. Scholes, O. Sirotenko, M. Howden, T. McAllister, G. Pan, V. Romanenkov, U. Schneider, S. Towprayoon, M. Wattenbach, and J. U. Smith. 2009. "Greenhouse Gas Mitigation in Agriculture." *Philosophical Transactions of the Royal Society B* 363: 789–813.

Sohi, S., E. Lopez-Capel, E. Krull, and R. Bol. 2009. *Biochar, Climate Change, and Soil: A Review to Guide Future Research*. Australia: CSIRO Land and Water Science Report 05/09.

Steinfeld, H., P. Gerber, T. Wassenaar, V. Castel, M. Rosales, and C. De Haan. 2006. *Livestock's Long Shadow: Environmental Issues and Options*. Rome: Food and Agriculture Organization.

Struhsaker, T. T., P. J. Struhsaker, and K. S. Siex. 2005. "Conserving Africa's Rain Forests: Problems in Protected Areas and Possible Solutions." *Biological Conservation* 123 (1): 45–54.

Strzepek, K., G. Yohe, R. S. J. Tol, and M. W. Rosegrant. 2004. "Determining the Insurance Value of the High Aswan Dam for the Egyptian Economy." International Food Policy Research Institute, Washington, DC.

Su, Z., J. Zhang, W. Wu, D. Cai, J. Lv, G. Jiang, J. Huang, J. Gao, R. Hartmann, and D. Gabriels. 2007. "Effects of Conservation Tillage Practices on Winter Wheat Water-Use Efficiency and Crop Yield on The Loess Plateau, China." *Agricultural Water Management* 87 (3): 307–14.

Sullivan, P., D. Hellerstein, L. Hansen, R. Johansson, S. Koenig, R. Lubowski, W. McBride, D. McGranahan, M. Roberts, S. Vogel, and S. Bucholtz. 2004. *The Conservation Reserve Program: Economic Implications for Rural America*. Washington, DC: United States Department of Agriculture.

Sundby, S., and O. Nakken. 2008. "Spatial Shifts in Spawning Habitats of Arcto-Norwegian Cod Related to Multidecadal Climate Oscillations and Climate Change." *ICES Journal of Marine Sciences* 65 (6): 953–62.

Swift, M. J., and K. D. Shepherd, ed. 2007. *Saving Africa's Soils: Science and Technology for Improved Soil Management in Africa*. Nairobi: World Agroforestry Centre.

Tacon, A. G. J., M. R. Hasan, and R. P. Subasinghe. 2006. "Use of Fishery Resources as Feed Inputs for Aquaculture Development: Trends and Policy." FAO Fisheries Circular 1018, Rome.

Tal, Y., H. Schreier, K. R. Sowers, J. D. Stubblefield, A. R. Place, and Y. Zohar. 2009. "Environmentally Sustainable Land-Based Marine Aquaculture." *Aquaculture* 286 (1–2): 28–35.

Thierfelder, C., E. Amezquita, and K. Stahr. 2005. "Effects of Intensifying Organic Manuring and Tillage Practices on Penetration Resistance and Infiltration Rate." *Soil and Tillage Research* 82 (2): 211–26.

Thornton, P. 2009. "The Inter-Linkage between Rapid Growth in Livestock Production, Climate Change, and the Impacts on Water Resources, Land Use, and Reforestation." Background paper for the WDR 2010.

Tilman, D., J. Hill, and C. Lehman. 2006. "Carbon-Negative Biofuels from Low-Input High-Diversity Grassland Biomass." *Science* 314: 1598–1600.

Tschakert, P. 2004. "The Costs of Soil Carbon Sequestration: An Economic Analysis for Small-Scale Farming Systems in Senegal." *Agricultural Systems* 81: 227–53.

Turner, W., S. Spector, N. Gardiner, M. Fladeland, E. Sterling, and M. Steininger. 2003. "Remote Sensing for Biodiversity Science and Conservation." *Trends in Ecology and Evolution* 18 (6): 306–14.

UNEP (United Nations Environment Programme). 1990. *Global Assessment of Soil Degradation*. New York: UNEP.

UNEP-WCMC (World Conservation Monitoring Centre). 2008. *State of the World's Protected Areas 2007: An Annual Review of Global Conservation Progress*. Cambridge, UK: UNEP-WCMC.

UNESCO. 2007. "A Global Perspective On Research And Development." Institute for Statistics Fact Sheet 5, UNESCO, Montreal.

United Nations. 2004. *Guidelines for Reducing Flood Losses*. Geneva: United Nations Department of Economic and Social Affairs, United Nations International Strategy for Disaster Reduction, and the National Oceanic and Atmosphere Administration.

———. 2009. *World Population Prospects: The 2008 Revision*. New York: UN Department of Economic and Social Affairs.

Van Buskirk, J., and Y. Willi. 2004. "Enhancement of Farmland Biodiversity within Set-Aside Land." *Conservation Biology* 18 (4): 987–94.

van der Werf, G. R., J. Dempewolf, S. N. Trigg, J. T. Randerson, P. S. Kasibhatla, L. Giglio, D. Murdiyarso, W. Peters, D. C. Morton, G. J. Collatz, A. J. Dolman, and R. S. DeFries. 2008. "Climate Regulation of Fire Emissions and Deforestation in Equatorial Asia." *Proceedings of the National Academy of Sciences* 105 (51): 20350–55.

Vassolo, S., and P. Döll. 2005. "Global-Scale Gridded Estimates of Thermoelectric Power and Manufacturing Water Use." *Water Resources Research* 41: W04010– doi:10.1029/2004WR003360.

Venter, O., E. Meijaard, H. Possingham, R. Dennis, D. Sheil, S. Wich, L. Hovani, and K. Wilson. 2009. "Carbon Payments as a Safeguard for Threatened Tropical Mammals." *Conservation Letters* 2: 123–29.

von Braun, J., A. Ahmed, K. Asenso-Okyere, S. Fan, A. Gulati, J. Hoddinott, R. Pandya-Lorch, M. W. Rosegrant, M. Ruel, M. Torero, T. van Rheenen, and K. von Grebmer. 2008. "High Food Prices: The What, Who, and How of Proposed Policy Actions." Policy brief, International Food Policy Research Institute, Washington, DC.

Ward, F. A., and M. Pulido-Velazquez. 2008. "Water Conservation in Irrigation Can Increase Water Use." *Proceedings of the National Academy of Sciences* 105 (47):18215–20.

Wardle, D. A., M-C. Nilsson, and O. Zackrisson. 2008. "Fire-derived Charcoal Causes Loss of Forest Humus." *Science* 320 (5876): 629–29.

West, P. O., and W. M. Post. 2002. "Soil Organic Carbon Sequestration Rates by Tillage and Crop Rotation: A Global Data Analysis." *Soil Science Society of America Journal* 66: 1930–46.

Williams, A. G., E. Audsley, and D. L. Sandars. 2006. *Determining the Environmental Burdens and Resource Use in the Production of Agricultural and Horticultural Commodities.* London: Department for Environmental Food and Rural Affairs.

Wise, M. A., K. V. Calvin, A. M. Thomson, L. E. Clarke, B. Bond-Lamberty, R. D. Sands, S. J. Smith, A. C. Janetos, and J. A. Edmonds. 2009. "Implications of Limiting CO_2 Concentrations for Land Use and Energy." *Science* 324 (5931): 1183–86.

Woelcke, J., and T. Tennigkeit. 2009. "Harvesting Agricultural Carbon in Kenya." *Rural 21* 43 (1): 26–27.

Wolf, D. 2008. "Biochar as a Soil Amendment: A Review of the Environmental Implications." Swansea University School of the Environment and Society, http://www.orgprints.org/13268/01/Biochar_as_a_soil_amendment_-_a_review.pdf (accessed July 15, 2009).

World Bank. 2005. *Agriculture Investment Sourcebook.* Washington, DC: World Bank.

———. 2006. *Aquaculture: Changing the Face of the Waters: Meeting the Promise and Challenge of Sustainable Aquaculture.* Washington, DC: World Bank.

———. 2007a. "India Groundwater AAA Midterm Review" (internal document), World Bank, Washington, DC.

———. 2007b. *Making the Most of Scarcity: Accountability for Better Water Management Results in the Middle East and North Africa.* Washington, DC: World Bank.

———. 2007c. *World Development Report 2008. Agriculture for Development.* Washington, DC: World Bank.

———. 2008a. *Biodiversity, Climate Change and Adaptation: Nature-Based Solutions from the World Bank Portfolio.* Washington, DC: World Bank.

———. 2008b. *China Water AAA: Addressing Water Scarcity.* Washington, DC: World Bank.

———. 2008c. *Framework Document for a Global Food Crisis Response Program.* Washington, DC: World Bank.

———. 2008d. *The Sunken Billions. The Economic Justification for Fisheries Reform.* Washington, DC: World Bank and FAO.

———. 2008e. *World Development Report 2009. Reshaping Economic Geography.* Washington, DC: World Bank.

———. 2009. *Improving Food Security in Arab Countries.* Washington, DC: World Bank.

———. Forthcoming a. *Agriculture and Climate Change in Morocco.* Washington, DC: World Bank.

———. Forthcoming b. *Deep Wells and Prudence: Towards Pragmatic Action for Addressing Groundwater Overexploitation in India.* Washington, DC: World Bank.

———. Forthcoming c. *Projet de Modernisation de l'Agriculture Irriguee Dans le Bassin de l'Oum Er Rbia. Mission d'Évaluation Aide Memoire.* Washington, DC: World Bank.

———. Forthcoming d. *Water and Climate Change: Understanding the Risks and Making Climate-Smart Investment Decisions.* Washington, DC: World Bank.

World Commission on Dams. 2000. *Dams and Development: A New Framework for Decision Making.* London and Sterling, VA: Earthscan.

WMO (World Meteorological Organization). 2000. "Fifth WMO Long-term Plan

2000-2009: Summary for Decision Makers." Geneva: WMO.

———. 2007. *Climate Information for Adaptation and Development Needs*. Geneva: WMO.

World Water Assessment Programme. 2009. *The United Nations World Water Development Report 3: Water in a Changing World*. Paris and London: UNESCO and Earthscan.

Xiaofeng, X. 2007. *Report on Surveying and Evaluating Benefits of China's Meteorological Service*. Beijing: China Meteorological Administration.

Yan, X., H. Akiyama, K. Yagi, and H. Akimoto. 2009. "Global Estimations of the Inventory and Mitigation Potential of Methane Emissions from Rice Cultivation Conducted Using the 2006 Intergovernmental Panel on Climate Change Guidelines." *Global Biogeochemical Cycles* 23: 1–15.

Young, M., and J. McColl. 2005. "Defining Tradable Water Entitlements and Allocations: A Robust System." *Canadian Water Resources Journal* 30 (1): 65–72.

———. Forthcoming. "A Robust Framework for the Allocation of Water in an Ever Changing World." In H. Bjornlund, ed., *Incentives and Instruments for Sustainable Irrigation*. Southampton: WIT Press.

Zhang, G. S., K. Y. Chan, A. Oates, D. P. Heenan, and G. B. Huang. 2007. "Relationship between Soil Structure and Runoff/Soil Loss After 24 Years of Conservation Tillage." *Soil and Tillage Research* 92: 122–28.

Zilberman, D., T. Sproul, D. Rajagopal, S. Sexton, and P. Hellegers. 2008. "Rising Energy Prices and the Economics of Water in Agriculture." *Water Policy* 10: 11–21.

Ziska, L. H. 2008. "Three-year Field Evaluation of Early and Late 20th Century Spring Wheat Cultivars to Projected Increases in Atmospheric Carbon Dioxide." *Field Crop Research* 108 (1): 54–59.

Ziska, L. H., and A. McClung. 2008. "Differential Response of Cultivated and Weedy (Red) Rice to Recent and Projected Increases in Atmospheric Carbon Dioxide." *Agronomy Journal* 100 (5): 1259–63.

CHAPTER 4

Energizing Development without Compromising the Climate

With the global economy set to quadruple by mid-century, energy-related carbon dioxide (CO_2) emissions would, on current trends, more than double, putting the world onto a potentially catastrophic trajectory that could lead to temperatures more than 5°C warmer than in preindustrial times. That trajectory is not inevitable. With concerted global action to adopt the right policies and low-carbon technologies, the means exist to shift to a more sustainable trajectory that limits warming to close to 2°C. In the process, there is an opportunity to produce enormous benefits for economic and social development through energy savings, better public health, enhanced energy security, and job creation.

Such a sustainable energy path requires immediate action by all countries to become much more energy efficient and achieve significantly lower carbon intensity. The path requires a dramatic shift in the energy mix from fossil fuels to renewable energy and possibly nuclear power, along with widespread use of carbon capture and storage (CCS). This, in turn, requires major cost reductions in and widespread diffusion of renewable energy technologies, safeguards for containment of nuclear waste and weapons proliferation, and breakthroughs in technologies from batteries to carbon capture and storage. And it also requires fundamental shifts in economic development and lifestyles. If even one of these requirements is not met, keeping temperature increases close to 2°C above preindustrial levels may be impossible.

In order to limit warming to 2°C, global emissions would have to peak no later than 2020 and then decline by 50–80 percent from today's levels by 2050, with further reductions continuing to 2100 and beyond. Delaying actions by 10 years would make it impossible to reach this goal. The inertia in energy capital stocks means that investments over the next decade will largely determine emissions through 2050 and beyond. Delays would lock the world into high-carbon infrastructure, later requiring costly retrofitting and premature scrapping of existing capital stocks.

Governments should not use the current financial crisis as an excuse to delay climate change actions. The future climate crisis is likely to be far more damaging to the world economy. The economic downturn may delay business-as-usual growth in emissions by a few years, but it is unlikely to fundamentally change that path over the long

Key messages

Solving the climate change problem requires immediate action in all countries and a fundamental transformation of energy systems—significant improvement in energy efficiency, a dramatic shift toward renewable energy and possibly nuclear power, and widespread use of advanced technologies to capture and store carbon emissions. Developed countries must lead the way and drastically cut their own emissions by as much as 80 percent by 2050, bring new technologies to market, and help finance developing countries' transition onto clean energy paths. But it is also in developing countries' interests to act now to avoid locking into high-carbon infrastructure. Many changes—such as removing distortionary price signals and increasing energy efficiency—are good both for development and the environment.

term. Instead, the downturn offers opportunities for governments to direct stimulus investment toward efficient and clean energy to meet the twin goals of revitalizing economic growth and mitigating climate change (box 4.1).

Governments can adopt climate-smart domestic policies now to deploy existing low-carbon technologies while a global climate deal is negotiated. Energy efficiency is the largest and lowest-cost source of emission reductions and is fully justified by development benefits and future energy savings. The potential is huge on both the energy supply side (as in the burning of coal, oil, and gas and the production, transmission, and distribution of electricity) and on the demand side (use of energy in buildings, transport, and manufacturing). But the fact that so much efficiency potential remains untapped suggests that it is not easily realized. Achieving significant energy savings requires price increases and the removal of fossil-fuel subsidies as well as a concerted strategy to tackle market failures and non-market barriers with effective regulations, financial incentives, institutional reforms, and financing mechanisms.

The second-largest source of potential emission reductions comes from use of low- to zero-emission fuels for power generation—particularly renewable energy. Many of these technologies are commercially available today, have benefits for development, and can be deployed much more widely under the right policy frameworks. Scaling them up requires putting a price on carbon and providing financial incentives to deploy low-carbon technologies. Large-scale deployment will help reduce their costs and make them more competitive.

But these win-wins, good for both development and climate change, are simply not enough to stay on a 2°C trajectory. Not-yet-proven advanced technologies, such as carbon capture and storage, are needed urgently and on a large scale. Accelerating their widespread availability and use will require greatly enhanced research, development, and demonstration as well as technology sharing and transfer.

An economywide, market-based mechanism, such as a carbon cap-and-trade program or a carbon tax (see chapter 6), is essential to unleash robust private sector investment and innovation to achieve deep emission cuts at least cost. Within governments, coordinated and integrated approaches are needed to achieve low-carbon economies while minimizing the risks of social and economic disruptions.

Developed countries must take the lead in committing to deep emission cuts, pricing carbon, and developing advanced technologies. That is the surest way to trigger development of the needed technologies and ensure their availability at a competitive price. But unless developing countries also start transforming their energy systems as they grow, limiting warming to close to 2°C above preindustrial levels will not be achievable. That transformation requires transfers of substantial financial resources and low-carbon technologies from developed to developing countries.

Energy mitigation paths, and the mix of policies and technologies necessary to reach them, differ among high-, middle-, and low-income countries, depending on their economic structures, resource endowments, and institutional and technical capabilities. A dozen high- and middle-

---

BOX 4.1 *The financial crisis offers an opportunity for efficient and clean energy*

The financial crisis brings both challenges and opportunities to clean energy. Sharply falling fossil-fuel prices discourage energy conservation and make renewable energy less competitive. The weak macroeconomic environment and tight credit have led to lower demand and declining investment, and renewable energy is hard hit because of its capital-intensive nature (renewable energy is characterized by high up-front capital costs but low operating and fuel costs). By the final quarter of 2008 clean energy investments dropped by more than half from their peak at the end of 2007.[a]

Yet the financial crisis should not be an excuse to delay climate-change action, for it offers opportunities to shift to a low-carbon economy (see chapter 1). First, stimulus investments in energy efficiency, renewable energy, and mass transit can create jobs and build an economy's productive capacity.[b] Second, falling energy prices provide a unique opportunity to implement programs to eliminate fossil-fuel subsidies in emerging economies and adopt fuel taxes in advanced economies in ways that are politically and socially acceptable.

Sources: WDR team based on
a. World Economic Forum 2009.
b. Bowen and others 2009.

income countries account for two-thirds of global energy-related emissions, and their emission reductions are essential to avoid dangerous climate change. This chapter analyzes the mitigation paths and challenges facing some of these countries. It also presents a portfolio of policy instruments and clean energy technologies that can be used to follow the 2°C trajectory.

Balancing competing objectives

Energy policies have to balance four competing objectives—sustain economic growth, increase energy access for the world's poor, enhance energy security, and improve the environment—tall orders. Fossil-fuel combustion produces around 70 percent of greenhouse gas emissions[1] and is the primary source of harmful local air pollution. Many win-win options can mitigate climate change and abate local air pollution through reducing fossil-fuel combustion (box 4.2). Other options present tradeoffs that need to be weighed. For example, sulfates emitted when coal is burned damage human health and cause acid rain, but they also have local cooling effects that offset warming.

Developing countries need reliable and affordable energy to grow and to extend service to the 1.6 billion people without electricity and the 2.6 billion without clean cooking fuels. Increasing access to electricity services and clean cooking fuels in many low-income developing countries, particularly in South Asia and Sub-Saharan Africa, would add less than 2 percent to global CO_2 emissions.[2] Replacing traditional biomass fuels used for cooking and heating with modern energy supplies can also reduce emissions of black carbon—an important contributor to global warming[3]—improve the health of women and children otherwise exposed to high levels of indoor air pollution from traditional biomass, and reduce deforestation and land degradation (see chapter 7, box 7.10).[4]

Energy supplies also face adaptation challenges. Rising temperatures are likely to increase demand for cooling and reduce demand for heating.[5] Higher demand for cooling strains electricity systems, as in the European heat wave of 2007. Climate

extremes accounted for 13 percent of the variation in energy productivity in developing countries in 2005.[6] Unreliable or changing precipitation patterns affect the reliability of hydropower. And droughts and heat waves that affect the availability and temperature of water hamper thermal and nuclear energy production,[7] because the plants require substantial quantities of water for cooling—as in the case of power shortages in France during the 2007 heat wave.

The challenge then is to provide reliable and affordable energy services for economic growth and prosperity without compromising the climate. Low-income countries now account for only 3 percent of global energy demand and energy-related emissions. While their energy demand will increase with rising income, their emissions are projected to remain a small share of global emissions in 2050. But middle-income countries, many with expanding economies and a large share of heavy industry, face huge energy needs. And developed countries demand enormous amounts of energy to maintain their current lifestyles.

Low-carbon energy choices can substantially improve energy security by reducing price volatility or exposure to disruptions in energy supplies.[8] Energy efficiency can reduce energy demand, and renewable energy diversifies the energy mix and reduces exposure to fuel price shocks.[9]

But coal, the most carbon-intensive fossil fuel, is abundant near many high-growth areas and provides low-cost and secure energy supplies. Recent oil price swings and uncertainty about gas supplies are leading to increased interest in new coal-fired power plants in many countries (developed and developing). Reducing reliance on oil and gas imports by turning to coal-to-liquid and coal-to-gas production would substantially increase CO_2 emissions. Global coal consumption has grown faster than consumption of any other fuel since 2000, presenting a formidable dilemma between economic growth, energy security, and climate change.

Faced with such challenges and competing objectives, the market alone will not deliver efficient and clean energy in the time and at the scale required to prevent

BOX 4.2   *Efficient and clean energy can be good for development*

Valuing the co-benefits of energy efficiency and clean energy for development—more energy savings, less local air pollution, greater energy security, more employment in local industry, and greater competitiveness from higher productivity—can justify part of the mitigation cost and increase the appeal of green policies. Energy savings could offset a significant share of mitigation costs.[a] The actions needed for the 450 parts per million (ppm) CO_2e concentrations associated with keeping warming at 2°C could reduce local air pollution (sulfur dioxide and nitrogen oxides) by 20–35 percent compared with business as usual in 2030.[b] In

2006 the renewable energy industry created 2.3 million jobs worldwide (directly or indirectly), and energy efficiency added 8 million jobs in the United States.[c] The energy-efficiency and technology-innovation programs in California over the past 35 years have actually increased gross state product.[d]

Many countries, both developed and developing, are setting targets and policies for clean energy technologies (see table). Many of these initiatives are driven by domestic development benefits, but they can also reduce CO_2 emissions substantially. The Chinese government's target of a 20 percent reduction in energy

intensity from 2005 to 2010 would reduce annual CO_2 emissions by 1.5 billion tons by 2010, the most aggressive emission reduction target in the world, five times the 300-million-ton reduction of the European Union's Kyoto commitment and eight times the 175-million-ton reduction of the California emission reduction target.[e]

Sources:
a. IEA 2008b; McKinsey & Company 2009a.
b. IEA 2008c.
c. EESI 2008;
d. Roland-Holst 2008.
e. Lin 2007.

Many countries have national plans or proposals for energy and climate change

Country	Climate change	Renewable energy	Energy efficiency	Transport
European Union	20 percent emission reduction from 1990 to 2020 (30 percent if other countries commit to substantial reductions); 80 percent reduction from 1990 to 2050	20 percent of primary energy mix by 2020	20 percent energy savings from the reference case by 2020	10 percent transport fuel from biofuel by 2020
United States	Emission reduction to 1990 levels by 2020; 80 percent reduction from 1990 to 2050	25 percent of electricity by 2025		Increase fuel economy standard to 35 miles a gallon by 2016
Canada	20 percent reduction from 2006 to 2020			
Australia	15 percent reduction from 2000 to 2020			
China	National Climate Change Plan and White Paper for Policies and Actions for Climate Change, a leading group on energy conservation and emission reduction established, chaired by the prime minister	15 percent of primary energy by 2020	20 percent reduction in energy intensity from 2005 to 2010	35 miles a gallon fuel economy standard already achieved; plan to be the world leader in electric vehicles; and mass construction of subways under way
India	National Action Plan on Climate Change: per capita emissions not to exceed developed countries', an advisory council on climate change created, chaired by the prime minister	23 gigawatts of renewable capacity by 2012	10 gigawatts of energy savings by 2012	Urban transport policy: increase investment in public transport
South Africa	Long-term mitigation scenario: emissions peak in 2020 to 2025, plateau for a decade, and then decline in absolute terms	4 percent of the power mix by 2013	12 percent energy-efficiency improvement by 2015	Plan to be the world leader in electric vehicles; and expand bus rapid transit
Mexico	50 percent emission reduction from 2002 to 2050; national strategy on climate change: intersecretariat commission on climate change set up for coordination	8 percent of the power mix by 2012	Efficiency standards, cogeneration	Increase investment in public transport
Brazil	National plan on climate change: reducing deforestation 70 percent by 2018	10 percent of the power mix by 2030	103 terawatt hours of energy savings by 2030	World leader in ethanol production

Sources: Government of China 2008; Government of India 2008; Government of Mexico 2008; Brazil Interministerial Committee on Climate Change 2008; Pew Center 2008a; Pew Center 2008b; Project Catalyst 2009.

Note: Some of the above goals represent formal commitments, while others are still under discussion.

dangerous climate change. Pollution needs to be priced. Achieving the needed progress in energy efficiency requires price incentives, regulations, and institutional reforms. And the risks and scale of the investments in unproven technologies call for substantial public support.

Breaking the high-carbon habit

Carbon emissions from energy are determined by the combination of total energy consumption and its carbon intensity (defined as the units of CO_2 produced by a unit of energy consumed). Energy consumption increases with income and population but with sizable variation depending on economic structure (manufacturing and mining are more energy intensive than agriculture and services), climate (which affects the need for heating or cooling), and policies (countries with higher energy prices and more stringent regulations are more energy efficient). Similarly, the carbon intensity of energy varies depending on domestic energy resources (whether a country is rich in coal or hydro potential) and policies. So the policy levers for a low-carbon growth path include reducing energy intensity (defined as energy consumed per dollar of gross domestic product, or GDP) by increasing energy efficiency and shifting to low-energy-consuming lifestyles—and reducing carbon intensity of energy by shifting to low-carbon fuels such as renewable energy.

A doubling of energy consumption since the 1970s combined with near-constant carbon intensity has resulted in a doubling of emissions (figure 4.1). Energy intensity has improved but far too little to offset the tripling in world income. And carbon intensity has remained relatively constant as achievements in producing cleaner energy have been largely offset by a massive increase in the use of fossil fuels. Fossil fuels dominate global energy supplies, accounting for more than 80 percent of the primary energy mix (figure 4.2).[10]

Developed countries are responsible for about two-thirds of the cumulative energy-related CO_2 now in the atmosphere.[11] They also consume five times more energy per capita, on average, than developing countries. But developing countries already

account for 52 percent of annual energy-related emissions, and their energy consumption is increasing rapidly—90 percent of the projected increases in global energy consumption, coal use, and energy-related CO_2 emissions over the next 20 years will likely be in developing countries.[12] Projections suggest that because such a large share of global population is in developing countries, they will use 70 percent more total

Figure 4.1　The story behind doubling emissions: improvements in energy and carbon intensity have not been enough to offset rising energy demand boosted by rising incomes

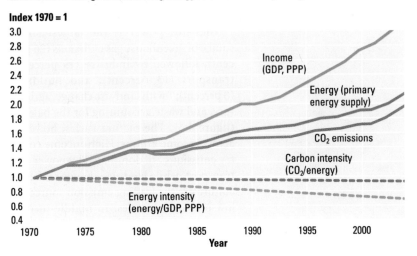

Index 1970 = 1

Source: IPCC 2007.
Note: GDP is valued using purchasing power parity (PPP) dollars.

Figure 4.2　Primary energy mix 1850–2006. From 1850 to 1950 energy consumption grew 1.5 percent a year, driven mainly by coal. From 1950 to 2006 it grew 2.7 percent a year, driven mainly by oil and natural gas.

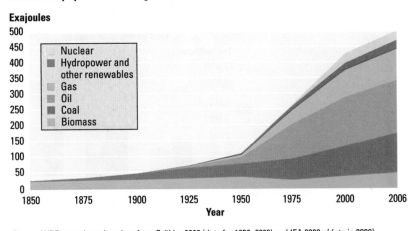

Exajoules

Source: WDR team, based on data from Grübler 2008 (data for 1850–2000) and IEA 2008c (data in 2006).
Note: To ensure consistency of the two data sets, the substitution equivalent method is used to convert hydropower to primary energy equivalent—assuming the amount of energy to generate an equal amount of electricity in conventional thermal power plants with an average generating efficiency of 38.6 percent.

energy annually than developed countries by 2030, even though their energy use per capita will remain low (figure 4.3).

Globally, power is the largest single source of greenhouse gas emissions (26 percent), followed by industry (19 percent), transport (13 percent), and buildings (8 percent),[13] with land-use change, agriculture, and waste accounting for the balance (figure 4.4). The picture varies, however, across income groups. High-income country emissions are dominated by power and transport, while land-use change and agriculture are the leading emission sources in low-income countries. In middle-income countries, power, industry, and land-use change are the largest contributors—but with land-use change emissions concentrated in a handful of countries (Brazil and Indonesia account for half the global land-

use change emissions). Power will most likely continue to be the largest source, but emissions are expected to rise faster in transport and industry.

As major centers of production and concentrations of people, the world's cities now consume more than two-thirds of global energy and produce more than 70 percent of CO_2 emissions. The next 20 years will see unprecedented urban growth—from 3 billion people to 5 billion, mostly in the developing world.[14] From now to 2050 building stocks will likely double,[15] with most new construction in developing countries. If cities grow through sprawl rather than densification, demand for travel will increase in ways not easily served by public transport.

Car ownership rates increase rapidly with rising incomes. On current trends 2.3 billion cars will be added between 2005 and 2050, more than 80 percent of them in developing countries.[16] But if the right policies are in place, increased rates of ownership do not have to translate into similar increases in car use (figure 4.5).[17] Because car use drives energy demand and emissions from transport, pricing policies (such as road pricing and high parking fees), public transport infrastructure, and urban form can make a big difference.

Developing countries can learn from Europe and developed Asia to decouple car ownership from car use. European and Japanese drivers travel 30–60 percent fewer vehicle kilometers than drivers in the United States with comparable incomes and car ownership. Hong Kong, China, has one-third the car ownership of New York, the American city with the lowest ratio of cars per capita.[18] How? Through a combination of high urban density, high fuel taxes and road-pricing policies, and well-established public transport infrastructure. Similarly, Europe has four times the public transport routes per 1,000 persons as the United States.[19] But in many developing countries, public transport has not kept up with urban growth, so the move to individual car ownership is causing chronic and increasing problems of congestion.

Transport infrastructure also affects settlement patterns, with a high volume of roads facilitating low-density settlements

Figure 4.3   Despite low energy consumption and emissions per capita, developing countries will dominate much of the future growth in total energy consumption and CO₂ emissions

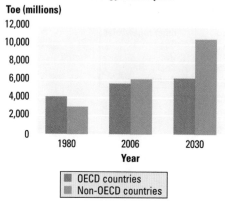

a. Per capita energy consumption

Toe/person

b. Total energy consumption

Toe (millions)

■ OECD countries
■ Non-OECD countries

Source: WDR team, based on data from IEA 2008c.

Note: Toe = tons of oil equivalent

Figure 4.4   Greenhouse gas emissions by sector: world and high-, middle-, and low-income countries

a. World

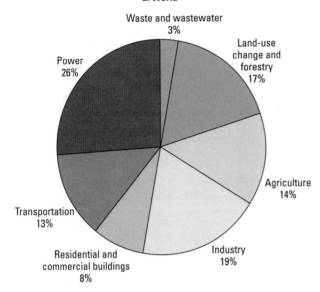

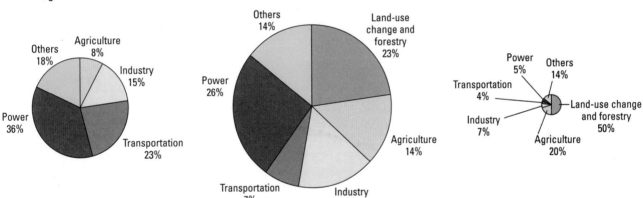

b. High-income countries   c. Middle-income countries   d. Low-income countries

Source: WDR team, based on data from Barker and others 2007 (figure 4a) and WRI 2008 (figures 4b, c, and d).

Note: The sectoral share of global emissions in figure 4.4a is for 2004. The sectoral share of emissions in high-, middle-, and low-income countries in figures 4.4b, 4.4c, and 4.4d are based on emissions from the energy and agriculture sectors in 2005 and from land-use changes and forestry in 2000. The size of each pie represents contributions of greenhouse gas emissions, including emissions from land-use changes, from high-, middle-, and low-income countries; the respective shares are 35, 58, and 7 percent. Looking only at CO₂ emissions from energy, the respective shares are 49, 49, and 2 percent. In Figure 4.4a, emissions from electricity consumption in buildings are included with those in the power sector. Figure 4.4b does not include emissions from land-use change and forestry, because they were negligible in high-income countries.

and an urban form that mass transit systems cannot easily serve. Low-density settlements then make it more difficult to adopt energy-efficient district heating for buildings.[20]

Where the world needs to go: Transformation to a sustainable energy future

Achieving sustainable and equitable growth and prosperity requires that high-income countries significantly reduce their emissions—and their emissions per capita (blue arrows in figure 4.6). It also depends on developing countries avoiding the carbon-intensive path followed by developed countries such as Australia or the United States, taking instead a low-carbon growth path (orange arrow). It thus requires fundamental changes in lifestyles for developed countries and a leapfrogging to new development models for developing countries.

Achieving these goals requires reconciling what is adequate to prevent dangerous climate change with what is technically

Figure 4.5 Car ownership increases with income, but pricing, public transport, urban planning, and urban density can contain car use

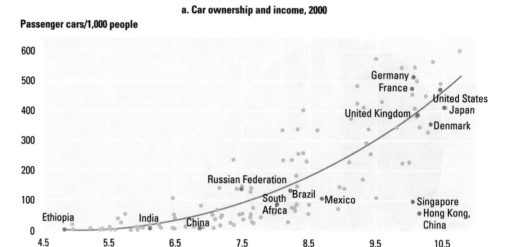

a. Car ownership and income, 2000

Passenger cars/1,000 people

b. Car use and income, 1970–2005

Vehicle-km/capita (thousands)

Sources: Schipper 2007; World Bank 2009c.

Note: In figure 4.5b, data are from West Germany through 1992 and for all of unified Germany from 1993 onward. Notice the similarity in rates of car ownership among, the United States, Japan, France, and Germany (panel a) but the large variation in distance traveled (panel b).

achievable at acceptable costs. Limiting warming to not much more than 2°C above preindustrial temperatures means that global emissions must peak no later than 2020, then decline by 50–80 percent from current levels by 2050, with perhaps even negative emissions required toward 2100.[21] This is an ambitious undertaking: only about half of the energy models reviewed find it feasible (figure 4.7), and even then most require all countries to start taking action immediately.

More specifically, staying close to a 2°C warming requires greenhouse gas concentrations in the atmosphere to stabilize at no more than 450 parts per million (ppm) CO_2 equivalent (CO_2e).[22] Current greenhouse gas concentrations are already at 387 ppm CO_2e and are rising at about 2 ppm a year.[23] Thus, there is little room for emissions to grow if warming is to stabilize around 2°C. Most models assume that achieving 450 ppm CO_2e will require overshooting that concentration for a few decades and then coming back to 450 ppm CO_2e toward the end of the century (table 4.1). Faster reductions of short-lived greenhouse gas emissions, such as methane and

Figure 4.6   Where the world needs to go: Energy-related CO₂ emissions per capita

CO₂ emissions per capita (metric tons)

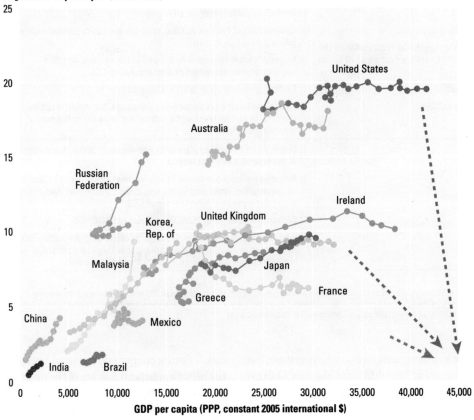

Source: Adapted from NRC 2008, based on data from World Bank 2008e.
Note: Emissions and GDP per capita are from 1980 to 2005.

Figure 4.7   Only half the energy models find it possible to achieve the emission reductions necessary to stay close to 450 ppm CO₂e (2°C)

CO₂ emissions change in 2050 relative to 2000 (%)

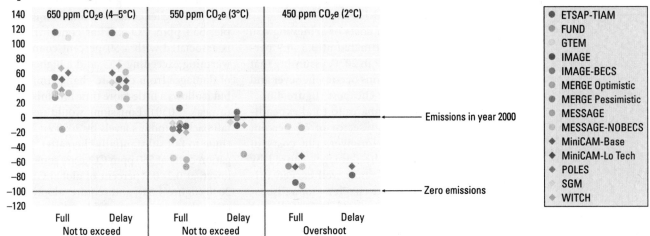

Source: Clarke and others, forthcoming.

Note: Each dot represents the emissions reduction that a particular model associates with a concentration target—450, 550, 650 parts per million (ppm) of CO₂ equivalent (CO₂e)—in 2050. The number of dots in each column signals how many of the 14 models and model variants were able to find a pathway that would lead to a given concentration outcome. "Overshoot" describes a mitigation path that allows concentrations to exceed their goal before dropping back to their goal by 2100, while "not to exceed" implies the concentration is not to be exceeded at any time. "Full" refers to full participation by all countries, so that emission reductions are achieved wherever and whenever they are most cost-effective. "Delay" means high-income countries start abating in 2012, Brazil, China, India, and the Russian Federation start abating in 2030, and the rest of the world in 2050.

Table 4.1   What it would take to achieve the 450 ppm CO_2e concentration needed to keep warming close to 2°C—an illustrative scenario

	Not-to-exceed	Overshoot
Immediate participation	1) Immediate participation by all regions 2) 70% dramatic emissions reductions by 2020 3) Substantial transformation of the energy system by 2020, including the construction of 500 new nuclear reactors, and the capture of 20 billion tons of CO_2 4) Carbon price of \$100/tCO_2 globally in 2020 5) Tax on land-use emissions beginning in 2020	1) Immediate participation by all regions 2) Construction of 126 new nuclear reactors and the capture of nearly a billion tons of CO_2 in 2020 3) Negative global emissions by the end of the century, and thus requires broad deployment of biomass-based CCS 4) Carbon prices escalate to \$775/tCO_2 in 2095 5) Possible without a tax on land-use emissions, but would result in a tripling of carbon taxes and a substantial increase in the cost of meeting the target.
Delayed participation		1) Dramatic emissions reductions for non-Annex I (developing countries) at the time of their participation 2) Negative emissions in Annex I (high-income) countries by 2050 and negative global emissions by the end of the century, and thus requires broad deployment of biomass-based CCS 3) Carbon prices begin at \$50/tCO_2, and rise to \$2,000/tCO_2 4) Results in significant carbon leakage, because crop production is outsourced to nonparticipating regions resulting in a substantial increase in land-use change emissions in those regions

Source: Clarke and others, forthcoming.

Note: Maintaining emissions at 450 ppm CO_2e or less at all times is almost impossible to attain. If concentrations are allowed to exceed 450 ppm CO_2e before 2100, keeping warming close to 2°C still poses tremendous challenges, as the right-hand column outlines. Annex I countries are the OECD and transition economies committed to reducing emissions under the Kyoto Protocol. The non-Annex I countries did not take on any commitment to reduce emissions.

black carbon, could reduce the overshoot but not avoid it.[24] In addition, 450 ppm CO_2e trajectories rely on biomass-based carbon capture and storage[25] for negative emissions.[26] But given the competition for land and water for food production and carbon storage (see chapter 3), sustainable biomass supplies will be an issue.[27] Limiting warming to 2°C will thus require fundamental changes in the global energy mix (box 4.3 and box 4.4; see endnote 28 for model details).[28]

The mitigation costs of achieving 450 ppm CO_2e are estimated at 0.3–0.9 percent of global GDP in 2030, assuming that all mitigation actions occur whenever and wherever they are cheapest (figure 4.8).[29] This estimate compares to total expenditures in the energy sector of 7.5 percent of GDP today. Moreover, the costs of inaction—from the damages caused by greater warming—may well exceed this mitigation cost (see chapter 1 for a discussion of the cost-benefit analysis of climate policy).

Achieving 450 ppm CO_2e requires the adoption of technologies with marginal costs of \$35 to \$100 a ton of CO_2 in 2030, for a global annual mitigation investment of \$425 billion to \$1 trillion in 2030 (table

4.2).[30] Future energy savings would eventually offset a substantial share of the up-front investment.[31] But much of this investment is needed within the next 10 years in financially constrained developing countries. And removing obstacles to reform and directing capital to low-carbon investments where and when they are needed will be challenging.

A less challenging option would be to aim for a higher concentration—for example, 550 ppm CO_2e. That concentration is associated with a 50-percent chance of warming exceeding 3°C, and a higher risk of damages from climate change impacts, but it allows a little more time for emissions to peak (2030). Emissions would need to fall back to today's levels by 2050 and continue to fall substantially thereafter. Mitigation costs of 550 ppm CO_2e are somewhat lower, at 0.2–0.7 percent of global GDP in 2030 (figure 4.8a), and require adoption of technologies with marginal costs up to \$25 to \$75 a ton of CO_2 in 2030 (figure 4.8b), for average annual additional investments of some \$220 billion a year over the next 20 years.[32] Achieving this more modest goal would still require far-reaching policy reforms.

Action—immediate and global

Delaying global actions for more than 10 years makes stabilization at 450 ppm CO_2e impossible.[33] There is little flexibility on the time when emissions peak. To achieve 450 ppm CO_2e, global energy-related CO_2 emissions will need to peak at 28–32 gigatons in 2020 from 26 gigatons in 2005, and then fall to 12–15 gigatons by 2050.[34] This trajectory requires a 2–3 percent cut in emissions each year from 2020 onward. If emissions increase for 10 years beyond 2020, emissions would have to be reduced 4–5 percent a year. In contrast, emissions increased 3 percent a year from 2000 to 2006, so most countries are on their way to a high-carbon path, with total global CO_2 emissions outpacing the worst-case scenario projected by the Intergovernmental Panel on Climate Change (IPCC).[35]

New additions of power plants, buildings, roads, and railroads over the next decade will lock in technology and largely determine emissions through 2050 and beyond. Why? Because the energy capital stock has a long life—it can take decades to turn over power plants, a century to turn over urban infrastructure.[36] Delaying action would substantially increase future mitigation costs, effectively locking the world into carbon-intensive infrastructure for decades to come. Even existing low-cost clean energy technologies will take decades to fully penetrate the energy sector. And given the long lead times for new technology development, deploying advanced technologies on a large scale beginning in 2030 requires aggressive action today.

Delaying action would, in addition, lead to costly retrofitting and early retirement of energy infrastructure. Building to current standards and then retrofitting existing capacity, whether power plants or buildings, would be far more costly than building new, efficient, and low-carbon infrastructure in the first place. The same is true for the forced early retirement of inefficient energy capital. Energy savings often justify the higher up-front investments in new capital, but they are less likely to cover premature replacement of capital stock. Even a high CO_2 price may be insufficient to change this picture.[37]

Figure 4.8   Estimates of global mitigation costs and carbon prices for 450 and 550 ppm CO_2e (2°C and 3°C) in 2030 from five models

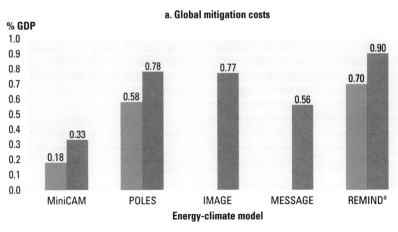

a. Global mitigation costs

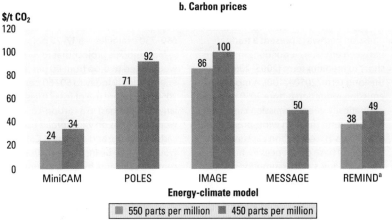

b. Carbon prices

Sources: WDR team, based on data from Knopf and others, forthcoming; Rao and others 2008; Calvin and others, forthcoming.

Note: This graphic compares mitigation costs and carbon prices from five global energy-climate models—MiniCAM, IMAGE, MESSAGE, POLES, and REMIND (see note 28 for model assumptions and methodology). MiniCAM, POLES, IMAGE, and MESSAGE report abatement costs for the transformation of energy systems relative to the baseline as a percent of GDP in 2030, where GDP is exogenous.

a. The mitigation costs from REMIND are given as macroeconomic costs expressed in GDP losses in 2030 relative to baseline, where GDP is endogenous.

Table 4.2   Investment needs to limit warming to 2°C (450 ppm CO_2e) in 2030
(constant 2005$ billion)

Region	IEA	McKinsey	MESSAGE	REMIND
Global	846	1013	571	424
Developing countries	565	563	264	384
North America		175	112	
European Union		129	92	
China		263	49	
India		75	43	

Sources: IEA 2008b; Knopf and others, forthcoming and additional data provided by B. Knopf; Riahi, Grübler, and Nakićenović 2007; IIASA 2009 and additional data provided by V. Krey; McKinsey & Company 2009a with further data breakdown provided by McKinsey (J. Dinkel).

BOX 4.3   *A 450 ppm CO₂e (2°C warmer) world requires a fundamental change in the global energy system*

For this Report the team examined five global energy-climate models that differ in methodology, assumptions about baseline, technology status, learning rates, costs, and inclusion of greenhouse gases (in addition to CO_2). Attainability of a 450 ppm CO_2e trajectory is dependent on the characteristics of the baseline. Some integrated assessment models can not reach a 450 ppm CO_2e trajectory from a fossil-fuel-intensive and high-energy-growth baseline.

A number of models can achieve 450 ppm CO_2e at moderate costs, but each follows different emissions pathways and energy mitigation strategies.[a] Different emission pathways present a tradeoff between emission reductions in the short to medium term (2005–2050) and the long term (2050–2100). A modest emission reduction before 2050 requires dramatically deeper emission cuts over the long term through widespread use of biomass-based carbon capture and storage.[b] These differences in model methodologies and assumptions also result in varying investment needs in the short term (2030), as shown in table 4.2. The models also vary significantly on the energy mix from now to 2050 (see the figure on the facing page), although the stark conclusion does not vary. The policy

implication is that a mix of technology options that varies by country and over time is needed—the least-cost strategies all rely on a broad portfolio of energy technologies.

Global energy mix for 450 ppm CO₂e

The 450 ppm CO_2e trajectory requires a global energy revolution—large reductions in total energy demand and major changes in the energy mix. To achieve this, global climate-energy models call for aggressive energy-efficiency measures that dramatically reduce global energy demand from around 900 exajoules by 2050 under a business-as-usual scenario to 650–750 exajoules—a 17–28 percent cut.

Most models project that fossil fuels would need to drop from 80 percent of energy supply today to 50–60 percent by 2050. The future use of fossil fuels (particularly coal and gas) in a carbon-constrained world depends on widespread use of carbon capture and storage (CCS), which would have to be installed in 80–90 percent of coal plants by 2050, assuming that capture-and-storage technology becomes technically and economically feasible for large-scale applications in the next decade or two (table below).[c]

This significant reduction in fossil-fuel use would need to be offset by

Cutting energy-related emissions in half by 2050 requires deep decarbonization of the power sector

Sector	Estimated % of carbon that must be removed by sector, 2005–2050	
	IEA	MiniCAM
Power	−71	−87
Building	−41	−50
Transport	−30	+47
Industry	−21	−71
Total	−50	−50

Sources: WDR team based on data from IEA 2008b; Calvin and others, forthcoming.

renewables and nuclear energy. The largest increase would be in renewable energy, which would jump from 13 percent today (mainly traditional biomass fuel and hydropower) to around 30–40 percent by 2050, dominated by modern biomass with and without carbon capture and storage, with the remainder from solar, wind, hydropower, and geothermal (see the figure). Nuclear would also need a boost—from 5 percent today to around 8–15 percent by 2050.[d]

The magnitude of the required effort is substantial: it amounts to an additional 17,000 wind turbines (producing 4 megawatts each), 215 million square meters of solar photovoltaic panels, 80 concentrated solar power plants (producing 250 megawatts each), and 32 nuclear plants (producing 1,000 megawatts each) per year over the next 40 years compared to the baseline.[e] The power sector would need to be virtually decarbonized, followed by the industrial and building sectors (table above).

Sources:
a. Knopf and others, forthcoming; Rao and others 2008.
b. Riahi, Grübler, and Nakićenović 2007; IIASA 2009.
c. IEA 2008b; Calvin and others, forthcoming; Riahi, Grübler, and Nakićenović 2007; IIASA 2009; van Vuuren and others, forthcoming; Weyant and others 2009.
d. IEA 2008b; Calvin and others, forthcoming; Riahi, Grübler, and Nakićenović 2007; IIASA 2009; van Vuuren and others, forthcoming.
e. IEA 2008b.

The energy mix to achieve 450 ppm CO₂e can vary, but we must make use of all options

Energy type	Current energy mix — Global	Energy mix in 2050				
		Global	United States	European Union	China	India
		% of total				
Coal without CCS	26	1–2	0–1	0–2	3–5	2–3
Coal with CCS	0	1–13	1–12	2–9	0–25	3–26
Oil	34	16–21	20–26	11–23	18–20	18–19
Gas without CCS	21	19–21	20–21	20–22	9–13	5–9
Gas with CCS	0	8–16	6–21	7–31	1–29	3–8
Nuclear	6	8	8–10	10–11	8–12	9–11
Biomass without CCS	10	12–21	10–18	10–11	9–14	16–30
Biomass with CCS	0	2–8	1–7	3–9	1–12	2–12
Non-biomass renewables	3	8–14	7–12	7–12	10–13	5–19
Total (exajoules a year)	493	665–775	87–121	70–80	130–139	66–68

Sources: WDR team, based on data from Riahi, Grübler, and Nakićenović 2007; IIASA 2009; Calvin and others, forthcoming; IEA 2008b.

(continued)

450 ppm CO₂e requires a fundamental change in the global primary energy mix

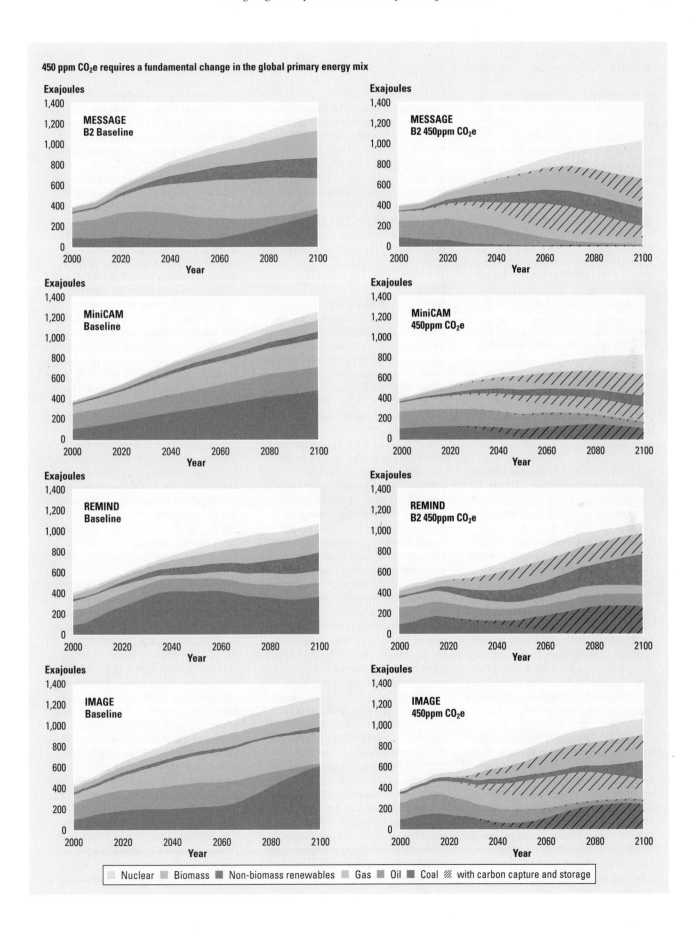

BOX 4.4   *Regional energy mix for 450 ppm CO_2e (to limit warming to 2°C)*

It is important for national policy makers to understand the implications of a 450 ppm CO_2e trajectory for their energy systems. Most integrated assessment models follow a "least-cost" approach, where emission reductions occur wherever and whenever they are cheapest in all sectors and in all countries.[a] But the country in which mitigation measures are taken is not necessarily the one that bears the costs (see chapter 6). It is not the purpose of this chapter to advocate any particular approach to burden sharing or to allocate emission reductions among countries; that is a matter for negotiation.

The United States, the European Union, and China now account for nearly 60 percent of the world's total emissions. India currently contributes only 4 percent of global emissions despite representing 18 percent of the world's population, but its share is projected to increase to 12 percent by 2050 in the absence of mitigation policy. So, these countries' contributions to global emission reductions will be essential to stabilize the climate.

United States and European Union
Energy efficiency could reduce total energy demand in developed countries by 20 percent in 2050 relative to business as usual. This would require an annual decline in energy intensity of 1.5–2 percent over the next four decades, continuing the current trend of the past two decades. To achieve 450 ppm CO_2e the United States and the European Union would need to cut oil consumption significantly by 2050, a substantial challenge because they now consume almost half of global oil production. They would also need to dramatically reduce coal use—a daunting task for the United States, the world's second-largest coal producer and consumer—and widely deploy carbon capture and storage.

The United States and the European Union have the resources to realize these measures and overcome the challenges. Both have abundant renewable energy potential. Some models project that carbon capture and storage would have to be installed for 80–90 percent of coal and gas plants and 40 percent of biomass plants in the United States by 2050 (see lower table of box 4.3). This is potentially feasible given the estimated CO_2 storage

capacity. But doubling the share of natural gas in the European primary energy mix from 24 percent today to 50 percent by 2050, assumed by some 450 ppm CO_2e scenarios, may pose energy security risks, particularly given the recent disruption of gas supplies to Europe. The 450 ppm CO_2e scenario requires an additional annual investment of $110 billion to $175 billion for the United States (0.8–1 percent of GDP) and $90 billion to $130 billion for the European Union (0.6–0.9 percent of GDP) in 2030 (see table 4.2).

China
Significantly reducing emissions below current levels is a formidable goal for China, the world's largest coal producer and consumer. China, relies on coal to meet 70 percent of its commercial energy needs (compared with 24 percent in the United States and 16 percent in Europe). To meet 450 ppm CO_2e, total primary energy demand would have to be 20–30 percent below the projected business-as-usual level by 2050. Energy intensity would have to decline by 3.1 percent a year over the next four decades.

Impressively, Chinese GDP quadrupled from 1980 to 2000 while energy consumption only doubled. After 2000, however, the trend reversed, even though energy intensity continues to fall within industrial subsectors. The main reason: a sharp rise in the share of heavy industry, driven by strong demand from domestic and export production.[b] China produces 35 percent of the world's steel, 50 percent of its cement, and 28 percent of its aluminum. This development stage, when energy-intensive industries dominate the economy, presents great challenges to decoupling emissions from growth.

China has increased the average efficiency of coal-fired power plants by 15 percent over the last decade to an average of 34 percent. A policy that requires closing small-scale coal-fired power plants and substituting large-scale efficient ones over the last two years reduces annual CO_2 emissions by 60 million tons. A majority of new coal-fired plants are equipped with state-of-the-art supercritical and ultrasupercritical technologies.[c]

Despite these advances, China would still have to reduce the share of coal in the primary energy mix dramatically to

achieve 450 ppm CO_2e (see the lower table of box 4.3). Renewable energy could meet up to 40 percent of total energy demand in 2050. Several scenarios have extremely ambitious nuclear programs, in which China would build nuclear power plants three times faster than France ever achieved, and nuclear capacity in 2050 would reach seven times France's current nuclear capacity. Given China's limited gas reserves, increasing the percentage of gas in the primary energy mix from the current 2.5 percent to 40 percent by 2050, as assumed by some models, is problematic.

Given the large domestic reserves, coal will likely remain an important energy source in China for decades. Carbon capture and storage is essential for China's economic growth in a carbon-constrained world. Some 450 ppm CO_2e scenarios project that carbon capture and storage would have to be installed for 85–95 percent of coal plants in China by 2050—more than can be accommodated by the current projections of economically available CO_2 storage capacity of 3 gigatons a year within 100 kilometers of the emission sources. But further site assessment, technology breakthrough, and future carbon pricing could change this situation. The 450 ppm CO_2e scenario requires an additional annual investment for China of $30 billion to $260 billion (0.5–2.6 percent of GDP) by 2030.

India and other developing countries
India faces tremendous challenges in substantially altering its emissions path given its limited potential for alternative energy resources and for carbon storage sites. Like China, India heavily relies on coal (which accounts for 53 percent of its commercial energy demand). Achieving 450 ppm CO_2e would require a veritable energy revolution in India. Total primary energy demand would have to decline relative to the business-as-usual projections by around 15–20 percent by 2050 and energy intensity by 2.5 percent a year from now to 2050, doubling the efforts of the past decade. A large potential exists, however, for improving energy efficiency and reducing the 29 percent losses in transmission and distribution, to a level closer to the world average of 9 percent. And while the efficiency of coal-fired power plants in India has improved in

(continued)

recent years, the average efficiency is still low at 29 percent, and nearly all the coal-fired plants are subcritical.

As in China, coal's share in India's primary energy mix would have to be reduced dramatically to achieve 450 ppm CO_2e. The potential for hydropower (150 gigawatts) and onshore wind power (65 gigawatts) is large in absolute terms but small in relation to future energy needs (12 percent in the power mix by 2050 in the 450 ppm CO_2e scenario). Considerable untapped possibilities exist for importing natural gas and hydropower from neighboring countries, but difficulties remain in establishing transboundary energy trade agreements. For solar to play a large role, costs would have to come down significantly. Some models suggest that India would need to rely on biomass to supply 30 percent of its primary energy by 2050 under the 450 ppm CO_2e scenario. But this may exceed India's sustainable biomass potential because biomass production competes with agriculture and forests for land and water.

India has limited economically available carbon storage sites, with a total storage capacity of less than 5 gigatons of CO_2, enough to store only three years of carbon if 90 percent of coal plants were equipped with carbon capture and storage by 2050, as some 450 ppm CO_2e scenarios project. Additional site assessments and technology breakthroughs could change this. The 450 ppm CO_2e scenario requires an additional annual investment of $40 billion to $75 billion for India (1.2–2.2 percent of GDP) in 2030.

Sub-Saharan Africa (excluding South Africa) contributes 1.5 percent of global annual energy-related CO_2 emissions today, an amount projected to grow to only 2–3 percent by 2050. Providing basic modern energy services to the poor should be the top priority and will only slightly increase global greenhouse gas emissions. But a global clean energy revolution is relevant to the low-income countries, which may be able to leapfrog to the next generation of technologies. Clean energy can play a large role in increasing access to energy, and pursuing energy efficiency is a cost-effective short-term solution to power outages.

According to climate-energy models, under the 450 ppm CO_2e scenarios, most developing countries would need to boost their production of renewable energy. Africa, Latin America, and Asia could contribute by switching to modern biomass. And Latin America and Africa have substantial untapped hydropower, although the amount could be affected by a less reliable hydrological cycle resulting from climate change. These countries would also need a major boost in natural gas.

Sources: Calvin and others, forthcoming; Chikkatur 2008; Dahowski and others 2009; de la Torre, Fajnzylber, and Nash 2008; Dooley and others 2006; German Advisory Council on Global Change 2008; Government of India Planning Commission 2006; Holloway and others 2008; IEA 2008b; IEA 2008c; IIASA 2009; Lin and others 2006; McKinsey & Company 2009a; Riahi, Grübler, and Nakićenović 2007; Wang and Watson 2009; Weber and others 2008; World Bank 2008c; Zhang 2008.

a. They are based on an integrated global carbon market and do not consider any explicit burden sharing between countries. In reality, this is unlikely. Burden sharing is discussed in chapter 1, and the implication of delayed participation by non-Annex I countries is discussed in chapter 6. We also reviewed models from developing countries (China and India), but no public information is available for 450 ppm CO_2e scenarios.

b. Lin and others 2006. Production of exports accounted for around one-third of China's emissions in 2005 (Weber and others 2008).

c. Supercritical and ultrasupercritical plants use higher steam temperatures and pressures to achieve higher efficiency of 38–40 percent and 40–42 percent respectively, compared with large subcritical power plants with an average efficiency of 35–38 percent.

To avoid such lock-ins, the scale and rate of urbanization present an unrivaled opportunity, particularly for developing countries, to make major decisions today about building low-carbon cities with compact urban designs, good public transport, efficient buildings, and clean vehicles.

One beneficial feature of the inertia in energy infrastructure is that introducing efficient low-carbon technologies into new infrastructure offers an opportunity to lock in a low-carbon path. Developing countries will install at least half the long-lived energy capital stocks built between now and 2020.[38] For example, half of China's building stock in 2015 will have been built between 2000 and 2015.[39] There are fewer opportunities in developed countries, where residential buildings tend to have slow retirements—60 percent of France's expected residential building stock in 2050 has already been built. This fact constrains the potential for reductions in heating and cooling demand, which requires retrofitting and replacing building shells. But there are abundant opportunities over the next decade in both developed and developing countries to build new power plants with clean energy technologies, thereby avoiding further lock in to carbon-intensive fuels.

For the reasons outlined in the Bali Action Plan, which is shaping the current negotiations under the United Nations Framework Convention on Climate Change, developed countries must take the lead in cutting emissions (see chapter 5). But developed countries alone could not put the world onto a 2°C trajectory, even if they were able to reduce their emissions to zero (figure 4.9). By 2050, 8 billion of the world's 9 billion people will live in today's developing countries, producing 70 percent of projected global emissions.[40] Developed countries can, however, provide financial assistance and

Figure 4.9   Global actions are essential to limit warming to 2°C (450 ppm) or 3°C (550 ppm). Developed countries alone could not put the world onto a 2°C or 3°C trajectory, even if they were to reduce emissions to zero by 2050.

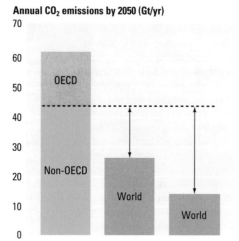

Annual CO_2 emissions by 2050 (Gt/yr)

Sources: Adapted from IEA 2008b; Calvin and others, forthcoming.

Note: If energy-related emissions from developed countries (orange) were to reduce to zero, emissions from developing countries (green) under business as usual would still exceed global emission levels required to achieve 550 ppm CO_2e and 450 ppm CO_2e scenarios (blue) by 2050.

Table 4.3   Different country circumstances require tailored approaches

Countries	Low-carbon technologies and policies
Low-income countries	Expand energy access through grid and off-grid options
	Deploy energy efficiency and renewable energy whenever they are the least cost
	Remove fossil-fuel subsidies
	Adopt cost-recovery pricing
	Leapfrog to distributed generation, where grid infrastructure does not exist
Middle-income countries	Scale up energy efficiency and renewable energy
	Integrate urban and transport approaches to low carbon use
	Remove fossil-fuel subsidies
	Adopt cost-recovery pricing including local externalities
	Conduct research, development, and demonstration in new technologies
High-income countries	Undertake deep emission cuts at home
	Put a price on carbon: cap-and-trade or carbon tax
	Remove fossil-fuel subsidies
	Increase research, development, and demonstration in new technologies
	Change high-energy-consuming lifestyle
	Provide financing and low-carbon technologies to developing countries

Source: WDR team.

low-carbon technology transfers to developing countries, while pursuing advanced low-carbon technologies and demonstrating that low-carbon growth is feasible (table 4.3).

Acting on all technical and policy fronts

What fundamental changes need to be made in the energy system to narrow the gap between where the world is headed and where it needs to go? The answer lies in a portfolio of efficient and clean energy technologies to reduce energy intensity and shift to low-carbon fuels. On current trends, global energy-related CO_2 emissions will increase from 26 gigatons in 2005 to 43–62 gigatons by 2050.[41] But a 450 ppm CO_2e trajectory requires that energy emissions be reduced to 12–15 gigatons, a 28–48 gigaton mitigation gap by 2050 (figure 4.10). Models rely on four technologies to close this gap—energy efficiency (the largest wedge), followed by renewable energy, carbon capture and storage, and nuclear.[42]

A portfolio of these technologies is needed to achieve the deep emission cuts required by the 450 ppm CO_2e trajectory at least cost, because each has physical and economic constraints, although these vary by country. Energy efficiency faces barriers and market failures. Wind, hydropower, and geothermal power are limited by the availability of suitable sites; biomass is constrained by competition for land and water from food and forests (see chapter 3); and solar is still costly (box 4.5). Nuclear power raises concerns about weapons proliferation, waste management, and reactor safety. Carbon capture and storage technologies for power plants are not yet commercially proven, have high costs, and may be limited by the availability of storage sites in some countries.

Sensitivity analysis incorporating these technology constraints suggests that 450 ppm CO_2e is not achievable without large-scale deployment of energy efficiency, renewable energy, and carbon capture and storage;[43] and that reducing the role of nuclear would require substantial increases of fossil-based carbon capture and storage and renewables.[44] Critical uncertainties include the availability of carbon capture and storage and the development of second-generation biofuels. With today's known

Biomass

Modern biomass as fuel for power, heat, and transport has the highest mitigation potential of all renewable sources.[a] It comes from agriculture and forest residues as well as from energy crops. The biggest challenge in using biomass residues is a long-term reliable supply delivered to the power plant at reasonable costs; the key problems are logistical constraints and the costs of fuel collection. Energy crops, if not managed properly, compete with food production and may have undesirable impacts on food prices (see chapter 3). Biomass production is also sensitive to the physical impacts of a changing climate.

Projections of the future role of biomass are probably overestimated, given the limits to the sustainable biomass supply, unless breakthrough technologies substantially increase productivity. Climate-energy models project that biomass use could increase nearly fourfold to around 150–200 exajoules, almost a quarter of world primary energy in 2050.[b] However, the maximum sustainable technical potential of biomass resources (both residues and energy crops) without disruption of food and forest resources ranges from 80–170 exajoules a year by 2050,[c] and only part of this is realistically and economically feasible. In addition, some climate models rely on biomass-based carbon capture and storage, an unproven technology, to achieve negative emissions and to buy some time during the first half of the century.[d]

Some liquid biofuels such as corn-based ethanol, mainly for transport, may aggravate rather than ameliorate carbon emissions on a life-cycle basis. Second-generation biofuels, based on ligno-cellulosic feedstocks—such as straw, bagasse, vegetative grass, and wood—hold the promise of sustainable production that is high-yielding and emits low levels of greenhouse gas, but they are still in the R&D stage.

Solar

Solar power, the most abundant energy source on Earth, is the fastest-growing renewable energy industry. Solar power has two major technologies—solar photovoltaic systems and concentrated solar power. Solar photovoltaic systems convert solar energy directly into electricity. Concentrated solar power uses mirrors to focus sunlight on a transfer fluid that generates steam to drive a conventional turbine. Concentrated solar power is much cheaper and offers the greatest potential to produce base-load, large-scale power to replace fossil power plants. But this technology requires water to cool the turbine—a constraint in the desert, where solar plants tend to be installed. So expansion is limited by geography (because concentrated solar power can only use direct beam sunlight) as well as by the lack of transmission infrastructure and large financing requirements. Solar photovoltaics are less location-sensitive, quicker to build, and suitable for both distributed generation and off-grid applications. Solar water heaters can substantially reduce the use of gas or electricity to heat water in buildings. China dominates the global market of solar water heaters, producing more than 60 percent of global capacity.

At current costs, concentrated solar would become cost competitive with coal at a price of $60 to $90 a ton of CO_2.[e] But with learning and economies of scale, concentrated solar power could become cost competitive with coal in less than 10 years, and the global installed capacity could rise to 45–50 gigawatts by 2020.[f] Similarly, solar photovoltaics have a learning rate of 15–20 percent cost reduction with each doubling of installed capacity.[g] Because global capacity is still small, potential cost reductions through learning are substantial.

Wind, hydro, and geothermal

Wind, hydro, and geothermal power are all limited by resources and suitable sites. Wind power has grown at 25 percent a year over the past five years, with installed capacity of 120 gigawatts in 2008. In Europe more wind power was installed in 2008 than any other type of electricity-generating technology. But climate change could affect wind resources, with higher wind speeds but more variable wind patterns.[h]

Hydropower is the leading renewable source of electricity worldwide, accounting for 16 percent of global power. Its potential is limited by availability of suitable sites (global economically exploitable potential of 6 million gigawatt-hours a year),[i] large capital requirements, long lead times to develop, concerns over social and environmental impacts, and climate variability (notably water resources). More than 90 percent of the unexploited economically feasible potential is in developing countries, primarily in Sub-Saharan Africa, South and East Asia, and Latin America.[j] Africa exploits only 8 percent of its hydropower potential.

For many countries in Africa and South Asia, regional hydropower trade could provide the least-cost energy supply with zero carbon emissions. But the lack of political will and trust and concerns about energy security constrain such trade. And greater climate variability will affect the hydrological cycle. Drought or glacial melting could make hydropower supplies unreliable in some regions. Nevertheless, after two decades of stagnation, hydropower is expanding, particularly in Asia. But the current financial crisis makes it more difficult to raise financing to meet the large capital requirements.

Geothermal can provide power, heating, and cooling. It meets 26 percent of Iceland's electricity needs and 87 percent of its building heating demand. But this power source requires major financial commitments in up-front geological investigations and expensive drilling of geothermal wells.

Smart grids and meters

With two-way digital communications between power plants and users, smart grids can balance supply and demand in real time, smooth demand peaks, and make consumers active participants in the production and consumption of electricity. As the share of generation from variable renewable resources such as wind and solar increases, a smart grid can better handle fluctuations in power.[k] It can allow electric vehicles to store power when needed or to sell it back to the grid. Smart meters can communicate with customers, who can then reduce costs by changing appliances or times of use.

Sources:

a. IEA 2008b.

b. IEA 2008b; Riahi, Grübler, and Nakićenović 2007; IIASA 2009; Knopf and others, forthcoming.

c. German Advisory Council on Global Change 2008; Rokityanskiy and others 2006; Wise and others 2009.

d. Riahi, Grübler, and Nakićenović 2007; IIASA 2009.

e. IEA 2008b; Yates, Heller, and Yeung 2009.

f. Yates, Heller, and Yeung 2009.

g. Neij 2007.

h. Pryor, Barthelmie, and Kjellstrom 2005.

i. IEA 2008b.

j. World Bank 2008b.

k. Worldwatch Institute 2009.

technologies, there is limited room for flexibility in the technology portfolio.

Historically, however, innovation and technology breakthroughs have reduced the costs of overcoming formidable technical barriers, given effective and timely policy action—a key challenge facing the world today. Acid rain and stratospheric ozone depletion are two of many examples demonstrating that estimates of environmental protection costs based on technology extant before regulation are dramatically overstated.[45]

Climate-smart development policies need to be tailored to the maturity of each technology and the national context and can accelerate the development and deployment of these technologies (figure 4.11 and table 4.4).

Figure 4.10   The emissions gap between where the world is headed and where it needs to go is huge, but a portfolio of clean energy technologies can help the world stay at 450 ppm CO₂e (2°C)

a. CO₂ emissions from the energy sector: wedge analysis for IEA Blue Scenario (450 ppm CO₂e)

Annual emissions (Gt CO₂)

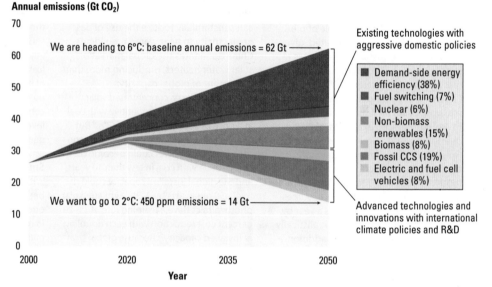

b. CO₂ emissions from the energy sector: wedge analysis for MESSAGE B2 (450 ppm CO₂e)
Annual emissions (Gt CO₂)

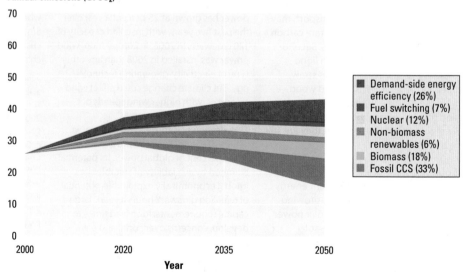

Sources: WDR team, based on data from Riahi, Grübler, and Nakićenović 2007; IIASA 2009; IEA 2008b.

Note: Fuel switching is changing from coal to gas. Non-biomass renewables include solar, wind, hydropower, and geothermal. Fossil CCS is fossil fuels with carbon capture and storage. While the exact mitigation potential of each wedge may vary under different models depending on the baseline, the overall conclusions remain the same.

Figure 4.11   The goal is to push low-carbon technologies from unproven concept to widespread deployment and to higher emission reductions

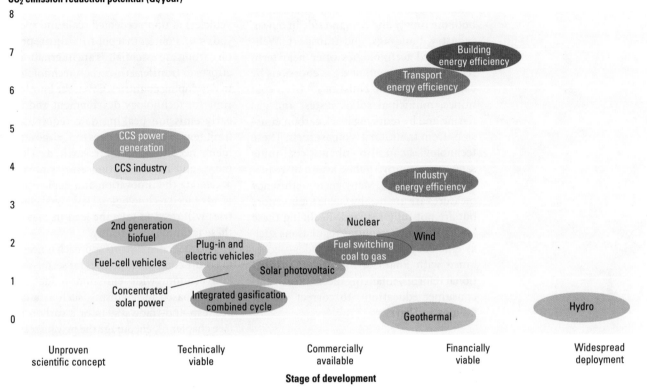

CO_2 emission reduction potential (Gt/year)

Source: WDR team, based on data from World Bank 2008a and IEA 2008a (mitigation potential from IEA Blue Scenario in 2050).

Note: See table 4.4 for detailed definitions of technology development stage. A given technology group can be progressing through different stages at the same time but in different country settings and at different scales. Wind, for example, is already cost competitive with gas-fired power plants in most of the United States (Wiser and Bolinger 2008). But in China and India wind may be economically but not financially viable against coal-fired power plants. So for clean technologies to be adopted in more places and at larger scales, they must move from the top to bottom in table 4.4.

Table 4.4   Policy instruments tailored to the maturity of technologies

Maturity level	Status	Issues to address to move to next stage	Policy support
Technically viable	The basic science is proven and tested in the lab or on a limited scale. Some technical and cost barriers remain.	Development and demonstration to prove operational viability at scale and to minimize costs. Internalize global externalities.	Technology development policies: Substantial public and private R&D, and large-scale demonstration. Internalize global externalities through carbon tax or cap-and-trade. Technology transfer.
Commercially available and economically viable	The technology is available from commercial vendors. Projected costs are well understood. Technology is economically viable, justified by country's development benefits. But it cannot yet compete against fossil fuels without subsidy and/or internalization of local externality.	Leveling the playing field between clean energy and fossil fuels.	Domestic policies to provide a level playing field: Remove fossil-fuel subsidies and internalize local externalities. Provide financial incentives for clean energy technologies.
Financially viable	Technology is financially viable for project investors—cost competitive with fossil fuels, or has high financial returns and short payback period for demand options.	Market failures and barriers hamper accelerating adoption through the market.	Regulations, with financial incentives to remove market failures and barriers. Support for delivery mechanisms and financing programs to expand adoption. Consumer education.
Widespread	Technology is being adopted widely through market operation.		

Source: WDR team.

Energy efficiency. In the short term the largest and cheapest source of emission reductions is increased energy efficiency on both the supply and demand side in power, industry, buildings, and transport. Well-established technologies offer near-term reductions in greenhouse gas emissions by capturing methane emissions[46] from coal mines, municipal solid wastes, and gas flaring and by reducing black carbon emissions from traditional biomass fuels. These technologies can also enhance coal mine safety and improve public health by reducing air pollution.[47] Many energy-efficiency measures are financially viable for investors but are not fully realized. Realizing these low-cost savings requires regulations such as efficiency standards and codes—combined with financial incentives, institutional reforms, financing mechanisms, and consumer education—to correct market failures and barriers.

Existing supply-side low-carbon technologies. In the short to medium term, low- or zero-emission fuels for the power sector—renewable energy and nuclear power—are commercially available and could be deployed much more widely under the right policy and regulatory frameworks. Smart and robust grids can enhance the reliability of electric networks and minimize the downside of relying on variable renewable energy and distributed generation (see box 4.5). Fuel switching from coal to natural gas also has great mitigation potential but increases energy security risks for gas-importing countries. Most renewable energy technologies are economically viable but not yet financially viable, so some form of subsidy (to internalize the externalities) is needed to make them cost competitive with fossil fuels. Adopting these technologies on a larger scale will require that fossil-fuel prices reflect the full cost of production and externalities, plus financial incentives to adopt low-carbon technologies.

Advanced technologies. While commercially available technologies can provide a substantial share of the abatement needed in the short to medium term,[48] limiting warming to 2°C requires developing and deploying advanced technologies (carbon capture and storage in power and industry, second-generation biofuels, and electric vehicles) at unprecedented scale and speed (box 4.6). Policies that put an adequate price on carbon are essential, as are international efforts to transfer low-carbon technologies to developing countries. Given the long lead time for technology development and the early emission peaking date required to limit temperature increases to 2°C, governments need to ramp up research, development, and demonstration efforts now to accelerate the innovation and deployment of advanced technologies. Developed countries will need to take the lead in making these technologies a reality.

An integrated systems approach is needed to ensure compatible policies for sector-wide and economywide emission reductions. Market-based mechanisms, such as a carbon cap-and-trade system or a carbon tax (see chapter 6), encourage the private sector to invest in least-cost, low-carbon technologies to achieve deep emission cuts.

Integrated urban and transport approaches combine urban planning, public transport, energy-efficient buildings, distributed generation from renewable sources, and clean vehicles (box 4.7). Latin America's pioneering experiences with rapid bus transit—dedicated bus lanes, prepayment of bus fares, and efficient intermodal connections—are examples of a broader urban transformation.[49] Modal shifts to mass transit have large development co-benefits of time savings in traffic, less congestion, and better public health from reduced local air pollution.

Changing behaviors and lifestyles to achieve low-carbon societies will take a concerted educational effort over many years. But by reducing travel, heating, cooling, and appliance use and by shifting to mass transit, lifestyle changes could reduce annual CO_2 emissions by 3.5–5.0 gigatons by 2030—8 percent of the reduction needed (see chapter 8).[50]

Governments do not have to wait for a global climate deal—they can adopt domestic efficient and clean energy policies now, justified by development and financial co-benefits. Such domestic win-win measures

BOX 4.6 *Advanced technologies*

Carbon capture and storage (CCS) could reduce emissions from fossil fuels by 85–95 percent and is critical in sustaining an important role for fossil fuels in a carbon-constrained world. It involves three main steps:

- CO_2 capture from large stationary sources, such as power plants or other industrial processes, before or after combustion.

- Transport to storage sites by pipelines.

- Storage through injection of CO_2 into geological sites, including: depleted oil and gas fields to enhance oil and gas recovery, coal beds to enhance coal bed methane recovery, deep saline formations, and oceans.

Currently, CCS is competitive with conventional coal only at a price of $50 to $90 a ton of CO_2.[a] Still at the R&D stage, it is technologically immature. The number of economically available geological sites close to carbon emission sources varies widely from country to country. Early opportunities to lower costs are at depleted oil fields and enhanced oil recovery sites, but storage in deep saline aquifers would also be required for deep emission cuts. CCS also significantly reduces efficiency of power plants and has the potential for leakage.

The near-term priority should be spurring large-scale demonstration projects to reduce costs and improve reliability. Four large-scale commercial CCS demonstration projects are in operation—in Sleipner (Norway); Weyburn (Canada–United States); Salah (Algeria); and Snohvit (Norway)—mostly from gas or coal gasification. Together these projects capture 4 million tons of CO_2 per year. A 450 ppm CO_2e trajectory requires 30 large-scale demonstration plants by 2020.[b] Capturing CO_2 from low-efficiency power plants is not economically viable, so new power plants should be built with highly efficient technologies for retrofitting with CCS later. Legal and regulatory frameworks must be established for CO_2 injection and to address long-term liabilities. The European Union has adopted a directive on the geological storage of CO_2, and the United States has proposed CCS rules. Detailed assessments of potential carbon storage sites are also needed, particularly in developing countries. Without a massive international effort, resolving the entire chain of technical, legal, institutional, financial, and environmental issues could require a decade or more before applications go to scale.

Plug-in hybrids offer a potential near-term option as a means of transition to full electric vehicles.[c] They combine batteries with smaller internal combustion engines, which allow them to travel part-time on electricity provided by the grid through recharging at night. When running on electricity generated from renewable energy, they emit 65 percent less CO_2 than a gasoline-powered car.[d] However, they increase electricity consumption, and the net emission reductions depend on the electricity source. Significant improvements and cost reductions in energy storage technology are required. Electric vehicles are solely battery-powered, but they require much greater battery capacity than plug-in hybrids and are more expensive.

Sources:
a. IEA 2008b.
b. IEA 2008b.
c. IEA 2008b.
d. NRDC 2007.

---

can go a long way to close the mitigation gap,[51] but they must be supplemented with international climate agreements to bridge the remaining gap.

Realizing the savings from energy efficiency

Globally an additional dollar invested in energy efficiency avoids more than two dollars in investment on the supply side, and the payoffs are even higher in developing countries.[52] So energy efficiency (*nega*watts) should be considered on a par with traditional supply-side measures (megawatts) in energy resource planning. Energy efficiency reduces energy bills for consumers, increases the competitiveness of industries, and creates jobs. Energy efficiency is essential for the 2°C trajectory, because it buys time by delaying the need to build additional capacity while advanced clean energy technologies are being developed and brought to market.

Buildings consume nearly 40 percent of the world's final energy,[53] about half for heating space and water, and the rest for running electric appliances, including lighting, air conditioning, and refrigeration.[54] Opportunities to improve energy efficiency lie in the building envelope (roof, walls, windows, doors, and insulation), in space and water heating, and in appliances. Buildings present one of the most cost-effective mitigation options, with more than 90 percent of potential mitigation achievable with a CO_2 price of less than $20 a ton.[55] Studies find that existing energy-efficiency technologies can cost-effectively save 30 to 40 percent of energy use in new buildings, when evaluated on a life-cycle basis.[56]

While most of these studies are based on high-income country data, the potential for energy-efficiency savings in developing countries can be larger because of the low baseline. For example, the current space-

BOX 4.7 *The role for urban policy in achieving mitigation and development co-benefits*

Urbanization is often cited as a major driver of global emissions growth[a] but is better understood as a major driver of development.[b] It is therefore a crucial nexus of climate and development policy making. Most emissions occur in cities precisely because that is where most production and consumption occur. And the high concentration of population and economic activity in cities can actually increase efficiency—if the right policies are in place. A number of factors call for an urban climate agenda.

First, denser cities are more energy and emission efficient (for example, in the transport sector; see the figure below), and local policies are essential for encouraging densification.[c] Second, the strong and persistent influence of infrastructure on long-term residential and commercial citing decisions reduces the responsiveness of emissions to price signals. Complementary regulation and land-use planning are therefore needed. Third, the interdependence of the systems that constitute the urban form—roads and public transit lines; water, wastewater, and

power services; and residential, commercial, and industrial buildings—and that are not easily changed once the initial patterns are set, increases the urgency of designing low-emissions cities in rapidly urbanizing countries.

As discussed in chapter 8, cities have already become a source of political momentum and will advance mitigation actions on the international stage even as they pursue their own initiatives at home. Contrary to a general presumption that local decision making focuses on local issues, more than 900 U.S. cities have signed on to meet or exceed Kyoto Protocol targets to reduce greenhouse gas emissions,[d] while the C40 Cities Climate Leadership Group that aims to promote action to combat climate change includes major cities on all continents.[e]

Cities have the unique ability to respond to a global issue like climate change at a tangible local level. Many cities have legislated to limit the use of plastic bags, disposable cups, or bottled water. These initiatives may be important for social messaging, but their

environmental impact has so far been minimal. Deeper, higher-impact efforts—such as congestion charging, green building incentives, support for urban design requiring less automobile dependence, and incorporation of carbon pricing in land taxes and development rights—will ultimately require a more comprehensive cultural momentum to overcome entrenched (or aspirational) high-carbon lifestyle preferences. Fortunately, many city-led measures needed for mitigation have benefits for adaptation to climate change, which will reduce tradeoffs.

Sources: WDR team.

a. Dodman 2009.

b. World Bank 2008f.

c. World Bank 2009b.

d. U.S. Conference of Mayors Climate Change Protection Agreement.

e. See http://www.c40cities.org/. In addition, the United Cities and Local Governments and International Council for Local Environmental Initiatives have a joint resolution requesting a greater voice for cities in the UNFCCC negotiating process.

Emissions from transport are much lower in denser cities

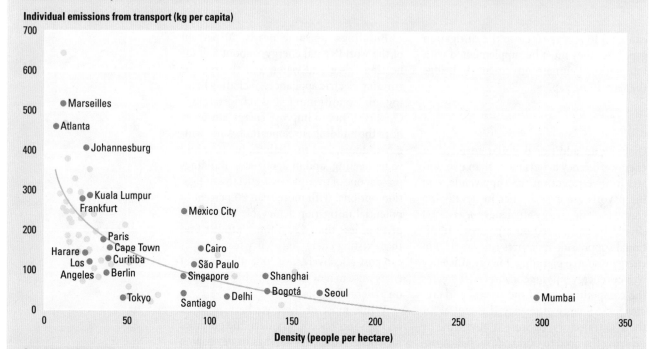

Source: World Bank 2009b.
Note: The figure does not correct for income because a regression of transport emissions on density and income reveals that density, not income, is a key factor. Data are for 1995.

heating technology used in Chinese buildings consumes 50 to 100 percent more energy than that used in Western Europe. Making buildings in China more energy efficient would add 10 percent to construction costs but would save more than 50 percent on energy costs.[57] Technology innovations such as advanced building materials can further increase the potential energy savings (see chapter 7). Integrated zero-emission building designs, combining energy-efficiency measures with on-site power and heat from solar and biomass, are technically and economically feasible—and the costs are falling.[58]

Manufacturing accounts for one-third of global energy use, and the potential for energy savings in industry is particularly large in developing countries. Key opportunities include improving the efficiency of energy-intensive equipment such as motors and boilers and of energy-intensive industries such as iron, steel, cement, chemicals, and petrochemicals. One of the most cost-effective measures is combined heat and power. Existing technologies and best practices could reduce energy consumption in the industrial sector by 20–25 percent, helping reduce carbon footprints without sacrificing growth.[59] In Mexico cogeneration in the refineries of Pemex, the large state-owned petroleum company, could provide more than 6 percent of the country's installed power capacity at a negative mitigation cost (meaning that the sale of previously wasted electricity and heat would generate sufficient revenue to more than offset the required investments).[60]

Improving vehicle fuel efficiency, for example by shifting to hybrid cars, is the most cost-effective means of cutting emissions in the transport sector in the near to medium term. Improving power-train systems (for example, by downsizing conventional internal combustion engines) and making other design changes, such as lower vehicle weight, optimized transmissions, and start-stop systems with regenerative braking, can also improve fuel efficiency.

In addition, smart urban planning—denser, more spatially compact, and with mixed-use urban design that allows growth near city centers and transit corridors to prevent urban sprawl—can substantially reduce energy demand and CO_2 emissions. It reduces the vehicle kilometers traveled and makes it possible to rely on district and integrated energy systems for heating.[61] In Mexico, for example, dense urban development is expected to reduce total emissions by 117 million tons of CO_2e from 2009 to 2030, with additional social and environmental benefits.[62]

Market and nonmarket barriers and failures

The large untapped potential for greater energy efficiency demonstrates that low-cost energy savings are not easy. Small-scale, fragmented energy-efficiency measures, involving multiple stakeholders and tens of millions of individual decision makers, are fundamentally more complex than large-scale, supply-side options. Energy-efficiency investments need cash up front, but future savings are less tangible, making such investment risky compared with asset-based energy-supply deals. Many market failures and barriers, as well as nonmarket barriers, to energy efficiency exist and tackling them requires policies and interventions that entail additional costs (box 4.8). Another concern is the rebound effect: acquiring efficient equipment lowers energy bills, so consumers tend to increase energy consumption, eroding some of the energy reductions. But empirically the rebound is small to moderate, with long-run effects of 10–30 percent for personal transport and space heating and cooling,[63] and these can be mitigated with price signals.

Price should reflect true cost

Many countries channel public subsidies, implicit and explicit, to fossil fuels, distorting investment decisions for clean energy. Energy subsidies in the 20 highest-subsidizing developing countries are estimated at around $310 billion a year, or around 0.7 percent of world GDP in 2007.[64] The lion's share of the subsidies artificially lowers the prices of fossil fuels, providing disincentives to save energy and making clean energy less attractive financially.[65]

Removing fossil-fuel subsidies would reduce energy demand, encourage the supply of clean energy, and lower CO_2 emissions.

BOX 4.8   *Energy efficiency faces many market and nonmarket barriers and failures*

- *Low or underpriced energy*. Low energy prices undermine incentives to save energy.
- *Regulatory failures*. Consumers who receive unmetered heat lack the incentive to adjust temperatures, and utility rate-setting can reward inefficiency.
- *A lack of institutional champion and weak institutional capacity*. Energy-efficiency measures are fragmented. Without an institutional champion to coordinate and promote energy efficiency, it becomes nobody's priority. Moreover, there are few energy-efficiency service providers, and their capacity will not be established overnight.
- *Absent or misplaced incentives*. Utilities make a profit by generating and selling more electricity, not by saving energy.

For most consumers, the cost of energy is small relative to other expenditures. Because tenants typically pay energy bills, landlords have little or no incentive to spend on efficient appliances or insulation.

- *Consumer preferences*. Consumer decisions to purchase vehicles are usually based on size, speed, and appearance rather than on efficiency.
- *Higher up-front costs*. Many efficient products have higher up-front costs. Individual consumers usually demand very short payback times and are unwilling to pay higher up-front costs. Preferences aside, low-income customers may not be able to afford efficient products.
- *Financing barriers and high transaction costs*. Many energy-efficiency projects

have difficulty obtaining financing. Financial institutions usually are not familiar with or interested in energy efficiency, because of the small size of the deal, high transaction costs, and high perceived risks. Many energy service companies lack collateral.

- *Products unavailable*. Some efficient equipment is readily available in high- and middle-income countries but not in low-income countries, where high import tariffs reduce affordability.
- *Limited awareness and information*. Consumers have limited information on energy-efficiency costs, benefits, and technologies. Firms are unwilling to pay for energy audits that would inform them of potential savings.

Source: WDR team.

Ample evidence shows that higher energy prices induce substantially lower demand.[66] If Europe had followed the U.S. policy of low fuel taxes, its fuel consumption would be twice as large as it is now.[67] Removing fossil-fuel subsidies in power and industry could reduce global CO_2 emissions by as much as 6 percent a year and add to global GDP.[68]

But removing those subsidies is no simple matter—it requires strong political will. Fuel subsidies are often justified as protecting poor people, even though most of the subsidies go to better-off consumers. As chapters 1 and 2 discuss, effective social protection targeted at low-income groups, in conjunction with the phased removal of fossil-fuel subsidies, can make reform politically viable and socially acceptable. It is also important to increase transparency in the energy sector by requiring service companies to share key information, so that the governments and other stakeholders can make better-informed decisions and assessments about removing subsidies.

Energy prices should reflect the cost of production and incorporate local and global environmental externalities. Urban air pollution from fossil-fuel combustion increases health risks and causes premature deaths. Lower-respiratory disease resulting from air pollution is a top cause of mortality in low-

income countries and a leading contributor to the global burden of disease.[69] A 15 percent greenhouse gas reduction below business as usual by 2020 in China would result in 125,000–185,000 fewer premature deaths annually from pollution emitted by power generation and household energy use.[70] Pricing local air pollution can be very effective in reducing the related health costs.

Pricing carbon, through a carbon tax or cap-and-trade system (see chapter 6), is fundamental to scaling up advanced clean energy technologies and leveling the playing field with fossil fuels.[71] It provides incentives and reduces risks for private investments and innovations in efficient and clean energy technologies on a large scale (see chapter 7).[72] Developed countries should take the lead in pricing carbon. Legitimate concerns include protecting the poor from high energy prices and compensating the losing industries, particularly in developing countries. Social safety nets and nondistortionary income support, possibly from revenues generated by the carbon tax or permit auction, can help (see chapters 1 and 2).

Pricing policy alone is not enough; energy-efficiency policies are also critical

Carbon-pricing policies alone will not be enough to ensure large-scale development and deployment of energy efficiency and low-carbon technologies (box 4.9). Energy efficiency faces distinct barriers in different sectors. For power, where a small number of decision makers determine whether energy-efficiency measures are adopted, financial incentives are likely to be effective. For transport, buildings, and industry—where adoption is a function of the preferences of, and requires action by, many decentralized individuals—energy demand is less responsive to price signals, and regulations tend to be more effective. A suite of policy instruments can replicate proven successes in removing barriers to energy efficiency.

Regulations. Economywide energy-intensity targets, appliance standards, building codes, industry performance targets (energy consumption per unit of output), and fuel-efficiency standards are among the most cost-effective measures. More than 35 countries have national energy-efficiency targets. France and the United Kingdom have gone a step further in energy-efficiency obligations by mandating that energy companies meet energy-saving quotas. In Japan energy-efficiency performance standards require utilities to achieve electricity savings equal to a set percentage of their baseline sales or load.[73] Brazil, China, and India have energy-efficiency laws, but as in all contexts, effectiveness depends on enforcement. Other options include the mandatory phasing out of incandescent lights.

Complying with efficiency standards can avoid or postpone adding new power plant capacity and reduce consumer prices. And industrial energy performance targets can spur innovation and increase competitiveness. For new buildings in Europe the cumulative energy savings from building codes is about 60 percent over those built before the first oil shock in the 1970s.[74] Refrigerator efficiency standards in the United States have saved 150 gigawatts in peak power demand over the past 30 years, more than the installed capacity of the entire U.S. nuclear program.[75] Efficiency standards and labeling programs cost about 1.5 cents a kilowatt-hour, much cheaper than any electricity supply option.[76] The average price of refrigerators in America has fallen by more

---

BOX 4.9　*Carbon pricing alone is not enough*

Carbon pricing alone cannot guarantee large-scale deployment of efficient and clean energy, because it cannot fully overcome the market failures and nonmarket barriers to the innovation and diffusion of low-carbon technologies.[a]

First, price addresses only one of many barriers. Others, such as a lack of institutional capacity and financing, block the provision of energy-saving services.

Second, while the price elasticity of energy demand is high over the long term, it is generally quite inelastic in the short term, because people have few short-run options for reducing their transport needs and household energy use in response to fuel price changes. Automobile fuel prices have an historical short-term elasticity ranging from only –0.2 to –0.4,[b] with a much smaller response of –0.03 to –0.08 in recent years,[c] but a long-

term elasticity ranging between –0.6 and –1.1.

Third, the low price elasticity of adoptiing many energy-efficiency measures may also be a result of high opportunity costs in rapidly growing developing countries like China. A return of 20 percent for an efficiency measure is attractive, but investors may not invest in efficiency if other investments with equivalent risks have higher returns.

So, strong pricing policies are important but not enough. They need to be combined with regulations to correct market failures, remove market and nonmarket barriers, and foster clean technology development.

Sources:
a. ETAAC 2008.
b. Chamon, Mauro, and Okawa 2008.
c. Hughes, Knittel, and Sperling 2008.

---

than half since the 1970s, even as their efficiency has increased by three-quarters.[77]

Financial incentives. In many developing countries weak enforcement of regulations is a concern. Regulations need to be supplemented with financial incentives for consumers and producers. Low-income consumers are most sensitive to the higher up-front costs of efficient products. Financial incentives to offset these up-front costs, such as consumer rebates and energy-efficient mortgages,[78] can change consumer behavior, increase affordability, and overcome barriers to market entry by new, efficient producers. In addition, regulations are also vulnerable to rebound effects, so pricing policies are needed to discourage consumption. Fuel taxes have proved one of the most cost-effective ways to reduce transport energy demand, along with congestion charges and insurance or tax levies on vehicles based on kilometers traveled, and higher taxes on light trucks and sports utility vehicles (table 4.5).

Utility demand-side management has produced large energy savings. Key to success is decoupling utility profits from electricity sales to give utilities incentives to save. Regulators forecast demand and allow utilities to charge a price that would recoup their costs and earn a fixed return based on that forecast. If demand turns out to be lower than expected, the regulator lets prices rise so that the utility can make the mandated profit; if it is higher, the regulator cuts prices to return the excess to customers (box 4.10).

Institutional reform. An institutional champion, such as a dedicated energy-efficiency agency, is essential to coordinate multiple stakeholders and promote and manage energy-efficiency programs. More than 50 countries, developed and developing, have a national energy-efficiency agency. It can be a government agency with a focus on clean energy or energy efficiency (the most common), such as the Department of Alternative Energy Development and Efficiency in Thailand, or an independent corporation or authority, such as the Korea Energy Management Corporation. To achieve successful results, they require adequate resources, the ability to engage multiple stakeholders, independence in decision making, and credible monitoring of results.[79]

Energy service companies (ESCOs) provide energy-efficiency services such as

Table 4.5   Policy interventions for energy efficiency, renewable energy, and transport

Policy area	Energy efficiency and demand-side management interventions	Renewable energy interventions	Barriers addressed
Economywide	Removal of fossil-fuel subsidies Tax (fuel or carbon tax) Quantitative limits (cap-and-trade)		Environmental externalities not included in the price Regressive or demand-augmenting distortions from subsidies for fossil fuels
Regulations	Economywide energy-efficiency targets Energy-efficiency obligations Appliance standards Building codes Industry energy-performance targets Fuel economy standards	Mandatory purchase, open and fair grid access Renewable portfolio standards Low-carbon fuel standards Technology standards Interconnection regulations	Lack of legal framework for renewable independent power producers Lack of transmission access by renewable energy Lack of incentives and misplaced incentives to save Supply-driven mentality Unclear interconnection requirements
Financial incentives	Tax credits Capital subsidies Profits decoupled from sales Consumer rebates Time-of-use tariffs Fuel taxes Congestion tolls Taxes based on engine size Insurance or tax levies on vehicle miles traveled Taxes on light trucks, SUVs	Feed-in tariff, net metering Green certificates Real-time pricing Tax credits Capital subsidies	High capital costs Unfavorable pricing rules Lack of incentives for utilities and consumers to save
Institutional arrangements	Utility Dedicated energy-efficiency agencies Independent corporation or authority Energy service companies (ESCOs)	Utility Independent power producers	Too many decentralized players
Financing mechanisms	Loan financing and partial loan guarantees ESCOs Utility energy-efficiency, demand-side management program, including system benefit fund	System benefit fund Risk management and long-term financing Concessional loans	High capital cost, and mismatch with short-term loans ESCOs' lack of collateral and small deal size Perceived high risks High transaction costs Lack of experience and knowledge
Promotion and education	Labeling Installing meters Consumer education	Education about renewable energy benefits	Lack of information and awareness Loss of amenities

Source: WDR team.

BOX 4.10   *California's energy-efficiency and renewable energy programs*

A U.S. leader in energy efficiency, California has kept its electricity consumption per capita flat for the past 30 years, substantially below the U.S. national average (figure, panel a). Appliance standards and building codes, along with financial incentives for utility demand-side management programs, are estimated to be responsible for one-quarter of the difference (figure, panel b). California decoupled utility profits from sales in 1982 and recently went a step further with "decoupling-plus"—utilities earn additional money if they meet or exceed savings goals.

The state's energy-efficiency program has an annual budget of $800 million, collected from tariff surcharges on electricity and used for utility procurements, demand-side management, and research and development. The average cost of the program is about 3 cents per kilowatt-hour, far lower than the cost of supply (figure, panel c). To promote renewable energy, the state is implementing renewable portfolio standards to increase renewable energy's share in power generation to 20 percent by 2010.

In June 2005 California became the first U.S. state to issue an executive order on climate change, setting a target for reducing greenhouse gas emissions to the 2000 level by 2010, to the 1990 level by 2020, and to 80 percent below the 1990 level by 2050. Energy efficiency is projected to contribute about 50 percent of this reduction.

Sources: California Energy Commission 2007a; Rosenfeld 2007; Rogers, Messenger, and Bender 2005; Sudarshan and Sweeney, forthcoming.

California's electricity consumption per capita has remained flat over the past 30 years, thanks largely to utility demand-side management and efficiency standards. The cost of energy efficiency is much lower than that of electricity supply

a. Electricity sales per capita

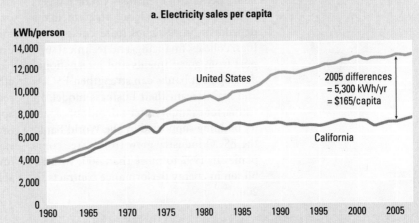

b. Annual energy savings from efficiency programs and standards

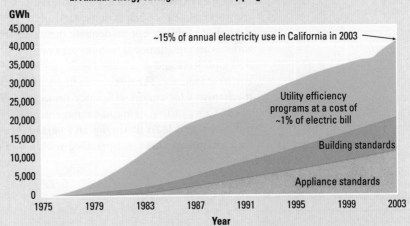

c. Comparison of California energy efficiency (EE) program costs to supply generation costs

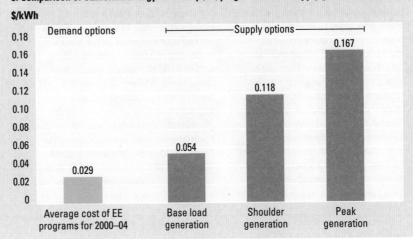

energy auditing, recommend energy saving measures, and provide financing to clients; they also serve as project aggregators. Most ESCOs have had difficulty in obtaining adequate financing from commercial banks because of their weak balance sheets and the perceived higher risks of loans dependent on revenues from energy savings. Policies, financing, and technical support from governments and international development banks can strengthen ESCOs and mainstream their business model. In China, for example, after a decade of capacity building supported by the World Bank, the ESCO industry grew from three companies in 1997 to more than 400, with $1 billion in energy performance contracts in 2007.[80]

Financing mechanisms. Developing and operating energy-efficiency services for investment in energy efficiency are primarily institutional issues. Lack of domestic capital is rarely a problem, but inadequate organizational and institutional systems for developing projects and accessing funds can be barriers to finance. The three main financing mechanisms for energy-efficiency projects are ESCOs, utility demand-management programs, and loan financing and partial loan guarantee schemes operating within

commercial banks, as specialized agencies, or as revolving funds.[81]

Lending through local commercial banks offers the best prospect for program sustainability and maximum impact. International financial institutions have supported partial-risk-guarantee programs to mitigate the risks of energy-efficiency projects for commercial banks, increasing the banks' confidence in jump-starting energy-efficiency financing (box 4.11). Dedicated revolving funds are another common approach, particularly in countries where investing in energy efficiency is in the early stages and banks are not ready to provide financing.[82] This approach is transitional, and sustainability is a major issue.

Utility demand-side management is usually funded through a system benefit fund (financed by a tariff surcharge on kilowatt-hours to all electricity customers), which is more sustainable than government budgets. Administered by either utilities or dedicated energy-efficiency agencies, the funds cover incremental costs of switching to renewable energy from fossil fuels, consumer rebates, concessional loans, research and development, consumer education, and low-income consumer assistance.

Public procurement. Mass procurement of energy-efficient products can substantially reduce costs, attract larger contracts and bank lending, and lower transaction costs. In Uganda and Vietnam the bulk procurement of 1 million compact fluorescent lamps in each country substantially reduced the cost of the lamps and improved product quality through technical specifications and warranty; once installed, they cut peak demand by 30 megawatts.[83] Public procurement through government agencies, usually one of the biggest energy consumers in an economy, can reduce costs and demonstrate government's commitment and to leadership in energy efficiency. But mandates, incentives, and procurement and budgeting rules have to be in place.[84]

Consumer education. Consumer education can promote lifestyle changes and more informed choices—examples include energy-efficiency labeling and increased use of elec-

---

BOX 4.11 *World Bank Group experience with financing energy efficiency*

The World Bank and the International Finance Corporation (IFC) have financed a series of energy-efficiency financial intermediary projects, mostly in Eastern Europe and East Asia. The IFC pioneered the use of a guarantee mechanism through selected domestic banks with the Hungary Energy Efficiency Guarantee Fund. A Global Environment Facility grant of $17 million was used to guarantee $93 million worth of loans for energy-efficient investments. No guarantee has been called, giving local banks confidence in and familiarity with energy-efficiency lending.

One of the key lessons of the experience is the importance of

technical assistance, particularly at the beginning, to raise awareness of energy efficiency, to provide training and advisory services to the banks in developing financial mechanisms, and to build the capacity of project developers. While in Bulgaria the transaction cost of institutional capacity building for both financial institutions and energy service companies—from project concept to financial closure—has been around 10 percent of total project costs at the beginning, it is expected to decline to around 5–6 percent later on.

Sources: WDR team; Taylor and others 2008.

tricity and heat meters, particularly smart meters. Consumer awareness campaigns are most effective in conjunction with regulations and financial incentives. Based on experience in the public health field, interventions to change behaviors need to occur at multiple levels—policy, physical environment (design of walkable cities and green buildings), sociocultural (media communications), interpersonal (face-to-face contacts), and individual (see chapter 8).[85]

Scaling up existing low-carbon technologies

Renewable energy could contribute around 50 percent to the power mix by 2050.[86] With costs of renewable energy declining over the past two decades, wind, geothermal, and hydro power are already or nearly cost-competitive with fossil fuels.[87] Solar is still costly, but costs are expected to decline rapidly along the learning curve over the next few years (box 4.12). With rising fossil-fuel prices, the cost gap is closing. Biomass, geothermal power, and hydropower can provide base-load power, but solar and wind are intermittent.

A large share of intermittent resources in the grid system may affect reliability, but this can be addressed in a variety of ways— through hydropower or pumped storage, load management, energy storage facilities, interconnection with other countries, and smart grids.[88] Smart grids can enhance

---

BOX 4.12 *Difficulties in comparing energy technology costs: A matter of assumptions*

Comparing costs of different energy technologies is a tricky business. A frequently used approach for comparing electricity generation technologies is based on costs per kilowatt-hour (kWh). A levelized-cost method is commonly used to compare the life-cycle economic costs of energy alternatives that deliver the same energy services. First, capital costs are calculated using a simple capital recovery factor method.[a] This method divides the capital cost into an equal payment series—an annualized capital cost—over the lifetime of the equipment. Then the annualized capital costs are added to the annual operation and maintenance (O&M) costs and the fuel costs to obtain the levelized costs. So capital costs, O&M costs, fuel costs, the discount rate, and a capacity factor are key determinants of levelized costs.

In reality, costs are time and site specific. The costs of renewable energy are closely linked to local resources and sites. Wind costs, for example, vary widely depending on site-specific wind resources. Labor costs and construction time are also key factors, particularly for fossil-fuel and nuclear plants. Chinese coal-fired power plants, for example, cost about one-third to one-half of the international prices for similar plants. The long lead time to construct nuclear power plants contributes to the high costs in the United States.

Second, sensible integrated comparative assessment of different energy technologies compares all the economic attributes along the primary fuel cycle for a unit of energy benefits. Comparing renewable energy costs with fossil fuel and nuclear should take into account the different services they provide (base-load or intermittent energy). On the one hand, solar and wind energy produce variable outputs, although outputs can be enhanced in various ways, usually at an additional cost. On the other hand, solar and wind energy technologies can typically be licensed and built in much less time than large-scale fossil or nuclear plants.

Third, externalities such as environmental costs and portfolio diversification values should be incorporated when comparing fossil-fuel costs and clean energy costs. A carbon price will make a big difference in pushing up the costs of fossil fuels. Fossil-fuel price volatility creates additional negative externalities. Increasing fuel prices by 20 percent increases the costs of generation by 16 percent for gas and 6 percent for coal, while leaving renewable energy practically untouched. Adding renewable energy sources provides portfolio diversification value because it hedges against the volatility of fossil fuel prices and supplies. Including this portfolio diversification value in the evaualtion of renewables increases their attractiveness.[b]

When dealing with new technologies, the potential for cost reduction should also be factored in. Dynamic analysis of future costs of new technologies depends on the assumptions made about the learning rate—the cost reductions associated with a doubling of capacity. The cost of wind energy has dropped nearly 80 percent over the past 20 years. Technology breakthroughs and economies of scale can lead to more rapid cost reductions, a phenomenon some experts now expect will lead to dramatic near-term reductions in solar cell prices.[c]

In financial analysis, differences in institutional context (whether public or private financing) and government policies (taxes and regulations) are often the deciding factors. Differences in financing costs are particularly important for the most capital-intensive technologies like wind, solar, and nuclear. A California study shows that the cost of a wind power plant varies much more than the cost of a gas combined cycle plant, with different financing terms for private ("merchant"), investor-owned, and publicly owned utilities.[d]

Sources:

a. The capital recovery factor = $[i(1+i)^n]/[(1+i)^n - 1]$ where i is the discount rate and n is the lifetime or period of capital recovery of the systems.
b. World Economic Forum 2009.
c. Deutsche Bank Advisors 2008 (projected photovoltaic cost reductions).
d. California Energy Commission 2007b.

reliability of electricity networks when incorporating variable renewable energy and distributed generation. High-voltage, direct-current lines can make long-range transmission possible with low line losses, which reduces the common problem of renewable energy sources located far from consumption centers. And further cost reduction and performance improvement of energy storage will be needed for large-scale deployment of solar and wind power and electric vehicles. So, while the required magnitude of renewable energy is vast, the transformation is achievable. For example, wind already accounts for 20 percent of Danish power production (box 4.13).

Renewable energy policies: financial incentives and regulations

Transparent, competitive, and stable pricing through long-term power purchase agreements has been most effective in attracting investors to renewable energy, and an enabling legal and regulatory framework can ensure fair and open grid access for independent power producers. Two major mandatory policies for renewable power generation are operating worldwide: feed-in laws that mandate a fixed price, and renewable portfolio standards that mandate a set target for the share of renewable energy (box 4.14).[89]

Feed-in laws require mandatory purchases of renewable energy at a fixed price. Feed-in laws such as those in Germany, Spain, Kenya, and South Africa produce the highest market penetration rates in a short period. They are considered most desirable by investors because of their price certainty and administrative simplicity and because they are conducive to creating local manufacturing industries. Three methods are commonly used to set prices for feed-in tariffs—avoided costs of conventional power generation, costs of renewable energy plus reasonable returns, and average retail prices (net metering allows consumers to sell excess electricity generated from their homes or businesses, usually through solar photovoltaics, to the grid at retail market prices). The main risk is in setting prices either too high or low, so feed-in tariffs need periodic adjustment.

Renewable portfolio standards require utilities in a given region to meet a minimum share of power in or level of installed capacity from renewable energy, as in many U.S. states, the United Kingdom, and Indian states. The target is met through utilities' own generation, power purchases from other producers, direct sales from third parties to the utility's customers, or purchases of tradable renewable energy certificates. But unless separate technology targets or tenders are in place, renewable portfolio standards lack price certainty and tend to favor established industry players and least-cost technologies.[90] They are also more complex to design and administer than feed-in laws.

BOX 4.13   *Denmark sustains economic growth while cutting emissions*

Between 1990 and 2006 Denmark's GDP grew at roughly 2.3 percent a year, more than Europe's average of 2 percent. Denmark also reduced carbon emissions by 5 percent.

Sound policies decoupled emissions from growth. Denmark, along with other Scandinavian countries, implemented the world's first carbon tax on fossil fuels in the early 1990s. At the same time Denmark also adopted a range of policies to promote the use of sustainable energy. Today around 25 percent of Denmark's electricity generation and 15 percent of its primary energy consumption come from renewable energy,

mainly wind and biomass, with a goal to raise the use of renewable energy to at least 30 percent by 2025. Membership in the Nordic power pool, with more than 50 percent hydropower, provides the additional flexibility of exporting surplus wind power and importing Norwegian hydropower during periods of low wind resources. Vestas, the major Danish wind company, has 15,000 employees and accounts for a quarter of the global market for wind turbines. In 15 years Danish renewable technology exports have soared to $10.5 billion.

In addition to its low carbon-intensity of energy, Denmark has the lowest

energy intensity in Europe, a result of stringent building and appliance codes and voluntary agreements on energy savings in industry. Combined heat- and power-based district heating networks provide 60 percent of the country's winter heating, with over 80 percent of it coming from heat previously wasted in electricity production.

Sources: WDR team based on WRI 2008; Denmark Energy Mix Fact Sheet, http://ec.europa.eu/energy/energy_policy/doc/factsheets/mix/mix_dk_en.pdf (accessed August 27, 2009).

BOX 4.14 *Feed-in laws, concessions, tax credits, and renewable portfolio standards in Germany, China, and the United States*

Developing countries account for 40 percent of global renewable energy capacity. By 2007, 60 countries, including 23 developing countries, had renewable energy policies.[a] The three countries with the largest installed capacity of new renewable energy are Germany, China, and the United States.

Germany's feed-in law
In the early 1990s Germany had virtually no renewable energy industry. Today it has become a global renewable energy leader, with a multibillion-dollar industry and 250,000 new jobs.[b] The government passed the Electricity Feed-in Law in 1990, requiring utilities to purchase the electricity generated from all renewable technologies at a fixed price. In 2000 the German Renewable Energy Act set feed-in tariffs for various renewable energy technologies for 20 years, based on their generation costs and generation capacity. To encourage cost reductions and innovation, prices will decline over time based on a predetermined formula. The law also distributed the incremental costs between wind

power and conventional power among all utility customers in the country.[c]

China's renewable energy law and wind concession
China was one of the first developing countries to pass a renewable energy law, and it now has the world's largest renewable energy capacity, accounting for 8 percent of its energy and 17 percent of its electricity.[d] The law set feed-in tariffs for biomass power, but wind power tariffs are established through a concession process. The government introduced wind concessions in 2003 to ramp up wind power capacity and drive down costs. The winning bids for the initial rounds were below average costs and discouraged both wind developers and domestic manufacturers. Improvements in the concession scheme and provincial feed-in tariffs put China at no. 2 in newly installed wind capacity in 2008. The government's target of 30 gigawatts of wind by 2020 will likely be reached ahead of time. The domestic wind manufacturing industry has been boosted by the government's requirement of 70

percent local content and new technology transfer models to hire and acquire international design institutes.

U.S. federal production tax credits and state renewable portfolio standards
A federal tax credit for producing electricity from renewable energy has encouraged significant capacity increases, but the uncertainty of its extension from year to year has led to boom-and-bust cycles in U.S. wind development. And twenty-five states now have renewable portfolio standards. As a result, wind accounted for 35 percent of new generation capacity in 2007, and the United States now has the world's largest installed wind capacity.[e]

Sources:
a. REN 21 2008.
b. Federal Ministry for the Environment 2008.
c. Beck and Martinot 2004.
d. REN 21 2008.
e. Wiser and Bolinger 2008.

An alternative approach for achieving renewable energy targets is competitive tendering, where power producers bid on providing a fixed quantity of renewable power, with the lowest-price bidder winning the contract, as is done in China and Ireland. Tendering is effective at reducing costs, but a main risk has been that some bidders underbid and obligations have not always translated into projects on the ground.

Several financial incentives are available to encourage renewable energy investments: reducing up-front capital costs through subsidies; reducing capital and operating costs through investment or production tax credits; improving revenue streams with carbon credits; and providing financial support through concessional loans and guarantees. Output-based incentives are generally preferable to investment-based incentives for grid-connected renewable energy.[91] Investment incentives per kilowatt of installed capacity do not necessarily provide incentives to

generate electricity or maintain the performance of plants. But output incentives per kilowatt-hour of power produced promote the desired outcome—generating electricity from renewable energy. Any incremental costs of renewable energy over fossil fuels can be passed on to consumers or financed through a system benefits charge, a carbon tax on fossil-fuel use, or a dedicated fund from government budgets or donors.

Nuclear power and natural gas

Nuclear power is a significant option for mitigating climate change, but it suffers from four problems: higher costs than coal-fired plants,[92] risks of nuclear weapon proliferation, uncertainties about waste management, and public concerns about reactor safety. Current international safeguards are inadequate to meet the security challenges of expanded nuclear deployment.[93] However, the next generation of nuclear reactor designs offer improved safety characteristics and better economics than the reactors currently in operation.

Nuclear power has large requirements for capital and highly trained personnel, with long lead times before it comes on line, thus reducing its potential for reducing carbon emissions in the short term. Planning, licensing, and constructing a single nuclear plant typically takes a decade or more. And because of the dearth of orders in recent decades, the world has limited capacity to manufacture many of the critical components of nuclear plants, and rebuilding that capacity will take at least a decade.[94]

Natural gas is the least carbon-intensive fossil fuel for power generation and for residential and industrial use. There is a large potential to reduce carbon emissions by substituting natural gas for coal in the short term. Some 2°C scenarios project that the share of natural gas in the primary energy mix will increase from 21 percent currently to 27–37 percent by 2050.[95] But the costs of natural gas-fired power depend on gas prices, which have been highly volatile in recent years. And, like oil, more than 70 percent of the world's gas reserves are in the Middle East and Eurasia. Security of gas supply is a concern for gas-importing countries. So energy diversification and supply security concerns could limit the share of natural gas in the global energy mix to less than indicated in some climate-energy models.[96]

Accelerating innovation and advanced technologies

Accelerating innovation and advanced technologies requires adequate carbon pricing; massive investment in research, development and demonstration; and unprecedented global cooperation (see chapter 7). Coupling technology push (by increasing research and development, for example) with demand pull (to increase economies of scale) is critical to substantially reduce the cost of advanced technologies (figure 4.12).

Utility-scale power generation technologies require policies and approaches different from those for small-scale technologies. An international Manhattan Project is likely to be needed to develop the former, such as power-plant-based carbon capture and storage, on a scale large enough to allow substantial cost reductions as the technology moves along the learning curve. Developers—utilities or independent power producers—usually have sufficient resources and capacity. But adequate carbon pricing and investment subsidies are required to overcome the high capital cost barrier. In contrast, decentralized, smaller-scale, clean energy technologies require that "a thousand flowers bloom" to address the needs of many small local players, with seed and venture capital and, in developing countries, business development advisory services.

To achieve the 2°C trajectory, a different technology path is required for developing countries. Energy and emissions growth are projected to come largely from developing countries, but developed countries attract much more investment in clean energy technology. Traditionally, new technologies are produced first in developed economies, followed by commercial roll-outs in developing countries, as has been the case with wind energy.[97] But for emissions to peak in 10 years to stay on the 2°C trajectory, both developed and developing countries would need to introduce large-scale demonstrations of advanced technologies now and in parallel. This pattern is fortunately emerging with the rapid advent of research and development in Brazil, China, India, and a few other technology leaders in the developing world. The lowest-cost manufacturers of

Figure 4.12   **Solar photovoltaic power is getting cheaper over time, thanks to R&D and higher expected demand from larger scale of production**

Cost reduction by factor ($/watt)

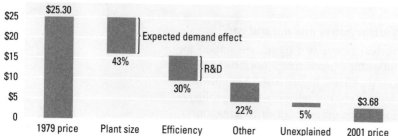

Source: Adapted from Nemet 2006.

Note: Cost reduction is expressed in 2002 $. Bars show the portion of the reduction in the cost of solar photovoltaic power, from 1979 to 2001, accounted for by different factors such as plant size (which is determined by expected demand) and improved efficiency (which is driven by innovation from R&D). The "other" category includes reductions in the price of the key input silicon (12 percent) and a number of much smaller factors (including reduced quantities of silicon needed for a given energy output, and lower rates of discarded products due to manufacturing error).

solar cells, efficient lighting, and ethanol are all in developing countries.

One of the major barriers facing developing countries is the high incremental cost of developing and demonstrating advanced clean energy technologies. It is essential that developed countries substantially increase financial assistance and transfers of low-carbon technologies to the developing world through mechanisms such as a global technology fund. Developed countries will also need to take the lead in encouraging technological breakthroughs (see chapter 7). The Mediterranean Solar Plan is an example of cooperation between developed and developing countries on the large-scale demonstration and deployment of concentrated solar power (box 4.15).

BOX 4.15 *Concentrated solar power in the Middle East and North Africa*

The Mediterranean Solar Plan would create 20 gigawatts of concentrated solar power and other renewable energy capacity by 2020 to meet energy needs in the Middle Eastern and North African countries and export power to Europe. This ambitious plan could bring down the costs of concentrated solar power enough to make it competitive with fossil fuels. Concentrated solar power on less than 1 percent of Saharan desert area (see the map below) would meet Europe's entire power needs.

Financing this solar initiative will be a major challenge but offers an excellent opportunity for a partnership between developed and developing countries to scale up renewable energy for the benefit of both Europe and North Africa.

First, the demand for green electricity and the attractive renewable energy feed-in tariffs in Europe can significantly improve the financial viability of concentrated solar power.

Second, bilateral and multilateral funds—such as the Global Environment Facility, Clean Technology Fund, and carbon financing—would be required for investment subsidies, concessional financing, and revenue enhancement to cover the incremental costs of concentrated solar power, particularly for the portion meeting demand in domestic markets in the Middle East and North Africa.

Third, a successful program also calls for policy actions by the region's governments, creating an enabling environment for renewable energy and removing subsidies to fossil fuels.

Source: WDR team.

Global direct normal solar radiation (kilowatt-hours a square meter a day)

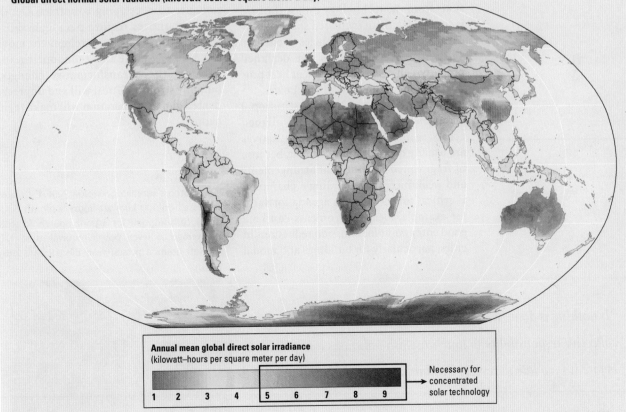

Source: United Nations Environmental Program, Solar and Wind Energy Resource Assessment, http://swera.unep.net/index.php?id=metainfo&rowid=277&metaid=386 (accessed July 21, 2009).

Policies have to be integrated

Policy instruments need to be coordinated and integrated to complement each other and reduce conflicts. A reduction of emissions in transport, for example, requires integration of a three-legged approach. In the order of difficulty, they are transforming vehicles (fuel efficient, plug-in hybrid, and electric cars), transforming fuels (ethanol from sugarcane, second generation biofuels, and hydrogen), and transforming mobility (urban planning and mass transit).[98] Biofuel policies need to coordinate energy and transport policies with agriculture, forestry, and land-use policies to manage the competing demands for water and land (see chapter 3). If energy crops take land away from agriculture in poor nations, the "medicine" of the requisite interventions might be worse than the "disease" in the sense that mitigation might increase vulnerability to climate impacts.[99] Large-scale deployment of plug-in hybrid and electric vehicles would substantially increase power demand, threatening the anticipated lower emissions from the technology unless the grid is supplied with an increased share of low-carbon energy sources. Policies to encourage renewable energy, if not designed properly, can discourage efficient heat production for combined heat and power.

Policies, strategies, and institutional arrangements also have to be aligned across sectors. Cross-sectoral initiatives are usually difficult to implement, because of fragmented institutional arrangements and weak incentives. Finding a champion is critical for moving the agenda forward; for example, local governments can be a good entry point for emission reductions in cities, particularly for buildings and modal shifts in transport. It is also important to align policies and strategies in national, provincial, and local governments (see chapter 8).

In conclusion low-carbon technology and policy solutions can put the world onto a 2°C trajectory, but a fundamental transformation is needed to decarbonize the energy sector. This requires immediate action, and global cooperation and commitment from developed and developing countries. There are win-win policies that governments can adopt now, including regulatory and institutional reforms, financial incentives, and financing mechanisms to scale up existing low-carbon technologies, particularly in the areas of energy efficiency and renewable energy.

Adequate carbon pricing and increased technology development are essential to accelerate development and deployment of advanced low-carbon technologies. Developed countries must take the lead in demonstrating their commitment to significant change at home, while also providing financing and low-carbon technologies to developing countries. Developing countries require paradigm shifts in new climate-smart development models. The technical and economic means exist for these transformative changes, but only strong political will and unprecedented global cooperation will make them happen.

Notes

1. IPCC 2007.

2. Authors' estimates; Socolow 2006. Estimates are based on 100 kilowatt-hours a month electricity consumption for a poor household with an average of seven people, equivalent to 170 kilowatt-hours a person-year. Electricity is pro-

> *"If nothing is done, we shall lose our beloved planet. It is our collective responsibility to find 'unselfish' solutions and fast before it's too late to reverse the damage caused every day."*
>
> —Maria Kassabian, Nigeria, age 10

vided at the current world average carbon intensity of 590 grams of CO_2 a kilowatt-hour for 1.6 billion people, equivalent to 160 million tons of CO_2. Socolow (2006) assumed providing 35 kilograms of clean cooking fuels (liquefied petroleum gas) for each of the 2.6 billion people would emit 275 million tons of CO_2. So a total of 435 million tons of CO_2 accounts for only 2 percent of current global emissions of 26,000 million tons of CO_2.

3. Black carbon, which is formed through the incomplete combustion of fossil fuels, contributes to global warming by absorbing heat in the atmosphere and, when deposited on snow and ice, by reducing their reflective power and accelerating melting. Unlike CO_2, black carbon remains in the atmosphere for only a few days or weeks, so reducing these emissions will have almost immediate mitigation impacts. In addition, black carbon is a major air pollutant and a leading cause of illness and premature death in many developing countries.

4. SEG 2007.

5. Wilbanks and others 2008.

6. McKinsey & Company 2009b.

7. Ebinger and others 2008.

8. The meaning and importance of energy security vary by country depending on its income, energy consumption, energy resources, and trading partners. For many countries dependence on imported oil and natural gas is a source of economic vulnerability and can lead to international tensions. The poorest countries (with per capita income of $300 or less) are particularly vulnerable to fuel price fluctuations, with an average 1.5 percent decrease in GDP associated with every $10 increase in the price of a barrel of oil (World Bank 2009a).

9. Increasing fuel prices by 20 percent increases the costs of generation by 16 percent for gas and 6 percent for coal, while leaving renewable energy practically untouched; see World Economic Forum 2009.

10. IEA 2008b.

11. WRI 2008; see also presentation of historical emissions in the overview.

12. IEA 2008c.

13. IPCC 2007.

14. United Nations 2007.

15. IEA 2008b.

16. Chamon, Mauro, and Okawa 2008.

17. Schipper 2007.

18. Lam and Tam 2002; 2000 U.S. Census, http://en.wikipedia.org/wiki/List_of_U.S._cities _with_most_households_without_a_car (accessed May 2009).

19. Kenworthy 2003.

20. District heating distributes heat for residential and commercial buildings that is supplied at a centralized location by efficient cogeneration plants or large-scale heating boilers.

21. Negative emissions can be achieved by sequestering carbon in terrestrial ecosystems (for example, by planting more forests). It could also be achieved by applying carbon capture and storage to biomass-produced energy.

22. A 450 ppm concentration of greenhouse gases translates into a 40–50 percent chance of temperatures not exceeding 2°C above preindustrial temperatures. Schaeffer and others 2008; Hare and Meinshausen 2006.

23. Tans 2009.

24. Rao and others 2008.

25. Biomass obtained from plants can be a carbon-neutral fuel, because carbon is taken up out of the atmosphere as the plants grow and is then released when the plants are burned as fuel. Biomass-based carbon capture and storage could result in large-scale "negative emissions" by capturing the carbon emitted from biomass combustion.

26. Weyant and others 2009; Knopf and others, forthcoming; Rao and others 2008; Calvin and others, forthcoming.

27. German Advisory Council on Global Change 2008; Wise and others 2009.

28. These five models (MESSAGE, MiniCAM, REMIND, IMAGE, and IEA ETP) are the global leading energy-climate models from Europe and the United States, with a balance of top-down and bottom-up approaches and different mitigation pathways. MESSAGE, developed by the International Institute for Applied Systems Analysis (IIASA), adopts the MESSAGE modeling system, which comprises energy systems engineering optimization model MESSAGE and the top-down macroeconomic equilibrium model MACRO, in addition to forest management model DIMA and agricultural modeling framework AEZ-BLS. This analysis considers the B2 scenarios, because they are intermediary between A2 (a high population growth case) and B1 (a plausible "best case" to achieve low emissions in the absence of vigorous climate policies), characterized by "dynamics as usual" rates of change (Riahi, Grübler, and Nakićenović 2007; Rao and others 2008). MiniCAM, developed at the Pacific Northwest National Laboratory, combines a technologically detailed global energy–economy–agricultural-land-use model with a suite of coupled gas-cycle, climate and ice-melt models (Edmonds and others 2008). REMIND, developed by Potsdam Institute for Climate Impact Research, is an optimal growth model that combines a top-down macroeconomic model with a bottom-up energy model, aiming at welfare maximization (Leimbach and others, forthcoming). IMAGE model, developed

by the Netherlands Environmental Assessment Agency, is an integrated assessment model including the TIMER 2 energy model coupled with the climate policy model FAIR-SiMCaP (Bouwman, Kram, and Goldewijk 2006). The fifth model is the IEA Energy Technology Perspective, a linear programming optimization model based on the MARKAL energy model (IEA 2008b).

29. Mitigation costs include additional capital investment costs, operation and maintenance costs, and fuel costs, compared to the baseline. Rao and others 2008; Knopf and others, forthcoming; Calvin and others, forthcoming; Riahi, Grübler, and Nakićenović 2007; IIASA 2009.

30. Riahi, Grübler, and Nakićenović 2007; IIASA 2009; Knopf and others, forthcoming; IEA 2008c.

31. IEA 2008b; McKinsey & Company 2009a.

32. Knopf and others, forthcoming; Calvin and others, forthcoming; IEA 2008c.

33. Rao and others 2008; IEA 2008b; Mignone and others 2008. This is true in the absence of effective and acceptable geoengineering technology (see chapter 7 for a discussion).

34. IEA 2008b; IEA 2008c; Riahi, Grübler, and Nakićenović 2007; IIASA 2009; Calvin and others, forthcoming.

35. Raupach and others 2007.

36. Shalizi and Lecocq 2009.

37. Philibert 2007.

38. McKinsey & Company 2009b.

39. World Bank 2001.

40. IEA 2008b; Calvin and others, forthcoming; Riahi, Grübler, and Nakićenović 2007; IIASA 2009.

41. IEA 2008b; Calvin and others, forthcoming; Riahi, Grübler, and Nakićenović 2007; IIASA 2009. The size of emission reductions required is critically dependent on the baseline scenarios, which vary greatly among different models.

42. IEA 2008b; Riahi, Grübler, and Nakićenović 2007; IIASA 2009; IAC 2007. It should be noted that land-use changes and methane reductions are also critical measures in nonenergy sectors (see chapter 3) to achieve a 450 ppm CO_2e trajectory, particularly to buy some time in the short term for new technology development.

43. Knopf and others, forthcoming; Rao and others 2008.

44. Rao and others 2008; Calvin and others, forthcoming; Knopf and others, forthcoming.

45. Barrett 2003; Burtraw and others 2005.

46. A molecule of methane, the major component of natural gas, has 21 times more global warming potential than a molecule of CO_2.

47. SEG 2007.

48. IEA 2008b; McKinsey & Company 2009b.

49. de la Torre and others 2008.

50. McKinsey & Company 2009a.

51. The Mexico Low Carbon Study identified nearly half of the total potential for emissions reduction to be from interventions with positive net benefits (Johnson and others 2008).

52. Bosseboeuf and others 2007.

53. IEA 2008b; Worldwatch Institute 2009.

54. UNEP 2003.

55. IPCC 2007.

56. Brown, Southworth, and Stovall 2005; Burton and others 2008. A comprehensive review of empirical experience based on 146 green buildings in 10 countries concluded that green buildings cost on average about 2 percent more to build than conventional buildings and could reduce energy use by a median of 33 percent (Kats 2008).

57. Shalizi and Lecocq 2009.

58. Brown, Southworth, and Stovall 2005.

59. IEA 2008b.

60. Johnson and others 2008.

61. Brown, Southworth, and Stovall 2005; ETAAC 2008.

62. Johnson and others 2008.

63. Sorrell 2008.

64. IEA 2008c.

65. Stern 2007. A small share of the subsidies supports clean energy technologies, such as the $10 billion a year for renewables.

66. World Bank 2008a.

67. Sterner 2007.

68. UNEP 2008.

69. Ezzati and others 2004.

70. Wang and Smith 1999.

71. A carbon tax of $50 a ton of CO_2 translates to a tax on coal-fired power of 4.5 cents a kilowatt-hour, or a tax on petroleum of 45 cents a gallon (12 cents a liter).

72. Philibert 2007.

73. WBCSD 2008.

74. World Energy Council 2008.

75. Goldstein 2007.

76. Meyers, McMahon, and McNeil 2005.

77. Goldstein 2007.

78. An energy-efficient mortgage allows borrowers to qualify for a larger mortgage by including energy savings gleaned from home energy-efficiency measures.

79. ESMAP 2008.

80. World Bank 2008d.

81. Taylor and others 2008.

82. World Bank 2008b.

83. Each lamp costs about $1 under these bulk procurement programs, instead of $3–$5, plus another dollar of transaction costs for distribution, awareness and promotion, monitoring and verification, and testing.

84. ESMAP 2009.

85. Armel 2008.

86. IEA 2008b; Riahi, Grübler, and Nakićenović 2007; IIASA 2009.

87. The costs of wind, geothermal, and hydro power vary greatly depending on resources and sites.

88. IEA 2008a.

89. ESMAP 2006.

90. For example, renewable portfolio standards tend to favor wind energy but discourage solar energy.

91. World Bank 2006.

92. MIT 2003; Keystone Center 2007.

93. MIT 2003.

94. Worldwatch Institute 2008; IEA 2008b.

95. Calvin and others, forthcoming; Riahi, Grübler, and Nakićenović 2007; IIASA 2009.

96. Riahi, Grübler, and Nakićenović 2007; IIASA 2009.

97. Gibbins and Chalmers 2008.

98. Sperling and Gordon 2008.

99. Weyant and others 2009.

References

Armel, K. C. 2008. "Behavior, Energy and Climate Change: A Solutions-Oriented Approach." Paper presented at the Energy Forum, Stanford University, Palo Alto, CA.

Barker, T., I. Bashmakov, L. Bernstein, J. E. Bogner, P. R. Bosch, R. Dave, O. R. Davidson, B. S. Fisher, S. Gupta, K. Halsnaes, B. Heij, S. Khan Ribeiro, S. Kobayashi, M. D. Levine, D. L. Martino, O. Masera, B. Metz, L. A. Meyer, G.-J. Nabuurs, A. Najam, N. Nakićenović, H.-H. Rogner, J. Roy, J. Sathaye, R. Schock, P. Shukla, R. E. H. Sims, P. Smith, D. A. Tirpak, D. Urge-Vorsatz, and D. Zhou. 2007. "Technical Summary." In *Climate Change 2007: Mitigation. Contribution of Working Group III to the Fourth Assessment Report of the Intergovernmental Panel on Climate Change,* ed. B. Metz, O. R. Davidson, P. R. Bosch, R. Dave, and L. A. Meyer. Cambridge, UK: Cambridge University Press.

Barrett, S. 2003. *Environment and Statecraft: The Strategy of Environmental Treaty-Making.* Oxford, UK: Oxford University Press.

Beck, F., and E. Martinot. 2004. "Renewable Energy Policies and Barriers." In *Encyclopedia of Energy,* ed. C. J. Cleveland. Amsterdam: Elsevier.

Bosseboeuf, D., B. Lapillonne, W. Eichhammer, and P. Boonekamp. 2007. *Evaluation of Energy Efficiency in the EU-15: Indicators and Policies.* Paris: ADEME/IEEA.

Bouwman, A. F., T. Kram, and K. K. Goldewijk. 2006. *Integrated Modelling of Global Environmental Change: An Overview of IMAGE 2.4.* Bilthoven: Netherlands Environmental Assessment Agency.

Bowen, A., S. Fankhauser, N. Stern, and D. Zenghelis. 2009. *An Outline of the Case for a "Green" Stimulus.* London: Grantham Research Institute on Climate Change and the Environment and the Centre for Climate Change Economics and Policy.

Brazil Interministerial Committee on Climate Change. 2008. *National Plan on Climate Change.* Brasilia: Government of Brazil.

Brown, M. A., F. Southworth, and T. K. Stovall. 2005. *Towards a Climate-Friendly Built Environment.* Arlington, VA: Pew Center on Global Climate Change.

Burton, R., D. Goldston, G. Crabtree, L. Glicksman, D. Goldstein, D. Greene, D. Kammen, M. Levine, M. Lubell, M. Savitz, D. Sperling, F. Schlachter, J. Scofield, and J. Dawson. 2008. "How America Can Look Within to Achieve Energy Security and Reduce Global Warming." *Reviews of Modern Physics* 80 (4): S1–S109.

Burtraw, D., D. A. Evans, A. Krupnick, K. Palmer, and R. Toth. 2005. "Economics of Pollution Trading for SO_2 and NO_x." Discussion Paper 05-05, Resources for the Future, Washington, DC.

California Energy Commission. 2007a. "2007 Integrated Energy Policy Report." California Energy Commission, Sacramento, CA.

———. 2007b. "Comparative Costs of California Central Station Electricity Generation Technologies." California Energy Commission, Sacramento, CA.

Calvin, K., J. Edmonds, B. Bond-Lamberty, L. Clarke, P. Kyle, S. Smith, A. Thomson, and M. Wise. Forthcoming. "Limiting Climate Change to 450 ppm CO2 Equivalent in the 21st Century." *Energy Economics.*

Chamon, M., P. Mauro, and Y. Okawa. 2008. "Cars: Mass Car Ownership in the Emerging Market Giants." *Economic Policy* 23 (54): 243–96.

Chikkatur, A. 2008. *Policies for Advanced Coal Technologies in India (and China).* Cambridge, MA: Kennedy School of Government, Harvard University.

Clarke, L., J. Edmonds, V. Krey, R. Richels, S. Rose, and M. Tavoni. Forthcoming. "International Climate Policy Architectures: Overview of the EMF 22 International Scenarios." *Energy Economics.*

Dahowski, R. T., X. Li, C. L. Davidson, N. Wei, J. J. Dooley, and R. H. Gentile. 2009. "A Preliminary Cost Curve Assessment of Carbon Dioxide Capture and Storage Potential in China." *Energy Procedia* 1 (1): 2849–56.

de la Torre, A., P. Fajnzylber, and J. Nash. 2008. *Low Carbon, High Growth: Latin American Responses to Climate Change.* Washington, DC: World Bank.

Deutsche Bank Advisors. 2008. *Investing in Climate Change 2009: Necessity And Opportunity In Turbulent Times.* Frankfurt: Deutsche Bank Group.

Dodman, D. 2009. "Blaming Cities for Climate Change? An Analysis of Urban Greenhouse Gas Emissions Inventories." *Environment and Urbanization* 21 (1): 185–201.

Dooley, J. J., R. T. Dahowski, C. L. Davidson, M. A. Wise, N. Gupta, S. H. Kim, and E. L. Malone. 2006. *Carbon Dioxide Capture and Geologic Storage: A Core Element of a Global Energy Technology Strategy to Address Climate Change—A Technology Report from the Second Phase of the Global Energy Technology Strategy Program (GTSP).* College Park, MD: Battelle, Joint Global Change Research Institute.

Ebinger, J., B. Hamso, F. Gerner, A. Lim, and A. Plecas. 2008. "Europe and Central Asia Region: How Resilient Is the Energy Sector to Climate Change?" Background paper for Fay, Block, and Ebinger, 2010, World Bank, Washington, DC.

Edmonds, J., L. Clarke, J. Lurz, and M. Wise. 2008. "Stabilizing CO_2 Concentrations with Incomplete International Cooperation." *Climate Policy* 8 (4): 355–76.

EESI (Environmental and Energy Study Institute). 2008. *Jobs from Renewable Energy and Energy Efficiency.* Washington, DC: EESI.

ESMAP (Energy Sector Management Assistance Program). 2006. *Proceedings of the International Grid-Connected Renewable Energy Policy Forum.* Washington, DC: World Bank.

————. 2008. *An Analytical Compendium of Institutional Frameworks for Energy Efficiency Implementation.* Washington, DC: World Bank.

————. 2009. *Public Procurement of Energy Efficiency Services.* Washington, DC: World Bank.

ETAAC (Economic and Technology Advancement Advisory Committee). 2008. *Technologies and Policies to Consider for Reducing Greenhouse Gas Emissions in California.* Sacramento, CA: ETAAC.

Ezzati, M., A. Lopez, A. Rodgers, and C. Murray, eds. 2004. *Climate Change. Comparative Quantification of Health Risks: Global and Regional Burden of Disease Due to Selected Major Risk Factors, vol. 2.* Geneva: World Health Organization.

Federal Ministry for the Environment, Nature Conservation and Nuclear Safety. 2008. *Renewable Energy Sources in Figures: National and International Development.* Berlin: Federal Ministry for the Environment, Nature Conservation and Nuclear Safety.

German Advisory Council on Global Change. 2008. *World in Transition: Future Bioenergy and Sustainable Land Use.* London: Earthscan.

Gibbins, J., and H. Chalmers. 2008. "Preparing for Global Rollout: A 'Developed Country First' Demonstration Programme for Rapid CCS Deployment." *Energy Policy* 36 (2): 501–07.

Goldstein, D. B. 2007. *Saving Energy, Growing Jobs: How Environmental Protection Promotes Economic Growth, Profitability, Innovation, and Competition.* Berkeley, CA: Bay Tree Publishing.

Government of China. 2008. *China's Policies and Actions for Addressing Climate Change.* Beijing: Information Office of the State Council of the People's Republic of China.

Government of India. 2008. *India National Action Plan on Climate Change.* New Delhi: Prime Minister's Council on Climate Change.

Government of India Planning Commission. 2006. *Integrated Energy Policy: Report of the Expert Committee.* New Delhi: Government of India.

Government of Mexico. 2008. *National Strategy on Climate Change.* Mexico City: Mexico Intersecretarial Commission on Climate Change.

Grübler, A. 2008. "Energy Transitions." *Encyclopedia of Earth*, ed. C. J. Cleveland. Washington, DC: Environmental Information Coalition, National Council for Science and Environment.

Hare, B., and M. Meinshausen. 2006. "How Much Warming Are We Committed to and How Much Can Be Avoided?" *Climatic Change* 75 (1–2): 111–49.

Holloway, S., A. Garg, M. Kapshe, A. Deshpande, A. S. Pracha, S. R. Kahn, M. A. Mahmood, T. N. Singh, K. L. Kirk, and J. Gale. 2008. "An Assessment of the CO_2 Storage Potential of the Indian Subcontinent." *Energy Procedia* 1 (1): 2607–13.

Hughes, J. E., C. R. Knittel, and D. Sperling. 2008. "Evidence of a Shift in the Short-Run Price Elasticity of Gasoline Demand." *Energy Journal* 29 (1): 113–34.

IAC (InterAcademy Council). 2007. *Lighting the Way: Toward a Sustainable Energy Future.* IAC Secretariat: The Netherlands.

IEA (International Energy Agency). 2007. *Renewables for Heating and Cooling: Untapped*

Potential. Paris: IEA and Renewable Energy Technology Development.

———. 2008a. *Empowering Variable Renewables: Options for Flexible Electricity Systems.* Paris: IEA.

———. 2008b. *Energy Technology Perspective 2008: Scenarios and Strategies to 2050.* Paris: IEA.

———. 2008c. *World Energy Outlook 2008.* Paris: IEA.

IIASA (International Institute for Applied Systems Analysis). 2009. "GGI Scenario Database." IIASA, Laxenburg, Austria.

IPCC (Intergovernmental Panel on Climate Change). 2007. "Summary for Policymakers." In *Climate Change 2007: Mitigation. Contribution of Working Group III to the Fourth Assessment Report of the Intergovernmental Panel on Climate Change,* ed. B. Metz, O. R. Davidson, P. R. Bosch, R. Dave, and L. A. Meyer. Cambridge, UK: Cambridge University Press.

Johnson, T., F. Liu, C. Alatorre, and Z. Romo. 2008. "Mexico Low-Carbon Study—México: Estudio Para la Disminución de Emisiones de Carbono (MEDEC)." World Bank, Washington, DC.

Kats, G. 2008. *Greening Buildings and Communities: Costs and Benefits.* London: Good Energies.

Kenworthy, J. 2003. "Transport Energy Use and Greenhouse Gases in Urban Passenger Transport Systems: A Study of 84 Global Cities." Paper presented at the third International Conference of the Regional Government Network for Sustainable Development, Fremantle, Australia.

Keystone Center. 2007. *Nuclear Power Joint Fact-Finding.* Keystone, CO: The Keystone Center.

Knopf, B., O. Edenhofer, T. Barker, N. Bauer, L. Baumstark, B. Chateau, P. Criqui, A. Held, M. Isaac, M. Jakob, E. Jochem, A. Kitous, S. Kypreos, M. Leimbach, B. Magné, S. Mima, W. Schade, S. Scrieciu, H. Turton, and D. van Vuuren. Forthcoming. "The Economics of Low Stabilisation: Implications for Technological Change and Policy." In *Making Climate Change Work for Us,* ed. M. Hulme and H. Neufeldt. Cambridge, UK: Cambridge University Press.

Lam, W. H. K., and M.-L. Tam. 2002. "Reliability of Territory-Wide Car Ownership Estimates in Hong Kong." *Journal of Transport Geography* 10 (1): 51–60.

Leimbach, M., N. Bauer, L. Baumstark, and O. Edenhofer. Forthcoming. "Mitigation Costs in a Globalized World." *Environmental Modeling and Assessment.*

Lin, J. 2007. *Energy in China: Myths, Reality, and Challenges.* San Francisco, CA: Energy Foundation.

Lin, J., N. Zhou, M. Levine, and D. Fridley. 2006. *Achieving China's Target for Energy Intensity Reduction in 2010: An Exploration of Recent Trends and Possible Future Scenarios.* Berkeley, CA: Lawrence Berkeley National Laboratories, University of California–Berkeley.

McKinsey & Company. 2009a. *Pathways to a Low-carbon Economy: Version 2 of the Global Greenhouse Gas Abatement Cost Curve.* McKinsey & Company.

———. 2009b. "Promoting Energy Efficiency in the Developing World." *McKinsey Quarterly,* February.

Meyers, S., J. McMahon, and M. McNeil. 2005. *Realized and Prospective Impacts of U.S. Energy Efficiency Standards for Residential Appliances: 2004 Update.* Berkeley, CA: Lawrence Berkeley National Laboratory, University of California–Berkeley.

Mignone, B. K., R. H. Socolow, J. L. Sarmiento, and M. Oppenheimer. 2008. "Atmospheric Stabilization and the Timing of Carbon Mitigation." *Climatic Change* 88 (3–4): 251–65.

MIT (Massachusetts Institute of Technology). 2003. *The Future of Nuclear Power: An Interdisciplinary MIT Study.* Cambridge, MA: MIT Press.

Neij, L. 2007. "Cost Development of Future Technologies for Power Generation: A Study Based on Experience Curves and Complementary Bottom-Up Assessments." *Energy Policy* 36 (6): 2200–11.

Nemet, G. 2006. "Beyond the Learning Curve: Factors Influencing Cost Reductions in Photovoltaics." *Energy Policy* 34 (17): 3218–32.

NRC (National Research Council). 2008. *The National Academies Summit on America's Energy Future: Summary of a Meeting.* Washington, DC: National Academies Press.

NRDC (National Resources Defense Council). 2007. *The Next Generation of Hybrid Cars: Plug-in Hybrids Can Help Reduce Global Warming and Slash Oil Dependency.* Washington, DC: NRDC.

Pew Center. 2008a. "Climate Change Mitigation Measures in India." International Brief 2, Washington, DC.

———. 2008b. "Climate Change Mitigation Measures in South Africa." Pew Center on Global Climate Change International Brief 3, Arlington, VA.

Philibert, C. 2007. *Technology Penetration and Capital Stock Turnover: Lessons from IEA Scenario Analysis.* Paris: Organisation for Economic Co-operation and Development and International Energy Agency.

Project Catalyst. 2009. *Towards a Global Climate Agreement: Project Catalyst.* Synthesis briefing paper, ClimateWorks Foundation.

Pryor, S., R. Barthelmie, and E. Kjellstrom. 2005. "Potential Climate Change Impacts on Wind Energy Resources in Northern Europe: Analyses Using a Regional Climate Model." *Climate Dynamics* 25 (7–8): 815–35.

Rao, S., K. Riahi, E. Stehfest, D. van Vuuren, C. Cho, M. den Elzen, M. Isaac, and J. van Vliet. 2008. *IMAGE and MESSAGE Scenarios Limiting GHG Concentration to Low Levels.* Laxenburg, Austria: International Institute for Applied Systems Analysis.

Raupach, M. R., G. Marland, P. Ciais, C. Le Quere, J. G. Canadell, G. Klepper, and C. B. Field. 2007. "Global and Regional Drivers of Accelerating CO_2 Emissions." *Proceedings of the National Academy of Sciences* 104 (24): 10288–93.

REN 21. 2008. *Renewables 2007 Global Status Report.* Paris and Washington: Renewable Energy Policy Network for the 21st Century Secretariat and Worldwatch Institute.

Riahi, K., A. Grübler, and N. Nakićenović. 2007. "Scenarios of Long-Term Socio-Economic and Environmental Development under Climate Stabilization." *Technological Forecasting and Social Change* 74 (7): 887–935.

Rogers, C., M. Messenger, and S. Bender. 2005. *Funding and Savings for Energy Efficiency Programs for Program Years 2000 through 2004.* Sacramento, CA: California Energy Commission.

Rokityanskiy, D., P. C. Benitez, F. Kraxner, I. McCallum, M. Obersteiner, E. Rametsteiner, and Y. Yamagata. 2006. "Geographically Explicit Global Modeling of Land-Use Change, Carbon Sequestration, and Biomass Supply." *Technological Forecasting and Social Change* 74 (7): 1057–82.

Roland-Holst, D. 2008. *Energy Efficiency, Innovation, and Job Creation in California.* Berkeley, CA: Center for Energy, Resources, and Economic Sustainability, University of California–Berkeley.

Rosenfeld, A. H. 2007. "California's Success in Energy Efficiency and Climate Change: Past and Future." Paper presented at the Electricite de France, Paris.

Schaeffer, M., T. Kram, M. Meinshausen, D. P. van Vuuren, and W. L. Hare. 2008. "Near-Linear Cost Increase to Reduce Climate-Change Risk." *Proceedings of the National Academy of Sciences* 105 (52): 20621–26.

Schipper, L. 2007. *Automobile Fuel, Economy and CO_2 Emissions in Industrialized Countries: Troubling Trends through 2005/6.* Washington, DC: EMBARQ, the World Resources Institute Center for Sustainable Transport.

SEG (Scientific Expert Group on Climate Change). 2007. *Confronting Climate Change: Avoiding the Unmanageable and Managing the Unavoidable.* Washington, DC: Sigma Xi and United Nations Foundation.

Shalizi, Z., and F. Lecocq. 2009. "Economics of Targeted Mitigation Programs in Sectors with Long-lived Capital Stock." Policy Research Working Paper 5063, World Bank, Washington, DC.

Socolow, R. 2006. "Stabilization Wedges: Mitigation Tools for the Next Half-Century." Paper presented at the World Bank Energy Week, Washington, DC.

Sorrell, S. 2008. "The Rebound Effect: Mechanisms, Evidence and Policy Implications." Paper presented at the Electricity Policy Workshop, Toronto.

Sperling, D., and D. Gordon. 2008. *Two Billion Cars: Driving Towards Sustainability.* New York: Oxford University Press.

Stern, N. 2007. *The Economics of Climate Change: The Stern Review.* Cambridge, UK: Cambridge University Press.

Sterner, T. 2007. "Fuel Taxes: An Important Instrument for Climate Policy." *Energy Policy* 35: 3194–3202.

Sudarshan, A., and J. Sweeney. Forthcoming. "Deconstructing the 'Rosenfeld Curve.'" *Energy Journal.*

Tans, P. 2009. "Trends in Atmospheric Carbon Dioxide." National Oceanic and Atmospheric Administration, Boulder, CO.

Taylor, R. P., C. Govindarajalu, J. Levin, A. S. Meyer, and W. A. Ward. 2008. *Financing Energy Efficiency: Lessons from Brazil, China, India and Beyond.* Washington, DC: World Bank.

UNEP (United Nations Environment Programme). 2003. "Energy and Cities: Sustainable Building and Construction." Paper presented at the UNEP Governing Council Side Event, Osaka.

———. 2008. *Reforming Energy Subsidies: Opportunities to Contribute to the Climate Change Agenda.* Nairobi: UNEP Division of Technology, Industry and Economics.

United Nations. 2007. *State of the World Population 2007: Unleashing the Potential of Urban Growth.* New York: United Nations Population Fund.

van Vuuren, D. P., E. Stehfest, M. den Elzen, J. van Vliet, and M. Isaac. Forthcoming. "Exploring Scenarios that Keep Greenhouse Gas Radiative Forcing Below 3 W/m^2 in 2100 in the IMAGE Model." *Energy Economics.*

Wang, T., and J. Watson. 2009. *China's Energy Transition: Pathways for Low Carbon Development.* Falmer and Brighton, UK: Sussex Energy Group and Tyndall Centre for Climate Change Research.

Wang, X., and K. R. Smith. 1999. "Near-term Benefits of Greenhouse Gas Reduction: Health Impacts in China." *Environmental Science and Technology* 33 (18): 3056–61.

WBCSD (World Business Council for Sustainable Development). 2008. *Power to Change: A Business Contribution to a Low Carbon Economy.* Geneva: WBCSD.

Weber, C. L., G. P. Peters, D. Guan, and K. Hubacek. 2008. "The Contribution of Chinese Exports to Climate Change." *Energy Policy* 36 (9): 3572–77.

Weyant, J., C. Azar, M. Kainuma, J. Kejun, N. Nakićenović, P. R. Shukla, E. La Rovere, and G. Yohe. 2009. *Report of 2.6 Versus 2.9 Watts/m^2 RCPP Evaluation Panel.* Geneva: Intergovernmental Panel on Climate Change.

Wilbanks, T. J., V. Bhatt, D. E. Bilello, S. R. Bull, J. Ekmann, W. C. Horak, Y. J. Huang, M. D. Levine, M. J. Sale, D. K. Schmalzer, and M. J. Scott. 2008. *Effects of Climate Change on Energy Production and Use in the United States.* Washington, DC: U.S. Climate Change Science Program.

Wise, M. A., L. Clarke, K. Calvin, A. Thomson, B. Bond-Lamberty, R. Sands, S. Smith, T. Janetos, and J. Edmonds. 2009. "The 2000 Billion Ton Carbon Gorilla: Implication of Terrestrial Carbon Emissions for a LCS." Paper presented at the Japan Low-Carbon Society Scenarios Toward 2050 Project Symposium, Tokyo.

Wiser, R., and M. Bolinger. 2008. *Annual Report on U.S. Wind Power Installation, Cost, and Performance Trends: 2007.* Washington, DC: U.S. Department of Energy, Energy Efficiency and Renewable Energy.

World Bank. 2001. *China: Opportunities to Improve Energy Efficiency in Buildings.* Washington, DC: World Bank Asia Alternative Energy Programme and Energy & Mining Unit, East Asia and Pacific Region.

———. 2006. *Renewable Energy Toolkit: A Resource for Renewable Energy Development.* Wahington, DC: World Bank.

———. 2008a. *An Evaluation of World Bank Win-Win Energy Policy Reforms.* Washington, DC: World Bank.

———. 2008b. *Energy Efficiency in Eastern Europe and Central Asia.* Washington, DC: World Bank.

———. 2008c. *South Asia Climate Change Strategy.* Washington, DC: World Bank.

———. 2008d. *The Development of China's ESCO Industry, 2004–2007.* Washington, DC: World Bank.

———. 2008e. *World Development Indicators 2008.* Washington, DC: World Bank.

———. 2008f. *World Development Report 2009: Reshaping Economic Geography.* Washington, DC: World Bank.

———. 2009a. *Energizing Climate-Friendly Development: World Bank Group Progress on Renewable Energy and Energy Efficiency in Fiscal 2008.* Washington, DC: World Bank.

———. 2009b. "World Bank Urban Strategy." World Bank. Washington, DC.

———. 2009c. *World Development Indicators 2009.* Washington, DC: World Bank.

World Economic Forum. 2009. *Green Investing: Towards a Clean Energy Infrastructure.* Geneva: World Economic Forum.

World Energy Council. 2008. *Energy Efficiency Policies around the World: Review and Evaluation.* London: World Energy Council.

Worldwatch Institute. 2008. *State of the World 2008: Innovations for a Sustainable Economy.* New York: W.W. Norton & Company.

———. 2009. *State of the World 2009: Into a Warming World.* New York: W.W. Norton & Company.

WRI (World Resources Institute). 2008. "Climate Analysis Indicators Tool (CAIT)." Washington, DC.

Yates, M., M. Heller, and L. Yeung. 2009. *Solar Thermal: Not Just Smoke and Mirrors.* New York: Merrill Lynch.

Zhang, X. 2008. *Observations on Energy Technology Research, Development and Deployment in China.* Beijing: Tsinghua University Institute of Energy, Environment and Economy.

united nations climate change conference

Nusa Dua - Bali, Indonesia, 3-14 December 2007

CHAPTER 5

Integrating Development into the Global Climate Regime

The past two decades have seen the creation and evolution of an international climate regime, with the United Nations Framework Convention on Climate Change (UNFCCC) and the Kyoto Protocol as the main pillars (box 5.1). Kyoto set binding international limits on the greenhouse gas emissions of developed countries. It created a carbon market to drive private investment and lower the cost of emission reductions. And it prompted countries to prepare national climate-change strategies.

But the existing global regime has major limitations. It has failed to substantially curb emissions, which have increased by 25 percent since Kyoto was negotiated.[1] It has delivered only very limited support to developing countries. Its Clean Development Mechanism (CDM) has so far brought little transformational change in countries' overall development strategies (see chapter 6 on the strengths and weaknesses of the CDM). The Global Environment Facility has invested $2.7 billion in climate projects,[2] well short of the flows

needed. The global regime has so far failed to spur countries to cooperate on research and development or to mobilize significant funding for the technology transfer and deployment needed for low-carbon development (see chapter 7). Aside from encouraging poor countries to prepare National Adaptation Programs of Action, it has delivered little concrete support for adaptation efforts. And the Adaptation Fund, slow to get started, falls far short of the projected needs (see chapter 6).

In 2007 the Bali Action Plan launched negotiations to achieve an "agreed outcome" during the UNFCCC 15th session in Copenhagen in 2009. These negotiations present an opportunity to strengthen the climate regime and address its shortcomings.

Building the climate regime: Transcending the tensions between climate and development[3]

If we are to meaningfully address climate change, there is no option but to integrate development concerns and climate change. The climate problem arises from the joint evolution of economic growth and greenhouse gas emissions. An effective regime must thus provide the incentives to reconsider trajectories of industrialization and unravel the ties that have bound development to carbon. However, for ethical and practical reasons, this rethinking must include meeting development aspirations and forging an equitable climate regime.

Until recently, climate change was not seen as an opportunity to rethink industrial

Key messages

A global problem on the scale of climate change requires international coordination. Nevertheless, implementation depends on actions within countries. Therefore, an effective international climate regime must integrate development concerns, breaking free of the environment-*versus*-equity dichotomy. A multitrack framework for climate action, with different goals or policies for developed countries and developing countries, may be one way to move forward; this framework would need to consider the process for defining and measuring success. The international climate regime will also need to support the integration of adaptation into development.

BOX 5.1 *The climate regime today*

The United Nations Framework Convention on Climate Change (UNFCCC), which was adopted in 1992 and entered into force in 1994, set an ultimate objective of stabilizing atmospheric concentrations of greenhouse gases at levels that would prevent "dangerous" human interference with the climate system. It divided countries into three main groups with different types of commitments:

Annex I parties include the industrial countries that were members of the OECD (Organisation for Economic Co-operation and Development) in 1992, plus countries with economies in transition (the EIT Parties), including the Russian Federation, the Baltic states, and several Central and Eastern European states. They commit to adopt climate-change policies and measures with the aim of reducing their greenhouse gas emissions to 1990 levels by the year 2000.

Annex II parties consist of the OECD members of Annex I, but not the EIT Parties. They are required to provide financial resources to enable developing countries to undertake emissions reduction activities under the UNFCCC and to help them adapt to adverse effects of climate change. In addition, they have to "take all practicable steps" to promote the development and transfer of environmentally friendly technologies to EIT parties and developing countries.

Non–Annex I parties are mostly developing countries. They undertake general obligations to formulate and implement national programs on mitigation and adaptation.

The ultimate decision-making body of the convention is its Conference of the Parties, which meets every year and reviews the implementation of the convention, adopts decisions to further develop the convention's rules, and negotiates substantive new commitments.

The Kyoto Protocol supplements and strengthens the convention. Adopted in 1997, it entered into force in February 2005, with 184 parties as of January 14, 2009.

At the heart of the protocol lie its legally binding emissions targets for Annex I parties, which have individual emissions targets, decided in Kyoto after intensive negotiation.

In addition to emissions targets for Annex I parties, the Kyoto Protocol contains a set of general commitments (mirroring those in the UNFCCC) that apply to all parties, such as

- Taking steps to improve the quality of emissions data,
- Mounting national mitigation and adaptation programs,
- Promoting environmentally friendly technology transfer,
- Cooperating in scientific research and international climate observation networks, and
- Supporting education, training, public awareness, and capacity-building initiatives.

The protocol broke new ground with three innovative mechanisms—Joint Implementation, the Clean Development Mechanism, and emissions trading[a]—designed to boost the cost-effectiveness of climate-change mitigation by opening ways for parties to cut emissions, or enhance carbon sinks, more cheaply abroad than at home.

The Bali Action Plan, adopted in 2007 by the parties to the UNFCCC, launched a comprehensive process to enable the full, effective, and sustained implementation of the convention through long-term cooperative action, now, up to, and beyond 2012 in order to reach an agreed outcome at the UNFCCC's 15th session in Copenhagen in December 2009.

The Bali Action Plan centered negotiations on four main building blocks—mitigation, adaptation, technology, and financing. Parties also agreed that the negotiations should address a shared vision for long-term cooperative action, including a global goal for emission reductions.

Source: Reproduced from UNFCCC 2005; UNFCCC decision 1/CP.13, http://unfccc.int/resource/docs/2007/cop13/eng/06a01.pdf (accessed July 6, 2009).

a. Parties with commitments under the Kyoto Protocol have accepted targets for limiting or reducing emissions. Joint Implementation allows a country with a target to implement projects counted toward meeting their own target, but conducted in other countries that also have targets. The Clean Development Mechanism (CDM) allows a country with commitments to implement an emission-reduction project in developing countries that do not have targets. Emissions trading allows countries that have emission units to spare—emissions permitted them but not used—to sell this excess capacity to countries that are over their targets. (Adapted from http://unfccc.int/kyoto_protocol/mechanisms/items/1673.php, accessed August 5, 2009.)

development. The climate debate was isolated from mainstream decision making on financing, investment, technology, and institutional change. That time has substantially, if not entirely, passed. Awareness of climate change among leaders and publics has grown to the level that there is now readiness to integrate climate change into development decision making.

Turning this readiness into an effective climate regime requires simultaneously addressing multiple goals involving equity, climate, and social and economic development. It would be naïve to suggest that there are no tensions among these objectives. Indeed, the very perception of tradeoffs can prove a potent political barrier to integrating climate change and development. Differences in perceptions and conceptual frameworks across high-income and developing countries can and do get in the way of a meaningful discussion on how climate action can be integrated with development. Many of these tensions emerge along North-South lines.

To ensure a climate regime that speaks to development concerns, it is useful to identify and engage opposing perspectives and then seek to transcend them. This chapter discusses four points of tension between a climate perspective and a development perspective: environment and equity; burden sharing and opportunistic early action; a predictable climate outcome and an unpredictable development process; and conditionality in financing and ownership. These points of tension are characterizations using broad brush strokes to bring out the disagreements and their possible resolution, knowing that in practice individual country positions, in both the North and the South, are far more nuanced than the extremes described here. The second part of the chapter explores alternative approaches to integrating developing countries into the international architecture.

Mitigating climate change: Environment and equity

Since its beginning the climate regime has framed both equity and environmental goals as core elements. Over time, though, the articulation of these goals has turned their complementarities into opposition, deadlocking the progress of climate negotiations. Equity and environment have been increasingly perceived as competing ways of thinking about the problem, with countries arrayed behind these positions along predictable North-South lines.

For much of the past two decades, climate change has been construed mainly as an environmental problem. This perspective follows directly from the underlying science: greenhouse gases are accumulating in the atmosphere and causing climate impacts because of growing anthropogenic emissions, combined with limits to the ocean's and biosphere's ability to absorb greenhouse gases. In this perspective the problem is one of global collective action, and the instrument of choice is negotiated commitments for absolute reductions in emissions.

This strict focus on the environment forced the rise of a competing perspective, which construes climate change as essentially a problem of equity. Adherents to this position agree that there are environmental limits, but they see the problem as wealthy countries disproportionately occupying the finite ecological space available. In this perspective, allocation principles based on equity, such as those centered on per capita and historical emissions, should provide the basis of a fair climate regime.

Equity and environmental goals have thus become polar elements of the debate. High-income countries argue that newly industrializing countries are already large emitters and will contribute an increasing share of emissions in the future—hence the need for absolute emission reductions.[4] Industrializing and developing economies view a regime based on negotiated absolute reductions as locking in unequal emissions in perpetuity, a situation that is not viable for them. Concerns about equity have been heightened by evidence that emissions from many high-income countries have increased over the past two decades, since the initiation of climate negotiations. As the urgency of finding a solution has increased, many developing countries, particularly the large, rapidly industrializing countries, fear that attention and responsibility for mitigating emissions will be increasingly displaced onto them. The notion of "major emitters," including the large, rapidly industrializing countries, as primary drivers of the problem feeds this perception.

An effective and legitimate global climate regime will have to find a way around these opposing framings—and speak to both perspectives. To begin with, global negotiations need to be approached in a spirit of pluralism. Given the history of entrenched politics and the kernel of truth in each, neither the environmental nor the equity framing of the climate problem can, practically, be an absolute guide to negotiations, even though both are essential. Hybrid approaches seek to relocate discussions within a development frame and could usefully broaden the debate. One approach seeks to reformulate the problem around the right to develop rather than the right to emit and identifies country "responsibility" and "capacity" to act on climate change.[5] Another strand of thinking suggests the articulation of "sustainable development policies and measures" (meaning measures to place a country on a low-carbon trajectory that are fully compatible with domestic development priorities) by developing countries, combined with absolute reductions by high-income countries.[6] While the specifics of any proposal may be debated, the climate regime would be well served by a politics of pragmatism built around the careful integration of climate and development.

But for developing countries to believe that integrating climate and development is not a slippery slope toward ever greater mitigation responsibility being displaced onto them, it will be necessary to have the backstop of an equity principle in the global regime. One example might be a long-term goal of per capita emissions across countries converging to a band; this principle could serve as a moral compass and a means of ensuring that the regime does not lock in grossly unequal emission futures. Again, while the specifics may be debated, a legitimate climate regime will need anchoring in some form of equity principle.

Given the North's historical responsibility for stocks of greenhouse gases, already supported by strong statements in the framework convention, it is hard to imagine an effective global regime that is not led by early and strong mitigation action by the developed world. The combination of early action by the North, a robust equity principle, and a spirit of pluralism in negotiations could provide the basis for transcending the environment-equity dichotomy that has plagued global climate negotiations.

Burden sharing and opportunistic early action

The environmental and equity constructions of the climate challenge share a common assumption that the challenge is a problem of burden sharing. The burden sharing language suggests that climate mitigation is going to impose considerable costs on national economies. Because current infrastructure and economic production are built on the assumption of costless carbon, building economies and societies around costly carbon will impose considerable adjustment costs. The difficult North-South politics around climate is closely tied to the burden sharing assumption, because environment and equity constructions of the problem imply very different ways of sharing a burden and therefore different political costs.

Recognizing how burden sharing contributes to entrenched politics, advocates for early climate mitigation have sought to develop a counternarrative of climate mitigation as an opportunity to be seized rather

than a burden to be shared. They point out that the history of environmental regulation is littered with examples of responses to regulation that have proved less costly than feared—acid rain and ozone depletion are two well-known examples.[7] Even if climate mitigation imposes costs in the aggregate, there are relative advantages to first movers in mitigation technologies. First movers will be well placed to seize new markets that emerge as carbon is priced. Many climate-mitigation opportunities—notably energy efficiency—can be harvested at negative economic cost and bring other co-benefits for development. And in the medium term, moving first allows societies to cultivate the positive feedbacks among institutions, markets, and technology as their economies are reoriented around a low-carbon future. In its strongest variant the opportunity narrative is one of seizing advantage by moving first on climate mitigation, independent of what other countries do.

But it is important not to overplay this narrative. Conceptually the tightness of the weave between the climate and industrial development suggests that adjustment costs are likely to be substantial—and that past comparisons such as acid rain and ozone depletion are of limited relevance. Neither the stock of industrial capital built around costless carbon nor the dependence on endowments of fossil fuels can simply be wished away. Skeptics will note that, so far, the narrative of climate opportunity has not been matched by concrete actions by any major high-income country to enable developing countries to realize this opportunity.

Moreover, even if countries believe the language of opportunity, they are likely to act strategically by maintaining a public stance based on burden sharing to win a better negotiating deal, even while privately organizing to seize available opportunities. So, opportunity-seizing is unlikely to entirely dethrone burden sharing as a dominant narrative in the short run—it provides only a limited opening to change the entrenched politics of climate change.

It is important, however, that this limited opening be seized. The prospect of a silver lining of economic opportunity to the climate cloud could tip the political balance toward getting started with the hard task of turning economies and societies toward a low-carbon future. Getting started with no prospect of an upside is a much harder sell. And starting is important, because it creates constituencies with a stake in a low-carbon future, begins the process of experimentation, and increases the costs to others of being left behind, thus generating a pull effect. That the language of opportunity seizing is not watertight does not negate its potential to counter burden sharing as the prominent construct in the climate debate (box 5.2).

Predictable climate outcome and unpredictable development process

Burden sharing is linked to the environment framing of the climate problem, from which the need emerges to set absolute reduction targets to avoid catastrophic climate change. Drawing on the recommendations of the Intergovernmental Panel on Climate Change (IPCC), some countries and advocates have urged a global goal of restricting global temperature rise to not more than 2°C, which will require reducing global emissions by at least 50 percent (the lower bound of the IPCC's range of 50–85 percent) by 2050 from their 1990 levels.[8] In response several high-income countries have submitted proposed national reduction targets (for 2050 and in some cases for interim years).[9] The underlying idea is to measure and benchmark progress toward meeting the climate challenge.

A global goal is particularly useful as a way to assess the commitment offers of the high-income world against the magnitude of the challenge. But, as discussed in chapter 4, simple arithmetic suggests that a global goal also carries implications for developing countries; the gap in reductions between the global goal and the sum of high-income country targets will have to be met by the developing world. Several developing countries therefore resist this approach as a back door into forcing commitments by the developing world or insist on a simultaneous discussion of an allocation framework.[10] This resistance stems less from opposition to the global goal and more from a sense that the language of predictability will prove a slippery slope toward translating all actions into absolute emission reductions, leading to an implicit cap on developing-country emissions.

The climate challenge looks quite different through a development lens. Building on a rich and complex intellectual history, a recent strand of development thinking focuses on institutions and institutional inertia in development (chapter 8). In this perspective formal "rules of the game" and informal norms, including those embedded in culture, are important determinants of economic incentives, institutional transformation, technological innovation, and social change. Politics is central to this process, as different actors organize to change institutions and transform incentives. Also central are the mental maps of what actors can bring to their engagement with development processes. Three key ideas are relevant here. First, development is a process of change, largely driven from below. Second, history and the past patterns of institutions matter a great deal, so common templates are of only limited use—one size does not fit all. Third, this characterization of change applies equally to high-income countries, even though the challenge of imperfect and incomplete institutions appears less daunting, and top-down policy and price signals are considered to be the main drivers of change.

In this perspective the task of low-carbon development in developing countries is a long-term process, one less amenable to being driven from above by targets and timetables than in high-income countries. Instead, changes in the direction of low-carbon development can be brought about only by internalizing this objective in the larger development processes in which bureaucracies, entrepreneurs, civil society, and citizens are already engaged. In other words, climate has to be integrated with development. An example of this approach might be rethinking urban planning in a low-carbon future, ensuring the colocation of work and residence to reduce the need for transport, designing more sustainable buildings, and devising solutions to public transport (see chapter 4). This contrasts with a target-led short-run approach, which might emphasize more fuel-efficient cars within existing urban infrastructures.

As highlighted in chapter 4, both approaches are necessary, one to yield results in the short run and the other to permit the necessary long-run transformation. The

BOX 5.2   *Some proposals for burden sharing*

Contraction and convergence

The contraction-and-convergence approach assigns every human being an equal entitlement to greenhouse gas emissions. All countries would thus move toward the same per capita emissions. Total emissions would contract over time, and per capita emissions would converge on a single figure. The actual convergence value, the path toward convergence, and the time when it is to be reached would all be negotiable.

Greenhouse Development Rights

The Greenhouse Development Rights Framework argues that those struggling against poverty should not be expected to focus their limited resources on averting climate change. Instead it argues for wealthier countries with greater capacity to pay and more responsibility for the existing stock of emissions to take on the bulk of the costs of a global mitigation and adaptation program.

The novelty of the Greenhouse Development Rights approach is that it defines and calculates national obligations on the basis of individual rather than national income. A country's capacity (resources to pay without sacrificing necessities) and responsibility (contribution to the climate problem) are thus determined by the amount of national income or emissions above a "development threshold." This is estimated at about $20 a person a day ($7,500 a person a year), with emissions assumed proportional to income. The index of capacity and responsibility under the Greenhouse Development Rights Framework would assign to the United States 29 percent of the global emission reductions needed by 2020 for 2°C stabilization, followed by the European Union (23 percent) and China (10 percent). India's share of global emission reductions would be around 1 percent.

Brazil proposal: historical responsibility

In 1997, in the negotiations leading to the Kyoto Protocol, the government of Brazil proposed that "historical responsibility" be used as the basis for apportioning the burden of mitigation among Annex I countries (meaning the countries with firm targets). The proposal sought to address "the relationship between the emissions of greenhouse gases by Parties over a period of time and the effect of such emissions in terms of climate change, as measured by the increase in global mean surface temperature." The notable feature of the proposal was the method used to distribute emission reduction burdens among countries, according to which an Annex I country's emission targets should be set on the basis of that country's relative responsibility for the global temperature rise.

The proposal included a "policy maker model" for determining emission targets for countries and suggested the need for an "agreed climate-change model" for estimating a country's contribution to global temperature increase.

Carbon budget

A research group at the Chinese Academy of Social Sciences argues that

- Greenhouse gas emission rights are a human right that ensures survival and development. Equality means ensuring equality among individuals, not among nations.
- The crux of promoting equality between individuals is to ensure the rights of the current generation. Controlling population growth is a policy option to promote sustainable development and to slow climate change.
- Given the wealth accumulated during development, which was accompanied by greenhouse gas emissions,

equality today includes equity acquired in historical, current, and future development.

- Giving priority to basic needs means that the allocation of emission entitlements should reflect differences in natural environments.

If only CO_2 emissions from fossil fuels are considered and emissions peak in 2015 and fall to 50 percent of 2005 levels by 2050, the annual per capita carbon budget for 1900 to 2050 would 2.33 metric tons of CO_2. Initial carbon budget allocations for each country should be proportional to base-year population, with adjustments for natural factors such as climate, geography, and natural resources.

Developing nations, despite often being historically under budget and therefore having the right to grow and to create emissions, have no choice but to transfer their carbon budgets to developed nations in order to cover the historical excesses of developed nations and ensure basic future needs.

This historical debt amounts to some 460 gigatons of CO_2. At the current cost of $13 a ton, the value of this debt would be $59 trillion—substantially more than is currently provided to developing countries in financial assistance to combat climate change.

Continued high per capita emissions in high-income countries could partly be offset through the carbon market. But progressive carbon taxes are likely to be necessary, with the excess carried over to the next round of commitments.

Sources: Contraction and convergence: Meyer 2001. Greenhouse development rights: Baer, Athanasiou, and Kartha 2007. Brazil: submission from the government of Brazil to the UNFCCC in 1997 (http://unfccc.int/cop3/resource/docs/1997/agbm/misc01a3.htm, accessed July 7, 2009). Carbon budget: reproduced from Jiahua and Ying 2008.

two perspectives are, thus, complementary. A climate-oriented perspective can throw up a series of short-term policy prescriptions that can, in substantial measure, be implemented across countries with minimal adjustment while also yielding development benefits. Many of them are in the realm of energy efficiency, such as improved building

codes, appliance standards, and the like.[11] And these approaches can be embedded in a longer-term process aimed at rethinking development through a climate lens.

But concern with the short term and the predictable should not crowd out or exclude longer-term but more fundamental transformations toward low-carbon development.

And there are risks that overly enthusiastic benchmarking of developing-country efforts to a long-term global target will do just that. As described above, many transformational measures are not subject to top-down planning and so are not subject to prediction and easy measurement. Indeed, an insistence on measurement and predictability will encourage only modest measures to minimize risks of noncompliance. In addition, any hint of an implicit target reached by subtracting high-income-country emissions from a global target encourages strategic gaming; under these conditions, countries have an incentive to persuade the international community that little can be done at home and only at high cost.

Reconciling these two perspectives may require a nested two-track approach for the short-to-medium term, at least until 2020. Consonant with the UNFCCC principle of "common but differentiated responsibility," high-income countries could agree to prioritize predictability of action aimed at carbon mitigation, to provide some assurance that the world is on track to meet the climate challenge. Here, short- and medium-term targets, for 2020 and 2030, are as significant as a target for 2050, because carbon reductions are more useful now than later and because they can win the confidence of the developing world. The developing countries could follow a second track, as discussed later in this chapter, that sets priorities for reorienting their economies and societies to low-carbon development.

These approaches, it should be clear, need not and should not compromise living standards—they should instead aggressively explore the co-benefits of development for climate. Nested within this longer-term objective, developing countries could agree to short-term "best-practice" measures—notably for energy efficiency—that bring both developmental and climate benefits. Agreeing to aggressively pursue these measures would provide some reassurance that some predictable climate gains will be realized in the short term.

The problem of financing—conditionality and ownership

The foregoing tensions are closely tied to the problematic issue of financing climate actions. There is broad agreement that high-income countries will transfer some funds to the developing world to assist specifically with adaptation—and provide separate funding for mitigation. But questions remain about how much financing will be available, its source, how its expenditure will be controlled, and on what basis it will be monitored; those questions are discussed here.

Governments of high-income countries are anxious that any funds provided be well targeted to climate mitigation or adaptation and produce real and measurable reductions (in emissions or vulnerability). To this end they envision having oversight of these funds, particularly in the current tight fiscal climate, where domestic constituencies may have little appetite for sending money overseas. This is particularly true for mitigation finance. Indeed, many high-income countries see public funds as playing a limited role in supporting climate financing in the developing world, instead envisioning that a greater proportion of funds be harnessed through market mechanisms.

Developing countries envision these funds entirely differently, as paying to help them adjust to and contribute to the mitigation of a problem not of their making. As a result, they eschew any overtones of aid and strongly resist any mechanisms of conditionality. To the contrary, they envision the use of these funds as guided by recipient-country priorities.

Elements in both positions appear reasonable. There are good arguments for not considering transfers of climate-related funds within an aid umbrella because of high-income-country responsibility for a substantial part of the climate problem. But it would appear politically difficult for high-income countries to sign a blank check without some mechanism of accountability for the funds. One way forward might be to focus on what the past teaches about conditionality as a tool.

Developing-country positions in the climate debate are, in part, shaped by the fraught history of conditionality in development debates. Civil society and other actors came to see conditionality as an instrument that undercuts democracy and forced through unpopular reforms. Because the conditions imposed did not prove particularly effective in helping governments undertake politically difficult reforms, conditionality gave way within a decade to the almost opposite concept of borrower "ownership" of a reform agenda as a precondition for policy reform loans.[12] The lesson for climate change appears to be that—even purely on pragmatic grounds, putting aside principles connected with responsibility for the problem—conditionality is simply not an effective tool for getting governments to take measures with little domestic support.

Fortunately, there is a more productive way to conceptualize how climate funds might be used. A first step requires redirecting attention from implementing actions predetermined by a donor to organizing funding around a process to encourage recipient-country development and ownership of a low-carbon development agenda. This is similar to the poverty reduction strategy approach discussed in chapter 6, whereby donors align around a strategy designed and owned by the recipient government. Such an approach would place the emphasis on the governance mechanism for fund providers and fund recipients to collectively scrutinize and oversee climate finance.

A second step is for mitigation financing to support both low-carbon development and well-specified mitigation actions in developing countries. The concrete actions should be collectively agreed on by those providing and those receiving funds as serving the dual functions of climate mitigation and development gains. As discussed earlier, many energy-efficiency measures would be good candidates for easy agreement.

Coming to agreement on supporting low-carbon development is more amorphous and challenging. But the lesson from conditionality is that the path for low-carbon development should be developed through a process that builds considerable recipient-country ownership. The efforts of a number of governments, such as Mexico and South Africa among others, to develop a long-term carbon mitigation strategy as a basis for identifying concrete actions and seeking international support are one interesting model. The rest of this chapter discusses avenues for developing these alternative approaches.

Options for integrating developing-country actions into the global architecture

Developing countries need to be persuaded that there is a feasible route to integrating climate change and development if they are to rapidly start the transition to a low-carbon development path. If the international climate regime is to promote stronger action by developing countries, it must incorporate new approaches appropriate to their circumstances. Any mitigation effort required for the developing countries must be grounded on "a clear understanding of the economic and governance context for their development choices and their overriding development priorities."[13] The future regime must be designed in a way that recognizes their efforts to reduce their emissions while achieving their development objectives.

So far, the primary vehicle for mitigation action within the regime has been economywide emission targets pegged to historical base-year emission levels, as in the Kyoto Protocol. Such an output-based approach (focused on the emission "output") is driven by the core objective of achieving and maintaining a tolerable level of greenhouse gas concentrations in the atmosphere.[14] Fixed economywide emission targets have two advantages. They provide certainty about the environmental outcome (assuming they are met). And they allow countries considerable flexibility to choose the most suitable and cost-effective means of implementation. This target-driven approach remains appropriate for developed countries.

But such a climate-centric approach is perceived as problematic for developing countries, at least at this stage of the climate regime. Many developing countries see a cap on total emissions as a cap on economic growth. Having demonstrated their competitive success, the countries fear that the climate agenda will hold them back. These concerns spring from the fact that the principal driving forces of emissions growth in developing countries are the development imperatives of energy and economic growth. And as a practical matter, setting and adhering to an economywide emission target requires the ability to accurately measure and reliably project emissions across a country's economy, a capacity that many developing countries now lack.

So engaging developing countries more fully in the climate regime may require alternative approaches deemed more appropriate to their circumstances. These approaches could build on the types of actions and strategies already being developed or implemented at the national level. Unlike emission targets, these actions can generally be characterized as "policy-based," centering on activities that generate emissions, rather than on emissions themselves. To achieve energy efficiency, a country could introduce a standard or incentive to shift behavior or technology. Lower greenhouse gas emissions would be one outcome, but the policy also would produce benefits more closely related to a country's core development objectives, such as greater energy affordability and access. Depending on their circumstances, countries could put forward different sets of policies or actions that address such development objectives as economic growth, energy security, and improved mobility while also delivering the co-benefit of reduced emissions.

A key question, however, is how to reconcile this approach with the urgency imparted in chapter 4—the notion that unless mitigation is immediate and global it will not be possible to maintain warming anywhere close to 2°C. New analysis, presented below, on multitrack frameworks and the impact of advance commitments suggests that a flexible approach could be effective.

An integrated multitrack climate framework

To better integrate development concerns into climate change efforts, the global climate regime must become more flexible and accommodate different national circumstances and strategies, especially for mitigation efforts. The Kyoto Protocol establishes a single type of mitigation commitment—a binding, absolute, economywide limit on emissions. This is sound from the perspectives of environmental effectiveness and economic efficiency, but as a political and practical matter it is an unlikely avenue for developing countries at this stage.

A more flexible regime integrating different approaches by different countries can be conceptualized as an "integrated multi-track" framework.[15] Many international regimes have the characteristics of such an approach. For example, the multilateral trade regime includes agreements accepted by all World Trade Organization members and plurilateral agreements among smaller groupings of members. Europe's Long-Range Transboundary Air Pollution regime and the International Convention for the Prevention of Pollution from Ships include core agreements setting forth common terms and annexes establishing differential obligations. Experiences within these arenas provide valuable lessons for climate policy makers, but the climate regime requires a distinct architecture matching a unique set of political and policy imperatives.

In broad terms, a multitrack climate regime could include at a minimum two distinct mitigation tracks:

- *Target track.* For developed countries and other countries that may be prepared to undertake such commitments, the target track would establish binding, absolute, economywide emission targets succeeding those established under the Kyoto Protocol's first commitment period. Countries with such targets would have full access to the agreement's international emissions-trading mechanisms.

- *Policy-based track.* On this track, other countries would agree to undertake nationally driven policies and actions that would have the effect of reducing emissions or emissions growth. Such policies could be sector based or economywide and could include, for example, energy-efficiency standards, renewable energy targets, fiscal measures, and land-use policies. Countries could propose individual policies or put forward comprehensive low-carbon development strategies identifying priority sectors and policies and the support needed for their implementation.

Recent modeling of such hybrid frameworks suggests that multitrack approaches score well on environmental effectiveness and equity and that the efficiency losses may be a reasonable tradeoff to achieve broad participation in policies that put countries collectively on track to greenhouse

BOX 5.3 *Multitrack approaches score well on effectiveness and equity*

Recent modeling by Battelle Memorial Institute's Joint Global Change Research Institute, in collaboration with the Pew Center on Global Climate Change, indicates that an "integrated multitrack" climate framework, in which developed countries undertake economywide emission targets and developing countries undertake nontarget policies, can produce global emission reductions by midcentury consistent with achieving atmospheric greenhouse gas concentrations of 450 ppm CO_2 by 2100.[a]

In the global policy scenarios, developed regions reduce their emissions 20 percent below 2005 levels by 2020, and 80 percent below by 2050; developing regions adopt a range of policies in the energy, transportation, industry, and buildings sectors, such as carbon-intensity goals, efficiency standards, and renewable energy targets. The specific policies, and their stringency, vary among the developing-country regions. "Policy-based crediting" awards developing regions tradable emission credits for a portion of the reductions their policies achieve (starting at 50 percent in 2020 and declining to zero in 2050).

The analysis shows global emission reductions in 2050 nearly as steep as those under an idealized "efficient" 450 ppm pathway in which full global emissions trading achieves reductions wherever and whenever they are least expensive. Globally, costs through 2050 are higher than in the efficient case, emphasizing the importance of moving toward full emissions coverage and full global trading by midcentury. But even with this loss in efficiency, costs remain below 2 percent of global gross domestic product (GDP) in 2050. Further, the policy-based crediting approach redistributes costs globally so that costs as a share of GDP are significantly lower in developing regions. In the early years, revenue from the sale of emission credits exceeds domestic mitigation costs in some developing regions, producing net economic gains.

Source: Calvin and others 2009.

a. The model does not specifically look at temperature increases. However 450 ppm CO_2 corresponds to concentrations of about 550 ppm CO_2e (a measure of all greenhouse gases, not just CO_2), hence possible temperature increases of around 3°C. At the time this report went to press, this exercise had not been conducted for 450 ppm CO_2e, which corresponds to a 40 to 50 percent probability of warming remaining below 2°C.

gas concentrations of 450 parts per million (ppm) CO_2 or 550 ppm of CO_2e (box 5.3).

Other modeling has also convincingly shown that a multitrack framework can be very effective if it provides some certainty as to when a country may commit to a binding agreement.[16] This, in fact, reduces the cost for any country of joining a binding agreement in the future because it spreads the transition over a longer period of time and investors can factor eventual policy changes into their investment choices, a process that reduces the amount of stranded assets or expensive retrofits a country can be left with.

In addition to the mitigation tracks, a comprehensive agreement would need to include

- An adaptation track to assist vulnerable countries with adaptation planning and implementation
- Cross-cutting enabling elements on technology, finance, and capacity-building support to developing countries
- Means to measure, report, and verify mitigation actions and support for the mitigation actions of developing countries, as specified under the Bali Action Plan.

Chapter 4 showed that it would be almost impossible to remain close to 2°C warming with delayed participation of developing countries. Instead multitrack frameworks permit early action but emphasize win-win options. And the models and the approaches discussed here suggest that multitrack approaches and forward-looking, predictable policies are worthwhile approaches to reconciling the need for urgent action and the priority that must be granted to development and poverty alleviation.

A policy-based mitigation track

To recognize and advance developing-country mitigation efforts, the major new element needed in the climate regime is a new category of mitigation action that is broad and supple enough to incorporate a wide variety of actions. Many developing countries have begun to identify existing and potential policies and actions at the national level that, while not driven exclusively or primarily by climate-change concerns, contribute to climate-mitigation efforts. As these policies and actions arise within national contexts, they inherently reflect a country's national circumstances and its development objectives and priorities. Indeed many of these policies are driven by development objectives such as energy access and security, better air quality, improved transportation services, and sustainable forestry, with mitigation an incidental co-benefit.

A mechanism that allows the integration of such nationally driven policies into the international framework offers four advantages to developing countries. First, it enables developing countries to contribute to the climate effort in ways that, by their own determination, are compatible with their development agendas. Second, it allows each country to come forward with a nationally defined package tailored to its circumstances, capabilities, and mitigation potential. Third, if it is coupled with a robust support mechanism, policies can be scaled or tiered to provide for stronger action on the provision of stronger support. Fourth, while providing a clear pathway for stronger mitigation efforts by developing countries, it does not bind them to quantified emission limits, which they perceive as undue constraints on their growth and development.

The case for a policy-based track has been advanced in the academic literature in different guises. One formulation, called "sustainable development policies and measures" (SD-PAMs), envisions voluntary pledges by developing countries.[17] Another proposal describes "policy-based commitments" in which the policy content might be identical to that under an SD-PAMs approach but would be reflected in the international framework as a commitment rather than a voluntary action.[18] Since the adoption of the Bali Action Plan, governments have put forward proposals addressing various aspects of how a policy-based approach could be made operational in a future climate agreement.[19]

In fashioning a new policy-based track as part of an evolving international climate framework, governments would need to consider several interrelated issues, including

- The process for countries to bring forward policies and actions and have them reflected in the international framework
- The legal character of these policies and actions
- The links to other mechanisms providing incentives and support for their implementation
- The standards and mechanisms for measuring, reporting, and verifying the policies and actions and the support for them.

Process for introducing policy actions. For country policy actions to be recognized within the international framework, governments would need to establish a process to bring them forward and, possibly, to have other parties consider and accept them. Within the negotiations, some parties have proposed the establishment of a "registry" for countries to record nationally appropriate mitigation actions they plan or propose to undertake.[20]

One critical issue is whether the process of bringing actions forward occurs in the course of negotiating a new agreement or is an outcome of those negotiations. The latter may be preferable for most developing countries. In this scenario a new agreement would establish binding emission targets for developed countries, mechanisms to support developing-country mitigation and adaptation efforts, and a process for developing countries to then define their mitigation actions. But developed countries may be reluctant to enter into binding emission targets unless the major developing countries are prepared to indicate at the same time the actions they will undertake. In that case the process of specifying those actions could be structured as part of the negotiating process, with the aim of arriving at a comprehensive agreement integrating binding targets for developed countries and specified policy actions for developing countries.

In either case, parties also need to consider whether the process should be completely open-ended, with countries free to propose any type of policy or action, or circumscribed in some way. One option proposed in the negotiations is a menu, or "tool box," of mitigation actions for developing countries to choose from.[21] The menu could identify broad categories of action, with parties invited to put forward detailed policies or action plans within the categories they choose. For consistency or comparability it may be useful to establish some form of template for countries to follow in describing their mitigation actions.

Another important consideration is quantifying the expected emission impacts of mitigation actions. Although countries participating in a policy-based track would not be committing to specific emission outcomes, other parties will want to know what impact their actions are likely to have on their future emissions. At a minimum countries should be prepared to offer such projections. Depending on the type of process established, emission projections also could be prepared or verified by an intergovernmental body or an independent third party.

Legal character. The Bali Action Plan distinguishes between "nationally appropriate mitigation commitments or actions" by developed countries and "nationally appropriate mitigation actions" by developing countries, implying that the actions of developing countries are not to take the form of legally binding commitments. Indeed, proposals put forward by developing countries in the post-Bali negotiations, including proposals for a registry of developing-country actions, emphasize the voluntary nature of these actions.

But the Bali Action Plan does not expressly preclude commitments by developing countries, contrary to the 1995 Berlin Mandate that framed the negotiations that led to the Kyoto Protocol. In the current round of negotiations some developed countries have taken the position that actions by some developing-countries should be binding.[22] Developing countries, however, have been reluctant to take on binding commitments, at least at this stage.

Links to support. Robust efforts by developing countries will be feasible only with stronger international support. Indeed, under the Bali Action Plan, the mitigation actions of developing countries are to be "supported and enabled by technology, financing, and capacity building." Potential mechanisms to generate such support are discussed below. If parties were to establish a policy-based mitigation track for developing countries, a related question is how actions under that track would be linked to specific flows of support.

Any process to enable countries to bring forward proposed actions could, in addition, identify means and levels of support for those actions. For example, in entering a proposed action in a mitigation-action registry, a country could indicate the type and level of support needed to implement the action. Or a country might specify the level of effort it is prepared to deliver on its own, and a higher level of effort it would be prepared to undertake with support. Or recording an action in the registry could initiate a review by a designated body, using agreed criteria, to evaluate the need for support, taking into account a country's circumstances and capacities. All of these approaches could lead to a determination of support commensurate with the proposed action.

Measurement, reporting, and verification. Parties agreed in Bali that the mitigation efforts of developed and developing countries—as well as the support for developing-country efforts—are to be "measurable, reportable, and verifiable" (MRV). Effective approaches to MRV can establish and maintain parties' confidence in one another's respective efforts and in the overall regime. To be workable, MRV terms and mechanisms must balance the need for transparency and accountability against the parties' traditional concerns about sovereignty.

Reporting requirements for developing countries under the existing regime are fairly minimal—national "communications" (including emission inventories) are submitted infrequently and are not subject to review. In a future agreement the MRV of developing-country actions on a policy-based mitigation track would likely require a more rigorous approach. Parties first must consider what actions are subject to measurement and verification. Some developing countries have taken the view that MRV should apply only to actions for which they are receiving support. A second issue is whether verification is performed by the country, an international body, or a third party. In some international regimes parties verify their own actions under national systems that must conform to international guidelines. In others expert teams review parties' submissions (as for national communications and emission inventories submitted by developed countries under the UNFCCC and the Kyoto Protocol).

Third is the metrics to be employed, regardless of the means of verification. One rationale for a policy-based track is that it allows parties to pursue the types of action most appropriate to their circumstances and development objectives. This diversity presents challenges for MRV, however, because different metrics are needed to measure and verify different types of actions (efficiency standards, renewable energy targets, carbon levies). How MRV is structured will therefore depend very heavily on how the actions are defined. In turn, the need for actions to be measurable and verifiable could strongly influence the way parties choose to define them. Somehow bounding the types of actions allowable in a policy-based track—say, by establishing a menu for parties to choose from—could make MRV more manageable.

Measurement and verification of developed-country support will likewise depend heavily on the specific types and mechanisms of support. If a new agreement were to recognize support provided through bilateral channels, criteria would be needed to determine what flows are "climate related" and "new and additional." As a general matter, support generated through a multilateral instrument, such as an international carbon levy or an auction of international emission allowances, would be more readily verifiable.

Support for developing-country mitigation efforts

The ability of developing countries to develop and effectively implement mitigation actions will depend in part on the availability of adequate and predictable support from the international community. General areas of support include finance, technology, and capacity building. These could include analyzing mitigation potentials to identify opportunities to reduce greenhouse gases with the lowest cost and highest co-benefits, developing and implementing greenhouse gas mitigation policies, disseminating and deploying the best available technologies, and measuring and verifying mitigation actions and their associated sustainable development benefits.

Adequate support will require a range of mechanisms to generate and channel public resources and to do so in a way that leverages private investment, which under any scenario will be the majority of flows available for a low-carbon transition (see chapter 6). The climate regime has two broad forms of support—public finance and market-based

mechanisms—and both must be substantially scaled up in a future agreement.

Public finance

A new multilateral effort must scale up public finance in support of developing countries. Among the key issues are funding sources, funding criteria, funding instruments, links to private finance, and managing and governing any new funding mechanisms (all discussed extensively in chapter 6). This section highlights a few findings.

Most of the funds under the climate regime have relied on pledging by donor countries, resulting in inadequate and unpredictable flows. Several proposals now under discussion could produce more reliable funding streams. These include funding commitments based on agreed assessment criteria, a levy on international aviation or other greenhouse gas–generating activities, or an auction of a portion of developed countries' international emission allowances. Another option—pressed by developing countries at the UN Climate Change Conference in Poznań, Poland, in December 2008—is an extension of the existing levy on CDM transactions to the Kyoto Protocol's other market-based flexibility mechanisms (international emissions trading and Joint Implementation).[23]

Any new fund could deploy an array of funding instruments, including grants, concessional loans, loan guarantees or other risk mitigation instruments, depending on the types of activity to be supported. For technology the options include payments for access to and use of intellectual property and the associated technological know-how. Important criteria in selecting activities for funding could include the projected emission reduction per dollar of investment, a project's contribution to a host country's sustainable development objectives, or its ability to leverage carbon finance or other private investment.

Market-based mechanisms

The Kyoto Protocol's Clean Development Mechanism has generated substantial flows supporting clean energy and other greenhouse gas-reducing projects in developing countries. While the CDM has had many successes, experience has also highlighted many concerns and areas for potential improvement (chapter 6). Beyond the reform of the original CDM model, however, parties have also begun to consider alternative approaches to emission crediting to provide incentives for investment and emission reduction on a broader scale.

As initially conceived and currently operating, the CDM generates emission credits from individual projects proposed and certified case by case. In the view of many, this project-based approach excludes many strategies with greater mitigation potential and imposes high transaction costs and administrative burdens, significantly limiting the CDM's potential to transform long-term emission trends. In an initial attempt to address these concerns, parties have authorized a "programmatic" CDM, which allows an aggregation of multiple activities over space and time as a single project. But emission reductions are still measured on the basis of discrete activities.

Alternative models now under discussion include sectoral or policy-based crediting. By allowing the generation of credits on the basis of policies or other broad programs, such approaches would help drive and support larger-scale emission-reduction efforts. Under a sectoral approach, for instance, emissions would be measured across an entire sector, and a country could earn credits for any reductions below an agreed emissions baseline. (This approach is sometimes described as "no-lose sectoral crediting," because a country faces no consequences if emissions rise above the agreed baseline.) The baseline could be set at business as usual, rewarding any deviation from projected emission levels. Or it could be set below business as usual, requiring that a country undertake some reductions on its own before qualifying for credits. Given the uncertainties in any projection of future emissions, however, the determination of business as usual is somewhat subjective and potentially quite contentious.

Under policy-based crediting a country could earn credits for verifiable reductions achieved by implementing mitigation policies recognized within the climate regime or by deploying technology action. This approach fits well with the notion of a policy-based mitigation track, providing a market-based incentive for countries to develop, put forward, and implement mitigation policies aligned with their development objectives. Methodologies could be established to quantify the reductions from different types of policy approaches. Crediting countries for all the reductions generated by their policy actions could cause an excessive supply of credits; developed countries might also object on the grounds that developing countries should bear some of the cost of their policy actions. These concerns could be addressed by issuing credits only after a certain reduction has been achieved or by discounting credits (say, by issuing one ton of credit for every two tons reduced).

Promoting international efforts to integrate adaptation into climate-smart development

Stronger international support for adaptation is a matter of need, because climate impacts are already being felt and because the poor who contribute least to the problem face the gravest risks. But adaptation efforts must extend well beyond the climate framework. As chapters 2 and 3 suggest, adaptation concerns and priorities must be integrated across the full breadth of economic and development planning and decision making, both national and international. The role of the international climate regime in particular lies with catalyzing international support and facilitating national adaptation efforts. The focus here is on how adaptation can be best promoted and facilitated under the international climate regime.

Adaptation efforts under the current climate regime

Under the UNFCCC all parties commit to undertake national adaptation measures and to cooperate in preparing for the impacts of climate change. Special consideration is given to the least developed countries for their special needs to cope with adverse effects of climate change.[24] The least developed countries are encouraged and supported under the convention to prepare a National Adaptation Program of Action identifying priority activities that respond to their urgent and immediate needs to adapt to climate change (see chapter 8). To date, 41 least developed countries have submitted national action programs.[25] The five-year Nairobi Work Program adopted in 2005 aims to help these countries improve their understanding and assessment of the impacts of climate change and to make informed decisions on practical adaptation actions and measures.[26]

Current funding for adaptation under the UNFCCC process is mainly through the Global Environment Facility's Strategic Priority on Adaptation initiatives; additional funding will come from the UNFCCC Adaptation Fund when it is fully operational.

The international effort to date has delivered some information and capacity building on adaptation, but it has yet to facilitate significant implementation at the domestic level, access to technology, or the building of national institutions to carry the adaptation agenda forward. The effort is constrained by limited funding (see chapter 6) and the limited engagement of national planning and development agencies. The UNFCCC process has traditionally involved environment agencies; its focus on climate change may not easily lead to a comprehensive, multisectoral effort addressing adaptation.

Strengthening action on adaptation under the UNFCCC

Working through the national development process is essential to encourage early planning to strengthen climate resilience and discourage investments that heighten climate vulnerability. The UNFCCC process can complement and facilitate this process by

- *Supporting comprehensive national adaptation strategies in vulnerable countries.* These strategies would establish frameworks for action and strengthen national capacities. They would build on the National Adaptation Programs of Action, which target urgent priorities, to map out comprehensive long-term plans identifying climate risks, existing and needed adaptation capacities, and national policies and measures to fully integrate climate risk management into development decision making. In addition to organizing national adaptation efforts, the strategies could serve as a basis for targeting implementation assistance through the climate regime or through other channels.

- *Exchanging experiences and best practices, and coordinating programmatic approaches to support national, regional, and international systems for adaptation and resilience.*[27] This effort would provide guidance to countries on vulnerability assessments and on how to integrate adaptation activities into sectoral and national development planning and policies, as well as help in accessing technology for adaptation. The universal membership of the UNFCCC provides a unique forum for countries, organizations, and private entities to exchange experiences and learn from each other. Bringing national development agencies to participate in this process is essential to success. Apart from using the UNFCCC process to disseminate information, it may be useful to establish regional centers of excellence for catalyzing local, national, and regional activities. The direct impacts of climate change are felt locally, and response measures need to be tailored to local circumstances. Regional centers, with international support, can promote capacity building, coordinate research activities, and exchange experiences and best practices.

- *Providing reliable funding to assist countries in implementing high-priority measures identified in their national adaptation strategies.* Funding for adaptation largely relies on public financing (see chapter 6). Finding additional sources of adaptation finance and packaging them with existing development finance are essential for effective adaptation. Funds could come from donors, a levy on the CDM, and the tax or auction revenues from emission allowances. Equally important are defining criteria for allocating funds and setting up institutional arrangements to manage them (see chapter 6). Efficient and equitable allocation and use of adaptation finance is in everybody's interest, and wasteful use of resources can undermine public support for the whole climate agenda.

A new body under the UNFCCC may be needed to provide guidance to the parties, assess national adaptation strategies, and develop criteria for allocating resources. Such a body would need to coordinate closely with other international development agencies and have enough independence to credibly assess national strategies and resource allocation.

As mentioned early in this chapter, the current UNFCCC regime does not include adequate provisions for adaptation. The Bali Action Plan presents a great opportunity to streamline the adaptation process and mobilize adequate funding to support adaptation.

Notes

1. Energy-related emissions increased by 24 percent between 1997 (when the Kyoto Protocol was signed) and 2006; see CDIAC database (DOE 2009).

2. The Global Environment Facility (GEF) manages projects and investments through a number of multilateral organizations, in addition to functioning as the financial mechanism for international environmental conventions, including the UNFCCC. The GEF is providing $17.2 billion in cofinancing; see GEF 2009.

3. This section is drawn from Dubash 2009.

4. Absolute emission reduction entails a net decline in emissions relative to current levels, as opposed to a shift in projected emission trajectory.

5. Baer, Athanasiou, and Kartha 2007. See also box 5.2.

6. Baumert and Winkler 2005.

7. Burtraw and others 2005; Barrett 2006.

8. See focus A on science and chapter 4 for a discussion.

9. EU submission to UNFCCC, http://unfccc .int/files/kyoto_protocol/application/pdf/ ecredd191108.pdf (accessed August 5, 2009).

10. India and China's submissions to the UNFCCC, http://unfccc.int/files/kyoto_protocol/ application/pdf/indiasharedvisionv2.pdf and http:// unfccc.int/files/kyoto_protocol/application/pdf/ china240409b.pdf (accessed July 6, 2009). For a civil society perspective see Third World Network, "Understanding the European Commission's Climate Communication," http://www.twnside. org.sg/title2/climate/info.service/2009/climate. change.20090301.htm (accessed July 8, 2009).

11. For example, McKinsey Global Institute (2008) suggests that focused action in six policy areas could deliver about 40 percent of the abatement potential identified in their cost-curve approach.

12. Dollar and Pritchett 1998.

13. Heller and Shukla 2003.

14. Heller and Shukla 2003.

15. Bodansky and Diringer 2007.

16. Blanford, Richels, and Rutherford 2008; Richels, Blanford, and Rutherford, forthcoming.

17. Winkler and others 2002.

18. Lewis and Diringer 2007.

19. See, for instance, submissions to the UNFCCC from South Africa (http://unfccc.int/ files/meetings/dialogue/application/pdf/work- ing_paper_18_south_africa.pdf) and the Republic of Korea (http://unfccc.int/resource/docs/2006/ smsn/parties/009.pdf) (accessed June 2009).

20. Submissions to the UNFCCC from South Africa and the Republic of Korea: http://unfccc .int/resource/docs/2006/smsn/parties/009.pdf, (accessed June 2009).

21. Submission to the UNFCCC from South Africa: http://unfccc.int/files/meetings/dialogue/ application/pdf/working_paper_18_south_ africa.pdf (accessed June 2009).

"Let's put in a joint effort . . . now before it's too late to save our Mama Earth."

—Sonia R. Bhayani, Kenya, age 8

Tewanat Saypan, Thailand, age 12

22. For example, in their submissions to the UNFCCC, the United States and European Union indicate that major developing countries shall commit to formulate and submit low-carbon strategies to the UNFCCC. See UNFCCC/AWGLCA/2009/MISC.4 at http://unfccc.int/resource/docs/2009/awglca6/eng/misc04p02.pdf (accessed August 5, 2009).

23. Akanle and others 2008. See http://unfccc.int/kyoto_protocol/mechanisms/items/1673.php (accessed July 8, 2009) for information about the Kyoto Protocol's flexibility mechanisms.

24. Article 4.1 of the UNFCCC.

25. UNFCCC Secretariat, http://unfccc.int/cooperation_support/least_developed_countries_portal/submitted_napas/items/4585.php (accessed August 5, 2009).

26. Decision 2/CP.11 of the UNFCCC.

27. SEG 2007.

References

Akanle, T., A. Appleton, D. Bushey, K. Kulovesi, C. Spence, and Y. Yamineva. 2008. *Summary of the Fourteenth Conference of Parties to the UN Framework Convention on Climate Change and Fourth Meeting of Parties to the Kyoto Protocol.* New York: International Institute for Sustainable Development.

Baer, P., T. Athanasiou, and S. Kartha. 2007. *The Right to Development in a Climate Constrained World: The Greenhouse Development Rights Framework.* Berlin: Heinrich Böll Foundation, Christian Aid, EcoEquity, and Stockholm Environment Institute.

Barrett, S. 2006. "Managing the Global Commons." In *Expert Paper Series Two: Global Commons.* Stockholm: Secretariat of the International Task Force on Global Public Goods.

Baumert, K., and H. Winkler. 2005. "Sustainable Development Policies and Measures and International Climate Agreements." In *Growing in the Greenhouse: Protecting the Climate by Putting Development First,* ed. R. Bradley and K. Baumert. Washington, DC: World Resources Institute.

Blanford, G. J., R. G. Richels, and T. F. Rutherford. 2008. "Revised Emissions Growth Projections for China: Why Post-Kyoto Climate Policy Must Look East." Kennedy School Discussion Paper 08-06, Harvard Project on International Climate Agreements, Cambridge, MA.

Bodansky, D., and E. Diringer. 2007. "Towards an Integrated Multi-Track Framework." Pew Center on Global Climate Change, Arlington, VA.

Burtraw, D., D. A. Evans, A. Krupnick, K. Palmer, and R. Toth. 2005. "Economics of Pollution Trading for SO_2 and NO_x." Discussion Paper 05-05. Resources for the Future, Washington, DC.

Calvin, K., L. Clarke, E. Diringer, J. Edmonds, and M. Wise. 2009. "Modeling Post-2012 Climate Policy Scenarios." Pew Center on Global Climate Change, Arlington, VA.

DOE (U.S. Department of Energy). 2009. "Carbon Dioxide Information Analysis Center (CDIAC)." Oak Ridge, TN.

Dollar, D., and L. Pritchett. 1998. *Assessing Aid: What Works, What Doesn't and Why.* Oxford, UK: Oxford University Press.

Dubash, N. 2009. "Climate Change through a Development Lens." Background paper for the WDR 2010.

GEF (Global Environment Facility). 2009. "Focal Area: Climate Change," Fact Sheet, GEF, Washington, DC, June.

Heller, T., and P. R. Shukla. 2003. "Development and Climate Change: Engaging Developing Countries." In *Beyond Kyoto: Advancing the International Effort against Climate Change,* ed. J. E. Aldy, J. Ashton, R. Baron, D. Bodansky, S. Charnovitz, E. Diringer, T. C. Heller, J. Pershing, P. R. Shukla, L. Tubiana, F. Tudela, and X. Wang. Arlington, VA: Pew Center on Global Climate Change.

Jiahua, P., and C. Ying. 2008. "Towards a Global Climate Regime." *China Dialogue,* December 10. http://www.chinadialogue.net/article/show/single/en/2616.

Lewis, J., and E. Diringer. 2007. "Policy-Based Commitments in a Post-2012 Framework." Working paper, Pew Center on Global Climate Change, Arlington, VA.

McKinsey Gloabl Institute. 2008. *The Carbon Productivity Challenge: Curbing Climate Change and Sustaining Economic Growth.* McKinsey & Company.

Meyer, A. 2001. *Contraction and Convergence: The Global Solution to Climate Change.* Totnes, Devon: Green Books on behalf of the Schumacher Society.

Richels, R. G., G. J. Blanford, and T. F. Rutherford. Forthcoming. "International Climate Policy: A Second Best Solution for a Second Best World?" *Climate Change Letters.*

SEG (Scientific Expert Group on Climate Change). 2007. *Confronting Climate Change: Avoiding the Unmanageable and Managing the Unavoidable.* Washington, DC: Sigma Xi and The United Nations Foundation.

UNFCCC (United Nations Framework Convention on Climate Change). 2005. *Caring for Climate: A Guide to the Climate Change Convention and the Kyoto Protocol.* Bonn: UNFCCC.

Winkler, H., R. Spalding-Fecher, S. Mwaka-sonda, and O. Davidson. 2002. "Sustainable Development Policies and Measures: Starting from Development to Tackle Climate Change." In *Building on the Kyoto Protocol: Options for Protecting the Climate,* ed. K. A. Baumert, O. Blanchard, S. Llosa, and J. Perkaus. Washington, DC: World Resources Institute.

Trade and climate change

The interaction between the international trade and climate change regimes has potentially major implications for developing countries. While there are positive reasons for exploring synergies between the two regimes and for aligning policies that could stimulate production, trade, and investment in cleaner technology options, instead much focus has been on using trade measures as sanctions in the global climate negotiations.

This focus on sanctions stems mainly from competitiveness concerns in countries that are now racing to reduce greenhouse gas emissions to meet Kyoto 2012 targets and beyond. These concerns have led to proposals for tariff or border tax adjustments to offset any adverse impact of capping carbon dioxide (CO_2) emissions. There is also a concern about "leakage" of carbon-intensive industries into countries that are not implementing the Kyoto Protocol.

The broad objective of bettering current and future human welfare is shared by both global trade and climate regimes. Just as the World Trade Organization (WTO) recognizes the importance of seeking to "protect and preserve the environment,"[1] the Kyoto Protocol states that parties should "strive to implement policies and measures . . . in such a way as to minimize adverse effect on international trade." The United Nations Framework Convention on Climate Change (UNFCCC) features similar language in several places, and the Doha Communiqué specifically states that "the aims of upholding and safeguarding an open and non-discriminatory multilateral trading system, and acting for the protection of the environment and promotion of sustainable development can and must be mutually supportive."[2] Both treaties thus recognize and respect each other's mandate.

Yet both climate and trade agendas have evolved largely independently through the years, despite their mutually supporting objectives and the potential for synergies. While the implementation of the Kyoto Protocol may have brought to light some conflicts between economic growth and environmental protection, the objectives of the protocol also provide an opportunity for aligning development and energy policies in ways that could stimulate production, trade, and investment in cleaner technology options.

Recent attempts to bring together the two agendas have been received with a great deal of skepticism. While trade ministers meeting in 2007 at the UNFCCC Bali Conference of Parties widely shared the view that the trade and climate regimes could buttress each other in several areas, they noted that tension between the two could arise, especially in the context of negotiations on post-Kyoto climate commitments after 2012.

A general developing-country perception is that any discussion of climate change issues (and, more broadly, environmental issues) in trade negotiations could eventually lead to "green protectionism" by high-income countries, which would be detrimental to their growth prospects. They have resisted attempts to include climate issues in trade by stating that climate change issues primarily belong and have to be negotiated under the umbrella of the UNFCCC. Even within the WTO there has been a general reluctance to broaden the climate mandate in the absence of a directive from the UNFCCC. Interestingly, despite all the rhetoric, a growing number of regional trade agreements (many of which include developing countries) now have elaborate environmental provisions. However, there is little evidence to show that they have contributed in any meaningful way to achieving positive environmental outcomes.[3] Also, regional trade agreements may have limited value in addressing environmental issues that require global solutions, such as climate change.

New developments

The proposed use of punitive trade sanctions to support domestic climate action remains prominent and has gained ground in the midst of the current financial crisis. All the recent energy and climate policy bills introduced in the U.S. Congress provide for trade sanctions or tariffs (or equivalent instruments) on certain goods from those countries that do not impose controls on carbon emissions. Similarly, the European Commission's plans to tighten Europe's greenhouse gas reduction regime also recognizes the risk that new legislation could put European companies at a competitive disadvantage compared to those in countries with less stringent climate protection laws.

The issue of imposing border measures on environmental grounds has been much discussed in the economic and legal literature. The WTO and other trade agreements do allow for "exceptions" for trade measures that might otherwise violate free trade rules but that can be justified as necessary or related to an effort to protect the

Should carbon be taxed where it is emitted, or at the point where goods are consumed on the basis of their "embodied" or "virtual" carbon—the amount of carbon emitted in producing and delivering the good? Many major exporting countries argue that they would be penalized by taxing carbon at the point of emission, when in fact much of this carbon is emitted in the production of goods for export—goods that are enjoyed by consumers in other countries. Based on analysis of carbon flows within a multiregional input-output table, the figure shows that China and the Russian Federation are net exporters of virtual carbon, while the European Union, the United States, and Japan are net importers.

However, countries imposing a carbon tax will be concerned about competitiveness and carbon leakage effects if other countries do not follow suit, and may consider taxing virtual carbon imports to level the playing field. The table shows the effective tariff rates in addition to the existing tariffs that countries would face if a tax of $50 a ton of CO_2 were placed on the virtual carbon content of imported goods and services.

A carbon price of $50 a ton of CO_2 is in line with recent experience—emission permits in the European Emission Trading Scheme traded as high as €35 in 2008. The table therefore suggests that virtual carbon tariff rates faced by developing countries could be significant if countries go this route.

Unilateral imposition of virtual carbon tariffs would clearly be a source of trade friction, however, damaging an international trading system that is already being stressed by the current financial crisis. Opening the door to border taxes for climate could lead to a proliferation of trade measures dealing with other areas where the competitive playing field is viewed as uneven. Accurate measurement of virtual carbon would be highly complex and subject to dispute. Moreover, placing tariffs on virtual carbon could burden low-income countries that have contributed very little to the problem of climate change.

Source: Atkinson and others 2009.

Production- and consumption-based emissions (millions of tons of CO_2)

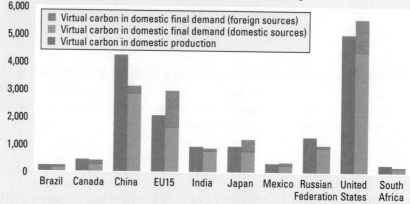

Source: Atkinson and others 2009.

Note: The height of the blue bar measures total emissions from production of goods and services; the green bar represents how much carbon is emitted domestically to support domestic final demand (virtual carbon from domestic sources); the orange bar represents how much carbon is emitted abroad to support domestic final demand (the virtual carbon from foreign sources). If the height of the blue bar is greater than the sum of the other two bars, then the country is a net exporter of virtual carbon.

Average tariff on imports of goods and services if virtual carbon is taxed at $50 a ton of CO_2
(percent)

		Importing countries										
		Brazil	Canada	China	EU15	India	Japan	Mexico	Russian Federation	United States	South Africa	Average
Exporting countries	Brazil	0.0	3.4	3.2	3.2	2.8	4.0	2.7	2.6	3.0	2.9	3.1
	Canada	4.5	0.0	3.4	3.4	3.7	3.2	2.8	2.8	2.6	3.0	2.8
	China	12.1	10.5	0.0	10.5	13.4	10.4	9.9	10.0	10.3	11.1	10.5
	EU15	1.6	1.1	1.1	0.0	1.3	1.2	1.1	1.1	1.2	1.2	1.2
	India	8.3	7.8	9.2	7.7	0.0	6.8	8.1	8.7	7.9	5.3	7.8
	Japan	1.4	1.3	1.5	1.4	1.6	0.0	1.4	1.4	1.2	1.3	1.4
	Mexico	3.5	2.1	4.2	4.0	10.8	4.0	0.0	4.1	1.7	3.5	2.1
	Russian Federation	18.0	14.3	12.4	11.8	12.8	11.3	14.7	0.0	10.4	15.9	11.7
	United States	3.3	3.0	3.1	3.1	3.3	3.0	2.8	2.8	0.0	3.2	3.0
	South Africa	15.9	10.1	10.6	9.8	11.5	11.4	16.6	7.9	8.9	0.0	10.1
	Average	3.7	2.9	2.2	5.0	4.5	4.8	3.3	2.6	3.0	2.9	

Source: Atkinson and others 2009.

Note: The last column is the trade-weighted average tariff faced by the exporting country; the last row is the trade-weighted average tariff applied by the importing country.

environment or conserve exhaustible natural resources and so long as they are "nondiscriminatory" and "least-trade-restrictive."[4] Trade measures are often justified as a mechanism to ensure compliance with multilateral environmental agreements (MEAs). Indeed MEAs such as the Convention on International Trade in Endangered Species and the Basel Convention use trade restrictions as a means to achieve MEA aims and these are accepted by all parties to the MEA. In case of climate change, however, a particularly thorny issue in assessing the compatibility of trade measures with climate change policy may arise from the application of unilateral measures based on national policies or product standards based on Processes and Production Methods, or both. The other issue with respect to "border tax adjustments" that has received little attention is what would happen to the revenue that is generated. If it is all given back to the country that is taxed it may have a very different political economy than if it stays in the country imposing the tax.

But legal experts remain divided on whether a tax on embodied carbon would be compatible with international trade regulations, because the WTO so far has not come out with clear provisions on the subject. Nonetheless, the recent proposals could have significant implications for trade in manufactures in developing countries (box FC.1).

Many high-income countries also express concern that any plan that exempts developing countries from emissions limits would not be effective because carbon-intensive industries would simply shift their operations to one of the exempt countries. Carbon leakage, as such a shift is called, not only would undercut the environmental benefits of the Kyoto Protocol but also would affect the competitiveness of high-income-country industries. For energy-intensive industries such as cement and chemicals, international competitiveness is an important con-

cern. This issue has a parallel to the "pollution havens" debate that dominated the trade and environment literature in the 1990s.

A recent World Bank study examined the evidence for any relocation of carbon-intensive industries attributable to more stringent climate policies, mostly in high-income countries. One of the factors influencing the operations of the energy-intensive sectors generally is the relative energy price in addition to land and labor costs. The study used import-export ratios of energy-intensive production in high-income countries and low- and middle-income countries as a proxy for any shift in production and trade patterns (figure FC.1).[5] The import-export ratios show an increasing trend for high-income countries and a declining trend for low- and middle-income countries. While not conclusive, this seems to suggest that some relocation of energy-intensive industries may already be happening to countries that do not face caps on their greenhouse gas emissions. However, the ratio is still less than 1 for high-income countries and more than 1 for developing economies, suggesting that high-income countries continue to

be net exporters and developing countries net importers of energy-intensive products.

In a similar vein, firms in some high-income countries are adopting "carbon labeling" as a mechanism for mitigating climate change. Carbon labeling involves measuring carbon emissions from the production of products or services and conveying that information to consumers and those making sourcing decisions within companies. It is possible that well-designed schemes would create incentives for production in different parts of the supply chain to move to lower-emission locations. Thus, carbon labeling could be an instrument that enables consumers to exercise their desire to join the battle against climate change by using their purchasing preferences.

The downside of carbon-labeling schemes is that they are likely to have a significant impact on exports from low-income countries.[6] Fears have been raised that low-income countries will face greater difficulties exporting in a climate-constrained world where carbon emissions need to be measured and certification obtained to enable participation in carbon-labeled trade. Exports

Figure FC.1   Import-export ratio of energy-intensive products in high-income countries and low- and middle-income countries

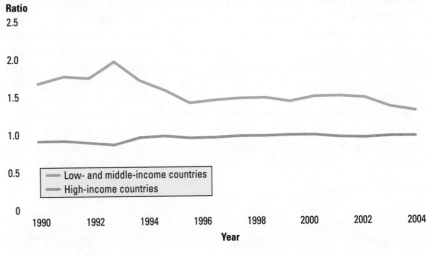

Source: World Bank 2008.

from low-income countries typically depend on long-distance transportation and are produced by relatively small firms and tiny farms that will find it difficult to participate in complex carbon-labeling schemes.

There is a significant knowledge gap to be filled regarding scientific studies of the structure of carbon emissions throughout international supply chains that include low-income countries. The small number of existing studies suggests that emissions patterns are highly complex, and an important finding is that geographic location alone is a poor proxy for emissions, because favorable production conditions may more than offset a disadvantage in transport. For example, Kenyan-produced roses airfreighted to and sold in Europe are associated with considerably lower carbon emissions than roses produced in the Netherlands.

The design and implementation of carbon labeling will also need to take into account a number of complex, technical challenges.[7] First, using secondary data from producers in rich countries to estimate the carbon emissions of producers in low-income countries will not capture the fact that the technologies being applied in rich and low-income countries are substantially different. A second technical issue relates to the use of emission factors—the amount of carbon emitted during particular parts of the manufacture and use of products—and how they should be calculated. A third issue is the choice of system boundaries, which define the extent of processes that are included in the assessment of greenhouse gas emissions. Estimates of the carbon footprint of a system, product, or activity will also depend on where the system boundary is drawn.

The positive agenda

The other area where trade and climate have recently overlapped relates to technology transfer. Given the limitations of the Clean Development Mechanism in delivering the kind and magnitude of technology transfer needed to deal with increasing greenhouse gas emissions in the developing world (see chapter 6), it has been suggested that broader trade and investment rules could be one way to speed up transfer of technology.[8] Liberalizing trade in environmental goods and services has been on the agenda of the WTO Doha Round since the beginning. All WTO members agree that environmental goods liberalization should be geared toward environmental protection. Yet very little has been achieved owing to the differing perceptions of high-income and developing countries on what goods are to be liberalized and how to liberalize.

Efforts have been made, including by the World Bank,[9] to move these negotiations forward by identifying climate-friendly goods and services that currently face tariff and nontariff barriers to trade, and making the removal of these barriers through the WTO negotiations a priority. This effort has proved challenging, because WTO members have yet to agree on a definition of "climate friendly" that both contributes to climate policy objectives and generates a balanced distribution of trade benefits among members. Two particular areas of controversy involve "dual use" technologies that may be used to reduce emissions as well as to meet other consumer needs, and agricultural products, which are mired in a very contentious part of the Doha negotiations.

The other issue that often goes unnoticed is the huge potential for trade between developing countries (South-South trade) in clean technology. Traditionally developing countries have been importers of clean technologies, while high-income countries have been exporters. However, as a result of their improving investment climate and huge consumer base, developing countries are increasingly becoming major players in the manufacture of clean technologies.[10] A key development in the global wind power market is the emergence of China as a significant player, both in manufacturing and in investing in additional wind power capacity. Similarly other developing countries have emerged as manufacturers of renewable energy technologies. India's solar photovoltaic manufacturing capacity has increased several times in the past four years, while Brazil continues to be a world leader in the production of biofuels. These developments call for liberalizing bilateral trade in clean technologies that could also facilitate buoyant South-South technology transfer in the future.

The way forward on trade and climate change

Countries have generally been reluctant to bring the trade and climate regimes closer for fear of one overwhelming the other. This is unfortunate because trade in clean energy technologies potentially offers an economic opportunity for developing countries that are emerging as major producers and exporters of these technologies.

Progress in the trade regime is possible even on very complex subjects. The success of the WTO's 1997 Information Technology Agreement suggests that implementation of any agreement on climate-friendly goods and technologies will certainly need to follow a phased approach to enable developing countries to deal gradually with implementing liberalization, including increasing the efficiency of customs administration and harmonizing customs classifications for climate-friendly goods. This should be supported through a package of financial and technical assistance measures. Postponing action on the trade and climate agenda until another lengthy round of WTO negotiations beyond the Doha Round is risky because of the imminent danger that climate-related trade sanctions of the variety proposed in the United States and the European Union could become a reality.

If climate-related trade measures bite deeply enough, developing countries can use the trade and climate negotiations to push back, or they may choose to adapt to the new policies and standards set by their major trading partners, in order to maintain access to their markets. In either case, developing countries will need to build their capacity to better understand and respond to these developments. Further, the need to push for financial and technology transfer as a part of any global deal on trade and climate change could not be more emphasized.

While there could be many benefits to bringing the trade and climate regimes closer, the potential for harm to the international trade regime from actions such as unilateral imposition of border taxes on carbon should not be underestimated, especially since the burden will fall disproportionately on developing countries. It is thus in the interest of developing countries to ensure that the pursuit of global climate objectives is compatible with maintaining a fair, open, and rule-based multilateral trading system as a foundation for their growth and development. Developed countries also have an important stake in the multilateral trading system and bear a major responsibility for ensuring that the system is maintained.

Notes

1. Preamble to the Marrakesh Agreement that established the WTO in 1995.

2. Quoted in World Bank 2008.

3. Gallagher 2004.

4. See article XX (b) and (g) of the 1947 General Agreement on Tariffs and Trade. WTO 1986.

5. World Bank 2008.

6. Brenton, Edwards-Jones, and Jensen 2009.

7. Brenton, Edwards-Jones, and Jensen 2009.

8. Brewer 2007.

9. World Bank 2008.

10. World Bank 2008.

References

Atkinson, G., K. Hamilton, G. Ruta, and D. van der Mensbrugghe. 2009. "Trade in 'Virtual Carbon': Empirical Results and Implications for Policy." Background paper for the WDR 2010.

Brenton, P., G. Edwards-Jones, and M. Jensen. 2009. "Carbon Labeling and Low Income Country Exports: An Issues Paper." *Development Policy Review* 27 (3): 243–267.

Brewer, T. L. 2007. "Climate Change Technology Transfer: International Trade and Investment Policy Issues in the G8+5 Countries." Paper prepared for the G8+5 Climate Change Dialogue, Georgetown University, Washington, DC.

Gallagher, K. P. 2004. *Free Trade and the Environment: Mexico, NAFTA and Beyond.* Palo Alto, CA: Stanford University Press.

World Bank. 2008. *International Trade and Climate Change: Economic, Legal and Institutional Perspectives.* Washington, DC: World Bank.

WTO (World Trade Organization). 1986. Text of the General Agreement on Tariffs and Trade 1947. Geneva: WTO.

CHAPTER 6

Generating the Funding Needed for Mitigation and Adaptation

Developed countries must take the lead in combating climate change. But mitigation will be neither effective nor efficient without abatement efforts in developing countries. Those are two key messages of earlier chapters. But there is a critical third dimension to meeting the climate challenge: equity. An equitable approach to limiting global emissions of greenhouse gases has to recognize that developing countries have legitimate development needs, that their development may be jeopardized by climate change, and that they have contributed little, historically, to the problem.

Flows of climate finance, both fiscal transfers and market transactions, from developed to developing countries represent the principal way to reconcile equity with effectiveness and efficiency in dealing with the climate problem. Financial flows can help developing countries reduce their greenhouse gas emissions and adapt to the effects of climate change. In addition, there will be financing needs related to

developing and diffusing new technologies. Mitigation, adaptation, and the deployment of technologies have to happen in a way that allows developing countries to continue their growth and reduce poverty. This is why additional financial flows to developing countries are so crucial.

The funding required for mitigation, adaptation, and technology is massive. In developing countries mitigation could cost $140 to $175 billion a year over the next 20 years (with associated financing needs of $265 to $565 billion); over the period 2010 to 2050 adaptation investments could average $30 to $100 billion a year (in round numbers). These figures can be compared with current development assistance of roughly $100 billion a year. Yet efforts to raise funding for mitigation and adaptation have been woefully inadequate, standing at less than 5 percent of projected needs.

At the same time, existing financing instruments have clear limits and inefficiencies. Contributions from high-income country governments are affected by fragmentation and the vagaries of political and fiscal cycles. Despite all its success, the Clean Development Mechanism (CDM), the main source of mitigation finance to date for developing countries, has design shortcomings and operational and administrative limits. The scope for raising adaptation funding through the CDM, now the main source of income for the Adaptation Fund, is thus also limited.

So new sources of finance will have to be tapped. Governments will have to step in, but it will be equally important to develop new innovative funding mechanisms and to leverage private finance. The private sector will have a key role in financing mitigation through carbon markets and related instruments. But official flows or other international funding will be an important complement to build capacity, correct market imperfections, and target areas overlooked by the market. Private finance will also be important for adaptation, because private agents—households and firms—will carry much of the adaptation burden. But good adaptation is very closely linked to good development, and those most in need of adaptation assistance are the poor and disadvantaged in the developing world. This means public finance will have a key role.

In addition to raising new funds, using available resources more effectively will be crucial. This calls both for exploiting synergies with existing financial flows, including development assistance, and for coordinating implementation. The scale of the financing gaps, the diversity of needs, and differences in national circumstances require a broad range of instruments. Concerns with effectiveness and efficiency mean that finance for climate change must be raised and spent coherently.

Financing needs are linked to the scope and timing of any international agreement on climate change. The size of the adaptation bill will depend directly on the effectiveness of the agreement. For mitigation, chapter 1 shows that delayed implementation of emission reductions, whether in developed or developing countries, risks hugely increasing the cost of limiting global warming. The overview chapter shows that on a global least-cost path for climate stabilization, a large fraction (65 percent or more)[1] of the needed mitigation would occur in developing countries. The cost of limiting global warming can thus be substantially reduced if high-income countries provide enough financial incentives for developing countries to switch to lower carbon paths. As other chapters emphasize, however, finance will need to be combined with access to technology and capacity building if developing countries are to shift to a lower-carbon development path.

This chapter deals with raising enough finance to reduce emissions and cope with the impacts of unavoidable changes. It assesses the gap between the projected needs for mitigation and adaptation finance compared with sources of finance available up to 2012. It looks at inefficiencies in the existing climate-finance instruments and discusses potential funding sources beyond the ones currently available (table 6.1). And it presents models for increasing the effectiveness of existing schemes, particularly the Clean Development Mechanism, and for allocating

Table 6.1   Existing instruments of climate finance

Type of instrument	Mitigation	Adaptation	Research, development, and diffusion
Market-based mechanisms to lower the costs of climate action and create incentives	Emissions trading (CDM, JI, voluntary), tradable renewable energy certificates, debt instruments (bonds)	Insurance (pools, indexes, weather derivatives, catastrophe bonds), payment for ecosystem services, debt instruments (bonds)	
Grant resources and concessional finance (levies and contributions including official development assistance and philanthropy) to pilot new tools, scale up and catalyze action, and act as seed money to leverage the private sector.	GEF, CTF, UN-REDD, FIP, FCPF	Adaptation Fund, GEF, LDCF, SCCF, PPCR and other bilateral and multilateral funds	GEF, GEF/IFC Earth Fund, GEEREF
Other instruments	Fiscal incentives (tax benefits on investments, subsidized loans, targeted tax or subsidies, export credits), norms and standards (including labels), inducement prizes and advanced market commitments, and trade and technology agreements		

Source: WDR team.

Note: CDM = Clean Development Mechanism; CTF = Clean Technology Fund; FCPF = Forest Carbon Partnership Facility; FIP = Forest Investment Program; GEEREF = Global Energy Efficiency and Renewable Energy Fund (European Union); GEF = Global Environment Facility; IFC = International Finance Corporation; JI = Joint Implementation; LDCF = Least Developed Country Fund (UNFCCC/GEF); PPCR = Pilot Program for Climate Resilience; SCCF = Strategic Climate Change Fund (UNFCCC/GEF); UN-REDD = UN Collaborative Program on Reduced Emissions from Deforestation and forest Degradation.

adaptation finance. Throughout the focus is on financing needs in developing countries, where the questions of effectiveness, efficiency, and equity all come together.

The financing gap

Successfully tackling climate change will cost trillions. How many depends on how ambitious the global response is, how it is structured, how the measures are timed, how effectively they are implemented, where mitigation takes place, and how the money is raised. Bearing the costs will be the international community, national governments, local governments, firms, and households.

The need for finance

According to the Intergovernmental Panel on Climate Change (IPCC), which reviewed cost estimates in its fourth assessment, the cost of cutting global greenhouse gas emissions by 50 percent by 2050 could be in the range of 1–3 percent of GDP.[2] That is the minimum cut most scientists believe is needed to have a reasonable chance of limiting global warming close to 2°C above preindustrial temperatures (see overview).

But mitigation costs are sensitive to policy choices. They increase steeply with the stringency of the emission reduction target and with the certainty of reaching it (figure 6.1). Global mitigation costs will also be higher if the world deviates from the least-cost emission reduction path. As earlier chapters explain, not including developing countries in the initial mitigation effort would increase global costs significantly (a consideration that led to the establishment of the Clean Development Mechanism under the Kyoto Protocol). Similarly, not considering all mitigation opportunities would markedly increase overall costs.

It is also important to distinguish between mitigation costs (the incremental costs of a low-carbon project over its lifetime) and incremental investment needs (the additional financing requirement created as a result of the project). Because many clean investments have high up-front capital costs, followed later by savings in operating costs, the incremental financing requirements tend to be higher than the lifetime costs reported in mitigation models. The difference could be as much as a factor of three (table 6.2).

Figure 6.1 Annual mitigation costs rise with the stringency and certainty of the temperature target

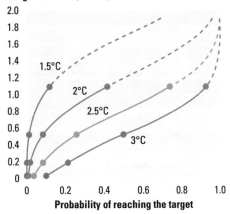

Mitigation costs (% GDP)

Source: Schaeffer and others 2008.

For fiscally constrained developing countries these high up-front capital costs can be a significant disincentive to invest in low-carbon technologies.

Table 6.2 reports both incremental costs and associated financing requirements for the mitigation efforts needed to stabilize atmospheric concentrations of CO_2e (all greenhouse gases summed up and expressed in terms of their carbon dioxide equivalent) at 450 parts per million (ppm) over the next decade, as well as the adaptation investments estimated to be required in 2030. Focusing on the 450 ppm target, mitigation costs in developing countries range between $140 billion and $175 billion a year by 2030 with associated financing needs of $265 to $565 billion a year. For adaptation the most comparable estimates are the medium-term figures produced by the United Nations Framework Convention on Climate Change (UNFCCC) and the World Bank, which range from $30 billion to $100 billion.

Many, but not all, of the identified adaptation needs would require public expenditures. According to the UNFCCC secretariat,[3] private funding would cover about a quarter of identified investment, although this estimate is unlikely to capture the full private investment in adaptation.

These numbers give a rough indication of the adaptation cost, but they are neither particularly accurate nor fully comprehensive. Most were derived from rules of

Table 6.2   Estimated annual climate funding needed in developing countries
2005 $ billions

Source of estimate	2010–20	2030	
Mitigation costs			
McKinsey & Company		175	
Pacific Northwest National Laboratory (PNNL)		139	
Mitigation financing needs	**2010–20**	**2030**	
International Institute for Applied Systems Analysis (IIASA)	63–165	264	
International Energy Agency (IEA) Energy Technology Perspectives	565[a]		
McKinsey & Company	300	563	
Potsdam Institute for Climate Impact Research (PIK)		384	
Adaptation costs	**2010–15**	**2030**	**Included measures**
Short term			
World Bank	9–41		Cost of climate-proofing development assistance, foreign and domestic investment
Stern Review	4–37		Cost of climate-proofing development assistance, foreign and domestic investment
United Nations Development Programme	83–105		Same as World Bank, plus cost of adapting Poverty Reduction Strategy Papers and strengthening disaster response
Oxfam	>50		Same as World Bank plus cost of National Adaptation Plan of Action and nongovernmental organization projects
Medium term			
United Nations Framework Convention on Climate Change (UNFCCC)		28–67	2030 cost in agriculture, forestry, water, health, coastal protection, and infrastructure
Project Catalyst		15–37	2030 cost for capacity building, research, disaster management and the UNFCCC sectors (most vulnerable countries and public sector only)
World Bank (EACC)		75–100	Average annual adaptation costs from 2010 to 2050 in the agriculture, forestry, fisheries, infrastructure, water resource management, and coastal zone sectors, including impacts on health, ecosystem services, and the effects of extreme-weather events.

Sources: For mitigation, IIASA 2009 and additional data provided by V. Krey; IEA 2008; McKinsey & Company 2009, and additional data provided by McKinsey (J. Dinkel) for 2030, using a dollar-to-Euro exchange rate of $1.25 to €1.00; PNNL figures from Edmonds and others 2008, and additional data provided by J. Edmonds and L. Clarke; PIK figures from Knopf and others, forthcoming, and additional data provided by B. Knopf; for adaptation, all figures from Agrawala and Fankhauser 2008, except World Bank EACC (Economics of Adaptation to Climate Change) from World Bank 2009; and Project Catalyst 2009.

Note: Estimates are for stabilization of greenhouse gases at 450 ppm CO_2e, which would provide a 40–50 percent chance of staying below 2°C warming by 2100.

a. IEA figures are annual averages through 2050.

thumb, dominated by the cost of climate-proofing future infrastructure. They underestimate the diversity of the likely adaptation responses and ignore changes in behavior, innovation, operational practices, or locations of economic activity. They also ignore the need for adaptation to nonmarket impacts such as those on human health and natural ecosystems. Some of the omitted options could reduce the adaptation bill (for example, by obviating the need for costly structural investments); others would increase it.[4] The estimates also do not consider residual damages beyond effective adaptation. A recent attempt to encompass

these complexities in measuring adaptation costs is reported in box 6.1.

Adaptation cost estimates also ignore the close links between adaptation and development. Although few studies are clear on this point, they measure the extra spending to accommodate climate change over and above what would have been spent on climate-sensitive investments anyway, such as those accommodating the consequences of income and population growth or correcting an existing adaptation deficit. But, in practice, the distinction between adaptation funding and development funding is not easy. Investments in education, health,

---

BOX 6.1 *Costing adaptation to climate change in developing countries*

A World Bank study published in 2009 on the economics of adaptation to climate change provides the most recent and comprehensive estimates of adaptation costs in developing countries, covering both country case studies and global estimates of adaptation costs. Key elements of the design of the study include:

Coverage. The sectors studied comprise agriculture, forestry, fisheries, infrastructure, water resource management, and coastal zones, including impacts on health and ecosystem services, and the effects of extreme weather events. Infrastructure is broken down into transport,

energy, water and sanitation, communications, and urban and social infrastructure.

Baseline. The estimates do not include the existing "adaptation deficit"—the extent to which countries are incompletely or suboptimally adapted to existing climate variability.

Level of adaptation. For most sectors the study estimates the cost of restoring welfare to the level that would exist without climate change.

Uncertainty. To capture the extremes of possible climate outcomes the study uses results from general circulation models

spanning the wettest and driest climate projections, under the IPCC's A2 scenario of possible socioeconomic and emissions trajectories.

Based on these design elements, the study arrives at bottom-line estimates of the global cost of adaptation to climate change in developing countries of $75 to $100 billion a year on average from 2010 to 2050.[a]

Source: World Bank 2009.
a. Expressed in constant 2005 dollars.

---

sanitation, and livelihood security, for example, constitute good development. They also help reduce socioeconomic vulnerability to both climatic and nonclimatic stress factors. Certainly in the short term, development assistance is likely to be a key complement to close adaptation deficits, to reduce climate risks, and to increase economic productivity. But new adaptation finance is also needed.

Mitigation finance available to date

Over the coming decades trillions of dollars will be spent to upgrade and expand the world's energy and transport infrastructure. These massive investments present an opportunity to decisively shift the global economy onto a low-carbon path—but they also raise the risk of a high-carbon lock-in if the opportunity is missed. As earlier chapters show, new infrastructure investments need to be steered to low-carbon outcomes.

Both public and private flows will be needed to fund these investments. Many instruments already exist (table 6.1). All will have a role in catalyzing climate action: mobilizing additional resources; reorienting public and private flows toward low-carbon and climate-resilient investments; and supporting the research, development, and deployment of climate-friendly technologies.

The public sector will provide capital mostly for big infrastructure projects, but a large part of the investment to create a low-carbon economy—from energy-efficient

machinery to cleaner cars to renewable energy—will come from the private sector. Currently, governments account for less than 15 percent of global economywide investment, although they largely control the underlying infrastructure investments that affect the opportunities for energy-efficient products.

There are various ways to encourage private investment in mitigation,[5] but the most prominent market instrument involving developing countries has been the Clean Development Mechanism. It has triggered more than 4,000 recognized emission reduction projects to date. Other similar mechanisms, such as Joint Implementation (the equivalent mechanism for industrial countries) and voluntary carbon markets, are important for some regions (transition countries) and sectors (forestry) but are much smaller. Under the CDM, emission reduction activities in developing countries can generate "carbon credits"—measured against an agreed baseline and verified by an independent entity under the aegis of the UNFCCC—and trade them on the carbon market. For example, a European power utility may acquire emission reductions (through direct purchase or financial support) from a Chinese steel plant embarking on an energy-efficiency project.

The financial revenues the CDM generates are modest relative to the amount of mitigation money that will have to be raised. But they constitute the largest source of mitigation finance to developing countries to date. Between 2001, the first year CDM projects could be registered, and 2012, the end of the Kyoto commitment period, the CDM is expected to produce some 1.5 billion tons of carbon dioxide equivalent (CO_2e) in emission reductions, much through renewable

Table 6.3　Potential regional CDM delivery and carbon revenues (by 2012)

By region	Millions of certified emission reductions[a]	$ millions	Percentage of total
East Asia and Pacific	871	10,453	58
China	786	9,431	52
Malaysia	36	437	2
Indonesia	21	252	2
Europe and Central Asia	10	119	1
Latin America and the Caribbean	230	2,758	15
Brazil	102	1,225	7
Mexico	41	486	3
Chile	21	258	1
Argentina	20	238	1
Middle East and North Africa	15	182	1
South Asia	250	3,004	17
India	231	2,777	16
Sub-Saharan Africa	39	464	3
Nigeria	16	191	1
Developed countries	85	1,019	6
By income			
Low income	46	551	3
Nigeria	16	191	1
Lower middle income	1,127	13,524	75
China	786	9,431	53
India	231	2,777	16
Indonesia	21	252	2
Upper middle income	242	2,906	16
Brazil	102	1,225	7
Mexico	41	486	3
Malaysia	36	437	2
Chile	21	258	1
Argentina	20	238	1
High income	85	1,019	6
Korea, Rep. of	54	653	4
Total	**1,500**	**18,000**	**100**

Source: UNEP 2008.

Note: Volumes include withdrawn and rejected projects.

a. 1 million certified emission reductions = 1 million tons of CO_2e.

energy, energy efficiency, and fuel switching. This could raise $18 billion ($15 billion to $24 billion) in direct carbon revenues for developing countries, depending on the price of carbon (table 6.3).[6] In addition each dollar of carbon revenue leverages on average $4.60 in investment and possibly up to $9.00 for some renewable energy projects. It is estimated that some $95 billion in clean energy investment benefited from the CDM over 2002–08.

In comparison, official development assistance for mitigation was about $19 billion over 2002–07,[7] and sustainable energy investment in developing countries totaled approximately $80 billion over 2002–08.[8]

Donors and international financial institutions are establishing new financing vehicles to scale up their support for low-carbon investment in the lead-up to 2012 (table 6.4). Total finance under these initiatives amounts to $19 billion up to 2012, although this figure combines mitigation and adaptation finance.

The current inadequacy of mitigation funding is obvious (figure 6.2). Combining the donor funds in table 6.4 (and counting them as if committed solely to mitigation) with the projected CDM finance to 2012 produces mitigation finance of roughly $37 billion up to 2012, or less than $8 billion a year. This falls far short of the estimated mitigation costs in developing countries of $140 to $175 billion a year in 2030, and even farther short of the associated financing requirements ($265 to $565 billion).

Adaptation finance available to date

Funding for adaptation started to flow only recently. The main existing source of adaptation funding is international donors, channeled either through bilateral agencies or through multilateral institutions like the Global Environment Facility (GEF) and the World Bank.

The establishment of the Adaptation Fund in December 2007, a funding mechanism with its own independent source of finance, was an important development. Its main income source is the 2 percent levy on the CDM, a novel financing source (discussed in more detail later) that could raise between $300 million and $600 million

Figure 6.2   The gap is large: Estimated annual climate funding required for a 2°C trajectory compared with current resources

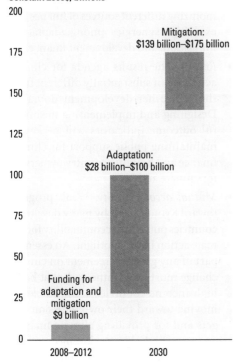

Source: For 2030 values, see table 6.2; for 2008–2012 values, see text.

Table 6.4   New bilateral and multilateral climate funds

Fund	Total amount ($ millions)	Period
Funding under UNFCCC		
Strategic Priority on Adaptation	50 (A)	GEF 3-GEF 4
Least Developed Country Fund	172 (A)	As of October 2008
Special Climate Change Fund	91 (A)	As of October 2008
Adaptation Fund	300–600 (A)	2008–12
Bilateral initiatives		
Cool Earth Partnership (Japan)	10,000 (A+M)	2008–12
ETF-IW (United Kingdom)	1,182 (A+M)	2008–12
Climate and Forest Initiative (Norway)	2,250	
UNDP-Spain MDG Achievement Fund	22 (A) / 92 (M)	2007–10
GCCA (European Commission)	84 (A) / 76 (M)	2008–10
International Climate Initiative (Germany)	200 (A) / 564 (M)	2008–12
IFCI (Australia)	160 (M)	2007–12
Multilateral initiatives		
GFDRR	15 (A) (of $83 million in pledges)	2007–08
UN-REDD	35 (M)	
Carbon Partnership Facility (World Bank)	500 (M) (140 committed)	
Forest Carbon Partnership Facility (World Bank)	385 (M) (160 committed)	2008–20
Climate Investment Funds, includes	6,200 (A+M)	2009–12
Clean Technology Fund	4,800 (M)	
Strategic Climate Fund, including	1,400 (A+M)	
Forest Investment Programme	350 (M)	
Scaling up renewable energy	200 (M)	
Pilot Program for Climate Resilience	600 (A)	

Source: UNFCCC 2008a plus updates by authors.

Note: For a number of bilateral initiatives, part of the funds will be distributed through multilateral initiatives (for example, some pledges to the Climate Investment Funds or the Forest Carbon Partnership Facility). This leads to some double counting and makes it difficult to draw an accurate picture of upcoming climate change resources in developing countries. The Climate Investment Funds are managed by the World Bank and implemented by all multilateral development banks. All data for the Climate Investment Funds are as of July 2009—$250 million of the Strategic Climate Fund was unallocated at that time, and the Scaling up Renewable Energy fund will require minimum pledges of $250 million before it becomes operational. A = funding devoted to adaptation; M = funding devoted to mitigation; ETF-IW = Environmental Transformation Fund-International Window; GCCA = Global Climate Change Alliance; IFCI = International Forest Carbon Initiative; UN-REDD = UN Collaborative Program on Reduced Emissions from Deforestation and forest Degradation; GFDRR = Global Facility for Disaster Reduction and Recovery. Pledges to the Climate and Forest Initiative (Norway) stood at $430 million in June 2009.

over the medium term, depending on the carbon price (see table 6.4 and endnote 7).

Excluding private finance, $2.2 billion to $2.5 billion is projected to be raised for adaptation from now to 2012, depending on what the Adaptation Fund raises. The potential adaptation finance now available is less than $1 billion a year, against funding requirements of $30 to $100 billion a year over the medium term (see table 6.2). Figure 6.2 compares the annual climate finance available over 2008–12 (both mitigation and adaptation, roughly $10 billion a year), with the projected medium-term financing needs.

Inefficiencies in existing climate-finance instruments

Inefficiency could take what is already projected to be a very large and costly endeavor and make it even more expensive. So there is an obvious case for ensuring that climate finance is generated and spent efficiently. Three aspects of the efficiency of climate finance are considered below: the fragmentation of climate finance into multiple funding sources, the limitations of carbon offset markets for mitigation, and the potential costs of taxing certified emission reductions (CERs) to finance the Adaptation Fund.

Fragmentation of climate finance

There is a risk of proliferation, illustrated in table 6.4, of special-purpose climate funds. Fragmentation of this sort threatens to reduce the overall effectiveness of climate finance, because as transaction costs increase, recipient country ownership lags, and alignment with country development objectives becomes more difficult. Each new source of finance, whether for development or climate change, carries with it a set of costs. These include transaction costs (which rise in aggregate as the number of funding sources increases), inefficient allocation (particularly if funds are narrowly defined), and limitations on scaling up. The current fragmentation and the low level of resources highlights the importance of the ongoing negotiations about a climate-financing architecture adequate to mobilize resources at scale and to deliver efficiently across a wide range of channels and instruments.

While there is not an exact parallel between climate finance and development aid, some of the lessons from the aid-effectiveness literature are highly relevant to climate finance. Concern about the negative effects of aid fragmentation was one of the key drivers of the Paris Declaration on Aid Effectiveness. In that declaration, most recently reaffirmed in the Accra Agenda for Action, both aid donors and recipients committed to incorporate the key tenets of ownership, alignment, harmonization, results orientation, and mutual accountability into their development activities.

The Paris Declaration raises important issues for financing climate investments in developing countries, many of which are widely accepted and reflected in negotiation documents, such as the Bali Action Plan:[9]

- *Ownership*. Building a shared consensus that climate change is a development issue, a central tenet of this Report, will be key in building country ownership. This consensus view must then be built into country development strategies.
- *Alignment*. Ensuring alignment between climate actions and country priorities is the second critical step in increasing the effectiveness of climate finance. Moving from the project to the sector and program level can facilitate this process. Predictability and sustainability of finance is another key aspect of alignment. Stop-start climate-action programs, driven by the volatility of finance, will reduce overall effectiveness.

- *Harmonization*. To the extent that the various climate funds have divergent purposes, this fragmentation of climate finance presents a great challenge to harmonizing different sources of finance and exploiting synergies among adaptation, mitigation, and development finance.
- *Results*. The results agenda for climate action is not substantially different from those of other development domains. Designing and implementing meaningful outcome indicators will be key to maintaining public support for climate finance and building country ownership for climate action.
- *Mutual accountability*. Weak progress toward Kyoto targets by many developed countries puts their accountability for climate action in the spotlight. An essential part of any global agreement on climate change must be a framework that holds high-income countries accountable for moving toward their own emission targets and for providing climate finance, and that also holds developing countries accountable for climate actions and uses of climate finance, as established in the Bali Action Plan. Beyond provision of resources, monitoring and reporting of climate finance flows and verification of results are a central topic of the ongoing climate negotiations.

In addition to the sources of finance, an important question is what investments climate funds should finance and the associated financing modalities. While some climate investments will be for individual projects— low-carbon power plants, for example— efficiencies can, in many instances, be gained by moving to the sector or program level. For adaptation, finance at the country level should in most cases be commingled with overall development finance, not used for specific adaptation projects.

More generally, rather than being overly prescriptive, climate finance could emulate the poverty reduction strategy approach now implemented in many low-income countries. This entails linking aid resources targeted at reducing poverty to a poverty reduction strategy prepared by the recipient country. Based on an analysis of poverty and a definition of country priorities, as validated by participatory processes with civil society, the strategy becomes the basis for broad budget support by donors to finance a program of action aimed at reducing poverty. Individual projects become the exception rather than the rule. If countries integrate climate action into their development strategies, a similar approach to climate finance should be feasible.

Inefficiencies of the Clean Development Mechanism

The principal instrument for catalyzing mitigation in developing countries is the CDM. It has grown beyond initial expectations, demonstrating the ability of markets to stimulate emission reductions, provide essential learning, raise awareness, and build capacity. But the CDM contains some inherent inefficiencies, raising questions about the overall process and its efficiency as a financing instrument:

Questionable environmental integrity. The long-term success of the CDM can be best assessed by its contribution to measurably reducing greenhouse gas emissions. In order not to dilute the environmental effectiveness of the Kyoto Protocol, CDM emission reductions must be additional to the reductions that would have occurred otherwise. The extent of additionality provided by the CDM has been debated vigorously.[10] The additionality of individual projects is difficult to prove and even more difficult to validate, because the point of reference is by definition a counterfactual reality that can never be incontrovertibly argued or conclusively proven. Because debates on baseline and additionality concerns continue to plague the CDM process, it is time to explore alternative, and simpler, approaches to demonstrate additionality. Approaches such as benchmarks and a positive list of specific desired activities should be explored further to streamline project preparation and monitoring. Revisiting additionality will not only address major inefficiencies in CDM operation but can also help to increase the credibility of the mechanism.

Insufficient contribution to sustainable development. The CDM was created with two objectives: the global mitigation of

climate change; and the sustainable development of developing countries. But the CDM has been more effective in reducing mitigation costs than in advancing sustainable development.[11] A project is deemed to contribute to sustainable development if national authorities sign off on it, acknowledging a wide range of local co-benefits in line with their development priorities (box 6.2). While many critics accept this broad definition,[12] some nongovernmental organizations have found flaws both in the acceptance of certain project types (such as hydropower, palm oil plantations, and the destruction of industrial gases) and in implementation. A closer look at the CDM project pipeline suggests that the treatment of sustainable development in project documents is sketchy and uneven and that project developers display only a rudimentary concern for or understanding of the concept.

Weak governance and inefficient operation. The CDM is unique in regulating a market dominated by private players through an executive board—essentially a United Nations committee—that approves the calculation methods and projects that create the market's underlying asset. The credibility of the CDM depends largely on the robustness of its regulatory framework and the private sector's confidence in the opportunities the mechanism provides.[13] Complaints are mounting about the continuing lack of transparency and predictability in the board's decision making.[14] At the same time, the CDM architecture has begun to show some weaknesses that are signs of it being a victim of success. There have been copious complaints about yearlong delays in the approval of methodologies[15] and the one- to two-year time lag in the assessment of projects.[16] These are significant constraints to the continuing growth of the CDM as a key instrument to support mitigation efforts in developing countries.

Limited scope. CDM projects are not evenly distributed. A full 75 percent of sales revenues from offsets accrue to Brazil, China, and India (see table 6.3). The CDM has pretty much bypassed low-income countries, which have received only 3 percent of carbon revenues, a third of them for

BOX 6.2   *Assessing the co-benefits of the CDM*

The Clean Development Mechanism produces three broad categories of potential host-country co-benefits (apart from the financial flow from carbon credit sales): the transfer and dissemination of technologies; the contribution to employment and economic growth; and the contribution to environmentally and socially sustainable development.

The extent to which projects contribute to these three objectives can be gauged by looking at project design documents, which can be searched for keywords associated with different co-benefits. This approach was used by Haites, Maosheng, and Seres to assess the technology transfer benefits of the CDM and by Watson and Fankhauser to assess contributions to economic growth and sustainable development.

Haites, Maosheng, and Seres found that only about a third of CDM projects claim to transfer technology, by passing on equipment, know-how, or both. A closer look reveals that they are predominantly projects involving foreign sponsors.

Only a quarter of projects developed unilaterally by the host country claim to transfer technology. Technology transfer is also associated with larger projects. Although only a third of projects transfer technology, they account for two-thirds of emission reductions. Projects explicitly labeled and processed as "small" projects lead to technology transfer in only 26 percent of the cases.

But technology transfer is a difficult concept to define. For mitigation, it tends to be not so much proprietary technology that is shared but operational and managerial know-how of how to run a particular process. A study by Dechezleprêtre and colleagues that specifically looked at the transfer of technologies protected by patent found that the Kyoto Protocol did not accelerate technology flows, though it may have stimulated innovation more generally.

Watson and Fankhauser found that a full 96 percent of projects claim to contribute to environmental and social sustainability, but most of these claims relate

to contributions to economic growth and employment in particular. Just over 80 percent of projects claim some employment impact, and 23 percent contribute to a better livelihood. There are relatively lower employment benefits from industrial gas projects (hydrofluorocarbon, perfluorocarbon, and nitrous oxide reduction—18 percent) and fossil-fuel switching projects (43 percent) than with other sectors, where at least 65 percent of projects state employment benefits.

Applying a more traditional and narrower definition of sustainable development, 67 percent of projects claim training or education benefits (increasing human capital), 24 percent reduce pollution or produce environmental co-benefits (increasing natural capital), and 50 percent have infrastructural or technology benefits (increasing manmade capital).

Sources: Haites, Maosheng, and Seres 2006; Watson and Fankhauser 2009; Dechezleprêtre and others 2009.

three gas-flaring projects in Nigeria. There is a similar concentration in sectors, with much of the abatement action concentrated in a fairly small number of industrial gas projects. The CDM has not supported any increased efficiencies in the built and household environments or transportation systems, which produce 30 percent of global carbon emissions[17] and are the fastest-growing sources of carbon emissions in the emerging markets.[18] Nor has the CDM supported sustainable livelihoods or catalyzed energy access for the rural and peri-urban poor.[19] The exclusion of deforestation emissions from the CDM leaves the largest emission source of many tropical developing countries untapped.[20]

Weakness of the incentive, reinforced by uncertainty about market continuity.   The CDM has not moved developing countries onto low-carbon development paths.[21] The incentive of the CDM has been too weak to foster the necessary transformation in the economy, without which carbon intensities in developing countries will continue

to increase.[22] The CDM's project approach structure and lack of leverage have restricted it to a fairly small number of projects. Uncertainty about the continuation of the carbon offset market beyond 2012 is also having a chilling effect on transactions.

The efficiency cost of adaptation funding

An important source of adaptation finance, and the key revenue source of the Adaptation Fund, is a 2 percent levy on the CDM, a tax that could be extended to include other trading schemes, such as Joint Implementation. This is a promising route to raising financial resources for the Adaptation Fund, which offers clear additionality. But it also raises some basic economic issues. Perhaps the most important objection is that the CDM levy is taxing a good (mitigation finance) rather than a bad (emissions). More generally, the levy raises two basic questions:

- What is the scope for raising additional adaptation finance through the levy, and what is the loss in economic efficiency (or deadweight loss, in economic jargon) associated with the tax?

- How is the tax burden distributed between the sellers (developing countries) and buyers (developed countries)?

Analysis based on the U.K. government's GLOCAF model shows that the ability of an extended carbon trading scheme to raise additional adaptation revenues will depend on the type of global climate deal that is agreed.[23] Revenues will vary depending on the expected demand, particularly whether demand will be constrained by supplementary restrictions to promote domestic abatement, and to a lesser extent on the expected supply, including whether a future regime could encompass credits from avoided deforestation and from other sectors and regions that currently produce little carbon trade.

Revenues will also depend on the tax rate. At the current rate of 2 percent the levy could be expected to raise around $2 billion a year in 2020 if demand is unconstrained but less than half that amount if restrictions are placed on the purchase of credits (table 6.5). To raise $10 billion a year the tax rate would have to increase to 10 percent and all supplementary restrictions would have to be abolished. Even at this higher rate the economic cost of the tax would be fairly minor, particularly in relation to the overall gains from trade.

Like all taxes, the cost of the levy is shared between the buyers and sellers of carbon credits depending on their responsiveness to price changes (the price elasticities of supply and demand). In the scenarios where demand is constrained, buyers do not respond strongly to the tax, and much of the tax burden is thus passed on to them. But this response changes if constraints on demand are eased. At that point the tax incidence shifts decidedly against developing countries, which have to shoulder more than two-thirds of the tax burden to keep the price of their credits competitive. That is, developing countries would make the main contribution to the Adaptation Fund (through forgone carbon market revenues). Rather than transferring funds from developed to developing countries, the CDM

levy would transfer resources from the big CDM host countries (Brazil, China, India —see table 6.3) to the vulnerable countries eligible for adaptation funding.

Increasing the scale of climate-change finance

To close the financing gap, financing sources have to be diversified, and the existing instruments have to be reformed to increase their efficiency and permit the required scale-up. This section highlights some of the main challenges in this respect, arguing for the following:

- Harnessing new sources of revenue to support adaptation and mitigation by national governments, international organizations, and dedicated financing mechanisms like the Adaptation Fund.

- Increasing the efficiency of carbon markets by reforming the CDM as a key vehicle to promote private mitigation funding.

- Expanding performance-based incentives to land use, land-use change, and forestry to change the balance between private and public funding in this important area.

- Leveraging private sector funding for adaptation.

Countries will also have to consider the fiscal framework for climate action. Government action on climate mitigation and adaptation can have important fiscal

Table 6.5　The tax incidence of an adaptation levy on the Clean Development Mechanism (2020)
$ millions

Tax rate	Revenue raised	Deadweight loss	Burden to developing countries
2 percent			
Restricted demand and low supply	996	1	249
Unrestricted demand and high supply	2,003	7	1,257
10 percent			
Restricted demand and low supply	4,946	20	869
Unrestricted demand and high supply	10,069	126	6,962

Source: Fankhauser, Martin, and Prichard, forthcoming.

Note: Under restricted demand, regions can buy up to 20 percent of their target through credits; there is completely free trading in the unrestricted demand scenario. In the low-supply scenario the CDM operates in the same sectors and regions as it does now. In the high-supply scenario carbon trading is expanded in regional and sectoral scope, including credits from Reduced Emissions from Deforestation and forest Degradation (although, as noted, the latter emissions are not currently in the CDM). The total market volume (excluding secondary transactions) is around $50 billion in the restricted-demand, low-supply case and around $100 billion in the unrestricted-demand, high-supply case.

BOX 6.3   *Carbon taxes versus cap-and-trade*

The principal market-based instruments used for climate mitigation are carbon taxes and cap-and-trade schemes. By eschewing fixed quotas or technology standards (the usual regulatory instruments employed by governments), these instruments leave individual firms and households free to find the least-cost way to meet a climate target.

A carbon tax is a price instrument and typically operates by taxing the carbon content of fuel inputs, thus creating an incentive either to switch to lower-carbon fuels or to use fuel more efficiently. However, because governments have imperfect information about the costs of fuel switching or increasing energy efficiency, there is corresponding uncertainty about how much abatement will actually occur for a given tax level. If a government has an emission cap under a global agreement, then it may need to adjust the tax rate iteratively to keep emissions within the cap.

Under a cap-and-trade scheme, governments issue emission permits representing a legal right to emit carbon—these permits are freely tradable between scheme participants. Because firms and sectors will differ in their marginal costs of fuel switching or energy efficiency, the potential for gains from trade exists. For example, if one firm has a high marginal cost of mitigation while another has a much lower cost, then the firm with the lower cost can sell a permit at a price above its marginal cost of mitigation, reduce its emissions accordingly, and make a profit—and as long as the price of the permit is below the marginal mitigation cost of the buyer, then this is a profitable trade for the buyer as well. Because cap-and-trade is a quantitative instrument, there is high certainty that a country will stay within its cap (assuming that enforcement is effective), but there may be a corresponding uncertainty about the level and stability of permit prices.

The two instruments differ in important ways:

Efficiency
Because of imperfect information about mitigation costs, there is a risk with any market instrument of abating emissions, either too much or not enough, engendering either excess costs or excess damages. A famous result by Weitzman shows that the choice of instrument under uncertainty depends on the relative slope of the damage and abatement cost functions. What this means in the case of climate change is unclear, since the shape of the damage function is highly uncertain. However, because greenhouse gases are stock pollutants, many have argued that, in the short-term, damages are likely to be fairly constant per marginal ton, which would favor a tax.

Price volatility
While cap-and-trade creates certainty about the quantity of emissions, it may lead to uncertainty about price. For example, if there is a shift in the business cycle or in the relative prices of low-carbon and high-carbon fuels, then permit prices will be directly affected. Price volatility not only makes it difficult to plan abatement strategies, it also reduces the incentive to invest in research and development on new abatement technologies. Banking and borrowing of allowances are two simple mechanisms that can help dampen price volatility.

Recycling revenues
A carbon tax is a direct source of fiscal revenue, and governments have the option of either using the tax to finance expenditures or recycling the revenues by lowering or eliminating other taxes. To the extent that recycling increases the overall efficiency of the tax system, there is a "double dividend"—but a double dividend is not guaranteed if the carbon taxes themselves exacerbate existing inefficiencies in the tax system. If emission permits are auctioned by the government, then these too become a source of fiscal revenue.

Political economy
Because the world has a fixed carbon budget for any chosen climate target, the certainty associated with a quantitative instrument may be appealing to some groups. And everyone, whether firms or individuals, dislikes taxes. This line of reasoning may seem to favor cap-and-trade, but tax aversion also means that firms will resist auctioning of permits and may instead lobby for their allocation of free permits. In general the process of allocating permits, if not done through auction, leads to rent seeking and potentially corrupt behavior.

Administrative efficiency
The cost of administering climate policy and the institutional and human capital required are particularly important considerations in developing countries. A tax on the carbon content of fuels is potentially very cost-effective because it could piggyback on existing administrative systems for levying excise taxes on fuels. In contrast setting up a market for auctioning and trading permits could be highly complex, and a regulator would be required to monitor the exercise of market power by participants. In addition, a permit system would require monitoring and enforcement at the level of individual emitters, while monitoring of a carbon tax potentially could be done much more cheaply at the level of fuel wholesalers.

Carbon taxes and cap-and-trade are not necessarily mutually exclusive. The European Union has opted for emissions trading to address emissions from large sources (utilities, heat production, large energy-intensive industrial facilities, and aviation, to be phased in in 2011), covering about 40 percent of EU emissions. Other instruments (including a carbon tax in several European countries) target emissions from other sectors, notably residential and services, transport, waste management, and agriculture. In contrast in Australia and the United States cap-and-trade is emerging as the main instrument to regulate economywide greenhouse gas emissions (with a set of accompanying policies and measures, like renewable energy portfolio standards).

Sources: Bovenberg and Goulder 1996; Weitzman 1974; Aldy, Ley, and Parry 2008; Newell and Pizer 2000.

consequences for revenues, subsidies, and flows of international finance. Key elements of this framework include the following.

Choice of mitigation instrument. Taxes or tradable permits will be more efficient instruments than regulation, and each can generate significant fiscal revenues (assuming that permits are auctioned by the government). Box 6.3 highlights the key characteristics of carbon taxes versus cap-and-trade approaches.

Fiscal neutrality. Countries have the option of using carbon fiscal revenues to reduce other distorting taxes, which could have major growth and welfare consequences. But treasuries in developing countries typically have a weak revenue base, which may reduce the incentives for complete fiscal neutrality.

Administrative simplicity and cost. Carbon taxes, because they can be placed on the carbon content of fuels, offer the simplicity of building on existing fuel excise regimes. Cap-and-trade systems can entail large administrative costs for allocating permits and ensuring compliance.

Distributional impacts. Any price instrument for mitigation will have distributional consequences for different income groups depending on the carbon intensity of their consumption and whether they are employed in sectors that shrink as a result of carbon taxes or caps; offsetting fiscal actions may be required if low-income households are disproportionately affected.

Policy coherence. Existing subsidy schemes, particularly on energy and agriculture, may run counter to actions to mitigate and adapt to climate change. Subsidies on goods that will become scarcer under climate change, such as water, also risk perverse effects.

Box 6.4 highlights the efforts of the Indonesian Ministry of Finance to incorporate climate issues into overall macroeconomic and fiscal policy.

Generating new sources of finance for adaptation and mitigation

Public institutions—national governments, international organizations, and the official financing mechanisms of the UNFCCC—are among the key drivers of climate-smart

---

BOX 6.4 *Indonesian Ministry of Finance engagement on climate change issues*

Indonesia's Finance Ministry has recognized that mitigating and adapting to climate change require macroeconomic management, fiscal policy plans, revenue-raising alternatives, insurance markets, and long-term investment options. With development as the priority, Indonesia is trying to balance economic, social, and environmental goals. The country could benefit from investing in development with climate-friendly technology for a cleaner, more efficient growth path. Benefits would include potential payments from carbon markets for the reductions in emissions achieved from a cleaner energy path or from reductions in the annual rate of deforestation. The Ministry of Finance will play an essential role in the financing, development, and implementation of climate-change policies and programs. To mobilize the financing needed, Indonesia

envisions a mix of mechanisms paired with integrated national policies, a strong enabling framework, and long-term incentives to attract investment.

The Finance Ministry's comparative advantage is in considering the allocation and incentive decisions that affect the whole economy. In managing climate-financing opportunities, the ministry acknowledges the importance of investor and donor confidence in its approaches and institutions. Recognizing that donor funds—whether grants or soft loans—will always be small relative to private investment in energy sector development, infrastructure, and housing, Indonesia will continue to need sound policies and incentives to attract and leverage private investment toward sustainable development and lower-carbon outcomes.

Indonesia has already taken steps to rationalize energy pricing by reducing fossil-fuel subsidies in 2005 and 2008, to reduce deforestation through improved enforcement and monitoring programs, and to provide incentives for import and installation of pollution control equipment through tax breaks. The Finance and Development Planning ministries have established a national blueprint and budget priorities for integrating climate change into the national development process. The Finance Ministry is examining fiscal and financial policies to stimulate climate-friendly investment, move toward lower-carbon energy options including renewables and geothermal, and improve fiscal incentives in the forestry sector.

Source: Ministry of Finance (Indonesia) 2008.

development. So far they have relied almost exclusively on government revenues to finance their activities. But it is unlikely that climate-change costs rising into the tens or hundreds of billions of dollars a year could be predominantly covered through government contributions. Although additional funds will be forthcoming, the experience with development assistance suggests that there are constraints on the amount of traditional donor finance that can be raised. Moreover, there is a worry from developing countries that contributions from developed countries may not be fully additional to existing development assistance.

Other sources of finance will therefore have to be tapped, and there are several proposals, particularly for adaptation. These include:

Internationally coordinated carbon tax. Proposals for a nationally administered but globally levied carbon tax have the appeal that the tax base would be broad and the revenue flow fairly secure. Moreover, unlike the CDM levy, the tax would be aimed at emissions rather than emission reductions. Rather than impose a deadweight loss, the tax would have a desirable and beneficial corrective effect. The main drawback is that an internationally coordinated tax could impinge on the tax authority of sovereign governments. Gaining international consensus for this option may thus be difficult.

Tax on emissions from international transport. A tax more narrowly focused on international aviation or shipping would have the advantage of targeting two sectors that so far have not been subject to carbon regulation and whose emissions are growing fast. The international nature of the sector might make a tax more palatable for national finance ministers, and the tax base would be large enough to raise considerable amounts. But the global governance of the sectors is complex, with considerable power in the hands of international bodies, such as the International Maritime Organization. So the administrative hurdles of setting up such a tax might be considerable.

Auctioning assigned amount units. The emission reduction commitments of par-

ties under the Kyoto Protocol are expressed in assigned amount units (AAUs)—the amount of carbon a country is permitted to emit. An innovative approach, put forward originally by Norway, would set aside a fraction of each country's AAU allocation and auction it to the highest bidder, with revenues earmarked for adaptation.

Domestic auction revenues. Earmarking auction revenues relies on the assumption that most developed countries will soon have fairly comprehensive cap-and-trade schemes and that most of the permits issued under the schemes would be auctioned rather than handed out for free. With schemes already running or under consideration in practically all developed countries, this is a reasonable expectation. But earmarking auction revenues would encroach on the fiscal autonomy of national governments just as much as an internationally coordinated carbon tax and may therefore be similarly difficult to implement.

Each of these options has its advantages and disadvantages.[24] What is important is that the chosen options provide a secure, steady, and predictable stream of revenues of sufficient size. This suggests that finance will have to come from a combination of sources. Table 6.6 presents a range of potential sources of finance as proposed by developed and developing countries.

In the short term some impetus may also come from international efforts to overcome the current economic slump and kick-start the economy through a fiscal stimulus (see chapter 1).[25] Globally, well over $2 trillion has been committed in various fiscal packages, chief among them the $800 billion U.S. package and the $600 billion Chinese plan. Some 18 percent of this, or about $400 billion, is green investment in energy efficiency and renewable energy, and also, in the Chinese plan, adaptation.[26] Deployed over the next 12–18 months these investments could do much to shift the world toward a low-carbon future. At the same time, the packages are by their very nature geared toward stimulating domestic activity. Their effect on international climate finance to developing countries will at best be indirect.

Generating the Funding Needed for Mitigation and Adaptation

Table 6.6 Potential sources of mitigation and adaptation finance

Proposal	Source of funding	Note	Annual funding ($ billions)
Group of 77 and China	0.25–0.5 percent of gross national product of Annex I Parties	Calculated for 2007 gross domestic product	201–402
Switzerland	$2 a ton of CO_2 with a basic tax exemption of 1.5 ton CO_2e per inhabitant	Annually (based on 2012 projections)	18.4
Norway	2 percent auctioning of AAUs	Annually	15–25
Mexico	Contributions based on GDP, greenhouse gases, and population and possibly auctioning permits in developed countries	Annually, scaling up as GDP and emissions rise	10
European Union	Continue 2 percent levy on share of proceeds from CDM	Ranging from low to high demand in 2020	0.2–0.68
Bangladesh, Pakistan	3–5 percent levy on share of proceeds from CDM	Ranging from low to high demand in 2020	0.3–1.7
Colombia, least developed countries	2 percent levy on share of proceeds from Joint Implementation and emissions trading	Annually, after 2012	0.03–2.25
Least developed countries	Levy on international air travel (IATAL)	Annually	4–10
Least developed countries	Levy on bunker fuels (IMERS)	Annually	4–15
Tuvalu	Auction of allowances for international aviation and marine emissions	Annually	28

Source: UNFCCC 2008a.

Note: AAU: assigned amount unit; IATAL: international air travel adaptation levy; IMERS: international maritime emission reduction scheme. Annex I Parties include the high-income countries that were members of the OECD in 1992, plus countries with economies in transition. Annex I countries have committed themselves specifically to the aim of returning individually or jointly.

It takes more than finance: Market solutions are essential but additional policy tools are needed

With more national or regional initiatives exploring emissions trading, the carbon market will likely be significant in catalyzing and financially supporting the needed transformation of investment patterns and lifestyles. Through purchasing offsets in developing countries, cap-and-trade systems can finance lower-carbon investments in developing countries. Carbon markets also provide an essential impetus to finding efficient solutions to the climate problem.

Looking forward, stabilizing temperatures will require a global mitigation effort. At that point carbon will have a price worldwide and will be traded, taxed, or regulated in all countries. Once an efficient carbon price is in place, market forces will direct most consumption and investment decisions toward low-carbon options. With global coverage many of the complications affecting the current carbon market—additionality, leakage, competitiveness, scale—will fall

away. They matter enormously today, and in addressing them the need for a smooth transition to an ultimately global carbon market must not be forgotten. However, some market failures will remain, and governments will need to intervene to correct them.

Decisions that help the emergence of a long-term, predictable, and adequate carbon price are necessary for effective mitigation but, as chapter 4 shows, not sufficient. Some activities, such as risky research and development or energy-efficiency improvements, are hindered by market or regulatory failures; others, such as urban planning, are not directly price sensitive. The forest and agriculture sectors present significant additional potential for emission reduction and sequestration in developing countries but are too complex, with intricate social issues, to rely exclusively on market incentives. Many climate actions will require complementary finance and policy interventions—for example, to overcome energy-efficiency barriers, reduce perceived risks, deepen domestic financial and capital markets, and accelerate the diffusion of climate-friendly technologies.

Increasing the scale and efficiency of carbon markets

The absence of market continuity beyond 2012 is the biggest risk to the momentum of today's carbon market. Considerable uncertainties remain about the very existence of a global carbon market beyond 2012, with questions about the ambition of mitigation targets, the resulting demand for carbon credits, the degree of linking of different trading schemes, and the role for offsets across various existing and upcoming regimes. Defining a global mitigation goal for 2050 supported by intermediate targets (to be determined through the UNFCCC process) would provide long-term carbon price signals and certainty to the private sector as major investment decisions with long-lasting impact on emission trajectories are made over the coming years.

The next phase in constructing a global carbon market must put developed countries onto a low-carbon path and provide the financial and other resources needed to assist the transition of developing countries to a lower-carbon development path. One of the main challenges for a climate agreement is to define a framework that supports and promotes this transformation and facilitates the transition to a more comprehensive system where more countries assume emission reduction targets. As discussed in chapter 5, a gradual incorporation process can be envisaged, with transitions toward more stringent steps depending on responsibility and capacity: adopting climate-friendly policies (a stage many developing countries have already reached), limiting emissions growth, and setting emission reduction targets. To support this gradual progress, various models using carbon finance have been proposed.[27]

But demand for international offsets from Annex I countries will likely remain for quite some time at levels well below what would be needed to reward all mitigation achievements in developing countries while simultaneously maintaining a sufficiently high carbon price. Setting more ambitious targets for Annex I countries[28] will create the incentive for greater cooperation with developing countries in scaling up mitigation, provided a credible supply of offsets can be built at scale.

Concern about the effectiveness and efficiency of the CDM has led to a broad array of proposals on how to enhance, expand, or evolve the mechanism. Broadly speaking, these could be organized along two lines of suggestions. One track would aim at streamlining the CDM to make it more appropriate for a growing market dominated by the private sector by improving efficiency and governance along the project cycle as well as by reducing transaction costs. Another track would aim at scaling up the transformational impact of CDM and carbon finance beyond the limited scope of a project approach, focusing on investment trajectories and affecting emission trends.

It is probably not realistic to attain anything more than incremental changes to the CDM by 2012. Some practitioners clamor for big improvements. But many countries are still learning the ropes of the instrument, and their first projects have just begun to enter the pipeline in the past few months. Others are focused on the agreement and tools for scaling up post-2012 mitigation. There is little or no political space to undertake immediate major revisions to the CDM before 2012, a point emphasized by developing countries that have argued that most of those revisions would require an amendment to the Kyoto Protocol. So, to organize the steps in a possible evolution, it may help to distinguish two levels of improvements or changes to the current CDM, which would ultimately result in two financial mechanisms, operating in parallel and complemented by a nonmarket mechanism funded by public sources.

An activity-based CDM. There is a case to continue operating the current activity-based CDM within its existing rules, with some targeted improvements. In the current system the baseline and additionality are determined for the individual project activity, and the rules seek to differentiate and reward individual efforts that are better than the norm (rather than promoting a better norm). Most medium-to-large installations in small countries can be effectively submitted as individual CDM projects, and microtechnologies such as light bulbs and cooking stoves now have the option of being registered as organized programs of activities under the current CDM (thus cutting down on transaction costs through aggregation). Most small or least developed countries have more urgent demands on scarce institutional capacity than the development of complex greenhouse gas accounting schemes. This means that for some developing countries, perhaps most, there is no need for another set of rules to supply their mitigation potential into the market.

Key administrative improvements would target, for example, improving the quality, relevance, and consistency of information flows within the CDM community; engagement of a professional, full-time staff for the CDM Executive Board and consideration of how to make it more representative of practitioners; and increasing the accountability of the process, potentially including a mechanism that provides an opportunity for project participants to appeal board decisions. In parallel, countries would have to create a business environment conducive to low-carbon investment in general.

A trend-changing market mechanism. This new mechanism would seek to reduce long-term emission trends much more comprehensively. Set up either in or outside the current CDM, it would support the enactment of policy changes that put developing countries onto a low-carbon path. It would recognize and promote emission reductions achieved by adopting particular policies or programs that lead to emission reductions at multiple sources. A programmatic CDM could be a first step toward a trend-changing market mechanism, allowing for the aggregation of unlimited similar activities resulting from the implementation of a policy across time and space. Proposals to support a sectoral shift can be classified in two broad groups: those that stem from an agreement among industries that operate in the same sector but are located across different countries; and those that evolve from a national government's decision to implement a specific policy or program.

There have been many thoughts on how CDM and carbon finance could support climate-friendly policies in developing countries. The proposed options all consider a mechanism for carbon finance to reward the measurable outcomes of a policy (in reduced emissions). Variants pertain to the policy and country commitment under an international agreement (mandatory or flexible), the geographical scale (regional or national), or the sectoral scope (sectoral or cross-sectoral). Among these options sectoral no-lose targets, whereby a country could sell carbon credits for emission reductions below an agreed target (which would lie below business-as-usual levels), while not being penalized for not achieving the target, have attracted a great deal of interest. Such a mechanism would be adapted to developing countries needing to significantly scale up private sector investment—beyond the reach of the CDM in its current form—in line with their sustainable development priorities.

Creating financial incentives for REDD

A particular concern for developing countries is the lack of financial incentives for Reduced Emissions from Deforestation and forest Degradation (REDD). In 2005, nearly one fourth of emissions in developing countries came from land-use change and forestry, so this is a substantial exclusion.[29] But land use, land-use change, and forestry have always been problematic and contentious in the climate negotiations. There was great opposition to their inclusion in the Kyoto Protocol. As a result,

Table 6.7 National and multilateral initiatives to reduce deforestation and degradation

Initiative	Total estimated funding ($ millions)	Period
International Forest Carbon Initiative (Australia)	160	2007–12
Climate and Forest Initiative (Norway)	2,250	2008–12
Forest Carbon Partnership Facility (World Bank)	300	2008–18
Forest Investment Program (part of Climate Investment Funds)	350	2009–12
UN-REDD Program	35	2008–12
Amazon Fund	1,000	2008–15
Congo Basin Forest Fund	200	Uncertain

Source: UNFCCC 2008b.

Note: Names in parentheses are countries or institutions that championed the proposal.

The mitigation potential in the agricultural sector could be significant, estimated to be around 6 gigatons of carbon dioxide equivalent (CO_2e) a year by 2030, with soil carbon sequestration being the main mechanism. Many mitigation opportunities (including cropland management, grazing land management, management of organic soils, restoration of degraded land, and livestock management) use current technologies and can be implemented immediately. In addition, these options are also cost competitive: assuming a price of less than $20 a ton of CO_2e, the global economic mitigation potential in the agricultural sector is close to 2 gigatons of CO_2e a year by 2030.

Extending the scope of carbon markets to include agricultural soil carbon would allow carbon finance to play more of a role in sound land management practices. Agricultural carbon sequestration can help increase agricultural productivity and enhance farmers' capacity to adapt to climate change. Increased soil carbon improves soil structure, with corresponding reduction in soil erosion and nutrient depletion. Soils with increased carbon stocks retain water better, thereby improving the resilience of agricultural systems to drought. These positive biophysical impacts of soil carbon sequestration lead directly to increased crop, forage, and plantation yields and land productivity. However, issues of monitoring and verification of the increased storage and the permanence of the carbon sequestration need to be resolved.

Source: IPCC 2007.

only afforestation and reforestation were allowed within the CDM, but the European Union Emission Trading Scheme excludes them.

Initial attention to REDD was focused on countries where deforestation is occurring (table 6.7). But some heavily forested countries have little deforestation, and they seek support to manage and conserve their forests sustainably, especially if REDD activities in other countries shift logging and agricultural expansion across national borders (leakage). Other countries already have policies and measures to bring their forests under sustainable management, and they seek recognition of their efforts in reducing emissions through market-based solutions akin to payments for environmental services. As discussed in chapter 3, conserving soil carbon (box 6.5) through performance-based mechanisms is also gaining traction, but discussions are at a less advanced stage than for REDD.

REDD touches on many groups and other societal goals, often with a mix of potential positive and negative effects. It could provide a new source of income to indigenous peoples, but they are rightly concerned that REDD mechanisms may be used to threaten their rights of access and their use of traditional lands. REDD may provide resources to bring areas of high biodiversity value under better protection, but it could also displace logging and land clearing across international borders to high biodiversity areas (another example of leakage).

It is generally recognized that before forest countries can receive financial incentives for REDD, they need to establish building blocks in the policy, legal, institutional, and technical areas—referred to as REDD-readiness. The key components of REDD-readiness ought to be carried out at the national level (not at the project level) to respond to the systemic causes of deforestation and forest degradation and to contain leakage.

The Forest Carbon Partnership Facility (FCPF) has been designed to help forest countries in tropical and subtropical regions prepare for REDD and pilot performance-based incentives. In the FCPF, REDD-readiness consists of a national REDD strategy and implementation framework; a national reference scenario for emissions from deforestation and forest degradation; and a national monitoring, reporting, and verification system. The UN-REDD, a joint initiative of the Food and Agriculture Organization, the United Nations Development Programme, and the United Nations Environment Programme, is a similar program.

In its national REDD strategy a country would assess its land use and forest policy to date, identifying the drivers of deforestation and forest degradation. Next, it would conceive strategic options to address these drivers and would assess these options from the point of view of cost-effectiveness, fairness, and sustainability. This would be followed by an assessment of the legal and institutional arrangements needed to implement the REDD strategy, including the body (or bodies) responsible for coordinating REDD at the national level, promoting REDD, and raising funds; benefit-sharing mechanisms for the financial flows expected from REDD; and a national carbon registry to manage REDD activities (both the emission reductions generated and the corresponding revenue flows). In addition, the country would evaluate the investment and capacity building needed to implement the strategy and would assess the environmental and social impacts of the various strategy and implementation options (the benefits, risks, and risk-mitigation measures).

REDD-ready countries need to develop a national reference scenario. The scenario should include a retrospective part, calculating a recent historical average of emissions, and could also include a forward-looking component, forecasting future emissions based on economic growth trends and national development plans.

A national monitoring, reporting, and verification (MRV) system is central to a system of performance-based payments. The MRV system could include the payments' impacts on biodiversity and livelihoods as well as on carbon levels. The roles of remote-sensing technology and ground-based measurements must be defined as part of the MRV system. Experience from community-based natural resource management initiatives has shown that involvement of local people, including indigenous peoples, in participatory monitoring of natural resources can also provide accurate, cost-effective, and locally anchored information on forest biomass and natural resource trends.[30] Natural resource stocks, benefit sharing, and wider social and ecological effects of REDD schemes can be monitored by local communities. Participatory approaches have the potential to greatly improve the governance and management of REDD schemes.

Before large-scale, performance-based payments for REDD can begin, most forest countries will need to adopt policy reforms and undertake investment programs. Investments may be needed to build institutional capacity, improve forest governance and information, scale up conservation and sustainable management of forests, and relieve pressure on forests through, say, relocating agribusiness activities away from forests or improving agricultural productivity. To assist countries in these activities several initiatives have been launched or are under design (see table 6.7). In addition the World Bank has proposed a forest investment program under the Climate Investment Funds, and the Prince's Rainforest Project and the Coalition for Rainforest Nations have recently proposed that financial institutions issue bonds to raise significant resources to help forest countries finance forest conservation and development programs. This example illustrates how a mix of instruments is required to steer a transformation of behaviors and investment decisions: a combination of up-front finance (concessional and innovative finance) and performance-based incentives are needed to promote policy reforms, build capacity, and undertake investment programs. The example also highlights the crucial role of public finance as a catalyst for climate action.

Leveraging private finance for adaptation

Compared with mitigation, where the emphasis has been on private finance from carbon markets, adaptation finance has a strong focus on official flows. This is not surprising, given that adaptation is closely linked to good development and that many adaptation measures are public goods—for example, the protection of coastal zones (a local public good) and the provision of timely climate information (a national public good).

Despite the emphasis on public finance, much of the adaptation burden will fall on individuals and firms. Insurance against climate hazards, for example, is provided primarily by the private sector. Similarly, the task of climate-proofing the world's capital stock—private dwellings, factory buildings, and machinery—will fall predominantly on private owners, although the state will have to provide flood protection and disaster relief. Private companies also own or operate some of the public infrastructure that will have to be adapted to a warmer world—seaports, electric power plants, and water and sewage systems.

For governments the challenge of involving the private sector in adaptation finance is threefold: getting private players to adapt; sharing the cost of adapting public infrastructure; and leveraging private finance to fund dedicated adaptation investments.

Getting private players to adapt effectively.

Most consumption and business decisions

are affected, directly or indirectly, by climate factors—from the clothes people wear to the planting decisions farmers make to the way buildings are designed. People are used to making these implicit adaptation decisions. The main role for governments will be to provide an economic environment that facilitates these decisions. This can take the form of economic incentives (tax breaks for adaptation investments, property taxes differentiated by risk, differentiated insurance premiums), regulation (zone planning, building codes) or simply education and better information (long-term weather forecasts, agricultural extension services).

These measures will entail an economic cost, such as meeting stricter building regulation, using different seed varieties, or paying higher insurance premiums. That cost will be borne by the economy and spread across sectors as producers pass on higher costs to their clients and as insurance schemes help to pool risks. There will be little need to draw on dedicated adaptation funding, except perhaps to meet the government's administrative costs or to protect vulnerable groups from the adverse effects of a policy.

Sharing the costs of adapting public infrastructure. A large part of the public adaptation bill involves climate-proofing a country's transport infrastructure, electric power networks, water systems, and communication networks. Whether these services are provided by public, private, or commercialized public entities, the bill will need to be funded either by taxpayers (domestic, or foreign if adaptation assistance is provided) or by users (through higher tariffs).

For infrastructure service providers climate change (and climate policy) will become another risk factor to take into account alongside other regulatory, commercial, and macroeconomic risks.[31] It would therefore be wise to build responsibility for adaptation into the regulatory regime as early and predictably as possible. The greater physical uncertainty also requires building more flexibility into the regulatory system because ex ante regulation is ill suited to situations with unpredictable changes. New and innovative approaches to regulation offer promising

alternatives. A good example is the model adopted by the U.K. energy regulator, which can act as an auditor and leave investment decisions to the key actors in the government and the private sector.[32]

Leveraging private finance to fund dedicated adaptation investments. For several reasons the scope for private participation in dedicated adaptation infrastructure is probably limited. Given that dedicated adaptation investments typically do not create commercial revenues for private operators, they must be remunerated from the public purse. This creates a debt-like liability for the government that needs to be recorded in the public accounts. Nor does the efficiency argument look compelling.[33] Adaptation structures such as flood defenses are fairly cheap and simple to operate and so offer little scope for operational efficiency gains by a private manager. There may be more scope for efficiency gains in the construction and design phase, but these can be captured equally well through appropriate procurement mechanisms.

More generally private flows have amounted to a small share of the overall infrastructure funding needs of developing countries and are likely to remain modest for the duration of the current financial crisis.[34] For this and the reasons discussed above, infrastructure experts have warned not to expect too much from public-private partnerships in raising climate-change finance.[35]

Ensuring the transparent, efficient, and equitable use of funds

However successful the attempts at raising additional funds may be, climate finance will be scarce, so funds have to be used effectively and allocated transparently and equitably.

On the mitigation side, fund allocation will be dominated by efficiency considerations. Mitigation is a global public good, and its benefits are the same wherever abatement takes place (although the allocation of mitigation costs raises equity issues). With the right framework in place—essentially a carbon market that allows the exploration of abatement opportunities on a global scale while protecting host-country interests—a combination of carbon markets, other performance-based systems, and public funds aimed at niches overlooked by the market can allocate capital fairly effectively.

The allocation of adaptation finance, by contrast, raises important questions of fairness as well as efficiency. Unlike that for mitigation the allocation of adaptation resources has strong distributional implications. Money spent protecting small island states is no longer available for African farmers. The question of how to classify adaptation finance is still debated, and the controversy spills over to how to allocate this finance. Developing countries are inclined to view adaptation finance as compensation for damages, invoking a global polluter-pays principle. From the developing-country viewpoint, therefore, the question of how adaptation finance is used is beyond the purview of high-income countries. But the latter countries feel strongly that scarce financial resources should be used efficiently, whatever the justification for or provenance of the funds.

It can certainly be argued that the efficient and equitable allocation and use of adaptation finance are in everybody's interest. Wasteful use of resources can undermine public support for the whole climate agenda. That makes the transparent, efficient, and equitable allocation of adaptation funding paramount. As an example of how development institutions have handled the allocation of finance, consider the approach taken by the International Development Association (IDA), which constructs an index combining the need for finance, the absorptive capacity of the government, and the performance of the central government (box 6.6). The IDA approach is not without its faults. Because the formula is uniform across countries, it essentially imposes the same development model on all countries.[36] This is already problematic for standard development issues and may be even more so for climate change, where much less is known about the right adaptation model. Even so, an empirical approach to allocating adaptation finance that aims to address these concerns could serve at least three purposes: it could reduce transaction costs if lobbying and negotiation

---

BOX 6.6   *Allocating concessional development finance*

The International Development Association (IDA) allocation formula offers a possible model for allocating concessional finance in a transparent and empirically driven way. This evolving model of resource allocation, with 10 years of progressive refinement, has allocated roughly $10 billion of concessional finance a year to the world's poorest countries.

The IDA allocation formula breaks down into three basic indexes, one of *need* for concessional finance, one of *absorptive capacity,* and one of *performance of the central government.* On need, the basic criterion is the average poverty level in each country, weighted to favor the poorest countries, times the number of people in the country. Absorptive capacity is measured by World Bank portfolio performance—delays in disbursement and cancellations of loans or credits are clear indicators of poor ability to absorb additional finance. Based on results from the aid-effectiveness literature, the formula is weighted toward countries with the strongest governance because the evidence suggests that these countries most successfully translate aid resources into economic growth. Performance of central government in turn has two subindexes: *quality of macroeconomic, structural, and social policies and institutions* and *quality of governance,* derived from the World Bank Country Policy and Institutional Assessment.

The formula gives weights of 68 percent to governance; 24 percent to macroeconomic, social, and structural policies; and 8 percent to absorptive capacity. The composite of these scores is then multiplied by the number of people in the country, weighted by the average income of the population (to capture need) to derive the final score that drives the allocation of concessional finance.

Because this formula could penalize some of the neediest countries, a portion of the annual supply of finance is allocated off the top: each country receives a minimum allocation; countries coming out of conflict and with extremely fragile institutions are given additional assistance; and allowance is made for natural disasters. In addition IDA finance is capped for "blend" countries, which have access to commercial finance.

Sources: IDA 2007; Burnside and Dollar 2000.

---

are not part of the allocation process; it could support the results agenda with an allocation process based on empirical measures; and it could support mutual accountability through transparency in allocations.

The measure of need for finance should be closely related to the concept of climate vulnerability. As conceived by the IPCC, vulnerability is a function of the capacity to adapt, the sensitivity to climate factors, and the exposure to climate change.[37] The measure of need for finance could thus be some population-weighted index of sensitivity and exposure, perhaps with a poverty weight as well. For large countries in particular, the distribution of impacts and differences in vulnerability between localities would also have to be taken into account.

Central government performance and absorptive capacity for flows of finance clearly determine a country's capacity to adapt, but they are not the only critical performance factors in climate adaptation. What might be called "social capacity" would appear important in determining the severity of local climatic impacts, including such factors as inequality (Gini coefficient), depth of financial markets, dependency ratio, adult literacy rate, and female education.

In sum, an allocation index for adaptation finance could consist of the following factors:

Allocation index =
Central government performance
× Absorptive capacity
× Lack of social capacity
× Climate sensitivity
× Climate change exposure
× Population weight
× Poverty weight

Actually constructing such an index presents several challenges. Information about the vulnerability of developing countries is still sketchy. Difficulties emerge from the complicated, and often undefined, pathways that translate potential impacts, themselves uncertain, into vulnerability. Compounding the uncertainty in linking environmental to socioeconomic impacts is the further uncertainty inherent in future climate scenarios. Models rely on a limited number of defined socioeconomic predictions, and each model has a range of potential changes. So most studies relating to future climatic scenarios focus on expected impacts within sectors or relate to specific outcomes, such as changes in health and losses because of sea-level rise. Few studies have attempted to translate these outputs into an assessment of vulnerability on the ground.[38]

As with IDA allocations, there is a risk that a climate adaptation allocation index will penalize poor countries with high climate sensitivity and exposure but very weak institutions. If an allocation formula is pursued, allowances for extremely fragile countries should be part of the overall allocation framework.

Some tentative first steps toward constructing a vulnerability index are shown in box 6.7, which plots a composite index of projected physical impacts against a composite index of social capacity. The results of this stylized exercise are indicative only, but they suggest that the countries with the highest vulnerability are predominantly in Sub-Saharan Africa.[39] Box 6.8 scatters the same projected impact index against a measure of country performance (combined central government capacity and ability to absorb finance) derived from the IDA allocation formula. Again Sub-Saharan Africa exhibits the combination of projected high impacts and low capacity to adapt.

Matching financing needs and sources of funds

Combating climate change is a massive socioeconomic, technological, institutional, and policy challenge. Particularly for developing countries it is also a financing challenge. By about 2030 the incremental investment needs for mitigation in developing countries could be $140 to $175 billion (with associated financing requirements of $265 to $565 billion) a year. The financing needs for adaptation by that time could be $30 to $100 billion a year. This is additional funding beyond baseline development finance needs, which also remain essential and will help in part to close existing adaptation gaps.

Though growing, current climate-related financial flows to developing countries cover only a tiny fraction of the estimated needs. No single source will provide that much additional revenue, and so a combination of funding sources will be required. For adaptation funding might come from the current adaptation levy on the CDM, which could raise around $2 billion a year by 2020 if extended to a wider set of carbon transactions. Proposals like the sale of AAUs, a levy on international transport emissions, and a global carbon tax could each raise around $15 billion a year.

For mitigation at the national level the majority of funding will have to come from the private sector. But public policy will need to create a business environment conducive to low-carbon investment, including but not limited to an expanded,

BOX 6.7   *Climate vulnerability versus social capacity*

The figure plots a composite index of physical impact (taken as a function of climate sensitivity and climate-change exposure and derived from a number of global impact studies) against a composite index of social capacity (derived from a number of socioeconomic indicators).

Social capacity and vulnerability, as measured by projected impacts, are composite indexes of the indicators described in the table below.

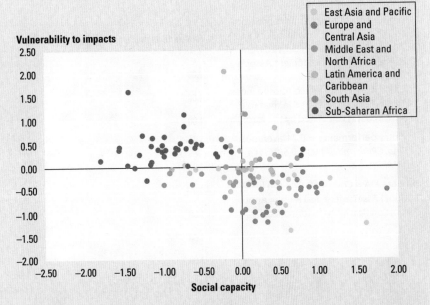

	Indicator	Metric	Source	Assumptions
Impact	Sea-level rise	Percent population affected by 1 meter rise	Dasgupta and others 2007	Landlocked countries assumed to experience zero impact
	Agriculture	Percent yield loss in 2050, IPCC SRES scenario A2b	Parry and others 2004	Decreasing yields represent decreasing welfare for country. Increased yields from climate change represent increasing welfare. Farm-level adaptation present
	Health	Percent additional deaths in 2050	Bosello, Roson, and Tol 2006	Additional deaths representative of all health impacts from climate change
	Disaster	Percent population killed by disasters (historical data set)	CRED 2008	Current disaster patterns to represent future areas at risk
Social capacity	Literacy	Percent population, aged >15 years, literate (1991–2005)	World Bank 2007c	The higher the literacy rate, the higher the social capacity
	Age dependency ratio	Ratio of dependent population to working population (2006)	World Bank 2007c	The lower the age dependency ratio, the higher the social capacity
	Primary completion rate (female)	Percent female population completing primary education (1991–2006)	World Bank 2007c	The higher the completion rate, the higher the social capacity
	Gini	Gini coefficient (latest available year)	World Bank 2007c	The lower the inequality, the higher the social capacity
	Domestic credit to private sector	Domestic credit to private sector, as percent of GDP (1998–2006)	World Bank 2007c	The greater the investment, the higher the social capacity
	Governance	WGI (World Governance Indicator) voice and accountability	Kaufman, Kraay, and Mastruzzi 2008	The higher the WGI score, the higher the social capacity

BOX 6.8 *Climate vulnerability versus capacity to adapt*

The figure plots the impact index against a measure of country performance (combined central government capacity and ability to absorb finance) derived from the International Development Association allocation formula.

Capacity to adapt is a composite index of the indicators described in the table below, and it is calculated by the formula:

Country performance = 0.24*average (CPIAa, CPIAb and CPIAc) + 0.68*CPIAd + 0.08*ARPP,

where CPIA = Country Policy and Institutional Assessment and ARPP = Annual Report on Portfolio Performance.

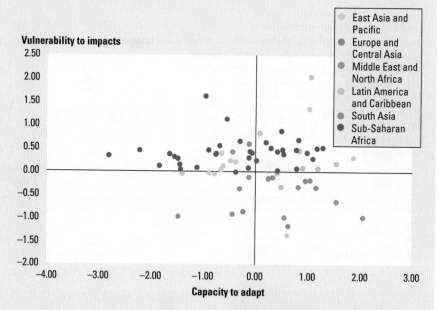

	Indicator	Metric (year)	Source	Assumptions
Capacity to adapt	Economic management	CPIAa (2007)	World Bank	The higher the country performance, the higher the capacity to adapt
	Structural policies	CPIAb (2007)	World Bank	
	Policies for social inclusion and equity	CPIAc (2007)	World Bank	
	Public sector management and institutions (governance)	CPIAd (2007)	World Bank	
	Capacity to absorb finance	ARPP (2007) World Bank portfolio at risk (age-discounted)	World Bank	

Sources: CPIA figures http://go.worldbank.org/S2THWI1X60. For details on the calculation of CPIA scores, see World Bank 2007b. ARPP scores are reported in World Bank 2007a.

efficient, and well-regulated carbon market. Complementary public funding—most likely from fiscal transfers—may be required to overcome investment barriers (such as those related to risk) and to reach areas the private sector is likely to neglect. Stringent emission targets will also be required—initially in high-income countries, eventually for many others—to create enough demand for offsets and to support the carbon price.

Once the majority of countries have emission caps under an international climate agreement, markets can autonomously generate much of the needed national mitigation finance as consumption and production decisions respond to carbon prices, whether through taxes or cap-and-trade. But national carbon markets will not automatically generate international flows of finance. Flows of mitigation finance to developing countries can come from fiscal flows, from linking national emission trading schemes, or potentially from trading AAUs. Flows from developed to developing countries can thus be achieved in several ways. But these flows are central to ensuring that an effective and efficient solution to the climate problem is also an equitable solution.

Notes

1. See the overview chapter for details.

2. Barker and others 2007.

3. UNFCCC 2008a.

4. Agrawala and Fankhauser (2008) review the adaptation cost literature; Klein and Persson (2008) discuss the link between adaptation and development. Parry and others (2009) critique the UNFCCC adaptation cost estimate, suggesting that the true costs could be 2–3 times higher.

5. Besides carbon markets, tradable green and white certificates schemes (targeting respectively the expansion of renewable energy sources or the improvement of energy efficiency through demand-side management measures) are other examples of market-based mechanisms with potential mitigation benefits. Other instruments include financial incentives (taxes or subsidies, price support, tax benefits on investment, or subsidized loans) and other policy and measures (norms, labels).

6. The financial benefit to host countries is lower than the overall size of the CDM market for two reasons. First a vast majority of CDM transactions on the primary market are forward purchase agreements with payment on delivery of emission reductions. Depending on project performance, the amount and schedule of carbon delivery may prove quite different. Project developers tend to sell forward credits at a discount that reflects these delivery risks. Second CDM credits are bought and sold several times on a secondary market until they reach the end user. The financial intermediaries active on the secondary market that take on the delivery risk are compensated with a higher sell-on price if the risk does not materialize. These trades do not directly give rise to emission reductions, unlike transactions in the primary market. The secondary CDM market continued to grow in 2008 with transactions in excess of $26 billion (a fivefold increase over 2007). In contrast the primary CDM market declined in value for the first time, to $ 7.2 billion (down 12 percent from 2007 levels), under the weight of the economic downturn and amid lingering uncertainty about market continuity after 2012. See Capoor and Ambrosi 2009.

7. OECD/DAC, Rio Marker for climate change, http://www.oecd.org/document/11/0,33 43,en_2649_34469_11396811_1_1_1_1,00.html (accessed May 2009).

8. UNEP 2009. Estimates of clean energy investments that benefit from CDM tend to be higher than actual sustainable energy investment in developing countries because many CDM projects are at an early stage (not operational or commissioned or at financial closure) when certified emission reductions are transacted.

9. See Decision 1/CP.13 reached at the 13th Conference of the Parties of the UNFCCC in Bali, December 2007, http://unfccc.int/resource/ docs/2007/cop13/eng/06a01.pdf#page=3 (accessed July 3, 2009).

10. Michaelowa and Pallav (2007) and Schneider (2007), for example, claim that a number of projects would have happened anyway. In contrast, business organizations complain about an excessively stringent additionality test (IETA 2008; UNFCCC 2007).

11. Olsen 2007; Sutter and Parreno 2007; Olsen and Fenhann 2008; Nussbaumer 2009.

12. Cosbey and others 2005; Brown and others 2004; Michaelowa and Umamaheswaran 2006.

13. Streck and Chagas 2007; Meijer 2007; Streck and Lin 2008.

14. IETA 2005; Stehr 2008.

15. IETA 2008.

16. Michaelowa and Pallav 2007; IETA 2008.

17. Barker and others 2007.

18. Sperling and Salon 2002.

19. Figueres and Newcombe 2007.

20. Eliasch 2008.

"*The ice is melting because of rising temperature. The boy sits upset. A bird has fallen—another victim of polluted air. Flowers grow near the trash can. They die before the boy could take them to the bird. To reverse these phenomena my appeal to world leaders is keep nature clean, use solar and wind energies, and improve technologies.*"

—Shant Hakobyan, Armenia, age 12

21. Figueres, Haites, and Hoyt 2005; Wara 2007; Wara and Victor 2008.

22. Sterk 2008.

23. See Fankhauser, Martin, and Prichard, forthcoming.

24. See Müller 2008 for a discussion.

25. Barbier 2009; Bowen and others 2009.

26. Robins, Clover, and Magness 2009, as discussed in chapter 1.

27. These include models under which emission reductions would be rewarded in relation to particular sectors or that are built on various forms of targets, such as intensity or absolute or relative emission reduction. Crediting achievements could take place on the national level only or involve project activities. Crediting could be based on an initial allocation of allowances (cap-and-trade) or ex post (baseline-and-credit). And it could be linked or separated from existing carbon markets. Mechanisms that build on emissions trading can be directly or indirectly linked to other carbon markets and can create credits that are fully, partly, or not fungible with existing carbon markets.

28. If achieved, the total reductions of the various proposals of high-income countries would reduce emissions in aggregate only 10–15 percent below 1990 emissions levels by 2020. This is far short of the 25–40 percent reductions below 1990 levels that have been called for by the IPCC in the 2020 time frame; see Howes 2009.

29. WRI 2008; Houghton 2009.

30. Danielsen and others 2009.

31. Vagliasindi 2008.

32. Pollitt 2008.

33. Agrawala and Fankhauser 2008.

34. Investment commitments through public-private partnerships have amounted to 0.3–0.4 percent of developing countries' GDP over the 2005–07 period (Private Participation in Infrastructure Database, http://ppi.worldbank.org/). In contrast, infrastructure investment needs are estimated to range from 2 percent to 7 percent of GDP, with fast-growing countries like China and Vietnam investing upward of 7 percent of GDP a year. Estache and Fay 2007.

35. Estache 2008.

36. Kanbur 2005.

37. Füssel 2007.

38. Impact and vulnerability studies include, for instance, Bättig, Wild, and Imboden (2007); Deressa, Hassan, and Ringler (2008); Diffenbaugh and others (2007); and Giorgi (2006). Other studies have focused on sectoral losses or case study/country specific vulnerability: see Dasgupta and others (2007) on coastal zones; Parry and others (1999) and Parry and others (2004) on changes in global agricultural yields; Arnell (2004) and Alcamo and Henrichs (2002) for water availability changes; Tol, Ebi, and Yohe (2006) and Bosello, Roson, and Tol (2006) for health.

39. In boxes 6.7 and 6.8, composite indexes are calculated by transforming individual indicators to z-scores then taking an unweighted average of the resulting scores.

References

Agrawala, S., and S. Fankhauser. 2008. *Economic Aspects of Adaptation to Climate Change: Costs, Benefits and Policy Instruments*. Paris: Organisation for Economic Co-operation and Development.

Alcamo, J., and T. Henrichs. 2002. "Critical Regions: A Model-based Estimation of World Water Resources Sensitive to Global Changes." *Aquatic Sciences* 64 (4): 352–62.

Aldy, J. E., E. Ley, and I. Parry. 2008. *A Tax-Based Approach to Slowing Global Climate Change*. Washington, DC: Resources for the Future.

Arnell, N. W. 2004. "Climate Change and Global Water Resources: SRES Emissions and Socio-Economic Scenarios." *Global Environmental Change* 14 (1): 31–52.

Bättig, M. B., M. Wild, and D. M. Imboden. 2007. "A Climate Change Index: Where Climate Change May Be Prominent in the 21st Century." *Geophysical Research Letters* 34 (1): 1–4.

Barbier, E. B. 2009. *A Global Green New Deal*. Geneva: United Nations Environment Programme.

Barker, T., I. Bashmakov, L. Bernstein, J. E. Bogner, P. R. Bosch, R. Dave, O. R. Davidson, B. S. Fisher, S. Gupta, K. Halsnaes, B. Heij, S. Khan Ribeiro, S. Kobayashi, M. D. Levine, D. L. Martino, O. Masera, B. Metz, L. A. Meyer, G.-J. Nabuurs, A. Najam, N. Nakićenović, H.-H. Rogner, J. Roy, J. Sathaye, R. Schock, P. Shukla, R. E. H. Sims, P. Smith, D. A. Tirpak, D. Urge-Vorsatz, and D. Zhou. 2007. "Technical Summary." In *Climate Change 2007: Mitigation. Contribution of Working Group III to the Fourth Assessment Report of the Intergovernmental Panel on Climate Change*, ed. B. Metz, O. R. Davidson, P. R. Bosch, R. Dave, and L. A. Meyer. Cambridge, UK: Cambridge University Press.

Bosello, F., R. Roson, and R. S. J. Tol. 2006. "Economy-Wide Estimates of the Implications of Climate Change: Human Health." *Ecological Economics* 58 (3): 579–91.

Bovenberg, A. L., and L. Goulder. 1996. "Optimal Environmental Taxation in the Presence of Other Taxes: General Equilibrium Analyses." *American Economic Review* 86 (4): 985–1000.

Bowen, A., S. Fankhauser, N. Stern, and D. Zenghelis. 2009. *An Outline of the Case for a "Green" Stimulus*. London: Grantham Research Institute on Climate Change and the Environment and the Centre for Climate Change Economics and Policy.

Brown, K., W. N. Adger, E. Boyd, E. Corbera-Elizalde, and S. Shackley. 2004. "How Do CDM Projects Contribute to Sustainable Development?" Tyndall Centre for Climate Change Research Technical Report 16, Norwich, UK.

Burnside, C., and D. Dollar. 2000. "Aid, Policies and Growth." *American Economic Review* 90 (4): 847–68.

Capoor, K., and P. Ambrosi. 2009. *State and Trends of the Carbon Market 2009*. Washington, DC: World Bank.

Cosbey, A., J. Parry, J. Browne, Y. D. Babu, P. Bhandari, J. Drexhage, and D. Murphy. 2005. *Realizing the Development Dividend: Making the CDM Work for Developing Countries*. Winnipeg: International Institute for Sustainable Development.

CRED (Centre for Research on the Epidemiology of Disasters). 2008. "EM-DAT: The International Emergency Disasters Database." Université Catholique de Louvain, Ecole de Santé Publique, Louvain.

Danielsen, F., N. D. Burgess, A. Balmford, P. F. Donald, M. Funder, J. P. Jones, P. Alviola, D. S. Balete, T. Blomley, J. Brashares, B. Child, M. Enghoff, J. Fieldsa, S. Holt, H. Hubertz, A. E. Jensen, P. M. Jensen, J. Massao, M. M. Mendoza, Y. Nqaqa, M. K. Poulsen, R. Rueda, M. Sam, T. Skielboe, G. Stuart-Hill, E. Topp-Jorgensen, and D. Yonten. 2009. "Local Participation in Natural Resource Monitoring: a Characterization of Approaches." *Conservation Biology* 23 (1): 31–42.

Dasgupta, S., B. Laplante, C. Meisner, D. Wheeler, and J. Yan. 2007. "The Impact of Sea Level Rise on Developing Countries: A Comparative Analysis." Policy Research Working Paper 4136, World Bank, Washington, DC.

Dechezleprêtre, A., M. Glachant, I. Hascic, N. Johnstone, and Y. Meniérè. 2008. *Invention and Transfer of Climate Change Mitigation Technologies on a Global Scale: A Study Drawing on Patent Data*. Paris: CERNA.

Deressa, T., R. M. Hassan, and C. Ringler. 2008. "Measuring Ethiopian Farmers' Vulnerability to Climate Change Across Regional States." Discussion Paper 00806, International Food Policy Research Institute, Washington, DC.

Diffenbaugh, N. S., F. Giorgi, L. Raymond, and X. Bi. 2007. "Indicators of 21st Century Socio-climatic Exposure." *Proceedings of the National Academy of Sciences* 104 (51): 20195–98.

Edmonds, J., L. Clarke, J. Lurz, and M. Wise. 2008. "Stabilizing CO_2 Concentrations with Incomplete International Cooperation." *Climate Policy* 8 (4): 355–76.

Eliasch, J. 2008. *Climate Change: Financing Global Forests: The Eliasch Review*. London: Earthscan.

Estache, A. 2008. *Public-Private Partnerships for Climate Change Investments: Learning from the Infrastructure PPP Experience*. Brussels: European Center for Advanced Research in Economics and Statistics.

Estache, A., and M. Fay. 2007. "Current Debates on Infrastructure Policy." Policy Research Working Paper 4410, World Bank, Washington, DC.

Fankhauser, S., N. Martin, and S. Prichard. Forthcoming. "The Economics of the CDM Levy: Revenue Potential, Tax Incidence, and Distortionary Effects." Working paper, London School of Economics.

Figueres, C., E. Haites, and E. Hoyt. 2005. *Programmatic CDM Project Activities: Eligibility, Methodological Requirements and Implementation*. Washington, DC: World Bank Carbon Finance Business Unit.

Figueres, C., and K. Newcombe. 2007. "Evolution of the CDM: Toward 2012 and Beyond." Climate Change Capital, London, UK.

Füssel, H. M. 2007. "Vulnerability: A Generally Applicable Conceptual Framework for Climate Change Research." *Global Environmental Change* 17 (2): 155–67.

Giorgi, F. 2006. "Climate Change Hot-Spots." *Geophysical Research Letters* 33(8):L08707–doi:10.1029/2006GL025734.

Haites, E., D. Maosheng, and S. Seres. 2006. "Technology Transfer by CDM Projects." *Climate Policy* 6: 327–44.

Houghton, R. A. 2009. "Emissions of Carbon from Land Management." Background note for the WDR 2010.

Howes, S. 2009. *Finding a Way Forward: Three Critical Issues for a Post-Kyoto Global Agreement on Climate Change*. Canberra: Crawford School of Economics and Government, Australian National University.

IDA (International Development Association). 2007. *IDA's Performance Based Allocation System: Simplification of the Formula and Other Outstanding Issues*. Washington, DC.

IEA (International Energy Agency). 2008. *Energy Technology Perspective 2008: Scenarios and Strategies to 2050*. Paris: IEA.

IETA (International Emissions Trading Association). 2005. *Strengthening the CDM: Position Paper for COP 11 and COP/MoP 1*. Geneva: IETA.

————. 2008. *State of the CDM 2008: Facilitating a Smooth Transition into a Mature Environmental Financing Mechanism.* Geneva: IETA.

IIASA (International Institute for Applied Systems Analysis). 2009. "GGI Scenario Database." Laxenburg, Austria.

IPCC (Intergovernmental Panel on Climate Change). 2007. *Climate Change 2007: Mitigation. Contribution of Working Group III to the Fourth Assessment Report of the Intergovernmental Panel on Climate Change.* Cambridge, UK: Cambridge University Press.

Kanbur, R. 2005. "Reforming the Formula: A Modest Proposal for Introducing Development Outcomes in IDA Allocation Procedures." Centre for Economic Policy Research Discussion Paper 4971, London.

Kaufman, D., A. Kraay, and M. Mastruzzi. 2008. *World Governance Indicators 2008.* Washington, DC: World Bank.

Klein, R. J. T., and A. Persson. 2008. "Financing Adaptation to Climate Change: Issues and Priorities." European Climate Platform Report 8, Centre for European Policy Studies, Brussels.

Knopf, B., O. Edenhofer, T. Barker, N. Bauer, L. Baumstark, B. Chateau, P. Criqui, A. Held, M. Isaac, M. Jakob, E. Jochem, A. Kitous, S. Kypreos, M. Leimbach, B. Magné, S. Mima, W. Schade, S. Scrieciu, H. Turton, and D. van Vuuren. Forthcoming. "The Economics of Low Stabilisation: Implications for Technological Change and Policy." In *Making Climate Change Work for Us,* ed. M. Hulme and H. Neufeldt. Cambridge, UK: Cambridge University Press.

McKinsey & Company. 2009. *Pathways to a Low-carbon Economy: Version 2 of the Global Greenhouse Gas Abatement Cost Curve.* McKinsey & Company.

Meijer, E. 2007. "The International Institutions of the Clean Development Mechanism Brought before National Courts: Limiting Jurisdictional Immunity to Achieve Access to Justice." *NYU Journal of International Law and Politics* 39 (4): 873–928.

Michaelowa, A., and P. Pallav. 2007. *Additionality Determination of Indian CDM Projects. Can Indian CDM Project Developers Outwit the CDM Executive Board?* Zurich: University of Zurich.

Michaelowa, A., and K. Umamaheswaran. 2006. "Additionality and Sustainable Development Issues Regarding CDM Projects in Energy Efficiency Sector." HWWA Discussion Paper 346, Hamburg.

Ministry of Finance (Indonesia). 2008. *Climate Change and Fiscal Policy Issues: 2008 Initiatives.* Jakarta: Working Group on Fiscal Policy for Climate Change.

Müller, B. 2008. "International Adaptation Finance: The Need for an Innovative and Strategic Approach." Economic Working Paper 42, Oxford Institute for Energy Studies, Oxford, UK.

Newell, R. G., and W. A. Pizer. 2000. "Regulating Stock Externalities Under Uncertainty." Working Paper 99-10, Resources for the Future, Washington, DC.

Nussbaumer, P. 2009. "On the Contribution of Labelled Certified Emission Reductions to Sustainable Development: A Multi-criteria Evaluation of CDM Projects." *Energy Policy* 37 (1): 91–101.

Olsen, K. H. 2007. "The Clean Development Mechanism's Contribution to Sustainable Development: A Review of the Literature." *Climatic Change* 84 (1): 59–73.

Olsen, K. H., and J. Fenhann. 2008. "Sustainable Development Benefits of Clean Development Mechanism Projects. A New Methodology for Sustainability Assessment Based on Text Analysis of the Project Design Documents Submitted for Validation." *Energy Policy* 36 (8): 2819–30.

Parry, M., C. Rosenzweig, A. Iglesias, G. Fischer, and M. Livermore. 1999. "Climate Change and World Food Security: A New Assessment." *Global Environmental Change* 9 (S1): S51-S67.

Parry, M., C. Rosenzweig, A. Iglesias, M. Livermore, and G. Fischer. 2004. "Effects of Climate Change on Global Food Production Under SRES Emissions and Socio-Economic Scenarios." *Global Environmental Change* 14 (1): 53–67.

Parry, M., N. Arnell, P. Berry, D. Dodman, S. Fankhauser, C. Hope, S. Kovats, R. Nicholls, D. Satterthwaite, R. Tiffin, and T. Wheeler. 2009. *Assessing the Costs of Adaptation to Climate Change: A Review of the UNFCCC and Other Recent Estimates.* London: International Institute for Environment and Development and Grantham Institute for Climate Change.

Pollitt, M. 2008. "The Arguments For and Against Ownership Unbundling of Energy Transmission Networks." *Energy Policy* 36 (2): 704–13.

Project Catalyst. 2009. *Adaptation to Climate Change: Potential Costs and Choices for a Global Agreement.* London: Climate Works and European Climate Foundation.

Robins, N., R. Clover, and J. Magness. 2009. *The Green Rebound: Clean Energy to Become an Important Component of Global Recovery Plans.* London: HSBC.

Schaeffer, M., T. Kram, M. Meinshausen, D. P. van Vuuren, and W. L. Hare. 2008. "Near-linear Cost Increase to Reduce Climate Change Risk." *Proceedings of the National Academy of Sciences* 105 (52): 20621–26.

Schneider, L. 2007. *Is the CDM Fulfilling Its Environmental and Sustainable Development Objective? An Evaluation of the CDM and Options for Improvement.* Berlin: Institute for Applied Ecology.

Sperling, D., and D. Salon. 2002. *Transportation in Developing Countries: An Overview of Greenhouse Gas Reduction Strategies.* Arlington, VA: Pew Center on Global Climate Change.

Stehr, H. J. 2008. "Does the CDM Need and Institutional Reform?" In *A Reformed CDM: Including New Mechanisms for Sustainable Development,* ed. K. H. Olsen and J. Fenhann. Roskilde, Denmark: United Nations Environment Programme, Risoe Centre Perspective Series 2008.

Sterk, W. 2008. "From Clean Development Mechanism to Sectoral Crediting Approaches: Way Forward or Wrong Turn?" JIKO Policy Paper 1/2008, Wuppertal Institute for Climate, Environment and Energy, Wuppertal, Germany.

Streck, C., and T. B. Chagas. 2007. "The Future of the CDM in a Post-Kyoto World." *Carbon & Climate Law Review* 1 (1): 53–63.

Streck, C., and J. Lin. 2008. "Making Markets Work: A Review of CDM Performance and the Need for Reform." *European Journal of International Law* 19 (2): 409–42.

Sutter, C., and J. C. Parreno. 2007. "Does the Current Clean Development Mechanism (CDM) Deliver Its Sustainable Development Claim? An Analysis of Officially Registered CDM Projects." *Climatic Change* 84 (1): 75–90.

Tol, R. S. J., K. L. Ebi, and G. W. Yohe. 2006. "Infectious Disease, Development, and Climate Change: A Scenario Analysis." *Environment and Development Economics* 12: 687–706.

UNEP (United Nations Environment Programme). 2008. "UNEP Risoe CDM/JI Pipeline Analysis and Database." Roskilde, Denmark.

———. 2009. *Global Trends in Sustainable Energy Investment 2009: Analysis of Trends and Issues in the Financing of Renewable Energy and Energy Efficiency.* Paris: UNEP and New Energy Finance.

UNFCCC (United Nations Framework Convention on Climate Change). 2007. *Call for Input on Non-Binding Best-Practice Examples on the Demonstration of Additionality to Assist the Development of PDDs, Particularly for SSC Project Activities.* Bonn: UNFCCC.

———. 2008a. *Investment and Financial Flows to Address Climate Change: An Update.* Bonn: UNFCCC.

———. 2008b. *Mechanisms to Manage Financial Risk from Direct Impacts of Climate Change.* Bonn: UNFCCC.

Vagliasindi, M. 2008. "Climate Change Uncertainty, Regulation and Private Participation in Infrastructure." Background note for the WDR 2010.

Wara, M. 2007. "Is the Global Carbon Market Working?" *Nature* 445: 595–96.

Wara, M., and D. Victor. 2008. "A Realistic Policy on International Carbon Markets." Working Paper 74, Program on Energy and Sustainable Development, Stanford University, Stanford, CA.

Watson, C., and S. Fankhauser. 2009. "The Clean Development Mechanism: Too Flexible to Produce Sustainable Development Benefits?" Background paper for the WDR 2010.

Weitzman, M. L. 1974. "Prices vs. Quantities." *Review of Economic Studies* 41 (4): 477–491.

World Bank. 2007a. "Annual Report On Portfolio Performance, Fiscal Year 2006." Quality Assurance Group, World Bank, Washington, DC.

———. 2007b. "Country Policy And Institutional Assessments 2007: Assessment Questionnaire." Operations Policy And Country Services, World Bank, Washington, DC.

———. 2007c. *World Development Indicators 2007.* Washington, DC: World Bank.

———. 2009. *The Economics of Adaptation to Climate Change.* Washington, DC: World Bank.

WRI (World Resources Institute). 2008. "Climate Analysis Indicators tool (CAIT)." Washington, DC.

CHAPTER 7

Accelerating Innovation and Technology Diffusion

Windmills peppered European landscapes to provide energy for agricultural activities long before the discovery of electricity. Thanks to the forces of innovation and technology diffusion, wind is now powering the first stages of what could become a veritable energy revolution. Between 1996 and 2008 the global installed wind capacity increased twentyfold to stand at more than 120 gigawatts, displacing an estimated 158 million tons of carbon dioxide (CO_2) a year while creating some 400,000 jobs (figure 7.1).[1] Much of this growth is attributable to government incentives and to publicly and privately funded research, driving down the cost of wind technology and driving up efficiency.

And although most installed capacity is in Europe and the United States, the pattern is shifting. In 2008 India and China each installed more wind capacity than any other country except the United States,

and together they host nearly 20 percent of the world's capacity. An Indian company, Suzlon, is one of the world's leading wind turbine manufacturers, employing 13,000 people across Asia. So the global takeoff of wind technology is setting an early precedent for climate-smart development. And complementary advances, such as global geospatial wind resource information, are making siting decisions easier (map 7.1).

Technological innovation and its associated institutional adjustments are key to managing climate change at reasonable cost. Strengthening national innovation and technology capacity can become a powerful catalyst for development.[2] High-income economies, the world's major emitters, can replace their stock of high-carbon technologies with climate-smart alternatives while massively investing in tomorrow's breakthrough innovations. Middle-income

Key messages

Meeting climate change and development goals requires significantly stepping up international efforts to diffuse existing technologies and develop and deploy new ones. Public and private investment—now in the tens of billions of dollars per year—need to be steeply ramped up to several hundreds of billions of dollars annually. "Technology-push" policies based on increasing public investments in R&D will not be sufficient. They need to be matched with "market-pull" policies that create public and private sector incentives for entrepreneurship, for collaboration, and to find innovative solutions in unlikely places. Diffusing climate-smart technology requires much more than shipping ready-to-use equipment to developing countries; it requires building absorptive capacity and enhancing the ability of the public and private sectors to identify, adopt, adapt, improve, and employ the most appropriate technologies..

Figure 7.1 Global cumulative installed wind capacity has soared in the past decade

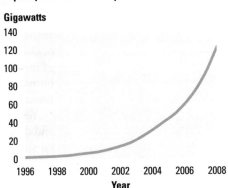

Gigawatts

Source: Global Wind Energy Council 2009.

Map 7.1   Advances in wind mapping open up new opportunities

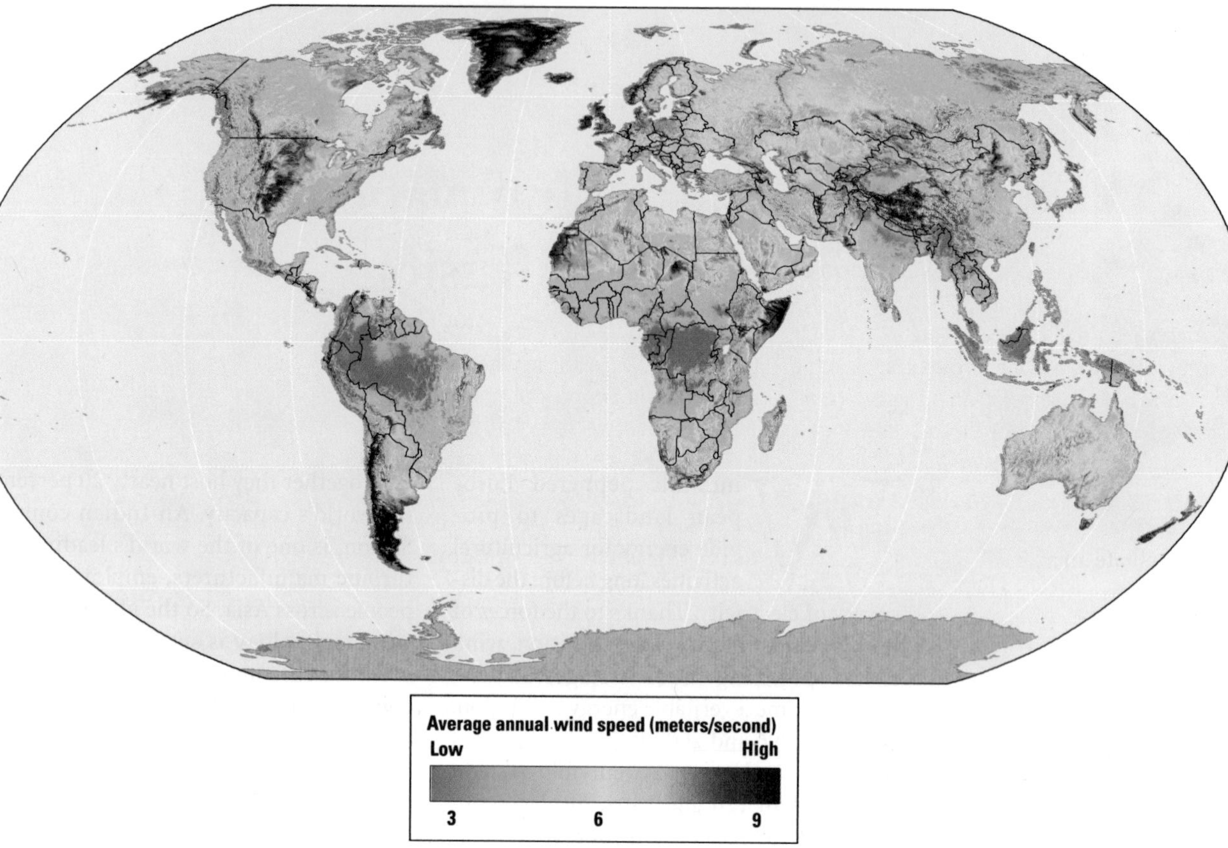

Source: Data provided by 3 Tier Inc.

Note: This is a 5-kilometer resolution map of average annual wind speed, with the average measured at a height of 80 meters (the height of some windmills), across the world's landmass.

countries can ensure that their investments take them in the direction of low-carbon growth and that their firms reap the benefits of existing technologies to compete globally. Low-income countries can ensure that they have the technological capacity to adapt to climate change, by identifying, assessing, adopting, and improving existing technologies with local knowledge and know-how. As chapter 8 points out, reaping the benefits of technological changes will require significant changes in human and organizational behavior, as well as a host of innovative supportive policies to reduce human vulnerability and manage natural resources.

Yet today's global efforts to innovate and diffuse climate-smart technologies fall far short of what is required for significant mitigation and adaptation in the coming decades. Investment in research, development, demonstration, and deployment

(RDD&D) is lacking, and the financial crisis is reducing private spending on climate-smart technology, delaying its diffusion. Mobilizing technology and fostering innovation on an adequate scale will require that countries not only cooperate and pool their resources but also craft domestic policies that promote a supportive knowledge infrastructure and business environment. And most developing countries, particularly low-income countries, have small market sizes which, taken individually, are unattractive to entrepreneurs wishing to introduce new technologies. But contiguous countries can achieve a critical mass through greater regional economic integration.

International cooperation must be scaled up to supply more financing and to formulate policy instruments that stimulate demand for climate-smart innovation, rather than simply focus on research subsidies. The international harmonization of regulatory incentives (such as carbon pricing) can have a multiplier effect on investment by creating economies of scale and by building momentum in the direction of climate-smart technologies. Innovation prizes and procurement subsidies can build demand and stimulate ingenuity. And where research priorities coincide with high costs, joint RDD&D can push out the technical frontiers. The concept of technology transfer needs to be broadened to include country capacities to absorb existing technologies. In this respect an international climate treaty with a focus on specific technological systems or subsystems presents a unique opportunity. Bundling in cost-sharing and technology transfer provisions could facilitate an accord.

Complementary domestic policies can ensure that technology is effectively selected, adapted, and absorbed. But identifying, evaluating, and integrating foreign technologies impose oft-overlooked learning costs, as do their modification and improvement. So the knowledge infrastructure of universities, research institutes, and firms has to be supported to build this capacity.

This chapter draws on the analysis of systems in which technology has withered or thrived and on the plethora of policies and factors that have acted as barriers or catalysts, suggesting what can be achieved if selected policies are combined and scaled up. It first describes the importance of technology in lowering greenhouse gas emissions, the needed tools to advance adaptation to climate change, and the role of both in creating competitive economies. It next assesses the gap between invention, innovation, and widespread diffusion in the marketplace. It then examines how international and domestic policies can bridge that gap.

The right tools, technologies, and institutions can put a climate-smart world well within our reach

To keep global temperatures from rising more than 2°C, global greenhouse gas emissions must come down by 50–80 percent in the coming decades. In the short term they can be drastically reduced by accelerating the deployment of existing mitigation technologies in high-emitting countries.

But to achieve the more ambitious medium-term emission objectives will require breakthrough technologies. Models show that four future key technology areas could be at the core of a solution: energy efficiency; carbon capture and storage; next-generation renewables, including biomass, wind and solar power; and nuclear power (see chapter 4).[3] All four need more research, development, and demonstration (RD&D) to determine whether they can be rapidly deployed in the marketplace without adverse consequences.

Despite their great promise, both short- and medium-term emission reduction strategies face major challenges. End-use technologies that improve efficiency and use sources with low emissions can dampen total energy demand, but they require changing the behavior of individuals and firms (see chapter 8). Carbon capture and storage could play a large role if geologically appropriate sites can be identified near power plants and if governments provide resources and policies to enable long-term sequestration.[4] Biotechnology and second-generation biofuels have great potential for mitigating carbon emissions but with increasing demands on land use (see chapter 3). Wind and solar power (both photovoltaic and solar thermal) could expand faster if energy storage and transmission improve. A new generation of nuclear power plants could be deployed extensively throughout the world but would have to overcome institutional constraints, safety and proliferation issues, and popular resistance in some countries. In addition, some have proposed that geoengineering options could not only decrease emissions rates but also temper the impacts of climate change (box 7.1).

The role of technology and innovation in adaptation has been much less studied than for mitigation, but it is clear that future climate conditions will be fundamentally different from the ones today. Responding to changes outside of historic experience will require increased institutional coordination on a regional scale, new tools for planning, and the ability to respond to multiple

BOX 7.1   *Geoengineering the world out of climate change*

Given the pace of climate change, current proposals for mitigation and adaptation may not be sufficient to avoid considerable impacts. Thus, possible geoengineering options are receiving increasing scrutiny. Geoengineering can be defined as actions or interventions taken for the primary purpose of limiting the causes of climate change or the impacts that result. They include mechanisms that could enhance carbon dioxide (CO_2) absorption or sequestration by the oceans or by vegetation, deflect or reflect incoming sunlight, or store CO_2 produced by energy use in reservoirs. The last of these is discussed in chapter 4, so this box focuses on the other two classes of options.

Possible options for sequestering additional carbon dioxide include terrestrial management practices that increase carbon held in soils or trees, as discussed in chapter 3. It may also be possible to stimulate phytoplankton growth and algal blooms in the oceans by adding needed nutrients such as iron or urea. As these tiny plants photosynthesize, they take up carbon dioxide from surface waters. The effectiveness of such enhanced approaches will depend on what happens to the CO_2 over the longer term; if it is integrated into the waste products from animals that eat the plankton and settles to the seafloor, then the CO_2 will essentially be removed from the system for millennia. However, recent research shows that previous quantifications of carbon removal capacity may have been greatly overestimated. Also, more experiments need to be done on the duration of sequestration as well as the potential toxicological impacts of sudden increases in iron or urea in marine ecosystems. If further studies confirm its potential, this is one geoengineering option that could be started quickly and at relevant scale.

Bringing cool, nutrient-rich water to the ocean's surface could also stimulate increased marine productivity and potentially remove CO_2 from the surface water. Such cooling would also be beneficial for coral, which are very sensitive to higher temperatures. Finally, cooling surface water could also dampen hurricane intensities. Initial research on a wave-powered pump to bring cool water to the surface suggests that the approach might work, but much more research and investigation is needed.

Other geoengineering options to remove greenhouse gases include scrubbing gases from the atmosphere with a CO_2 absorbing solution (and then sequestering the captured carbon below the land surface or in the deep ocean), or using lasers to destroy long-lived halocarbon molecules—best known as culprits in ozone depletion but also powerful greenhouse gases (see focus A on science). These options are still in the early experimental stage.

Several approaches to reflect incoming sunlight have been offered. Some of these could be targeted to particular regions, to prevent further melting of Arctic sea ice or the Greenland ice sheet, for example. One approach would be to inject sulfate aerosols into the atmosphere. This has shown to be an effective method for cooling—the 1991 eruption of Mount Pinatubo resulted in the earth cooling by nearly 1°C for about a year. To maintain this type of cooling, however, a constant stream or regular injections of aerosol must be released. Further, sulfate aerosols can exacerbate ozone depletion, increase acid rain, and cause adverse health impacts.

Alternatively, sea mist could be sprayed into the sky from a fleet of automated ships, thus "whitening" and increasing reflectivity of the low marine clouds that cover a quarter of the world's ocean. However, uneven cloud distribution could lead to regional cold and hot spots and droughts downwind of the spray vessels.

Increasing the reflectivity of the land surface would also help. Making roofs and pavements white or light-colored would help to reduce global warming by both conserving energy and reflecting sunlight back into space and would be the equivalent of taking all the cars in the world off the road for 11 years.

Another proposal would place a solar deflector disk between the Sun and Earth. A disk of approximately 1,400 kilometers in diameter could reduce solar radiation by approximately 1 percent, about equivalent to the radiative forcing of emissions projected for the 21st century.

But analysis shows that the most cost-effective approach for implementing this strategy is to set up a manufacturing plant for the deflector on the Moon, hardly a straightforward task. Similar ideas using multiple mirrors (such as 55,000 orbiting solar mirrors each roughly 10 square kilometers in size) have been discussed. However, when each of the orbiting mirrors passed between the Sun and Earth, they would eclipse the Sun, causing sunlight at the earth's surface to flicker.

There are even geoengineering proposals more akin to weather modification, such as attempting to push advancing tropical storms out to sea and away from human settlements to reduce damage. Although research on such ideas is in its very earliest stages, the newest climate models are becoming capable of analyzing the potential effectiveness of such proposals, something that was not possible when hurricane modification was first attempted several decades ago.

Although it may be possible for geoengineering to be undertaken by one nation, every nation would be affected by such actions taken. For this reason, it is essential that discussions begin on governance issues relating to geoengineering. Already, investor-funded experiments in support of iron fertilization have raised questions over what international entity or institution has jurisdiction. Questions about using geoengineering to limit the intensity of tropical cyclones or Arctic warming would add complexity. Thus, in addition to scientific research on possible approaches and their impacts, social, ethical, legal, and economic research should be supported to explore what geoengineering measures are and are not within the bounds of international acceptance.

Sources: S. Connor, "Climate Guru: 'Paint Roofs White.'" *New Zealand Herald*, May 28, 2009; American Meteorological Association, http://www.ametsoc.org/policy/2009geoengineeringclimate_amsstatement.html (accessed July 27, 2009); Atmocean, Inc., http://www.atmocean.com/ (accessed July 27, 2009); MacCracken 2009; "Geoengineering: Every Silver Lining Has a Cloud," *Economist,* January 29, 2009; see also U.S. Energy Secretary Steven Chu, http://www.youtube.com/watch?v=5wDlkKroOUQ.

environmental pressures occurring concomitantly with climate change. Greater investments are needed in understanding vulnerability, in conducting iterative assessments, and in developing strategies for helping societies cope with a changing climate.[5]

Integrating climate considerations into development strategies will foster thinking about adaptation.[6] Chapter 2 discusses how climate change will require designing appropriate physical infrastructure and protecting human health. Chapter 3 illustrates how adaptation will require new ways to manage natural resources. Promoting diversification—of energy systems, agricultural crops, and economic activities, for example—can also help communities cope with rapidly changing conditions. Innovation will be a necessary ingredient for all of these activities.

Research is also required to understand the effects of climate change and different adaptation options on individual countries. This research must characterize the effects of multiple stresses on natural and socioeconomic systems, biodiversity vulnerability and preservation, and changes in atmospheric and oceanic circulation. Such research has to produce new monitoring tools, new strategies to enhance resilience, and better contingency planning. Scientific capacity at the national level is thus required.

The capacity to tackle mitigation and adaptation will help build strong competitive economies

Many advanced technologies, such as information and communication technologies, can help specifically with climate change yet are generic enough for use across a wide range of productivity-enhancing areas. Sensors are valuable in industrial automation but can also help waste managers limit pollution. Mobile phones have helped in responding to impending disaster, as in the coastal village of Nallavadu, India, during the 2004 tsunami,[7] but they can also increase business productivity. In parts of Benin, Senegal, and Zambia mobile phones are used to disseminate information about food prices and innovations in farming techniques.[8]

Harnessing the technological opportunities arising from climate change concerns can also create opportunities for technological leadership and a new competitive edge. China, for example, has not yet locked in to carbon-intensive growth and has enormous (and economically attractive) potential for leapfrogging old inefficient technologies. Unlike in developed countries a large share of China's residential and industrial capital stock of the next decade is yet to be built. By using existing technologies, such as optimizing motor-driven systems (pumps and compressors), China could reduce its industrial energy demand in 2020 by 20 percent while increasing productivity.[9]

The current global recession can provide a platform for innovation and climate-smart growth. Crises can spur innovation because they cause an urgent focus on mobilizing resources and break down barriers that normally stand in the way of innovation.[10] And the opportunity cost of research and development (R&D), a long-term investment, is lower during an economic crisis.[11] In the early 1990s Finland's recovery from a severe economic recession was credited largely to its restructuring into an innovation-based economy, with sharp increases in government spending on R&D paving the way for the private sector. The same could be achieved with climate-smart R&D.

And with high rates of return, R&D presents untapped opportunities for economic growth. Most measures of rates of return on R&D are in the range of 20 to 50 percent, much higher than on investments in capital.[12] Estimates also show that developing countries could invest more than twice as much as they now do.[13] Yet, experience shows that R&D is procyclical, rising and falling with booms and busts, and firms tend to be short-sighted during recessions, limiting their investments in innovation, even though this is a suboptimal strategy.[14] The stimulus packages developed by many countries in reaction to the recession offer a timely opportunity for new investments in climate-smart innovation (see chapter 1).[15]

The current global recession also provides opportunities for economic restructuring in high-income countries that are locked into high-carbon lifestyles.

Overcoming technological inertia and institutional incumbency in these countries remains one of the most critical obstacles to the transition to a low-carbon economy.[16] Inertia and incumbency are themselves attributes of existing technoeconomic systems and cannot be wished away through diplomatic processes. Unseating them will entail actual changes in economic structures. Climate-smart policies will need to include mechanisms to identify those who stand to lose and to minimize socio-economic dislocations.

Although climate-smart innovation is concentrated mostly in high-income countries, developing countries are starting to make important contributions. Developing countries accounted for 23 percent ($26 billion) of the new investments in energy efficiency and renewable energy in 2007, up from 13 percent in 2004.[17] Eighty-two percent of those investments were concentrated in three countries—Brazil, China, and India. The world's best-selling developer and manufacturer of on-road electric cars is an Indian venture, the Reva Electric Car Company. As a first-mover it has penetrated the auto manufacturer market, including in high-income countries.[18]

BRIICS countries (Brazil, the Russian Federation, India, Indonesia, China, and South Africa) accounted for only 6.5 percent of global renewable energy patents in 2005,[19] but they are quickly catching up to high-income countries, with annual patenting growth rates more than twice those of the European Union (EU) or the United States. And they are developing a technological edge in renewable energy technologies, with roughly 0.7 percent of their patents filed in this sector from 2003 to 2005, compared with less than 0.3 percent in the United States. In 2005 China was seventh in overall renewable energy patenting and second only to Japan in geothermal and cement inventions, two major potential sources of emission reductions.[20]

All countries will need to step up their efforts to diffuse existing climate-smart technologies and create new ones

Neither public nor private funding of energy-related research, development, and deployment is remotely close to the amounts needed for transitioning to a climate-smart world. In absolute terms, global government energy RD&D budgets have declined since the early 1980s, falling by almost half from 1980 to 2007 (figure 7.2). Energy's share in government research and development budgets (not including demonstration) also plunged, from 11 percent in 1985 to less than 4 percent in 2007 (the green line in figure 7.2), heavily concentrated in nuclear power. Comparisons with public subsidies for energy or petroleum products are even more stark (figure 7.3). But recent calls for increases in energy research and development to $100 billion to $700 billion a year[21] are achievable. Japan is already taking the lead, spending 0.08 percent of its gross domestic product (GDP) on public energy RD&D, far ahead of the 0.03 average in the group of high-income and upper-middle-income-country members of the International Energy Agency.[22]

Given a recent upsurge, private spending on energy RD&D, at $40 billion to $60 billion a year, far exceeds public spending. Even so, at 0.5 percent of revenue, it remains an order of magnitude smaller than the 8 percent of revenue invested in RD&D in

Figure 7.2   Government budgets for energy RD&D are near their lows, and nuclear dominates

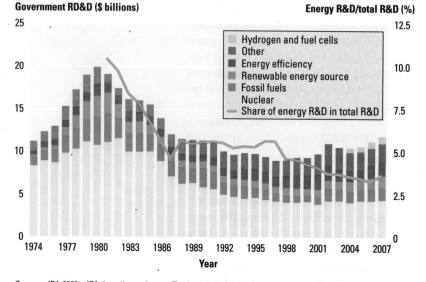

Sources: IEA 2008a; IEA, http://www.iea.org/Textbase/stats/rd.asp (accessed April 2, 2009); Organisation for Economic Co-operation and Development (OECD), http://www.oecd.org/statsportal (accessed April 2, 2009).

Note: RD&D calculated at 2007 prices and exchange rates. Values on left axis are for RD&D (that is, including demonstration in addition to research and development), as is typical in the energy sector. However because totals of cross-sectoral R&D alone are available, the right axis only includes R&D.

the electronics industry and the 15 percent in the pharmaceuticals sector.[23]

Progress in some technologies has just been too slow. Although patenting in renewable energy has grown rapidly since the mid-1990s, it was less than 0.4 percent of all patents in 2005, with only 700 applications.[24] Most growth in low-carbon technology patenting has been concentrated in the areas of waste, lighting, methane, and wind power, but improvement in many other promising technologies like solar, ocean, and geothermal power has been more limited (figure 7.4), with little of the needed progress toward steep cost reductions.

Developing countries are still lagging in innovation for adaptation. While it is more cost-effective to adopt technologies from abroad than to reinvent them, in some cases technological solutions for local problems do not exist.[25] So innovation is not only relevant to high-income economies. For example, advances in biotechnology offer potential for adapting to climate-related events (droughts, heat waves, pests, and diseases) affecting agriculture and forestry. But patents from developing countries still represent a negligible fraction of global biotechnology patents.[26] That will make it difficult to develop location-specific agricultural and health responses to climate change. Moreover, little spending on agricultural R&D—though on the rise since 1981—occurs in developing countries. High-income economies continue to account for more than 73 percent of investments in global agricultural R&D. In developing countries the public sector makes 93 percent of agricultural R&D investments, compared with 47 percent in high-income countries. But public sector organizations are typically less effective at commercializing research results than the private sector.[27]

International collaboration and cost sharing can leverage domestic efforts to promote innovation

Cooperation to drive technological change covers legislative and regulatory harmonization, knowledge sharing and coordination, cost sharing, and technology transfer

Figure 7.3   Annual spending for energy and climate change R&D pales against subsidies

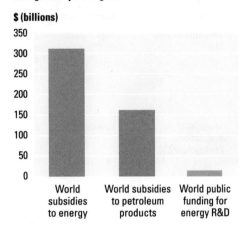

$ (billions)

Sources: IEA 2008a; IEA 2008b; IEA, http://www.iea.org/Textbase/stats/rd.asp (accessed April 2, 2009).

Note: Global subsidy estimates are based on subsidies shown for 20 highest-subsidizing non-OECD countries only (energy subsidies in OECD countries are minimal).

(table 7.1). Some efforts are under way, while other opportunities are as yet untapped.

Because of the mix of required technologies and their stages of development and because their global adoption rates are so widely varied, all these approaches to cooperation will be required. Moreover, climate-smart technology cannot be produced through fragmented efforts. Innovation has to be seen as a system of multiple interacting actors and technologies, path dependency, and learning processes, not just as a product of R&D (box 7.2).[28] Subsidies for research, development, demonstration, and deployment have to be combined with market incentives for firms to innovate and

Figure 7.4   The pace of invention is uneven across low-carbon technologies

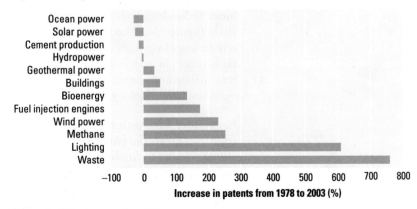

Source: Dechezleprêtre and others 2008.

Table 7.1   International technology-oriented agreements specific to climate change

Type of agreements	Subcategory	Existing agreements	Potential impact	Risk	Implementation	Target
Legislative and regulatory harmonization	Technology deployment and performance mandates	Very little (mainly EU)	High impact	Wrong technological choices made by government	Difficult	Energy technologies with strong lock-in effects (transport) and that are highly decentralized (energy efficiency)
Knowledge sharing and coordination	Knowledge exchange and research coordination	Many (such as International Energy Agency)	Low impact	No major risk	Easy	All sectors
	Voluntary standards and labels	Several (EnergyStar, ISO 14001)	Low impact	Limited adoption of standards and labeling by private sector	Easy	Industrial and consumer products; communication systems
Cost-sharing innovation	Subsidy-based "technology push" instruments	Very few (ITER)	High impact	Uncertainty of research outcomes	Difficult	Precompetitive RD&D with important economies of scale (carbon capture and storage, deep offshore wind)
	Reward-based "market pull" instruments	Very few (Ansari X-prize)	Medium impact	Compensation and required effort may result in inappropriate levels of innovation	Moderate	Specific medium-scale problems; solutions for developing-country markets; solutions not requiring fundamental R&D
	Bridge-the-gap instruments	Very few (Qatar-UK Clean Technology Investment Fund)	High impact	Funding remains unused due to lack of deal flow	Moderate	Technologies at the demonstration and deployment stage
Technology transfer	Technology transfer	Several (Clean Development Mechanism, Global Environment Facility)	High impact	Low absorptive capacities of recipient countries	Moderate	Established (wind, energy efficiency), region-specific (agriculture), and public sector (early-warning, coastal protection) technologies

Sources: Davis and Davis 2004; De Coninck and others 2007; Justus and Philibert 2005; Newell and Wilson 2005; Philibert 2004; World Bank 2008a.

move technologies along the innovation chain (figure 7.5).[29] And innovation has to rely on knowledge flows across sectors and on advances in such broad technologies as information and communications technologies and biotechnology.

Regulatory harmonization across countries forms the backbone of any climate-smart technology agreement

Harmonized incentives with a broad geographic reach can create large investor pools and markets for climate-smart innovation. Carbon pricing, renewable portfolio standards that regulate the share of energy coming from renewable sources, and performance mandates such as automobile fuel economy standards (see chapter 4) are cost-effective and can promote the development and diffusion of low-carbon technologies. For example, a number of countries have initiated measures to phase out incandescent light bulbs, because more efficient technologies such as compact fluorescent lamps as well as light emitting diodes now exist. Harmonized at a global scale, these regulations can drive the market for low-carbon products in the same way that the

BOX 7.2 *Innovation is a messy process and can be promoted only by policies that address multiple parts of a complex system*

In most countries, government policy is still driven by an outdated linear view of innovation, that perceives innovation as happening in four consecutive stages.

- R&D, to find solutions to specific technical problems and apply them to new technologies.
- Demonstration projects, to further adapt the technology and demonstrate its functioning in larger-scale and real-world applications.
- Deployment, once fundamental technical barriers have been resolved and the commercial potential of a technology becomes apparent.
- Diffusion, when technology becomes competitive in the market.

But experience shows that the process of innovation is much more complex.

Most innovations fail in one stage or another. Feedback from manufacturers in the deployment stage, or from retailers and consumers in the diffusion stage, trickles back to the earlier stages, completely modifying the course of innovation, leading to new, unexpected ideas and products and sometimes to unforeseen costs. Sometimes breakthrough innovations are driven not by R&D but by new business models that put together existing technologies. And learning curves, whereby unit costs decline as a function of cumulative production or cumulative RDD&D, are not well understood.

So why does this matter for policy? The linear view gives the misleading impression that innovation can be managed simply by supplying more research inputs

(technology push) and creating market demand (market pull). While both types of policy are extremely important, they ignore the contributions of the numerous interactions among the actors involved in the different stages of innovation: firms, consumers, governments, universities, and the like. Partnerships, learning by selling or buying a technology, and learning through imitation play critical roles. Equally critical are the forces that drive diffusion. The compatibility, perceived benefits, and learning costs of using a new product are all key factors for innovation. Effective policies must view innovation as part of a system and find ways to stimulate all these facets of the innovation process, particularly where there are market gaps.

Sources: Tidd 2006; World Bank 2008a.

---

harmonization of GSM communications standards for mobile phones created a critical mass for the mobile phone market in Europe in the 1990s.

Knowledge-sharing and coordination agreements are useful complements

Knowledge agreements can address market and system failures in innovation and diffusion. Such agreements coordinate national research agendas, information exchange systems, and voluntary standards and labeling schemes. Research coordination agreements include many of the International Energy Agency's 42 technology agreements, where countries finance and implement their individual contributions to different sector-specific projects, ranging from advanced fuel cells to electric vehicles.[30] Such agreements can avoid duplicating investments across countries. They allow countries to jointly decide on who works on what, thus ensuring that no key technologies are ignored, particularly those relevant to developing countries (such as biofuels from developing-country feedstocks and lower-capacity power generation). Information exchange systems include the Global Earth Observation System of Systems, which will make data available from

various observation and measurement systems (box 7.3). Prominent examples of international coordination in labels are the Energy Star program agreements, whereby government agencies in various countries

Figure 7.5   Policy affects every link of the innovation chain

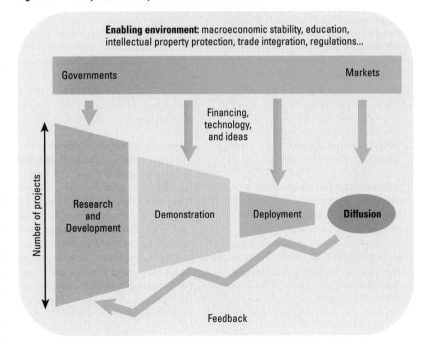

Source: Adapted from IEA 2008a.

BOX 7.3   *Innovative monitoring: Creating a global climate service and a "system of systems"*

Demand for sustained and reliable data and information on trends, unusual events, and long-range predictions has never been greater than it is today. A number of public and private entities in sectors as diverse as transportation, insurance, energy, water, agriculture, and fisheries are increasingly incorporating climate information into their planning. Such forecasting has become a critical component of their adaptation strategies.

A global climate services enterprise (GCS) could provide the climate-relevant information that society needs to better plan for and anticipate climate conditions on timescales from months to decades. Such an enterprise would build on existing observation systems but must go far beyond them. A GCS would provide information to help answer questions about appropriate city infrastructure to cope with the 100-year extreme precipitation and storm surge events that will now occur at higher magnitude and greater frequency, help farmers decide on appropriate crops and water management during droughts, monitor changing stocks and flows of carbon in forests and soils, and evaluate efficacy of disaster response strategies under changing climate conditions.

A GCS will require innovative partnerships across governments, the private sector, and other institutions, and its design will be quite critical. Beginning with today's observations and modeling capacity, a connected multi-hub-and-spoke design should be developed whereby global services are provided to regional service providers that in turn deliver information to local providers. This eliminates the requirement that every community develop very sophisticated information on their own.

Building the Components of a GCS
Some of the necessary information to develop a GCS is being provided by United States National Meteorological and Hydrologic Service Centers and increasingly by Global Climate Observing System contributions through various government agencies and nongovernmental institutions. Also, a number of other institutions, such as the World Data Centers and the International Research Institute, regularly provide climate-related data and products including forecasts on monthly to annual timescales.

There are also a few examples of fledgling regional climate services. One such example is the Pacific Climate Information System (PaCIS), which provides a regional framework to integrate ongoing and future climate observations, operational forecasting services, and climate projections. PaCIS facilitates the pooling of resources and expertise, and the identification of regional priorities. One of the highest priorities for this effort is the creation of a Web-based portal that will facilitate access to climate data, products, and services developed by the U.S. National Oceanic and Atmospheric Administration and its partners across the Pacific region.

Another example is the formation of regional climate centers, which the World Meteorological Organization (WMO) has formally sought to define and establish since 1999. The WMO has been sensitive to the idea that the responsibilities of regional centers should not duplicate or replace those of existing agencies but instead support five key areas: operational activities, including the interpretation of output from global prediction centers; coordination efforts that strengthen collaboration on observing, communication, and computing networks; data services involving providing data, archiving it and ensuring its quality; training and capacity building; and research on climate variability, predictability, and impacts in a region.

Integrating climate services with other innovative monitoring systems
Building a comprehensive and integrated system to monitor environmental changes across the planet is beyond the means of any single country, as is analyzing the wealth of data it would generate. That is why the Group on Earth Observation (GEO), a voluntary partnership of governments and international organizations, developed the concept of a Global Earth Observation System of Systems (GEOSS). Providing the institutional mechanisms to ensure the coordination, strengthening, and supplementation of existing global Earth observation systems, GEOSS supports policy makers, resource managers, scientific researchers, and a broad spectrum of decision makers in nine areas: disaster risk mitigation; adaptation to climate change; integrated water resource management; management of marine resources; biodiversity conservation; sustainable agriculture and forestry; public health; distribution of energy resources; and weather monitoring. Information is combined from oceanic buoys, hydrological and meteorological stations, remote-sensing satellites, and internet-based Earth-monitoring portals.

Some early progress:

- In 2007 China and Brazil jointly launched a land-imaging satellite and committed to distribute their Earth observation data to Africa.

- The United States recently made available 40 years of data from the world's most extensive archive of remotely sensed imagery.

- A regional visualization and monitoring system for Mesoamerica, SERVIR, is the largest open-access repository of environmental data, satellite imagery, documents, metadata, and online mapping applications. SERVIR's regional node for Africa in Nairobi is predicting floods in high-risk areas and outbreaks of Rift Valley Fever.

- GEO is beginning to measure forest-related carbon stocks and emissions through integrated models, in situ monitoring, and remote sensing.

Sources: Global Earth Observation System of Systems, http://www.epa.gov/geoss (accessed January 2009); Group on Earth Observations, http://www.earthobservations.org (accessed January 2009); IRI 2006; note from Tom Karl, National Oceanic and Atmospheric Administration, National Climatic Data Center, 2009; Pacific Region Integrated Climatology Information Products, http://www.pricip.org/ (accessed May 29, 2009); Rogers 2009; Westermeyer 2009.

unify certain voluntary energy-efficiency labeling schemes by providing a single set of energy-efficiency qualifications.[31]

The Montreal Protocol's Technology and Economic Assessment Panels offer a model for a technology agreement on climate change, in this case the effects of ozone depletion. The panels brought together governments, businesses, academic experts, and nongovernmental organizations into work groups to establish the technical feasibility of specific technologies and timetables for phasing out the production and use of chlorofluorocarbons and other ozone-depleting chemicals. The panels showed that technology coordination agreements work best when linked to emission mandates, which provided incentives for industry to participate.[32] One challenge to replicating this model for climate change is that a large number of panels would be required to tackle the wide range of technologies that affect climate change. A more feasible approach would be to initially limit this approach to several strategic sectors.

The European Union's "New Approach" to standardization also offers a model for harmonization of climate-smart standards. Goods traded within the EU must comply with basic safety, public health, consumer protection, and environmental protection rules. The EU first tackled this issue by requiring member states to harmonize legislation containing detailed technical specifications. But this approach caused deadlocks in the European Council and updating legislation to reflect technological progress was difficult. In 1985, the New Approach was designed to overcome this problem. Goods classified under the New Approach must simply comply with very broad, technology-neutral "essential requirements" enshrined in legislation that must be adopted by every EU member state. To meet the New Approach requirements, products can comply with harmonized European standards developed by one of the three regional voluntary standardization bodies. There, technical committees representing a mix of industry, governments, academia, and consumers from different EU countries agree on standards by consensus. Technical committees are open to any stakeholder from any EU member state wishing to participate. A similar approach could harmonize broad climate-smart regulations across countries through a climate treaty supported by voluntary standards developed separately through an open-consensus process.[33]

Voluntary standards, labels, and research coordination are lower-cost means of technology cooperation, but it is difficult to assess whether they generate additional technology investments.[34] It is unlikely that they alone could address the massive investment needs, urgency, and learning-by-doing required for such technologies as carbon capture and storage.

Cost-sharing agreements have the highest potential payoffs, if they can surmount implementation barriers

Cost-sharing agreements can be "technology-push" agreements, where the joint development of promising technologies is subsidized by multiple countries (the top-down, leftmost, orange arrow in figure 7.5) before knowing whether they will succeed. Or they can be "market-pull" agreements, where funding, pooled from multiple countries, rewards technologies that have demonstrated commercial potential—providing market signals through feedback loops. They can also bridge the gaps in the innovation chain between research and the market.

Research agreements. Only a few international cost-sharing programs support climate-change innovation, among them the $12 billion ITER fusion reactor (box 7.4) and several technology agreements coordinated by the International Energy Agency, with budgets of several million dollars. Another partnership model of research institutions is the Inter-American Institute for Global Change Research, an intergovernmental organization supported by 19 countries in the Americas, with a focus on the exchange of scientific information among scientists and between scientists and policymakers. The mission of the center is to encourage a regional, rather than national, approach.

There is potential for massively scaling up cost-sharing research agreements for

BOX 7.4 *ITER: A protracted start for energy R&D cost sharing*

ITER is an international research and development project to demonstrate the scientific and technical feasibility of nuclear fusion to generate electricity without producing the radioactive waste associated with nuclear fission. The partners in the project are China, the European Union, India, Japan, the Republic of Korea, the Russian Federation, and the United States.

ITER was proposed in 1986, and the design of its facilities was finalized in 1990. The initial schedule anticipated construction of an experimental reactor beginning in 1997, but this was postponed by negotiations over experimental design, cost sharing, the design site, the construction site,

and staffing. Several countries pulled out of ITER, some later rejoined, and some temporarily withdrew their funding.

ITER shows the difficulties in negotiating a more than $12 billion research project with uncertain outcomes. Funding for construction was finally approved in 2006. ITER is expected to be operational for 20 years, once construction is completed around 2017.

Source: http://www.iter.org (accessed December 12, 2008).

Note: ITER originally stood for International Thermonuclear Experimental Reactors but now is simply known as ITER.

fundamental research and demonstration projects, where expenses and uncertainty are high. Research consortia are also well suited to conduct long-term research with economies of scale and economies of learning, such as carbon capture and storage (box 7.5), third-generation photovoltaic, deep offshore wind, second-generation biofuels, and climate-monitoring technologies. The scope for cooperation is narrower for technologies closer to commercialization, when intellectual property rights become more problematic and when individual countries may want a first-mover advantage.

Cost-sharing agreements can focus on a few high-priority areas and be negotiated through centralized international institutions with existing negotiation structures. The ITER project shows that large-scale cost-sharing agreements are difficult to implement when countries can renege on their commitments or disagree on implementation. Ensuring the sustainability of funding for such agreements will require added incentives, such as withdrawal penalties or contractual commitments by each party to increase their funding (up to a cap) when new parties join, in order to discourage free-riding and lock cost-sharing agreements into a climate treaty.[35] Most of the technological efforts can be borne

by high-income countries. But to be effective, collaborative research agreements must subsidize the involvement of developing countries, particularly fast-growing middle-income countries that must start early to build technological capacity that will be essential for their long-term climate-smart development. The private sector must also be included in research partnerships to ensure technologies can later be diffused through the market.

Market-pull, reward-based agreements. Many breakthrough innovations come from unlikely places that can be easily missed by grant funding programs. In 1993 Shuji Nakamura, a lone engineer working with a limited budget in a small company in the Japanese countryside, astonished the scientific community with the first successful blue-light-emitting diodes. This was the critical step for creating today's brilliant high-efficiency white-light-emitting diodes.[36] Many of the leading global innovators—including the computer giant Dell—spend much less than their industry peers on R&D as a share of sales.[37] But they are uniquely skilled at scoping the horizon for high-potential technologies and ideas, at collaborating with others on R&D, and at bringing new technologies to the market.[38] Some of the most promising climate-smart technologies are likely to come out of sectors that are typically not associated with climate change. For example, super-water-absorbent polymers could play a key role in promoting revegetation of drylands and other degraded ecosystems by holding water in the soil. But much of the interest in this technology is concentrated among manufacturers of products such as diapers. Similarly, producers of water repellent materials could manufacture clothing that requires less washing, with significant reductions in water and energy use.

Financial instruments that reward risk taking, rather than picking winners from the start, represent a tremendous unexploited opportunity. Solutions to technological problems can come from rapid advances in unexpected places or from new business models that traditional R&D subsidy programs can easily overlook. New

BOX 7.5 *Technologies on the scale of carbon capture and storage require international efforts*

For carbon capture and storage to achieve a fifth of the emission reductions needed to limit atmospheric concentrations to, for example, 550 parts per million, the technology has to ramp up from the 3.7 million tons of carbon sequestered today[a] to more than 255 million tons by 2020 and at least 22 billion tons by the end of the century, or about the same amount of current global emissions from energy use today (figure). Each capture and storage plant costs between \$1.5 and \$2.5 billion to construct, and deploying the 20–30 needed by 2020 to prove the commercial viability of the technology would be prohibitive for a single country. There are only four commercial end-to-end carbon capture and storage projects, and their storage capacity is one to two orders of magnitude smaller than the capacity a commercial 1,000 megawatt plant would need over its expected operational lifetime.

Sources: Edmonds and others 2007; IEA 2006; IEA 2008b.

a. To convert tons of carbon to CO_2, multiply by 3.67.

Carbon capture and storage technology requires massive additional efforts

CO_2 removed/year (millions of tons)

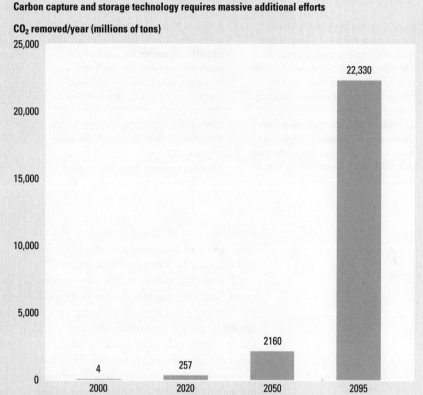

Note: Observed data for 2000. For all other years, projections based on needs in order to limit greenhouse gas concentrations to 550 ppm.

global financial instruments give markets the flexibility to find innovative solutions.

Inducement prizes and advanced market commitments are two closely related market-pull incentives for rewarding innovations that attain prespecified technological targets in a competition. Inducement prizes involve a known reward; advanced market commitments are financial commitments to subsidize future purchases of a product or service up to predetermined prices and volumes.

Although there are no examples of internationally funded climate-smart prizes, other recent national public and private initiatives have gathered growing interest. The \$10 million Ansari X-Prize was established in the mid-1990s to encourage nongovernmental space flight. The competition induced \$100 million of private research investments across 26 teams, leveraging 10 times the prize investment, before the winner was announced in 2004.[39] In March 2008 the X-Prize Foundation and a commercial partner announced a new \$10 million international competition to design, build, and bring to market high-fuel-mileage vehicles. One hundred and eleven teams from 14 countries have registered in the competition.[40]

Advanced market commitments, which encourage innovation by guaranteeing some minimum market demand to reduce uncertainty, have promoted climate-smart technologies through the U.S. Environmental Protection Agency, in partnership with nonprofit groups and utilities (box 7.6). A more recent international initiative is a pilot program for pneumococcal vaccines designed by the GAVI Alliance and the World Bank.[41] In 2007 donors pledged \$1.5 billion in advanced market commitments to the pilot. Vaccines are bought with donor-committed funds and with minor funding from recipient countries if they meet specified performance objectives. It is still too early to judge probable success.[42]

Market-pull inducements can complement but not replace technology-push incentives. Market-pull techniques can multiply public financial resources and foster competition to develop proof-of-concept and working prototypes. They have low barriers to entry—because funding is not awarded on past research credentials, small organizations and organizations from developing countries can compete. But these incentives cannot reduce risk to a point that private investors would be willing to finance large-scale or very early stage research.

Prizes and advanced market commitments offer good potential for multilateral

funding. Since prizes do not entail commercialization, they could be offered to solve precommercial research problems in such technologies as battery storage or photovoltaics. Private and public organizations in search of technology solutions could post competitions for designated cash prizes in a global technology marketplace. The World Bank Group is exploring prize competitions for early-stage clean technology innovations supported by the new Earth Fund launched by the Global Environment Facility and the International Finance Corporation.

Advanced market commitments could be useful where deployment learning costs are prohibitive, where there are no lead users willing to pay initial premiums for the technology, or where the market is too small or risky. These include energy generation and use but also adaptation technologies (such as malaria treatments and drought-resistant crop varieties), where the demand side of the market is fragmented (individual governments), financial resources are limited (particularly for developing countries), and the potential size of the market is blurred (by long-term policy uncertainty).[43]

Agreements to bridge the commercialization gap.   A major obstacle for innovation is the "valley of death," the lack of financing for bringing applied research to the market (figure 7.6). Governments are typically willing to fund R&D for unproven technologies, and the private sector is willing to finance technologies that have been demonstrated in the marketplace—the R&D block in figure 7.3—but there is little funding for technologies at the demonstration and deployment stages.[44] Governments are often reluctant to fund early-stage ventures for fear of distorting the market, and private investors consider them too risky, with the exception of a limited number of independent investors termed "business angels" and some corporations. Venture capitalists, who typically only fund firms with demonstrated technologies, were able to deploy no more than 73 percent of capital available in the clean technology sector in 2006 because so few firms in this sector had survived the valley of death.[45]

Figure 7.6   The "valley of death" between research and the market

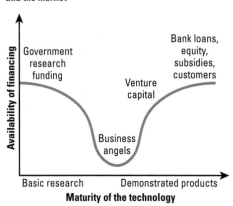

Source: WDR team.

Venture capital funding is also lacking for many types of climate-smart technologies. Investors are unlikely to be attracted to market segments involving particularly high-risk and capital-intensive energy technologies where demonstration costs can be massive. And it is expected that today's financial crisis will slow corporate venture capital, given the higher cost of debt.[46] Moreover, the bulk of the global venture capital industry is in a few developed countries, far from opportunities in several rapidly growing middle-income countries.[47]

Programs to commercialize technology can also support links with potential users of climate-smart technologies, particularly for small firms where breakthrough innovations often occur but which face the greatest financial and market access constraints. To commercialize ideas that meet its technology needs, the U.S. Environmental Protection Agency provides funding to small firms through the Small Business Innovation Research Program.[48] The French government's Passerelle program provides cofunding to large enterprises willing to invest in innovation projects of potential interest in small firms.[49] Other programs provide special grants to collaborative projects to encourage technology spillovers.

Because the gap between research and the market is particularly wide in developing countries and because many solutions to local problems may come from foreign countries, special multilateral funding can support research projects that include developing-country participants. This funding can create incentives for conducting research relevant to developing-country needs such as drought-resistant crops. Multilateral efforts can also promote climate-smart venture capital funds in high-income countries and in the several rapidly growing middle-income countries that have the critical mass of innovative activity and financial infrastructure to attract venture capital investors. This latter group includes China and India. In Israel, the Republic of Korea, and Taiwan, China, the government provided venture capital, acting as a core investor and attracting other funds.[50] Such strategies can provide the "valley of life" needed to nurture nascent technologies to levels where they can take root in the global economy.

The scale and scope of international efforts are far short of the challenge

Technology transfer comprises the broad processes to support flows of information, know-how, experience, and equipment to governments, enterprises, nonprofits, and research and educational institutions. The absorption of foreign technologies depends on much more than financing physical equipment and technology licenses. It requires building national capacity to identify, understand, use, and replicate useful technology. As discussed below, international policies can work hand in hand with national efforts to improve national institutions and create an enabling environment for technology transfer.

International organizations. Many international organizations dealing with environmental challenges are mainly mission focused; these include the World Health Organization, the Food and Agriculture Organization, and the UN Environment Programme. But these entities can be encouraged to collectively enhance the adequacy and coherence of the existing institutions for addressing climate change.

Similarly, many international agreements exist to address particular environmental problems but as these are operationalized, they should be mutually reinforcing.[51] These can be evaluated in terms of goals and means to achieve them in relation to their ability to support mitigation and adaptation of the magnitude expected under a 2°C world or a 5°C or beyond world.

Financing mechanisms. The Clean Development Mechanism (CDM), the main channel for financing investments in low-carbon technologies in developing countries, has leveraged public and private capital to finance over 4,000 low-carbon projects. But the majority of its projects do not involve either knowledge or equipment transfer from abroad.[52] (Chapter 6 discusses the limits of scaling up the CDM to accelerate technology transfers.)

The Global Environment Facility (GEF) is today the largest funder of projects that promote environmental protection while supporting national sustainable development goals. The GEF functions as the financial arm of the UNFCCC and provides support for technology needs assessments for more than 130 countries. Most GEF mitigation funding between 1998 to 2006—about $250 million a year—was directed at removing barriers to the diffusion of energy-efficient technologies.[53] The GEF's adaptation efforts focus on building capacity to identify the urgent and immediate needs of least developed countries. But its impact is limited by its modest proposed adaptation budget of $500 million for the 2010–14 period.[54]

The new Carbon Partnership Facility will provide complementary assistance to developing countries by supporting large and risky investments in clean energy and infrastructure with good potential for long-term emission reductions.[55] The Clean Technology Fund, a $5.2 billion multidonor initiative established in 2008, is another effort to provide low-interest financing for demonstration, deployment, and transfer of low-carbon technologies. In 2009 the Arab Republic of Egypt, Mexico, and Turkey are to be the first countries to benefit from a combined $1 billion of financing from this fund.

The Montreal Protocol shows how sustained multilateral funding can be achieved by making the financing of incremental costs of upgrading technology an obligation of an environmental treaty. The Multilateral Fund for Implementation of the Montreal Protocol provided developing countries with incentives to join the protocol by committing funds for incremental compliance costs.[56] In exchange, developing countries agreed to gradually phase out ozone-depleting substances. The fund provided grants or loans to cover the costs of facilities conversion, training, personnel, and licensing technologies. While the protocol is considered a successful model of technology diffusion, the sources of emissions of greenhouse gases are orders of magnitude larger than chlorofluorocarbons, and many greenhouse gas reduction technologies are not commercially available. A climate change fund similar to the Multilateral Fund would need to be scaled up appropriately.[57]

Financial and technological resources. As chapter 6 emphasizes, substantially more financing for developing countries is necessary. Estimates for additional required investments for mitigation and adaptation range from $170 billion to $765 billion annually by 2030. But financial transfers alone will not be enough. Acquiring technology, far from easy, is a long, costly, and risky process ridden with market failures. Adaptation technologies depend on local technical skills and indigenous knowledge because they involve designing systems tailored to local needs (box 7.7).

Even when technology can be imported, it involves a search process, prior technical knowledge, and the skills and resources necessary to use the technology efficiently. That capacity rests on various forms of knowledge, many of which are tacit and cannot be easily codified or transferred. Large-scale energy projects that can be contracted out to foreign firms, for example, require local capacity for policy makers to evaluate their merits, and for operation and maintenance. The European Union is developing legislation for managing risks associated with carbon capture and storage,[58] but few countries have the technical capacity to design such legislation, another barrier to deploying the technology.

BOX 7.7 *A promising innovation for coastal adaptation*

Bangladesh's coastal regions expect more frequent storm surges and tidal floods as a result of climate change. The University of Alabama at Birmingham is working with Bangladeshi researchers on home foundations and frames built of a lightweight composite material that bends—but does not break—in a hurricane and that can float on the rising tide of a coastal surge. Fibers from jute, one of Bangladesh's common plants, are woven with recycled plastics to form an ultrastrong building material. Jute does not require fertilizer, pesticides, or irrigation; is biodegradable; is inexpensive; and is already widely used to produce cloth, ropes, and other items in Bangladesh. Local architects are helping to incorporate the technology in local house designs. Bangladeshi researchers will contribute their expertise on the mass-manufacturing of jute products.

Sources: University of Alabama at Birmingham, http://main.uab.edu/Sites/MediaRelations/articles/55613/ (accessed February 17, 2009); interview with Professor Nassim Uddin, University of Alabama at Birmingham, on March 4, 2009.

Multilateral funding can have a greater impact on technology transfer and absorption by extending its scope from transferring physical and codified technology to enhancing human and organizational absorptive capacities in developing countries. Technology absorption is about learning: learning by investing in foreign technologies, learning through training and education, learning by interacting and collaborating with others outside and inside one's country, and learning through R&D. Multilateral funding can support technology transfer in three ways: by subsidizing investments in homegrown or foreign technologies in developing countries; by subsidizing the involvement of developing countries in the types of knowledge exchange, coordination, and cost-sharing agreements as discussed above; and by

supporting national knowledge infrastructures and private sectors, as discussed in the following section.

Public programs, policies, and institutions power innovation and accelerate its diffusion

Innovation is the outcome of a complex system that relies on the individual capacity of a multitude of actors, ranging from governments, universities, and research institutes to businesses, consumers, and nonprofits. Strengthening the capacity of this diverse set of actors, and how these actors interact, is a difficult but necessary task for tackling both development and climate change. Table 7.2 describes key policy priorities for encouraging innovation in countries of different income levels.

Table 7.2   Key national policy priorities for innovation

Countries	Main policies
Low-income	Invest in engineering, design, and management skills
	Increase funding to research institutions for adaptation research, development, demonstration, and diffusion
	Increase links between academic and research institutions, the private sector, and public planning agencies
	Introduce subsidies for adopting adaptation technologies
	Improve the business environment
	Import outside knowledge and technology whenever possible
Middle-income	Introduce climate-smart standards
	Create incentives for imports of mitigation technologies and, in rapidly industrializing countries, create long-term conditions for local production
	Create incentives for climate-smart venture capital in rapidly industrializing countries with a critical density of innovation (such as China and India)
	Improve the business environment
	Strengthen the intellectual property rights regime
	Facilitate climate-smart foreign direct investment
	Increase links between academic and research institutions, the private sector, and public planning agencies
High-income	Introduce climate-smart performance standards and carbon pricing
	Increase mitigation and adaptation innovation and diffusion through subsidies, prizes, venture capital incentives, and policies to encourage collaboration among firms and other sources and users of climate-smart innovation
	Assist developing countries in enhancing their technological absorptive and innovative capacities
	Support transfers of know-how and technologies to developing countries
	Support middle-income-country participation in long-term energy RDD&D projects
	Share climate change–related data with developing countries
All countries	Remove barriers to trade in climate-smart technologies
	Remove subsidies to high-carbon technologies
	Redefine knowledge-based institutions, especially universities, as loci of the diffusion of low-carbon practices

Source: WDR team.

Skills and knowledge constitute a key pillar for building a climate-smart economy. Basic education provides the foundation of any technology absorption process and reduces economic inequity, but a large enough pool of qualified engineers and researchers is also crucial. Engineers, in particularly short supply in low-income countries, play a role in implementing context-specific technologies for adaptation and are critical to rebuilding efforts after natural disasters (figure 7.7). Bangladesh, particularly prone to hurricanes and sea-level rise, is an extreme example: university students enrolled in engineering represented barely 0.04 percent of the population in 2006, compared with 0.43 percent in the Kyrgyz Republic, a country with a very similar per capita GDP.[59] Equally important are the management and entrepreneurial skills that channel technical knowledge into practical applications in the private sector. And in the public sector, skills are required in a wide range of areas including utility regulation, communication, urban planning, and climate policy development.

Skills and knowledge can be acquired by investing in the institutions and programs that make up a country's knowledge infrastructure. Institutions such as universities, schools, training institutes, R&D institutions, and laboratories, and such technological services as agricultural extension and business incubation[60] can support the private and public capacity to use climate-smart technologies and make decisions on the basis of sound science.

Another pillar for building a climate-smart economy is to create incentives for the private sector to invest in climate-smart technologies. This means creating not only regulatory incentives but also an enabling environment paired with public support programs for business innovation and technology absorption.

Knowledge infrastructure is a key to creating and adapting local mitigation and adaptation systems

Research institutes in developing countries can help governments better prepare for the consequences of climate change. In Indonesia and Thailand, for example, they are using NASA satellites to monitor environmental characteristics affecting malaria transmission in Southeast Asia, such as rainfall patterns and vegetation status.[61] Research institutes can partner with government agencies and private contractors to identify and design appropriate coastal adaptation technologies and to implement, operate, and maintain them. They can help devise adaptation strategies for farmers by combining local knowledge with scientific testing of alternative agroforestry systems or support forestry management by combining indigenous peoples' knowledge of forest conservation with genetically superior planting material.[62] And they can help firms improve the energy efficiency of their processes through consultancy, testing, troubleshooting, and training.

In middle-income countries research institutions can also solve longer-term mitigation challenges. Mastering the energy technologies that will be useful involves a learning process that can take decades. Agriculture and health depend on biotechnology to develop new technologies

Figure 7.7   Enrollment in engineering remains low in many developing countries

Enrollment in engineering, manufacturing, and construction in tertiary education as a share of the total population (%)

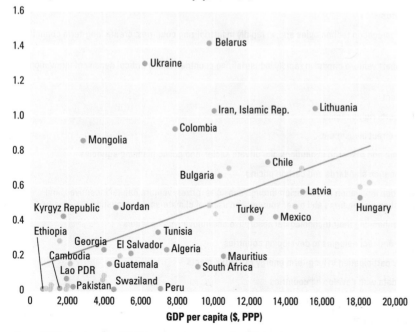

Source: WDR team based on UNESCO Institute for Statistics, http://stats.uis.unesco.org/unesco/ReportFolders/ReportFolders.aspx (accessed August 30, 2009).

and climate science for planning purposes. Development of smart grids for national electricity distribution relies on mastering integrated communications, sensing, and measurement technologies.

Yet after investing in research and academic institutions, many governments have found the contributions to development minimal.[63] The reasons: the research typically is not demand-driven, and there are few links between research institutes, universities, the private sector, and the communities in which they operate (box 7.8).[64] In addition universities in many developing countries have historically focused on teaching and do little research.

Shifting the balance of government funding in favor of competitive research funding, instead of guaranteed institutional funding, can go a long way to increase the effectiveness of public research institutions. In Ecuador the government's Program for Modernization of Agricultural Services finances a competitive research grant program that supports strategic work on innovations to open new export markets by controlling fruit flies, reducing production costs for new export products, and controlling disease and pests in traditional exports crops. The program introduced a new research culture and brought new organizations into the research system. Cofinancing requirements helped increase

national research funding by 92 percent.[65] Institutional reforms that give the private sector a greater voice in the governance of research institutions and that reward transfer of knowledge and technology to external clients can also help.[66] In some cases "bridging institutions" such as business incubators can facilitate knowledge spillovers from research institutions. In 2007, 283 clean technology companies were under incubation worldwide (even before including China), twice as many as in 2005.[67]

High-income countries can support the global development and diffusion of climate-smart systems by helping build capacity and partnering with research institutions in developing countries. An example is the International Research Institute for Climate and Society at Columbia University in the United States, which collaborates with local institutions in Africa, Asia, and Latin America.

Another example is the Consultative Group on International Agricultural Research (CGIAR). A donor-funded, decentralized, and cooperative global structure of research institutions, the CGIAR already targets a number of topics relevant to climate adaptation (box 7.9). A similar approach can be used for other climate technologies. Lessons from CGIAR suggest that regional research centers can be funded in developing countries to focus on a limited number

---

BOX 7.8 *Universities need to be innovative: The case of Africa*

Most donor assistance to Africa does not address the need to harness the world's existing fund of knowledge for long-term development. Higher education enrollments in Africa average close to 5 percent, compared with typical figures of more than 50 percent in developed economies. The challenge, however, is not only to increase access to African universities but also to make them function as engines of development.

There are opportunities for universities to forge closer links with the private sector, train more graduates for professional careers, and diffuse knowledge into the economy. As a model, the United States has a long tradition of land grant colleges,

which since the 19th century have been working directly with their communities to diffuse agricultural knowledge. The task ahead requires qualitative change in the goals, functions, and structure of the university. As part of this process, fundamental reforms will be needed in curriculum design, teaching, location, student selection, and university management.

Training will have to become more interdisciplinary to address the interconnected problems that transcend traditional disciplinary boundaries. South Africa's Stellenbosch University offers a shining example of how to adjust curricula to the needs of R&D organizations. It was the first university in the world to design and

launch an advanced microsatellite as part of its training. The aim for the program was to build competence in new technologies in the fields of remote sensing, spacecraft control, and earth sciences. Uganda's Makerere University has new teaching approaches that allow students to solve public health problems in their communities as part of their training. Similar approaches can be adopted by students in other technical fields, such as infrastructure development and maintenance.

Sources: Juma 2008; Land grant colleges, https://www.aplu.org/NetCommunity/Page.aspx?pid=183; sea grant colleges, http://www.seagrant.noaa.gov/ (accessed August 31, 2009).

BOX 7.9   *CGIAR: A model for climate change?*

The Consultative Group on International Agricultural Research (CGIAR) is a strategic partnership of 64 members from developing and industrial countries, foundations, and international organizations including the World Bank. Founded in 1971 in response to widespread concern that many developing countries were in danger of succumbing to famine, it has contributed significantly to agricultural productivity gains through improved crop varieties and played a pivotal role in bringing about the Green Revolution. Over time the CGIAR's mandate has expanded to include policy and institutional matters, conservation of biodiversity, and management of natural resources including fisheries, forests, soil, and water.

The CGIAR supports agricultural research by assisting 15 research centers, independent institutions with their own staff and governance structures, mostly in developing countries—and by running challenge programs. These are independently governed broad-based research partnerships designed to confront global or regional issues of vital importance,

such as genetic resource conservation and improvement, water scarcity, micronutrient deficiency, and climate change. In 2008 the CGIAR implemented an independent review of its governance, scientific work, and partnerships. The review concluded that CGIAR research has produced high overall returns since its inception, with benefits far exceeding costs. The benefit of yield-enhancing and yield-stabilizing crop varieties produced by the centers and their national partners is estimated at more than $10 billion annually, attributable largely to improved staple crops such as wheat, rice, and maize. Natural resource management research also shows substantial benefits and high returns on investment. However, the impact of these efforts has varied geographically because of a complex of factors such as local collective action, extension services, or assignment of property rights. The review deemed the CGIAR "one of the world's most innovative development partnerships," thanks to its multidisciplinary research activities and range of collaborations. But it also

found that the CGIAR has lost focus on its comparative advantages and that its growing mandate has diluted its impact. At the same time volatile food prices, more extreme weather patterns, growing global demand for food, and increasingly stressed natural resources are challenging the CGIAR like never before.

In December 2008 the CGIAR adopted a new business model. The reform entails a programmatic approach that will focus on a limited number of strategic "megaprograms" on key issues. The reforms also emphasize results-oriented research agenda setting and management, clear accountabilities, streamlined governance and programs, and stronger partnerships. The changes are expected to strengthen the CGIAR so that it can more effectively address many complex global issues, including climate change, but it is still too early to gauge their success.

Sources: Consultative Group on International Agricultural Research, http://www.cgiar .org/ (accessed March 5, 2009); CGIAR Independent Review Panel 2008; CGIAR Science Council 2008; World Bank 2008a.

---

of well-defined, region-specific topics, such as biomass, bioenergy, energy-efficient buildings, methane mitigation, and forest management.

Knowledge institutions can help inform and coordinate policy, particularly context-specific adaptation policies. As adaptations to climate change begin to be considered within policy processes, it becomes important to share solutions and experiences.[68] When planners, managers, and policy makers begin to recognize how their individual decisions can combine to reduce vulnerability to climate change, there is a tremendous opportunity to enhance coordination among sectors to improve the use of resources and to share this valuable information with other nations, regions, and localities.[69] Establishing and managing a "clearinghouse" that processes and makes available adaptation success stories and options from around the world will help communities faced with adaptation decisions.[70]

Carbon pricing and regulations to mobilize the private sector

As chapter 4 discusses, carbon pricing is essential for catalyzing market-driven innovation and adoption of mitigation technologies.[71] As relative prices change firms are likely to respond with new types of technological investments to economize on the factor that has become more expensive.[72] There is strong evidence that pricing can induce technological change.[73] One study found that if energy prices had remained at their low 1973 level until 1993, the energy efficiency of air conditioners would have been 16 percent lower in the United States.[74]

Regulation and its proper enforcement can also induce innovation. Performance standards for emissions or energy efficiency can induce technological change in much the same way as carbon pricing, because they can be associated with implicit prices that firms face in emitting pollutants.[75] In the United States patenting activity in sulfur dioxide (SO_2) emissions technology started to increase only in the late 1960s in anticipation of new national standards on SO_2 control. From 1975 to 1995 technological improvements reduced the capital costs for removing SO_2 from power plant emissions by half, and the share of SO_2 removed rose from less than 75 percent to above 95 percent.[76] Regulations can also provide firms with niche markets to develop new technologies and allow countries to gain a competitive edge. A ban on gasoline-propelled motorbikes in several urban areas of China in 2004—which coincided with technological improvements in electric motor and battery technologies, faster urbanization, higher gasoline prices, and increases in purchasing power—boosted the electric bicycle market from a mere 40,000 in 1998 to 21 million in 2008. E-bikes are now cheaper and cleaner than other motorized modes of transportation, including buses (figure 7.8), and China is exporting these low-carbon vehicles to developed countries.[77]

But regulation alone can have its drawbacks. Unlike price signals, regulations can limit the flexibility of firms, especially when they are technology-specific. They can also result in mitigation options that are more costly for society. But they are a necessary complement to carbon pricing (see chapter 4). Studies have analyzed the comparative effects of environmental regulations and market-based incentives on innovation: the general view is that combining different policy instruments may be the most effective, so long as their development and enforcement are predictable to stakeholders.[78]

An enabling business environment provides the basic framework for climate-smart technology diffusion and innovation

Markets need to function properly to ensure that firms do not face unnecessary risk, have access to information, operate within a well-defined legal framework, and have supportive

Figure 7.8   E-bikes are now among the cheapest and cleanest travel mode options in China

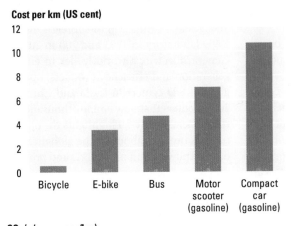

Cost per km (US cent)

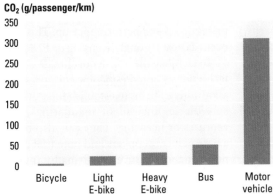

CO_2 (g/passenger/km)

Sources: Cherry 2007; Weinert, Ma, and Cherry 2007; photograph from the Wikipedia Foundation.

Note: E-bike emissions refer to full life-cycle, which, in this case, includes production, energy production, and use. For the regular bicycle only emissions from production are included.

market institutions. Securing land tenure, documenting land rights, strengthening land rental and sale markets, and broadening access to financial services can create incentives for technology transfer for rural smallholders (see chapter 3).[79] But an enabling business environment needs to recognize the basic rights of vulnerable groups, particularly indigenous peoples, heavily dependent on land and natural resources. Many of them have become landless, live on small parcels of land, or do not have secure tenure.[80]

Reducing entry barriers for firms and offering a flexible labor market supports technology start-ups that can create breakthrough innovations and agribusinesses that can bring new types of fertilizers or seeds to farmers.[81] The case of hybrid pearl millet in India shows that market liberalization in the late 1980s increased not only the role of private companies in seed development and distribution but also the rates of innovation.[82] Macroeconomic stability is another pillar of the enabling environment, along with a well-functioning financial sector. Basic infrastructure services, such as continuous energy and water supplies, are also indispensable.

Eliminating tariff and nontariff barriers on clean energy technologies—such as cleaner coal, wind power, solar photovoltaics, and energy-efficient lighting—could increase their traded volume by 14 percent in the 18 developing countries that emit high levels of greenhouse gases.[83] Trade barriers on imports, such as quotas, rules of origin, or unclear customs code specifications, can impede the transfer of climate-smart technologies by raising their domestic prices and making them cost-ineffective. In Egypt the average tariffs on photovoltaic panels are 32 percent, 10 times the 3 percent tariff imposed in high-income members of the Organisation for Economic Co-operation and Development (OECD). In Nigeria potential users of photovoltaic panels face nontariff barriers of 70 percent in addition to a 20 percent tariff.[84] Biofuels are hit particularly hard by tariffs. Tariffs on ethanol and on some biodiesel feedstocks, including import and export duties on Brazilian ethanol, totaled $6 billion in 2006. OECD country subsidies to their domestic biofuels producers came to $11 billion in 2006.

As a result, investments are not being made where technology is the most cost-effective. Brazil, the world's lowest-cost ethanol producer, saw a modest 6 percent increase in its ethanol production between 2004 and 2005, whereas the United States and Germany saw production increases of 20 and 60 percent respectively, protected by tariffs of over 25 percent in the United States and over 50 percent in the EU.[85] Removing these tariffs and subsidies would likely reallocate production to the most efficient biofuel producers.[86]

An attractive investment climate for foreign direct investment (FDI) is critical to accelerating technology transfer and absorption.[87] In 2007 FDI accounted for 12.6 percent of total gross fixed capital formation in electricity, gas, and water in developing countries, three times the amount of multilateral and bilateral aid.[88] Transnational corporations based in high-income countries have invested massively in photovoltaic production in India (BP Solar), ethanol in Brazil (Archer Daniels Midland and Cargill), and wind power in China (Gamesa and Vestas). China had one foreign-owned R&D laboratory in 1993 and 700 in 2005.[89] General Electric, a world leader in energy generation and efficiency products, opened global R&D centers in India and China in 2000, centers that now employ thousands of researchers. Figure 7.9 highlights the opportunities brought about by the globalization of wind power equipment R&D and production in middle-income countries.

Developing local production capacity can help these countries ensure their long-term uptake of climate-smart technologies and compete in global markets, driving prices down and performance up. This will occur fastest through licensing or FDI.

To facilitate the transfer of climate-smart technologies, middle-income countries can allow foreign firms to establish fully owned subsidiaries instead of mandating joint ventures or licensing. They can also build a base of local suppliers and potential partners for foreign-invested firms by investing in training and capacity building.[90] And they can ensure that their intellectual property rights adequately protect foreign technology transfer and R&D.

When enforcement of intellectual property rights (IPR) is perceived to be weak (see figure 7.9), foreign firms may not be willing to license their most sophisticated technologies, for fear that competitors will use it—which is the situation for wind equipment in China.[91] Weak IPR enforcement also discourages foreign subsidiaries from increasing the scale of their R&D activities and foreign venture capitalists from investing in promising domestic enterprises.[92] Despite their investments in local manufacturing and R&D, foreign subsidiaries of global wind equipment producers register very few patents in Brazil, China, India, or Turkey. All these countries have weak IPR regimes that could discourage scaling up R&D.[93]

Figure 7.9 **Middle-income countries are attracting investments from the top five wind equipment firms, but weak intellectual property rights constrain technology transfers and R&D capacity**

a. Intellectual property rights performance

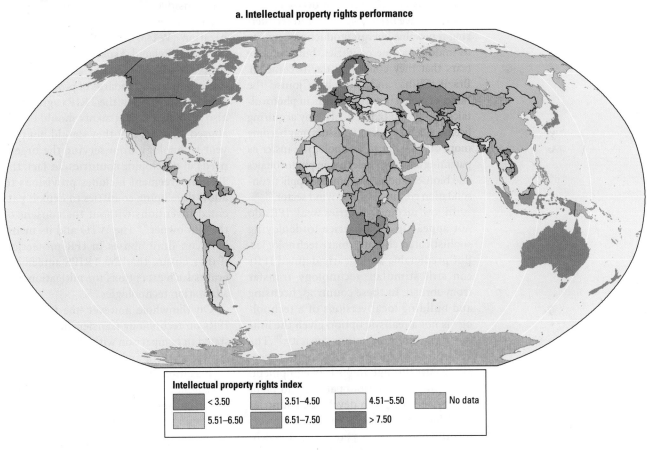

Intellectual property rights index
- < 3.50
- 3.51–4.50
- 4.51–5.50
- No data
- 5.51–6.50
- 6.51–7.50
- > 7.50

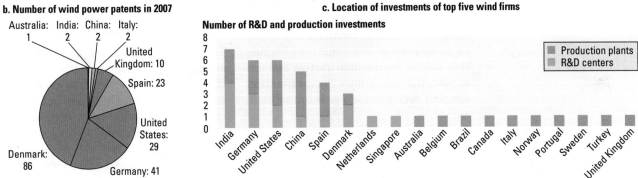

b. Number of wind power patents in 2007

Australia: 1 India: 2 China: 2 Italy: 2
United Kingdom: 10
Spain: 23
United States: 29
Germany: 41
Denmark: 86

c. Location of investments of top five wind firms

Number of R&D and production investments

- Production plants
- R&D centers

(India, Germany, United States, China, Spain, Denmark, Netherlands, Singapore, Australia, Belgium, Brazil, Canada, Italy, Norway, Portugal, Sweden, Turkey, United Kingdom)

Sources: Published patent data from U.S., Japanese, European, and international patent application databases, annual reports, and Web sites of Vestas, General Electric, Gamesa, Enercon, and Suzlon (accessed on March 4, 2009); Dedigama 2009.

Note: A country's IPR score reflects its ranking according to an IPR index based on the strength of its intellectual property protection policies and their enforcement.

Yet IPRs may also hamper innovation if a patent blocks other useful inventions because it is too broad in scope. Some patent claims on synthetic biology products and processes with promise for synthetic biofuels are perceived by critics to be so broad that scientists fear they may halt scientific progress in related fields.[94] Strong IPRs can also hamper technology transfer if firms refuse to license their technology to keep their market power.

There is no evidence that overly restrictive IPRs have been a big barrier to transferring renewable energy production capacity to middle-income countries, but there are fears that they could one day become so. Brazil, China, and India have joined the ranks of global industry leaders in photovoltaics, wind, and biofuels, often by acquiring licensed technologies. IPR issues may become more of a barrier to technology transfer as patenting activity accelerates in photovoltaics and biofuels and as equipment supplier consolidation continues in the wind sector.[95]

In low-income countries weak IPRs do not appear to be a barrier to deploying sophisticated climate-smart technologies. But predictable and clearly defined IPRs can still stimulate technology transfer from abroad. In these countries, licensing and building local versions of a technology is not a realistic option given the limited domestic production capacity.[96] The absorption of energy technologies generally occurs through imports of equipment. For climate adaptation, patents and plant variety rights held in developed countries are seldom a problem in small and lower-income countries. A patent registered in a specific country can only be protected in that market, and foreign companies do not register their intellectual property in many low-income countries, because they do not represent attractive markets or potential competitors. Poorer countries can thus decide to use a gene or tool from abroad.[97]

High-income countries can ensure that excessive industry consolidation in climate-smart sectors does not reduce incentives to license technology to developing countries. They can also ensure that national policies do not prevent foreign firms from licensing publicly funded research for climate-smart technologies of global importance. In many countries, universities are not allowed to license technology funded by their national government to foreign firms.[98] Other proposals include patent buyouts and the transfer of climate-smart IPRs to the public domain by international organizations.

High-income countries can also ensure that concerns over IPRs and transfer and innovation of climate-smart technologies are considered in international treaties such as those of the World Trade Organization (WTO). The WTO's agreement on Trade-Related Aspects of Intellectual Property Rights (TRIPS) establishes the minimum legal standards of protection for WTO members. But the TRIPS agreement also recognizes that patents should not be abused, namely, that they should not prevent technology from serving the urgent needs of developing countries. In fact, the TRIPS agreement includes provisions to allow developing countries to exploit patented inventions without the consent of the IPR owner.[99] The WTO and its members can limit abuses in IPR protection if they ensure that the TRIPS agreement grants such exceptions for mitigation and adaptation technologies.

On the whole however, the impact of IPRs on technology transfer may be overstated in comparison with other costs such as management and training and barriers such as limited absorptive capacity. Building engineering competence could go a long way in enhancing the absorptive capacity of developing countries.

Public funding can help firms overcome market failures associated with innovation and technology diffusion

There is a limit to how much carbon prices and emission standards can increase investments in low-carbon technology and innovation. New technologies are not always rapidly adopted even when they become economically attractive to potential users (see box 4.5 in chapter 4). Accelerating technological change requires supplementing carbon pricing and regulations with public funding to explore a wide portfolio of technological options.[100] Well-known market failures leading to private underinvestment in innovation and diffusion have provided the basis for public funding policies for decades.[101]

In middle-income countries with industrial capacity, financial support can go to the local design, production, and export of climate-smart systems. Public funding policies can broadly define innovation to include adapting, improving, and developing products, processes, and services that are new to a firm, irrespective of whether they are new to their markets. This takes into account the spillover effects of R&D in helping build technological absorptive capacity.[102] For example, the Technology Development Foundation of Turkey provides zero-interest loans of up to $1 million to companies that adopt or develop systems for energy efficiency, renewable energy, or cleaner production.[103] In small and low-income countries where there are even more market barriers to technology absorption, public financial support can selectively finance technology absorption in firms, along with related technical consulting and training.

Publicly supported technology diffusion programs bridge gaps in information and know-how among firms, farmers, and public agencies. The most effective programs respond to real demand, address multiple barriers, and include community institutions from the beginning. This creates local buy-in, builds sustainability, and ensures that the programs are compatible with local development goals.[104] In South Africa the Clean Production Demonstration project for metal finishers was successful precisely because it targeted a wide range of issues in parallel—from the lack of information about the advantages of cleaner technologies to the lack of legislation or its enforcement. The demand-driven project obtained the buy-in of all stakeholders—a broad range of company owners, managers, staff, consultants, regulators, and suppliers—and combined awareness campaigns, training, technical consulting, and financial assistance.[105] In China the government's strategy to improve and diffuse biomass cook stove technology was equally successful because it recognized the systems nature of

innovation and was largely demand-driven (box 7.10).

As already pointed out in chapter 4, government procurement is another market-pull instrument that can create market niches for climate-smart technology, but it relies on good governance and a sound institutional environment. Public purchasing preferences can stimulate climate-smart innovation and technology adoption when the government is a major customer in areas such as wastewater management, construction, and transport equipment and services. Germany and Sweden already include "green" criteria in more than 60 percent of their tenders.[106]

Preventing unmanageable climate change, coping with its unavoidable impacts on society, and meeting global development objectives requires significantly stepping up international efforts at diffusing existing technologies and deploying new ones. For ambitious high-priority initiatives, such as carbon capture and storage, countries can pool their resources, share the risks and share the learning benefits of joint RDD&D. They can create new global funding mechanisms. "Technology-push" policies based on increasing public investments in R&D will not be sufficient to reach our technological objectives. They need to be matched with "market-pull" policies that create public and private sector incentives for entrepreneurship, for collaboration, and to find innovative solutions in unlikely places.

The world must ensure that technological advances find their ways rapidly to countries that have the least ability to adopt them but the most need. Diffusing climate-smart technology will require much more than shipping ready-to-use equipment to developing countries. Namely, it will require building technological absorptive capacity—the ability of the public and private sectors to identify, adopt, adapt, improve, and employ the most appropriate technologies. It will also require creating environments that facilitate the transfer of mitigation and adaptation technologies from one country to the next through channels of trade and investment.

BOX 7.10 *Improved cook stoves designs can reduce soot, producing important benefits for human health and for mitigation*

About 2 billion people in developing countries depend on biomass for heating and cooking. Rudimentary cookstoves in rural areas from Central America to Africa, India, and China release CO_2 along with black carbon (tiny particles of carbon in soot) and products of incomplete combustion (carbon monoxide, nitrogen compounds, methane, and volatile organic compounds). These products pose a serious health hazard. Inhalation of indoor smoke from burning of solid biomass is thought to contribute to the deaths of 1.6 million people a year globally, about 1 million of them children under five years of age.

Recent studies suggest that the power of black carbon as a driver for climate change could be as much as twice what the Intergovernmental Panel on Climate Change previously estimated. New analyses suggest that black carbon could have contributed more than 70 percent of the warming of the Arctic since 1976 and could have been a strong factor in the retreat of Himalayan glaciers.

Given that household solid fuel used in cookstoves in the developing world is responsible for 18 percent of the emissions of black carbon, new cookstove technologies that improve combustion and thus reduce soot and emissions of other gases can have benefits not only for human health but also for mitigation.

A lot of funding has been devoted to support the use of liquefied petroleum gas (LPG) stoves as a cleaner alternative to biomass stoves, mostly by subsidizing LPG, but that has proved ineffective at diffusing the technology widely in developing countries. Even with subsidies, most poor people cannot afford the fuel.

Public programs to introduce improved biomass cook stoves over the past two decades have produced mixed results. In India the government subsidized 50 percent of the cost of 8 million stoves that it distributed. Initially, the program encountered some difficulties because the stove design was not appropriate for the tools and foods used by the population, but during the past five years the government has launched new research to correct these problems. Improved cook stoves are gaining some ground in other countries. In China the government recognized that success hinged on meeting people's needs, and that this could not be achieved through a supply-driven top-down approach. It confined its role to research, technical training, setting manufacturing standards, and reducing bureaucratic impediments to the production and diffusion of new stoves. The enterprise sector was mobilized for local distribution.

Given recent technological progress in biomass cookstoves, their impact on health, and their recently revealed impact on climate change, it is appropriate to massively scale up and commercialize high-quality biomass-based cookstoves. The most effective stoves will be affordable to the poor, adaptable to local cooking needs, durable, and appealing to customers. Project Surya, a pilot evaluation program, is going to undertake the most comprehensive and rigorous scientific evaluation to date on the efficacy of improved cookstoves on climate warming and people's health. The project will support the introduction of new cookstove models in 15,000 households in three different regions of India. By monitoring

A woman cooks with her Envirofit G-3300 cookstove

Photo credit: Envirofit India.

pollutants through cutting edge sensor technologies, measuring solar heating of the air, and combining these data with measurements from NASA satellites, the project team hopes to observe a "black carbon hole"—the absence of the usual black carbon particles—in the atmosphere over the areas of intervention, and to measure how this impacts regional temperatures and people's health. The study will also improve understanding of how future cookstove programs should address households' needs and behaviors.

Sources: Bond and others 2004; Columbia Earthscape, http://www.earthscape.org/r1/kad09/ (accessed May 14, 2009); Forster and others 2007; Hendriksen, Ruzibuka, and Rutagambwa 2007; Project Surya, http://www-ramanathan.ucsd.edu/ProjectSurya.html (accessed August 31, 2009); Ramanathan and Carmichael 2008; Ramanathan, Rehman, and Ramanathan 2009; Shindell and Faluvegi 2009; Smith, Rogers, and Cowlin 2005; UNEP 2008b; Watkins and Ehst 2008.

Notes

1. Global Wind Energy Council, http://www.gwec.net/fileadmin/documents/PressReleases/PR_stats_annex_table_2nd_feb_final_final.pdf (accessed April 2009).

2. Metcalfe and Ramlogan 2008.

3. Edmonds and others 2007; Stern 2007; World Bank 2008a.

4. Most integrated assessment models show a demand for no more than 600 gigatons of carbon (2,220 gigatons of carbon dioxide) storage capac-

ity over the course of this century. Published estimates place the potential global geologic storage capacity at about 3,000 gigatons of carbon (11,000 gigatons of carbon dioxide). Dooley, Dahowski, and Davidson 2007.

5. SEG 2007. See, in particular, appendix B, "Sectoral Toolkit for Integrating Adaptation into Planning/Management and Technology/R&D."

6. Heller and Zavaleta 2009.

7. Hulse 2007.

8. Commonwealth Secretariat 2007.

9. McKinsey Global Institute 2007.

10. Leadbeater and others 2008.

11. Aghion and others 2005.

12. Salter and Martin 2001.

13. De Ferranti and others 2003.

14. Barlevy 2007.

15. Robins and others 2009.

16. Berkhout 2002.

17. UNEP 2008a.

18. A. Gentleman, "Bangalore Turning into a Power in Electric Cars." *International Herald Tribune*, August 14, 2006; Maini 2005; S. Nagrath, "Gee Whiz, It's A Reva! The Diminutive Indian Electric Car Is a Hit on the Streets of London." *Businessworld*, Dec. 19, 2008.

19. The number of patents is often used as a measure of inventive activity, but there can be drawbacks to comparing patents across countries because certain types of inventions are less suited to patenting than others.

20. OECD 2008; Dechezleprêtre and others 2008.

21. IEA 2008a; SEG 2007; Stern 2007; Nemet and Kammen 2007; Davis and Owens 2003; PCAST 1999.

22. Based on International Energy Agency (IEA) RD&D statistics including high- and upper-middle-income IEA countries except for Australia, Belgium, the Czech Republic, Greece, Luxembourg, Poland, the Slovak Republic, and Spain.

23. IEA 2008a.

24. OECD 2008.

25. For example, crops and growing methods often need to be adapted to local climatic, soil, and technological conditions.

26. OECD 2008.

27. Beintema and Stads 2008.

28. Carlsson 2006; Freeman 1987; Lundvall 1992; Nelson 1996; OECD 1997.

29. PCAST 1999.

30. IEA, http://www.iea.org/Textbase/techno/index.asp (accessed December 15, 2008).

31. http://www.energystar.gov/ (accessed December 15, 2008).

32. Milford, Ducther, and Barker 2008; Stern 2007.

33. Guasch and others 2007.

34. De Coninck and others 2007.

35. De Coninck and others 2007.

36. The Millennium Technology Prize, http://www.millenniumprize.fi (accessed February 16, 2009).

37. Jaruzelski, Dehoff, and Bordia 2006.

38. Chesbrough 2003.

39. Newell and Wilson 2005; X Prize Foundation, http://www.xprize.org/ (accessed December 15, 2008).

40. Progressive Automotive X Prize, http://www.progressiveautoxprize.org/ (accessed April 19, 2009).

41. Pneumonia is the leading infectious cause of childhood mortality worldwide; World Bank 2008a.

42. World Bank 2008a.

43. World Bank 2008a.

44. Branscomb and Auerswald 2002.

45. DB Advisors 2008.

46. UNEP 2008a.

47. Nemet and Kammen 2007.

48. National Center for Environmental Research, http://www.epa.gov/ncer/sbir/ (accessed April 2009).

49. Passerelles Pacte PME, http://www.oseo.fr/a_la_une/actualites/passerelles_pacte_pme (accessed November 30, 2008).

50. Goldberg and others 2006.

51. Among the pertinent framework conventions are those on climate change (United Nations Framework Convention on Climate Change, or UNFCCC), biodiversity (Convention on Biological Diversity), desertification (Convention to Combat Desertification), the Ramsar Convention on Wetlands, shared international

"Through my painting I would like to transmit to all the people, including world's leaders, my hope to stop global warming promoting the use of our sun because it is powerful, clean, and practically endless. . . . If we want, we could turn it to be our everyday energy source. Governments and companies should support the use of solar energy and scientists to find the best way so the people can easily use it in their homes, appliances, machines, factories, and vehicles."

—Laura Paulina Tercero Araiza, Mexico, age 10

watercourses, and the Plant Genetic Resources for Food and Agriculture.

52. Brewer 2008; De Coninck, Haake, and van der Linden 2007; Dechezleprêtre, Glachant, and Meniérè 2007.

53. Doornbosch, Gielen, and Koutstaal 2008; Global Environment Facility, http://www.gefweb.org/ (accessed December 4, 2008).

54. GEF 2008; GEF 2009.

55. The World Bank Carbon Finance Unit, http://wbcarbonfinance.org/ (accessed December 4, 2008).

56. Barrett 2006.

57. De Coninck and others 2007.

58. CCS in Europe, http://ec.europa.eu/environment/climat/ccs/work_en.htm (accessed July 2, 2009).

59. UNESCO Institute for Statistics, http://www.uis.unesco.org (accessed January 18, 2009).

60. Lundvall 2007.

61. Humanitarian Practice Network, http://www.odihpn.org/report.asp?id=2522 (accessed January 14, 2009); Kiang 2006.

62. IPCC 2000.

63. Goldman and Ergas 1997; World Bank 2007a.

64. Juma 2006.

65. World Bank 2005.

66. Watkins and Ehst 2008.

67. UNEP 2008a.

68. Huq, Reid, and Murray 2003.

69. See ecosystems-based management in chapter 3.

70. SEG 2007.

71. Schneider and Goulder 1997; Popp 2006; also see chapter 4.

72. Hicks 1932.

73. Hayami and Ruttan 1970; Hayami and Ruttan 1985; Ruttan 1997; Jaffe, Newell, and Stavins 2003; Popp 2002.

74. Newell, Jaffe, and Stavins 1999.

75. Jaffe, Newell, and Stavins 2003.

76. Taylor, Rubin, and Hounshell 2005.

77. Weinert, Ma, and Cherry 2007; the Climate Group 2008; Hang and Chen 2008; C. Whelan, "Electric Bikes Are Taking Off." *New York Times*, March 14, 2007, http://www.time.com/time/world/article/0,8599,1904334,00.html (accessed July 5, 2009).

78. Bernauer and others 2006.

79. World Bank 2007b.

80. de Chavez and Tauli-Corpuz 2008.

81. World Bank 2008b; Scarpetta and Tressel 2004.

82. Matuschke and Qaim 2008.

83. These countries are Argentina, Bangladesh, Brazil, Chile, China, Colombia, Arab Republic of Egypt, India, Indonesia, Kazakhstan, Malaysia, Mexico, Nigeria, the Philippines, South Africa, Thailand, República Bolivariana de Venezuela, and Zambia. World Bank 2008c.

84. World Bank 2008c.

85. Steenblik 2007.

86. IMF 2008.

87. Goldberg and others 2008.

88. Brewer 2008.

89. UNCTAD 2005.

90. Maskus 2004; Hoekman, Maskus, and Saggi 2004; Lewis 2007.

91. Barton 2007.

92. Branstetter, Fisman, and Fritz Foley 2005; Deloitte 2007.

93. Dedigama 2009.

94. ICTSD 2008.

95. Barton 2007; Lewis 2007; ICTSD 2008.

96. Hoekman, Maskus, and Saggi 2004.

97. World Bank 2007b.

98. Barton 2007.

99. ICTSD 2008.

100. Baker and Shittu 2006; Jaffe, Newell, and Stavins 2003; Schneider and Goulder 1997; Popp 2006.

101. Nelson 1959; Arrow 1962.

102. Cohen and Levinthal 2009.

103. Technology Development Foundation of Turkey, http://www.ttgv.org.tr/en/page.php?id=35 (accessed March 5, 2009).

104. IPCC 2000.

105. Koefoed and Buckley 2008.

106. Bouwer and others 2006.

References

Aghion, P., G. M. Angeletos, A. Banerjee, and K. Manova. 2005. "Volatility and Growth: Credit Constraints and Productivity-Enhancing Investments." Department of Economics Working Paper 05-15. Massachusetts Institute of Technology, Cambridge, MA.

Arrow, K. J. 1962. "Economic Welfare and the Allocation of Resources for Invention." In *The Rate and Direction of Inventive Activity: Economic and Social Factors*, ed. R. Nelson. Princeton, NJ: Princeton University Press.

Baker, E., and E. Shittu. 2006. "Profit-Maximizing R&D in Response to a Random Carbon Tax." *Resource and Energy Economics* 28 (2): 160–180.

Barlevy, G. 2007. "On the Cyclicality of Research and Development." *American Economic Review* 97 (4): 1131–1164.

Barrett, S. 2006. "Managing the Global Commons." In *Expert Paper Series Two: Global Commons.* Stockholm: Secretariat of the International Task Force on Global Public Goods.

Barton, J. H. 2007. "Intellectual Property and Access to Clean Energy Technologies in Developing Countries: An Analysis of Solar Photovoltaic, Biofuels and Wind Technologies." Trade and Sustainable Energy Series Issue Paper 2, International Centre for Trade and Sustainable Development, Geneva.

Beintema, N. M., and G. J. Stads. 2008. "Measuring Agricultural Research Investments: A Revised Global Picture." Agricultural and Technology Indicators Background Note, International Food Policy Research Institute, Washington, DC.

Berkhout, F. 2002. "Technological Regimes, Path Dependency and the Environment." *Global Environmental Change* 12 (1): 1–4.

Bernauer, T., S. Engel, D. Kammerer, and J. Seijas. 2006. "Explaining Green Innovation." Working Paper 17, Center for Comparative and International Studies, Zurich.

Bond, T. C., D. G. Streets, K. F. Yarber, S. M. Nelson, J.-H. Woo, and Z. Klimont. 2004. "A Technology-Based Global Inventory of Black and Organic Carbon Emissions from Combustion." *Journal of Geophysical Research* 109: D14203–doi:10.1029/2003JD003697.

Bouwer, M., M. Jonk, T. Berman, R. Bersani, H. Lusser, V. Nappa, A. Nissinen, K. Parikka, P. Szuppinger, and C. Vigano. 2006. *Green Public Procurement in Europe 2006—Conclusions and Recommendations.* Haarlem: Virage Milieu & Management.

Branscomb, L. M., and P. E. Auerswald. 2002. *Between Invention and Innovation: An Analysis of Funding for Early-Stage Technology Development.* Gaithersburg, MD: National Institute of Standards and Technology.

Branstetter, L., R. Fisman, and C. F. Foley. 2005. "Do Stronger Intellectual Property Rights Increase International Technology Transfer? Empirical Evidence from U.S. Firm-Level Data." Working Paper 11516, National Bureau of Economic Research, Cambridge, MA.

Brewer, T. L. 2008. "International Energy Technology Transfer for Climate Change Mitigation: What, Who, How, Why, When, Where, How Much . . . and the Implications for International Institutional Architecture." Working Paper 2048, CESifo, Venice.

Carlsson, B. 2006. "Internationalization of Innovation Systems: A Survey of the Literature." *Research Policy* 35 (1): 56–67.

CGIAR Independent Review Panel. 2008. *Bringing Together the Best of Science and the Best of Development: Independent Review of the CGIAR System: Report to the Executive Council.* Washington, DC: Consultative Group on International Agricultural Research.

CGIAR Science Council. 2008. *Report of the First External Review of the Generation Challenge Program.* Rome: Consultative Group on International Agricultural Research.

Cherry, C. R. 2007. "Electric Two-Wheelers in China: Analysis of Environmental, Safety, and Mobility Impacts." Ph.D. thesis. University of California, Berkeley, CA.

Chesbrough, H. W. 2003. *Open Innovation: The New Imperative for Creating and Profiting from Technology.* Boston, MA: Harvard Business School Press.

Climate Group. 2008. *China's Clean Revolution.* London: The Climate Group.

Cohen, W. M., and D. A. Levinthal. 2009. "Innovation and Learning: The Two Faces of R&D." *Economic Journal* 99 (397): 569–96.

Commonwealth Secretariat. 2007. *Commonwealth Ministers Reference Book 2007.* London: Henley Media Group.

Davis, G., and B. Owens. 2003. "Optimizing the Level of Renewable Electric R&D Expenditures Using Real Option Analysis." *Energy Policy* 31 (15): 1589–1608.

Davis, L., and J. Davis. 2004. "How Effective Are Prizes as Incentives to Innovation? Evidence from Three 20th Century Contests." Paper presented at the Danish Research Unit for Industrial Dynamics Summer Conference on Industrial Dynamics, Innovation and Development. Elsinore, Denmark.

DB Advisors. 2008. "Investing in Climate Change 2009 Necessity And Opportunity In Turbulent Times." Global team, DB Advisors, Deutsche Bank Group, Frankfurt.

de Chavez, R., and V. Tauli-Corpuz. 2008. *Guide on Climate Change and Indigenous Peoples.* Baguio City, Philippines: Tebtebba Foundation.

de Coninck, H. C., C. Fisher, R. G. Newell, and T. Ueno. 2007. *International Technology-Oriented Agreements to Address Climate Change.* Washington, DC: Resources for the Future.

de Coninck, H. C., F. Haake, and N. J. van der Linden. 2007. *Technology Transfer in the Clean Development Mechanism.* Petten, The Netherlands: Energy Research Centre of the Netherlands.

de Ferranti, D. M., G. E. Perry, I. Gill, J. L. Guasch, W. F. Maloney, C. Sanchez-Paramo, and N. Schady. 2003. *Closing the Gap in Education and Technology.* Washington, DC: World Bank.

Dechezleprêtre, A., M. Glachant, I. Hascic, N. Johnstone, and Y. Meniérè. 2008. *Invention and Transfer of Climate Change Mitigation Technologies on a Global Scale: A Study Drawing on Patent Data.* Paris: CERNA.

Dechezleprêtre, A., M. Glachant, and Y. Meniérè. 2007. "The Clean Development Mechanism and the International Diffusion of Technologies: An Empirical Study." Working Paper 2007.105, Fondazione Eni Enrico Mattei, Milan.

Dedigama, A. C. 2009. *International Property Rights Index (IPRI): 2009 Report.* Washington, DC: Property Rights Alliance.

Deloitte. 2007. *Global Trends in Venture Capital 2007 Survey.* New York: Deloitte Touche Tohmatsu.

Dooley, J. J., R. T. Dahowski, and C. Davidson. 2007. "CCS: A Key to Addressing Climate Change." In *Fundamentals of the Global Oil and Gas Industry 2007.* London: Petroleum Economist.

Doornbosch, R., D. Gielen, and P. Koutstaal. 2008. *Mobilising Investments in Low-Emissions Technologies on the Scale Needed to Reduce the Risks of Climate Change.* Paris: OECD Round Table on Sustainable Development.

Edmonds, J., M. A. Wise, J. J. Dooley, S. H. Kim, S. J. Smith, P. J. Runci, L. E. Clarke, E. L. Malone, and G. M. Stokes. 2007. *Global Energy Technology Strategy Addressing Climate Change: Phase 2 Findings from an International Public-Private Sponsored Research Program.* Washington, DC: Battelle Pacific Northwest Laboratories.

Forster, P., V. Ramaswamy, P. Artaxo, T. Bernsten, R. Betts, D. W. Fahey, J. Haywood, J. Lean, D. C. Lowe, G. Myhre, J. Nganga, R. Prinn, G. Raga, M. Schulz, and R. Van Dorland. 2007. "Changes in Atmospheric Constituents and in Radiative Forcing." In *Climate Change 2007: The Physical Science Basis. Contribution of Working Group I to the Fourth Assessment Report of the Intergovernmental Panel on Climate Change,* ed. S. Solomon, D. Qin, M. Manning, Z. Chen, M. Marquis, K. B. Averyt, M. Tignor, and H. L. Miller. Cambridge, UK: Cambridge University Press.

Freeman, C. 1987. *Technology Policy and Economic Performance: Lessons from Japan.* London: Pinter.

GEF (Global Environment Facility). 2008. *Transfer of Environmentally Sound Technologies: The GEF Experience.* Washington, DC: GEF.

———. 2009. *Draft Adaptation to Climate Change Programming Strategy.* Washington, DC: GEF.

Global Wind Energy Council. 2009. *Global Wind 2008 Report.* Brussels: Global Wind Energy Council.

Goldberg, I., L. Branstetter, J. G. Goddard, and S. Kuriakose. 2008. *Globalization and Technology Absorption in Europe and Central Asia.* Washington, DC: World Bank.

Goldberg, I., M. Trajtenberg, A. B. Jaffe, J. Sunderland, T. Muller, and E. Blanco Armas. 2006. "Public Financial Support for Commercial Innovation." Europe and Central Asia Chief Economist's Regional Working Paper 1, World Bank, Washington, DC.

Goldman, M., and H. Ergas. 1997. "Technology Institutions and Policies: Their Role in Developing Technological Capability in Industry." Technical Paper 383, World Bank, Washington, DC.

Guasch, J. L., J. L. Racine, I. Sanchez, and M. Diop. 2007. *Quality Systems and Standards for a Competitive Edge.* Washington, DC: World Bank.

Hang, C. C., and J. Chen. 2008. "Disruptive Innovation: An Appropriate Innovation Approach for Developing Countries." ETM Internal Report 1/08. National University of Singapore, Division of Engineering and Technology Management, Singapore.

Hayami, Y., and V. W. Ruttan. 1970. "Factor Prices and Technical Change in Agricultural Development: The United States and Japan." *Journal of Political Economy* 78: 1115–41.

———. 1985. *Agricultural Development: An International Perspective.* Baltimore: John Hopkins University Press.

Heller, N. E., and E. S. Zavaleta. 2009. "Biodiversity Management in the Face of Climate Change: A Review of 22 Years of Recommendations." *Biological Conservation* 142 (1): 14–32.

Hendriksen, G., R. Ruzibuka, and T. Rutagambwa. 2007. *Capacity Building for Science, Technology and Innovation for Sustainable Development and Poverty Reduction.* Washington, DC: World Bank.

Hicks, J. R. 1932. *The Theory of Wages.* London: Macmillan.

Hoekman, B. M., K. E. Maskus, and K. Saggi. 2004. "Transfer of Technology to Developing Countries: Unilateral and Multilateral Policy Options." Policy Research Working Paper 3332, World Bank, Washington, DC.

Hulse, J. H. 2007. *Sustainable Development at Risk: Ignoring the Past*. Ottawa: Foundation Books/IDRC.

Huq, S., H. Reid, and L. Murray. 2003. "Mainstreaming Adaptation to Climate Change in Least Developed Countries." Working Paper 1: Country by Country Vulnerability to Climate Change, International Institute for Environment and Development, London.

ICTSD (International Centre for Trade and Sustainable Development). 2008. "Climate Change, Technology Transfer and Intellectual Property Rights." Paper presented at the Trade and Climate Change Seminar. Copenhagen.

IEA (International Energy Agency). 2006. *Energy Technology Perspectives: In Support of the G8 Plan of Action. Scenarios and Strategies to 2050*. Paris: IEA.

———. 2008a. *Energy Technology Perspective 2008: Scenarios and Strategies to 2050*. Paris: IEA.

———. 2008b. *World Energy Outlook 2008*. Paris: IEA.

IMF (International Monetary Fund). 2008. *Fuel and Food Price Subsidies: Issues and Reform Options*. Washington, DC: IMF.

IPCC (Intergovernmental Panel on Climate Change). 2000. *Special Report: Methodological and Technological Issues in Technology Transfer: Summary for Policymakers*. Cambridge, UK: Cambridge University Press.

IRI (International Research Institute for Climate and Society). 2006. "A Gap Analysis for the Implementation of the Global Climate Observing System Programme in Africa." Technical Report IRI-TR/06/1, IRI, Palisades, N.Y.

Jaffe, A., R. G. Newell, and R. N. Stavins. 2003. "Technological Change and the Environment." In *Handbook of Environmental Economics, vol. 1*, ed. K. G. Maler and J. R. Vincent. Amsterdam: Elsevier.

Jaruzelski, B., K. Dehoff, and R. Bordia. 2006. *Smart Spenders: The Global Innovation 1000*. McLean, VA: Booz Allen Hamilton.

Juma, C. 2006. *Reinventing African Economies: Technological Innovation and the Sustainability Transition: 6th John Pesek Colloquium on Sustainable Agriculture*. Ames, IA: Iowa State University.

———. 2008. "Agricultural Innovation and Economic Growth in Africa: Renewing International Cooperation." *International Journal of Technology and Globalisation* 4 (3): 256–75.

Justus, D., and C. Philibert. 2005. *International Energy Technology Collaboration and Climate Change Mitigation*. Paris: OECD/IEA.

Kiang, R. 2006. *Malaria Modeling and Surveillance Verification and Validation Report, Part 1: Assessing Malaria Risks in Thailand Provinces Using Meteorological and Environmental Parameters*. Greenbelt, MD: NASA Goddard Space Flight Center.

Koefoed, M., and C. Buckley. 2008. "Clean Technology Transfer: A Case Study from the South African Metal Finishing Industry 2000–2005." *Journal of Cleaner Production* 16S1: S78–S84.

Leadbeater, C., J. Meadway, M. Harris, T. Crowley, S. Mahroum, and B. Poirson. 2008. *Making Innovation Flourish*. Birmingham, UK: National Endowment for Science, Technology, and the Arts.

Lewis, J. I. 2007. "Technology Aquisition and Innovation in the Developing World: Wind Turbine Development in China and India." *Studies in Comparative International Development* 42: 208–232.

Lundvall, B. A., ed. 1992. *National Systems of Innovation: Towards a Theory of Innovation and Interactive Learning*. London: Pinter.

———. 2007. "National Innovation-Systems: Analytical Concept and Development Tool." *Industry and Innovation* 14 (1): 95–119.

MacCracken, M. 2009. "Beyond Mitigation: Potential Options for Counter-Balancing the Climatic and Environmental Consequences of the Rising Concentrations of Greenhouse Gases." Policy Research Working Paper Series 4938, World Bank, Washington, DC.

Maini, C. 2005. "Development of a Globally Competitive Electric Vehicle In India." *Journal of the Indian Insitute of Science* 85: 83–95.

Maskus, K. E. 2004. "Encouraging International Technology Transfer." Project on Intellectual Property Rights and Sustainable Development 7, United Nations Conference on Trade and Development and International Centre for Trade and Sustainable Development, Chavanod, France.

Matuschke, I., and M. Qaim. 2008. "Seed Market Privatisation and Farmers' Access to Crop Technologies: The Case of Hybrid Pearl Millet Adoption in India." *Journal of Agricultural Economics* 59 (3): 498–515.

McKinsey Global Institute. 2007. *Leapfrogging to Higher Productivity in China*. McKinsey & Company.

Metcalfe, S., and R. Ramlogan. 2008. "Innovation Systems and the Competitive Process in

Developing Economies." *Quarterly Review of Economics and Finance* 48 (2): 433–46.

Milford, L., D. Ducther, and T. Barker. 2008. *How Distributed and Open Innovation Could Accelerate Technology Development and Deployment.* Montpelier, VT: Clean Energy Group.

Nelson, R. R. 1959. "The Simple Economics of Basic Scientific Research." *Journal of Political Economy* 67: 297–306.

———. 1996. *National Innovation Systems.* New York: Oxford University Press.

Nemet, G., and D. M. Kammen. 2007. "U.S. Energy Research and Development: Declining Investment, Increasing Need, and the Feasibility of Expansion." *Energy Policy* 35: 746–55.

Newell, R. G., A. B. Jaffe, and R. N. Stavins. 1999. "The Induced Innovation Hypothesis and Energy-saving Technological Change." *Quarterly Journal of Economics* 114: 941–75.

Newell, R. G., and N. E. Wilson. 2005. "Technology Prizes for Climate Change Mitigation." Discussion Paper 05-33, Resources for the Future, Washington, DC.

OECD (Organisation for Economic Co-operation and Development). 1997. *National Innovation Systems.* Paris: OECD.

———. 2008. *Compendium on Patent Statistics 2008.* Paris: OECD.

PCAST (President's Committee of Advisors on Science and Technology). 1999. *Powerful Partnerships: The Federal Role in International Cooperation on Energy Innovation.* Washington, DC: PCAST.

Philibert, C. 2004. *International Energy Technology Collaboration and Climate Change Mitigation.* Paris: Organisation for Economic Co-operation and Development and International Energy Agency.

Popp, D. 2002. "Induced Innovation and Energy Prices." *American Economic Review* 92 (1): 160–80.

———. 2006. "R&D Subsidies and Climate Policy: Is There a Free Lunch?" *Climatic Change* 77: 311–41.

Ramanathan, N., I. H. Rehman, and V. Ramanathan. 2009. "Project Surya: Mitigation of Global and Regional Climate Change: Buying the Planet Time by Reducing Black Carbon, Methane and Ozone." Background note for the WDR 2010.

Ramanathan, V., and G. Carmichael. 2008. "Global and Regional Climate Changes Due to Black Carbon." *Nature Geoscience* 1: 221–27.

Robins, N., R. Clover, and C. Singh. 2009. *A Climate for Recovery: The Colour of Stimulus Goes Green.* London, UK: HSBC.

Rogers, D. 2009. "Environmental Information Services and Development." Background note for the WDR 2010.

Ruttan, V. W. 1997. "Induced Innovation, Evolutionary Theory and Path Dependence: Sources of Technical Change." *Economic Journal* 107 (444): 1520–29.

Salter, A. J., and B. R. Martin. 2001. "The Economic Benefits of Publicly Funded Basic Research: A Critical Review." *Research Policy* 30 (3): 509–32.

Scarpetta, S., and T. Tressel. 2004. "Boosting Productivity Via Innovation and Adoption of New Technologies: Any Role for Labor Market Institutions?" Policy Research Working Paper 3273, World Bank, Washington, DC.

Schneider, S. H., and L. H. Goulder. 1997. "Achieving Low-Cost Emissions Targets." *Nature* 389 (6646): 13–14.

SEG (Scientific Expert Group on Climate Change). 2007. *Confronting Climate Change: Avoiding the Unmanageable and Managing the Unavoidable.* Washington, DC: Sigma Xi and the United Nations Foundation.

Shindell, D., and G. Faluvegi. 2009. "Climate Response to Regional Radiative Forcing during the Twentieth Century." *Nature Geoscience* 2: 294–300.

Smith, K. R., J. Rogers, and S. C. Cowlin. 2005. "Household Fuels and Ill-Health in Developing Countries: What Improvements Can be Brought by LP Gas?" Paper presented at 18th World LP Gas Foum, Sept. 14–16, Shanghai.

Steenblik, R., eds. 2007. *Biofuels: At What Cost? Government Support for Ethanol and Biodiesel in Selected OECD Countries.* Geneva: International Institute for Sustainable Development, Global Subsidies Initiative.

Stern, N. 2007. *The Economics of Climate Change: The Stern Review.* Cambridge, UK: Cambridge University Press.

Taylor, M. R., E. S. Rubin, and D. A. Hounshell. 2005. "Control of SO_2 Emissions from Power Plants: A Case of Induced Technological Innovation in the U.S." *Technological Forecasting and Social Change* 72 (6): 697–718.

Tidd, J. 2006. *Innovation Models.* London: Imperial College London.

UNCTAD (United Nations Conference on Trade and Development). 2005. *World Investment Report 2005: Transnational Corporations and the Internationalization of R&D.* New York: United Nations.

UNEP (United Nations Environment Programme). 2008a. *Global Trends in Sustainable*

Energy Investments. Paris: UNEP Sustainable Energy Finance Initiative.

———. 2008b. *Reforming Energy Subsidies: Opportunities to Contribute to the Climate Change Agenda*. Nairobi: UNEP Division of Technology, Industry and Economics.

Watkins, A., and M. Ehst, eds. 2008. *Science, Technology and Innovation Capacity Building for Sustainable Growth and Poverty Reduction*. Washington, DC: World Bank.

Weinert, J., C. Ma, and C. Cherry. 2007. "The Transition to Electric Bikes in China: History and Key Reasons for Rapid Growth." *Transportation* 34 (3): 301–18.

Westermeyer, W. 2009. "Observing the Climate for Development." Background note for the WDR 2010.

World Bank. 2005. *Agricultural Investment Sourcebook*. Washington, DC: World Bank.

———. 2007a. *Building Knowledge Economies: Advanced Strategies for Development*. Washington, DC: World Bank Institute.

———. 2007b. *World Development Report 2008: Agriculture for Development*. Washington, DC: World Bank.

———. 2008a. "Accelerating Clean Technology Research, Development and Deployment: Lessons from Nonenergy Sector." Working Paper 138, World Bank, Washington, DC.

———. 2008b. *Doing Business 2008 Report*. Washington, DC: World Bank.

———. 2008c. *International Trade and Climate Change: Economic, Legal and Institutional Perspectives*. Washington, DC: World Bank.

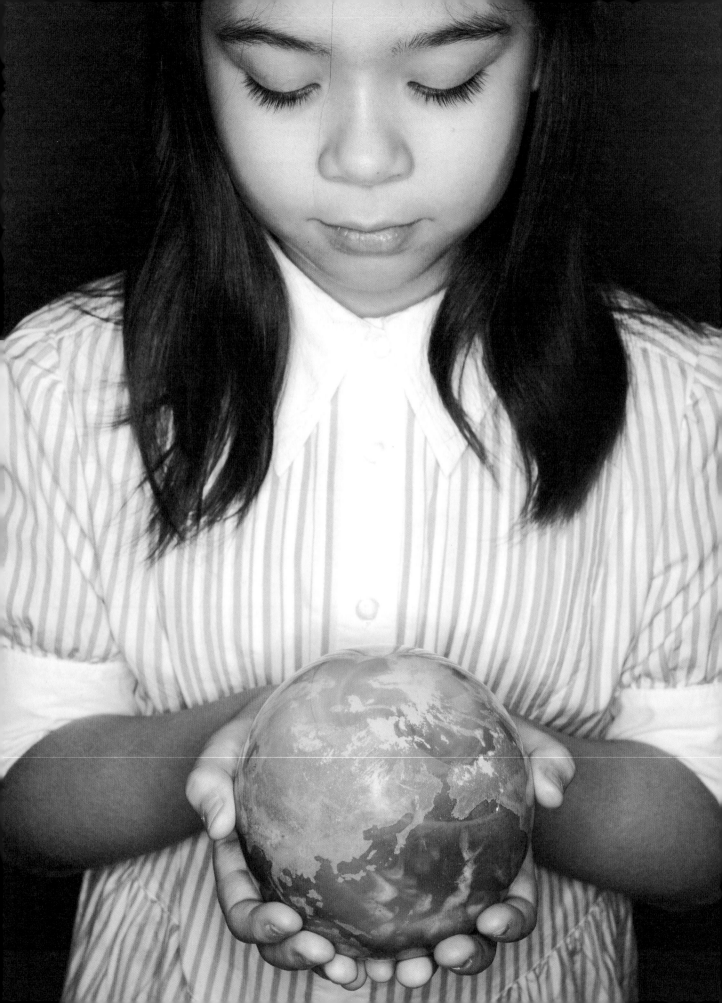

CHAPTER 8

Overcoming Behavioral and Institutional Inertia

Many policies to address adaptation and mitigation are already known. Secure property rights, energy-efficient technologies, market-based eco-taxes and tradable permits—all have been piloted and studied over decades. But implementing them still proves difficult. Their success relies not just on new finance and new technology but also on complex and context-specific social, economic, and political factors normally called institutions—the formal and informal rules affecting policy design, implementation, and outcomes.[1]

Values, norms, and organizational arrangements can make policy change hard. Experiences frame current and future action. Patterns of individual and organizational behavior die hard even in the face of new challenges. And political traditions constrain policy choices. Some examples.

Most countries still gear policies and regulatory institutions to ensure the supply of energy—not to manage demand. Pollution taxes in economies where pollution is not considered a public bad will generate resistance from decision makers and the public alike. And economic interests can hinder the deployment of energy-efficient technologies.[2]

The examples show another dimension of the urgency of tackling climate change. In addition to the inertia of climate, technology, and capital stocks, policy has to overcome institutional inertia. Institutions tend to be sticky—once in place and accepted, they can limit policy change and future choices.[3]

Institutional inertia has three implications for climate-smart development policy. First, institutional change should be a priority. Success will hinge on reshaping the institutional framework supporting interventions. Second, institutional reform pays off. Addressing the institutional determinants of climate policy can ensure the effectiveness and sustainability of interventions, maximize the impact of finance and technology, and yield additional development payoffs. Third, institutional change is feasible. Increasing gender inclusion, recognizing indigenous peoples' rights, reforming property rights, and shaping individual incentives can be demanding, but they are not impossible. Many of these changes can be accomplished without technological

Key messages

Achieving results in tackling the climate challenge requires going beyond the international mobilization of finance and technology, by addressing the psychological, organizational, and political barriers to climate action. These barriers stem from the way people perceive and think about the climate problem, the way bureaucracies work, and the interests shaping government action. Policy change requires shifting political incentives and even organizational responsibilities. And it requires the active marketing of climate policies, tapping into social norms and behaviors, in order to translate the public's concern into understanding and understanding into action—starting at home.

breakthrough or additional finance. More important, many of these interventions fall within the realm of national or even local policy—there is no need for a global climate deal to enhance press freedom, for example, or the voice of civil society.[4]

This chapter discusses the behavioral, organizational, and political determinants of the institutional inertia hindering climate-smart development. It shows how these forces affect the implementation of new policies and hamper their success in both developed and developing countries. And it argues that overcoming inertia requires reconsidering the scope and quality of government's role. We start with individuals' minds.

Harnessing individuals' behavioral change

Understanding the drivers of human behavior is essential for climate-smart development policy. First, myriad private acts of consumption are at the root of climate change. As consumers, individuals hold a reservoir of mitigation capacity. A large share of emissions in developed countries results directly from decisions by individuals—for travel, heating, food purchases. U.S. households account for roughly 33 percent of the nation's carbon dioxide (CO_2) emissions—more than U.S. industry and any other country bar China

(figures 8.1 and 8.2).[5] If fully adopted, existing efficiency measures for households and motor vehicles could produce energy savings of almost 30 percent—10 percent of total U.S. consumption.[6] Second, individuals drive the larger processes of change in organizations and political systems. Particularly in democratic countries, much government action is the result of citizen and voter pressures to act. Third, when designing and implementing policy, decision makers apply the same mental processes as other individuals.

The debate about changing individual behavior has focused on market mechanisms. Better pricing of energy and costing of scarce resources can steer individuals away from carbon-intensive consumption and encourage them to preserve endangered habitats and manage ecosystems better. But the drivers of consumption by individuals and groups go beyond prices. Many cost-effective energy-efficient technologies have been available for years. "No-regret" investments such as improving building insulation, addressing water leaks, and limiting building in flood-prone areas yield benefits beyond mitigation and adaptation. So, why haven't they been adopted? Because concern does not mean understanding, and understanding does not necessarily lead to action.

Concern does not mean understanding

Over the past decade, awareness of climate change has grown without translating into widespread individual action.[7] Indeed, flying, driving, holidaying abroad, and using household appliances have increased globally.[8]

What explains the disconnect between perception and action? Concern about climate change does not necessarily mean understanding its drivers and dynamics or the responses needed. Polls show that the public admits to remaining confused over climate change's causes and solutions.[9] This "green gap" in public attitudes stems partly from how climate science is communicated and how our minds (mis)understand climate dynamics (box 8.1).[10]

Standard information-deficit models assume that when people "know" more, they

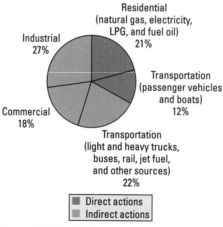

Figure 8.1   The direct actions of U.S. consumers produce up to one-third of total U.S. CO_2 emissions

Residential (natural gas, electricity, LPG, and fuel oil) 21%

Industrial 27%

Transportation (passenger vehicles and boats) 12%

Commercial 18%

Transportation (light and heavy trucks, buses, rail, jet fuel, and other sources) 22%

■ Direct actions
■ Indirect actions

Sources: EIA 2009; EPA 2009.
Note: LPG = liquified petroleum gas.

act differently.[11] People today are exposed to lots of information on the causes, dynamics, and effects of climate change. This information has clearly increased concern, but it has not led to action.[12] Why? Because information can produce misleading feelings of "empowerment," which then turns into ambivalent powerlessness when paired with more "realistic" messages. Conveying urgency by stressing the unprecedented nature and scale of the problems can result in paralysis.[13] Similarly, playing up the multistakeholder nature of mitigation and adaptation is a reminder that the solution rests with no single actor, resulting in a general feeling of helplessness and disempowerment.[14] This might explain why, in developed countries where information on climate change is more readily available, people are less optimistic about a possible solution (figure 8.3).

To produce action, awareness needs to be grounded in clear information from trustworthy sources. The way climate change science is communicated to the public can complicate things. Scientific debate evolves through testing and cross-checking of theories and findings. News coverage can veer from one extreme to another, resulting in more confusion for the public, which may perceive the debate not as scientific progress but as a proliferation of contradictory opinions.[15] Moreover, the media's need to present "balanced" stories has given disproportionate coverage to climate science contrarians lacking scientific expertise and standing.[16]

Figure 8.2   Small local adjustments for big global benefits: Switching from SUVs to fuel-efficient passenger cars in the United States alone would nearly offset the emissions generated by providing energy to 1.6 billion more people

Emissions (million tons of CO_2)

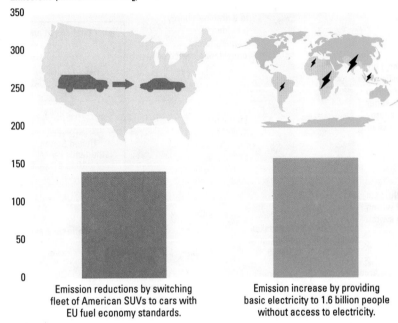

Emission reductions by switching fleet of American SUVs to cars with EU fuel economy standards.

Emission increase by providing basic electricity to 1.6 billion people without access to electricity.

Source: WDR team calculations based on BTS 2008.

Note: Estimates are based on 40 million SUVs (sports utility vehicles) in the United States traveling a total of 480 billion miles (assuming 12,000 miles a car) a year. With average fuel efficiency of 18 miles a gallon, the SUV fleet consumes 27 billion gallons of gasoline annually with emissions of 2,421 grams of carbon a gallon. Switching to fuel-efficient cars with the average fuel efficiency of new passenger cars sold in the European Union (45 miles a gallon; see ICCT 2007) results in a reduction of 142 million tons of CO_2 (39 million tons of carbon) annually. Electricity consumption of poor households in developing countries is estimated at 170 kilowatt hours a person-year and electricity is assumed to be provided at the current world average carbon intensity of 160 grams of carbon a kilowatt-hour, equivalent to 160 million tons of CO_2 (44 million tons of carbon). The size of the electricity symbol in the global map corresponds to the number of people without access to electricity.

Figure 8.3   Individuals' willingness to respond to climate change differs across countries and does not always translate into concrete actions

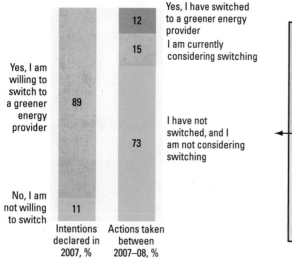

a. Globally, individual intentions to act
do not yet translate into concrete action

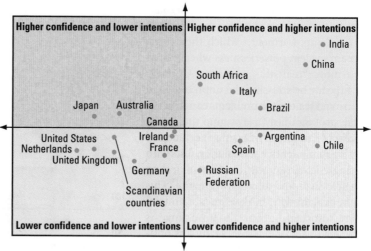

b. In emerging markets people are more confident that climate change
will be solved have higher intentions to act

Source: Accenture 2009.

Note: The 2009 Accenture Climate Change Survey was conducted with a sample of 10,733 individuals in 22 developed and emerging economies. The sample was representative of the general population in developed countries and urban populations in developing countries. Panel a: Respondents were asked about their willingness to switch to a greener energy provider if the provider offered services that help reduce carbon emissions. Intentions did not translate into action, with most respondents staying with their old energy provider. Panel b: Based on the questionnaire, countries were ranked on two criteria—confidence and intention. Confidence measured the individual's optimism about the ability of individuals, politicians, and energy providers to find a solution. Respondents in emerging economies generally were more optimistic about humankind's ability to take action to solve global climate change.

The media, in search of punchy stories, tend to shy away from the scientific community's careful wording to express uncertainty. Readers then face messages lacking scientific caution and containing strong appeals that might then be refuted by other similarly strongly worded statements, hampering the perceived reliability of the information source. In addition to confusing the public (and policy makers) about causes, impacts, and potential solutions, different types of framing can antagonize individuals and induce a sense of guilt, and even of being vilified, when the problem of consumption is characterized as a problem of consumers.[17] This can lead people to reject the message rather than act on it.

An added challenge in moving from concern to understanding has to do with how the mind perceives the problem. The dynamics of climate change stretch our mental capacities in several ways.[18] Psychological research shows that individuals are ill equipped to deal with multiple-cause problems.[19] Simplifying problems by adopting single-cause explanations in turn leads to searching for individual solutions and

focusing on (often nonexistent) technological silver bullets. The inertia affecting our responses can be linked to a limited understanding of stock-and-flow relationships, which characterize the concentration, removal, and stabilization of greenhouse gases. The fact that even the most drastic and sudden emission reductions will not prevent further warming, or make the need for adaptation disappear in the short and medium term, is something we struggle with and, without careful explanation, simply do not understand (box 8.2).[20]

Understanding does not necessarily lead to action

Knowledge is mediated through value systems shaped by psychological, cultural, and economic factors that determine whether we act or not. Again the idea here is not that we are irrational but that we need to understand better how we make decisions. Our evolution as a species has shaped the way our brains work. We are particularly good at acting on threats that can be linked to a human face; that present themselves as unexpected, dramatic, and immediate; that involve obvious links to human health; that challenge our moral framework, provoking visceral reactions; or that evoke recent personal experience.[21] The slow pace of climate change as well as the delayed, intangible, and statistical nature of its risks, simply do not move us (box 8.3).

Behavioral economics shows that features of human decision making under uncertainty constrain our natural instinct to adapt.[22] We tend to underestimate cumulative probabilities (the sum of the probabilities of an event occurring over a period of time), which explains why building continues in areas prone to fires, flooding, and earthquakes. People strongly favor the status quo and prefer to make only small incremental adjustments to it. They are at a loss when measuring achievements is difficult, as in disaster preparedness, where there are no clear counterfactuals. We are "myopic decision makers" who strongly discount future events and assign higher priorities to problems closer in space and time. For instance, the public tends to be mobilized by visible environmental problems (urban air pollution) but not by less visible ones (species extinction). Individuals rank climate change lower than other

environmental issues perceived as closer to home (figure 8.4).[23]

Even if people were indeed fully rational, knowledge would not necessarily lead to action. Their "finite pool of worries" might prevent them from acting on existing information because they prioritize basic needs such as security, shelter, and the like.[24] They

---

BOX 8.2 *Misunderstandings about the dynamics of climate change encourage complacency*

Support for policies to control greenhouse gas emissions is hampered by people's limited understanding of climate change's dynamics. Experiments show that a majority of people misunderstand the basic stock-and-flow nature of the problem: they believe that stabilizing emissions near the current rates would stabilize concentrations of greenhouse gases in the atmosphere and halt climate change. Instead the flow of emissions is best compared to the flow of water entering a bathtub: as long as the inflow is greater than the outflow, the level of water in the tub will rise. As long as emissions exceed the amounts that can be taken up by terrestrial and aquatic systems, concentrations of greenhouse gases will rise. Even for those who consider climate change a priority, a misunderstanding of the stock-and-flow process favors wait-and-see policies, limiting public pressure and political will for active policy to stabilize the climate. These misperceptions can be corrected through communication strategies that use analogies, such as the bathtub example.

Sources: Sternman and Sweeney 2007; Moxnes and Saysel 2009.

BOX 8.3 *How risk perceptions can sink policies: Flood risk management*

The impulse to address risk is fundamentally related to perceptions of the seriousness and likelihood of impacts.

The perception of probabilities and the methods people tend to use to estimate those probabilities can be misleading. For example, people evaluate the likelihood of an event occurring in a given place based on how similar the latter is to locations where such events normally occur.[a] The availability of recent and vivid memories of an event also leads people to overestimate its probability. It has been observed that often people overestimate the likelihood of low-probability events and underestimate the likelihood of high-probability events. People are notoriously more scared of sitting in a plane than in a car (although the risk of a deadly car accident event is significantly higher). Similarly, rare natural disasters such as tsunamis, generate more concern than more frequent events such as storm surges.[b]

These behavior patterns were identified among farmers and policy makers in Mozambique after the 2000 floods and during the subsequent resettlement program implemented by the government. Farmers (more than policy makers) showed a bias toward the status quo: for farmers, actions to adapt to climate factors are often weighted against risks of negative outcomes. The decision to move to a safe area on higher ground, for example, entails the risk of losing one's livelihood or community. The decision to plant a drought-tolerant crop can lead to the risk of having a lower harvest, if the rains are plentiful. Farmers wanting to avoid personal responsibility for negative outcomes will avoid making new choices. By contrast, policy makers can gain personal credit for avoiding a negative outcome, but only if they take visible action—say, by helping farmers survive through resettlement.

Different stakeholders view probabilities differently. Policy makers in Maputo tend to associate the Limpopo River floodplain with flood risk alone. For the people living there, however, life in the floodplain is defined by many other factors in addition to climate risks. Relative to local farmers, these policy makers have a propensity to overestimate climate-related risks. Unless risk analysis and communication are adequately factored in, major differences in perceptions of risk can impede successful policy design and implementation.

Sources: Patt and Schröter 2008.
a. Tversky and Kahneman 1974.
b. Kahneman and Tversky 1979.

also assess both the market and nonmarket costs of decisions. The nonmarket costs of acting on information that challenges core value systems (such as calls for resettlement and migration or for limiting consumption patterns) can be high. Indeed, the very act of interpreting or mediating additional information is costly. For a household having to decide whether to keep rebuilding on a flood-prone area, or for a local official designing and enforcing building codes in low-lying coastal areas, the transaction costs can be substantial. Moreover, both mitigation—and, very often, adaptation—present themselves as tragedies of the commons requiring collective action. Rational and self-interested individuals face structural disincentives to cooperate in solving these problems.[25] Cooperation in these conditions requires the payoffs to be clear—obviously not the case with climate-change impacts and responses.[26]

Understanding barriers to behavior change also requires going beyond psychological explanations based on the individual as a unit of analysis—and embracing the way social factors influence perceptions, decisions, and actions. People naturally tend to resist and deny information that contradicts their cultural values or ideological beliefs. This includes information that challenges notions of belonging and identity as well as of rights to freedom and consumption. Notions of needs and the priorities deriving from them are socially and culturally constructed.[27] This might explain why awareness of environmental problems normally increases with wealth, but concern about climate change does not (figure 8.5).[28] Individuals (and nations) with higher incomes (and higher carbon dioxide emissions) may disregard global warming as a way to avoid incurring the potential costs of solutions associated with lower levels of consumption and lifestyle changes.[29]

People also construct and reconstruct information to make it less uncomfortable, leading to strategies of socially organized denial that shape the way societies and governments interpret and respond to climate change.[30] The evolution of standard narratives about climate change provides an example. Focusing on country emissions rather than per capita emissions can lead people living outside the big emitters to minimize their responsibility and rationalize their failure to act. Drastic calls for the need for an international response tend to play down the fact that domestic action will be required in any case. And uncertainty about dynamics and impacts can be overplayed to justify inaction.

These forms of denial are not abstract—nor are they confined to climate policy. Similar processes operate at various levels of day-to-day decision making, and addressing them is part of solving crucial development challenges, such as reducing the spread of HIV-AIDS or the incidence of common water- and sanitation-related diseases. Rather than an aberration, denial needs to be considered a coping strategy deployed by individuals and communities facing unmanageable and uncomfortable events. Resistance to change is never simply the result of ignorance—it derives from individual perceptions, needs, and wants based on material and cultural values.

Figure 8.4   Climate change is not a priority yet

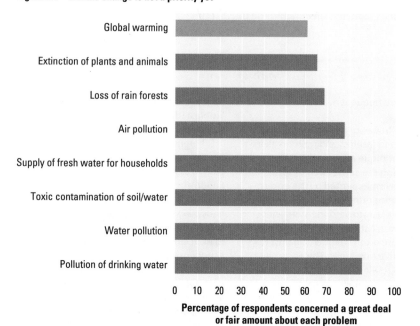

Percentage of respondents concerned a great deal or fair amount about each problem

Source: Gallup Poll, www.gallup.com/poll/106660/Little-Increase-Americans-Global-Warming-Worries.aspx (accessed March 6, 2009).

Note: Respondents were asked the following question: " I'm going to read you a list of environmental problems. As I read each one, please tell me if you personally worry a great deal, a fair amount, only a little, or not at all." Results are based on phone interviews on March 5–8, 2009. The sample comprised 1,012 U.S. citizens aged 18 and older.

Encouraging behavioral change

Policy makers need to be aware of these barriers to action and treat policy options accordingly. Three policy areas are relevant here: communications, institutional measures, and social norms.

From information to communication.

Information, education, and awareness raising, as carried out so far, are at best not enough to spur people to action and at worst counterproductive. This calls for a different approach to providing information about climate change.[31] First, the information-driven approach must shift to an audience-centric one in communicating climate change. Both scientists and the media need to work together to enhance the salience of their messages. Second, as in other policy areas, such as AIDS prevention, this shift should entail a marketing approach to communication, where the individual is considered not merely the passive receiver of information but an active agent in both causes and solutions (box 8.4).

Well-designed communication campaigns that address individuals as members of a local community—and not as powerless members of an unmanageably large group—can empower them to act. This treatment can help make a global phenomenon personally relevant and immediate, and accentuate the local and individual ownership of the solutions. It is important to limit "greenwash" in business and government—the gap between agreeing publicly on the reality of climate change while doing nothing about it—to avoid confusion and public backlash (box 8.5).

A controversial question is whether detailed public understanding of highly complex issues such as climate change is feasible, even necessary, for effective policy making. The answer is no, or at least not always. Much policy making is based on technicalities fully ignored by the public. Few people understand the intricacies of trade policies affecting the price of the food they buy and eat, or produce and sell. Where buy-in is necessary, it is often encouraged through other means.

Yet discounting information and public awareness as unnecessary would be a

Figure 8.5 Concern about climate change decreases as wealth goes up

Percentage of respondents who consider climate change a serious problem

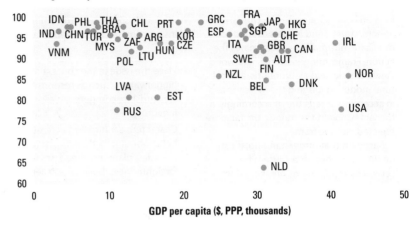

Source: Sandvik 2008.

Note: Public concern about global warming is expressed as percentage based on respondents who consider climate change a serious problem. It was taken from a global online survey conducted by ACNielsen in 2007 on consumer attitudes toward global warming. Respondents from 46 different countries were asked how serious a problem (on a scale from 1 to 5) they thought global warming was. The base population is respondents who have heard or read about global warming.

mistake. Recent work has highlighted that information is key for the public to back costly measures. The benefits of providing more accurate information about people's consumption decisions—say, through

---

BOX 8.4 *End-to-end community engagement for landslide risk reduction in the Caribbean*

A new way of delivering real landslide-risk reduction to vulnerable communities was piloted by MoSSaiC, a program aimed at improving the management of slopes in communities in the eastern Caribbean. MoSSaiC identifies and implements low-cost, community-based approaches to landslide-risk reduction, in which community residents indicate areas of perceived drainage problems before assessing options for reducing landslide risk by managing surface water.

The activities? Managing surface water in all forms (roof water, grey water, and overland flow of rainfall water), monitoring shallow groundwater conditions, and constructing low-cost drain systems. All the work is bid out to contractors in the community. This end-to-end community engagement encourages participation in planning, executing, and maintaining surface water management on high-risk slopes. It produces a program owned by the community rather than imposed by the agency or government.

MoSSaiC has lowered landslide risk by offering the community employment and risk awareness—and has taken a participatory approach to rolling out the program to other communities. The program shows that changing community views of hazard mitigation can enhance community perceptions about climate risks. It also establishes a feedback loop between project inputs and outputs, with more than 80 percent of funds spent in the communities, allowing communities and governments to establish a clear link between risk perceptions, inputs, and tangible outputs.

Source: Anderson and Holcombe 2007.

BOX 8.5 *Communicating climate change*

How an issue is framed—the words, metaphors, stories, and images used to communicate information—determines the action. Frames trigger deeply held world views, widely held assumptions, and cultural models in judging the message and in accepting or rejecting it accordingly. If the facts don't fit the frames, the facts are rejected, not the frame.

Based on that understanding, it can be decided whether a cause is best served by repeating or breaking dominant discourse, or by reframing an issue using different concepts, languages, and images to evoke a different way of thinking and facilitate alternative choices.

Applying this approach to communications on climate change could take many forms:

- Place the issue in the context of higher values, such as responsibility, stewardship, competence, vision, and ingenuity.
- Characterize mitigation actions as being about new thinking, new technologies, planning ahead, smartness, farsightedness, balance, efficiency, and prudent caring.
- Simplify the model, analogy, or metaphor to help the public understand how global warming works—a

conceptual hook to make sense of information and set up appropriate reasoning (instead of the "greenhouse gas effect" call it a "heat trap").

- Refocus communications to underscore the human causes of the problem and the solutions that exist to address it, suggesting that humans can and should act to prevent the problem now.
- Evoke the existence and effectiveness of solutions upfront.

Source: Lorenzoni, Nicholson-Cole, and Whitmarsh 2007.

---

carbon labeling and smart meters—have long been proven. A U.S.-based survey found that one of the main factors responsible for the public's negative perceptions of cap-and-trade schemes is not the fear of additional costs but the limited knowledge of their effectiveness, reducing public trust in them.[32] Similarly, opposition to environmental taxes seems to fall once the public fully understands that they are a way not simply to raise money but to change behavior.[33]

Institutional measures. Beyond communication, a key issue for climate policy is designing interventions that take into account the social and psychological constraints to positive action. Effective adaptation interventions should reduce the transaction costs for individuals in making decisions and enhance the ownership of the information available. This requires that adaptation strategies be informed by community perceptions of risk, vulnerability, and capacity (see box 8.5). Institutionalizing participatory self-assessments for national and local disaster preparedness, adaptation planning, and mitigation can be useful here.

Limiting the tendency of individuals to discount the value of the future is another area for action. Although discounting the future is an innate mental propensity, it

varies with social characteristics and external pressures. Evidence from Peru shows that farmers with limited access to credit and insurance and with weak property rights have higher discount rates—and that steeper discounting increases individuals' incentives to deforest.[34] Institutional reforms to improve credit access and property rights can affect inner behavioral drivers of discounting. So can education (box 8.6).

Similarly, interventions that rely on individuals and businesses facing up-front costs but gaining long-term benefits (such as those deriving from energy-efficiency investments) should consider providing immediate payoffs in tax rebates or subsidies. Giving private actors a sense of long-term policy direction is also useful. An international survey of business leaders conducted in 2007 found that 81 percent of those polled believed that the government needs to provide clear long-term policy signals to help companies find the incentives to change and plan investments.[35] (Ways for government to signal long-term direction are explored below.)

Climate policy should also heed the tendency of individuals to favor local, visible, and privately securable outcomes. Mitigation actions produce benefits that are global and diffuse, and the direct benefits of adaptation measures may or may not be immediately apparent, based on the type of climate event under consideration and on the rate of change. The public at large may perceive these benefits as distant and uncertain. It is the role of institutions to communicate clearly the direct benefits and co-benefits of both adaptation and mitigation, particularly emphasizing those that involve human health, a subject that moves people.

Improved cost-benefit tools can encourage public and private decision makers to act more decisively. The estimation of costs and benefits of energy-efficiency projects often does not include nonenergy co-benefits. These include the public health benefits from cleaner air and water, the possibly greater comfort of building occupants, and higher labor productivity.[36] Switching from fossil to renewable energy can create jobs.[37] Case studies in manufacturing conclude that these benefits can be considerable, sometimes equivalent to the value of the energy savings alone.[38] So the time frame for investment paybacks can be substantially shortened, providing better incentives to invest. Similarly, earmarking revenues from carbon or energy taxes can increase the visibility of benefits of mitigation. Although fiscal earmarking is deemed economically inefficient, it can increase political acceptance of new taxes, because the public sees clearly where the money goes.

Social norms. Social norms are the patterns of behavior that most people approve of—the yardsticks they use to assess the appropriateness of their own conduct. In shaping human action, social norms can achieve socially desirable outcomes, generally at a fairly low cost. The basic idea is that people want to act in a socially acceptable way and tend to follow the lead of others, particularly when the others are numerous and are perceived as similar.

Social norms have a particularly strong impact under conditions of uncertainty.[39] When looking for clues about how to behave, people rely on what others do. Appeals for proenvironmental behavior based on social norms are superior to traditional persuasion. Not littering is an example.

A climate-relevant example comes from a psychological experiment on California residents to test the impact of social norms on energy consumption.[40] The average household energy consumption was communicated through energy bills to one group of high-energy households and two groups of low-energy households. This set the social norm. One group of low-energy households received positive feedback for their energy consumption statement (a smiley face), conveying approval of their energy footprint. High-energy households were shown their use coupled with negative feedback (a sad face) to convey disapproval. The result: high-energy households reduced consumption, and low-energy ones maintained their lower-than-average consumption. The third group—low-energy households initially exposed to the social norm but receiving no positive feedback about their behavior—increased their consumption to reach the average. Utilities eager to reduce energy use have adopted the approach in 10 major metropolitan areas in the United States, including Chicago and Seattle.

Harnessing the power of social norms implies increasing the visibility of behavior and its implications. Individual decisions and actions that have a bearing on energy consumption today are largely invisible to the public and even to restricted circles of family and friends. In these cases human action cannot benefit from patterns of reciprocity, peer pressure, and group behavior normally at play in more visible cases of behavior change and compliance, such as compliance with traffic control.

Research on cooperation leads to the same conclusion. Unless information about other players' behavior is available, people tend not to cooperate.[41] Farmers within a river basin should receive information not only about their water use but also about whether they are below or above the standard set by their peers. Residents of flood-prone areas can be encouraged to adopt protection measures by exposing them to the rapid uptake of such measures by others in their community. Conversely, appeals stressing that too many people have not yet installed basic energy-efficiency measures are bound to lead to even less adoption of such measures, not more.

Social norms can complement traditional public policy approaches and measures, such as regulation, taxation, and pricing. Thinking about group behavior can ameliorate the impact of these measures, opening opportunities for combining different instruments. But some policies based on economic incentives might do more harm than good by weakening the effect of social norms. Pricing pollution or emissions might give polluters the impression that it is all right to pollute, as long as they pay their fair share. Similarly, imperfectly enforced regulation, or perceptions that formal rules can be eluded, can favor more self-interested behavior and weaken cooperation.[42]

More radical calls for social norms focus on alternative parameters of progress, such as stressing a shift toward notions of well-being decoupled from consumption.[43] And political opposition to instruments such as green taxes can be overcome through tax-rebate schemes—in Sweden, for example, very high tax rates on nitrogen oxide emissions from power producers were politically acceptable because taxes were fully rebated to producers on the basis of how much electricity they produced.[44]

These measures are obviously not enough to ensure the success of climate policy. But they might well prove necessary. Encouraging behavior change for mitigation and adaptation goes beyond providing additional information, finance, or technology. Traditional measures can be complemented by alternative interventions, often at low cost. Rather than simply treat these social and psychological drivers of behavior as barriers to adaptation and mitigation, policy makers can use them to build more effective and sustainable policy.

Bringing the state back in

Over the past 30 years the role of the state has been cut back in various domains key to addressing the climate challenge, such as energy research. The retreat from direct intervention occurred with a switch from "government" to "governance" and an emphasis on the state's role in steering and enabling the private sector.[45] This general trend hides a complex picture. Twentieth-century Europe saw various forms and degrees of state capitalism. The rise of East Asian economies, including China's, demonstrated the preeminence of the state in "governing the market" to deliver the most successful example of accelerated development.[46] Most recently, the 2008 financial crisis showed the pitfalls of deregulation and unrestrained markets—and triggered renewed emphasis on bringing back the state.

Climate change requires public interventions to address the multiple market failures driving it—the failures of pricing; of research and technology development; and of coordination and collective action, global, national, and local.[47] As providers of public goods and correctors of externalities, governments are expected to address these market failures. But there are more specific drivers of government intervention.

First, the private sector's role in solving the climate challenge is crucial, but overplaying it would be unwise. Despite the enthusiasm for the private sector's contribution to major investment projects in the 1980s and 1990s, private participation in infrastructure remains limited. Although the bulk of the additional investment and financing needed for climate-change mitigation and adaptation is expected to come from the private sector, government policies and incentives will be fundamental.[48] Moreover, energy providers and electric utilities are usually government-owned or government-regulated private corporations. Changing the mix of generation facilities may require subsidies and up-front fixed-capital investments. Business certainly has an incentive to secure the attractive returns from investments in energy efficiency, but, as discussed in chapter 4, market barriers are likely to require government action. Where high costs of new technology (low-emission vehicles or solar electricity generation, for example) are constraining supply and demand, a range of government incentives may be required to expand markets.

Second, mitigation and adaptation are both likely to increase public spending. Auctioning emission permits or taxing carbon generates revenues. Keeping expenditure flat would require government to deliver complete tax rebates or full revenue recycling. But such fiscal neutrality might be perceived as a luxury in countries looking for cash to fund new public investments for adaptation and for new energy infrastructure while containing their fiscal deficits. As chapter 7 highlights, governments need to expand their already significant role in technology research, development, and demonstration. Governments can change incentives, either by subsidizing investments with wider social benefits that markets tend to undersupply (such as risky energy R&D) or by taxing or regulating actions that are socially harmful.

Third, the greater frequency and severity of extreme weather events will pressure governments to enhance their insurance function. As chapter 2 notes, insurance markets can go only so far in securitizing climate risks. Developed-world insurance systems are already stretched in dealing with rising hazards along the U.S. and Japanese coasts, in upper-middle-income Caribbean islands, and on floodplains in northern Europe.

Climate change is expected to exacerbate insurability problems, requiring renegotiation of the boundary between private and public insurance systems. Governments will face pressures to become insurers of last resort for more of the population and for more damages. In parallel, they will need to address the moral hazards inducing people to make bad choices because of insurance.

Fourth, governments will have to do more as knowledge and learning platforms, particularly around adaptation.[49] As chapter 7 argues, this will require more investments in R&D and more effective markets for technology innovation. It will also require transforming meteorological services into climate services, overseeing the distribution of information at different levels, and using international regimes and organizations as policy-learning arenas for governments to learn from each other and adapt policy to local circumstances.

Fifth, as the prime repositories of political legitimacy, governments will be expected to steer the private sector, facilitate community action, and establish the optimal decentralization of adaptation and mitigation decision making and action. On top of steering, governments will be expected to play an "ensuring" function: guaranteeing that targets and goals are achieved through new emphasis on regulation, taxation, long-term planning, and communication.[50]

None of this means that the size of the state needs to expand—government size is not always associated with better provision of public goods.[51] Instead, it is about recognizing, as chapter 2 points out, that the added challenges of climate change will also increase the cost of government failures. Addressing these challenges will require broadening government objectives and agendas and stepping up the type, scope, and quality of government interventions.

Toward climate-smart government

Governments will need to review the way they operate if they are to successfully address the climate challenge. As attention shifts from identifying the causes and impacts of climate change to devising responses, government setups will need rearranging.[52]

In most countries no single government agency can fully control climate-change policy; relevant mandates, responsibilities, and constituencies are spread over different ministries. Yet few governments have an agency capable of enforcing carbon budgets. In addition, the time frames of climate impacts and required responses go well beyond those of any elected administration. And bureaucracies are not quick learners.[53] Because of the novelty of climate change as a public policy domain and because of the urgency of action, policy makers need to prepare for a degree of failure—and to learn from it. These problems have been identified in the literature as the main drivers of failures to act in organizations.[54]

Government effectiveness will be critical to leveraging the impact of adaptation funding. As chapter 6 notes, most adaptation activities today are implemented through stand-alone and disconnected projects. Fragmented adaptation finance hampers mainstreaming and scaling up in planning and development processes, increases transaction costs for recipients and donors, and diverts the time and attention of politicians and government officials away from domestic priorities to manage aid-related activities. The tens of billions of dollars required for adaptation may put additional pressure on developing countries' already limited absorptive capacity. Many of the developing countries most in need of adaptation support are those with weaker capacity to manage and absorb funding. When a recipient's capacity to manage funds is limited, donors engage in tighter controls of funds and project-based modalities, putting further strains on country systems and leading to vicious cycles of lower capacities, fiscal shortfalls, and fragmentation.[55]

Enhancing the capacity of central government

When political leaders take an active interest, focusing the minds of officials, public opinion, and external stakeholders, countries move forward. Conversely, when leaders fail to act, countries lag behind. This is hardly surprising. Decision makers are individuals, and the failures in the way individuals make decisions also affect the way organizations, including governments, work.[56] However, leadership is not just an individual issue; it is also institutional and has to do with the way responsibility, coordination, and accountability for climate policy are organized (figure 8.6).

Assigning responsibility for climate policy. In most countries climate change is still the preserve of the environment ministry. But climate policy spills over into domains that transcend the boundaries of environmental protection and include trade, energy, transport, and fiscal policy. Environment agencies are normally weaker than departments such as treasury, commerce, or economic development. They tend to have fewer resources and to be represented in cabinets by junior politicians.

Although there is no single recipe for assigning the climate remit, reconsolidating responsibility is key (box 8.7). Bureaucratic consolidation—based on budgetary independence, expert personnel, and the authority to propose and enforce legislation—concentrates authority and avoids diffusion of responsibility that can lead to failures to act. The creation of ministerial-level agencies led by senior cabinet ministers, or the inclusion of climate policy on the agenda of already-established key

Figure 8.6   Effective governance goes hand in hand with good environmental performance

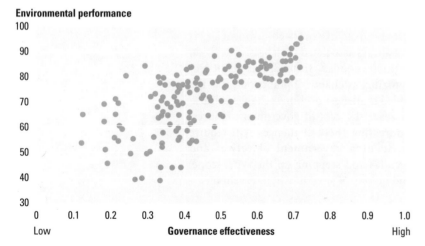

Environmental performance

Sources: Kaufman, Kraay, and Mastruzzi 2007; Esty and others 2008.

Note: Environmental performance is measured by an environmental performance index (http://epi.yale.edu/). Governance effectiveness ranges between 0 and 1 and is derived using log transformation of the governance effectiveness indicator from the World Governance Indicators database for 212 countries for 1996–2007. It combines the views of a large number of enterprise, citizen, and expert survey respondents in high-income and developing countries.

agencies are signs of a trend toward bureaucratic consolidation.

Facilitating integration and interagency coordination.

Bureaucratic consolidation, though important, may not be enough. And the mere creation of a separate agency might even be counterproductive. Policy coherence throughout an administration requires integrating climate planning across government. Here, the challenge is the typical compartmentalization of government work and the tendency to treat multidimensional problems in organizational silos. Approaches for integration include establishing climate units in each ministry or agency complemented by sectoral plans at national and local levels for mitigation and adaptation. In addition to a revision of their mandates, relevant public agencies—such as those involved in public health, energy, forestry and land-use planning, and natural resource management—can coordinate their work under a lead climate-change agency. Achieving this type of coordination is likely to require rethinking the role of hydrometeorological services (see chapter 7).

New coordination bodies—a cabinet committee on climate change, one explicitly linking climate with an already recognized and critical issue area such as energy, or an intragovernmental coordinating committee chaired by the lead agency—can bring together officials working on climate change across government. Coordination of climate policy can also be the prime minister's remit—say, by creating an advisory function directly within the prime minister's office.

For both integration and coordination, particular attention should go to developing sector policies and strategies. As chapter 4 shows, energy policy in many countries emphasizes market reform and pricing, introducing competition to the energy sector, and developing regulatory institutions to deliver low prices and reliable supplies to consumers.[57] Until very recently, mitigation was not even a tangential preoccupation of energy policy. As climate change moves up the political agenda, the mandates of energy agencies and the policies and strategies

---

BOX 8.7 *China's and India's path to institutional reform for climate action*

China shows how responsibility for climate policy has moved from the fringes to the core of government activity. The government initially set up special institutions to address climate change in 1990. Recognizing the relevance and intersectoral nature of the issue, it established a National Coordination Committee on Climate Change in 1998.

In 2007 the committee was transformed into the National Leading Group to Address Climate Change. Headed by the Chinese premier, the leading group coordinates strategies, policies, and measures among 28 member units within government agencies. During the 2008 government reform, the general office of the leading group was placed within the National Development and Reform Commission, which undertakes the general work on climate change, supported by an expert committee providing scientific information to inform decision making.

India is another developing-country example. Its Council on Climate Change is chaired by the Prime Minister. It developed the National Action Plan on Climate Change and is responsible for monitoring its implementation. The Plan encompasses eight National Missions that span sectoral ministries since they include Solar Energy, Enhanced Energy Efficiency, Sustainable Habitat, Conserving Water, Sustaining the Himalayan Ecosystem, the creation of a "Green India," Sustainable Agriculture, and the establishment of a Strategic Knowledge Platform for Climate Change. The vision of the National Action Plan is a graduated shift from fossil fuels to non-fossil fuels and renewable sources of energy.

Similar institutional reform measures have already been adopted by a range of other countries, developed and developing.

Source: WDR team.

---

guiding them will be updated to include low-carbon supply and energy-efficiency as core responsibilities.

Strategy documents can increase the coordination of adaptation activities. Consider the National Adaptation Programs of Action (NAPAs) of least developed countries. Born as a technical priority-setting exercise, NAPAs determine country-specific impacts and design locally tailored responses by engaging different agencies and levels of government as well as broad constituencies of business and civil society actors. In this sense, they can provide an institutional framework for placing adaptation at the center of government's priorities. But to consolidate their strategic function, they will require more attention from internal and external stakeholders (box 8.8).

Reinforcing government accountability.

Governments can fail to act on specific policy issues when accountability lines are not clear, either because of the nature of the

---

BOX 8.8 *National adaptation programs of action*

National Adaptation Programs of Action (NAPAs), the most prominent national efforts by the least developed countries to identify priority areas for adapting to climate change, have been subjected to three criticisms. First, the NAPA process puts in place similar projects across different countries, without paying attention to their specific adaptation needs. Second, many adaptation projects are difficult to distinguish from standard development projects. Third, the NAPA process fails to involve the major ministries and decision makers in the country or to pay enough attention to subnational and local institutional requirements.

In light of these criticisms, the World Development Report team sponsored two meetings of high-level NAPA officials in Asian and African countries, one in Bangkok in October 2008 and one in Johannesburg in November 2008. The meetings showed a more complicated picture and suggested that some criticisms may be misplaced.

Although adaptation needs and projects may appear similar when viewed collectively, they vary substantially across countries depending on the climate hazards and threats identified as most relevant. The standard NAPA guidelines explain some of the similarities in the language used to defend the identified projects as the most urgent adaptation needs. The preponderance of agricultural, natural resource, and disaster management projects reflects the fact that the impacts of climate change will be felt first in sectors related to primary goods and disaster management. Finally, the NAPAs were prepared on a shoestring, so the planning could not extend beyond the national level or across multiple ministries and decision makers.

But there is another side to the criticisms—the way the least developed countries view the NAPAs that they have prepared.

Little financial support: The total cost of all projects identified as urgent in 38 NAPA documents is less than $2 billion.

Despite this low price tag, little financial support has been available, raising valid concerns about donor assistance and widening the trust gap.

Poor architecture: Institutional arrangements for adaptation need to be more permanent and better linked to different ministries with support from ministries of finance and planning and stronger connections to provinces and districts. A dedicated body can do the planning, but implementation will have to be undertaken through existing institutional and governmental structures because many projects are sectoral.

Low capacity: Capacity for adaptation planning and implementation continues to be very low in most of the least developed countries. Improvements are needed in technical capacity, knowledge, training, equipment, and modeling; some capacity in these areas could be gained from experts in universities and civil society.

Source: WDR team.

---

issue or because of institutional flaws. Take responses to natural disaster. Unless a country is regularly hit by severe weather events, disaster avoidance and response usually fall through the cracks of the government agenda. Leaders find it unlikely they will be scrutinized, rewarded, or sanctioned for actions that the public did not even know their governments were supposed to take (avoiding disasters). If the relationship between efforts and outcomes is not clear to the public, governments lack clear incentives for action.

Government accountability for climate policy can be enhanced by making line agencies more accountable to core government ministries, such as the treasury or the prime minister—and by making the entire government more accountable to parliament, the public, and autonomous bodies (box 8.9). Parliaments can conduct hearings, monitor performance, educate the public, and require government to engage in regular reporting on climate objectives, policy, and achievements. Inscribing climate policy targets and objectives into law can be a potent tool for greater government accountability—and to ensure continuity of action beyond a government's short time frame. An independent expert advisory body can make recommendations to government and report to parliament.

Leveraging local government action

Local and regional governments can provide political and administrative space closer to the sources of emissions and the impacts of climate change. Charged with implementing and articulating national policies, they have policy-making, regulatory, and planning functions in sectors key to mitigation (transportation, construction, public service provision, local advocacy) and adaptation (social protection, disaster risk reduction, natural resource management). Closer to citizens, subnational governments can raise public awareness and mobilize nonstate actors. And because they are at the intersection of government and the public, they become the space where government accountability for appropriate responses plays out.[58]

Probably for these reasons, local authorities often precede national governments in taking climate action. As chapter 2 shows, the regional and local levels are often more appropriate for the design and implementation of adaptation measures in agriculture, infrastructure planning, training, and water management. But local governments can also lead in mitigation. States on both U.S. coasts have developed locally owned strategies and targets and then coalesced to pilot regional carbon markets (box 8.10). Cities worldwide have their own climate action plans and strategies, adopting Kyoto targets to compensate for the inaction of national governments and becoming active members of national and transnational city initiatives, such as the C40 network of the world's largest cities committed to tackling climate change.

The relevance of local governments requires their inclusion in climate policy. Decentralizing climate policy has pros and cons, and its optimal level and scope are context specific.[59] Local governments suffer from the same limitations as central governments, though usually more severely. The climate policy remit at the local level is usually with an environment unit, with integration and coordination problems. Subnational governments usually face resource and skill gaps and have less fiscal power, which prevents them from using environmental taxes. Despite their proximity to citizens, local governments often lack the same legitimacy as national governments, because of low turnouts in local elections and weak electoral mandates or weak capacities to deliver. All this makes devolution of climate policy particularly tricky.

To enhance vertical collaboration, national governments can engage in enabling, provision, and authority measures. Enabling measures include transferring knowledge and best practice. Of interest are benchmarking initiatives linked to competition and awards for the best-performing local authorities—the provincial competitiveness index in Vietnam is a good example of such subnational benchmarking. Provision measures include performance-based public sector agreements that link funding

BOX 8.9 *Enhancing government accountability for climate change in the United Kingdom*

By restructuring and establishing the institutional machinery for climate action, the United Kingdom has also deployed measures that increase the government's accountability for delivering results. The United Kingdom

- Passed a climate change bill that provided a statutory foundation for the official UK CO_2 emissions targets in the short, medium, and long terms, through five-year carbon budgets that set annual levels for permissible emissions. Three budgets spanning 15 years will be active at any given time, presenting a medium-term perspective for the evolution of carbon emissions throughout the economy.

- Designated a lead agency for climate change—the Department of Energy and Climate Change.

- Formalized in Public Sector Agreement 27 the accountability of the Department of Energy and Climate Change to the Treasury for various policy objectives and set delivery targets to measure performance in implementing them. The targets include specific steps to reduce the total U.K. emissions, increase the sustainable withdrawal of water, reduce the CO_2 intensity of the U.K. economy.

- Established a committee on climate change as an independent expert advisory body that can recommend to government ways to achieve targets. The committee reports annually to Parliament, and government is required to reply formally. Every five years the committee will offer a comprehensive assessment of the country's overall progress toward the long-term targets.

Source: WDR team.

not only to the number of inhabitants and geographical coverage of the authority but also to the achievement of targets. Authority measures include national laws requiring local governments to develop strategic plans in relevant sectors or regulation schemes to make local government officials accountable to central government, as with land-use planning.

Thinking politically about climate policy

Shaping the design and outcomes of any public policy are the strength, density, and extent of civil society; the bureaucratic culture and budget laws; and the factors driving the articulation and organization of political interests.[60] Fossil fuels, in addition to powering the economies of developed and developing countries, feed some of the special interests driving their politics. In many developing countries, carbon is not only unpriced, it is subsidized (see chapter 4). At the end of 2007 roughly a fifth of countries were subsidizing gasoline, and

Green federalism and climate change policy

Subnational jurisdictions in federalist systems have long been recognized as laboratories of policy experimentation and reform.[a] State, provincial, and local governments have had varying degrees of success when it comes to efficiency and effectiveness of "green federalism" policies—those environmental policies where subnational governments take the lead.[b]

Arguments supporting green federalism include the ability of lower-level governments to tailor policies to their unique resources and demographics, as well as the opportunity to drive slower-moving national policy with innovative subnational experimentation and learning.[c] Critics of green federalism cite risks of carbon leakage, as well as the incentive for businesses to relocate in less restrictive jurisdictions. This process is often termed the race to the bottom, since it reduces environmental quality and underprovides public goods and services.[d]

But for climate policy, green federalism has shown promising results. One of the most visible examples is the United States (box map). Despite the national government's decision not to ratify the

Green federalism in the United States: State and regional action

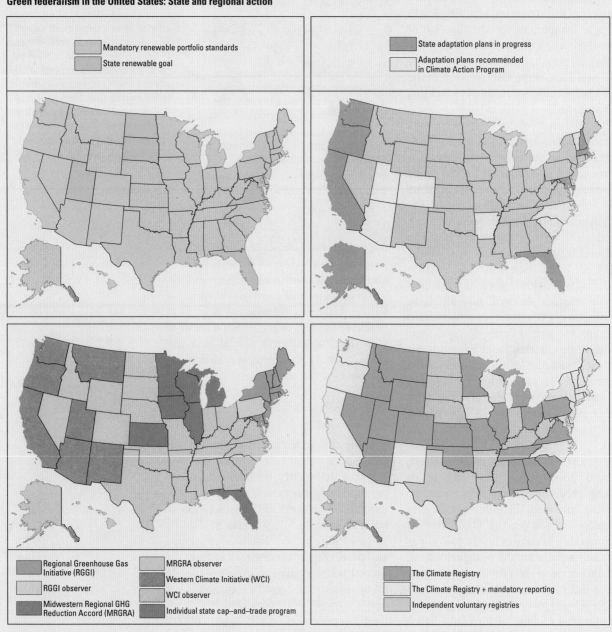

Mandatory renewable portfolio standards
State renewable goal

State adaptation plans in progress
Adaptation plans recommended in Climate Action Program

Regional Greenhouse Gas Initiative (RGGI)
RGGI observer
Midwestern Regional GHG Reduction Accord (MRGRA)
MRGRA observer
Western Climate Initiative (WCI)
WCI observer
Individual state cap–and–trade program

The Climate Registry
The Climate Registry + mandatory reporting
Independent voluntary registries

(continues)

Kyoto Protocol, and in the absence of overarching federal climate-change policy, subnational governments have taken the lead.[e] Many regions have greenhouse gas monitoring and registering programs as well as emissions reduction goals. And dozens of individual states have crafted and implemented mitigation and adaptation plans or instituted renewable portfolio standards and reduction targets. Cities and

municipalities have also initiated comprehensive climate change auditing and planning programs, setting emissions reduction goals of their own.

These actions add up to significant reductions, and some claim that such efforts have led to a race to the top.[f] If the handful of states with firm emissions targets achieve their 2020 goals, U.S. national emissions could be stabilized at 2010 levels by 2020.[9]

Source: State actions are tracked by the Pew Center on Global Climate Change (www.pewclimate.org).

a. Osborne 1988.

b. Oats and Portney 2003.

c. Lutsey and Sperling 2008.

d. Kunce and Shogren 2005.

e. Rabe 2002.

f. Rabe 2006.

g. Lutsey and Sperling 2008.

slightly more than a third were subsidizing diesel fuel. More than two-thirds of low- and lower-middle-income countries were subsidizing kerosene.[61] Clearly, countries with large fossil-based energy sectors or highly energy-intensive economies face major resistance to change.[62] The result is that worldwide the sources and drivers of carbon emissions are often tied to governments' political legitimacy.

Each political system presents advantages and obstacles in addressing climate change. Take democracy. Strong evidence shows that democracies outperform autocracies in environmental policy.[63] Political freedoms improve environmental performance, particularly in poorer nations.[64] Greater civil liberties are linked with better air and water quality, such as reduced sulfur dioxide and particulates in air and lower coliform and dissolved oxygen levels in water.[65] Democracies are more likely to join international environmental regimes and treaties, are generally faster at ratifying them, and have a track record of solving global commons problems such as ozone depletion.[66]

Yet democracies sometimes do better in policy outputs (signing up to international commitments) than policy outcomes (actual emission reductions), as with Kyoto.[67] As with individual consumers and voters, democracies prove more responsive in committing to solving a problem than in actually solving it, with the "green gap" in consumer attitudes translating into a words-deeds gap in government behavior (figure 8.7).[68] There are several reasons for this. Despite rising public concern about climate change,

politicians keep fearing the electorate, assuming that voters are likely to be less supportive of climate action once policies affect them personally through direct and visible personal costs (carbon and energy taxes, price increases, job losses).[69] This might explain why it is harder to achieve emissions reductions through restrictions that affect individual choices. Intervening in personal mobility choices is politically tougher than targeting power plants.[70]

In political terms, climate action faces a "proximity limit." People's tendency to first address visible and direct concerns translates into a political bias favoring the solution of local environmental problems (sanitation infrastructure, water and air quality, risks associated with toxic releases, and local habitat protection) over transboundary issues (such as biodiversity loss, overfishing, or climate change).[71] The proximity limit has a temporal dimension too. Problems with long time horizons, particularly those involving public goods, are tricky to resolve. Climate change is no exception.[72] Intergenerational problems require long-term policy frameworks at odds with government time frames and electoral cycles.

When policy issues are left without a public to champion them, shortsightedness can produce perverse incentives. Disaster risk management is an example of how standard adaptation measures can fail because the public (the voter) often fails to think in preventive terms. So decision makers neglect prevention and preparedness because these issues do not win votes. In turn, decision makers' realization that

Figure 8.7   Democracies do better in climate policy outputs than policy outcomes

Output: policies, laws, and international agreements

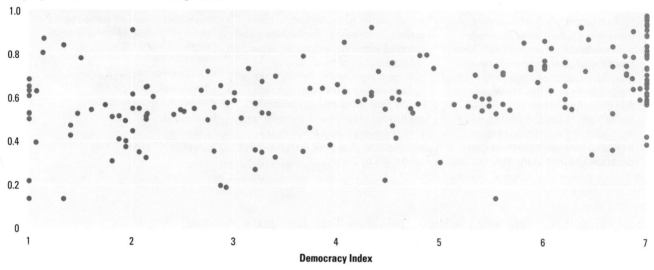

Outcome: emission reductions

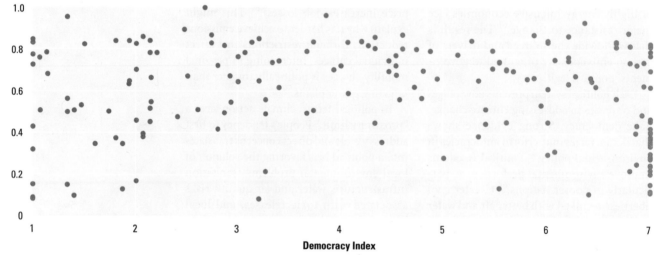

Source: Bättig and Bernauer 2009.

Note: Output is an index of cooperative behavior in climate change policy, spanning ratification of agreements, reporting, and financing—it ranges between 0 and 1, with higher values indicating more cooperation. Outcome is an index of cooperative behavior in climate change policy, spanning emission trends and emission levels—it ranges between 0 and 1, with higher values indicating more cooperation. The Political Rights Index by Freedom House is a measure of democracy encompassing the degree of freedom in the electoral process, political pluralism and participation, and functioning of government. Numerically, Freedom House rates political rights on a scale of 1 to 7, with 1 representing the most free and 7 representing the least free. However, in this figure the scale of original data has been inverted and higher values indicate a higher level of democracy. Data are 1990–2005 averages. The figure shows that there is a positive relationship between output and level of democracy, as represented by the Freedom House political rights index; democratic countries have, in general, better output. Conversely no significant relationship has been found between level of democracy and climate outcomes in the form of emission reductions (using emissions reductions in 2003 compared to 1990 levels).

disaster relief has higher political payoffs than preparedness closes the circle of moral hazard. This is far from purely theoretical. If the costs of disasters have increased dramatically, it is partly because governments realize that providing compensation to groups and areas struck by severe weather events provides major electoral benefits.[73] This realization works against policy change and reinforces bad policies.

Government crop insurance reduces farmers' incentives to avoid weather damage. Disaster relief leads citizens and local governments to expect compensation as an entitlement rather than take preventive measures.[74]

Climate reforms depend on political support. Any policy change generally meets resistance, particularly when it involves visible costs to large and diverse actors. Climate policy is a perfect example, because its costs are going to be clearly visible to various economic groups and the population at large. Building public support for climate policy can take many avenues.

Devise interventions that a maximum number of (key) political actors can agree on

Design policies that yield co-benefits. Countries abiding by and implementing international environmental obligations tend do so because of local incentives: air pollution, water quality degradation, direct and visible environmental threats.[75] Individuals contribute to public goods more easily when they see a direct benefit. Actively seeking overlapping goals and benefits should be a core part of a politically sustainable climate policy.[76] Not all climate-smart development policies are climate specific, and a range of actions can overcome the (perceived) tradeoffs between economic development and climate action. The challenge is to frame climate action in terms of local, private, and near-term goals and co-benefits—such as energy security, energy efficiency, public health, pollution abatement, and disaster risk reduction.

Target key constituencies. The co-benefits of climate policy can win over opposing vested interests. Take labor. Where the short-term employment effect of climate policy is negative, offsetting payoffs for organized labor should be made clear. Unions can be brought round by demonstrating to them how a low-carbon economy is more labor intensive than a conventional one; how energy savings can be turned into higher, labor-intensive expenditures; how investments in technology development and deployment will create jobs; and how the revenues from energy taxes can offset taxes on labor, increasing the demand for workers. It is important to carefully assess whether policies are perceived to be unduly favorable to one key group or the other. Support for climate policy is strong among groups that see a low-carbon economy as a business opportunity, but legacy industries remain opposed. Grandfathering emission

permits is often cited as a strategic measure to get the longer-term buy-in of business, but the scheme also generates public resistance (box 8.11).

Rely on consensus processes and instruments. Obtaining the prior agreement of the main stakeholders on specific measures can reduce political damage. In addition to identifying co-benefits, consensus policies involve setting up consultative systems and voluntary schemes that bind key actors such as industry groups to the principles of climate policy. Consultative political systems seem to be more effective in environmental policy.[77]

Increase the public's acceptance of reforms

Pursue equity, fairness, and inclusion. A decision maker's aversion to inequity is a product of both ethics and politics, because redistributional outcomes normally lead to political payoffs or sanctions by voters. The public is more likely to accept policy change if it is seen as tackling a severe problem and if its costs and benefits are perceived as equitably distributed. This calls for designing progressive and equitable climate policies involving transparent compensatory measures for the poorest. Green fiscal policies can be progressive and play a strong equity role.[78] Revenue recycling from carbon taxes or auctioned permits can support tax cuts and provide economic stimulus. Earmarking the proceeds of carbon permits and taxes for social protection schemes can increase

---

BOX 8.11 *Garnering support for cap-and-trade*

The European Union recently created an emissions trading system to meet its Kyoto obligations. Overall, the system has many good features. One peculiarity is that EU countries are required to grandfather credits (give them freely) to firms despite the potentially huge rents associated with them and the clear economic gains to be had from auctioning credits. In part because of this grandfathering rule and the implicit recognition of the large rents associated with it, the allocation mechanism is set only for five-year periods.

These short allocation periods avoid giving away too much wealth through rent creation and capture. But the massive windfalls for major polluters drew media attention and alienated the public. The five-year system also created perverse incentives for strategic behavior to influence the next allocation rule and was protested by firms aiming to enter the industry.

Source: WDR team.

the acceptance of energy-pricing reforms. In several European countries revenues raised from charges on air pollutants, hazardous wastes, and toxic chemicals reduce income taxes and social security contributions.

Lead by example.   Policy makers can set social norms by changing the behavior of government. The greening of government can play an important communication role in addition to providing immediate benefits in reducing emissions and catalyzing research and investments in new technologies. Where feasible, government can also revise instruments such as public procurement to support green objectives.

Use weather-related natural disasters as teaching moments.   Disasters can provide "focusing events" that lead to rapid policy change, although the window of opportunity is usually short.[79] The 2003 heat wave in Europe, Hurricane Katrina in 2005, and Australia's 2009 wildfires all increased attention to climate change. Such events can provide an opening for government to take actions unpopular in normal times.[80] Postdisaster reconstruction also provides opportunities to depart from past practices and build more resilient communities and societies.

Increase the acceptability of policies.   Swift and sudden government actions can circumvent groups that want to maintain the status quo and create a feeling of inevitability, if momentum is maintained.[81] But gradualism can also increase the acceptability of policies, because incremental policy changes usually draw less attention and resistance. This could explain why major economies have been slow in starting to reduce emissions. Small, incremental changes can establish platforms for advancing larger changes later on. Here, establishing predictability— setting the long-term orientation of government policy—allows stakeholders (in and outside government) to identify the incentives they need to reorient their activities.[82]

Improve communication.   Well-designed communication strategies not only can help change behaviors—they can also mobilize political support for reform. Pub-

lic information campaigns have been key to successful subsidy reforms, even where groups capturing the subsidies were better organized and more powerful than the beneficiaries of reform (consumers and taxpayers). Communication should focus on filling the knowledge gap and addressing what can be rationally based opposition to reforms. For instance, demystifying some of the unsubstantiated perceptions of the negative sides of climate policies can reduce uncertainty and opposition. Research shows that fears of racing to the bottom and losing competitiveness are exaggerated and that investing in new green technology can lead to the development of markets for environmental goods and services.[83] Similarly, stressing that environmental taxes are not simply a source of revenue for the state but a key to changing behavior is central to enhancing public acceptability.

Address structural deficiencies of political systems

Reinforce political pluralism.   Vested interests, including those that fear climate policies would harm their business or industry, may have a stake in limiting the scope and impact of climate policy. Measures to reduce interest group activity aimed at capturing or hijacking climate policy include reinforcing political pluralism. This can have varying impacts on policy change. A large number of veto players can produce a policy gridlock.[84] But political pluralism generally reduces behind-closed-door lobbying and corruption by giving access and voice to countervailing interests.[85] Environmental interests have overwhelmed business interests trying to curtail the stringency of environmental policies in food safety, renewable portfolio standards, and waste regulation.[86] Political pluralism can also foster coalitions of environmental and business interests as drivers of change.

Promote transparency.   Clarifying the cost of energy and its components (production, imports, distribution subsidies, and taxes) can build support for reform of energy markets. In mitigation policy one major advantage of transparent reporting of the cost of energy is that the additional cost of carbon is

BOX 8.12 *The private sector is changing practices even without national legislation*

Private sector actors have stepped up their actions to reduce greenhouse gas emissions, even in countries lacking comprehensive climate-change legislation. An increasing number of firms have developed voluntary emissions targets and reporting standards. In 2008 a record 57 climate-related shareholder resolutions were filed in U.S. boardrooms—double the number five years earlier. Support for these measures averaged more than 23 percent among shareholders—another all-time high.

Carbon-intensive firms have also come together to discuss strategy for mitigating climate change. In early 2009 the U.S. Climate Action Partnership, an alliance of more than two dozen major greenhouse-gas-emitting companies and several nongovernmental organizations, put forth a unified plan for federal legislative action that calls for an 80 percent reduction of 2005 emission levels by 2050. The Business Roundtable, an association of leading U.S. companies, has mapped ways to improve conservation, efficiency, and domestic energy production between now and 2025. The Prince of Wales International Business Leaders Forum, an independent organization that supports more than 100 of the world's leading businesses, launched the Business and the Environment program in recognition of the impact of climate change on business operations and liabilities.

This drive is pushing entire industries to shift their practices. In March 2009 the U.S. insurance association implemented a first-of-its-kind requirement that all insurers must evaluate the climate-change risks posed to the companies they insure and disclose their plans for managing such risks. These include direct risks posed by climate-change impacts and indirect risks posed by policy initiatives to mitigate climate change. Similarly, the financial investment industry is moving to increase the disclosure of climate risks in publicly traded companies, while promoting climate-smart investments.

Source: WDR team.

put in relative terms. Transparency has been particularly useful in raising public awareness about the costs of energy subsidies, assessing the tradeoffs, and identifying winners and losers. Some countries have subsidy reporting systems to enhance public understanding of their costs and benefits.[87]

Make it difficult to reverse policy. Political and institutional arrangements can help avoid shifting action on climate change from the living to the unborn by making it difficult to reverse climate policy. Such arrangements could include constitutional amendments and climate-change laws.[88] But they can also involve the establishment of independent institutions that take a longer-term view, in the same way that monetary institutions control inflation.

Climate-smart development starts at home

The quest for appropriate responses to climate change has long focused on the need for an international agreement—a global deal. Although important, a global deal is only a part of the answer. Climate change is certainly a global market failure, but one articulated according to locally defined causes and effects and mediated by context-specific circumstances.

This means that climate policy—for both mitigation and adaptation—has local

determinants. A study on the adoption of renewable portfolio standards across U.S. states shows that political liberalism, renewable energy potential, and concentrations of local air pollutants all increase the probability that a state will adopt such standards. On the other hand, carbon intensity tends to decrease this probability.[89] International regimes influence domestic policies, but the reverse also holds. A country's behavior in shaping, adhering to, and implementing a climate deal depends on domestic incentives. Political norms, institutional structures, and vested interests influence the translation of international norms into domestic political dialogue and policy, while shaping the international regime by driving the national actions.[90] A country's wealth, its energy mix, and its economic preferences—such as the propensity for state-driven or market-driven responses—will shape mitigation policy. Cultural and political traditions are added to economic and administrative considerations in choosing taxes or cap-and-trade. And because of the lack of an international sanctioning mechanism, the incentives for meeting global commitments need to be found domestically, through concentrated local benefits such as cleaner air, technology transfer, and energy security.

Climate action is already taking place. Countries have shown different levels of commitment and performance in reducing emissions. Small countries—which in theory should have incentives to free ride, given their negligible role in global emission reductions—have so far undertaken more aggressive actions than the big players. In some countries subnational measures and homegrown policy responses are already affecting national policy and the position of countries in the international arena. And the private sector is showing that old practices can give way to new visions (box 8.12).

Reversing the institutional inertia that constrains climate policy requires fundamental changes in interpreting information and making decisions. A range of actions can be taken domestically by national and subnational governments as well as by the private sector, the media, and the scientific community. Although establishing an effective international climate regime is a justified preoccupation, it should not lead to a wait-and-see attitude, which can only add to the inertia and constrain the response.

Notes

1. North 1990.
2. Soderholm 2001.
3. Sehring 2006.
4. Foa 2009.
5. Gardner and Stern 2008.
6. Gardner and Stern 2008.
7. Bannon and others 2007; Leiserowitz 2007; Brechin 2008; Sternman and Sweeney 2007.
8. IPPR 2008; Retallack, Lawrence, and Lockwood 2007.
9. Wimberly 2008; Accenture 2009.
10. Norgaard 2006; Jacques, Dunlap, and Freeman 2008.
11. Bulkeley 2000.
12. Kellstedt, Zahran, and Vedlitz 2008.
13. Immerwahr 1999.
14. Krosnick and others 2006.
15. Boykoff and Mansfield 2008.
16. Oreskes 2004; Krosnick 2008.
17. Miller 2008.
18. Bostrom and others 1994.
19. Bazerman 2006.
20. Sternman and Sweeney 2007.
21. Ornstein and Ehrlich 2000; Weber 2006.
22. Repetto 2008.
23. Moser and Dilling 2007; Nisbet and Myers 2007.
24. Maslow 1970.
25. Olson 1965; Hardin 1968; Ostrom 2009.
26. Irwin 2009.
27. Winter and Koger 2004.
28. Sandvik 2008.
29. O'Connor and others 2002; Kellstedt, Zahran, and Vedlitz 2008; Norgaard 2006; Moser and Dilling 2007; Dunlap 1998.
30. Norgaard 2009.
31. Ward 2008.
32. Krosnick 2008.
33. Kallbekken, Kroll, and Cherry 2008.
34. Swallow and others 2007.
35. Clifford Chance 2007.
36. Romm and Ervin 1996.
37. Roland-Holst 2008.
38. Laitner and Finman 2000.
39. Cialdini and Goldstein 2004; Griskevicius 2007.
40. A. Corner, "Barack Obama's Hopes of Change Are All in the Mind." *The Guardian*, November 27, 2008.
41. Irwin 2009.
42. Irwin 2009.
43. Layard 2005.
44. Sterner 2003.
45. World Bank 1992; World Bank 1997; World Bank 2002.
46. Wade 1990.

"Ever think of emigration outside the world? To the Moon, Mars, or Venus? But our Earth is known to be the most beautiful planet of all. I still want to live in this wonderful place—with birds singing everywhere, the aroma of flowers in the air, green mountains, and blue icebergs. So everybody, please start to work together to conserve the beauty of Mother Earth. Join me now in making the world better."

—Giselle Lau Ching Yue, China, age 9

47. Stern 2006.

48. Haites 2008.

49. Janicke 2001.

50. Giddens 2008.

51. Bernauer and Koubi 2006.

52. Meadowcroft 2009.

53. Birkland 2006.

54. Bazerman 2006.

55. OECD 2003.

56. Bazerman 2006.

57. Doern and Gattinger 2003.

58. Alber and Kern 2008.

59. Estache 2008.

60. Kunkel, Jacob, and Busch 2006.

61. IMF 2008.

62. Kunkel, Jacob, and Busch 2006.

63. Congleton 1992; Congleton 1996.

64. Barrett and Graddy 2000.

65. Torras and Boyce 1998.

66. Congleton 2001; Schneider, Leifeld, and Malang 2008.

67. Rowell 1996; Vaughn-Switzer 1997.

68. Bättig and Bernauer 2009.

69. Compston and Bailey 2008.

70. Bättig and Bernauer 2009.

71. Bättig and Bernauer 2009.

72. Sprinz 2008.

73. Schmidtlein, Finch, and Cutter 2008; Garrett and Sobel 2002.

74. Birkland 2006.

75. Dolsak 2001.

76. Agrawala and Fankhauser 2008.

77. Compston and Bailey 2008.

78. Ekins and Dresner 2004.

79. Birkland 2006.

80. Compston and Bailey 2008.

81. Kerr 2006.

82. "A Major Setback for Clean Air," *New York Times*, July 16, 2008.

83. Janicke 2001.

84. Tsebelis 2002.

85. Dolsak 2001.

86. Vogel 2005; Bernauer and Caduff 2004; Bernauer 2003.

87. IMF 2008.

88. Kydland and Prescott 1977; Sprinz 2008.

89. Matisoff 2008.

90. Davenport 2008; Kunkel, Jacob, and Busch 2006; Dolsak 2001; Cass 2005.

References

Accenture. 2009. *Shifting the Balance from Intention to Action: Low Carbon, High Opportunity, High Performance*. New York: Accenture.

Agrawala, S., and S. Fankhauser. 2008. *Economic Aspects of Adaptation to Climate Change: Costs, Benefits and Policy Instruments*. Paris: Organisation for Economic Co-operation and Development.

Alber, G., and K. Kern. 2008. "Governing Climate Change in Cities: Modes of Urban Climate Governance in Multi-level Systems." Paper presented at the OECD Conference on Competitive Cities and Climate Change, Milan, October 9–10.

Anderson, M. G., and E. A. Holcombe. 2007. "Reducing Landslide Risk in Poor Housing Areas of the Caribbean: Developing a New Government-Community Partnership Model." *Journal of International Development* 19: 205–21.

Bannon, B., M. DeBell, J. A. Krosnick, R. Kopp, and P. Aldous. 2007. "Americans' Evaluations of Policies to Reduce Greenhouse Gas Emissions." Technical paper, Stanford University, Palo Alto, CA.

Barrett, S., and K. Graddy. 2000. "Freedom, Growth and the Environment." *Environment and Development Economics* 5 (4): 433–56.

Bättig, M. B., and T. Bernauer. 2009. "National Institutions and Global Public Goods: Are Democracies More Cooperative in Climate Change Policy?" *International Organization* 63 (2): 1–28.

Bazerman, M. 2006. "Climate Change as a Predictable Surprise." *Climatic Change* 77: 179–93.

Bernauer, T. 2003. *Genes, Trade, and Regulation: The Seeds of Conflict in Food Biotechnology*. Princeton, NJ: Princeton University Press.

Bernauer, T., and L. Caduff. 2004. "In Whose Interest? Pressure Group Politics, Economic Competition and Environmental Regulation." *Journal of Public Policy* 24 (1): 99–126.

Bernauer, T., and V. Koubi. 2006. "States as Providers of Public Goods: How Does Government Size Affect Environmental Quality?" Working Paper 14, Center for Comparative and International Studies, Zurich.

Birkland, T. A. 2006. *Lessons from Disaster: Policy Change after Catastrophic Events*. Washington, DC: Georgetown University Press.

Bostrom, A., M. G. Morgan, B. Fischhoff, and D. Read. 1994. "What Do People Know about Global Climate Change? Mental Models." *Risk Analysis* 14 (6): 959–70.

Boykoff, M., and M. Mansfield. 2008. "Ye Olde Hot Aire: Reporting on Human Contributions to Climate Change in the U.K. Tabloid Press." *Environmental Research Letters* 3: 1–8.

Brechin, S. R. 2008. "Ostriches and Change: A Response to Global Warming and Sociology." *Current Sociology* 56 (3): 467–74.

BTS (Bureau of Transportation Statistics). 2008. *Key Transportation Indicators November 2008.* Washington, DC: U. S. Department of Transportation.

Bulkeley, H. 2000. "Common Knowledge? Public Understanding of Climate Change in Newcastle, Australia." *Public Understanding of Science* 9: 313–33.

Cass, L. 2005. "Measuring the Domestic Salience of International Environmental Norms: Climate Change Norms in German, British, and American Climate Policy Debates." Paper presented at the International Studies Association, Honolulu.

Cialdini, R. B., and N. J. Goldstein. 2004. "Social Influence: Compliance and Conformity." *Annual Review Psychology* 55: 591–621.

Clifford Chance. 2007. *Climate Change: A Business Response to a Global Issue.* London: Clifford Chance.

Compston, H., and I. Bailey. 2008. *Turning Down the Heat: The Politics of Climate Policy in Affluent Democracies.* Basingstoke, UK: Palgrave Macmillan.

Congleton, R. D. 1992. "Political Regimes and Pollution Control." *Review of Economics and Statistics* 74: 412–21.

———. 1996. *The Political Economy of Environmental Protection.* Ann Arbor, MI: University of Michigan Press.

———. 2001. "Governing the Global Environmental Commons: The Political Economy of International Environmental Treaties and Institutions." In *Globalization and the Environment,* ed. G. G. Schulze and H. W. Ursprung. New York: Oxford University Press.

Davenport, D. 2008. "The International Dimension of Climate Policy." In *Turning Down the Heat: The Politics of Climate Policy in Affluent Democracies,* ed. H. Compston and I. Bailey. Basingstoke, UK: Palgrave Macmillan.

Doern, G. B., and M. Gattinger. 2003. *Power Switch: Energy Regulatory Governance in the 21st Century.* Toronto: University of Toronto Press.

Dolsak, N. 2001. "Mitigating Global Climate Change: Why Are Some Countries More Committed than Others?" *Policy Studies Journal* 29 (3): 414–36.

Dunlap, R. E. 1998. "Lay Perceptions of Global Risk: Public Views of Global Warming in Cross-National Context." *International Sociology* 13: 473–98.

EIA (Energy Information Administration). 2009. *Annual Energy Outlook 2009.* Washington, DC: EIA.

Ekins, P., and S. Dresner. 2004. *Green Taxes and Charges: Reducing their Impact on Low-income Households.* York, UK: Joseph Rowntree Foundation.

EPA (Environmental Protection Agency). 2009. *Draft Inventory of U.S. Greenhouse Gas Emissions and Sinks: 1990-2007.* Washington, DC: EPA.

Estache, A. 2008. "Decentralized Environmental Policy in Developing Countries." World Bank, Washington, DC.

Esty, D. C., M. A. Levy, C. H. Kim, A. de Sherbinin, T. Srebotnjak, and V. Mara. 2008. *Environmental Performance Index.* New Haven, CT: Yale Center for Environmental Law and Policy.

Foa, R. 2009. "Social and Governance Dimensions of Climate Change: Implications for Policy." Policy Research Working Paper 4939, World Bank, Washington, DC.

Gardner, G. T., and P. C. Stern. 2008. "The Short List: The Most Effective Actions U.S. Households Can Take to Curb Climate Change." *Environment Magazine.*

Garrett, T. A., and R. S. Sobel. 2002. "The Political Economy of FEMA Disaster Payments." Working Paper 2002-01 2B, Federal Reserve Bank of St. Louis.

Gautier, C., K. Deutsch, and S. Rebich. 2006. "Misconceptions about the Greenhouse Effect." *Journal of Geoscience Education* 54 (3): 386–95.

Giddens, A. 2008. *The Politics of Climate Change: National Responses to the Challenge of Global Warming.* Cambridge, UK: Polity Press.

Griskevicius, V. 2007. "The Constructive, Destructive, and Reconstructive Power of Social Norms." *Psychological Science* 18 (5): 429–34.

Haites, E. 2008. "Investment and Financial Flows Needed to Address Climate Change." Breaking the Climate Deadlock Briefing Paper, The Climate Group, London.

Hardin, G. 1968. "The Tragedy of the Commons." *Science* 162: 1243–48.

Hungerford, H., and T. Volk. 1990. "Changing Learner Behavior through Environmental Education." *Journal of Environmental Education* 21: 8–21.

ICCT (International Council on Clean Transportation). 2007. *Passenger Vehicle Greenhouse Gas and Fuel Economy Standard: A Global Update.* Washington, DC: San Francisco: ICCT.

IMF (International Monetary Fund). 2008. *Fuel and Food Price Subsidies: Issues and Reform Options.* Washington, DC: IMF.

Immerwahr, J. 1999. *Waiting for a Signal: Public Attitudes toward Global Warming, the Environment and Geophysical Research.* New York: Public Agenda.

IPPR (Institute for Public Policy Research). 2008. *Engagement and Political Space for Policies on Climate Change.* London: IPPR.

Irwin, T. 2008. "Implications for Climate Change Policy of Research on Cooperation in Social Dilemma." Policy Research Working Paper 5006, World Bank, Washington, DC.

Jacques, P., R. Dunlap, and M. Freeman. 2008. "The Organisation of Denial: Conservative Think Tanks and Environmental Skepticism." *Environmental Politics* 17 (3): 349–85.

Janicke, M. 2001. "No Withering Away of the Nation State: Ten Theses on Environmental Policy." In *Global Environmental Change and the Nation State: Proceedings of the 2001 Berlin Conference on the Human Dimensions of Global Environmental Change,* ed. F. Biermann, R. Brohm, and K. Dingwert. Berlin: Potsdam Institute for Climate Impact Research.

Kahneman, D., and A. Tversky. 1979. "Prospect Theory: An Analysis of Decision under Risk." *Econometrica* 47: 263–91.

Kallbekken, S., S. Kroll, and T. L. Cherry. 2008. "Do You Not Like Pigou, or Do You Not Understand Him? Tax Aversion and Earmarking in the Lab." Paper presented at the Oslo Seminars in Behavioral and Experimental Economics, Department of Economics, University of Oslo.

Kastens, K. A., and M. Turrin. 2006. "To What Extent Should Human/Environment Interactions Be Included in Science Education?" *Journal of Geoscience Education* 54 (3): 422–36.

Kaufman, D., A. Kraay, and M. Mastruzzi. 2007. *World Governance Indicators 2007.* Washington, DC: World Bank.

Kellstedt, P., S. Zahran, and A. Vedlitz. 2008. "Personal Efficacy, the Information Environment, and Attitudes toward Global Warming and Climate Change in the United States." *Risk Analysis* 28 (1): 113–26.

Kerr, S. 2006. "The Political Economy of Structural Reform in Natural Resource Use: Observations from New Zealand." Paper presented at the National Economic Research Organizations meeting, Paris.

Krosnick, J. 2008. "The American Public's Views of Global Climate Change and Potential Amelioration Strategies." *World Development Report 2010* Seminar Series, presentation, World Bank, Washington, DC.

Krosnick, J., A. Holbrook, L. Lowe, and P. Visser. 2006. "The Origins and Consequences of Democratic Citizen's Policy Agendas: A Study of Popular Concern about Global Warming." *Climate Change* 77: 7–43.

Kunce, M., and J. F. Shogren. 2005. "On Interjurisdictional Competition and Environmental Federalism." *Journal of Environmental Economics and Management* 50: 212–24.

Kunkel, N., K. Jacob, and P.-O. Busch. 2006. "Climate Policies: (The Feasibility of) a Statistical Analysis of their Determinants." Paper presented at the Human Dimensions of Global Environmental Change, Berlin.

Kydland, F. E., and E. C. Prescott. 1977. "Rules rather than Discretion: The Inconsistency of Optimal Plan." *Journal of Political Economy* 85 (3): 473–91.

Laitner, J., and H. Finman. 2000. *Productivity Benefits from Industrial Energy Efficiency Investments.* Washington, DC: EPA Office of the Atmospheric Programs.

Layard, R. 2005. *Happiness: Lessons from a New Science.* London: Penguin.

Leiserowitz, A. 2007. "Public Perception, Opinion and Understanding of Climate Change: Current Patterns, Trends and Limitations." Occasional Paper for the *Human Development Report 2007/2008*, United Nations Development Programme, New York.

Lorenzoni, I., S. Nicholson-Cole, and L. Whitmarsh. 2007. "Barriers Perceived to Engaging with Climate Change among the UK Public and Their Policy Implications." *Global Environmental Change* 17: 445–59.

Lutsey, N., and D. Sperling. 2008. "America's Bottom-up Climate Change Mitigation Policy." *Energy Policy* 36: 673–85.

Maslow, A. H. 1970. *Motivation and Personality.* New York: Harper & Row.

Matisoff, D. C. 2008. "The Adoption of State Climate Change Policies and Renewable Portfolio Standards." *Review of Policy Research* 25: 527–46.

Meadowcroft, J. 2009. "Climate Change Governance." Policy Research Working Paper 4941, World Bank, Washington, DC.

Miller, D. 2008. "What's Wrong with Consumption?" University College London, London.

Moser, S. C., and L. Dilling. 2007. *Creating a Climate for Change: Communicating Climate Change and Facilitating Social Change.* New York: Cambridge University Press.

Moxnes, E., and A. K. Saysel. 2009. "Misperceptions of Global Climate Change: Information Policies." *Climatic Change* 93 (1–2): 15–37.

Nisbet, M. C., and T. Myers. 2007. "Twenty Years of Public Opinion about Global Warming." *Public Opinion Quarterly* 71 (3): 444–70.

Norgaard, K. M. 2006. "People Want to Protect Themselves a Little Bit: Emotions, Denial, and Social Movement Nonparticipation." *Sociological Inquiry* 76: 372–96.

———. 2009. "Cognitive and Behavioral Challenges in Responding to Climate Change." Policy Research Working Paper 4940, World Bank, Washington, DC.

North, D. C. 1990. *Institutions, Institutional Change and Economic Performance.* Cambridge, UK: Cambridge University Press.

Oats, W. E., and P. R. Portney. 2003. "The Political Economy of Environmental Policy." In *Handbook of Environmental Economics,* ed. K. G. Maler and J. R. Vincent. Amsterdam: Elsevier Science B.V.

O'Connor, R., R. J. Bord, B. Yarnal, and N. Wiefek. 2002. "Who Wants to Reduce Greenhouse Gas Emissions?" *Social Science Quarterly* 83 (1): 1–17.

OECD (Organisation for Economic Cooperation and Development). 2003. *Harmonizing Donor Practices for Effective Aid Delivery.* Paris: OECD.

Olson, M. 1965. *The Logic of Collective Action.* Cambridge, MA: Harvard University Press.

Oreskes, N. 2004. "Beyond the Ivory Tower: The Scientific Consensus on Climate Change." *Science* 306 (5702): 1686.

Ornstein, R., and P. Ehrlich. 2000. *New World, New Mind: Moving toward Conscious Evolution.* Cambridge, MA: Malor Books.

Osborne, D. 1988. *Laboratories of Democracy: A New Breed of Governor Creates Models for National Growth.* Boston: Harvard Business School Press.

Ostrom, E. 2009. "A Polycentric Approach for Coping with Climate Change." Background paper for the WDR 2010.

Patt, A. G., and D. Schröter. 2008. "Climate Risk Perception and Challenges for Policy Implementation: Evidence from Stakeholders in Mozambique." *Global Environmental Change* 18: 458–67.

Rabe, B. G. 2002. *Greenhouse and Statehouse: The Evolving State Government Role in Climate Change.* Arlington, VA: Pew Center on Global Climate Change.

———. 2006. *Race to the Top: The Expanding Role of U.S. State Renewable Portfolio Standards.* Arlington, VA: Pew Center on Global Climate Change.

Repetto, R. 2008. "The Climate Crisis and the Adaptation Myth." Yale School of Forestry and Environmental Studies Working Paper 13, Yale University, New Haven, CT.

Retallack, S., T. Lawrence, and M. Lockwood. 2007. *Positive Energy: Harnessing People Power to Prevent Climate Change.* London: Institute for Public Policy Research.

Roland-Holst, D. 2008. *Energy Efficiency, Innovation, and Job Creation in California.* Berkeley, CA: Center for Energy, Resources, and Economic Sustainability, University of California at Berkeley.

Romm, J. J., and C. A. Ervin. 1996. "How Energy Policies Affect Public Health." *Public Health Reports* 111 (5): 390–99.

Rowell, A. 1996. *Green Backlash: Global Subversion of the Environmental Movement.* London: Routledge.

Sandvik, H. 2008. "Public Concern over Global Warming Correlates Negatively with National Wealth." *Climatic Change* 90 (3): 333–41.

Schmidtlein, M. C., C. Finch, and S. L. Cutter. 2008. "Disaster Declarations and Major Hazard Occurrences in the United States." *Professional Geographer* 60 (1): 1–14.

Schneider, V., P. Leifeld, and T. Malang. 2008. "Coping with Creeping Catastrophes: The Capacity of National Political Systems in the Perception, Communication and Solution of Slow-moving and Long-term Policy Problems." Paper presented at the Berlin Conference on the Human Dimensions of Global Environmental Change: "Long-Term Policies: Governing Social-Ecological Change," Berlin, Feb. 22–23.

Sehring, J. 2006. "The Politics of Water Institutional Reform: A Comparative Analysis of Kyrgyzstan and Tajikistan." Paper presented at the Berlin Conference on the Human Dimensions of Global Environmental Change: "Resource Policies: Effectiveness, Efficiency and Equity," Berlin, November 17–18.

Soderholm, P. 2001. "Environmental Policy in Transition Economies: Will Pollution Charges Work?" *Journal of Environment Development* 10 (4): 365–90.

Sprinz, D. F. 2008. "Responding to Long-term Policy Challenges: Sugar Daddies, Airbus Solution or Liability?" *Ökologisches Wirtschaften* 2: 16–19.

Stern, N. 2006. *The Economics of Climate Change: The Stern Review.* Cambridge, UK: Cambridge University Press.

Sterner, T. 2003. *Policy Instruments for Environmental and Natural Resources Management.* Washington, DC: Resources for the Future.

Sternman, J. D., and L. B. Sweeney. 2007. "Understanding Public Complacency about Climate Change: Adults' Mental Models of Climate Change Violate Conservation of Matter." *Climatic Change* 80 (3–4): 213–38.

Swallow, B., M. van Noordwijk, S. Dewi, D. Murdiyarso, D. White, J. Gockowski, G. Hyman, S. Budidarsono, V. Robiglio, V. Meadu, A. Ekadinata, F. Agus, K. Hairiah, P. Mbile, D. J. Sonwa, and S. Weise. 2007. *Opportunities for Avoided Deforestation with Sustainable Benefits.* Nairobi: ASB Partnership for the Tropical Forest Margins.

Torras, M., and J. K. Boyce. 1998. "Income, Inequality and Pollution: A Reassessment of the Environmental Kuznets Curve." *Ecological Economics* 25 (2): 147–60.

Tsebelis, G. 2002. *Veto Players: How Political Institutions Work.* Princeton, NJ: Princeton University Press.

Tversky, A., and D. Kahneman. 1974. "Judgment under Uncertainty: Heuristics and Biases." *Science* 211: 1124–31.

Vaughn-Switzer, J. 1997. *Environmental Politics.* London: St. Martin's Press.

Vogel, D. 2005. *The Market for Virtue: The Potential and Limits of Corporate Social Responsibility.* Washington, DC: Brookings Institution Press.

Wade, R. 1990. *Governing the Market.* Princeton, NJ: Princeton University Press.

Ward, B. 2008. *Communicating on Climate Change: An Essential Resource for Journalists, Scientists, and Educators.* Narragansett, RI: Metcalf Institute for Marine and Environmental Reporting, University of Rhode Island Graduate School of Oceanography.

Weber, E. U. 2006. "Experience-Based and Description-Based Perceptions of Long-Term Risk: Why Global Warming Does Not Sare Us (Yet)." *Climatic Change* 77: 103–20.

Wimberly, J. 2008. *Climate Change and Consumers: The Challenge Ahead.* Washington, DC: EcoAlign.

Winter, D. D., and S. M. Koger. 2004. *The Psychology of Environmental Problems.* Mahwah, NJ: Lawrence Erlbaum Associates.

World Bank. 1992. *World Development Report 1992. Development and the Environment.* New York: Oxford University Press.

———. 1997. *World Development Report 1997. The State in a Changing World.* Washington, DC: World Bank.

———. 2002. *World Development Report 2002. Building Institutions for Markets.* Washington, DC: World Bank.

Bibliographical note

Many people inside and outside the World Bank gave comments to the team. Valuable comments, guidance and contributions were provided by Shardul Agrawala, Montek Singh Ahluwalia, Nilufar Ahmad, Kulsum Ahmed, Sadiq Ahmed, Ahmad Ahsan, Ulrika Åkesson, Mehdi Akhlaghi, Mozaharul Alam, Vahid Alavian, Harold Alderman, Sara Amiri, David Anderson, Simon Anderson, Ken Andrasko, Juliano Assunçao, Giles Atkinson, Varadan Atur, Jessica Ayers, Abdulhamid Azad, Sushenjit Bandyopadhyay, Ian Bannon, Ellysar Baroudy, Rhona Barr, Scott Barrett, Wim Bastiaanssen, Daniel Benitez, Craig Bennett, Anthony Bigio, Yvan Biot, Jeppe Bjerg, Brian Blankespoor, Melinda Bohannon, Jan Bojo, Benoît Bosquet, Aziz Bouzaher, Richard Bradley, Milan Brahmbhatt, Carter Brandon, Gernot Brodnig, Marjory-Anne Bromhead, Andrew Burns, Anil Cabraal, Duncan Callaway, Simon Caney, Karan Capoor, Jean-Christophe Carret, Rafaello Cervigni, Rita E. Cestti, Muyeye Chambwera, Vandana Chandra, David Chapman, Joelle Chassard, Flávia Chein Feres, Ashwini Chhatre, Kenneth Chomitz, David A. Cieslikowski, Hugh Compston, Luis Constantino, Jonathan Coony, Charles Cormier, Christophe Crepin, Richard Damania, Stephen Danyo, Michael Davis, Melissa Dell, Shantayanan Devarajan, Charles E. Di Leva, William J. Dick, Simeon Djankov, Carola Donner, Diletta Doretti, Krystel Dossou, Navroz Dubash, Hari Bansha Dulal, Mark Dutz, Jane Olga Ebinger, M. Willem van Eeghen, Nada Eissa, Siri Eriksen, Antonio Estache, James Warren Evans, Mandy Ewing, Pablo Fajnzylber, Charles Feinstein, Gene Feldman, Erick C. M. Fernandes, Daryl Fields, Christiana Figueres, Cyprian F. Fisiy, Ariel Fiszbein, Richard Fix, Paolo Frankl, Vicente Fretes Cibils, Alan Gelb, Francis Ghesquiere, Dolf Gielen, Indermit S. Gill, Habiba Gitay, Barry Gold, Itzhak Goldberg, Jan von der Goltz, Bernard E. Gomez, Arturo Gomez Pompas, Christophe de Gouvello, Chandrasekar Govindarajalu, Margaret Grosh, Michael Grubb, Arnulf Grübler, José Luis Guasch, Eugene Gurenko, Stéphane Hallegatte, Tracy Hart, Marea Eleni Hatziolos, Johannes Heister, Rasmus Heltberg, Fernando L. Hernandez, Jason Hill, Ron Hoffer, Daniel Hoornweg, Chris Hope, Nicholas Howard, Rafael de Hoyos, Veronika Huber, Vijay Iyer, Michael Friis Jensen, Peter Johansen, Todd Johnson, Torkil Jonch-Clausen, Benjamin F. Jones, Ben Jones, Frauke Jungbluth, John David Kabasa, Ravi Kanbur, Tom Karl, Benjamin S. Karmorh, George Kasali, Roy Katayama, Andrzej Kędziora, Michael Keen, Kieran Kelleher, Claudia Kemfert, Karin E. Kemper, Qaiser Khan, Euster Kibona, Richard Klein, Masami Kojima, Auguste Tano Kouamé, Jarl Krausing, Holger A. Kray, Alice Kuegler, Norman Kuring, Yevgeny Kuznetsov, Christina Lakatos, Julian A. Lampietti, Perpetua Latasi, Judith Layzer, Danny Leipziger, Robert Lempert, Darius Lilaoonwala, James A. Listorti, Feng Liu, Bertrand Loiseau, Laszlo Lovei, Magda Lovei, Susanna Lundstrom, Kathleen Mackinnon, Marília Magalhães, Olivier Mahul, Ton Manders, McKinsey & Company (Jeremy Oppenheim, Jens Dinkel, Per-Anders Enkvist, and Biniam Gebre), Marília Telma Manjate, Michael Mann, Sergio Margulis, Will Martin, Ursula Martinez, Michel Matera, J. M. Mauskar, Siobhan McInerney-Lankford, Robin Mearns, Malte Meinshausen, Abel Mejía, Stephen Mink, Rogerio de Miranda, Lucio Monari, Paul Moreno López, Roger Morier, Richard Moss, Valerie Müller, Robert Muir-Wood, Enrique Murgueitio Restrepo, Siobhan Murray, Everhart Nangoma, Mudit Narain, John Nash, Vikram Nehru, Dan Nepstad, Michele de Nevers, Ken Newcombe, Brian Ngo, Carlo del Ninno, Andy Norton, Frank Nutter, Erika Odendaal, Ellen Olafsen, Ben Olken, Sanjay Pahuja, Alessandro Palmieri, Gajanand Pathmanathan, Nicolas Perrin, Chris Perry, Djordjija Petkoski, Tanyathon Phetmanee, Henry Pollack, Joanna Post, Neeraj Prasad, Tovondriaka Rakotobe, Nithya Ramanathan, V. Ramanathan, Nicola Ranger, Dilip Ratha, Keywan Riahi, Richard Richels, Brian Ricketts, Jeff Ritchie, Konrad von Ritter, David Rogers, Mattia Romani, Joyashree Roy, Eduardo Paes Saboia, Claudia Sadoff, Salman Salman, Jamil Salmi, Klas Sandler, Apurva Sanghi, Shyam Saran, Ashok Sarkar, John Scanlon, Hartwig Schäfer, Imme Scholz, Sebastian Scholz, Claudia Sepúlveda, Diwesh Sharan, Bernard Sheahan, Susan Shen, Xiaoyu Shi, Jas Singh, Emmanuel Skoufias, Leopold Some, Richard Spencer, Frank Sperling, Sir Nicholas Stern, Thomas Sterner, Andre Stochniol, Rachel Strader, Charlotte Streck, Ashok Subramanian, Vivek Suri, Joanna Syroka, Mark Tadross, Patrice Talla Takoukam, Robert P. Taylor, Dipti Thapa, Augusto de la Torre, Jorge E.

Uquillas Rodas, Maria Vagliasindi, Hector Valdes, Rowena A. Valmonte-Santos, Trond Vedeld, Victor Vergara, Walter Vergara, Tamsin Vernon, Juergen Voegele, Paul Waide, Alfred Jay Watkins, Kevin Watkins, Charlene Watson, Sam Wedderburn, Bill Westermeyer, David Wheeler, Johannes Woelcke, Henning Wuester, Winston Yu, Shahid Yusuf, N. Robert Zagha, Sumaya Ahmed Zakieldeen, and Jürgen Zattler.

We are grateful to persons in locations across the world who participated in consultations and provided comments. In addition, we thank guest bloggers and members of the public who commented on our blog, "Development in a Changing Climate."

Other valuable assistance was provided by Gytis Kanchas, Polly Means, Nacer Mohamed Megherbi, Swati Mishra, Prianka Nandy, Rosita Najmi, and Kaye Schultz. Anita Gordon, Merrell J. Tuck-Primdahl, and Kavita Watsa assisted the team with consultations and dissemination.

Despite efforts to compile a comprehensive list, some who contributed may have been inadvertently omitted. The team apologizes for any oversights and reiterates its gratitude to all who contributed to this Report.

This Report draws on a wide range of World Bank documents and on numerous outside sources. Background papers commissioned for the Report are available either on the World Wide Web www.worldbank.org/wdr2010 or through the World Development Report office. The views expressed in these papers are not necessarily those of the World Bank or of this Report.

Background papers

Atkinson, Giles, Kirk Hamilton, Giovanni Ruta, and Dominique van der Mensbrugghe. "Trade in 'Virtual Carbon': Empirical Results and Implications for Policy."

Barnett, Jon, and Michael Webber. "Accommodating Migration to Promote Adaptation to Climate Change."

Benitez, Daniel, Ricardo Fuentes Nieva, Tomas Serebrisky, and Quentin Wodon. "Assessing the Impact of Climate Change Policies in Infrastructure Service Delivery: A Note on Affordability and Access."

Brown, Casey, Robyn Meeks, Yonas Ghile, and Kenneth Hunu. "An Empirical Analysis of the Effects of Climate Variables on National Level Economic Growth."

Caney, Simon. "Ethics and Climate Change."

Dubash, Navroz. "Climate Change Through a Development Lens."

Figueres, Christiana, and Charlotte Streck. "Great Expectations: Enhanced Financial Mechanisms for Post-2012 Mitigation."

Foa, Roberto. "Social and Governance Dimensions of Climate Change: Implications for Policy."

Hallegatte, Stéphane, Patrice Dumas, and Jean-Charles Hourcade. "A note on the economic cost of climate change and the rationale to limit it below 2°K."

Hourcade, Jean-Charles, and Franck Nadaud. "Long-run Energy Forecasting in Retrospect."

Irwin, Tim. "Implications for Climate-change Policy of Research on Cooperation in Social Dilemmas."

Liverani, Andrea. "Climate Change and Individual Behavior: Considerations for Policy."

MacCracken, Mike. "Beyond Mitigation: Potential Options for Counter-Balancing the Climatic and Environmental Consequences of the Rising Concentrations of Greenhouse Gases."

Meadowcroft, James. "Climate Change Governance."

Mechler, Reinhard, Stefan Hochrainer, Georg Pflug, Keith Williges, and Alexander Lotsch. "Assessing Financial Vulnerability to Climate-Related Natural Hazards."

Norgaard, Kari. "Cognitive and Behavioral Challenges in Responding to Climate Change."

Ostrom, Elinor. "A Polycentric Approach for Coping with Climate Change."

Ranger, Nicola, Robert Muir-Wood, and Satya Priya. "Assessing Extreme Climate Hazards and Options for Risk Mitigation and Adaptation in the Developing World."

Shalizi, Zmarak, and Franck Lecocq. "Climate Change and the Economics of Targeted Mitigation in Sectors with Long-lived Capital Stock."

Strand, Jon. "'Revenue Management' Effects of Climate Policy-Related Financial Flows."

Thornton, Philip. "The Inter-linkages between Rapid Growth in Livestock Production, Climate Change, and the Impacts on Water Resources, Land Use, and Deforestation."

Watson, Charlene, and Samuel Fankhauser. "The Clean Development Mechanism: Too Flexible to Produce Sustainable Development Benefits?"

Background notes

Benitez, Daniel, and Natsuko Toba. "Transactional Costs and Marginal Abatement Costs." "Review of Energy Efficiency Policies." "Promoting Energy Efficiency: Issues and Lessons Learned."

Beringer, Tim, and Wolfgang Lucht. "Second Generation Bioenergy Potential."

Estache, Antonio. "Public Private Partnerships for Climate Change Investments: Learning from the Infrastructure PPP Experience."

———. "What Do We Know Collectively about the Need to Deal with Climate Change?"

———. "How Should the Nexus between Economic and Environmental Regulation Work for Infrastructure Services?"

Füssel, Hans-Martin. "Review and Quantitative Analysis of Indices of Climate Change Exposure, Adaptive Capacity, Sensitivity, and Impacts."

———. "The Risks of Climate Change: A Synthesis of New Scientific Knowledge Since the Finalization of the IPCC Fourth Assessment Report."

Gerten, Dieter, and Stefanie Rost. "Climate Change Impacts on Agricultural Water Stress and Impact Mitigation Potential."

Haberl, Helmut, Karl-Heinz Erb, Fridolin Krausmann, Veronika Gaube, Simone Gingrich, and Christof Plutzar. "Quantification of the Intensity of Global Human Use of Ecosystems for Biomass Production."

Hamilton, Kirk. "Delayed Participation in a Global Climate Agreement."

Harris, Nancy, Stephen Hagen, Sean Grimland, William Salas, Sassan Saatchi, and Sandra Brown. "Improvement in Estimates of Land-Based Emissions."

Heyder, Ursula. "Ecosystem Integrity Change as Measured by Biome Change."

Hoornweg, Daniel, Perinaz Bhada, Mila Freire, and Rutu Dave. "An Urban Focus—Cities and Climate Change."

Houghton, Richard. "Emissions of Carbon from Land Management."

Imam, Bisher. "Waters of the World."

Lotze-Campen, Hermann, Alexander Popp, Jan Philipp Dietrich, and Michael Krause. "Competition for Land between Food, Bioenergy, and Conservation."

Louati, Mohamed El Hedi. "Tunisia's Experience in Water Resource Mobilization and Management."

Meinzen-Dick, Ruth. "Community Action and Property Rights in Land and Water Management."

Müller, Christoph, Alberte Bondeau, Alexander Popp, Katharina Waha, and Marianela Fader. "Climate Change Impacts on Agricultural Yields."

Rabie, Tamer, and Kulsum Ahmed. "Climate Change and Human Health."

Ramanathan, N., I. H. Rehman, and V. Ramanathan. "Project Surya: Mitigation of Global and Regional Climate Change: Buying the Planet Time by Reducing Black Carbon, Methane, and Ozone."

Rogers, David. "Environmental Information Services and Development."

Vagliasindi, Maria. "Climate Change Uncertainty, Regulation and Private Participation in Infrastructure."

Westermeyer, William. "Observing the Climate for Development."

Glossary

Abatement / see mitigation

Adaptation: Adjustment in natural or human systems, in response to actual or expected climatic stimuli or their effects, which moderates harm or exploits beneficial opportunities. Various types of adaptation can be distinguished, including anticipatory and reactive, autonomous and planned, public and private.

Adaptation Fund: The Adaptation Fund was established to finance concrete adaptation projects and programs in developing countries that are Parties to the Kyoto Protocol. The Fund is financed with a share of proceeds from the Clean Development Mechanism (CDM) and receives funds from other sources.

Adaptive capacity: The ability of a system to adjust to climate change (including climate variability and extremes) in order to take advantage of opportunities, moderate potential damages, or cope with the consequences.

Adaptive management: A systematic process for continually improving management policies and practices by learning from the outcomes of previously employed policies and practices, through an explicitly experimental approach.

Additionality: In the CDM context this refers to whether the carbon offsets generated by a project are backed up by emission reductions additional to those that otherwise would occur without the financial and technical incentive of the CDM mechanism. An activity's emissions as they would have been in the absence of the CDM project constitute the baseline against which additionality is measured. The creation and

sale of offsets from a CDM project lacking additionality may lead to an increase in emissions to the atmosphere, relative to the emissions released if the potential purchaser of the offset instead directly reduced their own emissions at home.

Afforestation: Planting a new forest on land that has either never or not recently been forested.

Annex I parties: Annex I parties include the industrial countries that were members of the OECD (Organization for Economic Co-operation and Development) in 1992, plus countries with economies in transition (the EIT Parties), including the Russian Federation, the Baltic states, and several Central and Eastern European states. They have committed to limit their greenhouse gas emissions. *Non-Annex-I parties:* The group of primarily developing countries without such commitments, which instead have acknowledged general obligations to formulate and implement national programs on mitigation and adaptation.

Anthropogenic: Directly caused by human actions. For example, burning fossil fuels to supply energy leads to anthropogenic GHG emissions, whereas natural decay of vegetation leads to non-anthropogenic emissions.

Assigned amount units (AAUs): The total volume greenhouse gases—measured in tons CO_2e—that each Annex I country is allowed to emit during the first phase of the Kyoto Protocol.

Bali Action Plan: The two year plan launched at the 2007 United Nations Climate Change Conference in Bali, Indonesia to negotiate long-term cooperative action on climate change beyond 2010 and to reach an agreed outcome in Denmark in late 2009. The plan has four pillars: mitigation, adaptation, finance, and technology.

Biodiversity: Biodiversity is the variety of all forms of life, including genes, populations, species, and ecosystems.

Biofuel: A fuel produced from organic matter or combustible oils produced by plants. Examples of biofuel include alcohol, black liquor from the paper-manufacturing process, wood, and soybean oil. *Second-generation biofuels:* Products such as ethanol and biodiesel derived from woody material by chemical or biological processes.

Cap and trade: An approach to controlling pollution emissions that combines market and regulation. An overall emissions limit (cap) is set for a specific time period and individual parties receive permits (either through grant or auction) giving them the legal right to emit pollution up to the quantity of permits they hold. Parties are free to trade emission permits, and there will be gains from trade if different parties have different marginal pollution abatement costs.

Carbon capture and storage (CCS): A process consisting of separation of CO_2 from industrial and energy-related sources, transport to a storage location, and long-term isolation from the atmosphere.

Carbon dioxide (CO_2): A naturally occurring gas that is also a by-product of burning fossil fuels (fossil carbon deposits such as oil, gas, and coal), of burning biomass, of land-use changes, and of several industrial processes. It is the principal anthropogenic greenhouse gas that affects the Earth's radiative balance. It is the reference gas against which other greenhouse gases are measured and therefore has a Global Warming Potential of 1.

Carbon dioxide equivalent (CO_2e): A way of expressing the quantity of a mixture of different greenhouse gases. Equal amounts of the different greenhouse gases produce different contributions to global warming; for example, an emission of methane to the atmosphere has about 20 times the warming effect as the same emission of carbon dioxide. CO_2e expresses the quantity of a mixture of greenhouse gases in terms of the quantity of CO_2 that would produce the same amount of warming as would the mixture of gases. Both emissions (flows) and concentrations (stocks) of greenhouse gases can be expressed in CO_2e. A quantity of greenhouse gases can also be expressed in terms of its carbon equivalent, by multiplying the quantity of CO_2e by 12/44.

Carbon fertilization: The enhancement of the growth of plants as a result of increased atmospheric carbon dioxide (CO_2) concentration. Depending on their mechanism of photosynthesis, certain types of plants are more sensitive to changes in atmospheric CO_2 concentration.

Carbon footprint: The amount of carbon emissions associated with a particular activity or all the activities of a person or organization. The carbon footprint can be measured in many ways, and may include indirect emissions generated in the whole chain of production of inputs into an activity.

Carbon intensity: Typically, the amount of economywide emissions of carbon or CO_2e per unit of GDP, that is, the carbon intensity of GDP. May also refer to the carbon emitted per dollar of gross production or dollar of value added by a given firm or sector. Also used to describe the amount of carbon emitted per unit of energy or fuels consumed, that is, the carbon intensity of energy, which depends on the energy sources, fuel mix, and efficiency of technologies. The carbon intensity of GDP is simply the product of the economywide average carbon-intensity of energy and energy-intensity of GDP.

Carbon lock-in: Actions which perpetuate a given level of carbon emissions. For example, expansion of roads and highways will tend to lock in carbon emissions from fossil fuels for decades unless there are countervailing policies to limit fuel use or control vehicle use.

Carbon sink: Any process, activity or mechanism which removes carbon dioxide from the atmosphere. Forests and other vegetation are considered sinks because they remove carbon dioxide through photosynthesis.

Clean Development Mechanism (CDM): A mechanism under the Kyoto Protocol through which developed countries may finance greenhouse-gas emission reduction or removal projects in developing countries, and thereby receive credits for doing so which they may apply towards meeting mandatory limits on their own emissions. The CDM allows greenhouse gas emission reduction projects to take place in countries that are signatories but have no emission targets under the Kyoto Protocol.

Climate sensitivity: The change in global mean surface temperature in response to a doubling of the atmospheric CO_2e concentration. A key parameter for translating projected emissions into projections of warming and thus impacts.

Consumptive use of water: Water removed from available supplies without return to a water resources system (for example, water used in manufacturing, agriculture, and food preparation that is not returned to a stream, river, or water treatment plant).

Coping capacity: The ability of people, organizations and systems, using available skills and resources, to face and manage adverse conditions, emergencies or disasters. Refers to short-term capacity in response to an event, whereas adaptive capacity refers to the long-term ability to make systematic changes to reduce the impact of climate change.

Damage function: In the climate change context, the relation between changes in the climate and reductions in production or consumption, or losses of assets (potentially including ecosystems or human health).

Deadweight loss: A cost that generates no benefit.

Discount rate: The rate at which individuals or enterprises trade off present versus future consumption or wellbeing, usually expressed as a percentage.

Downscaling: A method that derives local- to regional-scale (10 to 100 km) information from larger-scale (200+ km) climate-projection models or data analyses. Dynamic downscaling uses high resolution models for a particular region run within a large-scale global model; statistical downscaling uses statistical relationships that link the large-scale atmospheric variables with local or regional climate variables.

Early warning system: A mechanism to generate and disseminate timely and meaningful warning information to enable individuals, communities and organizations threatened by a hazard to prepare and to act appropriately and in sufficient time to reduce the possibility of harm or loss.

Ecosystem services: The ecosystem processes or functions that have value to individuals or society, for example, the provision of food, water purification, and recreational opportunities.

Evapotranspiration: An important part of the water cycle, it is the combined process of evaporation from the Earth's surface (from sources such as the soil and bodies of water) and transpiration from vegetation (loss of water as vapor from plants, primarily through their leaves).

Forest degradation: The reduction in forest biomass through unsustainable harvest or land-use practices including logging, fire, and other anthropogenic disturbances.

Geoengineering: Geoengineering is the large-scale engineering of our environment to combat or to counteract the effects of climate change. Proposed measures include injecting particles into the upper atmosphere to reflect sunlight and the fertilization of the oceans with iron to increase uptake of CO_2 by algae.

Gini coefficient: A commonly used measure of inequality of income or wealth distribution, varying between 0 (perfect equality) and 1.

Green tax: A tax that aims to increase environmental quality by taxing actions which harm the environment.

Greenhouse gas (GHG): Any of the atmospheric gases that cause climate change by trapping heat from the sun in Earth's atmosphere—producing the greenhouse effect. The most common greenhouse gases are carbon dioxide (CO_2), methane (CH_4), nitrous oxide (N_2O), ozone (O_3), and water vapor (H_2O).

Innovation: The creation, assimilation, or exploitation of a new or significantly improved good or service, process, or method.

Institutions: Structures and mechanisms of social order and cooperation governing the behavior of a set of individuals.

Integrated assessment: A method of analysis that combines results and models from the physical, biological, economic and social sciences, and the interactions between these components, in a consistent framework, to project the consequences of climate change and the policy responses to it.

Intellectual property rights (IPRs): Legal property rights over artistic and commercial creations of the mind, including patents on new technologies, and the corresponding fields of law.

Intergovernmental Panel on Climate Change (IPCC): Established in 1988 by the World Meteorological Organization and the United Nations Environment Program, the IPCC surveys worldwide scientific and technical literature and publishes assessment reports that are widely recognized as the most credible existing sources of information on climate change. The IPCC also prepares methodologies and responds to specific requests from the subsidiary bodies of the United Nations Framework Convention on Climate Change (UNFCCC). The IPCC is independent of the UNFCCC.

Kyoto Protocol: An agreement under the United Nations Framework Convention on Climate Change (UNFCCC) that was adopted in 1997 in Kyoto, Japan, by the parties to the UNFCCC. It contains legally binding commitments to reduce greenhouse gas emissions by developed countries.

Leakage: In the climate change context, the process whereby emissions outside of a mitigation project area increase as a result of emission reduction activities inside the project area, thus reducing the effectiveness of the project.

Land use, land-use change, and forestry (LULUCF): A set of activities including human-induced land use, land-use change, and forestry activities which lead to both emissions and removals of greenhouse gases from the atmosphere. A category used in reporting greenhouse gas inventories.

Maladaptation: Activities or actions that increase vulnerability to climate change.

Market-pull: The allocation of research and development (R&D) resources based on market demand for products and services, rather than scientific interest or top-down government policies.

Mitigation: A human intervention to reduce the emissions or enhance the sinks of greenhouse gases.

National Adaptation Programs of Action (NAPAs): Documents prepared by least developed countries (LDCs) identifying the activities to address urgent and immediate needs for adapting to climate change.

No regrets project: In the climate change context, a project that would generate net social and/or economic benefits irrespective of whether the project affects the climate or whether the climate affects the project.

Polluter pays principle: A principle in environmental law whereby the polluter must bear the cost of the pollution. Thus the polluter is responsible for the cost of measures to prevent and control pollution.

Positive feedback: When one variable in a system triggers changes in a second variable that in turn affect the original variable; a positive feedback intensifies the initial effect, and a negative feedback reduces the effect.

Precautionary principle: A principle that holds that, in the absence of scientific certainty that serious or irreversible harm would not occur as a result of an action or policy, the burden of proof lies with those that favor the action or policy. In the United Nations Framework on Climate Change (UNFCCC), it is a provision under Article 3 stipulating that the parties should take precautionary measures to anticipate, prevent, or minimize the causes of climate change and mitigate its adverse effects, and that a lack of full scientific certainty about possibly serious or irreversible damages should not be used as a reason to postpone such measures—taking into account that policies and measures to deal with climate change should be cost-effective in order to ensure global benefits at the lowest possible cost.

Public good: A good whose consumption is non-exclusive (so that it is impossible to prevent anyone from enjoying the benefit) and non-rival (so that the enjoyment of the benefit by one individual does not diminish the quantity of benefits available to others). Climate change mitigation is an example of a public good as it would be impossible to prevent any one individual or state from enjoying the benefit of a stabilized climate, and the enjoyment of this stabilized climate by one individual or state would not diminish the ability of others to benefit from it.

RDD&D: Research, development, demonstration, and deployment of new methods, technologies, equipment, and products.

Reduced Emissions from Deforestation and forest Degradation (REDD): REDD refers to a suite of actions aimed at reducing greenhouse gas emissions from forested land. Financial incentives for REDD are potentially a part of the policy response to climate change.

Reforestation: Planting of forests on lands that were previously forested but that have been converted to another use.

Reinsurance: The transfer of a portion of primary insurance risks to a secondary tier of insurers (reinsurers); essentially "insurance for insurers."

Resilience: The ability of a social or ecological system to absorb disturbances while retaining the same basic structure and ways of functioning, the capacity for self-organization, and the capacity to adapt to stress and change.

Return period: The average time between occurrences of a defined event.

Risk assessment: A standardized methodology consisting of risk identification, risk quantification, risk reduction, and risk mitigation.

Robust decision making: In the face of uncertainty, choosing not the measure or policy that would be optimal under the most likely future world, but the one that would be acceptable across a range of possible futures. The process involves evaluating options to minimize expected regret across a variety of models, assumptions, and loss functions, rather than to maximize returns under a unique likely future.

Safety net: Mechanisms that aim to protect people from the impact of shocks such as flood, drought, unemployment, illness, or the death of a household's primary income earner.

Sequestration: In the climate context, the process of removing carbon from the atmosphere and storing it in reservoirs such as new forests, soil carbon or underground storage. *Biological sequestration:* The removal of CO_2 from the atmosphere and storing it in organic matter through land-use change, afforestation, reforestation, carbon storage in landfills, and practices that enhance soil carbon in agriculture.

Social learning: Social learning is the process by which people learn new behavior through overt reinforcement or punishment, or via observing other social actors in their environment. If people observe positive, desired outcomes for others exhibiting a particular behavior, they are more likely to model, imitate, and adopt the behavior themselves.

Social norms: Implicit or explicit values, beliefs, and rules adopted by a group to self-regulate behavior through peer pressure; the yardstick individuals use to assess what is acceptable or unacceptable behavior.

Social protection: The set of public interventions aimed at supporting the poorer and more vulnerable members of society, as well as helping individuals, families, and communities manage risk—for example, unemployment insurance programs, income support, and social services.

Solar photovoltaics (PV): The field of technology and research related to the conversion of sunlight, including ultra violet radiation, directly into electricity; the technology applied in the creation and use of solar cells, which make up solar panels.

SRES scenarios: A set of descriptions or storylines of possible futures used in climate change related modeling developed for the IPCC. The scenarios are used to project future emissions based on assumptions about changes in population, technology, and societal development. Four scenario families comprise the SRES scenario set: A1, A2, B1 and B2. A1 represents a future world of very rapid economic growth, global population that peaks in mid-century and declines thereafter, and rapid introduction of new and more efficient technologies. A2 represents a very heterogeneous world with continuously increasing global population and regionally oriented economic growth that is more fragmented and slower than in other storylines. B1 represents a convergent world with the same global population as in the A1 storyline but with rapid changes in economic structures toward a service and information economy, reductions in material intensity, and the introduction of clean and resource-efficient technologies. Finally, B2 represents a world in which the emphasis is on local solutions to economic, social, and environmental sustainability, with continuously increasing population (lower than A2) and intermediate economic development.

Stationarity: The idea that natural systems fluctuate within an unchanging envelope of variability, delimited by the range of past experiences.

Supplementarity: The Kyoto Protocol states that emissions trading and Joint Implementation activities are to be supplemental to domestic policies (e.g. energy taxes, fuel efficiency standards) taken by developed countries to reduce their GHG emissions. Under some proposed definitions of supplementarity, developed countries could be required to achieve a given share of their reduction targets domestically. This is a subject for further negotiation and clarification by the parties.

Technology transfer: The process of sharing of skills, knowledge, technologies, and methods of manufacture to ensure that scientific and technological developments are accessible to a wider range of users.

Technology-push: The allocation of R&D resources motivated largely by inherent scientific interest, rather than market demand.

Threshold: In the climate change context, the level above which sudden or rapid change occurs.

Transaction costs: Costs associated with the exchange of goods or services that are additional to the monetary cost or price of the good or service. Examples include search and information costs or policing and enforcement costs.

Uncertainty: An expression of the degree to which a value (such as the future state of the climate system) is unknown. Uncertainty can result from lack of information or from disagreement about what is known or even knowable. It may have many types of sources, from quantifiable errors in the data to uncertain projections of human behavior. Uncertainty can therefore be represented by quantitative measures, for example, a range of values calculated by various models, or by qualitative statements, for example, reflecting expert judgment. However, in economics, uncertainty refers to Knightian uncertainty, which is immeasurable. This is in contrast to risk, wherein the occurrence of certain events is associated with a knowable probability distribution.

United Nations Framework Convention on Climate Change (UNFCCC): A convention adopted in May 1992 with the ultimate objective of the "stabilization of greenhouse gas concentrations in the atmosphere at a level that would prevent dangerous anthropogenic interference with the climate system."

Virtual water: The amount of water that is directly or indirectly consumed in the production of a good or service.

Vulnerability (also climate vulnerability): The degree to which a system is susceptible to, and unable to cope with, adverse effects of climate change, including climate variability and extremes. Vulnerability is a function of the character, magnitude, and rate of climate change and variability to which a system is exposed, as well as the system's sensitivity and adaptive capacity.

Weather derivatives: Financial instruments to reduce risk associated with adverse weather conditions by, for example, providing for payments associated with a specified weather event (such as an unusually cool or hot month of August).

Weather-index insurance: Insurance where the indemnity (or payout) is based on the realization of pre-agreed values of an index of a specific weather parameter, measured over a pre-specified period of time, at a particular weather station. The insurance can be structured to protect against index realizations that are either so high or so low that they are expected to cause crop losses. The indemnity is calculated based on a pre-agreed sum insured per unit of the index (e.g. US$/millimeter of rainfall).

Win-win-(win): In the Report, this refers to measures that are beneficial for adaptation and mitigation (and development).

Selected Indicators

Selected world development indicators

Table A1 Energy-related emissions and carbon intensity

	Carbon dioxide (CO_2) emissions							Non-CO_2 emissions (CH_4, N_2O)		Carbon intensity			
	Annual total		Change	Per capita		Share of annual world total	Cumulative emissions since 1850	Annual total		Energy		Income	
	Metric tons (millions)		%	Metric tons		%	Metric tons (billions)	Metric tons of CO_2 equivalent (millions)		Metric tons of CO_2 per ton of oil equivalent		Metric tons of CO_2 per thousand $ of GDP	
	1990	2005	1990–2005[a]	1990	2005	2005	1850–2005	1990	2005	1990	2005	1990	2005
Algeria	68	91	33.3	2.7	2.8	0.34	2.8	9.6	15.5	2.86	2.63	0.44	0.39
Argentina	105	142	35.3	3.2	3.7	0.54	5.6	10.0	19.1	2.28	2.24	0.43	0.34
Australia	260	377	45.0	15.2	18.5	1.42	12.5	27.5	38.8	2.97	3.12	0.65	0.58
Austria	58	77	33.6	7.5	9.4	0.29	4.3	1.4	1.4	2.31	2.27	0.28	0.28
Belarus	108	61	–43.8	10.6	6.2	0.23	4.0	2.9	3.3	2.55	2.26	1.65	0.73
Belgium	109	112	2.7	10.9	10.7	0.42	10.4	2.8	2.4	2.19	1.81	0.44	0.34
Brazil	195	334	70.8	1.3	1.8	1.26	8.8	10.9	14.7	1.40	1.54	0.18	0.21
Bulgaria	75	46	–38.7	8.6	6.0	0.17	3.0	6.0	4.8	2.61	2.30	1.13	0.64
Canada	433	552	27.5	15.6	17.1	2.08	23.8	41.0	57.8	2.07	2.02	0.58	0.49
Chile	32	59	81.7	2.5	3.6	0.22	1.8	2.4	3.4	2.30	1.99	0.37	0.30
China	2,211	5,060	128.9	1.9	3.9	19.06	94.3	192.9	218.7	2.56	2.94	1.77	0.95
Colombia	45	61	34.0	1.4	1.4	0.23	2.2	5.1	7.1	1.83	2.12	0.26	0.23
Czech Republic	154	118	–23.3	14.9	11.5	0.44	10.7[b]	10.9	7.2	3.14	2.61	0.92	0.57
Denmark	51	48	–5.9	9.9	8.8	0.18	3.4	0.9	1.6	2.84	2.43	0.39	0.26
Egypt, Arab Rep. of	81	149	83.3	1.5	2.0	0.56	3.2	8.5	16.0	2.54	2.43	0.45	0.45
Finland	55	55	0.7	11.0	10.6	0.21	2.3	1.4	1.8	1.92	1.61	0.47	0.35
France	355	388	9.3	6.3	6.4	1.46	31.7	16.3	13.2	1.56	1.41	0.25	0.21
Germany	968	814	–15.9	12.2	9.9	3.06	117.8[c]	47.8	28.9	2.72	2.36	0.49	0.32
Greece	71	96	35.6	6.9	8.6	0.36	2.6	4.6	5.8	3.18	3.08	0.34	0.29
Hungary	71	58	–18.3	6.8	5.7	0.22	4.1	6.0	5.4	2.47	2.07	0.55	0.34
India	597	1,149	92.6	0.7	1.1	4.33	28.6	53.1	89.2	1.87	2.14	0.58	0.47
Indonesia	151	349	131.7	0.8	1.6	1.31	6.8	41.2	58.8	1.46	1.98	0.41	0.49
Iran, Islamic Rep. of	178	431	142.3	3.3	6.2	1.62	8.6	24.4	64.9	2.58	2.73	0.52	0.67
Iraq	61	99	62.0	3.3	3.5	0.37	2.2	4.1	3.3	3.21	3.31	..	..
Ireland	31	44	41.7	8.8	10.5	0.16	1.6	1.3	1.8	3.00	2.89	0.50	0.28
Israel	34	60	78.3	7.2	8.6	0.23	1.5	0.2	0.4	2.77	2.83	0.41	0.38
Italy	398	454	14.0	7.0	7.7	1.71	17.9	16.8	18.5	2.69	2.44	0.30	0.28
Japan	1,058	1,214	14.8	8.6	9.5	4.57	46.1	10.0	7.1	2.38	2.30	0.33	0.31
Kazakhstan	233	155	–33.6	14.3	10.2	0.58	9.9[d]	28.8	13.2	3.17	2.73	2.01	1.17
Korea, Dem. Rep. of	114	73	–35.5	5.6	3.1	0.28	5.9[e]	26.9	27.3	3.43	3.42	..	..
Korea, Rep. of	227	449	97.6	5.3	9.3	1.69	9.0[e]	6.6	7.7	2.43	2.11	0.50	0.44
Kuwait	27	76	184.0	12.7	30.1	0.29	1.6	5.4	9.1	3.36	2.71	..	0.67
Libya	37	47	28.8	8.4	7.9	0.18	1.3	..	..	3.16	2.65	..	0.63
Malaysia	52	138	163.9	2.9	5.4	0.52	2.7[e]	..	..	2.24	2.09	0.43	0.46
Mexico	293	393	33.9	3.5	3.8	1.48	12.5	47.9	86.1	2.38	2.22	0.38	0.33
Morocco	20	41	111.2	0.8	1.4	0.16	0.9	..	..	2.72	3.08	0.29	0.39
Netherlands	158	183	15.6	10.6	11.2	0.69	8.3	3.3	2.6	2.36	2.22	0.41	0.32
Nigeria	68	97	43.0	0.7	0.7	0.36	2.3	25.8	66.2	0.95	0.92	0.49	0.39
Norway	30	38	27.9	7.0	8.2	0.14	1.9	0.9	1.7	1.39	1.15	0.22	0.17
Pakistan	61	118	94.1	0.6	0.8	0.45	2.4[e]	7.5	12.5	1.40	1.55	0.34	0.35
Philippines	36	77	113.1	0.6	0.9	0.29	1.9	3.6	2.6	1.38	1.76	0.24	0.31
Poland	349	296	–15.3	9.2	7.8	1.11	22.6	23.5	20.9	3.50	3.19	1.14	0.57
Portugal	40	63	59.1	4.0	6.0	0.24	1.7	1.1	1.7	2.30	2.32	0.26	0.30
Qatar	14	44	202.1	30.8	54.6	0.16	0.9	..	..	2.21	2.71	..	0.77
Romania	167	91	–45.5	7.2	4.2	0.34	6.9	24.5	13.2	2.67	2.37	0.91	0.45
Russian Federation	2,194	1,544	–29.6	14.8	10.8	5.81	92.5[d]	406.4	206.4	2.50	2.35	1.17	0.91
Saudi Arabia	169	320	89.6	10.3	13.8	1.21	7.4	2.3	3.9	2.75	2.28	0.54	0.65
Serbia	59	50	–14.3	7.8	6.8	0.19	..	..	..	3.02	3.13	..	0.78
Singapore	29	43	49.7	9.5	10.1	0.16	1.4	0.2	0.8	2.16	1.39	0.39	0.23
Slovak Republic	57	38	–32.8	10.8	7.1	0.14	3.2[b]	1.7	1.6	2.67	2.03	0.86	0.45
South Africa	255	331	29.9	7.2	7.1	1.25	14.1	10.6	12.5	2.79	2.59	0.93	0.83
Spain	208	342	64.7	5.3	7.9	1.29	10.0	5.3	6.6	2.28	2.36	0.27	0.29
Sweden	53	51	–4.5	6.2	5.7	0.19	4.1	2.1	2.2	1.12	0.98	0.25	0.18
Switzerland	41	45	9.0	6.2	6.1	0.17	2.4	0.7	0.6	1.67	1.67	0.18	0.17
Syrian Arab Republic	32	48	51.6	2.5	2.6	0.18	1.2	..	..	2.72	2.62	0.85	0.64
Thailand	79	214	172.6	1.4	3.4	0.81	3.9	13.0	19.2	1.79	2.13	0.35	0.48
Turkey	129	219	70.3	2.3	3.0	0.82	5.3	26.1	56.6	2.43	2.56	0.31	0.29
Turkmenistan	47	42	–11.3	12.8	8.6	0.16	2.1[d]	19.7	46.4	2.38	2.51	..	..
Ukraine	681	297	–56.4	13.1	6.3	1.12	22.6[d]	139.7	118.4	2.68	2.07	1.63	1.13
United Arab Emirates	52	112	114.1	28.0	27.3	0.42	2.2	20.1	40.0	2.26	2.45	0.60	0.57
United Kingdom	558	533	–4.4	9.7	8.8	2.01	68.1	36.9	27.0	2.63	2.27	0.42	0.28
United States	4,874	5,841	19.9	19.5	19.7	22.00	324.9	298.8	242.8	2.53	2.49	0.61	0.47
Uzbekistan	120	110	–8.4	5.9	4.2	0.41	6.9[d]	28.1	40.3	2.59	2.34	2.93	2.10
Venezuela, R. B. de	112	150	33.4	5.7	5.6	0.56	5.3	30.5	46.3	2.56	2.48	0.59	0.57
Vietnam	17	81	376.5	0.3	1.0	0.31	1.5[e]	3.5	4.9	0.70	1.58	0.28	0.45
World	20,693t	26,544t	28.3w	4.0w	4.2w	100.00w	1,169.1s	1,861.0t	1,978.9t	2.39w	2.35w	0.57w	0.47w
Low income	549	707	28.9	0.7	0.6	2.66	24.0	115.5	256.4	1.38	1.26	0.46	0.38
Middle income	9,150	12,631	38.0	2.6	3.0	47.59	395.1	1,168.3	1,279.4	2.41	2.49	0.80	0.61
High income	10,999	13,207	20.1	11.8	12.7	49.75	750.1	577.2	557.1	2.44	2.32	0.47	0.39
European Union 15	3,122	3,271	4.8	8.5	8.5	12.32	284.8	142.1	115.7	2.36	2.11	0.36	0.28
OECD	11,121	12,946	16.4	10.7	11.1	48.77	764.7	644.6	651.4	2.46	2.33	0.47	0.37

a. Denotes percent change in CO_2 emissions between 1990 and 2005. b. Share of cumulative emissions for Czech Republic and Slovak Republic prior to 1992 were calculated based on their share of total combined emissions in during 1992–2006. c. Share of cumulative emissions for Germany prior to 1991 were calculated based on total for German Democratic Republic and the Federal Republic of Germany and were combined with emissions for Germany between 1991 and 2006. d. Share of cumulative emissions for Belarus, Russian Federation, Kazakhstan, Turkmenistan, Ukraine, and Uzbekistan prior to 1992 were calculated based on the share of combined emissions of former Soviet Union countries during 1992–2006. e. Emissions for the Democratic Republic of Korea and the Republic of Korea are based on data for United Korea prior to 1950. Emissions for Pakistan and Bangladesh are based on data for East and West Pakistan before 1971. Emissions for Malaysia and include Malaysia's share of emissions from the Federation of Malaya. Emissions for Vietnam include emissions for the Democratic Republic of Vietnam and the Republic of South Vietnam.

Table A2 Land-based emissions

Table A2a CO$_2$ emissions from deforestation

	Annual average				Average share of total
	Total emissions		Per capita		
	Metric tons (millions)	Rank	Metric tons	Rank	%
	1990–2005[a]	1990–2005[a]	1990–2005[a]	1990–2005[a]	1990–2005[a]
Argentina	33	25	0.9	48	0.6
Bolivia	139	7	15.2	1	2.5
Brazil	1,830	1	9.8	5	32.4
Cambodia	84	10	6.0	13	1.5
Cameroon	70	12	3.9	18	1.2
Canada	70	12	2.2	29	1.2
China	57	18	0.0	83	1.0
Congo, Dem. Rep. of	176	4	3.0	24	3.1
Ecuador	84	10	6.5	12	1.5
Guatemala	62	16	4.9	17	1.1
Honduras	48	20	7.0	10	0.8
Indonesia	1,459	2	6.6	11	25.9
Malaysia	139	7	5.4	15	2.5
Mexico	40	23	0.4	63	0.7
Myanmar	158	5	3.3	20	2.8
Nigeria	158	5	1.1	40	2.8
Papua New Guinea	44	21	7.2	8	0.8
Peru	70	12	2.6	27	1.2
Philippines	70	12	0.8	50	1.2
Russian Federation	58	17	0.4	61	1.0
Tanzania	51	19	1.3	35	0.9
Turkey	34	24	0.5	58	0.6
Venezuela, R. B. de	187	3	7.0	9	3.3
Zambia	106	9	9.3	6	1.9
Zimbabwe	40	22	3.1	22	0.7

a. Data are an average for the period 1990–2005.

Table A2b Non-CO$_2$ emissions (Methane (CH$_4$), Nitrous Oxide (N$_2$O)) from agriculture

	Annual total		Share of total	Per capita			
	Metric tons of CO$_2$ equivalent (millions)		%	Metric tons of CO$_2$ equivalent		Rank	
	1990	2005	2005	1990	2005	1990	2005
Argentina	114	139	2.3	3.5	3.6	6	7
Australia	97	110	1.8	5.7	5.4	4	4
Bangladesh	60	80	1.3	0.5	0.5	77	70
Bolivia	22	46	0.8	3.3	5.0	7	5
Brazil	426	591	9.7	2.9	3.2	8	8
Canada	57	73	1.2	2.1	2.3	15	10
China	905	1,113	18.3	0.8	0.9	62	48
Colombia	61	89	1.5	1.8	2.1	19	11
Congo, Dem. Rep. of	36	75	1.2	0.9	1.3	53	21
Ethiopia	39	55	0.9	0.8	0.7	60	58
France	110	103	1.7	1.9	1.7	18	15
Germany	110	84	1.4	1.4	1.0	32	37
India	330	403	6.6	0.4	0.4	84	83
Indonesia	106	132	2.2	0.6	0.6	73	66
Mexico	67	77	1.3	0.8	0.7	61	57
Myanmar	50	78	1.3	1.2	1.6	38	16
Nigeria	75	115	1.9	0.8	0.8	63	52
Pakistan	58	79	1.3	0.5	0.5	76	73
Russian Federation	222	118	1.9	1.5	0.8	25	50
Thailand	79	89	1.5	1.4	1.4	27	18
Turkey	80	76	1.3	1.4	1.1	29	31
United Kingdom	54	48	0.8	0.9	0.8	57	54
United States	427	442	7.3	1.7	1.5	20	17
Venezuela, R. B. de	47	52	0.9	2.4	1.9	11	12
Vietnam	48	65	1.1	0.7	0.8	67	55

Table A3 Total primary energy supply

	Total primary energy supply (TPES)								Electricity consumption		
	Annual total		Share of fossil fuels in TPES			Share of renewable energy in TPES		Share of nuclear in TPES	Per capita		Electrification rate
			% of total			% of total					
	Tons of oil equivalent (millions)		Coal	Natural gas	Oil	Hydro, solar, wind, and geothermal	Biomass and waste	% of total	kilowatt-hours	% change	% of population
	1990	2006	2006	2006	2006	2006	2006	2006	2006	1990–2006[a]	2000–2006[b]
Albania	2.7	2.3	1.1	0.6	66.8	19.1	10.1	0.0	961	84.0	..
Algeria	23.9	36.7	1.9	65.2	32.6	0.1	0.2	0.0	870	60.6	98
Angola	6.3	10.3	0.0	6.4	27.5	2.2	63.9	0.0	153	155.5	15
Argentina	46.1	69.1	1.1	49.3	38.0	4.7	3.7	2.9	2,620	100.7	95
Armenia	7.9	2.6	0.0	53.1	15.2	6.1	0.0	26.6	1,612	−40.7	..
Australia	87.7	122.5	43.9	19.1	31.6	1.3	4.1	0.0	11,309	34.6	100
Austria	25.1	34.2	11.8	21.8	42.0	9.6	13.1	0.0	8,090	32.5	100
Azerbaijan	26.1	14.1	0.0	63.5	34.4	1.5	0.0	0.0	2,514	−2.7	..
Bahrain	4.8	8.8	0.0	75.4	24.6	0.0	0.0	0.0	12,627	92.1	99
Bangladesh	12.8	25.0	1.4	46.6	17.8	0.5	33.7	0.0	146	221.2	32
Belarus	42.3	28.6	0.1	60.3	31.5	0.0	4.9	0.0	3,322	−24.2	..
Belgium	49.7	61.0	7.8	24.6	40.1	0.1	5.9	19.9	8,688	36.2	100
Benin	1.7	2.8	0.0	0.0	37.1	0.0	61.1	0.0	69	104.5	22
Bolivia	2.8	5.8	0.0	27.5	55.5	3.2	13.8	0.0	485	76.9	64
Bosnia and Herzegovina	7.0	5.4	62.4	5.9	22.3	9.3	3.4	0.0	2,295	−24.6	..
Botswana	1.3	2.0	32.5	0.0	36.6	0.0	23.2	0.0	1,419	96.0	39
Brazil	140.0	224.1	5.7	7.8	40.2	13.4	29.6	1.6	2,060	41.5	97
Brunei Darussalam	1.8	2.8	0.0	73.1	26.9	0.0	0.0	0.0	8,173	87.7	99
Bulgaria	28.8	20.7	34.1	14.0	24.7	1.9	3.9	24.6	4,315	−9.3	..
Cambodia	0.0	5.0	0.0	0.0	28.4	0.1	71.3	0.0	88	..	20
Cameroon	5.0	7.1	0.0	0.0	16.3	4.5	79.2	0.0	186	−3.1	47
Canada	209.5	269.7	10.2	29.5	35.3	11.4	4.7	9.5	16,766	3.8	100
Chile	14.1	29.8	13.3	21.9	38.3	9.9	15.9	0.0	3,207	157.3	99
China	863.2	1,878.7	64.2	2.5	18.3	2.2	12.0	0.8	2,040	299.1	99
Hong Kong, China	10.7	18.2	38.6	13.2	44.9	0.0	0.3	0.0	5,883	40.8	..
Colombia	24.7	30.2	8.2	20.3	45.0	12.2	14.9	0.0	923	11.6	86
Congo, Dem. Rep. of	11.9	17.5	1.5	0.0	3.1	3.9	92.4	0.0	96	−19.9	6
Congo, Rep. of	0.8	1.2	0.0	1.6	35.2	2.7	57.5	0.0	155	−8.2	20
Costa Rica	2.0	4.6	0.9	0.0	47.6	35.8	15.5	0.0	1,801	65.7	99
Côte d'Ivoire	4.4	7.3	0.0	18.8	16.9	1.8	63.8	0.0	182	21.3	..
Croatia	9.1	9.0	7.0	26.2	51.5	5.8	4.1	0.0	3,635	21.5	..
Cuba	16.8	10.6	0.2	8.3	79.5	0.1	11.9	0.0	1,231	1.6	96
Cyprus	1.6	2.6	1.4	0.0	96.4	1.7	0.5	0.0	5,746	78.9	..
Czech Republic	49.0	46.1	45.2	16.4	21.4	0.5	4.0	14.8	6,511	16.6	..
Denmark	17.9	20.9	26.2	21.7	39.4	2.6	12.9	0.0	6,864	15.5	100
Dominican Republic	4.1	7.8	6.4	3.5	70.4	1.5	18.0	0.0	1,309	242.1	93
Ecuador	6.1	11.2	0.0	5.0	83.2	5.5	5.2	0.0	759	58.5	90
Egypt, Arab Rep. of	32.0	62.5	1.4	44.4	50.0	1.9	2.3	0.0	1,382	100.2	98
El Salvador	2.5	4.7	0.0	0.0	44.0	24.4	31.6	0.0	721	95.9	80
Eritrea	..	0.7	0.0	0.0	26.9	0.0	73.1	0.0	49	..	20
Estonia	9.6	4.9	57.0	16.5	15.1	0.2	10.7	0.0	5,890	0.0	..
Ethiopia	15.0	22.3	0.0	0.0	8.8	1.3	90.0	0.0	38	91.5	15
Finland	28.7	37.4	13.7	10.4	28.2	2.7	20.4	15.9	17,178	37.6	100
France	227.6	272.7	4.8	14.5	33.3	1.9	4.4	43.0	7,585	26.9	100
Gabon	1.2	1.8	0.0	5.8	33.4	4.5	56.4	0.0	1,083	13.9	48
Georgia	12.3	3.3	0.3	41.3	23.5	14.0	19.3	0.0	1,549	−42.1	..
Germany	355.6	348.6	23.6	22.8	35.4	1.4	4.6	12.5	7,175	8.0	100
Ghana	5.3	9.5	0.0	0.0	31.7	5.1	63.3	0.0	304	−1.1	49
Greece	22.2	31.1	27.0	8.8	57.3	2.5	3.3	0.0	5,372	69.0	100
Guatemala	4.5	8.2	4.8	0.0	39.7	4.0	51.6	0.0	529	136.8	79
Haiti	1.6	2.6	0.0	0.0	23.3	0.9	75.8	0.0	37	−36.2	36
Honduras	2.4	4.3	2.7	0.0	50.6	5.1	41.5	0.0	642	72.2	62
Hungary	28.6	27.6	11.1	41.5	27.6	0.4	4.3	12.8	3,883	13.2	..
Iceland	2.2	4.3	1.8	0.0	22.9	75.3	0.1	0.0	31,306	94.0	100
India	319.9	565.8	39.4	5.5	24.1	1.9	28.3	0.9	503	82.3	56
Indonesia	102.8	179.1	15.5	18.6	33.0	3.7	29.2	0.0	530	228.3	54
Iran, Islamic Rep. of	68.8	170.9	0.7	51.5	46.3	0.9	0.5	0.0	2,290	134.9	97
Iraq	19.1	32.0	0.0	8.9	90.5	0.1	0.1	0.0	1,161	−7.6	15
Ireland	10.3	15.5	11.0	26.0	54.8	1.3	1.4	0.0	6,500	72.1	100
Israel	12.1	21.3	36.0	8.8	52.4	3.4	0.0	0.0	6,893	65.1	97
Italy	148.1	184.2	9.1	37.6	44.1	4.6	2.6	0.0	5,762	39.0	100
Jamaica	2.9	4.6	0.5	0.0	88.7	0.3	10.5	0.0	2,450	178.8	87
Japan	443.9	527.6	21.3	14.7	45.6	2.1	1.3	15.0	8,220	26.7	100
Jordan	3.5	7.2	0.0	28.0	70.0	1.4	0.0	0.0	1,904	81.2	100
Kazakhstan	73.6	61.4	49.3	30.6	18.8	1.1	0.1	0.0	4,293	−27.3	..
Kenya	11.2	17.9	0.4	0.0	20.2	5.9	73.6	0.0	145	16.3	14
Korea, Dem. Rep. of	33.2	21.7	86.9	0.0	3.3	5.0	4.8	0.0	797	−36.1	22
Korea, Rep.	93.4	216.5	24.3	13.3	43.2	0.2	1.1	17.9	8,063	239.8	100
Kuwait	8.0	25.3	0.0	38.3	61.7	0.0	0.0	0.0	16,314	101.2	100
Kyrgyz Republic	7.6	2.8	18.3	22.9	20.8	45.5	0.1	0.0	2,015	−12.9	..
Latvia	7.9	4.6	1.8	30.5	31.9	5.1	25.9	0.0	2,876	−15.1	..
Lebanon	2.3	4.8	2.8	0.0	91.5	1.4	2.7	0.0	2,142	354.9	100
Libya	11.5	17.8	0.0	29.4	69.7	0.0	0.9	0.0	3,688	130.1	97
Lithuania	16.2	8.5	3.1	28.7	30.3	0.4	8.8	27.0	3,232	−19.7	..
Luxembourg	3.5	4.7	2.3	26.2	63.3	0.4	1.3	0.0	16,402	20.1	100

	Total primary energy supply (TPES)							Electricity consumption		
	Annual total	Share of fossil fuels in TPES % of total			Share of renewable energy in TPES % of total		Share of nuclear in TPES	Per capita		Electrification rate
	Tons of oil equivalent (millions)	Coal	Natural gas	Oil	Hydro, solar, wind, and geothermal	Biomass and waste	% of total	kilowatt-hours	% change	% of population
	1990	2006	2006	2006	2006	2006	2006	2006	2006	1990–2006[a]	2000–2006[b]
Macedonia, FYR	2.7	2.8	45.4	2.4	35.0	5.5	6.0	0.0	3,496	25.3	..
Malaysia	23.3	68.3	12.0	44.4	38.8	0.9	4.1	0.0	3,388	187.5	98
Malta	0.8	0.9	0.0	0.0	100.0	0.0	0.0	0.0	4,975	79.1	..
Mexico	123.0	177.4	4.9	27.4	56.8	4.8	4.6	1.6	1,993	50.3	..
Moldova	9.9	3.4	2.5	66.7	19.4	0.2	2.2	0.0	1,516	−44.4	..
Mongolia	3.4	2.8	71.7	0.0	24.0	0.0	3.8	0.0	1,297	−19.1	65
Morocco	7.2	14.0	27.8	3.4	63.3	1.1	3.2	0.0	685	85.8	85
Mozambique	6.0	8.8	0.0	0.3	6.6	14.4	81.6	0.0	461	1,040.4	6
Myanmar	10.7	14.3	0.8	12.4	12.7	2.0	72.1	0.0	93	104.5	11
Namibia	..	1.5	1.9	0.0	65.4	8.8	12.7	0.0	1,545	..	34
Nepal	5.8	9.4	2.7	0.0	8.6	2.4	86.2	0.0	80	129.2	33
Netherlands	67.1	80.1	9.7	42.7	40.4	0.3	3.3	1.1	7,057	35.2	100
Netherlands Antilles	1.5	1.7	0.0	0.0	100.0	0.0	0.0	0.0	5,651	59.2	..
New Zealand	13.8	17.5	11.9	18.7	39.4	24.0	6.0	0.0	9,746	14.5	100
Nicaragua	2.1	3.5	0.0	0.0	39.0	8.7	52.2	0.0	426	44.7	69
Nigeria	70.9	105.1	0.0	8.6	11.2	0.6	79.6	0.0	116	32.6	46
Norway	21.4	26.1	2.7	18.2	34.0	39.6	5.1	0.0	24,295	4.0	100
Oman	4.6	15.4	0.0	67.6	32.4	0.0	0.0	0.0	4,457	107.3	96
Pakistan	43.4	79.3	5.4	31.6	23.9	3.5	34.9	0.8	480	73.6	54
Panama	1.5	2.8	0.0	0.0	71.7	11.1	17.4	0.0	1,506	76.4	85
Paraguay	3.1	4.0	0.0	0.0	30.5	116.5	52.0	0.0	900	78.4	86
Peru	10.0	13.6	5.9	12.3	50.3	14.0	17.4	0.0	899	64.1	72
Philippines	26.2	43.0	13.4	5.8	31.8	22.9	26.1	0.0	578	60.7	81
Poland	99.9	97.7	58.5	12.7	24.1	0.2	5.5	0.0	3,586	9.3	..
Portugal	17.2	25.4	13.0	14.3	53.8	5.1	11.9	0.0	4,799	89.0	100
Qatar	6.5	18.1	0.0	82.2	17.8	0.0	0.0	0.0	17,188	75.7	71
Romania	62.5	40.1	23.5	36.4	25.3	4.0	8.1	3.7	2,401	−17.9	..
Russian Federation	878.9	676.2	15.7	53.0	20.6	2.3	1.1	6.1	6,122	−8.3	..
Saudi Arabia	61.3	146.1	0.0	36.7	63.3	0.0	0.0	0.0	7,079	77.8	97
Senegal	1.8	3.0	3.4	0.3	55.7	0.7	39.6	0.0	150	52.3	33
Serbia	19.5	17.1	51.0	11.7	27.5	5.5	4.7	0.0	4,026	13.9	..
Singapore	13.4	30.7	0.0	20.9	79.0	0.0	0.0	0.0	8,363	72.1	100
Slovak Republic	21.3	18.7	23.9	28.8	18.3	2.1	2.6	25.4	5,136	−7.3	..
Slovenia	5.6	7.3	20.3	12.4	36.5	4.3	6.5	19.9	7,123	39.9	..
South Africa	91.2	129.8	71.7	2.9	12.4	0.3	10.5	2.4	4,810	8.5	70
Spain	91.2	144.6	12.4	21.5	49.0	3.0	3.6	10.8	6,213	76.3	100
Sri Lanka	5.5	9.4	0.7	0.0	40.7	4.2	54.3	0.0	400	159.5	66
Sudan	10.7	17.7	0.0	0.0	21.8	0.7	77.5	0.0	95	91.5	30
Sweden	47.6	51.3	4.7	1.7	28.5	10.5	18.4	34.0	15,230	−3.8	100
Switzerland	24.8	28.2	0.6	9.6	46.0	10.1	7.2	25.8	8,279	11.7	100
Syrian Arab Republic	11.7	18.9	0.0	27.0	71.2	1.8	0.0	0.0	1,466	117.6	90
Tajikistan	5.6	3.6	1.3	13.4	44.7	39.1	0.0	0.0	2,241	−33.0	..
Tanzania	9.8	20.8	0.2	1.5	6.6	0.6	91.0	0.0	59	15.0	11
Thailand	43.9	103.4	12.1	25.8	44.4	0.7	16.6	0.0	2,080	181.4	99
Togo	1.3	2.4	0.0	0.0	13.4	0.3	84.5	0.0	98	12.6	17
Trinidad and Tobago	6.0	14.3	0.0	87.7	12.1	0.0	0.2	0.0	5,008	87.0	99
Tunisia	5.1	8.7	0.0	39.4	47.2	0.1	13.3	0.0	1,221	91.2	99
Turkey	52.9	94.0	28.1	27.6	33.4	5.5	5.5	0.0	2,053	130.2	..
Turkmenistan	19.6	17.3	0.0	71.3	29.4	0.0	0.0	0.0	2,123	−7.4	..
Ukraine	253.8	137.4	29.1	42.4	10.8	0.8	0.4	17.1	3,400	−29.0	..
United Arab Emirates	23.2	46.9	0.0	72.0	28.0	0.0	0.0	0.0	14,569	66.2	92
United Kingdom	212.3	231.1	17.9	35.1	36.3	0.3	1.7	8.5	6,192	15.6	100
United States	1,926.3	2,320.7	23.7	21.6	40.4	1.6	3.4	9.2	13,515	15.6	100
Uruguay	2.3	3.2	0.1	3.2	64.6	9.7	14.9	0.0	2,042	63.9	95
Uzbekistan	46.4	48.5	2.2	85.8	10.9	1.1	0.0	0.0	1,691	−29.1	..
Venezuela, R. B. de	43.9	62.2	0.1	37.6	50.6	11.0	0.9	0.0	3,175	28.9	99
Vietnam	24.3	52.3	16.8	9.5	23.4	3.9	46.4	0.0	598	511.2	84
Yemen, Rep. of	2.6	7.1	0.0	0.0	98.9	0.0	1.1	0.0	190	58.9	36
Zambia	5.5	7.3	1.4	0.0	9.7	11.0	78.2	0.0	730	−3.2	19
Zimbabwe	9.4	9.6	22.2	0.0	7.1	5.0	63.3	0.0	900	4.5	34
World	8,637.3t	11,525.2t	26.6w	21.0w	35.7w	2.8w	9.8w	6.3w	2,750w	29.6w	..
Low income	400.2	575.5	7.3	19.1	7.8	3.1	53.8	0.1	311	18.7	..
Middle income	3,797.2	5,348.7	35.8	19.2	29.9	3.2	12.3	2.0	1,647	58.2	..
High income	4,479.4	5,659.1	13.9	22.9	43.7	2.5	3.4	11.0	9,675	27.5	..
European Union 15	1,324.2	1,542.8	20.5	24.5	40.9	2.4	5.0	15.1	7,058	25.5	..
OECD	4,521.8	5,537.4	20.5	21.9	39.7	2.8	3.8	11.1	8,413	24.4	..

a. Denotes percent change in value of the variable within the given period.   b. Data are for the most recent year available.

Table A4　Natural disasters

	Mortality		People affected			Economic losses			Coastline	Population in low-elevation coastal zones	Area in low-elevation coastal zones
	Droughts	Floods and storms	Droughts	Floods and storms	Share of population	Droughts	Floods and storms	Largest per event loss	Coastline		
	Number of people		Number of people (thousands)		%	$ (thousands)		% of GDP	kilometers	%	%
	1971–2008[a]	1971–2008[a]	1971–2008[a]	1971–2008[a]	1971–2008[a]	1971–2008[a]	1971–2008[a]	1961–2008[b]	2008	2000	2000
Angola	2	7	69	18	2.2	0	263	..	1,600	5.3	0.3
Argentina	0	13	0	355	1.1	3,158	229,348	0.8	4,989	10.9	1.9
Australia	0	10	186	108	4.8	262,447	390,461	3.2	25,760	12.1	1.6
Bahamas, The	0	1	0	1	0.2	0	67,116	9.8	3,542	87.6	93.2
Bangladesh	0	5,673	658	8,751	9.1	0	445,576	9.8	580	45.6	40.0
Belize	0	2	0	8	3.6	0	14,862	200.2	386	40.3	15.6
Benin	0	3	58	56	5.3	17	214	..	121	21.0	1.6
Bolivia	0	22	92	62	2.4	25,411	43,050	18.7	0	0.0	0.0
Brazil	1	102	993	384	1.4	124,289	157,849	1.2	7,491	6.7	1.4
Cambodia	0	30	172	251	5.8	3,632	8,634	9.2	443	23.9	7.4
Chad	0	8	62	18	6.0	2,184	30	..	0	0.0	0.0
China	93	1,304	9,642	53,460	5.2	522,350	4,791,624	2.9	14,500	11.4	2.0
Costa Rica	0	5	0	39	1.0	632	19,668	2.4	1,290	2.4	3.5
Cuba	0	6	22	331	3.1	4,819	287,436	..	3,735	13.3	21.1
Czech Republic	0[c]	2[c]	0[c]	8[c]	0.1[c]	0[c]	122,263[c]	3.2	0	0.0	0.0
Djibouti	0	6	26	18	8.5	0	151	..	314	40.6	1.9
Dominica	0	1	0	3	3.5	0	7,412	100.8	148	6.7	4.5
Dominican Republic	0	75	0	111	1.6	0	71,240	36.4	1,288	3.3	4.7
Ecuador	0	21	1	43	0.5	0	40,972	3.3	2,237	14.0	3.2
Ethiopia	10,536	51	1,361	59	6.6	2,411	424	..	0	0.0	0.0
Fiji	0	8	8	26	4.8	789	18,078	17.1	1,129	17.6	10.6
Georgia	0	3	18	1	0.8	5,263	15,259	26.8	310	6.2	2.2
Ghana	0	7	329	94	8.1	3	882	4.5	539	3.7	1.0
Grenada	0	1	0	2	1.6	0	23,803	205.1	121	6.4	6.5
Guatemala	1	73	5	24	0.2	632	48,434	3.9	400	1.4	2.1
Guyana	0	1	16	12	5.7	763	16,692	56.3	459	54.6	3.7
Haiti	0	225	55	131	2.8	0	21,707	62.6	1,771	9.2	5.1
Honduras	0	621	19	109	2.9	447	130,421	72.9	820	4.6	5.6
India	8	2,489	25,294	22,314	7.2	61,608	1,055,375	2.5	7,000	6.3	2.5
Indonesia	35	182	121	206	0.3	4,216	62,572	9.3	54,716	19.6	9.3
Iran, Islamic Rep. of	0	102	974	101	4.8	86,842	202,133	3.5	2,440	2.1	1.6
Italy	0	8	0	2	0.1	21,053	597,289	2.7	7,600	9.3	6.3
Jamaica	0	7	0	56	2.4	158	68,304	26.1	1,022	7.9	6.9
Jordan	0	1	9	0	0.2	0	26	7.5	26	0.0	0.0
Kenya	5	23	960	56	9.7	39	588	..	536	0.9	0.4
Korea, Dem. Rep. of	0	49	0	314	1.4	0	622,156	..	2,495	10.2	3.8
Korea, Rep. of	0	116	0	76	0.2	0	391,754	1.2	2,413	6.2	5.0
Lao PDR	0	5	112	123	6.3	26	8,657	22.8	0	0.0	0.0
Lebanon	0	1	0	3	0.1	0	4,342	2.8	225	13.7	1.6
Madagascar	5	54	74	231	3.6	0	55,337	14.8	4,828	5.5	2.7
Malawi	13	16	518	50	12.3	0	837	..	0	0.0	0.0
Malaysia	0	12	0	15	0.1	0	28,039	0.9	4,675	23.5	6.2
Mauritius	0	1	0	26	2.9	4,605	16,352	21.3	177	9.4	6.1
Mongolia	0	5	12	53	3.7	0	2,376	145.3	0	0.0	0.0
Mozambique	2,633	65	455	328	13.8	1,316	22,846	9.9	2,470	11.8	3.2
Nepal	0	137	121	87	2.0	263	25,804	24.6	0	0.0	0.0
Nicaragua	0	105	15	53	1.4	474	46,256	27.7	910	2.1	6.2
Niger	0	3	335	10	13.2	0	295	..	0	0.0	0.0
Pakistan	4	273	58	1,163	1.3	6,500	120,942	10.5	1,046	2.9	2.8
Peru	0	55	87	75	0.7	7,526	1,916	5.2	2,414	1.8	0.5
Philippines	0	743	172	2,743	4.5	1,696	164,362	11.0	36,289	17.7	7.7
Puerto Rico	0	15	0	5	0.1	53	82,789	3.2	501	18.4	10.8
Russian Federation	0[c]	32[c]	26[c]	58[c]	0.1[c]	0[c]	147,461[c]	6.9	37,653	2.4	1.7
Samoa	0	1	0	7	4.6	0	13,858	248.4	403	23.6	8.4
Senegal	0	6	199	18	11.3	9,863	1,168	13.6	531	31.5	7.5
South Africa	0	34	460	22	1.1	26,316	50,502	0.7	2,798	1.0	0.1
Spain	0	22	158	21	2.5	280,526	245,471	2.4	4,964	7.7	1.3
Sri Lanka	0	45	165	282	3.1	0	12,049	3.7	1,340	11.8	8.3
St. Lucia	0	2	0	2	1.9	0	29,731	365.0	158	4.3	4.1
Sudan	3,947	19	611	155	6.0	0	14,505	1.1	853	0.6	0.1
Swaziland	13	1	43	24	18.3	46	1,426	10.7	0	0.0	0.0
Tajikistan	0[c]	39[c]	100[c]	19[c]	2.9[c]	1,500[c]	12,037[c]	15.7	0	0.0	0.0
Tanzania	0	15	210	22	2.0	0	179	..	1,424	2.3	0.3
Thailand	0	95	618	929	2.2	11,166	132,709	..	3,219	26.3	6.9
Tunisia	0	8	1	7	0.1	0	8,889	7.8	1,148	14.8	3.3
United States	0	272	0	672	0.1	187,763	12,104,146	1.0	19,924	8.1	2.6
Vanuatu	0	3	0	6	4.4	0	5,395	139.9	2,528	4.5	7.4
Venezuela, R. B. de	0	801	0	20	0.1	0	84,697	3.3	2,800	6.8	3.6
Vietnam	0	393	161	1,749	3.0	17,082	157,603	..	3,444	55.1	20.2
Zimbabwe	0	4	365	9	10.7	67,105	7,308	29.3	0	0.0	0.0

a. Denotes annual average values for variables during the period 1971–2008. b. Denotes largest per-event loss in the period 1961–2008. c. Data prior to 1990 are based on detailed EM-DAT disaster information in Yugoslavia, Czechoslovakia, and the Soviet Union.

Table A5 Land, water, and agriculture

	Arable land	Share irrigated land	Aquaculture production	Projected physical impacts by 2050				Projected agricultural impacts	
				Change in temperature	Change in heat wave duration	Precipitation	Precipitation intensity	Agricultural output	Agricultural yield
	hectares (millions)	% of cropland	$ (millions)	°C	number of days	% change		% change	
	2005	2003	2007	2000–2050	2000–2050	2000–2050ª	2000–2050ª	2000–2080ª	2000–2050ª
Algeria	7.5	6.9	0.9	1.9	22.2	–4.9	7.2	–36.0	–6.7
Argentina	28.5	..	16.7	1.2	5.9	0.7	3.5	–11.1	–13.8
Australia	49.4	5.0	478.8	1.5	10.9	–1.4	2.1	–26.6	–16.4
Bangladesh	8.0	56.1	1,522.6	1.4	8.7	1.4	5.4	–21.7	8.9
Belarus	5.5	2.0	1.8	1.7	28.8	2.7	4.9	..	29.6
Bolivia	3.1	4.1	2.0	1.6	16.4	–0.9	2.5	..	–13.7
Brazil	59.0	4.4	598.0	1.5	13.5	–2.0	3.0	–16.9	–16.1
Bulgaria	3.2	16.6	18.2	1.7	27.2	–4.3	3.0	..	–7.0
Burkina Faso	4.8	0.5	0.9	1.4	5.7	0.3	0.0	–24.3	–4.4
Cambodia	3.7	7.0	7.6	1.2	4.0	3.3	1.7	–27.1	–19.3
Cameroon	6.0	0.4	0.8	1.3	2.0	0.9	3.0	–20.0	–6.6
Canada	45.7	1.5	788.2	2.1	28.2	8.5	4.9	–2.2	19.5
Chile	2.0	81.0	5,314.5	1.2	4.9	–3.5	1.2	–24.4	47.7
China	143.3	35.6	44,935.2	1.7	16.1	4.5	5.4	–7.2	8.4
Colombia	2.0	24.0	277.2	1.4	4.0	1.2	2.4	–23.2	–3.3
Congo, Dem. Rep. of	6.7	0.1	7.4	1.4	2.0	0.8	3.1	–14.7	–7.0
Côte d'Ivoire	3.5	1.1	2.2	1.3	1.9	–0.3	–0.2	–14.3	–12.9
Cuba	3.7	19.5	35.0	1.1	2.0	–12.0	–0.9	–39.3	–18.1
Czech Republic	3.0	0.7	49.5	1.7	20.3	0.3	4.6	..	14.3
Denmark	2.2	9.0	11.4	1.4	11.0	5.0	5.8	..	16.1
Egypt, Arab Rep. of	3.0	100.0	1,192.6	1.6	14.7	–7.0	–1.6	11.3	–27.9
Ethiopia	13.1	2.5	..	1.4	3.1	2.4	5.0	–31.3	0.5
Finland	2.2	2.9	63.8	2.1	29.6	5.6	4.4	..	15.7
France	18.5	13.3	757.2	1.5	12.3	–3.5	3.2	–6.7	–2.6
Germany	11.9	4.0	191.1	1.5	14.8	2.4	5.0	–2.9	9.5
Ghana	4.2	0.5	2.5	1.3	1.3	–1.0	0.8	–14.0	–10.1
Greece	2.6	37.9	533.3	1.7	16.0	–10.9	1.8	–7.8	–3.5
Hungary	4.6	3.1	4.6	1.9	25.0	–1.3	6.5	..	–10.8
India	159.7	32.9	4,383.5	1.6	10.8	1.9	2.7	–38.1	–12.2
Indonesia	23.0	12.4	2,854.9	1.2	0.4	1.8	2.5	–17.9	–17.7
Iran, Islamic Rep. of	16.5	47.0	451.1	1.8	19.9	–15.6	4.2	–28.9	–7.3
Iraq	5.8	58.6	35.8	1.8	22.3	–13.3	6.1	–41.4	–18.5
Italy	7.7	25.8	757.4	1.5	12.3	–7.0	4.6	–7.4	–2.7
Japan	4.4	35.1	4,279.9	1.4	4.0	0.5	3.8	–5.7	0.6
Kazakhstan	22.4	15.7	0.9	1.8	28.5	5.6	5.0	11.4	7.7
Kenya	5.3	1.8	6.3	1.2	2.5	7.5	8.0	–5.5	6.1
Korea, Dem. Rep. of	2.8	50.3	32.6	1.7	10.0	6.0	7.0	–7.3	–0.7
Madagascar	3.0	30.6	47.5	1.2	2.1	–4.1	1.1	–26.2	–0.5
Malawi	2.6	2.2	3.6	1.4	7.5	–0.1	2.4	–31.3	–3.0
Mali	4.8	4.9	0.6	1.7	16.1	8.4	3.8	–35.6	–9.6
Mexico	25.0	22.8	535.5	1.6	16.8	–7.2	1.6	–35.4	–0.5
Morocco	8.5	15.4	6.9	2.1	21.1	–16.8	5.3	–39.0	–25.2
Mozambique	4.4	2.6	4.6	1.3	5.9	–2.7	1.4	–21.7	–10.4
Myanmar	10.1	17.0	1,862.4	1.3	8.6	1.9	3.7	–39.3	–15.4
Nepal	2.4	47.1	43.7	1.7	21.8	3.6	4.9	–17.3	–10.6
Niger	14.5	0.5	0.9	1.6	16.1	5.6	2.5	–34.1	–1.7
Nigeria	32.0	0.8	24.8	1.3	4.1	0.6	1.1	–18.5	–9.9
Pakistan	21.3	82.0	214.2	1.8	19.8	–3.0	3.5	–30.4	–32.9
Peru	3.7	27.8	271.8	1.5	5.0	1.2	3.3	–30.6	0.6
Philippines	5.7	14.5	1,371.4	1.2	1.3	2.1	1.7	–23.4	–14.3
Poland	12.1	..	15.0	1.7	21.6	1.8	4.4	–4.7	16.7
Romania	9.3	5.8	22.5	1.7	28.9	–4.2	5.3	–6.6	–8.1
Russian Federation	121.8	3.7	326.1	2.2	29.5	8.8	5.5	–7.7	11.0
Saudi Arabia	3.5	42.7	186.4	1.8	13.9	–10.5	1.8	–21.9	–28.3
Senegal	2.6	4.8	0.2	1.6	6.0	–1.9	3.1	–51.9	–19.3
South Africa	14.8	9.5	33.3	1.5	9.5	–4.5	1.4	–33.4	–5.2
Spain	13.7	20.3	384.2	1.6	15.2	–11.9	0.9	–8.9	–1.3
Sudan	19.4	10.2	3.8	1.6	9.5	–0.6	–0.1	–56.1	–7.0
Sweden	2.7	4.3	21.4	1.8	22.0	5.1	5.3	..	19.8
Syrian Arab Republic	4.9	24.3	24.8	1.7	23.4	–13.6	3.7	–27.0	–4.5
Tanzania	9.2	1.8	0.1	1.3	2.3	4.4	6.0	–24.2	–2.0
Thailand	14.2	28.2	2,432.8	1.2	8.1	2.7	2.2	–26.2	–15.9
Togo	2.5	0.3	12.0	1.3	1.5	–2.0	–0.5	..	–14.0
Turkey	23.8	20.0	64.6	1.7	24.3	–10.2	1.0	–16.2	–1.0
Uganda	5.4	0.1	115.7	1.3	1.7	3.4	6.6	–16.8	–5.0
Ukraine	32.5	6.6	76.9	1.7	28.5	–0.7	4.0	–5.2	–7.4
United Kingdom	5.7	3.0	927.9	1.1	5.1	2.5	3.7	–3.9	3.2
United States	174.4	12.5	944.6	1.8	24.4	2.7	4.0	–5.9	–1.7
Uzbekistan	4.7	84.9	2.4	1.7	21.5	–0.1	3.4	–12.1	–2.8
Venezuela, R. B. de	2.7	16.9	65.8	1.6	10.3	–6.4	1.1	–31.9	–9.8
Vietnam	6.6	33.7	4,544.8	1.2	7.3	3.6	1.7	–15.1	–11.4
Zambia	5.3	2.9	8.7	1.5	8.1	0.6	3.9	–39.6	1.3
Zimbabwe	3.2	5.2	5.1	1.5	12.3	–3.7	4.8	–37.9	–10.6

a. Denotes percentage change in the value of the variable within the given period.

Table A6　Wealth of nations

	Total wealth	Produced capital and urban land	Intangible capital	Natural capital	Pastureland	Cropland	Protected areas	Non-timber forest resources	Timber resources	Subsoil assets
	$ per capita	$ per capita	$ per capita	$ per capita	$ per capita	$ per capita	$ per capita	$ per capita	$ per capita	$ per capita
	2000	2000	2000	2000	2000	2000	2000	2000	2000	2000
Algeria	18,491	8,709	−3,418	13,200	426	859	161	16	68	11,670
Argentina	139,232	19,111	109,809	10,312	2,754	3,632	350	219	105	3,253
Australia	371,031	58,179	288,686	24,167	5,590	4,365	1,421	551	748	11,491
Austria	493,080	73,118	412,789	7,174	2,008	1,298	2,410	144	829	485
Bangladesh	6,000	817	4,221	961	52	810	9	2	4	83
Belgium	451,714	60,561	388,123	3,030	2,161	575	0	20	254	20
Bolivia	18,141	2,110	11,248	4,783	541	1,550	232	1,426	100	934
Brazil	86,922	9,643	70,528	6,752	1,311	1,998	402	724	609	1,708
Bulgaria	25,256	5,303	16,505	3,448	1,108	1,650	217	102	126	244
Burkina Faso	5,087	821	3,047	1,219	191	547	100	142	239	0
Cameroon	10,753	1,749	4,271	4,733	179	2,748	187	357	348	914
Canada	324,979	54,226	235,982	34,771	1,631	2,829	5,756	1,264	4,724	18,566
Chad	4,458	289	2,307	1,861	316	787	80	366	311	0
Chile	77,726	10,688	56,094	10,944	1,001	2,443	1,095	231	986	5,188
China	9,387	2,956	4,208	2,223	146	1,404	27	29	106	511
Colombia	44,660	4,872	33,241	6,547	978	2,911	253	266	134	3,006
Côte d'Ivoire	14,243	997	10,125	3,121	72	2,568	11	102	367	2
Dominican Republic	33,410	5,723	24,511	3,176	386	1,980	461	37	27	286
Ecuador	33,745	2,841	17,788	13,117	1,065	5,263	1,057	193	335	5,205
Egypt, Arab Rep. of	21,879	3,897	14,734	3,249	0	1,705	0	0	0	1,544
Ethiopia	1,965	177	992	796	197	353	167	16	63	0
France	468,024	57,814	403,874	6,335	2,091	2,747	1,026	77	307	87
Germany	496,447	68,678	423,323	4,445	1,586	1,176	1,113	39	263	269
Ghana	10,365	686	8,343	1,336	43	855	7	76	290	65
Greece	236,972	28,973	203,445	4,554	573	3,424	57	101	82	318
Guatemala	30,480	3,098	24,411	2,971	218	1,697	181	57	517	301
Haiti	8,235	601	6,840	793	112	668	3	3	8	0
Hungary	77,072	15,480	56,645	4,947	1,131	2,721	366	42	152	536
India	6,820	1,154	3,738	1,928	192	1,340	122	14	59	201
Indonesia	13,869	2,382	8,015	3,472	50	1,245	167	115	346	1,549
Iran, Islamic Rep. of	24,023	3,336	6,581	14,105	611	1,989	109	26	0	11,370
Italy	372,666	51,943	316,045	4,678	1,083	2,639	543	51	0	361
Japan	493,241	150,258	341,470	1,513	316	710	364	56	38	28
Kenya	6,609	868	4,374	1,368	529	361	113	129	235	1
Korea, Rep. of	141,282	31,399	107,864	2,020	275	1,241	441	30	0	33
Madagascar	5,020	395	2,944	1,681	345	955	36	171	174	0
Malawi	5,200	542	3,873	785	45	474	26	56	184	0
Malaysia	46,687	13,065	24,520	9,103	24	1,369	161	188	438	6,922
Mali	5,241	621	2,463	2,157	295	1,420	44	276	121	0
Mexico	61,872	18,959	34,420	8,493	721	1,195	176	128	199	6,075
Morocco	22,965	3,435	17,926	1,604	453	993	7	24	22	106
Mozambique	4,232	478	2,695	1,059	57	261	9	392	340	0
Nepal	3,802	609	1,964	1,229	111	767	81	38	233	0
Netherlands	421,389	62,428	352,222	6,739	3,090	1,035	527	7	27	2,053
Niger	3,695	286	1,434	1,975	187	1,598	152	28	9	1
Nigeria	2,748	667	−1,959	4,040	78	1,022	6	24	270	2,639
Pakistan	7,871	975	5,529	1,368	448	549	94	4	7	265
Peru	39,046	5,562	29,908	3,575	341	1,480	98	570	153	934
Philippines	19,351	2,673	15,129	1,549	45	1,308	59	17	90	30
Portugal	207,477	31,011	172,837	3,629	934	1,724	385	107	438	41
Romania	29,113	8,495	16,110	4,508	1,154	1,602	175	65	290	1,222
Russian Federation	38,709	15,593	5,900	17,217	1,342	1,262	1,317	1,228	292	11,777
Rwanda	5,670	549	3,055	2,066	98	1,849	27	9	81	2
Senegal	10,167	975	7,920	1,272	196	608	78	147	238	4
South Africa	59,629	7,270	48,959	3,400	637	1,238	51	46	310	1,118
Spain	261,205	39,531	217,300	4,374	971	2,806	360	105	81	50
Sri Lanka	14,731	2,710	11,204	817	84	485	166	24	58	0
Sweden	513,424	58,331	447,143	7,950	1,676	1,120	1,549	908	2,434	263
Syrian Arab Republic	10,419	3,292	−1,598	8,725	730	1,255	0	6	0	6,734
Thailand	35,854	7,624	24,294	3,936	96	2,370	855	55	92	469
Tunisia	36,537	6,270	26,328	3,939	736	1,546	8	12	27	1,610
Turkey	47,859	8,580	35,774	3,504	861	2,270	86	34	64	190
United Kingdom	408,753	55,239	346,347	7,167	1,291	583	495	14	44	4,739
United States	512,612	79,851	418,009	14,752	1,665	2,752	1,651	238	1,341	7,106
Venezuela, R. B. de	45,196	13,627	4,342	27,227	581	1,086	1,793	464	0	23,302
Zambia	6,564	694	4,091	1,779	98	477	78	716	276	134
Zimbabwe	9,612	1,377	6,704	1,531	258	350	70	341	211	301
World	95,860	16,850	74,998	4,011	536	1,496	322	104	252	1,302
Low income	7,532	1,174	4,434	1,925	189	1,143	111	48	109	325
Middle income	27,616	5,347	18,773	3,426	407	1,583	129	120	169	1,089
High income (OECD)	439,063	76,193	353,339	9,531	1,552	2,008	1,215	183	747	3,825

Table A7   Innovation, research, and development

	Research and development expenditure	Researchers in R&D	Triadic patent families	Knowledge Economy Index	Availability of latest technologies	Firm-level technology absorption
	% of GDP	per million people	per million people	Index	Index	Index
	2005–2006[a]	2005–2006[a]	2005	2008	2008–2009[a]	2007–2009[a]
Austria	2.4	3,473	39.7	8.9	6.2	6.2
Belgium	1.9	3,188	34.4	8.7	6.1	5.5
Canada	2.0	..	24.0	9.2	6.2	5.6
China	1.3	..	0.3	4.4	4.2	5.1
Czech Republic	1.4	2,371	..	7.8	5.1	5.4
Denmark	2.5	5,202	42.2	9.6	6.5	6.2
Estonia	0.9	2,478	..	8.3	5.8	5.5
Finland	3.5	7,545	53.0	9.4	6.6	6.1
France	2.1	3,353	39.4	8.5	6.2	5.6
Germany	2.5	3,359	76.4	8.9	6.2	6.0
Greece	0.5	1,744	..	7.4	4.7	4.4
Hungary	0.9	1,574	4.1	7.9	4.7	4.7
Iceland	2.8	7,287	..	8.9	6.7	6.6
India	..	..	0.1	3.1	5.2	5.5
Ireland	1.3	2,797	15.0	8.9	5.5	5.5
Israel	4.5	..	60.3	8.2	6.1	6.0
Italy	1.1	1,407	12.3	7.9	4.7	4.6
Japan	3.3	5,512	117.2	8.6	6.2	6.3
Korea, Rep. of	3.0	3,756	58.4	7.7	5.8	5.8
Kuwait	..	74	..	6.0	5.4	5.5
Lithuania	0.8	2,230	..	7.7	5.0	5.0
Luxembourg	1.6	4,877	50.5	8.7	5.7	5.5
Macedonia, FYR	0.2	547	..	5.3	3.6	3.4
Netherlands	1.7	2,477	66.9	9.3	6.2	5.5
New Zealand	1.2	4,207	15.3	8.9	..	5.5
Norway	1.5	4,668	25.6	9.3	6.4	6.1
Poland	0.1	1,627	..	7.4	4.4	4.7
Portugal	..	2,007	..	7.5	5.7	5.4
Russian Federation	1.1	3,227	0.4	5.4	3.9	4.1
Singapore	2.4	5,497	24.3	8.2	6.2	6.0
Slovak Republic	0.5	2,027	..	7.3	5.1	5.4
Slovenia	1.5	2,627	..	8.3	5.1	4.9
South Africa	0.9	361	0.6	5.6	5.4	5.5
Spain	1.1	2,528	4.5	8.2	5.2	5.0
Sweden	3.9	6,095	81.0	9.5	6.6	6.2
Switzerland	..	..	107.6	9.2	6.4	6.2
Tunisia	1.0	1,450	..	4.7	5.4	5.4
Ukraine	1.0	..	..	5.8	4.2	4.5
United Kingdom	1.8	2,995	27.4	9.1	6.2	5.6
United States	2.6	4,651	53.1	9.1	6.5	6.3

Note: The 40 countries shown in the table were chosen based on availability of data for at least four out of six variables.

a. Data are for the most recent year available.

Definitions and notes

Table A1   Energy-related emissions

Column	Indicator	Notes
	Carbon dioxide emissions	
1, 2	annual total (million metric tons)	Total CO_2 emissions from the energy sector, including electricity and heat production, manufacturing and construction, gas flaring, transportation, and other industries from WRI (2008). Emissions from industrial processes (primarily cement production) that amount to approximately 4% of global energy-related CO_2 emissions are not included. Annual CO_2 emissions in 2005 were used to truncate the table to the 65 economies that account for 96% of annual global CO_2 emissions in the energy sector. Aggregates are based on full 210-country list.
2, 3	change (%)	Percentage change in energy-related CO_2 emissions between 1990 (base year) and 2005.
4, 5	per capita (metric tons)	Annual emissions divided by midyear population (World Bank 2009) expressed in tons of CO_2 per person.
6	share of world total (%)	Share of world's total energy-related CO_2 emissions attributed to a given country, income group, or region.
7	cumulative since 1850 (billion metric tons)	Cumulative CO_2 emissions between 1850 and 2005 from DOE (2009). Sources of emissions include combustion of solid, liquid, and gaseous fuels, as well as cement production and gas flaring. For historical consistency, data on fuel-production was used rather than fuel consumption. CO_2 emissions do not include emissions from waste, agriculture, land-use change, or bunker fuels used in international transportation. Cumulative emissions are based on data availability—data coverage for the majority of the largest 25 emitters starts in 1850 and for smaller countries and island nations starts between 1900 and 1950.
8, 9	Annual total non-CO_2 emissions (million tons of CO_2 equivalent)	Total methane (CH_4) and nitrous oxide (N_2O) emissions in CO_2 equivalent from the energy sector based on WRI (2008). This indicator includes emissions from biomass combustion, oil and natural gas systems, coal mining and other stationary and mobile sources. CO_2 equivalent expresses the quantity of a mixture of greenhouse gases in terms of the quantity of CO_2 that would produce the same amount of warming as would the mixture of gases (see Glossary).
10, 11	Carbon intensity of energy (metric tons of CO_2 per ton of oil equivalent)	The ratio of carbon dioxide emissions to energy production. This ratio measures the greenness of energy production and is expressed in tons of CO_2 (WRI 2008) per ton of oil equivalents (IEA 2008a, 2008b).
12, 13	Carbon intensity of income (metric tons of CO_2 per thousand PPP $ of GDP)	The ratio of carbon dioxide emissions to gross domestic product. This measure is an indicator of the greenness of the economy and is expressed in tons of CO_2 per 1000 PPP dollars of GDP. Emissions are from WRI (2008), GDP data is from World Bank (2009).

Table A2   Land-based emissions
Table A2.a CO_2 emissions from deforestation

Column	Indicator	Notes
1, 2	Annual average CO_2 emissions (million metric tons) and rank	CO_2 emission estimates due to deforestation are based on Houghton (2009) and are derived from estimates of tropical forest cover change by the 2005 UN Forest Resources Assessment (FAO 2005). Estimates of CO_2 emissions from deforestation vary across time and also as a result of uncertain data: There is variation among estimates of deforestation rates and estimates of carbon stocks in the forests converted to other uses. To account for year-to-year trends and measurement uncertainty, the numbers reported here are based on average annual emissions between 1990 and 2005. The 25 largest contributors to CO_2 emissions from deforestation in 2005, shown in the table, account for approximately 95% of the world total. Net deforestation from high-income countries is estimated to be close to zero or slightly negative. The rank is based on the average annual emission for the period 1990-2005.
3, 4	Per capita CO_2 emissions (metric tons) and rank	Annual average emissions from deforestation divided by midyear population expressed in tons of CO_2 per person. Population numbers are from World Bank (2009). The ranking of per capita emissions is based on 186 countries (see chapter 1, Figure 1.1).
5	Average share of world total (%)	Share of CO_2 emissions based on average annual emissions between 1990 and 2005 as a percentage of global emissions due to deforestation.

Table A2.b   Non-CO_2 emissions from agriculture

Column	Indicator	Notes
1, 2	Annual emissions (million metric tons of CO_2 equivalent)	Total methane and nitrous oxide emissions from the agriculture sector measured in CO_2 equivalent from WRI (2008). CO_2 equivalent expresses the quantity of a mixture of greenhouse gases in terms of the quantity of CO_2 that would produce the same amount of warming as would the mixture of gases (see Glossary). Emissions in the agricultural sector result primarily from rice cultivation, agricultural soils, manure management and enteric fermentation (belching) from livestock. Consistent with IPCC categories for carbon sources and sinks, CO_2 associated with fuel combustion in the agricultural sector is included under the energy, not the agricultural sector. The 25 largest contributors to agricultural emissions shown in the table account for approximately 70 percent of the global total.
3	Share of world total (%)	Share of world's total emissions from the agriculture sector attributed to a given country or a region.
4–7	Per capita emissions (million metric tons of CO_2 equivalent) and rank	Annual emissions from the agriculture sector divided by midyear population in 1990 and 2005 (World Bank 2009) expressed in tons of CO_2 equivalent per person. Per capita emissions rank is based on the full set of more than 200 countries.

Table A3   **Total primary energy supply**

Column	Indicator	Notes
1, 2	Annual total primary energy supply (million metric tons of oil equivalent)	Total primary energy supply (TPES) is a measure of commercial energy consumption. TPES is the sum of indigenous production, imports, and stock changes, minus exports and international marine bunkers. A lower share of fossil fuels and higher share of renewable sources in TPES is an indicator of countries' path toward a green economy. Data for 135 OECD and non-OECD countries are from IEA (2008a) and IEA (2008b), respectively.
3–5	Share of fossil fuels in TPES (%)	Share of total primary energy derived from fossil fuels, including coal, oil, and natural gas. Share of coal includes coal and coal products (IEA 2008a, 2008b). Share of oil includes crude, natural gas liquids, feedstocks, and petroleum products. Share of natural gas includes natural gas only.
6, 7	Share of renewable energy in TPES (%)	Share of total primary energy derived from hydropower, solar, wind, geothermal, biomass, and waste (IEA 2008a, 2008b). Biomass, also referred to as traditional fuel, is comprised of animal and plant materials (wood, vegetal waste, ethanol, animal materials/wastes, and sulphite lyes). Waste is comprised of municipal waste (wastes produced by the residential, commercial, and public service sectors that are collected by local authorities for disposal in a central location for the production of heat and/or power) and industrial waste.
8	Share of nuclear in TPES (%)	Share of total energy derived from nuclear power (IEA 2008a, 2008b).
9, 10	Electricity consumption per capita (kilowatt-hours)	Electricity consumption per capita measures the average kilowatt-hours (kWh) of electrical power generated per person in a particular country or region from IEA (2008c) and IEA (2008d). It includes public and private electricity plants, and combined heat and power plants as well as production by nuclear and hydro (excluding pumped storage production), geothermal, hydro, wind, solar, and other renewables. Electricity produced by heat from chemical processes is not included here. Electricity consumption equals the sum of production and imports minus exports and distribution losses.
11	Electrification rate (%)	The share of population with access to electricity between 2000 and 2006 from IEA (2002, 2006).

Table A4   Natural disasters

Column	Indicator	Notes
1, 2	Mortality (number of people)	Number of people confirmed as dead and persons missing and presumed dead (official figures when available) during a disaster event (includes droughts, floods, and storms) based on CRED (2009). Numbers are annual averages for the period from 1971–2008.
3–5	People affected (thousands of people)	People injured, homeless and requiring immediate assistance during a disaster (includes droughts, floods, and storms); it can also include displaced or evacuated people based on CRED (2009). Numbers are annual averages for the period from 1971–2008.
6, 7	Economic losses (thousands of $)	Estimated damage cause by the disaster event in $ based on CRED (2009). Numbers are annual average damages for the period from 1971–2008.
8	Largest per-event loss (% of GDP)	Estimates of total damage caused by the single largest loss due to a slow or fast onset event between 1961 and 2008 (Mechler and others 2009). The table lists economies that had a at least one per-event loss exceeding 0.8% of GDP during this period. Event type includes droughts, floods, storms, cold waves and forest fires. The largest per-event loss is defined as the total loss from an event expressed in $ (CRED 2009) divided by the total GDP (World Bank 2009).
9	Coastline (kilometers)	The total length of the boundary between the land area (including islands) and the sea from CIA (2009).
10	Population in low-elevation coastal zones (%)	Share of total population living in low-elevation coastal zones (defined as land areas contiguous with the coast and 10 meters or less in elevation) from CIESIN (2006).
11	Area in low-elevation coastal zones (%)	Share of total area in low-elevation coastal zones (defined as land areas contiguous with the coast and 10 meters or less in elevation) from CIESIN (2006).

Table A5   Land, water and projected impacts of climate change

Column	Indicator	Notes
1	Arable land (million hectares)	Arable land is land fit for cultivation of crops that are replanted after each harvest like wheat, maize, and rice. From World Bank (2009).
2	Share of irrigated land (% of cropland)	Share of total cropland under irrigation from World Bank (2009).
3	Aquaculture production (millions $)	Aquaculture production includes farming of aquatic organisms including fish, molluscs, crustaceans, and aquatic plants in brackish water, freshwater, or marine environment; both in inland waters and marine areas. Aquaculture production specifically refers to output from aquaculture activities, which are designated for final harvest for consumption. Data is from FAO (2009).
4–7	Projected physical impacts	Projected physical impacts of climate change by the middle of the 21st century. Selected indicators include change in average annual temperature, change in precipitation and precipitation intensity, and change in heat wave duration. These projections estimates represent an ensemble mean of 19 general circulation models used for the IPCC Fourth Assessment (IPCC 2007). The changes are estimated for the future time period 2030–2049 relative to 1980–1999. Indicators are spatially-weighted averages for each country.
8, 9	Projected agricultural impacts	Percentage change in agricultural output (defined as revenue per hectare) between 2000 and 2080 based on "preferred estimates" from Cline (2007). Impacts in agricultural yield are defined as an average percentage change in crop yields between 2000 and 2050 for wheat, rice, maize, millet, field pea, sugar beet, sweet potato, soybean, groundnut, sunflower, and rapeseed based on Müller and others (2009).

Table A6 Wealth of nations

Column	Indicator	Notes
1	Total wealth ($ per capita)	The aggregate wealth nations have produced in the past, reflecting the value of all goods, resources, and services, including natural, produced, and intangible capital. Sub-categories of natural capital include forest, soil, and agricultural resources, which are indicative of a country's reliance on natural resources and vulnerability to climate change. All indicators are expressed in per capita US$ value obtained after dividing the total value by midyear population (World Bank 2005).
2	Produced capital ($ per capita)	Produced capital includes machinery, equipment, and structures and urban land.
3	Intangible capital ($ per capita)	Intangible capital includes raw labor, human capital, social capital, and other factors such as the quality of institutions. It is calculated as a residual, the difference between total wealth and the sum of produce and natural capital.
4	Natural capital ($ per capita)	Natural capital includes energy resources (oil, natural gas, hard coal, and lignite), mineral resources (bauxite, copper, gold, iron, lead, nickel, phosphate, silver, tin, and zinc), timber resources, nontimber forest resources, cropland, pastureland, and protected areas.
5	Pastureland ($ per capita)	Natural capital associated with pastureland reflects the annual value of pastureland for production of goods. Returns to pastureland are assumed to be 45 percent of output value, which is based on the production of beef, lamb, milk, and wool valued at international prices.
6	Cropland ($ per capita)	Natural capital associated with cropland reflects the annual value of agricultural production based on available cropland. Return to cropland is computed as the difference between the market value of crops and crop-specific production costs.
7	Protected areas ($ per capita)	Natural capital associated with protected area reflects the annual value of benefits associated with protected areas including recreational value, tourism and other existence values.
8	Nontimber forest resources ($ per capita)	Nontimber forest benefits include minor forest products, hunting, recreation, and watershed protection. Annual benefits were derived assuming that one-tenth of the forest area in each country is accessible with benefits ranging from $190 per hectare in developed countries to $145 per hectare in developing countries.
9	Timber resources ($ per capita)	Timber resources are based on coniferous and non-coniferous roundwood (wood in the rough) production. Since market values are used to estimate the value of standing timber a distinction is made between forests available and forests not available for wood supply. The area of forest available for wood supply is defined as within 50 kilometers of infrastructure.
10	Subsoil assets ($ per capita)	Subsoil assets are proven reserves of mineral deposits located on or below the earth's surface that are economically exploitable, given current technology and relative prices.

Table A7 Innovation, research, and development

Column	Indicator	Notes
1	Research and development expenditure (% of GDP)	Expenditures for research and development (R&D) are current and capital expenditures (both public and private) on creative work undertaken systematically to increase knowledge, including knowledge of humanity, culture, and society, and the use of knowledge for new applications. R&D covers basic research, applied research, and experimental development. Share of R&D expenditures is total R&D expenditures divided by GDP for a given year. Data are from the World Bank.
2	Researchers in R&D (per million people)	Number of researchers in R&D is expressed as a number per million people.
3	Triadic patent families (per million people)	Defined as a set of patents, for a single invention, granted by the European Patent Office, the Japan Patent Office, and the United States Patent and Trademark Office. It is a good indicator of the number of patents filed and patents per capita (OECD 2008).
4	Knowledge Economy Index	Knowledge Economy Index (World Bank 2008) is an aggregate index based on the World Bank Knowledge Assessment Methodology 2008 (KAM) and represents the overall preparedness of a country or region for the knowledge economy. The KEI is constructed as the simple average of 4 sub-indexes, which represent the following 4 pillars of the knowledge economy: (1) Economic Incentive and Institutional Regime, (2) Education and Training, (3) Innovation and Technological Adoption, and (4) Information and Communications Technologies Infrastructure.
5	Availability of latest technologies	Index defining the availability of latest technologies in the country. The index ranges between 1 (technologies are not widely available and used) and 7 (technologies are widely available and used). For a full list of countries see the World Economic Forum (2009).
6	Firm-level technology absorption index	Index defining the country's capacity to absorb new technologies. It ranges between 1 (not able to absorb technology) and 7 (aggressive in absorbing new technology). For a full list of countries see the World Economic Forum (2009).

Symbols and aggregates

..   Denotes that data are not available or that aggregates cannot be calculate because of missing data in the years shown.

0 or 0.0   Denotes zero or less than half the unit shown.

Aggregate measures for regions and income groups are calculated by simple addition when they are expressed in levels. Aggregate rates and ratios are computed as weighted averages.

Summary measures are either totals (indicated by **t** if the aggregates include estimates for missing data and non-reporting countries or by an **s** for simple sums of the data available), weighted averages (**w**), or median values (**m**) calculated for groups of economies. Data for the countries excluded from the main tables have been included while calculating the summary measures.

References

CIA. 2009. "The World Factbook 2009." Washington, DC: Central Intelligence Agency. Available at https://www.cia.gov/library/publications/the-world-factbook/index.html (accessed July 2009).

CIESIN. 2006. "Low Elevation Coastal Zone (LECZ) Urban-Rural Estimates, Global Rural-Urban Mapping Project (GRUMP), Alpha Version." Palisades, NY: Socioeconomic Data and Applications Center (SEDAC), Columbia University. Available at http://sedac.ciesin.columbia.edu/gpw/lecz (accessed July 2009).

Cline, W. R. 2007. *Global Warming and Agriculture: Impact Estimates by Country.* Washington, DC: Center for Global Development and Peterson Institute for International Economics.

CRED. 2008. "EM-DAT: The OFDA/CRED International Emergency Disaster Database." Brussels, Belgium: Centre for Research on the Epidemiology of Disasters (CRED), Université Catholique de Louvain - Ecole de Santé Publique.

DOE (U.S. Department of Energy). 2009. "Carbon Dioxide Information Analysis Center (CDIAC)." DOE, Oak Ridge, TN.

FAO. 2009. "Global Aquaculture Production 1950–2007." Rome, Italy: UN Food and Agriculture Organization Fisheries and Aquaculture Department. Available at http://www.fao.org/fishery/statistics/global-aquaculture-production/query/en (accessed July 2009).

Houghton, R. A. 2009. "Emissions of Carbon from Land Management." Background note for the WDR 2010.

IEA (International Energy Agency). 2002. *World Energy Outlook 2002.* Paris: IEA.

———. 2006. *World Energy Outlook 2006.* Paris: IEA.

———. 2008a. *Energy Balances of Non-OECD Countries—2008 Edition.* Paris: IEA.

———. 2008b. *Energy Balances of OECD Countries—2008 Edition.* Paris: IEA.

———. 2008c. *Energy Statistics of Non-OECD Countries—2008 Edition.* Paris: IEA.

———. 2008d. *Energy Statistics of OECD Countries—2008 Edition.* Paris: IEA.

Mechler, R., S. Hochrainer, G. Pflug, K. Williges, and A. Lotsch. 2009. "Assessing the Financial Vulnerability to Climate-Related Natural Hazards." Background paper for the WDR 2010.

Müller, C., A. Bondeau, A. Popp, K. Waha, and M. Fader. 2009. "Climate Change Impacts on Agricultural Yields." Background note for the WDR 2010.

OECD. 2008. *Compendium of Patent Statistics 2008.* Paris: Organisation for Economic Co-operation and Development.

———. 2009. "OECD Science and Technology Database - Main Science and Technology Indicators." Paris, Organisation for Economic Co-operation and Development. Available at http://www.sourceoecd.org (accessed July 2009).

World Bank. 2005. *Where is the Wealth of Nations? Measuring Capital for the 21st Century.* Washington, DC: World Bank.

———. 2008. "Knowledge Assessment Methodology - Knowledge Economy Index (KEI)." Washington, DC: World Bank. Available at http://info.worldbank.org/etools/kam2/KAM_page5.asp (accessed August 2009).

———. 2009. *World Development Indicators 2009.* Washington, DC: World Bank.

World Economic Forum. 2009. *Global Information Technology Report 2008–2009.* Geneva, Switzerland: World Economic Forum.

WRI. 2008. "Climate Analysis Indicators Tool (CAIT)." Washington, DC: World Resources Institute.

Selected World Development Indicators 2010

I n this year's edition, development data are presented in six tables presenting comparative socioeconomic data for more than 130 economies for the most recent year for which data are available and, for some indicators, for an earlier year. An additional table presents basic indicators for 78 economies with sparse data or with populations of less than 3 million.

The indicators presented here are a selection from more than 800 included in *World Development Indicators 2009.* Published annually, *World Development Indicators* (WDI) reflects a comprehensive view of the development process. The WDI's six sections recognize the contribution of a wide range of factors: progress on the Millennium Development Goals and human capital development, environmental sustainability, macroeconomic performance, private sector development and the investment climate, and the global links that influence the external environment for development. Note that this year's poverty table (table 2) includes poverty estimates using the international poverty lines of $1.25 a day and $2 a day that are based on new purchasing power parity (PPP) estimates benchmarked to 2005.

World Development Indicators is complemented by a separately published database that gives access to more than 800 time-series indicators for 227 economies and regions. This database is available through an electronic subscription (*WDI Online*) or as a CD-ROM.

Data sources and methodology

Socioeconomic and environmental data presented here are drawn from several sources: primary data collected by the World Bank, member country statistical publications; research institutes; and international organizations such as the United Nations (UN) and its specialized agencies, the International Monetary Fund (IMF), and the Organisation for Economic Co-operation and Development (OECD) (see the *Data Sources* following the *Technical notes* for a complete listing). Although international standards of coverage, definition, and classification apply to most statistics reported by countries and international agencies, there are inevitably differences in timeliness and reliability arising

from differences in the capabilities and resources devoted to basic data collection and compilation. For some topics, competing sources of data require review by World Bank staff members to ensure that the most reliable data available are presented. In some instances, where available data are deemed too weak to provide reliable measures of levels and trends or do not adequately adhere to international standards, the data are not shown.

The data presented are generally consistent with those in *World Development Indicators 2009.* However, data have been revised and updated wherever new information has become available. Differences may also reflect revisions to historical series and changes in methodology. Thus data of different vintages may be published in different editions of World Bank publications. Readers are advised not to compile data series from different publications or different editions of the same publication. Consistent time-series data are available on *World Development Indicators 2009* CD-ROM and through *WDI Online*.

All dollar figures are in current U.S. dollars unless otherwise stated. The various methods used to convert from national currency figures are described in the Technical notes.

Because the World Bank's primary business is providing lending and policy advice to its low- and middle-income members, the issues covered in these tables focus mainly on these economies. Where available, information on the high-income economies is also provided for comparison. Readers may wish to refer to national statistical publications and publications of the OECD and the European Union (EU) for more information on the high-income economies.

Classification of economies and summary measures

The summary measures at the bottom of most tables include economies classified by income per capita and by region. gross national income (GNI) per capita is used to determine the following income classifications: low-income, $975 or less in 2008; middle-income, $976 to $11,905; and high-income, $11,906 or more. A further division at GNI per capita $3,855 is made between lower-middle-income and upper-middle-income economies. The classification of economies based on per capita income occurs annually, so the country composition of the income groups may change annually. When these changes in classification are made based on the most recent estimates, aggregates based on the new income classifications are recalculated for all past periods to ensure that a consistent time series is maintained. See the table on classification of economies at the end of this volume for a list of economies in each group (including those with populations of less than 3 million).

Summary measures are either totals (indicated by **t** if the aggregates include estimates for missing data and nonreporting countries or by an **s** for simple sums of the data available), weighted averages (**w**), or median values (**m**) calculated for groups of economies. Data for the countries excluded from the main tables (those presented in table 6) have been included in the summary measures, where data are available, or by assuming that they follow the trend of reporting countries. This gives a more consistent aggregated measure by standardizing country coverage for each period shown. Where missing information accounts for a third or more of the overall estimate, however, the group measure is reported as not available. The section on *Statistical methods* in the *Technical notes* provides further information on aggregation methods. Weights used to construct the aggregates are listed in the technical notes for each table.

Terminology and country coverage

The term *country* does not imply political independence but may refer to any territory for which authorities report separate social or economic statistics. Data are shown for economies as they were constituted in 2008, and historical data are revised to reflect current political arrangements. Throughout the tables, exceptions are noted. Unless otherwise noted, data for China do not include data for Hong Kong, China; Macao, China; or Taiwan, China. Data for Indonesia include Timor-Leste through 1999 unless otherwise noted. Montenegro declared independence from Serbia and Montenegro on June 3, 2006. When available, data for each country are shown separately. However, some indicators for Serbia continue to include data for Montenegro through 2005; these data are footnoted in the tables. Moreover, data for most indicators from 1999 onward for Serbia exclude data for Kosovo, which in 1999 became a territory under international administration pursuant to UN Security Council Resolution 1244 (1999); any exceptions are noted.

Technical notes

Because data quality and intercountry comparisons are often problematic, readers are encouraged to consult the *Technical notes*, the table on Classification of Economies by Region and Income, and the footnotes to the tables. For more extensive documentation, see *World Development Indicators 2009*.

Symbols

.. means that data are not available or that aggregates cannot be calculated because of missing data in the years shown.

0 or **0.0** means zero or small enough that the number would round to zero at the displayed number of decimal places.

/ in dates, as in 2003/04, means that the period of time, usually 12 months, straddles two calendar years and refers to a crop year, a survey year, or a fiscal year.

$ means current U.S. dollars unless otherwise noted.

> means more than.

< means less than.

Data presentation conventions

- A blank means not applicable or, for an aggregate, not analytically meaningful.
- A billion is 1,000 million.
- A trillion is 1,000 billion.
- Figures in italics refer to years or periods other than those specified or to growth rates calculated for less than the full period specified.
- Data for years that are more than three years from the range shown are footnoted.

Readers may find more information on the WDI 2009, and orders can be made online, by phone, or fax as follows:

For more information and to order online: http://www.worldbank.org/data/wdi2009/index.htm.

To order by phone: 1-800-645-7247 or 703-661-1580; or by fax: 703-661-1501

To order by mail: The World Bank, P.O. Box 960, Herndon, VA 20172-0960, U.S.A.

Classification of economies by region and income, FY2010

East Asia and the Pacific		Latin America and the Caribbean		South Asia		High-income OECD
American Samoa	UMC	Argentina	UMC	Afghanistan	LIC	Australia
Cambodia	LIC	Belize	LMC	Bangladesh	LIC	Austria
China	LMC	Bolivia	LMC	Bhutan	LMC	Belgium
Fiji	UMC	Brazil	UMC	India	LMC	Canada
Indonesia	LMC	Chile	UMC	Maldives	LMC	Czech Republic
Kiribati	LMC	Colombia	UMC	Nepal	LIC	Denmark
Korea, Dem. People's Rep.	LIC	Costa Rica	UMC	Pakistan	LMC	Finland
Lao PDR	LIC	Cuba	UMC	Sri Lanka	LMC	France
Malaysia	UMC	Dominica	UMC			Germany
Marshall Islands	LMC	Dominican Republic	UMC	Sub-Saharan Africa		Greece
Micronesia, Federated	LMC	Ecuador	LMC	Angola	LMC	Hungary
States of	LMC	El Salvador	LMC	Benin	LIC	Iceland
Mongolia	LIC	Grenada	UMC	Botswana	UMC	Ireland
Myanmar	UMC	Guatemala	LMC	Burkina Faso	LIC	Italy
Palau	LMC	Guyana	LMC	Burundi	LIC	Japan
Papua New Guinea	LMC	Haiti	LIC	Cameroon	LMC	Korea, Rep. of
Philippines	LMC	Honduras	LMC	Cape Verde	LMC	Luxembourg
Samoa	LMC	Jamaica	UMC	Central African Republic	LIC	Netherlands
Solomon Islands	LMC	Mexico	UMC	Chad	LIC	New Zealand
Thailand	LMC	Nicaragua	LMC	Comoros	LIC	Norway
Timor-Leste	LMC	Panama	UMC	Congo, Dem. Rep. of	LIC	Portugal
Tonga	LMC	Paraguay	LMC	Congo, Rep. of	LMC	Slovak Republic
Vanuatu	LIC	Peru	UMC	Côte d'Ivoire	LMC	Spain
Vietnam		St. Kitts and Nevis	UMC	Eritrea	LIC	Sweden
		St. Lucia	UMC	Ethiopia	LIC	Switzerland
Europe and Central Asia	LMC	St. Vincent and the Grenadines	UMC	Gabon	UMC	United Kingdom
Albania	LMC	Suriname	UMC	Gambia, The	LIC	United States
Armenia	LMC	Uruguay	UMC	Ghana	LIC	
Azerbaijan	UMC	Venezuela, R. B. de	UMC	Guinea	LIC	Other high income
Belarus	UMC			Guinea-Bissau	LIC	Andorra
Bosnia and Herzegovina	UMC	Middle East and North Africa		Kenya	LIC	Antigua and Barbuda
Bulgaria	LMC	Algeria	UMC	Lesotho	LMC	Aruba
Georgia	UMC	Djibouti	LMC	Liberia	LIC	Bahamas, The
Kazakhstan	LMC	Egypt, Arab Rep. of	LMC	Madagascar	LIC	Bahrain
Kosovo	LIC	Iran, Islamic Rep. of	LMC	Malawi	LIC	Barbados
Kyrgyz Republic	UMC	Iraq	LMC	Mali	LIC	Bermuda
Latvia	UMC	Jordan	LMC	Mauritania	LIC	Brunei Darussalam
Lithuania	UMC	Lebanon	UMC	Mauritius	UMC	Cayman Islands
Macedonia, FYR	LMC	Libya	UMC	Mayotte	UMC	Channel Islands
Moldova	UMC	Morocco	LMC	Mozambique	LIC	Croatia
Montenegro	UMC	Syrian Arab Rep.	LMC	Namibia	UMC	Cyprus
Poland	UMC	Tunisia	LMC	Niger	LIC	Equatorial Guinea
Romania	UMC	West Bank and Gaza	LMC	Nigeria	LMC	Estonia
Russian Federation	UMC	Yemen, Republic of	LIC	Rwanda	LIC	Faeroe Islands
Serbia	LIC			São Tomé and Principe	LMC	French Polynesia
Tajikistan	UMC			Senegal	LIC	Greenland
Turkey	LMC			Seychelles	UMC	Guam
Turkmenistan	LMC			Sierra Leone	LIC	Hong Kong, China
Ukraine	LIC			Somalia	LIC	Isle of Man
Uzbekistan				South Africa	UMC	Israel
				Sudan	LMC	Kuwait
				Swaziland	LMC	Liechtenstein
				Tanzania	LIC	Macao, China
				Togo	LIC	Malta
				Uganda	LIC	Monaco
				Zambia	LIC	Netherlands Antilles
				Zimbabwe	LIC	New Caledonia
						Northern Mariana Islands
						Oman
						Puerto Rico
						Qatar
						San Marino
						Saudi Arabia
						Singapore
						Slovenia
						Taiwan, China
						Trinidad and Tobago
						United Arab Emirates
						Virgin Islands (U.S.)

This table classifies all World Bank member economies and all other economies with populations of more than 30,000. Economies are divided among income groups according to 2008 GNI per capita, calculated using the World Bank Atlas method. The groups are low income (LIC), $975 or less; lower middle income (LMC), $976–3,855; upper middle income (UMC), $3,856–11,905; and high income, $11,906 or more.

Source: World Bank data.

Table 1   Key indicators of development

	Population			Population age composition % ages 0–14 2008	Gross national income (GNI)[a]		PPP gross national income (GNI)[b]		Gross domestic product per capita % growth 2007–08	Life expectancy at birth		Adult literacy rate % ages 15 and older 2007
	Millions 2008	Average annual % growth 2000–08	Density people per sq. km 2008		$ billions 2008	$ per capita 2008	$ billions 2008	$ per capita 2008		Male Years 2007	Female Years 2007	
Afghanistan	..	..	..	..	9.8	..[c]	30.6[d]	..	..	..	..	..
Albania	3	0.3	115	24	12.1	3,840	25.0	7,950	5.6	73	80	99
Algeria	34	1.5	14	28	146.4	4,260	272.8[d]	7,940[d]	1.5	71	74	75
Angola	18	2.9	14	45	62.1	3,450	90.5	5,020	11.8	45	49	..
Argentina	40	1.0	15	25	287.2	7,200	559.2	14,020	6.0	72	79	98
Armenia	3	0.0	109	21	10.3	3,350	19.4	6,310	6.6	70	77	99
Australia	21	1.4	3	19	862.5	40,350	727.5	34,040	1.9	79	84	..
Austria	8	0.5	101	15	386.0	46,260	314.5	37,680	1.5	77	83	..
Azerbaijan	9	0.9	105	25	33.2	3,830	67.4	7,770	9.6	64	71	100
Bangladesh	160	1.6	1,229	32	82.6	520	230.6	1,440	4.7	65	67	53
Belarus	10	−0.4	47	15	52.1	5,380	117.6	12,150	10.2	65	76	100
Belgium	11	0.5	354	17	474.5	44,330	372.1	34,760	0.4	77	83	..
Benin	9	3.3	78	43	6.0	690	12.7	1,460	1.8	60	62	41
Bolivia	10	1.9	9	37	14.1	1,460	40.1	4,140	4.3	63	68	91
Bosnia and Herzegovina	4	0.3	74	16	17.0	4,510	32.5	8,620	6.2	72	78	..
Brazil	192	1.2	23	26	1,411.2	7,350	1,932.9	10,070	4.1	69	76	90
Bulgaria	8	−0.7	70	13	41.8	5,490	91.1	11,950	6.5	69	76	98
Burkina Faso	15	3.1	56	46	7.3	480	17.6	1,160	1.5	51	54	29
Burundi	8	2.8	314	39	1.1	140	3.1	380	1.4	49	52	..
Cambodia	15	1.7	83	34	8.9	600	26.8	1,820	3.4	57	62	76
Cameroon	19	2.2	41	41	21.8	1,150	41.3	2,180	1.9	50	51	..
Canada	33	1.0	4	17	1,390.0	41,730	1,206.5	36,220	−0.6	78	83	..
Central African Republic	4	1.7	7	41	1.8	410	3.2	730	0.9	43	46	..
Chad	11	3.4	9	46	5.9	530	12.9	1,160	−3.1	49	52	32
Chile	17	1.0	22	23	157.5	9,400	222.4	13,270	2.2	75	82	97
China	1,326	0.6	142	21	3,899.3	2,940	7,984.0	6,020	8.4	71	75	93
Hong Kong, China	7	0.6	6,696	13	219.3	31,420	306.8	43,960	1.6	79	85	..
Colombia	45	1.4	40	30	207.4	4,660	379.1	8,510	1.3	69	77	93
Congo, Dem. Rep. of	64	3.0	28	47	9.8	150	18.4	290	3.2	45	48	..
Congo, Rep. of	4	2.2	11	41	7.1	1,970	11.2	3,090	3.7	53	55	..
Costa Rica	5	1.8	89	26	27.5	6,060	49.6[d]	10,950[d]	1.5	76	81	96
Côte d'Ivoire	21	2.2	65	41	20.3	980	32.6	1,580	−0.1	56	59	..
Croatia	4	0.0	79	15	60.2	13,570	81.7	18,420	2.4	72	79	99
Czech Republic	10	0.2	135	14	173.2	16,600	237.6	22,790	2.3	74	80	..
Denmark	5	0.4	130	18	325.1	59,130	205.0	37,280	−1.8	76	81	..
Dominican Republic	10	1.5	203	32	43.2	4,390	77.6[d]	7,890[d]	4.1	69	75	89
Ecuador	13	1.1	49	31	49.1	3,640	104.7	7,760	5.4	72	78	84
Egypt, Arab Rep. of	82	1.9	82	32	146.9	1,800	445.4	5,460	5.1	68	72	66
El Salvador	6	0.4	296	33	21.4	3,480	40.9[d]	6,670[d]	2.1	67	76	82
Eritrea	5	3.8	49	42	1.5	300	3.1[d]	630[d]	−1.2	56	60	..
Ethiopia	81	2.6	81	44	22.7	280	70.2	870	8.5	54	56	..
Finland	5	0.3	17	17	255.7	48,120	189.5	35,660	0.4	76	83	..
France	62	0.7	113	18	2,702.2[e]	42,250[e]	2,134.4	34,400	−0.2	78	85	..
Georgia	4	−1.0	63	17	10.8	2,470	21.2	4,850	2.8	67	75	..
Germany	82	0.0	236	14	3,485.7	42,440	2,952.4	35,940	1.5	77	82	..
Ghana	23	2.2	103	39	15.7	670	33.4	1,430	4.0	56	57	65
Greece	11	0.4	87	14	322.0	28,650	320.0	28,470	2.5	77	82	97
Guatemala	14	2.5	126	42	36.6	2,680	64.2[d]	4,690[d]	1.5	67	74	73
Guinea	10	2.0	40	43	3.7	390	11.7	1,190	6.0	56	60	..
Haiti	10	1.6	355	37	6.5	660	11.5[d]	1,180[d]	−0.5	59	63	..
Honduras	7	1.9	65	38	13.0	1,800	28.0[d]	3,870[d]	2.2	67	74	84
Hungary	10	−0.2	112	15	128.6	12,810	178.6	17,790	0.8	69	77	99
India	1,140	1.4	383	32	1,215.5	1,070	3,374.9	2,960	5.7	63	66	66
Indonesia	228	1.3	126	27	458.2	2,010	875.1	3,830	4.9	69	73	92
Iran, Islamic Rep. of	72	1.5	44	24	251.5	3,540	769.7	10,840	4.2	69	73	82
Iraq	..	..	..	..	..[f]					..	..	..
Ireland	4	2.0	65	21	221.2	49,590	166.6	37,350	−4.4	77	82	..
Israel	7	1.9	338	28	180.5	24,700	200.6	27,450	2.3	79	83	..
Italy	60	0.6	204	14	2,109.1	35,240	1,810.6	30,250	−1.8	79	84	99
Japan	128	0.1	350	13	4,879.2	38,210	4,497.7	35,220	−0.7	79	86	..
Jordan	6	2.6	67	35	19.5	3,310	32.7	5,530	2.3	71	74	91
Kazakhstan	16	0.6	6	24	96.2	6,140	152.0	9,690	1.9	61	72	100
Kenya	39	2.6	68	43	29.5	770	60.9	1,580	0.9	53	55	..
Korea, Rep. of	49	0.4	492	17	1,046.3	21,530	1,366.9	28,120	1.9	76	82	..
Kyrgyz Republic	5	1.0	28	30	3.9	740	11.3	2,130	6.2	64	72	99
Lao PDR	6	1.7	27	38	4.7	750	12.8	2,060	5.6	63	66	73
Lebanon	4	1.2	405	26	26.3	6,350	45.0	10,880	6.9	70	74	90
Liberia	4	3.7	39	43	0.6	170	1.1	300	2.4	57	59	56
Libya	6	2.0	4	30	72.7	11,590	98.1[d]	15,630[d]	5.0	72	77	87
Lithuania	3	−0.5	54	15	39.9	11,870	61.1	18,210	3.6	65	77	100
Madagascar	19	2.8	33	43	7.8	410	19.9	1,040	4.1	59	62	..
Malawi	14	2.6	152	46	4.1	290	11.9	830	7.0	48	48	72
Malaysia	27	1.9	82	30	188.1	6,970	370.8	13,740	2.9	72	77	92
Mali	13	3.0	10	44	7.4	580	13.9	1,090	1.9	52	57	26
Mauritania	3	2.8	3	40	2.6	840	6.3	2,000	−0.6	62	66	56

Table 1 Key indicators of development

	Population			Population age composition % ages 0–14	Gross national income (GNI)[a]		PPP gross national income (GNI)[b]		Gross domestic product per capita % growth	Life expectancy at birth		Adult literacy rate % ages 15 and older
	Millions 2008	Average annual % growth 2000–08	Density people per sq. km 2008	2008	$ billions 2008	$ per capita 2008	$ billions 2008	$ per capita 2008	2007–08	Male Years 2007	Female Years 2007	2007
Mexico	106	1.0	55	29	1,061.4	9,980	1,517.2	14,270	0.8	73	77	93
Moldova	4	–1.5	111	17	5.3[g]	1,470[g]	11.7	3,210	8.2	65	72	99
Morocco	31	1.2	70	29	80.5	2,580	135.3	4,330	4.6	69	73	56
Mozambique	22	2.2	28	44	8.1	370	16.7	770	4.5	42	42	44
Myanmar	49	0.9	75	27	..	..[c]	63.1[d]	1,290[d]	11.7	59	65	..
Nepal	29	2.0	200	37	11.5	400	32.1	1,120	3.6	63	64	57
Netherlands	16	0.4	485	18	824.6	50,150	685.1	41,670	1.7	78	82	..
New Zealand	4	1.3	16	21	119.3	27,940	107.1	25,090	–2.5	78	82	..
Nicaragua	6	1.3	47	36	6.1	1,080	14.9[d]	2,620[d]	2.2	70	76	78
Niger	15	3.5	12	50	4.8	330	10.0	680	6.0	58	56	29
Nigeria	151	2.4	166	43	175.6	1,160	293.1	1,940	3.0	46	47	72
Norway	5	0.8	16	19	415.3	87,070	279.0	58,500	0.7	78	83	..
Pakistan	166	2.3	215	37	162.9	980	448.8	2,700	3.7	65	66	54
Panama	3	1.8	46	30	21.0	6,180	39.5[d]	11,650	7.5	73	78	93
Papua New Guinea	6	2.3	14	40	6.5	1,010	12.9[d]	2,000	3.7	55	60	58
Paraguay	6	1.9	16	34	13.6	2,180	30.0	4,820	4.0	70	74	95
Peru	29	1.3	23	31	115.0	3,990	230.0	7,980	8.6	71	76	90
Philippines	90	1.9	303	34	170.4	1,890	352.4	3,900	2.0	70	74	93
Poland	38	–0.1	124	15	453.0	11,880	659.7	17,310	4.8	71	80	99
Portugal	11	0.5	116	15	218.4	20,560	234.6	22,080	–0.2	75	82	95
Romania	22	–0.5	94	15	170.6	7,930	290.3	13,500	9.4	69	76	98
Russian Federation	142	–0.4	9	15	1,364.5	9,620	2,216.3	15,630	7.5	62	74	100
Rwanda	10	2.5	394	42	4.0	410	9.9	1,010	8.2	48	52	..
Saudi Arabia	25	2.2	11	33	374.3	15,500	554.4	22,950	2.1	71	75	85
Senegal	12	2.6	63	44	11.8	970	21.5	1,760	–0.2	54	57	42
Serbia	7	–0.3	83	18	41.9	5,710	81.9	11,150	6.1	71	76	..
Sierra Leone	6	3.4	78	43	1.8	320	4.2	750	2.4	46	49	38
Singapore	5	2.3	7,024	17	168.2	34,760	232.0	47,940	–4.1	78	83	94
Slovak Republic	5	0.0	112	16	78.6	14,540	115.2	21,300	6.2	71	78	..
Somalia	9	3.0	14	45	..	..[c]	..	..	..	47	49	..
South Africa	49	1.3	40	31	283.3	5,820	476.2	9,780	1.3	49	52	88
Spain	46	1.5	91	15	1,456.5	31,960	1,418.7	31,130	–0.3	78	84	98
Sri Lanka	20	0.9	310	24	35.9	1,790	89.9	4,480	5.8	69	76	91
Sudan	41	2.1	17	40	46.5	1,130	79.8	1,930	5.9	56	60	..
Sweden	9	0.5	22	17	469.7	50,940	352.0	38,180	–1.0	79	83	..
Switzerland	8	0.8	191	16	498.5	65,330	354.5	46,460	0.5	79	84	..
Syrian Arab Rep.	21	3.1	116	35	44.4	2,090	92.4	4,350	1.6	72	76	83
Tajikistan	7	1.3	49	38	4.1	600	12.7	1,860	6.2	64	69	100
Tanzania	42	2.7	48	45	18.4[h]	440[h]	52.1	1,230	4.4	55	56	72
Thailand	67	1.0	132	22	191.7	2,840	403.4	5,990	2.0	66	72	94
Togo	6	2.6	119	40	2.6	400	5.3	820	–1.4	61	64	..
Tunisia	10	1.0	66	24	34.0	3,290	73.0	7,070	4.1	72	76	78
Turkey	74	1.3	96	27	690.7	9,340	1,017.6	13,770	2.5	69	74	89
Turkmenistan	5	1.4	11	30	14.3	2,840	31.2[d]	6,210[d]	8.4	59	68	100
Uganda	32	3.2	161	49	13.3	420	36.1	1,140	6.0	52	53	74
Ukraine	46	–0.8	80	14	148.6	3,210	333.5	7,210	2.7	63	74	100
United Arab Emirates	4	4.0	54	19	..	..[i]	..	..	5.7	77	81	90
United Kingdom	61	0.5	254	18	2,787.2	45,390	2,218.2	36,130	0.1	77	82	..
United States	304	0.9	33	20	14,466.1	47,580	14,282.7	46,970	0.2	75	81	..
Uruguay	3	0.1	19	23	27.5	8,260	41.8	12,540	8.6	72	80	98
Uzbekistan	27	1.3	64	30	24.7	910	72.6[d]	2,660[d]	7.2	64	70	..
Venezuela, R. B. de	28	1.7	32	30	257.8	9,230	358.6	12,830	3.1	71	77	95
Vietnam	86	1.3	278	27	77.0	890	232.9	2,700	4.7	72	76	..
West Bank and Gaza	4	3.4	638	45	..	..[f]	..	..	..	72	75	94
Yemen, Republic of	23	3.0	44	44	21.9	950	50.9	2,210	0.9	61	64	59
Zambia	13	2.3	17	46	12.0	950	15.5	1,230	3.4	45	46	71
Zimbabwe	12	0.0	32	40	..	..	..	..	..	43	44	91
World	6,692s	1.2w	52w	27w	57,637.5t	8,613w	69,309.0t	10,357w	0.8w	67w	71w	84w
Low income	973	2.1	52	38	509.6	524	1,368.8	1,407	4.1	57	60	64
Middle income	4,651	1.1	60	27	15,159.6	3,260	28,619.5	6,154	5.0	67	71	83
Lower middle income	3,702	1.2	119	28	7,691.9	2,078	17,001.7	4,592	6.3	66	70	81
Upper middle income	948	0.8	21	25	7,471.9	7,878	11,663.5	12,297	3.8	68	75	93
Low and middle income	5,624	1.3	59	29	15,683.1	2,789	29,971.3	5,330	4.9	65	69	81
East Asia & Pacific	1,931	0.8	122	23	5,080.5	2,631	10,425.9	5,398	7.2	70	74	93
Europe & Central Asia	441	0.1	19	19	3,274.0	7,418	5,393.2	12,219	5.2	65	74	98
Latin America & the Caribbean	565	1.2	28	29	3,833.0	6,780	5,827.4	10,309	3.2	70	76	91
Middle East & North Africa	325	1.9	38	31	1,052.9	3,242	2,330.6	7,308	3.9	68	72	73
South Asia	1,543	1.6	323	33	1,521.6	986	4,217.6	2,734	5.3	63	66	63
Sub-Saharan Africa	818	2.5	35	43	885.3	1,082	1,628.3	1,991	2.5	51	53	62
High income	1,069	0.7	32	18	42,041.4	39,345	39,686.3	37,141	0.0	77	82	99

a. Calculated using the World Bank Atlas method. b. PPP is purchasing power parity; see Technical notes. c. Estimated to be low income ($975 or less). d. The estimate is based on regression; others are extrapolated from the latest International Comparison Program benchmark estimates. e. The GNI and GNI per capita estimates include the French overseas departments of French Guiana, Guadeloupe, Martinique, and Réunion. f. Estimated to be lower middle income ($976 to $3,855). g. Excludes data for Transnistria. h. Data refers to mainland Tanzania only. i. Estimated to be high income ($11,906 or more).

Table 2   Poverty

| | National poverty line | | | | International poverty line | | | | | | | |
| | Population below national poverty line | | | | | | | | | | | |
	Survey year	National %	Survey year	National %	Survey year	Population below $1.25 a day %	Poverty gap at $1.25 a day %	Population below $2 a day %	Survey year	Population below $1.25 a day %	Poverty gap at $1.25 a day %	Population below $2 a day %
Afghanistan	2007	42.0	..	..	..	..	..	..	..	..	..	..
Albania	2002	25.4	2005	18.5	2002[a]	<2.0	<0.5	8.7	2005[a]	<2.0	<0.5	7.8
Algeria	1988	12.2	1995	22.6	1988[a]	6.6	1.8	23.8	1995[a]	6.8	1.4	23.6
Angola	..	..	..	..	..	..	..	..	2000[a]	54.3	29.9	70.2
Argentina	1998	28.8[b]	2002	53.0[b]	2002[b,c]	9.9	2.9	19.7	2005[b,c]	4.5	1.0	11.3
Armenia	1998–99	55.1	2001	50.9	2002[a]	15.0	3.1	46.7	2003[a]	10.6	1.9	43.4
Australia	..	..	..	..								
Austria		..		..								
Azerbaijan	1995	68.1	2001	49.6	2001[a]	6.3	1.1	27.1	2005[a]	<2	<0.5	<2.0
Bangladesh	2000	48.9	2005	40.0	2000[a]	57.8[d]	17.3[d]	85.4[d]	2005[a]	49.6[d]	13.1[d]	81.3[d]
Belarus	2002	30.5	2004	17.4	2002[a]	<2.0	<0.5	<2.0	2005[a]	<2.0	<0.5	<2.0
Belgium		..		..								
Benin	1999	29.0	2003	39.0	..	..	..	..	2003[a]	47.3	15.7	75.3
Bolivia	1999	62.0	2002	64.6	2002[c]	22.8	12.4	34.2	2005[a]	19.6	9.7	30.3
Bosnia and Herzegovina	2001–02	19.5	..	..	2001[a]	<2.0	<0.5	<2.0	2004[a]	<2.0	<0.5	<2.0
Brazil	1998	22.0	2002–03	21.5	2005[c]	7.8	1.6	18.3	2007[c]	5.2	1.3	12.7
Bulgaria	1997	36.0	2001	12.8	2001[a]	2.6	<0.5	7.8	2003[a]	<2.0	<0.5	<2.0
Burkina Faso	1998	54.6	2003	46.4	1998[a]	70.0	30.2	87.6	2003[a]	56.5	20.3	81.2
Burundi	1998	68.0	..	..	1998[a]	86.4	47.3	95.4	2006[a]	81.3	36.4	93.4
Cambodia	1994	47.0	2004	35.0	1993–94[a,e]	48.6	13.8	77.8	2004[a]	40.2	11.3	68.2
Cameroon	1996	53.3	2001	40.2	1996[a]	51.5	18.9	74.4	2001[a]	32.8	10.2	57.7
Canada		..		..								
Central African Republic		..		..	1993[a]	82.8	57.0	90.7	2003[a]	62.4	28.3	81.9
Chad	1995–96	43.4	..	..	..	..	..	..	2002–03[a]	61.9	25.6	83.3
Chile	1996	19.9	1998	17.0	2003[c]	<2.0	<0.5	5.3	2006[c]	<2.0	<0.5	2.4
China	1998	4.6	2004	2.8	2002[a]	28.4[f]	8.7[f]	51.1[f]	2005[a]	15.9[f]	4.0[f]	36.3[f]
Hong Kong, China		..										
Colombia	1995	60.0	1999	64.0	2003[c]	15.4	6.1	26.3	2006[c]	16.0	5.7	27.9
Congo, Dem. Rep. of	2004–05	71.3	..	..	..	..	..	..	2005–06[a]	59.2	25.3	79.5
Congo, Rep. of	2005	42.3	..	..	..	..	..	..	2005[a]	54.1	22.8	74.4
Costa Rica	1989	31.7	2004	23.9	2003[c]	5.6	2.4	11.5	2005[c]	2.4	<0.5	8.6
Côte d'Ivoire		..		..	1998[a]	24.1	6.7	49.1	2002[a]	23.3	6.8	46.8
Croatia	2002	11.2	2004	11.1	2001[a]	<2.0	<0.5	<2.0	2005[a]	<2.0	<0.5	<2.0
Czech Republic		..		..	1993[c]	<2.0	<0.5	<2.0	1996[c]	<2.0	<0.5	<2.0
Denmark		..		..								
Dominican Republic	2000	27.7	2004	42.2	2003[c]	6.1	1.5	16.3	2005[c]	5.0	0.9	15.1
Ecuador	1998	46.0	2001	45.2	2005[c]	9.8	3.2	20.4	2007[c]	4.7	1.2	12.8
Egypt, Arab Rep. of	1995–96	22.9	1999–2000	16.7	1999–2000[a]	<2.0	<0.5	19.3	2004–05[a]	<2.0	<0.5	18.4
El Salvador	1995	50.6	2002	37.2	2003[c]	14.3	6.7	25.3	2005[c]	11.0	4.8	20.5
Eritrea	1993–94	53.0	..	..								
Ethiopia	1995–96	45.5	1999–2000	44.2	1999–2000[a]	55.6	16.2	86.4	2005[a]	39.0	9.6	77.5
Finland		..		..								
France		..		..								
Georgia	2002	52.1	2003	54.5	2002[a]	15.1	4.7	34.2	2005[a]	13.4	4.4	30.4
Germany		..		..								
Ghana	1998–99	39.5	2005–06	28.5	1998–99[a]	39.1	14.4	63.3	2006[a]	30.0	10.5	53.6
Greece		..		..								
Guatemala	1989	57.9	2000	56.2	2002[c]	16.9	6.5	29.8	2006[c]	11.7	3.5	24.3
Guinea	1994	40.0	..	..	1994[a]	36.8	11.5	63.8	2002–03[a]	70.1	32.2	87.2
Haiti	1987	65.0	1995	66.0[g]	..	..	..	..	2001[c]	54.9	28.2	72.1
Honduras	1998–99	52.5	2004	50.7	2005[c]	22.2	10.2	34.8	2006[c]	18.2	8.2	29.7
Hungary	1993	14.5	1997	17.3	2002[a]	<2.0	<0.5	<2.0	2004[a]	<2.0	<0.5	<2.0
India	1993–94	36.0	1999–2000	28.6	1993–94[a]	49.4[f]	14.4[f]	81.7[f]	2004–05[a]	41.6[f]	10.8[f]	75.6[f]
Indonesia	1996	17.6	2005	16.0	1998[a]	<2.0	<0.5	8.3	2005[a]	<2.0	<0.5	8.0
Iran, Islamic Rep. of		..		..								
Iraq		..		..								
Ireland		..		..								
Israel		..		..								
Italy		..		..								
Japan		..		..								
Jordan	1997	21.3	2002	14.2	2002–03[a]	<2.0	<0.5	11.0	2006[a]	<2.0	<0.5	3.5
Kazakhstan	2001	17.6	2002	15.4	2002[a]	5.2	0.9	21.5	2003[a]	3.1	<0.5	17.2
Kenya	1994	40.0	1997	52.0	1997[a]	19.6	4.6	42.7	2005–06[a]	19.7	6.1	39.9
Korea, Rep. of		..		..								
Kyrgyz Republic	2003	49.9	2005	43.1	2002[a]	34.0	8.8	66.6	2004[a]	21.8	4.4	51.9
Lao PDR	1997–98	38.6	2002–03	33.0	1997–98[a]	49.3[d]	14.9[d]	79.9[d]	2002–03[a]	44.0[d]	12.1[d]	76.8[d]
Lebanon		..		..								
Liberia		..		..						2007[a]	83.7	40.8	94.8
Libya		..		..								
Lithuania		..		..	2002[a]	<2.0	<0.5	<2.0	2004[a]	<2.0	<0.5	<2.0
Madagascar	1997	73.3	1999	71.3	2001[a]	76.3	41.4	88.7	2005[a]	67.8	26.5	89.6
Malawi	1990–91	54.0	1997–98	65.3	1997–98[a]	83.1	46.0	93.5	2004–05[a,h]	73.9	32.3	90.4
Malaysia	1989	15.5	..	..	1997[c]	<2.0	<0.5	6.8	2004–05[c]	<2.0	<0.5	7.8
Mali	1998	63.8	..	..	2001[a]	61.2	25.8	82.0	2006[a]	51.4	18.8	77.1
Mauritania	1996	50.0	2000	46.3	1995–96[a]	23.4	7.1	48.3	2000[a]	21.2	5.7	44.1
Mexico	2002	20.3	2004	17.6	2004[a]	2.8	1.4	7.0	2006[a]	<2.0	<0.5	4.8
Moldova	2001	62.4	2002	48.5	2002[a]	17.1	4.0	40.3	2004[a]	8.1	1.7	28.9
Morocco	1990–91	13.1	1998–99	19.0	2000[a]	6.3	0.9	24.3	2007[a]	2.5	0.5	14.0
Mozambique	1996–97	69.4	2002–03	54.1	1996–97[a]	81.3	42.0	92.9	2002–03[a]	74.7	35.4	90.0
Myanmar		..		..		..						

Table 2 Poverty

	National poverty line				International poverty line							
	Population below national poverty line					Population below $1.25 a day %	Poverty gap at $1.25 a day %	Population below $2 a day %		Population below $1.25 a day %	Poverty gap at $1.25 a day %	Population below $2 a day %
	Survey year	National %	Survey year	National %	Survey year				Survey year			
Nepal	1995–96	41.8	2003–04	30.9	1995–96[a]	68.4	26.7	88.1	2003–04[a]	55.1	19.7	77.6
Netherlands		..		..		..	..	..		..	..	..
New Zealand		..		..		..	..	..		..	..	..
Nicaragua	1998	47.9	2001	45.8	2001[c]	19.4	6.7	37.5	2005[c]	15.8	5.2	31.8
Niger	1989–93	63.0		..	1994[a]	78.2	38.6	91.5	2005[a]	65.9	28.1	85.6
Nigeria	1985	43.0	1992–93	34.1	1996–97[a]	68.5	32.1	86.4	2003–04[a]	64.4	29.6	83.9
Norway		..		..		..	..	..		..	..	..
Pakistan	1993	28.6	1998–99	32.6	2001–02[a]	35.9	7.9	73.9	2004–05[a]	22.6	4.4	60.3
Panama	1997	37.3		..	2004[c]	9.2	2.7	18.0	2006[c]	9.5	3.1	17.8
Papua New Guinea	1996	37.5		..		..	..	..	1996[a]	35.8	12.3	57.4
Paraguay	1990	20.5[i]		..	2005[c]	9.3	3.4	18.4	2007[c]	6.5	2.7	14.2
Peru	2001	54.3	2004	53.1	2005[c]	8.2	2.0	19.4	2006[c]	7.9	1.9	18.5
Philippines	1994	32.1	1997	25.1	2003[a]	22.0	5.5	43.8	2006[a]	22.6	5.5	45.0
Poland	1996	14.6	2001	14.8	2002[a]	<2.0	<0.5	<2.0	2005[a]	<2.0	<0.5	<2.0
Portugal		..		..		..	..	..		..	..	..
Romania	1995	25.4	2002	28.9	2002[a]	2.9	0.8	13.0	2005[a]	<2.0	<0.5	3.4
Russian Federation	1998	31.4	2002	19.6	2002[a]	<2.0	<0.5	3.7	2005[a]	<2.0	<0.5	<2.0
Rwanda	1993	51.2	1999–2000	60.3	1984–85[a]	63.3	19.7	88.4	2000[a]	76.6	38.2	90.3
Saudi Arabia		..		..		..	..	..		..	..	..
Senegal	1992	33.4		..	2001[a]	44.2	14.3	71.3	2005[a]	33.5	10.8	60.3
Serbia		..		..		..	..	..		..	..	..
Sierra Leone	1989	82.8	2003–04	70.2	1989–90[a]	62.8	44.8	75.0	2002–03[a]	53.4	20.3	76.1
Singapore		..		..		..	..	..		..	..	..
Slovak Republic	2004	16.8		..	1992[c]	<2.0	<0.5	<2.0	1996[c]	<2.0	<0.5	<2.0
Somalia		..		..		..	..	..		..	..	..
South Africa		..		..	1995[a]	21.4	5.2	39.9	2000[a]	26.2	8.2	42.9
Spain		..		..		..	..	..		..	..	..
Sri Lanka	1995–96	25.0	2002	22.7	1995–96[a]	16.3	3.0	46.7	2002[a]	14.0	2.6	39.7
Sudan		..		..		..	..	..		..	..	..
Sweden		..		..		..	..	..		..	..	..
Switzerland		..		..		..	..	..		..	..	..
Syrian Arab Rep.		..		..		..	..	..		..	..	..
Tajikistan	1999	74.9	2003	44.4	2003[a]	36.3	10.3	68.8	2004[a]	21.5	5.1	50.8
Tanzania	1991	38.6	2000–01	35.7	1991–92[a]	72.6	29.7	91.3	2000–01[a]	88.5	46.8	96.6
Thailand	1994	9.8	1998	13.6	2002[a]	<2.0	<0.5	15.1	2004[a]	<2.0	<0.5	11.5
Togo	1987–89	32.3		..		..	..	..	2006[a]	38.7	11.4	69.3
Tunisia	1990	7.4	1995	7.6	1995[a]	6.5	1.3	20.4	2000[a]	2.6	<0.5	12.8
Turkey	1994	28.3	2002	27.0	2002[a]	2.0	<0.5	9.6	2005[a]	2.7	0.9	9.0
Turkmenistan		..		..	1993[c]	63.5	25.8	85.7	1998[a]	24.8	7.0	49.6
Uganda	1999–2000	33.8	2002–03	37.7	2002[a]	57.4	22.7	79.8	2005[a]	51.5	19.1	75.6
Ukraine	2000	31.5	2003	19.5	2002[a]	<2.0	<0.5	3.4	2005[a]	<2.0	<0.5	<2.0
United Arab Emirates		..		..		..	..	..		..	..	..
United Kingdom		..		..		..	..	..		..	..	..
United States		..		..		..	..	..		..	..	..
Uruguay	1994	20.2[b]	1998	24.7[b]	2005[b,c]	<2.0	<0.5	4.5	2006[b,c]	<2.0	<0.5	4.2
Uzbekistan	2000–01	31.5	2003	27.2	2002[a]	42.3	12.4	75.6	2003[a]	46.3	15.0	76.7
Venezuela, R. B. de	1989	31.3	1997–99	52.0	2003[c]	18.4	8.8	31.7	2006[c]	3.5	1.2	10.2
Vietnam	1998	37.4	2002	28.9	2004[a]	24.2	5.1	52.5	2006[a]	21.5	4.6	48.4
West Bank and Gaza		..		..		..	..	..		..	..	..
Yemen, Republic of	1998	41.8		..	1998[a]	12.9	3.0	36.3	2005[a]	17.5	4.2	46.6
Zambia	1998	72.9	2004	68.0	2002–03[a]	64.6	27.1	85.1	2004–05[a]	64.3	32.8	81.5
Zimbabwe	1990–91	25.8	1995–96	34.9		..	..	..		..	..	..

a. Expenditure base. b. Covers urban area only. c. Income base. d. Adjusted by spatial consumer price index information. e. Due to security concerns, the survey covered only 56 percent of rural villages and 65 percent of the rural population. f. Weighted average of urban and rural estimates. g. Covers rural area only. h. Due to change in survey design, the most recent survey is not strictly comparable with the previous one. i. Survey covers Asunción metropolitan area.

Table 3 Millennium Development Goals: eradicating poverty and improving lives

	Eradicate extreme poverty and hunger			Achieve universal primary education	Promote gender equality	Reduce child mortality	Improve maternal health	Combat HIV/AIDS and other diseaes		Ensure environmental sustainability		Develop a global partnership for development
	Share of poorest quintile in national consumption or income % 1990–2007[b]	Vulnerable employment % of employment 2007	Prevalence of child malnutrition % of children under 5 2000–07[b]	Primary completion rate % 2007	Ratio of girls to boys enrollments in primary and secondary school % 2007	Under-five mortality rate per 1,000 2007	Maternal mortality rate per 100,000 live births 2005	HIV prevalence % of population ages 15–49 2007	Incidence of tuberculosis per 100,000 people 2007	Carbon dioxide emissions per capita metric tons 2005	Access to improved sanitation facilities % of population 2006	Internet users per 100 people[a] 2008
Afghanistan	..	..	32.9	38	58	257	1,800	..	168	..	30	1.9
Albania	7.8[c]	..	17.0	96	97	15	92	..	17	1.1	97	15.1
Algeria	6.9[c]	..	10.2	95	99	37	180	0.1	57	4.2	94	10.3
Angola	2.0[c]	..	27.5	..	..	158	1,400	2.1	287	0.5	50	3.1
Argentina	3.4[d,e]	20[f]	2.3	99	104	16	77	0.5	31	3.9	91	28.1
Armenia	8.6[c]	..	4.2	98	104	24	76	0.1	72	1.4	91	5.6
Australia	5.9[e]	9	..	..	97	6	4	0.2	6	18.1	100	55.7
Austria	8.6[e]	9	..	102	97	4	4	0.2	12	8.9	100	59.3
Azerbaijan	13.3[c]	53	14.0	113	97	39	82	0.2	77	4.4	80	10.8
Bangladesh	9.4[c]	85	39.2	56	107	61	570	..	223	0.3	36	0.3
Belarus	8.8[c]	..	1.3	92	101	13	18	0.2	61	6.5	93	29.0
Belgium	8.5[e]	10	..	86	98	5	8	0.2	12	9.8	..	65.9
Benin	6.9[c]	..	21.5	64	73	123	840	1.2	91	0.3	30	1.8
Bolivia	1.8[c]	..	5.9	98	99	57	290	0.2	155	1.0	43	10.5
Bosnia and Herzegovina	6.9[c]	..	1.6	..	99	14	3	<0.1	51	6.9	95	34.7
Brazil	3.0[e]	27	2.2	106	103	22	110	0.6	48	1.7	77	35.5
Bulgaria	8.7[c]	8	1.6	98	97	12	11	..	39	5.7	99	30.9
Burkina Faso	7.0[c]	..	35.2	37[g]	84[g]	191	700	1.6	226	0.1	13	0.9
Burundi	9.0[c]	..	38.9	39	90	180	1,100	2.0	367	0.0	41	0.8
Cambodia	7.1[c]	..	28.4	85	90	91	540	0.8	495	0.0	28	0.5
Cameroon	5.6[c]	..	15.1	55	85	148	1,000	5.1	192	0.2	51	3.0
Canada	7.2[c]	10[f]	..	96	99	6	7	0.4	5	16.6	100	72.8
Central African Republic	5.2[c]	..	21.8	30[g]	..	172	980	6.3	345	0.1	31	0.4
Chad	6.3[c]	..	33.9	30	64	209	1,500	3.5	299	0.0	9	1.2
Chile	4.1[c]	25	0.6	95	99	9	16	0.3	12	4.1	94	32.6
China	5.7[c]	..	6.8	101	100	22	45	0.1[h]	98	4.3	65	22.5
Hong Kong, China	5.3[e]	7	..	102	98	..	..	..	62	5.7	..	59.1
Colombia	2.3[e]	41	5.1	107	104	20	130	0.6	35	1.4	78	38.4
Congo, Dem. Rep. of	5.5[c]	..	33.6	51	73	161	1,100	..	392	0.0	31	0.5
Congo, Rep. of	5.0[c]	..	11.8	72	91	125	740	3.5	403	0.6	20	4.3
Costa Rica	4.2[e]	20	..	91	102	11	30	0.4	11	1.7	96	33.6
Côte d'Ivoire	5.0[c]	..	16.7	45	..	127	810	3.9	420	0.5	24	3.2
Croatia	8.7[c]	16	..	101	102	6	7	<0.1	40	5.2	99	50.6
Czech Republic	10.2[e]	12	2.1	93	101	4	4	..	9	11.7	99	48.3
Denmark	8.3[e]	..	..	101	102	4	3	0.2	8	8.5	100	84.2
Dominican Republic	4.0[e]	43	4.2	91[g]	103[g]	38	150	1.1	69	2.0	79	26.0
Ecuador	3.4[e]	34[f]	6.2	106	100	22	210	0.3	101	2.2	84	9.7
Egypt, Arab Rep. of	9.0[c]	25	5.4	98	95	36	130	..	21	2.2	66	15.4
El Salvador	3.3[e]	36	6.1	91	101	24	170	0.8	40	1.1	86	12.5
Eritrea	..	..	34.5	46	78	70	450	1.3	95	0.2	5	3.0
Ethiopia	9.3[c]	52[f]	34.6	46	83	119	720	2.1	378	0.1	11	0.4
Finland	9.6[e]	..	..	98	102	4	7	0.1	6	10.1	100	78.8
France	7.2[e]	6	..	..	100	4	8	0.4	14	6.2	..	51.2
Georgia	5.4[c]	62	..	92	98	30	66	0.1	84	1.1	93	8.2
Germany	8.5[e]	..	..	103	99	4	4	0.1	6	9.5	100	76.1
Ghana	5.2[c]	..	13.91	78[g]	95[g]	115	560	1.9	203	0.3	10	4.3
Greece	6.7[c]	28	..	101	97	4	3	0.2	18	8.6	98	32.3
Guatemala	3.4[e]	..	17.7	77	93	39	290	0.8	63	0.9	84	10.1
Guinea	5.8[c]	..	22.5	64	76	150	910	1.6	287	0.1	19	0.9
Haiti	2.5[e]	..	18.9	..	..	76	670	2.2	306	0.2	19	10.4
Honduras	2.5[e]	..	8.6	89	106	24	280	0.7	59	1.1	66	9.1
Hungary	8.6[c]	7	..	92	99	7	6	0.1	17	5.6	100	54.8
India	8.1[c]	..	43.5	86	91	72	450	0.3	168	1.3	28	7.2
Indonesia	7.1[c]	63	24.4	105	98	31	420	0.2	228	1.9	52	11.1
Iran, Islamic Rep. of	6.4[c]	43	..	105	105	33	140	0.2	22	6.5	..	32.0
Iraq	..	..	7.1	75	78	44	300	..	56	..	76	0.9
Ireland	7.4[e]	11	..	97	103	4	1	0.2	13	10.2	..	63.5
Israel	5.7[e]	7	..	102	101	5	4	0.1	8	9.2	..	27.9
Italy	6.5[e]	22	..	102	99	4	3	0.4	7	7.7	..	48.6
Japan	10.6[e]	11	..	..	100	4	6	..	21	9.6	100	69.0
Jordan	7.2[c]	..	3.6	102	102	24	62	..	7	3.8	85	25.4
Kazakhstan	7.4[c]	..	4.9	104[g]	99[g]	32	140	0.1	129	11.9	97	12.3
Kenya	4.7[c]	..	16.5	93	95	121	560	..	353	0.3	42	8.7
Korea, Rep. of	7.9[e]	25	..	102	96	5	14	<0.1	90	9.4	..	77.1
Kyrgyz Republic	8.1[c]	47	2.7	95	100	38	150	0.1	121	1.1	93	14.3
Lao PDR	8.5[c]	..	36.4	77	86	70	660	0.2	151	0.2	48	1.6
Lebanon	..	..	..	83[g]	103[g]	29	150	0.1	19	4.2	..	38.3
Liberia	6.4[c]	..	20.4	55[g]	..	133	1,200	1.7	277	0.1	32	0.6
Libya	..	..	..	..	105	18	97	..	17	9.5	97	4.7
Lithuania	6.8[c]	..	..	95	100	8	11	0.1	68	4.1	..	52.9
Madagascar	6.2[c]	86	36.8	62	96	112	510	0.1	251	0.2	12	1.7
Malawi	7.0[c]	..	18.4	55	100	111	1,100	11.9	346	0.1	60	2.2
Malaysia	6.4[e]	22	..	96	104	11	62	0.5	103	9.3	94	62.6
Mali	6.5[e]	..	27.9	52	76	196	970	1.5	319	0.0	45	1.4
Mauritania	6.2[c]	..	30.4	59	103	119	820	0.8	318	0.6	24	1.4

Table 3   Millennium Development Goals: eradicating poverty and improving lives

	Eradicate extreme poverty and hunger			Achieve universal primary education	Promote gender equality	Reduce child mortality	Improve maternal health	Combat HIV/AIDS and other diseaes		Ensure environmental sustainability		Develop a global partnership for development
	Share of poorest quintile in national consumption or income % 1990–2007[b]	Vulnerable employment % of employment 2007	Prevalence of child malnutrition % of children under 5 2000–07[b]	Primary completion rate % 2007	Ratio of girls to boys enrolllments in primary and secondary school % 2007	Under-five mortality rate per 1,000 2007	Maternal mortality rate per 100,000 live births 2005	HIV prevalence % of population ages 15–49 2007	Incidence of tuberculosis per 100,000 people 2007	Carbon dioxide emissions per capita metric tons 2005	Access to improved sanitation facilities % of population 2006	Internet users per 100 people[a] 2008
Mexico	4.6[c]	29	3.4	105	99	35	60	0.3	20	4.1	81	21.9
Moldova	7.3[c]	32	3.2	93	102	18	22	0.4	141	2.1	79	19.1
Morocco	6.5[c]	52	9.9	83	88	34	240	0.1	92	1.6	72	33.0
Mozambique	5.4[c]	..	21.2	46	85	168	520	12.5	431	0.1	31	1.6
Myanmar	..	..	29.6	..	..	103	380	0.7	171	0.2	82	0.1
Nepal	6.1[c]	..	38.8	78[g]	98[g]	55	830	0.5	173	0.1	27	1.4
Netherlands	7.6[e]	..	..	..	98	5	6	0.2	8	7.7	100	86.8
New Zealand	6.4[e]	12	..	..	102	6	9	0.1	7	7.2	..	69.2
Nicaragua	3.8[e]	45	7.8	74	103	35	170	0.2	49	0.7	48	2.8
Niger	5.9[c]	..	39.9	40	71	176	1,800	0.8	174	0.1	7	0.5
Nigeria	5.1[c]	..	27.2	72	84	189	1,100	3.1	311	0.8	30	7.3
Norway	9.6[e]	6	..	97	99	4	7	0.1	6	11.4	..	84.8
Pakistan	9.1[c]	62	31.3	63	80	90	320	0.1	181	0.9	58	11.1
Panama	2.5[c]	28	..	99	101	23	130	1.0	47	1.8	74	22.9
Papua New Guinea	4.5[c]	..	..	..	..	65	470	1.5	250	0.7	45	1.8
Paraguay	3.4[e]	47	..	95	99	29	150	0.6	58	0.7	70	8.7
Peru	3.9[e]	40[f]	5.2	104	102	20	240	0.5	126	1.3	72	24.7
Philippines	5.6[c]	45	20.7	94	102	28	230	..	290	0.9	78	6.0
Poland	7.3[c]	19	..	96	99	7	8	0.1	25	7.9	..	44.0
Portugal	5.8[e]	18	..	104	101	4	11	0.5	30	5.9	99	41.9
Romania	8.2[c]	32	3.5	120	99	15	24	0.1	115	4.1	72	23.9
Russian Federation	6.4[c]	6	..	93	98	15	28	1.1	110	10.5	87	21.1
Rwanda	5.3[c]	..	18.0	35	100	181	1,300	2.8	397	0.1	23	3.1
Saudi Arabia	..	..	..	93	94	25	18	..	46	16.5	99	29.2
Senegal	6.2[c]	..	14.5	50	94	114	980	1.0	272	0.4	28	8.4
Serbia	8.3[c,i]	23	1.8	..	102	8	..	0.1	32	6.5[j]	92	32.1
Sierra Leone	6.1[c]	..	28.3	81	86	262	2,100	1.7	574	0.2	11	0.3
Singapore	5.0[e]	10	3.3	..	..	3	14	0.2	27	13.2	100	67.7
Slovak Republic	8.8[e]	10	..	94	100	8	6	<0.1	17	6.8	100	51.3
Somalia	..	..	32.8	..	..	142	1,400	0.5	249	0.1	23	1.1
South Africa	3.1[c]	3	..	84	100	59	400	18.1	948	8.7	59	8.6
Spain	7.0[e]	12	..	..	103	4	4	0.5	30	7.9	100	57.4
Sri Lanka	6.8[c]	41[f]	22.8	104	..	21	58	..	60	0.6	86	5.7
Sudan	..	..	38.4	50	88	109	450	1.4	243	0.3	35	9.2
Sweden	9.1[e]	..	..	95	99	3	3	0.1	6	5.4	100	79.7
Switzerland	7.6[e]	10	..	88	97	5	5	0.6	6	5.5	100	75.2
Syrian Arab Rep.	..	..	..	114	96	17	130	..	24	3.6	92	16.8
Tajikistan	7.7[c]	..	14.9	95	89	67	170	0.3	231	0.8	92	7.2
Tanzania	7.3[c]	88[f]	16.7	112[g]	..	116	950	6.2	297	0.1	33	1.2
Thailand	6.1[c]	53	7.0	101	104[g]	7	110	1.4	142	4.1	96	20.0
Togo	7.6[c]	..	..	57	75	100	510	3.3	429	0.2	12	5.4
Tunisia	5.9[c]	..	..	100	104	21	100	0.1	26	2.2	85	27.1
Turkey	5.2[c]	36	3.5	97	90	23	44	..	30	3.5	88	33.1
Turkmenistan	6.0[c]	..	..	..	..	50	130	<0.1	68	8.6	..	1.4
Uganda	6.1	..	19.0	54	98	130	550	5.4	330	0.1	33	7.9
Ukraine	9.0[c]	..	4.1	101	100	24	18	1.6	102	6.9	93	22.4
United Arab Emirates	..	..	..	105	101	8	37	..	16	30.1	97	86.1
United Kingdom	6.1[e]	..	..	..	102	6	8	0.2	15	9.1	..	79.4
United States	5.4[e]	..	1.3	96	100	8	11	0.6	4	19.5	100	72.4
Uruguay	4.5[e]	25	6.0	104	98	14	20	0.6	22	1.7	100	40.2
Uzbekistan	7.1[c]	..	4.4	97	98	41	24	0.1	113	4.3	96	8.8
Venezuela, R. B. de	4.9[e]	30	..	95[g]	102[g]	19	57	..	34	5.6	..	25.6
Vietnam	7.1[c]	..	20.2	..	..	15	150	0.5	171	1.2	65	21.0
West Bank and Gaza	..	36	..	83	104	27	..	..	20	..	80	9.6
Yemen, Republic of	7.2[c]	..	..	60	66	73	430	..	76	1.0	46	1.4
Zambia	3.6[c]	..	23.3	88	96	170	830	15.2	506	0.2	52	5.5
Zimbabwe	4.6[c]	..	14.0	..	97	90	880	15.3	782	0.9	46	11.4
World		..w	23.1w	87w	95w	68w	400w	0.8w	139w	4.5w, k	60w	21.3w
Low income		..	27.8	65	91	120	790	2.3	275	0.5	38	3.7
Middle income		..	22.7	91	96	58	320	0.6	138	3.1	58	14.7
Lower middle income		..	25.8	90	94	65	370	0.4	147	2.6	52	11.7
Upper middle income		24	..	98	100	25	110	1.5	105	5.1	82	26.6
Low and middle income		..	24.0	86	95	74	440	0.9	162	2.7	55	12.8
East Asia & Pacific		..	12.6	100	100	27	150	0.2	136	3.6	66	23.3
Europe & Central Asia		19	..	98	97	23	45	0.6	84	7.0	89	23.4
Latin America & the Caribbean		31	4.5	97	101	26	130	0.5	50	2.5	78	26.6
Middle East & North Africa		37	..	91	93	38	200	0.1	41	3.6	74	24.2
South Asia		..	40.9	79	90	78	500	0.3	174	1.1	33	6.6
Sub-Saharan Africa		..	26.5	63	88	146	900	5.0	369	0.9	31	4.5
High income		..	..	98	99	7	10	0.3	16	12.6	100	67.1

a. Data are from the International Telecommunication Union's (ITU) World Telecommunication Development Report database. Please cite ITU for third-party use of these data. b. Data are for the most recent year available. c. Refers to expenditure shares by percentiles of population, ranked by per capita expenditure. d. Urban data. e. Refers to income shares by percentiles of population, ranked by per capita income. f. Limited coverage. g. Data are for 2008. h. Includes Hong Kong, China. i. Includes Montenegro. j. Includes Kosovo and Montenegro. k. Includes emissions not allocated to specific countries.

Table 4 Economic activity

	Gross domestic product		Agricultural productivity agricultural value added per worker 2000 $		Value added as % of GDP			Household final consumption expenditure % of GDP 2008	General government final consumption expenditure % of GDP 2008	Gross capital formation % of GDP 2008	External balance of goods and services % of GDP 2008	GDP implicit deflator average annual % growth 2000–08
	Millions of dollars 2008	Average annual % growth 2000–08	1990–92	2003–05	Agriculture 2008	Industry 2008	Services 2008					
Afghanistan	10,170	..	..	..	37	25	38	98	11	31	–39	7.1
Albania	12,295	5.4	778	1,449	21	20	59	85	10	32	–27	3.5
Algeria	173,882	4.3	1,911	2,225	9	69	23	22	7	37	35	9.4
Angola	83,383	13.7	165	174	10	86	4	37	..ᵃ	12	50	48.1
Argentina	328,385	5.3	6,767	10,072	9	34	57	59	13	24	4	12.8
Armenia	11,917	12.4	1,476ᵇ	3,692	18	45	37	75	12	38	–25	4.6
Australia	1,015,217	3.3	20,839	29,908	..	..	..	55	18	29	–2	3.8
Austria	416,380	2.1	12,048	21,920	2	31	67	54	18	21	7	1.8
Azerbaijan	46,259	18.1	1,084ᵇ	1,143	6	71	23	25	10	23	42	10.9
Bangladesh	78,992	5.9	254	338	19	29	52	79	5	24	–8	4.8
Belarus	60,302	8.6	1,977ᵇ	3,153	9	39	53	54	16	35	–6	25.5
Belgium	497,586	2.0	..	39,243	1	24	75	52	22	22	3	2.0
Benin	6,680	3.9	326	519	..	..	..	..	..	..	..	3.3
Bolivia	16,674	4.1	670	773	14	42	44	61	12	16	12	7.0
Bosnia and Herzegovina	18,452	5.5	..	8,270	..	..	..	85	22	23	–30	3.8
Brazil	1,612,539	3.6	1,507	3,119	7	28	65	61	20	19	0	8.1
Bulgaria	49,900	5.8	2,500	7,159	7	31	61	70	16	37	–23	5.6
Burkina Faso	7,948	5.6	110	173	33	22	44	75	22	18	–15	2.4
Burundi	1,163	2.9	108	70	..	..	..	91	29	16	–36	9.6
Cambodia	9,574	9.7	..	314	32	27	41	83	3	21	–8	4.7
Cameroon	23,396	3.5	389	648	20	33	48	68	13	19	1	2.2
Canada	1,400,091	2.5	28,243	44,133	..	..	..	56	19	23	3	2.0
Central African Republic	1,970	0.6	287	381	53	14	32	95	3	10	–9	2.2
Chad	8,361	10.4	173	215	23	42	35	69	6	15	10	8.3
Chile	169,458	4.4	3,573	5,309	4	47	49	55	10	21	14	6.6
China	4,326,187	10.4	258	407	11	49	40	37	14	43	7	4.3
Hong Kong, China	215,355	5.2	..	..	0	8	92	60	8	20	11	–1.7
Colombia	242,268	4.9	3,080	2,749	9	34	57	64	13	24	–1	6.9
Congo, Dem. Rep. of	11,588	5.5	184	149	41	27	31	82	11	17	–10	28.3
Congo, Rep. of	10,699	4.0	..	..	5	60	35	29	14	27	30	7.0
Costa Rica	29,834	5.5	3,143	4,506	7	29	64	69	13	27	–10	10.2
Côte d'Ivoire	23,414	0.6	598	795	24	25	51	77	8	10	5	3.4
Croatia	69,333	4.6	5,425ᵇ	11,354	6	28	65	59	19	31	–8	3.8
Czech Republic	216,485	4.6	..	5,521	2	38	60	48	20	27	5	2.2
Denmark	342,672	1.7	15,190	38,441	1	26	73	50	26	23	1	2.3
Dominican Republic	45,790	5.4	1,924	3,305	11	28	61	81	6	20	–7	15.0
Ecuador	52,572	5.0	1,686	1,676	7	36	57	67	12	24	–3	9.5
Egypt, Arab Rep. of	162,818	4.7	1,528	2,072	14	36	50	72	11	24	–7	7.8
El Salvador	22,115	2.9	1,633	1,638	13	28	58	98	9	15	–22	3.7
Eritrea	1,654	1.3	..	71	24	19	56	86	31	11	–28	18.0
Ethiopia	26,487	8.2	..	158	43	13	45	85	11	21	–17	8.7
Finland	271,282	3.0	18,818	31,276	3	32	65	52	21	22	5	1.1
France	2,853,062	1.7	22,234	44,080	2	21	77	57	23	22	–2	2.1
Georgia	12,793	8.1	2,443ᵇ	1,791	10	24	66	76	21	31	–28	7.3
Germany	3,652,824	1.2	13,724	25,657	1	30	69	57	18	18	7	1.1
Ghana	16,123	5.6	293	320	32	26	42	81	14	32	–26	18.7
Greece	356,796	4.2	7,536	8,818	4	23	73	71	17	26	–13	3.3
Guatemala	38,977	3.9	2,120	2,623	11	28	62	90	4	24	–18	5.2
Guinea	4,266	3.1	142	190	8	35	58	85	5	13	–2	20.2
Haiti	6,953	0.5	..	..	..	..	..	98	..ᵃ	26	–23	16.7
Honduras	14,077	5.3	1,193	1,483	13	27	61	83	14	30	–28	6.5
Hungary	154,668	3.6	4,122	6,922	4	29	66	67	9	22	1	5.0
India	1,217,490	7.9	324	392	18	29	53	56	11	39	–6	4.6
Indonesia	514,389	5.2	484	583	14	48	37	63	8	28	1	10.9
Iran, Islamic Rep. of	385,143	6.0	1,954	2,561	10	45	45	45	14	31	10	17.9
Iraq	..	..	..	1,756	..	..	..	..	..	..	..	..
Ireland	281,776	5.0	..	17,107	2	35	63	46	16	27	11	2.9
Israel	199,498	3.5	..	..	..	..	..	58	25	19	–2	1.1
Italy	2,293,008	0.9	11,528	23,967	2	27	71	59	20	21	0	2.6
Japan	4,909,272	1.6	20,445	35,668	1	30	68	57	18	24	1	–1.2
Jordan	20,013	6.7	1,892	1,360	4	32	64	108	18	19	–45	4.2
Kazakhstan	132,229	9.5	1,795ᵇ	1,557	6	42	52	35	10	35	20	15.1
Kenya	34,507	4.6	334	333	21	13	65	79	11	25	–14	6.5
Korea, Rep. of	929,121	4.5	..	11,451	3	37	60	55	15	31	–1	2.2
Kyrgyz Republic	4,420	4.4	675ᵇ	979	34	19	48	101	18	26	–45	6.8
Lao PDR	5,431	6.9	360	459	40	31	29	69	8	38	–15	9.4
Lebanon	28,660	2.8	..	29,950	5	22	73	91	14	20	–25	2.2
Liberia	870	–1.1	..	..	54	19	27	116	15	20	–51	10.5
Libya	99,926	4.1	..	..	..	..	..	..	..	..	..	22.2
Lithuania	47,341	7.7	..	3,790	4	33	63	66	18	27	–11	4.0
Madagascar	8,970	3.8	186	174	25	17	57	85	5	36	–25	11.5
Malawi	4,269	4.2	72	116	34	21	45	85	11	32	–28	19.3
Malaysia	194,927	5.5	386	525	10	48	42	46	12	22	20	4.4
Mali	8,740	5.2	208	241	37	24	39	76	11	23	–10	4.2
Mauritania	2,858	5.1	574	356	13	47	41	61	20	26	–7	11.3

Table 4   Economic activity

	Gross domestic product		Agricultural productivity agricultural value added per worker 2000$		Value added as % of GDP			Household final consumption expenditure % of GDP 2008	General government final consumption expenditure % of GDP 2008	Gross capital formation % of GDP 2008	External balance of goods and services % of GDP 2008	GDP implicit deflator average annual % growth 2000–08
	Millions of dollars 2008	Average annual % growth 2000–08	1990–92	2003–05	Agriculture 2008	Industry 2008	Services 2008					
Mexico	1,085,951	2.7	2,256	2,793	4	37	59	66	10	26	–2	8.2
Moldova	6,048	6.3	1,286[b]	816	11	15	74	97	19	37	–53	11.6
Morocco	86,329	5.0	1,430	1,746	16	20	64	61	16	33	–9	1.6
Mozambique	9,735	8.0	107	148	28	26	46	75	12	23	–10	8.1
Myanmar	..	..	..	..	..	..	..	..	..	..	..	..
Nepal	12,615	3.5	191	207	34	17	50	79	10	32	–21	6.2
Netherlands	860,336	1.8	24,914	42,049	2	24	74	47	25	20	8	2.2
New Zealand	130,693	3.0	19,155	27,189	..	..	..	60	19	23	–1	3.0
Nicaragua	6,592	3.5	..	2,071	19	30	51	90	12	32	–34	8.5
Niger	5,354	4.4	152	157[b]	..	..	..	..	..	..	..	2.6
Nigeria	212,080	6.6	..	..	31	41	28	..	..	..	13	17.0
Norway	449,996	2.5	19,500	37,039	1	43	56	42	20	23	16	4.7
Pakistan	168,276	5.8	594	696	20	27	53	80	9	22	–10	7.3
Panama	23,088	6.6	2,363	3,904	6	17	76	65	11	23	1	2.2
Papua New Guinea	8,168	2.8	500	595	33	48	19	44	10	19	27	7.3
Paraguay	15,977	3.7	1,596	2,052	23	20	57	69	9	20	3	10.5
Peru	127,434	6.0	930	1,481	7	38	55	61	9	27	2	3.5
Philippines	166,909	5.1	905	1,075	15	32	53	77	10	15	–2	5.2
Poland	526,966	4.4	1,502[b]	2,182	4	30	65	66	15	23	–3	2.6
Portugal	242,689	0.9	4,642	6,220	3	24	73	65	20	22	–7	2.9
Romania	200,071	6.3	2,196	4,646	8	34	58	73	11	26	–10	17.0
Russian Federation	1,607,816	6.8	1,825[b]	2,519	5	38	57	45	19	25	11	16.5
Rwanda	4,457	6.7	167	182	35	12	53	90	9	21	–19	10.0
Saudi Arabia	467,601	4.1	7,875	15,780	2	70	27	26	20	19	35	8.9
Senegal	13,209	4.4	225	215	15	23	62	82	10	30	–22	2.9
Serbia	50,061	5.7	..	..	13	28	59	84	17	23	–24	17.2
Sierra Leone	1,953	10.3	..	..	43	24	33	80	13	20	–12	9.3
Singapore	181,948	5.8	22,695	40,419	0	28	72	39	11	31	19	1.5
Slovak Republic	94,957	6.3	..	5,026	4	41	55	54	16	28	1	3.7
Somalia	..	..	..	..	..	..	..	..	..	..	..	..
South Africa	276,764	4.3	1,786	2,495	3	31	66	61	20	22	–4	7.1
Spain	1,604,174	3.3	9,511	18,619	3	30	67	57	18	31	–7	3.9
Sri Lanka	40,714	5.5	679	702	13	29	57	70	16	27	–13	10.6
Sudan	58,443	7.4	414	667	26	34	40	59	16	24	1	9.9
Sweden	480,021	2.8	22,533	35,378	2	29	70	47	26	20	8	1.7
Switzerland	488,470	1.9	19,884	23,588	1	28	71	59	11	22	8	1.0
Syrian Arab Rep.	55,204	4.4	2,344	3,261	20	35	45	75	12	14	0	8.4
Tajikistan	5,134	8.6	346[b]	409	18	23	59	114	8	20	–42	21.0
Tanzania[c]	20,490	6.8	238	295	45	17	37	73	16	17	–6	9.4
Thailand	260,693	5.2	497	624	12	46	43	51	13	28	8	2.4
Togo	2,823	2.5	312	347	..	..	..	..	16	..	–27	1.1
Tunisia	40,180	4.9	2,422	2,700	10	28	62	65	14	25	–3	2.9
Turkey	794,228	5.9	1,770	1,846	10	28	62	71	13	22	–5	16.9
Turkmenistan	18,269	14.5	1,222[b]	..	..	..	..	..	..	..	11	12.2
Uganda	14,529	7.5	155	175	23	26	52	82	12	24	–18	5.1
Ukraine	180,355	7.2	1,195[b]	1,702	8	37	55	64	17	25	–6	15.7
United Arab Emirates	163,296	7.7	10,454	25,841	2	59	39	45	10	21	24	7.7
United Kingdom	2,645,593	2.5	22,664	26,942	1	23	76	63	22	19	–4	2.7
United States	14,204,322	2.5	20,793	42,744	1	22	77	70	16	20	–6	2.6
Uruguay	32,186	3.8	6,304	8,797	11	27	63	69	12	23	–4	8.2
Uzbekistan	27,918	6.6	1,272[b]	1,800	23	33	43	55	16	19	10	25.5
Venezuela, R. B. de	313,799	5.2	4,483	6,331	..	..	..	53	10	23	14	26.3
Vietnam	90,705	7.7	214	305	20	42	38	66	6	42	–13	7.8
West Bank and Gaza	..	–0.9	..	..	..	..	..	..	..	..	..	3.4
Yemen, Republic of	26,576	3.9	271	328[b]	..	..	..	..	..	..	..	13.6
Zambia	14,314	5.3	159	204	21	46	33	66	9	22	3	17.1
Zimbabwe	..	–5.7	240	222	..	..	..	..	..	..	..	232.0
World	60,587,016t	3.2w	731w	908w	3w	28w	69w	61w	17w	22w	0w	
Low income	568,504	5.8	222	268	25	29	46	75	9	27	–11	
Middle income	16,826,866	6.4	470	650	10	37	53	56	14	30	1	
Lower middle income	8,377,130	8.3	359	499	14	41	45	50	13	36	1	
Upper middle income	8,445,380	4.6	1,998	2,721	6	33	61	61	15	23	1	
Low and middle income	17,408,313	6.4	432	577	11	37	53	57	14	29	1	
East Asia & Pacific	5,658,322	9.1	295	438	12	48	41	42	13	39	6	
Europe & Central Asia	3,860,600	6.3	1,749	2,076	7	34	60	60	15	24	0	
Latin America & the Caribbean	4,247,077	3.9	2,125	3,044	6	32	62	63	14	23	0	
Middle East & North Africa	1,117,198	4.7	1,583	2,204	12	41	48	57	12	28	3	
South Asia	1,531,499	7.4	335	406	18	29	53	61	11	36	–7	
Sub-Saharan Africa	987,120	5.2	263	279	14	32	54	67	16	23	–3	
High income	43,189,942	2.3	15,906	25,500	1	26	73	62	18	21	–1	

a. Data on general government final consumption expenditure are not available separately; they are included in household final consumption expenditure. b. Data for all three years are not available. c. Data refer to mainland Tanzania only.

Table 5 Trade, aid, and finance

| | Merchandise trade | | Manufactured exports % of total merchandise exports 2007 | High technology exports % of manufactured exports 2007 | Current account balance $ millions 2008 | Foreign direct investment net inflows $ millions 2007 | Net official development assistance[a] $ per capita 2007 | External debt | | Domestic credit provided by banking sector % of GDP 2008 | Net migration thousands 2000–05[b] |
	Exports $ millions 2008	Imports $ millions 2008						Total $ millions 2007	Present value % of GNI 2007		
Afghanistan	680	3,350	..	..	..	288	..	2,041	18[d]	0	..
Albania	1,353	5,230	70	12	−1,924	477	97	2,776	22	68	−100
Algeria	78,233	39,156	1	2	..	1,665	12	5,541	4	−12	−140
Angola	66,300	21,100	..	..	9,402	−893	14	12,738	32	10	175
Argentina	70,588	57,413	31	7	7,588	6,462	2	127,758	63	24	−100
Armenia	1,069	4,412	56	2	−1,356	699	114	2,888	38	17	−100
Australia	187,428	200,272	19	14	−44,040	39,596	..	..	..	151	641
Austria	182,158	184,247	82	11	14,269	30,717	..	..	..	129	220
Azerbaijan	31,500	7,200	6	4	16,454	−4,749	26	3,021	14	17	−100
Bangladesh	15,369	23,860	91	..	857	653	10	22,033	22	60	−700
Belarus	32,902	39,483	53	3	−5,050	1,785	9	9,470	25	31	20
Belgium	476,953	469,889	78	7[c]	−12,015	72,195	..	..	..	115	196
Benin	1,050	1,990	9	0	−217	48	56	857	12[d]	15	99
Bolivia	6,370	4,987	7	5	1,800	204	50	4,947	24[d]	48	−100
Bosnia and Herzegovina	5,064	12,282	61	3	−2,765	2,111	117	6,479	42	59	62
Brazil	197,942	182,810	47	12	−28,191	34,585	2	237,472	25	102	−229
Bulgaria	23,124	38,256	55	6	−12,577	8,974	..	32,968	100	67	−41
Burkina Faso	620	1,800	..	..	..	600	63	1,461	14[d]	16	100
Burundi	56	403	21	4	−116	1	59	1,456	97[d]	35	192
Cambodia	4,290	6,510	..	..	−1,060	867	46	3,761	46	16	10
Cameroon	4,350	4,360	3	3	−547	433	104	3,162	5[d]	6	−12
Canada	456,420	418,336	53	14	27,281	111,772	..	..	..	191	1,089
Central African Republic	185	310	36	0	..	27	41	973	48[d]	18	−45
Chad	4,800	1,700	..	..	..	603	33	1,797	19[d]	−3	219
Chile	67,788	61,901	10	7	−3,440	14,457	7	58,649	45	83	30
China	1,428,488	1,133,040	93	30	426,107	138,413	1	373,635	13	126	−2,058
Hong Kong, China	370,242[e]	392,962	68[e]	19	30,637	54,365	..	..	..	125	113
Colombia	37,626	39,669	39	3	−6,761	9,040	17	44,976	28	43	−120
Congo, Dem. Rep. of	3,950	4,100	..	..	..	720	20	12,283	111[d]	5	−237
Congo, Rep. of	9,050	2,850	..	..	−2,181	4,289	36	5,156	93[d]	−19	4
Costa Rica	9,675	15,374	63	45	−1,578	1,896	12	7,846	35	54	84
Côte d'Ivoire	10,100	7,150	18	32	−146	427	8	13,938	67[d]	20	−339
Croatia	14,112	30,728	68	9	−6,397	4,916	37	48,584	109	75	−13
Czech Republic	146,934	141,882	90	14	−6,631	9,294	..	..	..	58	67
Denmark	117,174	112,296	66	17	6,938	11,858	..	..	..	210	46
Dominican Republic	6,910	16,400	..	..	−2,068	1,698	13	10,342	33	39	−148
Ecuador	18,511	18,686	8	7	1,598	183	16	17,525	50	18	−400
Egypt, Arab Rep. of	25,483	48,382	19	0	412	11,578	14	30,444	25	78	−291
El Salvador	4,549	9,755	55	4	−1,119	1,526	14	8,809	50	45	−340
Eritrea	20	530	..	..	..	−3	32	875	41[d]	125	229
Ethiopia	1,500	7,600	13	3	−828	223	31	2,634	8[d]	47	−340
Finland	96,714	91,045	81	21	10,121	11,568	..	..	..	88	33
France	608,684	707,720	79	19	−52,911	159,463	..	..	..	126	761
Georgia	1,498	6,058	45	7	−2,851	1,728	87	2,292	20	33	−309
Germany	1,465,215	1,206,213	83	14	243,289	51,543	..	..	..	126	930
Ghana	5,650	10,400	11	1	−2,151	970	50	4,479	22[d]	33	12
Greece	25,311	77,970	52	8	−51,313	1,959	..	..	..	109	154
Guatemala	7,765	14,545	50	3	−1,697	724	34	6,260	21	37	−300
Guinea	1,300	1,600	..	..	−456	111	23	3,268	64[d]	..	−425
Haiti	490	2,148	..	..	−80	75	73	1,598	20[d]	23	−140
Honduras	6,130	9,990	29	1	−1,225	816	65	3,260	21[d]	50	−150
Hungary	107,904	107,864	81	25	−12,980	37,231	..	..	..	81	70
India	179,073	291,598	64	5	−9,415	22,950	1	220,956	20	70	−1,540
Indonesia	139,281	126,177	42	11	606	6,928	4	140,783	43	37	−1,000
Iran, Islamic Rep. of	116,350	57,230	10	6	..	755	1	20,577	8	51	−993
Iraq	59,800	31,200	0	0	2,681	383	..	..	..	..	..
Ireland	124,158	82,774	84	28	−12,686	26,085	..	..	..	194	230
Israel	60,825	67,410	76	8	1,596	9,664	..	..	..	81	115
Italy	539,727	556,311	84	7	−78,029	40,040	..	..	..	133	1,750
Japan	782,337	761,984	90	19	156,634	22,180	..	..	..	293	82
Jordan	7,790	16,888	76	1	−2,776	1,835	88	8,368	54	122	104
Kazakhstan	71,184	37,889	13	23	6,978	10,189	13	96,133	131	34	−200
Kenya	4,972	11,074	37	5	−1,102	728	34	7,355	26	35	25
Korea, Rep. of	422,007	435,275	89	33	−6,350	1,579	..	..	..	113	−65
Kyrgyz Republic	1,642	4,058	35	2	−631	208	52	2,401	43[d]	14	−75
Lao PDR	1,080	1,390	..	..	107	324	65	3,337	84	7	−115
Lebanon	4,454	16,754	..	..	−1,395	2,845	229	24,634	111	177	100
Liberia	262	865	..	..	−211	132	192	2,475	978[d]	161	62
Libya	63,050	11,500	..	..	28,454	4,689	3	..	..	−47	14
Lithuania	23,728	30,811	64	11	−5,692	2,017	..	..	..	64	−36
Madagascar	1,345	4,040	57	1	..	997	48	1,661	21[d]	9	−5
Malawi	790	1,700	11	2	..	55	53	870	9[d]	16	−30
Malaysia	199,516	156,896	71	52	28,931	8,456	8	53,717	34	115	150
Mali	1,650	2,550	3	7	−581	360	82	2,018	16[d]	13	−134
Mauritania	1,750	1,750	0	..	..	153	117	1,704	85[d]	..	30

Table 5 Trade, aid, and finance

	Merchandise trade		Manufactured exports % of total merchandise exports 2007	High technology exports % of manufactured exports 2007	Current account balance $ millions 2008	Foreign direct investment net inflows $ millions 2007	Net official development assistance[a] $ per capita 2007	External debt		Domestic credit provided by banking sector % of GDP 2008	Net migration thousands 2000–05[b]
	Exports $ millions 2008	Imports $ millions 2008						Total $ millions 2007	Present value % of GNI 2007		
Mexico	291,807	323,151	72	17	−15,957	24,686	1	178,108	20	37	−2,702
Moldova	1,597	4,899	32	5	−1,009	493	73	3,203	72	40	−320
Morocco	20,065	41,699	65	9	−122	2,807	35	20,255	29	98	−550
Mozambique	2,600	4,100	6	2	−975	427	83	3,105	15[d]	14	−20
Myanmar	6,900	4,290	..	..	802	428	4	7,373	46	..	−1,000
Nepal	1,100	3,570	..	..	6	6	21	3,645	22[d]	53	−100
Netherlands	633,974	573,924	60	26	65,391	123,609	..	..	..	198	110
New Zealand	30,586	34,366	25	10	−11,317	2,753	..	..	..	151	103
Nicaragua	1,489	4,287	10	4	−1,475	382	149	3,390	31[d]	66	−206
Niger	820	1,450	6	14	−314	27	38	972	12[d]	6	−29
Nigeria	81,900	41,700	1	8	21,972	6,087	14	8,934	6	26	−170
Norway	167,941	89,070	18	18	83,497	3,788	..	..	..	..	84
Pakistan	20,375	42,326	79	1	−8,295	5,333	14	40,680	25	46	−1,239
Panama	1,180	9,050	11	0	−2,792	1,907	−40	9,862	70	86	8
Papua New Guinea	5,700	3,550	..	..	..	96	50	2,245	42	26	0
Paraguay	4,434	10,180	14	6	−345	196	18	3,570	35	22	−45
Peru	31,529	29,981	12	2	1,505	5,343	9	32,154	42	19	−525
Philippines	49,025	59,170	51	54	4,227	2,928	7	65,845	51	46	−900
Poland	167,944	203,925	80	4	−29,029	22,959	..	195,374	53	60	−200
Portugal	55,861	89,753	74	9	−29,599	5,534	..	..	..	185	291
Romania	49,546	82,707	80	4	−24,642	9,492	..	85,380	67	41	−270
Russian Federation	471,763	291,971	17	7	102,331	55,073	..	370,172	39	27	964
Rwanda	250	1,110	5	16	−147	67	75	496	8[d]	6	6
Saudi Arabia	328,930	111,870	9	1	95,080	−8,069	−5	..	..	10	285
Senegal	2,390	5,702	36	4	−1,311	78	71	2,588	21[d]	25	−100
Serbia	10,973	22,999	66	4	−15,989	3,110	113	26,280	86	38	−339
Sierra Leone	220	560	..	..	−181	94	99	348	10[d]	14	336
Singapore	338,176[e]	319,780	76[e]	46	39,106	24,137	..	..	..	84	139
Slovak Republic	70,967	73,321	87	5	−4,103	3,363	..	..	..	54	10
Somalia	..	..	..	..	..	141	44	2,944	..	..	−200
South Africa	80,781	99,480	51[f]	6	−20,981	5,746	17	43,380	19	88	700
Spain	268,108	402,302	75	5	−154,184	60,122	..	..	..	213	2,504
Sri Lanka	8,370	14,008	70	2	−3,775	603	29	14,020	42	43	−442
Sudan	12,450	9,200	0	1	−3,268	2,426	52	19,126	93[d]	17	−532
Sweden	183,975	166,971	77	16	40,317	12,286	..	..	..	136	186
Switzerland	200,387	183,491	91	22	41,214	49,730	..	..	..	185	200
Syrian Arab Rep.	14,300	18,320	32	1	920	600	4	..	..	37	300
Tajikistan	1,406	3,270	..	..	−495	360	33	1,228	30	28	−345
Tanzania	2,870	6,954	17	1	−1,856	647	68	5,063	15[d,g]	17	−345
Thailand	177,844	178,655	76	27	15,755	9,498	−5	63,067	29	136	1,411
Togo	790	1,540	62	0	−340	69	19	1,968	80[d]	25	−4
Tunisia	19,319	24,612	70	5	−904	1,620	30	20,231	65	73	−81
Turkey	131,975	201,960	81	0	−41,685	22,195	11	251,477	47	51	−71
Turkmenistan	10,780	4,680	..	..	..	804	6	743	7	..	−25
Uganda	2,180	4,800	21	11	−1,088	484	56	1,611	9[d]	12	−5
Ukraine	67,049	84,032	74	4	−12,933	9,891	9	73,600	66	82	−173
United Arab Emirates	231,550	158,900	3	1	..	..	..	..	..	67	577
United Kingdom	457,983	631,913	74	20	−78,765	197,766	..	..	..	215	948
United States	1,300,532	2,165,982	77	28	−673,261	237,541	..	..	..	220	5,676
Uruguay	5,949	8,933	30	3	−1,119	879	10	12,363	69	33	−104
Uzbekistan	10,360	5,260	..	..	..	262	6	3,876	20	..	−400
Venezuela, R. B. de	93,542	49,635	5	3	39,202	646	3	43,148	26	20	40
Vietnam	62,906	80,416	51	6	−6,992	6,700	29	24,222	35	95	−200
West Bank and Gaza	..	..	..	..	..	..	504	..	..	..	11
Yemen, Republic of	9,270	9,300	1	1	−1,508	917	10	5,926	23	11	−100
Zambia	5,093	5,070	13	2	−505	984	85	2,789	7[d]	19	−82
Zimbabwe	2,150	2,900	48	3	..	69	37	5,293	121	..	−700
World	16,129,607t	16,300,527t	72w	18w		2,139,338s	16w	..s		158w	..w[h]
Low income	167,308	239,464	44	4		19,975	37	156,551		46	−3,728
Middle income	4,905,095	4,547,215	61	19		501,721	9	3,260,910		74	−14,512
Lower middle income	2,627,173	2,376,905	71	23		232,806	9	1,228,986		98	−11,119
Upper middle income	2,276,454	2,164,216	52	13		268,916	9	2,031,924		53	−3,393
Low and middle income	5,072,412	4,786,667	60	19		521,696	19	3,417,461		74	−18,240
East Asia & Pacific	2,081,208	1,762,013	77	31		175,340	4	741,471		117	−3,722
Europe & Central Asia	1,141,248	1,146,612	45	6		151,521	13	1,214,038		42	−2,138
Latin America & the Caribbean	873,299	896,683	54	12		107,270	12	825,697		62	−5,738
Middle East & North Africa	418,183	315,621	16	4		28,905	55	136,448		48	−1,850
South Asia	225,882	380,660	66	5		29,926	7	304,713		69	−3,181
Sub-Saharan Africa	336,637	296,944	30	8		28,734	44	195,094		41	−1,611
High income	11,060,159	11,522,679	75	18		1,617,642	0			191	18,091

a. The distinction between official aid, for countries on the Part II list of the Organisation for Economic Co-operation and Development Development Assistance Committee (DAC), and official development assistance was dropped in 2005. Regional aggregates include data for economies not listed in the table. World and income group totals include aid not allocated by country or region. b. Total for the five-year period. c. Includes Luxembourg. d. Data are from debt sustainability analysis for low-income countries. e. Includes reexports. f. Data on total exports and imports refer to South Africa only. Data on export commodity shares refer to the South African Customs Union (Botswana, Lesotho, Namibia, and South Africa). g. GNI refers to mainland Tanzania only. h. World total computed by the UN sums to zero, but because the aggregates shown here refer to World Bank definitions, regional and income group totals do not equal zero.

Table 6   Key indicators for other economies

	Population			Population age composition	Gross national income (GNI)[a]		PPP gross national income (GNI)[b]		Gross domestic product	Life expectancy at birth		Adult literacy rate
	Thousands 2008	Average annual % growth 2000–08	density people per sq. km 2008	% ages 0–14 2008	$ millions 2008	Per capita dollars 2008	$ millions 2008	Per capita dollars 2008	per capita % growth 2007–08	Male years 2007	Female years 2007	% ages 15 and older 2007
American Samoa	66	1.7	331	..	..	..[d]	..	..	..	..	..	..
Andorra	84	3.7[c]	178	..	..	..[e]	..	..	..	..	..	..
Antigua and Barbuda	86	1.3	194	..	1,165	13,620	1,760[f]	20,570[f]	1.6	..	..	..
Aruba	105	1.9	586	20	..	..[e]	..	..	..	72	77	98
Bahamas, The	335	1.3	33	26	..	..[e]	..	..	−0.2	71	76	..
Bahrain	767	2.1	1,080	27	..	..[e]	..	..	..	74	77	89
Barbados	255	0.2	594	18	..	..[e]	..	..	..	74	80	..
Belize	311	2.7	14	36	1,186	3,820	1,875[f]	6,040[f]	0.9	73	79	..
Bermuda	64	0.4	1,284	..	..	..[e]	..	..	4.3	76	82	..
Bhutan	687	2.5	15	31	1,302	1,900	3,349	4,880	12.0	64	68	53
Botswana	1,905	1.2	3	34	12,328	6,470	24,964	13,100	−2.2	50	51	83
Brunei Darussalam	397	2.2	75	27	10,211	26,740	19,540	50,200	−1.3	75	80	95
Cape Verde	499	1.6	124	37	1,561	3,130	1,720	3,450	4.5	68	74	84
Cayman Islands	54	3.7	209	..	..	..[e]	..	..	..	..	..	99
Channel Islands	149	0.2	787	16	10,241	68,640	..	..	5.7	77	81	..
Comoros	644	2.2	346	38[g]	483	750	754	1,170	−1.4	63	67	75
Cuba	11,247	0.1	102	18	..	..[d]	..	..	..	76	80	100
Cyprus	864	1.2	93	18	19,617[h]	22,950[h]	20,549	24,040	3.3	77	82	98
Djibouti	848	1.9	37	37	957	1,130	1,972	2,330	2.1	54	56	..
Dominica	73	0.3	98	..	349	4,770	607[f]	8,300[f]	2.9	..	..	..
Equatorial Guinea	659	2.8	24	41	9,875	14,980	14,305	21,700	8.4	49	51	..
Estonia	1,341	−0.3	32	15	19,131	14,270	25,848	19,280	−3.6	67	79	100
Faeroe Islands	49	0.7	35	..	..	..[e]	..	..	..	77	81	..
Fiji	839	0.6	46	32	3,300	3,930	3,578	4,270	−0.3	67	71	..
French Polynesia	266	1.5	73	26	..	..[e]	..	..	..	72	77	..
Gabon	1,448	2.0	6	37	10,490	7,240	17,766	12,270	0.2	59	62	86
Gambia, The	1,660	3.0	166	42	653	390	2,130	1,280	3.0	54	57	..
Greenland	57	0.1	0[i]	..	..	..[e]	..	..	..	..	..	..
Grenada	106	0.6	310	28	603	5,710	850[f]	8,060[f]	2.2	67	70	..
Guam	175	1.5	325	28	..	..[e]	..	..	..	73	78	..
Guinea-Bissau	1,575	2.4	56	43	386	250	832	530	0.5	46	49	..
Guyana	763	0.1	4	30	1,081	1,420	1,916[f]	2,510[f]	3.1	64	70	..
Iceland	317	1.5	3	21	12,702	40,070	7,993	25,220	−1.6	79	83	..
Isle of Man	81	0.6	141	..	3,516	43,710	..	..	7.3	..	..	..
Jamaica	2,689	0.5	248	30	13,098	4,870	19,785[f]	7,360[f]	−1.8	70	75	86
Kiribati	97	1.7	119	..	193	2,000	353[f]	3,660[f]	1.8	59	63	..
Korea, Dem. People's Rep. of	23,858	0.5	198	22	..	..[j]	..	..	..	65	69	..
Kosovo	..	..	..	..	..[k]		..	..	..	..	..	..
Kuwait	2,728	2.7	153	23	99,865	38,420	136,748	52,610	3.7	76	80	94
Latvia	2,266	−0.6	36	14	26,883	11,860	37,943	16,740	−4.2	66	77	100
Lesotho	2,017	0.8	66	39	2,179	1,080	4,033	2,000	3.4	43	42	..
Liechtenstein	36	1.1	222	..	..	..[e]	..	..	..	..	..	..
Luxembourg	488	1.4	188	18	41,406	84,890	31,372	64,320	−2.5	76	82	..
Macao, China	526	2.2	18,659	13	18,142	35,360	26,811	52,260	10.4	79	83	94
Macedonia, FYR	2,038	0.2	80	18	8,432	4,140	20,266	9,950	5.0	72	77	97
Maldives	310	1.6	1,035	29	1,126	3,630	1,639	5,280	4.0	68	69	97
Malta	411	0.7	1,286	16	6,825	16,680	9,192	22,460	3.1	77	82	92
Marshall Islands	60	1.9	331	..	195	3,270	..	..	−0.8	..	..	..
Mauritius	1,269	0.8	625	23	8,122	6,400	15,841	12,480	4.7	69	76	87
Mayotte	191	2.9l	511	40	..	..[d]	..	..	..	..	..	..
Micronesia, Federated States	111	0.5	159	37	260	2,340	334[f]	3,000[f]	−1.3	68	69	..
Monaco	33	0.3[c]	16,821	..	..	..[e]	..	..	..	..	..	..
Mongolia	2,632	1.2	2	27	4,411	1,680	9,158	3,480	7.9	64	70	97
Montenegro	622	−0.7	45	20	4,008	6,440	8,661	13,920	6.9	72	76	..
Namibia	2,114	1.5	3	37	8,880	4,200	13,248	6,270	1.0	52	53	88
Netherlands Antilles	194	0.9	242	21	..	..[e]	..	..	..	71	79	96
New Caledonia	246	1.8	13	26	..	..[e]	..	..	..	72	80	96
Northern Mariana Islands	85	2.3[c]	186	..	..	..[e]	..	..	..	..	..	..
Oman	2,785	1.8	9	32	32,755	12,270	55,126	20,650	5.1	74	77	84
Palau	20	0.7	44	..	175	8,650	..	..	−1.6	66	72	..
Puerto Rico	3,954	0.4	446	21	..	..[e]	..	..	..	74	83	..
Qatar	1,281	9.1	116	16	..	..[e]	..	..	..	75	77	93
Samoa	182	0.6	64	40	504	2,780	789[f]	4,340[f]	−3.6	69	75	99
San Marino	31	1.3[m]	517	..	1,430	46,770	..	..	3.1	79	85	..
São Tomé and Principe	161	1.7	168	41	164	1,020	286	1,780	3.9	64	67	88

Table 6   Key indicators for other economies

	Population			Population age composition % ages 0–14 2008	Gross national income (GNI)[a]		PPP gross national income (GNI)[b]		Gross domestic product per capita % growth 2007–08	Life expectancy at birth		Adult literacy rate % ages 15 and older 2007
	Thousands 2008	Average annual % growth 2000–08	density people per sq. km 2008		$ millions 2008	Per capita dollars 2008	$ millions 2008	Per capita dollars 2008		Male years 2007	Female years 2007	
Seychelles	86	0.8	188	..	889	10,290	1,707[f]	19,770[f]	1.3	69	78	..
Slovenia	2,039	0.3	101	14	48,973	24,010	54,875	26,910	2.5	74	82	100
Solomon Islands	507	2.5	18	39	598	1,180	1,309[f]	2,580[f]	4.9	63	64	..
St. Kitts and Nevis	49	1.3	189	..	539	10,960	746[f]	15,170[f]	8.8	..	..	..
St. Lucia	170	1.1	279	27	940	5,530	1,561[f]	9,190[f]	1.1	73	76	..
St. Vincent and the Grenadines	109	0.1	280	27	561	5,140	957[f]	8,770[f]	0.9	69	74	..
Suriname	515	1.2	3	29	2,570	4,990	3,674[f]	7,130[f]	6.0	65	73	90
Swaziland	1,168	1.0	68	40	2,945	2,520	5,852	5,010	1.1	46	45	..
Timor-Leste	1,098	3.7	74	45	2,706	2,460	5,150[f]	4,690[f]	9.6	60	62	99
Tonga	104	0.6	144	37	265	2,560	402[f]	3,880[f]	0.7	69	75	99
Trinidad and Tobago	1,338	0.4	261	21	22,123	16,540	32,033[f]	23,950[f]	3.0	68	72	99
Vanuatu	231	2.5	19	39	539	2,330	910[f]	3,940[f]	4.2	68	72	78
Virgin Islands (U.S.)	110	0.1	314	21	..	..[e]	..	..	..	76	82	..

a. Calculated using the World Bank Atlas method. b. PPP is purchasing power parity; see technical notes. c. Data are for 2003–07. d. Estimated to be upper middle ($3,856–$11,905). e. Estimated to be high income ($11,906 or more). f. The estimate is based on regression; others are extrapolated from the latest International Comparison Program benchmark estimates. g. Includes Mayotte. h. Excludes Turkish Cypriot side. i. Less than 0.5. j. Estimated to be low income ($975 or less). k. Estimated to be lower middle income ($976–$3,855). l. Data are for 2002–07. m. Data are for 2004–07.

Technical notes

These technical notes discuss the sources and methods used to compile the indicators included in this edition of Selected World Development Indicators. The notes follow the order in which the indicators appear in the tables.

Sources

The data published in the Selected World Development Indicators are taken from *World Development Indicators 2009*. Where possible, however, revisions reported since the closing date of that edition have been incorporated. In addition, newly released estimates of population and GNI per capita for 2008 are included in table 1 and table 6.

The World Bank draws on a variety of sources for the statistics published in the *World Development Indicators*. Data on external debt for developing countries are reported directly to the World Bank by developing member countries through the Debtor Reporting System. Other data are drawn mainly from the United Nations and its specialized agencies, from the IMF, and from country reports to the World Bank. Bank staff estimates are also used to improve currentness or consistency. For most countries, national accounts estimates are obtained from member governments through World Bank economic missions. In some instances these are adjusted by staff numbers to ensure conformity with international definitions and concepts. Most social data from national sources are drawn from regular administrative files, special surveys, or periodic censuses.

For more detailed notes about the data, please refer to the World Bank's *World Development Indicators 2009*.

Data consistency and reliability

Considerable effort has been made to standardize the data, but full comparability cannot be assured, and care must be taken in interpreting the indicators. Many factors affect data availability, comparability, and reliability: statistical systems in many developing economies are still weak; statistical methods, coverage, practices, and definitions differ widely; and cross-country and intertemporal comparisons involve complex technical and conceptual problems that cannot be unequivocally resolved. Data coverage may not be complete because of special circumstances or for economies experiencing problems (such as those stemming from conflicts) affecting the collection and reporting of data. For these reasons, although the data are drawn from the sources thought to be most authoritative, they should be construed only as indicating trends and characterizing major differences among economies rather than offering precise quantitative measures of those differences. Discrepancies in data presented in different editions reflect updates by countries as well as revisions to historical series and changes in methodology. Thus readers are advised not to compare data series between editions or between different editions of World

Bank publications. Consistent time series are available from the *World Development Indicators 2009* CD-ROM and in *WDI Online*.

Ratios and growth rates

For ease of reference, the tables usually show ratios and rates of growth rather than the simple underlying values. Values in their original form are available from the *World Development Indicators 2009* CD-ROM. Unless otherwise noted, growth rates are computed using the least-squares regression method (see *Statistical methods*). Because this method takes into account all available observations during a period, the resulting growth rates reflect general trends that are not unduly influenced by exceptional values. To exclude the effects of inflation, constant price economic indicators are used in calculating growth rates. Data in italics are for a year or period other than that specified in the column heading—up to two years before or after for economic indicators and up to three years for social indicators, because the latter tend to be collected less regularly and change less dramatically over short periods.

Constant price series

An economy's growth is measured by the increase in value added produced by the individuals and enterprises operating in that economy. Thus, measuring real growth requires estimates of GDP and its components valued in constant prices. The World Bank collects constant price national accounts series in national currencies and recorded in the country's original base year. To obtain comparable series of constant price data, it rescales GDP and value added by industrial origin to a common reference year, 2000 in the current version of the *World Development Indicators*. This process gives rise to a discrepancy between the rescaled GDP and the sum of the rescaled components. Because allocating the discrepancy would give rise to distortions in the growth rate, it is left unallocated.

Summary measures

The summary measures for regions and income groups, presented at the end of most tables, are calculated by simple addition when they are expressed in levels. Aggregate growth rates and ratios are usually computed as weighted averages. The summary measures for social indicators are weighted by population or subgroups of population, except for infant mortality, which is weighted by the number of births. See the notes on specific indicators for more information.

For summary measures that cover many years, calculations are based on a uniform group of economies so that the composition of the aggregate does not change over time. Group measures are compiled only if the data available for a given year account for at least two-thirds of the full group, as defined for the 2000 benchmark year. As long as this criterion is met, economies for which data are missing are assumed to behave like those that provide estimates. Readers should keep in mind that the summary measures are estimates of representative aggregates for each topic and that nothing meaningful can be deduced about behavior at the country level by working back from group indicators. In addition, the estimation process may result in discrepancies between subgroup and overall totals.

Table 1. Key indicators of development

Population is based on the de facto definition, which counts all residents, regardless of legal status or citizenship, except for refugees not permanently settled in the country of asylum, who are generally considered part of the population of the country of origin. The values shown are midyear estimates. (Eurostat, United Nations Population Division, and World Bank)

Average annual population growth rate is the exponential rate of change for the period (see the section on Statistical methods). (Eurostat, United Nations Population Division, and World Bank)

Population density is midyear population divided by land area *in square kilometers*. Land area is a country's total area, excluding area under inland water bodies. (Eurostat, United Nations Population Division, and World Bank)

Population age composition, ages 0–14 refers to the percentage of the total population that is ages 0–14. (Eurostat, United Nations Population Division, and World Bank)

Gross national income (GNI) is the broadest measure of national income. It measures total value added from domestic and foreign sources claimed by residents. GNI comprises GDP plus net receipts of primary income from foreign sources. Data are converted from national currency to current U.S. dollars using the World Bank Atlas method. This involves using a three-year average of exchange rates to smooth the effects of transitory exchange rate fluctuations. (See the section on Statistical methods for further discussion of the Atlas method.) (World Bank)

GNI per capita is GNI divided by midyear population. It is converted into current U.S. dollars by the Atlas method. The World Bank uses GNI per capita in U.S. dollars to classify economies for analytical purposes and to determine borrowing eligibility. (World Bank)

PPP gross national income is GNI converted into international dollars using purchasing power parity (PPP) conversion factors, is included. Because exchange rates do not always reflect differences in price levels between countries, this table converts GNI and GNI per capita estimates into international dollars using PPP rates. PPP rates provide a standard measure allowing comparison of real levels of expenditure between countries, just as conventional price indexes allow comparison of real values over time. The PPP conversion factors used here are derived from the 2005

round of price surveys covering 146 countries conducted by the International Comparison Program. For OECD countries, data come from the most recent round of surveys, completed in 2005. Estimates for countries not included in the surveys are derived from statistical models using available data. For more information on the 2005 International Comparison Program, go to www.worldbank.org/data/icp. (World Bank, Eurostat/OECD)

PPP GNI per capita is PPP GNI divided by midyear population. (World Bank, Eurostat/OECD)

Gross domestic product per capita growth is based on GDP measured in constant prices. Growth in GDP is considered a broad measure of the growth of an economy. GDP in constant prices can be estimated by measuring the total quantity of goods and services produced in a period, valuing them at an agreed set of base year prices, and subtracting the cost of intermediate inputs, also in constant prices. See the section on Statistical methods for details of the least-squares growth rate. (World Bank, Eurostat/OECD)

Life expectancy at birth is the number of years a newborn baby would live if patterns of mortality prevailing at its birth were to stay the same throughout its life. Data are presented for males and females separately. (Eurostat, United Nations Population Division, World Bank)

Adult literacy rate is the percentage of persons aged 15 and older who can, with understanding, read and write a short, simple statement about their everyday life. In practice, literacy is difficult to measure. To estimate literacy using such a definition requires census or survey measurements under controlled conditions. Many countries estimate the number of literate people from self-reported data. Some use educational attainment data as a proxy but apply different lengths of school attendance or level of completion. Because definition and methodologies of data collection differ across countries, data need to be used with caution. (UNESCO Institute for Statistics)

Table 2. Poverty

The World Bank periodically prepares poverty assessments of countries in which it has an active program, in close collaboration with national institutions, other development agencies, and civil society groups, including poor people's organizations. Poverty assessments report the extent and causes of poverty and propose strategies to reduce it. Since 1992 the World Bank has conducted about 200 poverty assessments, which are the main source of the poverty estimates using national poverty lines presented in the table. Countries report similar assessments as part of their Poverty Reduction Strategies.

The World Bank also produces poverty estimates using international poverty lines to monitor progress in poverty reduction globally. The first global poverty estimates for developing countries were produced for World Development

Report 1990: Poverty using household survey data for 22 countries (Ravallion, Datt, and van de Walle 1991). Since then there has been considerable expansion in the number of countries that field household income and expenditure surveys.

National and international poverty lines. National poverty lines are used to make estimates of poverty consistent with the country's specific economic and social circumstances and are not intended for international comparisons of poverty rates. The setting of national poverty lines reflects local perceptions of the level of consumption or income needed not to be poor. The perceived boundary between poor and not poor rises with the average income of a country and so does not provide a uniform measure for comparing poverty rates across countries. Nevertheless, national poverty estimates are clearly the appropriate measure for setting national policies for poverty reduction and for monitoring their results.

International comparisons of poverty estimates entail both conceptual and practical problems. Countries have different definitions of poverty, and consistent comparisons across countries can be difficult. Local poverty lines tend to have higher purchasing power in rich countries, where more generous standards are used, than in poor countries. International poverty lines attempt to hold the real value of the poverty line constant across countries, as is done when making comparisons over time, regardless of average income of countries.

Since World Development Report 1990 the World Bank has aimed to apply a common standard in measuring extreme poverty, anchored to what poverty means in the world's poorest countries. The welfare of people living in different countries can be measured on a common scale by adjusting for differences in the purchasing power of currencies. The commonly used $1 a day standard, measured in 1985 international prices and adjusted to local currency using PPPs, was chosen for World Development Report 1990 because it was typical of the poverty lines in low-income countries at the time. Later this $1 a day line was revised to be $1.08 a day measured in 1993 international prices. More recently, the international poverty lines were revised using the new data on PPPs compiled by the 2005 round of the International Comparison Program, along with data from an expanded set of household income and expenditure surveys. The new extreme poverty line is set at $1.25 a day in 2005 PPP terms, which represents the mean of the poverty lines found in the poorest 15 countries ranked by per capita consumption. The new poverty line maintains the same standard for extreme poverty—the poverty line typical of the poorest countries in the world—but updates it using the latest information on the cost of living in developing countries.

Quality and availability of survey data. Poverty estimates are derived using surveys fielded to collect, among other things, information on income or consumption from a sample of households. To be useful for poverty estimates, surveys must be nationally representative and include sufficient information to compute a comprehensive estimate of total household consumption or income (including consumption or income from own production), from which it is possible to construct a correctly weighted distribution of consumption or income per person. Over the past 20 years there has been considerable expansion in the number of countries that field surveys and in the frequency of the surveys. The quality of their data has improved greatly as well. The World Bank's poverty monitoring database now includes more than 600 surveys representing 115 developing countries. More than 1.2 million randomly sampled households were interviewed in these surveys, representing 96 percent of the population of developing countries.

Measurement issues using survey data. Besides the frequency and timeliness of survey data, other data issues arise in measuring household living standards. One relates to the choice of income or consumption as a welfare indicator. Income is generally more difficult to measure accurately, and consumption comes closer to the notion of standard of living. And income can vary over time even if the standard of living does not. But consumption data are not always available: the latest estimates reported here use consumption for about two-thirds of countries. Another issue is that even similar surveys may not be strictly comparable because of differences in number of consumer goods they identify, a difference in the length of the period over which respondents must recall their expenditures, or differences in the quality and training of enumerators. Selective nonresponse are also a concern in some surveys.

Comparisons of countries at different levels of development also pose a potential problem because of differences in the relative importance of the consumption of nonmarket goods. The local market value of all consumption in kind (including own production, particularly important in underdeveloped rural economies) should be included in total consumption expenditure, but may not be. Surveys now routinely include imputed values for consumption in-kind from own-farm production. Imputed profit from the production of nonmarket goods should be included in income, but is not always done (such omissions were a bigger problem in surveys before the 1980s). Most survey data now include valuations for consumption or income from own production, but valuation methods vary.

Definitions

Survey year is the year in which the underlying data were collected.

Population below national poverty line, National is the percentage of the population living below the national poverty line. National estimates are based on population-weighted subgroup estimates from household surveys. (World Bank)

Population below $1.25 a day and **population below $2 a day** are the percentages of the population living on less than $1.25 a day and $2 a day at 2005 international prices. As a result of revisions in PPP exchange rates, poverty rates for individual countries cannot be compared with poverty rates reported in earlier editions. (World Bank)

Poverty gap is the mean shortfall from the poverty line (counting the nonpoor as having zero shortfall), expressed as a percentage of the poverty line. This measure reflects the depth of poverty as well as its incidence. (World Bank)

Table 3. Millennium Development Goals: eradicating poverty and improving lives

Share of poorest quintile in national consumption or income is the share of the poorest 20 percent of the population in consumption or, in some cases, income. It is a distributional measure. Countries with more unequal distributions of consumption (or income) have a higher rate of poverty for a given average income. Data are from nationally representative household surveys. Because the underlying household surveys differ in method and type of data collected, the distribution data are not strictly comparable across countries. The World Bank staff have made an effort to ensure that the data are as comparable as possible. Wherever possible, consumption has been used rather than income. (World Bank)

Vulnerable employment is the sum of unpaid family workers and own-account workers as a percentage of total employment. The proportion of unpaid family workers and own-account workers in total employment is derived from information on status in employment. Each status group faces different economic risks, and unpaid family workers and own-account workers are the most vulnerable—and therefore the most likely to fall into poverty. They are the least likely to have formal work arrangements, are the least likely to have social protection and safety nets to guard against economic shocks, and are often incapable of generating sufficient savings to offset these shocks. (International Labour Organization)

Prevalence of child malnutrition is the percentage of children under five whose weight for age is less than minus two standard deviations from the median for the international reference population ages 0–59 months. The table presents data for the new child growth standards released by the World Health Organization (WHO) in 2006. Estimates of child malnutrition are from national survey data.

The proportion of children who are underweight is the most common indicator of malnutrition. Being underweight, even mildly, increases the risk of death and inhibits cognitive development in children. Moreover, it perpetuates the problem from one generation to the next, as malnourished women are more likely to have low-birthweight babies. (WHO)

Primary completion rate is the percentage of students completing the last year of primary school. It is calculated by taking the total number of students in the last grade of primary school, minus the number of repeaters in that grade, divided by the total number of children of official graduation age. The primary completion rate reflects the primary cycle as defined by the International Standard Classification of Education (ISCED), ranging from three or four years of primary education (in a very small number of countries) to five or six years (in most countries) and seven (in a small number of countries). Because curricula and standards for school completion vary across countries, a high rate of primary completion does not necessarily mean high levels of student learning. (UNESCO Institute for Statistics)

Ratio of girls to boys enrollments in primary and secondary school is the ratio of the female gross enrollment rate in primary and secondary school to the male gross enrollment rate.

Eliminating gender disparities in education would help to increase the status and capabilities of women. This indicator is an imperfect measure of the relative accessibility of schooling for girls. School enrollment data are reported to the UNESCO Institute for Statistics by national education authorities. Primary education provides children with basic reading, writing, and mathematics skills along with an elementary understanding of such subjects as history, geography, natural science, social science, art, and music. Secondary education completes the provision of basic education that began at the primary level and aims at laying foundations for lifelong learning and human development by offering more subject- or skill-oriented instruction using more specialized teachers. (UNESCO Institute for Statistics)

Under-five mortality rate is the probability per 1,000 that a newborn baby will die before reaching age five, if subject to current age-specific mortality rates. The main sources of mortality data are vital registration systems and direct or indirect estimates based on sample surveys or censuses. To make under-five mortality estimates comparable across countries and over time and to ensure consistency across estimates by different agencies, UNICEF and the World Bank developed and adopted a statistical method that uses all available information to reconcile differences. The method fits a regression line to the relationship between mortality rates and their reference dates using weighted least-squares. (Inter-agency Group for Child Mortality Estimation)

Maternal mortality rate is the number of women who die from pregnancy-related causes during pregnancy and childbirth per 100,000 live births. The values are modeled estimates. The modeled estimates are based on an exercise by WHO, United Nations Children's Fund (UNICEF), United Nations Population Fund (UNFPA), and World Bank. For countries with complete vital registration systems with good attribution of cause of death information, the data are used as reported. For countries with national data, either from complete vital registration systems with uncertain or poor attribution of cause of death information, or from household surveys, reported maternal mortality was adjusted usually by a factor of underenumeration and misclassification. For countries with no empirical national data (about 35 percent of countries), maternal mortality was estimated with a regression model using socioeconomic information, including fertility, birth attendants, and GDP. (WHO, UNICEF, UNFPA, World Bank)

Prevalence of HIV is the percentage of people ages 15–49 who are infected with HIV. Adult HIV prevalence rates reflect the rate of HIV infection in each country's population. Low national prevalence rates can be very misleading, however. They often disguise serious epidemics that are initially concentrated in certain localities or among specific population groups and threaten to spill over into the wider population. In many parts of the developing world, most new infections occur in young adults, with young women especially vulnerable. (Joint United Nations Programme on HIV/AIDS [UNAIDS] and WHO)

Incidence of tuberculosis is the estimated number of new tuberculosis cases (pulmonary, smear positive, and extrapulmonary). Tuberculosis is one of the main causes of death from a single infectious agent among adults in developing countries. In high-income countries tuberculosis has reemerged largely as a result of cases among immigrants. The estimates of tuberculosis incidence in the table are based on a approach in which reported cases are adjusted using the ratio of case notifications to the estimated share of cases detected by panels of 80 epidemiologists convened by the WHO. (WHO)

Carbon dioxide emissions are those stemming from the burning of fossil fuels and the manufacture of cement and include carbon dioxide produced during consumption of solid, liquid, and gas fuels and gas flaring divided by midyear population (Carbon Dioxide Information Analysis Center, World Bank).

Access to improved sanitation facilities is the percentage of the population with at least adequate access to excreta disposal facilities (private or shared, but not public) that can effectively prevent human, animal, and insect contact with excreta (facilities do not have to include treatment to render sewage outflows innocuous). Improved facilities range from simple but protected pit latrines to flush toilets with a sewerage connection. To be effective, facilities must be correctly constructed and properly maintained. (WHO and UNICEF)

Internet users are people with access to the worldwide network. (International Telecommunications Division)

Table 4. Economic activity

Gross domestic product is gross value added, at purchasers' prices, by all resident producers in the economy plus any taxes and minus any subsidies not included in the value of the products. It is calculated without deducting for depreciation of fabricated assets or for depletion or degradation of natural resources. Value added is the net output of an industry after adding up all outputs and subtracting intermediate inputs. The industrial origin of value added is determined by the International Standard Industrial Classification (ISIC) revision 3. The World Bank conventionally uses the U.S. dollar and applies the average official exchange rate reported by the IMF for the year shown. An alternative conversion factor is applied if the official exchange rate is judged to diverge by an exceptionally large margin from the rate effectively applied to transactions in foreign currencies and traded products. (World Bank, OECD, United Nations)

Gross domestic product average annual growth rate is calculated from constant price GDP data in local currency. (World Bank, OECD, United Nations)

Agricultural productivity is the ratio of agricultural value added, measured in 2000 U.S. dollars, to the number of workers in agriculture. Agricultural productivity is measured by value added per unit of input. Agricultural value added includes that from forestry and fishing. Thus interpretations of land productivity should be made with caution. (FAO)

Value added is the net output of an industry after adding up all outputs and subtracting intermediate inputs. The industrial origin of value added is determined by the ISIC revision 3. (World Bank)

Agriculture value added corresponds to ISIC divisions 1–5 and includes forestry and fishing. (World Bank)

Industry value added comprises mining, manufacturing, construction, electricity, water, and gas (ISIC divisions 10–45). (World Bank, OECD, United Nations)

Services value added correspond to ISIC divisions 50–99. (World Bank, OECD, United Nations)

Household final consumption expenditure is the market value of all goods and services, including durable products (such as cars, washing machines, and home computers), purchased by households. It excludes purchases of dwellings but includes imputed rent for owner-occupied dwellings. It also includes payments and fees to governments to obtain permits and licenses. Here, household consumption expenditure includes the expenditures of nonprofit institutions serving households, even when reported separately by the country. In practice, household consumption expenditure may include any statistical discrepancy in the use of resources relative to the supply of resources. (World Bank, OECD)

General government final consumption expenditure includes all government current expenditures for purchases of goods and services (including compensation of employees). It also includes most expenditures on national defense and security, but excludes government military expenditures that are part of government capital formation. (World Bank, OECD)

Gross capital formation consists of outlays on additions to the fixed assets of the economy plus net changes in the level of inventories and valuables. Fixed assets include land improvements (fences, ditches, drains, and so on); plant, machinery, and equipment purchases; and the construction of buildings, roads, railways, and the like, including commercial and industrial buildings, offices, schools, hospitals, and private dwellings. Inventories are stocks of goods held by firms to meet temporary or unexpected fluctuations in production or sales, and "work in progress." According to the 1993 SNA, net acquisitions of valuables are also considered capital formation. (World Bank, OECD)

External balance of goods and services is exports of goods and services less imports of goods and services. Trade in goods and services comprise all transactions between residents of a country and the rest of the world involving a change in ownership of general merchandise, goods sent for processing and repairs, nonmonetary gold, and services. (World Bank, OECD)

GDP implicit deflator reflects changes in prices for all final demand categories, such as government consumption, capital formation, and international trade, as well as the main component, private final consumption. It is derived as the ratio of current to constant price GDP. The GDP deflator may also be calculated explicitly as a Paasche price index in which the weights are the current period quantities of output. (National accounts indicators for most developing countries are collected from national statistical organizations and central banks by visiting and resident World Bank missions. Data for high-income economies come from the OECD.)

Table 5. Trade, aid, and finance

Merchandise trade exports show the free on board (f.o.b.) value of goods provided to the rest of the world valued in U.S. dollars.

Merchandise trade imports show the c.i.f. value of goods (the cost of the goods including insurance and freight) purchased from the rest of the world valued in U.S. dollars. (Data on merchandise trade come from the World Trade Organization (WTO) in its annual report.)

Manufactured exports comprise the commodities in Standard Industrial Trade Classification (SITC) sections 5 (chemicals), 6 (basic manufactures), 7 (machinery and transport equipment), and 8 (miscellaneous manufactured goods), excluding division 68 (United Nations Statistics Division Commodity Trade statistics database).

High technology exports are products with high R&D intensity. They include high-technology products such as in aerospace, computers, pharmaceuticals, scientific instruments, and electrical machinery. (United Nations Statistics Division Commodity Trade statistics database)

Current account balance is the sum of net exports of goods and services, net income, and net current transfers. (IMF)

Foreign direct investment net inflows (FDI) is net inflows of investment to acquire a lasting management interest (10 percent or more of voting stock) in an enterprise operating in an economy other than that of the investor. It is the sum of equity capital, reinvestment of earnings, other long-term capital, and short-term capital, as shown in the balance of payments. (Data on FDI are based on balance of payments data reported by the IMF, supplemented by World Bank staff estimates using data reported by the United Nations Conference on Trade and Development and official national sources.)

Net official development assistance (ODA) from the high-income members of the OECD is the main source of official external finance for developing countries, but ODA is also disbursed by some important donor countries that are not members of OECD's DAC. DAC has three criteria for ODA: it is undertaken by the official sector; it promotes economic development or welfare as a main objective; and it is provided on concessional terms, with a grant element of at least 25 percent on loans (calculated at a 10 percent discount rate).

Official development assistance comprises grants and loans, net of repayments, that meet the DAC definition of ODA and are made to countries and territories on the DAC list of aid recipients. The new DAC list of recipients is organised on more objective needs-based criteria than its predecessors and includes all low- and middle-income countries, except those that are members of the G8 or the European Union (including countries with a firm date for EU admission). (OECD DAC)

Total external debt is debt owed to nonresidents repayable in foreign currency, goods, or services. It is the sum of public, publicly guaranteed, and private nonguaranteed long-term debt, use of IMF credit, and short-term debt. Short-term debt includes all debt having an original maturity of one year or less and interest in arrears on long-term debt. (World Bank)

Present value of external debt is the sum of short-term external debt plus the discounted sum of total debt service payments due on public, publicly guaranteed, and private nonguaranteed long-term external debt over the life of existing loans. (Data on external debt are mainly from reports to the World Bank through its Debtor Reporting System from member countries that have received International Bank for Reconstruction and Development (IBRD) loans or International Development Association (IDA) credits, with additional information from the files of the World Bank, the IMF, the African Development Bank and African Development Fund, the Asian Development Bank and Asian Development Fund, and the Inter American Development Bank. Summary tables of the external debt of developing countries are published annually in the World Bank's *Global Development Finance.*)

Domestic credit provided by banking sector includes all credit to various sectors on a gross basis, with the exception of credit to the central government, which is net. The banking sector includes monetary authorities, deposit money banks, and other banking institutions for which data are available (including institutions that do not accept transferable deposits but do incur such liabilities as time and savings deposits). Examples of other banking institutions include savings and mortgage loan institutions and building and loan associations. (Data are from the IMF's *International Finance Statistics.*)

Net migration is the net total of migrants during the period. It is the total number of immigrants less the total number of emigrants, including both citizens and noncitizens. Data are five-year estimates. (Data are from the United Nations Population Division's *World Population Prospects: The 2008 Revision.*)

Table 6. Key indicators for other economies
See Technical notes for Table 1. Key indicators of development.

Statistical methods

This section describes the calculation of the least-squares growth rate, the exponential (endpoint) growth rate, and the World Bank's Atlas methodology for calculating the conversion factor used to estimate GNI and GNI per capita in U.S. dollars.

Least-squares growth rate

Least-squares growth rates are used wherever there is a sufficiently long-time series to permit a reliable calculation. No growth rate is calculated if more than half the observations in a period are missing.

The least-squares growth rate, r, is estimated by fitting a linear regression trendline to the logarithmic annual values of the variable in the relevant period. The regression equation takes the form

$$\ln X_t = a + bt,$$

which is equivalent to the logarithmic transformation of the compound growth equation,

$$X_t = X_o (1 + r)^t.$$

In this equation, X is the variable, t is time, and $a = \log Xo$ and $b = ln (1 + r)$ are the parameters to be estimated. If b^* is the least-squares estimate of b, the average annual growth rate, r, is obtained as $[\exp(b^*)-1]$ and is multiplied by 100 to express it as a percentage.

The calculated growth rate is an average rate that is representative of the available observations over the entire period. It does not necessarily match the actual growth rate between any two periods.

Exponential growth rate

The growth rate between two points in time for certain demographic data, notably labor force and population, is calculated from the equation

$$r = \ln (p_n/p_1)/n,$$

where p_n and p_1 are the last and first observations in the period, n is the number of years in the period, and ln is the natural logarithm operator. This growth rate is based on a model of continuous, exponential growth between two points in time. It does not take into account the intermediate values of the series. Note also that the exponential growth rate does not correspond to the annual rate of change measured at a one-year interval which is given by

$$(p_n - p_{n-1})/p_{n-1}.$$

World Bank Atlas method

In calculating GNI and GNI per capita in U.S. dollars for certain operational purposes, the World Bank uses the Atlas conversion factor. The purpose of the Atlas conversion factor is to reduce the impact of exchange rate fluctuations in the cross-country comparison of national incomes. The Atlas conversion factor for any year is the average of a country's exchange rate (or alternative conversion factor) for that year and its exchange rates for the two preceding years, adjusted for the difference between the rate of inflation in the country and that in Japan, the United Kingdom, the United States, and the Euro area. A country's inflation rate is measured by the change in its GDP deflator. The inflation rate for Japan, the United Kingdom, the United States, and the Euro area, representing international inflation, is measured by the change in the special drawing right (SDR) deflator. (SDRs are the IMF's unit of account.) The SDR deflator is calculated as a weighted average of these countries' GDP deflators in SDR terms, the weights being the amount of each country's currency in one SDR unit. Weights vary over time because both the composition of the SDR and the relative exchange rates for each currency change. The SDR deflator is calculated in SDR terms first and then converted to U.S. dollars using the SDR to dollar Atlas conversion factor. The Atlas conversion factor is then applied to a country's GNI. The resulting GNI in U.S. dollars is divided by the midyear population to derive GNI per capita.

When official exchange rates are deemed to be unreliable or unrepresentative of the effective exchange rate during a period, an alternative estimate of the exchange rate is used in the Atlas formula (see below).

The following formulas describe the calculation of the Atlas conversion factor for year t:

$$e_t^* = \frac{1}{3}\left[e_{t-2}\left(\frac{p_t}{p_{t-2}} \middle/ \frac{p_t^{s\$}}{p_{t-2}^{s\$}} \right) + e_{t-1}\left(\frac{p_t}{p_{t-1}} \middle/ \frac{p_t^{s\$}}{p_{t-1}^{s\$}} \right) + e_t \right]$$

and the calculation of GNI per capita in U.S. dollars for year t:

$$Y_t^\$ = (Y_t/N_t)/e_t^*$$

where e_t^* is the Atlas conversion factor (national currency to the U.S. dollar) for year t, e_t is the average annual exchange rate (national currency to the U.S. dollar) for year t, p_t is the GDP deflator for year t, $p_t^{s\$}$ is the SDR deflator in U.S. dollar terms for year t, $Y_t^\$$ is the Atlas GNI per capita in U.S. dollars in year t, Y_t is current GNI (local currency) for year t, and N_t is the midyear population for year t.

Alternative conversion factors

The World Bank systematically assesses the appropriateness of official exchange rates as conversion factors. An alternative conversion factor is used when the official exchange rate is judged to diverge by an exceptionally large margin from the rate effectively applied to domestic transactions of foreign currencies and traded products. This applies to only a small number of countries, as shown in primary data documentation table in *World Development Indicators 2009*. Alternative conversion factors are used in the Atlas methodology and elsewhere in the Selected World Development Indicators as single-year conversion factors.

Index

Boxes, figures, maps, notes, and tables are indicated by b, f, m, n, and t following page numbers.